SOCIAL SECURITY PENSIONS

Development and reform

SOCIAL SECURITY PENSIONS

Development and reform

Edited by

Colin Gillion • John Turner
Clive Bailey • Denis Latulippe

International Labour Office • Geneva

Gillion, C.; Turner, J.; Bailey, C.; Latulippe, D. (eds)
Social security pensions: Development and reform
Geneva, International Labour Office, 2000

/Pension scheme/, /Social security/, /Social security reform/, /Developed country/, /Developing country/.
02.04.1
ISBN 92-2-110859-7

ILO Cataloguing-in-Publication data

Printed in the United Kingdon   ALD

PREFACE

At the beginning of the twentieth century few workers possessed the security of an old-age pension. In the developed countries most either died early or worked until they were in their late sixties, spent a brief retirement living with their children, then died in their early seventies. To be old generally meant to be poor. Being disabled signified that poverty began earlier. To survive the wage earner implied that poverty lasted longer. No support from children meant being thrown back on charity or minimal public support. For developing and middle-income countries matters were a great deal worse: incomes were substantially closer to subsistence levels and the capacity of children to support their parents was less; death came earlier; life was nasty, brutish and short. But by the end of the century things changed dramatically. In developed countries the incidence of poverty in old age is now at comparable levels to that in the remainder of the population. Life expectancy is longer and most workers can expect a significant period of retirement with a reasonable income. Disability pensions and the possibility of early retirement have reduced the financial risks of incapacity to work. Almost all women are entitled to survivors' pensions, and a growing majority are entitled to pensions as workers in their own right. Alongside these changes, an increasing number of developing countries are beginning to emulate the experience of the developed countries, in terms of the extension of coverage and in the improvement of benefits.

A large part of this profound improvement in social conditions can be attributed to the creation of social security pensions, which must be counted as one of the great social developments of the last hundred years. After growing hesitantly in the first part of the century, they underwent an accelerated development in the second half. Pension outlays in the developed countries grew at twice the rate of GDP, and more and more developing and middle-income countries joined the number of countries attempting to provide pensions for their people.

But, as this book shows, the task is only half finished. Pension schemes throughout the world are in a state of upheaval. On one hand the developed countries are contemplating new architectures for the financing of pension outlays. This requires careful thought and the development of a new consensus. On the other hand the overwhelming majority of the world's population is still without some form of income security in old age or disability. To extend the security available to workers in the developed countries of the world to workers in all other countries remains a paramount task for the early years of the twenty-first century. It will require great effort, great imagination and an enlightened adaptation to the different circumstances of developing countries. It means extending the coverage of pension schemes (and all other forms of social security), improving their governance, and ensuring that the design of the schemes is both economically efficient and compatible with internationally accepted human and social values.

The International Labour Organization has been closely involved in these developments over the last three-quarters of a century: in its normative work and in the setting of international labour standards concerning pensions; in its research activities; and in its technical cooperation programmes. It intends to be equally involved in the twenty-first century.

Juan Somavia
Director General
International Labour Office

CONTENTS

Contents

Contents

Contents

Contents

Contents

ACKNOWLEDGEMENTS

This book reflects the collaboration, individual effort and ideas of many people. Colin Gillion initiated and organized the project and it was carried out under his supervision. Michael Cichon, Wouter van Ginneken and Warren McGillivray also contributed significantly to the project. Heather Mitches served as editorial assistant. Denis Latulippe, with the assistance of Patrick Milot-Daignault, prepared the statistical annex and many of the figures. José Tossa and Diane Vergnaud assisted in collecting data for the statistical annex. Thanks are due to John Turner, Heather Mitches and Dominique Blanvillain as well as to the editors and production staff of the ILO's Publications Bureau. Dominique Blanvillain assisted with administration of the project. Andreas Jesse contributed to the bibliography, which was prepared in final form by Helen Griffith. Guy Bezou assisted in checking the bibliography.

Regional conferences to present and discuss the material for the book, organized with the assistance of ILO regional offices, were held in Budapest (Hungary), Amman (Jordan), Abidjan (Côte d'Ivoire), Harare (Zimbabwe), Lima (Peru) and Bangkok (Thailand). In addition, a joint conference was held with the OECD and the World Bank in Paris (France). A conference to review the draft manuscript was held in Megève (France), which was attended by ILO staff and the following outside reviewers: Richard Burkhauser, Bernard Casey, Philip de Jong, David Lindeman, Carmelo Mesa-Lago, Warren McGillivray, Einar Overbye, Monika Queisser, Peter Scherer, Jules Theeuwes and Lawrence Thompson.

In addition to comments received at the regional conferences and the Megève conference, comments on sections of the book were provided by a number of people. Taoufik Bendahou read and commented on the entire manuscript. Detailed comments on sections relating to Latin America were provided by Carmelo Mesa-Lago, and Elaine Fultz, and David Rajnes commented on substantial parts of the book. Michael Cichon, Wouter van Ginneken, Warren McGillivray, Einar Overbye and Pierre Plamonton also provided comments on various chapters. Wouter van Ginneken, Peter Heller, Rüdiger Knop

Acknowledgements

and Lawrence Thompson commented on the chapter on public finance effects of social security pensions.

Colin Gillion co-authored with John Turner the introductory chapter, and wrote the chapter on the normative basis of pension reform, based in part on an earlier paper by Jean-Victor Gruat. Clive Bailey co-authored with Wouter van Ginneken the chapters on coverage, co-authored with John Turner the chapter on contribution evasion, and wrote the chapters on governance. He also wrote the chapter on invalidity and survivors' benefits, incorporating a major component on invalidity provided by Richard Burkhauser. Jonathan Bradshaw wrote the OECD section of the chapter on social assistance benefits. John Turner wrote the chapter on the public-private mix, co-authored with Sophie Korczyk the chapter on setting the retirement age, wrote the chapter on designing mixed systems, with David Rajnes co-authoring the section on privatizing social security and wrote the chapter on managing the reform process, based in part on papers by Pauline Barrett and Giovanni Tamburi. E. Philip Davis wrote the chapter on investment of mandatory funded systems with the section on regulation of pension fund managers written by Peter Kahn. John Turner, Sophie Korczyk and Denis Latulippe wrote the chapter on retirement benefits with the section on annuities written by Mark Warshawsky. Lawrence Thompson (savings) and John Turner and Wolfgang Scholz (labour markets) wrote the chapter on economic effects of social security. Denis Latulippe wrote the chapter on pension transfers and co-authored with Lawrence Thompson the chapter on risks. Michael Cichon wrote the chapter on the impact on public finances and wrote the chapter on social security pension financing, with sections written by John Turner.

The boxes and annexes on special topics were written by Leo J. M. Aarts and Philip M. DeJong ("The Dutch disability experience"); Emily Andrews ("Pension reform in Kazakhstan"); Debra Bailey ("Expanding coverage to the agricultural sector"); Vickie Bajtelsmit ("The effect of rebalancing retirement portfolios as retirement nears"; "Rate of return affects retirement income"); Clive Bailey ("The institutional framework for the governance of social security pensions in the United States", based on work done by Lawrence Thompson; "Extending coverage to groups outside the core labour force"; "Progress on extending coverage in the Republic of Korea"; "Comparison of advantages versus reality concerning the effects of defined contribution schemes on coverage, the Latin experience"; "Social security reform in Mexico"); Michael Cichon ("Two basic indicators for the development of pension cost"; "Summary of factors affecting the financial equilibrium of a pension scheme"); Bryn Davies ("The misselling of personal pensions: The United Kingdom experience"; "The effect of different governance traditions on the design and financing of pension systems"); Dennis Fredriksen ("Convergence of social security old-age benefits in Norway"); Teresa Ghilarducci ("Can government agencies invest pensions well"; "Labour unions' role in pension reform"); Colin Gillion ("Funding pensions: The individual and the economy"); Nabanita Datta Gupta ("Early retirement in Denmark: The Post-Employment Wage Plan"); Gerard Hughes ("Social security in Ireland"); Aidi Hu ("Disability benefits in China"); Sophie Korczyk ("Guarantees in defined contribution schemes"; "Administrative costs in public and private pension plans"; "Contribution evasion in Kazakhstan: The whole and its parts"; "National readiness for individual account plans"; "Invalidity benefits in Central and Eastern Europe"); Denis Latulippe ("Actuarial valuations and good governance"; "A success story of public funds management: The case of the Quebec Pension Plan"; "Immunizing defined benefit plans against demographic change: The Canadian case"; "Simulation of the impact of population ageing on the labour and capital markets"; "Retirement experience and the cost of providing pensions in developed countries"; "Partial retirement: Lessons to be drawn from OECD countries"); Pierre Plamondon ("Interest rates and the conversion of capital into an annuity"); Emmanuel Reynaud ("Virtual defined indicators for the development of pension cost"; "Summary of factors affecting the financial equilibrium of a pension scheme"); Annika Sundén ("The Swedish pension system"); John Turner ("Extending coverage to government employees and the military"; "Problems in the disability benefits programme in the Philippines"; "Unfunded occupational pension schemes"; "Tax expenditures"; "Effective contribution rates are lower than legislated ones"); Noriyasu Watanabe ("Contribution evasion in Japan"; "Funding Japanese social security pensions"); John Woodall ("Annuities in developing countries"; "Disability benefits in developing countries"); and Gretchen Young ("Cash balance plans").

The country boxes were written by Clive Bailey (Egypt), Anne Drouin (Bulgaria), Krzysztof Hagemejer (Poland), Aïdi Hu (China), Denis Latulippe (India), Ana Lagares (Argentina, Brazil), Amy Shannon (Tanzania) and John Turner (Chile).

Michael Cichon, Krzysztof Hagemejer and Markus Ruck wrote the regional brief on Central and Eastern Europe. Roger Beattie wrote the regional brief on Asia and the Pacific. John Turner wrote the regional brief on Latin America and the Caribbean, based largely on papers by Alejandro Bonilla Garcia and Alfredo H. Conte Grand and by Carmelo Mesa-Lago; Clive Bailey and John Turner wrote the regional brief on the Arab states, based in part on a paper by Hyam Mallat. John Turner and Lorna Dailey wrote the regional brief on the OECD region. Clive Bailey and Lambert Gbossa wrote the regional brief on Africa.

The technical briefs were written by Denis Latulippe ("The quantitative modelling of pension reform and development"), Ursula Kulke ("Summary of International Labour Standards on Social Security"), David Rajnes ("Pensions for public sector employees"), and Denis Latulippe, Michael Cichon and Karuna Pal ("The impact of demography"). The glossary was prepared by John Turner, based in part on a glossary compiled by Lorna Dailey and Judy Mayers which was published in Turner and Beller (1992).

Acknowledgements

To all these many contributors, to numerous other officials of the ILO who made the path easy for us, and to the International Labour Office itself, for its encouragement and financial support, we owe a profound debt of gratitude.

The Editors

THE INTERNATIONAL LABOUR ORGANIZATION

The International Labour Organization was founded in 1919, in the aftermath of the First World War and the Russian revolution, as an international organization with the mandate to promote industrial peace through the protection of workers and to advance social justice throughout the world. The Preamble to the ILO's constitution gives expression to these objectives by declaring "that universal and lasting peace can be established only if it is based upon social justice" and the Declaration of Philadelphia of 1944, which reaffirms the fundamental principles and objectives of the ILO, recalls succinctly that "poverty anywhere constitutes danger to prosperity everywhere".

To be able to follow its mandate, the ILO was created on the basis of a tripartite structure whose governing body comprises governments, employers' and workers' representatives and, although initially established by European and North American countries, it has now expanded to include almost all countries of the world, a total membership of 174 countries in 1998. Its headquarters, the International Labour Office, was established in Geneva, and it has regional and area offices throughout the world. One of the several departments at headquarters is the Social Security Department (SEC SOC) which deals exclusively with issues related to social security.

During its early years, roughly up to the end of the 1940s, the principal way in which the ILO followed its objectives was through the drafting and enacting of international labour standards – Conventions and Recommendations – which could then be ratified by its member governments and which, once ratified, are subject to control and verification by a committee of international legal experts (see also Technical Brief 2). These standard-setting activities made the ILO the only international organization which built up a series of legal instruments able to regulate working and social conditions all over the world and which are commonly accepted by all countries.

From the mid-1940s onwards, several developments greatly influenced the development of the ILO. The first of these was the creation of the United Nations and the absorption of the ILO as a specialized agency within the UN system. This not only placed the normative concerns of the ILO within a more general framework of human rights but also associated the ILO with some of the broader aims of the United Nations, especially those concerned with economic development. Second, the rapid but prolonged process of decolonization and the emergence of a number of developing countries not only increased the membership of the ILO but also introduced, in addition to the framing of International Labour Standards, technical cooperation activities, particularly those concerned with practical efforts towards the creation of employment opportunities, the protection of workers and the development of employers' and workers' associations. Third, the division of the industrialized countries into two large, and conflicting, power blocs, the western OECD countries and the Soviet bloc, deflected much of the ILO's attention away from its more fundamental concerns. This division has, of course, now disappeared and has resulted in a resurgence of ILO activity in Eastern and Central Europe as well as in a number of other formerly planned economies.

Currently the annual budget of the ILO is around US$500 million and it employs about 1,800 staff, divided between its headquarters in Geneva and 40 offices in all parts of the world. The latter include a number of multidisciplinary teams intended to provide the countries in the different regions with immediate specialized professional advice. But for many of its technical cooperation activities the ILO acts only as executing agency and not as financing agency. Finance for projects is obtained from outside donors: the United Nations Development Programme, individual donor countries, or other international agencies such as the World Bank, the European Union or the regional development banks. Although the sources and level of these external funds have varied considerably in recent years, they add about US$100 million a year to the level of ILO activity in member countries.

ABBREVIATIONS

ACTFU	All China Federation of Trade Unions
AFJP	*Administradoras de Fondos Jubilaciones y Pensiones* or Retirement Pension Fund (Argentina)
AFORES	*Administradoras de Fondos para le Retiro* or Retirement Pension Fund Management Companies (Mexico)
AFP	*Administradoras de Fondos de Pensiones* or Pension Fund Administrators (Chile)
AGIRC	*Association générale des institutions de retraite des cadres* or General Association of Pension Institutions for Managerial Staff (France)
AHV-IV/AVS-AI	*Alters- und Hinterlassenenversicherung und die Invaliden-Versicherung/Assurance vieillesse et survivants et Assurance Invalidité* or Old-age and survivors' insurance (Switzerland)
AMCs	Asset management companies
ANSeS	*Administración Nacional de Seguridad Social* or National Administration of Social Security (Argentina)
ARRCO	*Association des régimes de retraites complémentaires* or Association of Supplementary Pension Schemes (France)
ATP	National Supplementary Pension Scheme (Sweden)
BPS	*Banco de Previsión Social* or Social Security Institution (Uruguay)
BPU	Basic pension unit
BVG/LPP	*Berufliche Vorsorge/Loi sur la prévoyance professionelle* or Compulsory occupational pension
CDF	Cooperative Development Foundation (India)
CDU	Cooperation Development Union

CEFTA	Central European Free Trade Agreement
CFA	*Communauté financière africaine* or African Financial Community (composed of 15 African countries)
CIESS	Centro Interamericano de Estudios de Seguridad Social
CIFOCSS	*Centre ivoirien de Formation des Cadres de Sécurité sociale* or Ivorian Centre for the Training of Managerial Staff in Social Security (in Côte d'Ivoire)
CIS	Commonwealth of Independent States (composed of countries that were formerly part of the Soviet Union
CNESS	*Centre national d'Etudes supérieures de Sécurité sociale* or National Centre for Advanced Studies on Social Security
COLAs	Cost-of-living adjustments
DB	Defined benefit
DC	Defined contribution
EMU	European Monetary Union
EOBI	Employees' Old-Age Benefit Institution (Pakistan)
ESOP	Employee stock ownership plan
GDP	Gross domestic product
GNP	Gross national product
IBRD	International Bank for Reconstruction and Development
ILO	International Labour Organization, International Labour Office (the International Labour Office in Geneva, Switzerland, serves the International Labour Organization)
IMF	International Monetary Fund
IMSS	*Instituto Mexicano del Seguro Social* or Mexican Institute of Social Security
IRS	Internal Revenue Service (United States)
ISS	Social Security Institution (Colombia)
ISSA	International Social Security Association
MOLSP	Ministry of Labour and Social Protection
MRS	Mandatory retirement savings scheme
NBC	National defined contribution
NBK	National Bank of Kazakhstan
NGO	Non-governmental organization
NPA	National Pension Agency
NPF	National Provident Fund
NSAFs	Non-state Accumulation Funds

NSAP	National Social Assistance Programme (India)
NSC	National Securities Commission
OECD	Organization for Economic Cooperation and Development
PAP	Public Pension (Argentina)
PAYG	Pay-as-you-go
PBU	Basic Universal Pension (Argentina)
PC	Compensation benefits (Argentina)
PEW	Post-employment wage
PRIS	Pay-related social insurance
SAF	State Accumulation Fund
SAFJP	*Superintendencia de Administradoras de Fondos de Jubilaciones y Pensiones* or Superintendency of Pension Fund Companies (Argentina)
SAR	Supplementary private savings system
SERPS	State earnings-related pension scheme (United Kingdom)
SEWA	Self-Employed Women's Association
SIGMA	Management in Central and Eastern European Countries
SIJP	*Sistema Integrado de Jubilaciones y Pensiones* or Integrated System of Retirement and Pensions (Argentina)
SSAC	Social Security Advisory Committee
SSI	Social Security Income (United States)
SSK	Social Security Scheme (Turkey)
SSPTW	Social Security Programs Throughout the World
SSS	Social Security Scheme
UK	United Kingdom
UN	United Nations
UNDP	United Nations Development Programme
UNICEF	United Nations Children's Fund (formerly United Nations International Children's Educational Fund)
US	United States
VAT	Value added tax
VMBFs	Voluntary Mutual Benefit Funds
WAEMU	West African Economic and Monetary Union

GENERAL OVERVIEW AND MAIN ISSUES

1

ABOUT THIS BOOK

This book has three main purposes. Its first and principal intention is to act as a reference work for policy analysts and decision-makers in countries which are seeking to reform their existing pension programmes, or which are seeking to establish pension programmes for the first time. For this group of readers what is happening in other parts of the world and its implications are of critical relevance to the decisions which they themselves must take and implement. This is especially the case because few such countries possess their own prior experience on which to draw in shaping their decisions. A balanced assessment can only come from a factual review of what other countries have done, modified by its applicability to the particular circumstances and history of the country contemplating reform.

The second main intention of the book is to act as a textbook, mainly for graduate students or for undergraduate students in their last year who wish to find out about the structure of pension programmes on a global basis, and who wish to understand not only the current situation as far as pension schemes are concerned but also some of the analytical social and economic consequences which arise from different pension structures. These first two groups of readers are addressed mainly in the first part of the book which, as far as possible, is descriptive and which, again as far as possible, avoids taking sides in what has become a controversial and sometimes heated policy debate.

The third purpose of the book is frankly more prescriptive and, because of this, may be more controversial. It is concerned with making the right choice of policies. It should be of interest to all members of the general public, who will be affected by the choice of policy, as well as to those members of the international community whose task it is to set normative as well as economic standards for the reform and development of pension schemes. The second part of the book sets out the normative basis for pension programmes, in terms of the replacement incomes which they can generate, their desired universality, the extent to which they can assist in the avoidance of poverty, the extent to which they can guarantee an adequate retirement income and the degree to which they should be managed on a tripartite basis. This normative underpinning is largely taken as a set of self-evident axioms, although it has been endorsed by the international community and consecrated in International Labour Standards. It also raises the question of whether these Standards may require revision and whether the same set of Standards can be universally applied to all countries. This part goes on to discuss the views of the International Labour Office about the various policy options which are available to countries undertaking reform and development, especially in the areas of extending the coverage of pension schemes, improving their institutional structure and governance, adjusting the age of retirement, in setting the structure of benefits and contributions, in the broad question of the funding or non-funding of pension schemes, and of casting the whole in a pluralistic and flexible framework.

The subject matter of the book is social security pensions. This is an extraordinarily vast topic. Broadly it is taken here to mean those pension schemes (including invalidity and survivors', as well as retirement, benefits) which require mandatory participation by workers. On the benefit side it also includes social assistance for the elderly and, on the revenue side, pension schemes financed from general taxation as well as from earmarked social security contributions. Private pension schemes in which participation is voluntary are given a much slighter treatment, and are referred to only in so far as they supplement social security pension schemes. But these are not hard-and-fast definitions and, as the book itself shows, there are many areas where public social security schemes and private and/or personal pension or savings schemes interact, and cannot be considered one without the other.

Much of the book is concerned with detail – the practicalities of running a pension scheme which are the lifeblood of most pensions agencies – and it provides numerous examples, including institutional structure, of how things are managed across a wide range of countries. These illustrate what works in some countries and what does not work in other countries. They cover the administrative regulations and operational procedures used to collect contributions, to pay pensions, to invest any reserves and to set the various formulae which determine contribution and benefit rates. But pension issues are seldom open to black and white resolution. Except in a very few instances it is not possible to give a single categorical answer which fits all circumstances. This information is displayed throughout the book, but it can also be found in the regional and technical briefs which give summary accounts of the situation in the main regions of the world and deal with particular issues. It is backed up by a statistical annex which presents quantitative information concerning demography, capital markets and other features of social security pension schemes.

THE CLIMATE OF CHANGE

As a starting point, it is necessary to recognize the widespread turbulence which is affecting almost all social security pension schemes throughout the world. In retrospect, the 1980s and 1990s may appear as one of the great watersheds in the development of social policy. A large number of countries are at present contemplating, planning or implementing major changes to their existing schemes of retirement protection. Others are undertaking large-scale expansions of their schemes, frequently from a very limited base. A majority of countries, across all regions, now fall into one of these two categories and there is almost no country anywhere in the world (including the advanced countries) where the reform, development, adjustment, improvement or modification of pension schemes does not appear on the political agenda. By the early years of the twenty-first century, the international landscape of income protection in old age may have changed beyond recognition.

The list of countries affected is a long one. In China, the government is planning to introduce major reforms to pension schemes, as well as to employment injury insurance, unemployment compensation and health care. After decades of discussion, Thailand is establishing a social security pension scheme for employees. A number of countries in Africa are converting national provident funds into pension schemes; partial conversion was implemented in India in 1995, and is now also under consideration in Malaysia. Conversely, in Latin America many countries are contemplating a change to privately managed pension schemes based on individual accounts. In Central and Eastern Europe, most countries face an almost complete overhaul of their pension schemes, together with the installation of new programmes of unemployment compensation and social safety nets. Many schemes in Africa, such as that in Madagascar, are undertaking a basic reconstruction, both of their design and coverage and of their organization and management. Timing differs. Chile introduced major reforms nearly 20 years ago. Other countries, such as Tanzania, are in the middle of their transformation. Yet other countries, such as Mexico and Viet Nam, are just beginning the process of change. Waiting in the wings are countries such as Cuba, Nepal and South Africa.

PUBLIC AND NON-PUBLIC PENSION PROGRAMMES

In many developing countries, the social security retirement benefit programme provides benefits to only a small fraction of the population, primarily upper-income urban workers. For most workers, there is no public-private mix. There is only private provision for consumption in old age, which occurs through work, transfers from other family members and support from charities and other non-governmental organizations. In some countries low coverage is the result of widespread contribution evasion; in others it is the result of legislated exclusions of certain groups from coverage. Legislated exclusions, however, are often a pragmatic policy based on the realization that, if certain groups were covered in the legislation, these groups would have high contribution evasion. Low coverage may also be the result of the design of pension schemes which provide benefits that do not correspond to the priority needs of workers or for which contributions exceed the payment capacity of workers.

By contrast, in many of the countries making the transition from planned economies to market economies, the provision of retirement income remains largely a public sector responsibility. This situation is also in transition in some of these countries, however, as they are preparing and enacting reforms to shift responsibility to the private sector.

In developed countries, for the bottom 40 per cent of the income distribution, retirement income is provided almost exclusively by the public sector through social security retirement, disability and social assistance benefits. In these countries, the top 60 per cent of the income distribution also finance retirement consumption through private savings, occupational pensions and work.

In most developed countries the largest component of the provision of retirement benefits is the social security retirement benefits programme. This programme is generally a defined benefit pay-as-you-go programme providing monthly or biweekly benefits. In some middle-income and developing countries, the public sector retirement benefit programme is a provident fund, a funded defined contribution plan managed by the government. Provident funds generally provide benefits as a single lump-sum payment at retirement. In a small but growing number of countries social security defined contribution pension schemes are managed by private sector management companies. Other governmental components include benefits for disabled workers and for survivors of deceased workers, for the unemployed and for workers taking early retirement. Government provision or financing of health care in old age is an important benefit in some countries. In addition, most countries provide social assistance benefits for some low-income elderly. Often, in countries with a personal income tax, the elderly receive a government subsidy through preferential income tax treatment.

Government may influence the public-private mix in a number of ways. The most important way is by setting the generosity of the benefits it provides. It may allow voluntary privatization through contracting out, as is done in Japan and the United Kingdom. It can mandate provision of employer-provided benefits, as in Switzerland, or that workers contract with private pension fund management companies, as in Peru. It may offer incentives for private sector provision by providing preferential tax treatment for occupational pensions, as in Canada, or, as in the United States, affect the level of private sector provision through regulations as to the characteristics of benefits provided.

DEVELOPMENT: THE STRUCTURE OF PENSION SCHEMES AND THEIR PROBLEMS

Part I of the book begins by discussing benefits. The first three chapters discuss the major types of retirement pension benefits. A conclusion running across the three chapters is that the entitlement conditions – the requirements for qualifying to receive benefits – are an important aspect of the structure of benefits. Particularly for disability and social assistance benefits, the entitlement conditions may ease or tighten on the basis of bureaucratic interpretation or application of the rules. Because of budgetary pressures, many countries are seeking to reduce the generosity of benefits. This can be done as an equal percentage reduction for all beneficiaries or a selective reduction. A selective reduction that reduces benefits relatively more for upper-income workers may be fairer because they generally have other sources of income and consequently depend less on social security benefits than do lower-income workers.

Retirement benefits

While countries structure social retirement benefits in different ways, in all cases they need to decide the entitlement conditions under which benefits will be paid and the factors that determine the level of benefits. Retirement (old-age) benefits provided by social security defined benefit and defined contribution schemes are the main focus of the book. In defined benefit schemes the benefit formula determines the level of benefits the individual receives and the link between contributions and benefits. A number of countries have made changes in their defined benefit programmes to tie benefits more closely to contributions. Defined contribution schemes generally more closely link benefits to contributions than defined benefit schemes, but often have features that break the connection between contributions and capital market returns. These features include guaranteed minimum benefits, rate of return guarantees and benefits based on rates of return fixed by the pension fund, which are often lower but less variable than market rates of return. Thus social insurance features in both defined benefit and defined contribution schemes weaken the link between benefits and contributions, but serve to reduce risk faced by retirees.

The annuitization of benefits in defined contribution schemes is the conversion of the account balance at retirement into a flow of periodic benefit payments. Typically, defined contribution schemes do not automatically provide annuitized benefits and, when they do, those benefits generally are not price indexed. By contrast, defined benefit schemes typically provide annuitized benefits with indexation based on increases in prices or earnings.

Disability and survivors' benefits

All developed countries, and many others, have established disability benefit programmes. The level of protection against the hazards of job separation (i.e. job loss) that disability benefits provide varies dramatically across countries. In some countries, disability benefits are an important source of benefits for older workers who leave the workforce before reaching the minimum age for retirement benefits. This path to retirement is especially likely to be widely used if a high minimum age has been set for receipt of benefits through the retirement benefits programme.

In countries where welfare benefits are low or difficult to obtain compared to disability transfers, unemployment is high and unemployment benefits are of short duration and little is available in terms of rehabilitation and job protection, it is likely that the supply of applicants for disability benefits will be relatively large. This supply of applicants will increase as the unemployment rate increases, disability benefits increase, and as the period over which benefits can be received lengthens.

The generosity of survivors' benefits has an important influence on the well-being of older widows. Because women have a longer life expectancy than men, they are the principal recipients of survivors' benefits. While many countries still do not treat men and women equally with respect to the receipt of survivors' benefits, there is a trend towards equality of treatment.

Social assistance benefits

Social assistance benefits are provided by governments to low-income people. These benefits are not tied to previous work or contributions but are based solely on need. Thus a means test must be satisfied in order to qualify to receive them. They are important for some retirees who would receive low or no benefits through the retirement benefits programme, owing to low wages or not having substantial periods of work. Social assistance includes:

- *general assistance* – providing cash benefits for all or most people below a specified minimum income level;
- *categorical assistance* – providing cash benefits for specific groups (sometimes at a level above the minimum);
- *tied assistance* – providing free or subsidized access to specific goods or services, either in kind or in cash. Housing assistance is an example.

The financing of pension programmes

In most countries, social security retirement benefits are financed through contributions by both workers and employers. Generally employers finance 50 per cent or more of contributions in defined benefit schemes, but in many defined contribution schemes workers provide all the financing. In many countries the government provides partial financing out of general tax revenues, it being considered fair that the government, employers and workers share in financing social security retirement benefits. The government's share can be determined by a formula or can be a back-up source to cover deficits.

To encourage coverage through voluntary compliance by self-employed workers, and even in some cases to encourage self-employment, those workers have generally been charged a lower rate than the total rate charged to employees and employers. Numerous countries, however, charge self-employed workers a rate equal to the sum of the worker and employer rate, on the theory that ultimately employees bear, through reduced pay, the rate paid by the employer, and thus self-employed workers should also bear the full rate.

The management of investment

The difficulties facing pay-as-you-go social security pension schemes in both developing and OECD countries are leading to growing interest in the advance funding of pensions as a complement or even a substitute for pay-as-you-go. Most countries do not provide funded benefits, but for those that do particular issues relating to the management of investments arise. The investments financing funded benefits may be managed by employers, workers, financial institutions or the government.

If employers or financial institutions are given responsibility for managing pension funds, considerable government oversight is required to protect the interests of the workers. Placing responsibility for managing the considerable sums of money in mandatory defined contribution pension accounts in the hands of private pension fund managers requires some mechanism to ensure that those funds are not stolen or otherwise misused. Experience with the management of private pension funds in OECD countries suggests that the regulation of pension managers requires considerable care. Pension fund management presents notable and perhaps obvious opportunities for self-dealing whereby the managers improperly benefit themselves. In addition, managers may mismanage their funds, either through laziness or through excessively zealous pursuit of profit, to the detriment of beneficiaries who will often find it difficult to evaluate accurately the performance of the managers in whose funds they participate. There must be realistic and effective legal means of addressing these potential problems.

If pension policy gives individuals responsibility for managing the investments of their defined contribution retirement accounts, that policy should also ensure that workers have sufficient financial knowledge to make wise decisions. Experience has shown that workers tend to be conservative in their investment decisions, which causes them to receive low expected returns and thus low benefits compared to what they would have received had they invested in higher-risk assets. If government is given the responsibility, care needs to be taken to prevent the politicization of the investments. While there are numerous examples of poor management of investment by government, there are also examples, such as the Quebec Pension Plan, where government management of investment has been effective.

Whoever manages the investments, pension funding in capital markets requires that those markets are adequately regulated. This criterion is not met in many capital markets, where there is a lack of transparency as to the value of assets.

Coverage and its shortfalls

In 1944, the International Labour Conference recognized in the Declaration of Philadelphia that economic security should be a right for all people and that the nations of the world should develop programmes "which will achieve ... the extension of social security measures to provide a basic income to all in need of such protection and comprehensive medical care". More than 50 years later, however, that right is still denied to the vast majority of retired and disabled people, widows and orphans. For them the key issue concerning social protection is their lack of entitlement, and not the basis for determining benefit.

Lack of coverage tends to be a problem among workers with particular characteristics: informal sector, agriculture, rural, low-wage, household workers and the self-employed. While workers with these characteristics are likely not to be covered or to evade contributions in both developed and developing countries, they are a much larger percentage of the workforce in developing countries, which explains in part why the problem of lack of coverage is more severe in developing countries.

The extent of population coverage for social security pensions, however, depends on many factors, of which the following are particularly significant.

- *The method of financing:* universal, or social assistance, schemes are typically financed from general taxes rather than social security contributions. Provided that the tax base is broad and yields sufficient resources, coverage may be extensive and not directly dependent on individualized financing.

- *The age of the scheme:* generally the more established the scheme, the broader the coverage.

- *The level of economic development:* there is a close link between the level of coverage and the level of social protection resources available to finance it, with more developed countries generally having a higher level of coverage.

- *The size of the formal sector:* it is easier to collect contributions and taxes from those in formal sector employment than from those in the informal sector.

- *The capacity of the social security administration:* this affects both the credibility and viability of the scheme and has implications for existing coverage in that many schemes experience difficulty in ensuring compliance. It also limits the extension of coverage to excluded groups and contingencies.

- *Government policy:* the extent to which the government gives priority to extending coverage for social protection varies according to national priorities and may be sufficient to counteract other factors. Thus, for example, Costa Rica is less developed than Mexico but has considerably higher coverage as a result of government initiatives in the 1970s.

Governance and administration

The overall performance of social security pension schemes in many countries has been disappointing. This is attributable to a broad range of problems, some of which are outside the control of the social security administration. Some, however, reflect mismanagement, or are due to weaknesses in the design of the scheme. Good governance is the key to an effective social security scheme, but it is essential to be clear as to what this term means. The definition used here is broad and embraces the processes of consultation and decision making, the institutional arrangements, and the managerial and administrative functions relating to the implementation and supervision of social security schemes. It is also concerned with the interrelationship between national policy, national management and scheme management.

Many countries have had problems with poor functioning of their social security schemes. Frequently these problems are due to poor governance. Sometimes they arise because of politicization of the social security institution. Sometimes they result from the poor design of administrative procedures, or the benefit formula. Poor governance in some countries results in high administrative costs and poor service. These issues of coverage and governance are primarily relevant for developing countries because developed countries generally have high coverage and are fairly well governed.

The following are objectives for good governance, grouped according to whether they relate to strategic and macro policy issues, institutional arrangements or administrative obligations at the operational level.

Strategic and macro-policy objectives

1. Establish a process of policy formulation which takes account of the full range of social protection needs and which balances those needs against national resources.

2. Create a balance within national policy between public and social security schemes and individual and private provision which ensures widespread coverage and achieves the desired level of income redistribution.

3. Create a mechanism for the enactment of legislation to give effect to policy decisions.

Institutional arrangements

1. Establish institutional arrangements which are accountable for the implementation of social security programmes.

2. Ensure that contributors and beneficiaries have an opportunity to influence the decision-making process and to monitor the administration of social security schemes.

3. Establish financial control mechanisms to monitor the allocation and management of resources.

Administrative obligations

1. Ensure that contributions are collected and accounted for and that benefits are paid promptly and accurately and with appropriate explanation.

2. Minimize the cost of administration within the desired level of service.

3. Ensure that contributors and beneficiaries are aware of their rights and obligations.

4. Establish a mechanism for monitoring and reviewing administrative performance.

These objectives for good governance provide the basic framework for the conception, development and monitoring of a sound and viable social security scheme. The governance of social security has received increasing attention in recent years as part of a growing awareness that schemes are only as effective as they are administered. There has been a tendency in the debate on the reform of social security, however, to fail to distinguish governance issues from conceptual ones. This has led to criticism of social insurance principles when, often, the focus should have been on weaknesses in the way such schemes were administered.

Contribution evasion

Contribution evasion, or non-compliance, is a critical issue in the design and operation of contributory social security pension programmes. It influences the adequacy of benefit payments to participants as well as both the financial status and the political legitimacy of the entire programme. Contribution evasion occurs when employers, employees and the self-employed do not pay required social security contributions. It is a major problem in much of Central and Eastern Europe, Latin America, Africa and Asia. It has seriously undermined the social security scheme in some countries, with revenue falling far short of that needed to pay benefits. This shortfall has resulted in social security schemes failing to pay benefits or paying low benefits and in their receiving subsidies from general revenue. Even in OECD countries, many schemes lose considerable revenue because of this revenue gap.

Contribution evasion is one of the reasons why social security schemes are mandatory: some workers will not voluntarily save enough on their own to fund their retirement. The problem is compounded because employers generally act as a collection agent, and they may have even less interest in collecting contributions than some workers have in making them. However the causes of contribution evasion are more complex. In some countries contribution evasion is primarily a result of high inflation. In others corruption and lack of trust in the government are important reasons. While a loose connection between contributions paid and benefits received may be a factor in contribution evasion, it is certainly not the only factor and is probably not the most important one.

Contribution evasion can only occur if three conditions coincide: (a) employers wish to evade, or place a low priority on, making social security contributions relative to other expenses, (b) employees prefer non-payment of contributions, are reluctant to report non-payment to authorities or are unaware of the non-payment, and (c) government enforcement tolerates evasion or is inadequate to prevent it.

Pension transfers and the redistribution of income

Redistribution is an important feature of many social security pension schemes. Governments design pension schemes to be redistributive to guarantee adequate retirement income for retirees who were in low-paid employment while working, or whose accrual of pension benefits was reduced because they were temporarily out of work for reasons such as sickness, unemployment or family responsibilities. Redistribution between generations may also be desired to share the benefits of economic growth or to provide decent pensions for people who had low lifetime income owing to a depression or war.

Redistribution from upper-income to lower-income workers is generally seen as an essential feature of a pension scheme. The desire of governments to redistribute income raises questions about how this can be done equitably, both for those who contribute and for those entitled to benefits.

Pension schemes can be designed so as to be progressive, meaning that they provide low-income workers with a higher rate of return on their contributions than upper-income workers. While progressive features are commonly built into the structure of defined benefit schemes, that is rarely the case with defined contribution schemes. Defined benefit schemes often have features designed to reduce the inequality of income, although features that increase income inequality by benefiting privileged groups may also be present in some countries. In many countries, including countries with defined contribution schemes, the military and government employees are treated as privileged groups. Political pressure by powerful groups may result in redistribution favouring the military and the judiciary, or upper- and middle-class workers, rather than the poor. Defined benefit schemes may also adversely redistribute benefits to those workers whose earnings increase rapidly during their career and whose earnings just before retirement are disproportionately high. For both defined benefit and defined contribution schemes, the fact that higher-income workers tend to have higher life expectancy causes annuitization of benefits on a uniform basis to favour those workers in terms of lifetime benefits received.

The risks to individuals

The challenge in delivering stable and predictable retirement income is that the world is changing and is inherently unpredictable. Pension schemes are subject to a variety of risks. The economy may not behave as expected, demographic trends may alter, political systems may change, and private and public sector institutions important to the pension scheme may fail to execute the responsibilities they have been assigned. Moreover, at the beginning of a working career, the worker's own fortunes are not entirely predictable. He or she may experience prolonged unemployment, or have a promising career disrupted or prematurely ended by industrial restructuring. Each of these possibilities introduces risk that expected pension benefits may not be received.

No pension scheme in an unpredictable world can completely succeed in providing a predictable source of retirement income. Some threats to a predictable retirement income, however, have more serious consequences under one approach to pension provision than another. The following categories of risk affect pension benefits:

- demographic risk arising from unexpected changes in birth rates or mortality rates;
- economic risk arising from unexpected changes in the rate of growth of wages or prices or from unexpected changes in the rate of return earned in financial markets over the course of the worker's career;
- political risk arising from a breakdown in governmental decision processes which allow politicians to make benefit promises in excess of what society can afford to pay, cause benefits to be reduced at short notice owing to political changes, lead to other flaws in system design, or prevent the political system from making timely adjustments to meet changing economic and demographic trends;
- institutional risk arising from the possible failure of private financial institutions, or their government regulators, or from the inability to obtain retirement benefits as a result of inadequate record-keeping or other kinds of incompetence on the part of pension administrators; and
- individual risk arising out of uncertainties about the individual's future career.

The risks of social security pension schemes differ between pay-as-you-go defined benefit, funded defined contribution and unfunded notional account systems. Risks as to replacement rates provided by defined contribution schemes are affected both by unexpected changes in capital markets and by unexpected changes in the rate of growth of wages. For example, an unexpected rapid growth in real wages will lead to a low replacement rate in a defined contribution plan, just as will an unexpected decline in asset values in capital markets. Relying on defined contribution schemes may lead to considerable oversaving or undersaving in comparison to that needed to reach a target replacement rate, depending on the performance of capital markets and wage growth rates near the point of retirement. Fluctuations in interest rates also affect the value of annuitized benefits provided by defined contribution. For defined contribution schemes, a decrease in interest rates will cause a given account balance at retirement to provide lower annuitized benefits. However it will also affect the value of assets held by the pension fund, and the two effects may be partially offsetting. Neither of these effects of interest rates, however, directly affects the benefits provided by defined benefit schemes.

Economic effects

Social security retirement pensions are determined by the political process in democratic countries. Thus their effects are to some extent desired outcomes of conscious decisions concerning design. Some effects of social security, however, may be undesired, due either to inherent trade-offs in the design of systems or to consequences unanticipated when systems were designed.

Economists have extensively analysed the effects of defined benefit social security schemes. These schemes may affect hours employees work, their choice of work in the formal or informal sector, and the age they retire. They may also affect savings decisions of workers, national aggregate savings and the development of capital markets. In most cases, theory yields ambiguous predictions concerning these effects, empirical studies have failed to resolve the issues and controversy remains. However there is little support among economists for the idea that there would be large effects of retirement benefits programmes in either labour or capital markets. In many countries disability benefits programmes, and to a lesser extent special early retirement programmes and unemployment benefits, are the primary paths to early retirement. Empirical evidence suggests that even a relatively large change in the generosity of benefits would affect the average retirement age by only a few months. Evidence concerning effects of unfunded social security programmes on savings or effects of switching to funded programmes is mixed, but does not consistently indicate a negative effect of unfunding, or a positive effect of switching to funding. Other government policies, such as tax policies, aimed specifically at encouraging savings, are more appropriate tools for influencing national savings because they do not involve a sacrifice of social insurance goals in order to increase savings.

Because of the apparent simplicity of defined contribution schemes, economists have hardly analysed them. These schemes collect contributions, make investments and disburse payments. Policy analysts generally treat them as savings plans that do not affect the way workers behave. A closer look at the provisions of mandatory defined contribution pension schemes indicates that they may affect retirement age and other worker labour supply decisions. These effects occur because the schemes are mandatory. Any mandatory programme that induces people to change their behaviour, such as causing them to increase their savings, will cause distortions, as individuals act to minimize the consequences of the programme that is not desired by them. Defined contribution schemes also have behavioural effects because of their relationship to minimum benefit and poverty programmes, their sometimes high administrative expenses and the effects of capital market risks on account balances and interest rate risks on monthly benefits when they are annuitized.

The consequences for public finances

Social security pension revenues and benefit payments affect public finances but common accounting practices have weaknesses in recording these effects. Single period accounting methods commonly used to measure the effects of social security pensions on public finances do not indicate whether the long-term financing for social security is adequate. The commonly used definition of implicit pension debt, measured using private sector insurance concepts, is misleading for social insurance. Pension debt is created when benefits have been promised but not funded. Social security financing is adequate if projections indicate that in each period revenue plus reserves are sufficient to meet benefit payments. Standard accounting methods have difficulty incorporating the value of implicit and explicit contingent liabilities, such as for guaranteed minimum benefits, and thus understate the costs of social security defined contribution schemes where contingent liabilities may be relatively important.

The primary conclusion of Part I is that, for the majority of workers in the world, the most important social security pension issue is not how benefits are financed or determined, but the fact that they are not covered by a social security pension programme. This problem occurs primarily in developing countries. The second main conclusion of Part I is that governance is an important issue in many countries. A well-designed social security pension programme can fail to meet its goals if it is poorly governed. Many of the problems of social security schemes in developing countries result from poor governance and can be resolved by improvements in governance rather than major reforms.

REFORM: THE SEARCH FOR A NEW BALANCE

Recognizing that social security schemes need to adjust to their changing economic, demographic and social environments, Part II provides policy analysis and major policy prescriptions geared towards finding a new balance for social security schemes.

The normative basis for policy

Guidance on social security pension policy is always underpinned by the normative views or values of the policy adviser. The normative basis for policy concerns value judgements as to how social security retirement benefits ought to be structured. The general objectives for the benefit structure of pension schemes can be thought of in terms of five components:

- extension of coverage to all members of the population;

- protection against poverty in old age, during disability or on death of the wage earner for all members of the population;

- provision of an income, as replacement for earnings lost as the result of voluntary or involuntary retirement, for all those who have contributed;

- adjustment of this income to take account of inflation and, at least to some extent, of the general rise in living standards;

- creation of an environment for the development of additional voluntary provisions for retirement income.

In addition to these aspects, which affect the amount of benefits to be delivered and their universality, there are other considerations. These include:

- the principle of compulsory affiliation;

- equality of treatment between men and women and between nationals and non-nationals;

- the need to provide guaranteed and predictable benefits, at least up to a certain level;

- democratic management of the pension scheme, through the inclusion of workers' and employers' representatives on the controlling body;

- the responsibility of the state to ensure that the conditions for the delivery of benefits are fulfilled (although this does not mean that the state is obliged to carry out this task itself, only to ensure that it is done);

- the establishment of benefit (and contribution) ceilings which limit the state's responsibilities to high-income earners.

Most of these principles are contained in the various International Labour Standards established by the ILO, which also set out the minimum level of benefits: broadly speaking, these amount to a replacement rate of 40 per cent of previous earnings after 30 years of contributions, with safeguards and minima for those whose lifetime earnings were low, or who experienced significant periods of non-contribution.

Extending coverage to the informal sector

A number of common considerations lie behind the policy options for extending coverage:

- There is unlikely to be, in any country, only one solution to the goal of universal coverage.

- In developing countries it may be unrealistic to rely on an extension of a social insurance scheme designed for the formal sector as a means of covering the self-employed and those in the informal sector.

- High levels of coverage depend on a high degree of consensus and the latter depends on the scheme being related to the needs and circumstances of those that it seeks to cover.
- Achieving an extension of coverage is interdependent with good governance and scheme design.

Policy options include:

- extending, without a significant modification of the contribution and benefit structure, existing schemes to cover excluded groups;
- restructuring or adapting existing schemes to facilitate coverage of excluded groups;
- designing special schemes for excluded groups;
- introducing tax-based universal or selective schemes;
- encouraging the development of special schemes based on self-help or mutual insurance principles.

The first three approaches seek, each to a different extent, to bring the excluded within the scope of the existing system and imply the general application of at least some social security principles, particularly contribution-based entitlement and compulsory insurability and related obligations that ensure compliance. The fourth breaks the contributory link and presumes, with financing from general taxation, the payment of benefit based on evidence of a contingency such as old age or low income. The fifth presumes that, at least for some of those excluded, coverage under a public social security scheme is unrealistic and implies that private and group arrangements based on mutual support might be the only solution.

Extending coverage to the informal sector may require special programmes to be constructed or special treatment to be provided for those workers to make the programme better fit their needs and their limited capacity for contributing. This may involve providing them only with disability and survivors' benefits, or providing retirement benefits at a relatively high age, such as age 70. In some cases, special programmes need to be designed specifically to meet the needs of informal sector workers. Legislative restrictions on coverage in the retirement benefits programme may need to be eased: in some countries, for example, workers employed in small enterprises are excluded.

Improving governance, management and compliance

Some of the problems social security schemes have encountered can be addressed by policies to improve governance, management and compliance. Governance can be improved by involving workers and employers in the process. The way they would be involved depends on the circumstance of the country, but in some cases it would involve tripartite (worker, employer, government) participation in a management board. Management needs to be structured so that employers and workers have input into the structure of social security programmes. While in some cases it may be useful to have the formal input of these groups through their participation in management committees, in other cases participation could occur through lobbying, voting and their otherwise being involved in the political process.

Maintaining compliance requires an enforcement policy and mechanism. Compliance problems have occurred in both defined benefit and defined contribution schemes. Compliance needs to be a responsibility of the government. In some defined contribution schemes, compliance has been assigned as a responsibility of private sector pension providers. Because the small pension accounts of low-income workers tend to be as expensive to manage as the larger accounts of upper-income workers, and thus result in little profit, frequently private sector providers do not have an incentive to maintain compliance among low-income workers, where compliance problems tend to be found.

Influencing the age of retirement

The lower the minimum age at which retirement social security pension benefits can be received, the more expensive it is to finance a given replacement rate. Wealthier countries can afford to finance longer retirement periods, and as wealth increases workers tend to want to spend more years in retirement. With increases in life expectancy the retirement period tends to increase. Population ageing, however, raises the number of retirees relative to workers, which raises the cost of providing benefits through pay-as-you-go schemes. These are some of the factors that need to be considered in setting the minimum age at which benefits can be received.

Raising the minimum retirement age may cause people to retire later or it may have little effect on the actual age at which people retire but instead act as a cut in retirement benefits. When countries raise the minimum retirement age there tends to be an increase in demand by older workers for other types of benefits, such as disability and unemployment benefits, and that should be factored in when figuring any cost savings.

Developing pluralistic designs and flexible structures

There is no one perfect universal retirement income scheme. The level of economic development, the population age structure and political factors affect the retirement income scheme appropriate for different countries. As the economic, demographic and political situation in a country alters, changes in retirement income schemes may also be required. Because of the interaction between social security retirement benefit schemes and economic development, retirement income schemes evolve over time and different systems may operate more successfully in different countries and at different periods.

All countries need to develop pluralistic designs and flexible structures for their social security schemes. To meet the goals of alleviating poverty in old age and providing low-risk retirement benefits, generally multiple sources of benefits are needed. This book stresses the roles of the retirement income scheme in reducing poverty and providing low-risk retirement income. To do that, retirement income must have an element that is redistributive and it must be provided from diversified sources. The relative importance of the different sources will depend on the rate of return and risk of the different sources. Whether the sources are managed in the public or private sector will depend on political philosophies towards individual and private sector responsibilities versus the role of the government and views as to the relative governance capabilities of the private and public sectors.

To reduce risk through risk diversification, the best approach for developed countries can be characterized as a multi-tiered system, with the tiers being determined by their risk and redistributive characteristics. They would include a bottom, anti-poverty and means-tested tier, financed from general revenues; a second pay-as-you-go tier; a third tier which would be a mandatory defined contribution component; and an upper tier of voluntary retirement savings and non-pension sources of income. The essential aspect of this approach is not a particular number of tiers, however, but that retirement income be provided from different sources having different risk characteristics in order to diversify risk. This approach stresses the desirability of increasing complexity in retirement income schemes as they develop to allow for greater diversification of retirement income risks.

For developing countries with low coverage, priority needs to be given to expanding coverage. This could be done by having special programmes designed for workers in the informal sector, or by having a national programme that includes most workers while only higher-income workers are required to participate in a more expensive programme. In order to keep costs low for poor workers, the basic programme could provide only disability and survivors' benefits, or could provide retirement benefits starting at a relatively high age, such as 65 or 70.

The reform process and its political management

Managing the political aspects of the reform process is an essential aspect of successful social security reform. Strategies are needed for developing and reaching consensus on reforms. Because of difficulties in reaching consensus, many countries have found that it takes years to enact reforms once the need for reform has been agreed upon. Instituting reforms gradually, and allowing for options for workers, are strategies to reduce opposition to reform. However, for a country to be able to use these strategies, it needs to have long-term planning concerning the financing of its social security pension benefits; otherwise it may not be able to afford postponement of reform.

In planning reform, government consultation with workers and employers is needed at all stages. The government may need to educate the public about the problems and issues, and investments may be needed in strengthening the knowledge of staff and parliamentarians involved in the process. Once reform has been achieved, periodic review is needed of the social security scheme to evaluate what adjustments are required.

The main conclusion to Part II is that different types of retirement income schemes are appropriate for different countries. Typically, pluralistic programmes that diversify retirement income sources to reduce risk and have a redistributive function aimed at alleviating poverty are desirable.

For most developed countries, meeting the goal of providing low-risk retirement income requires a programme that has a pay-as-you-go element that is subject primarily to macroeconomic labour market risks and a funded element that is subject primarily to capital market risks. (Both types of programme are subject to risks as to the individual becoming unemployed, with the consequences typically being more serious in a defined contribution scheme than in a traditional defined benefit scheme.) These two elements could be in one or several programmes. Because of the fixed costs of individual accounts, it may be better for low-income workers to have a less complex system.

INTRODUCTION TO THE REGIONAL BRIEFS

The regional briefs discuss social security schemes and related policy issues around the world. They divide the world into six regions: Asia, Africa, Latin America and the Caribbean, the Arab states of the Middle East, Central and Eastern Europe and Central Asia, and the countries of the OECD. This division of the world is by geographic region, except for the OECD countries, which have as their unifying element that they are the most highly developed economies. Thus, for example, Japan is included in the OECD regional brief rather than the one for Asia.

Social security schemes vary greatly around the world. Even within regions, large variation reflects diversity in level of development, views towards policies of income redistribution and historical experience. Thus, while it is possible to generalize to some extent within regions, the division of the world into regions was not done on the basis of retirement income schemes being similar within a region: for many aspects of social security the briefs stress the variations within regions. Low coverage is a problem, however, in all the regions except the OECD region.

Asia and the Pacific

One striking feature of this region is the large number of countries with no mandatory pension scheme. Most of these countries are former British colonies and the main reason they do not have a pension scheme is that they have provident funds. Indonesia, Malaysia and Singapore provide benefits through provident funds. A provident fund does not fulfil the same function as a pension scheme, as it does not provide a replacement income for the length of retirement. A few countries, such as Thailand until 1998, have not had any statutory retirement benefits. Countries in the region less exposed to British influence have, for the most part, set up social insurance pension schemes to cover employees and sometimes also the self-employed. These include countries as diverse as the Republic of Korea, the Philippines and Viet Nam. Pakistan, despite its strong British connections, opted for a social insurance pension scheme in the 1970s. This may reflect the influence of the Arab countries, almost all of which have such schemes. India has also recently established a social insurance pension scheme, though this did not happen until half a century after the end of British rule. The funded schemes in the region have been hard hit by financial turmoil, arising in part from problems with the government regulation of the national financial systems in the region.

Africa

Some countries provide benefits through provident funds, but there is a trend towards ending those funds and converting them to defined benefit pay-as-you-go schemes, as was recently done by Tanzania. In general, and with certain exceptions, the coverage and effectiveness of existing social protection schemes relating to the contingencies of retirement, invalidity and death in Africa are weak. This is attributable to a number of factors, some political and economic, and others which reflect failures in governance at all levels from the design of schemes to their operation. The schemes introduced by the colonial countries often took insufficient account of the sociocultural context and thus proved limited and inappropriate. Since independence, this has been compounded by adverse economic and political circumstances as well as by mismanagement. Many African schemes have failed to provide effective social protection, even for the small minority of the population that they cover.

Latin America and the Caribbean

Most of the countries of this region provide benefits through defined benefit pay-as-you-go schemes. However, because of the poor functioning of their defined benefit social security schemes, an increasing number of countries – eight as of 1998 – have converted at least partially to defined contribution schemes. These schemes involve fully funded individual accounts that are managed by private sector pension fund managers, sometimes with the government also operating a pension fund management company that competes with the private companies to attract workers as clients. While it was thought that converting to a defined contribution scheme would reduce contribution evasion because benefits would be tied more closely to contributions, contribution evasion remains a problem in these countries, suggesting that, as discussed earlier, the causes of contribution evasion are more complex.

There has been a trend towards defined benefit schemes in the Caribbean, where countries have converted their provident fund defined contribution schemes into defined benefit pay-as-you-go schemes.

The Arab states of the Middle East

The Arab states of the Middle East include some of the world's wealthiest and poorest countries. Birth rates tend to be high in this region and population ageing is not viewed as a problem. In most countries, the schemes are relatively young; all have been established since 1950. All the programmes are traditional defined benefit social insurance programmes. In most cases, the schemes are financed by contributions from both employers and employees, with the state covering any deficit. Some of the wealthy countries provide very generous social security benefits.

Some of the countries in the region have workforces with a high percentage of foreign workers. The treatment of foreign workers is a social security issue in the region because some of the countries exclude them from coverage under the social security retirement benefits programme.

Central and Eastern Europe and Central Asia

The countries of Central and Eastern Europe and Central Asia are in the process of converting their economies from command-based to market economies. The social protection schemes in most of these countries have features inherited from the systems of the former planned economies, which consisted of a visible (explicit) and an invisible (implicit) component. The visible institutionalized system of social security provided pensions, short-term cash benefits and health care. The implicit component added security through specific socialist income redistribution mechanisms, such as guaranteed employment, the provision of low-cost housing and heavily subsidized basic goods and services (for example food and services for large families, educational supplies, books and cultural goods and services). There was also a system of cash and in-kind benefits provided by state enterprises for employees, their families and retirees, such as cash allowances, subsidized recreational facilities and vacations, and subsidized short- and long-term loans.

Many of these countries are rethinking their social security schemes, with some adopting defined contribution schemes. The defined contribution schemes in the region are just being instituted and it is too early to evaluate their performance.

The OECD countries

The OECD countries have the oldest populations, which is a motivating factor in their reforms. OECD countries spend on average 10 per cent of their gross domestic product (GDP) on old-age retirement benefits, exceeding their health care spending. OECD countries rely primarily on pay-as-you-go defined benefit schemes for providing social security retirement benefits. The pay-as-you-go social security schemes are frequently supplemented by voluntary funded schemes, mostly operated by the private sector.

Most OECD countries are considering changes in their retirement income schemes to ensure the financial viability of their systems in the face of population ageing. Many of them have legislated increases in the age for early or normal retirement in an attempt to reduce benefits and encourage workers to postpone retirement. A number of countries have reduced benefits by increasing the years used in the earnings averaging period, reducing the generosity of cost-of-living increases for retirees, or requiring more years of work to qualify for certain benefits.

INTRODUCTION TO THE TECHNICAL BRIEFS

This section contains four technical briefs that provide a variety of information relating to pension coverage, governance and pension reform. The first technical brief discusses quantitative modelling of pension reform and development. Quantitative modelling can be an important aspect of governance of social security. It allows social security institutions to have a clearer understanding of the long-term effects of proposed reform.

The second technical brief summarizes the principal aspects of the ILO social security conventions, the most significant of which is the Social Security (Minimum Standards) Convention, 1952 (No. 102). The setting of minimum labour standards is an important function of the ILO, especially for developing countries. A prominent aspect of the ILO social security minimum standards is that countries should provide guaranteed social security old-age benefits that provide a minimum replacement rate of 40 per cent after 30 years' work for lower- and middle-income workers. This standard is a minimum standard, and for low-wage workers the level of benefit may not even be sufficient to raise them out of poverty.

The third technical brief discusses the coverage of public sector employees by a government-provided occupational old-age benefits programme. In some developing countries with low coverage by old-age benefits programmes, government old-age benefits programmes for public sector employees are an important aspect of the total coverage provided. These programmes are typically defined benefit schemes.

The fourth technical brief simulates the performance of an African pension scheme with a relatively high birth rate and low life expectancy.

Throughout this book, and in addition to its attempt to provide a comprehensive and global view of pension schemes, a number of major themes will be apparent which in turn give rise to a number of important general issues. The approach to these issues is based on the International Labour Standards which have been established in the International Labour Office over many years, and which have been confirmed by the world community. These Standards heavily influence the ILO's view of what ought to be the guiding principles for the design of pension schemes. But that is not to say that they are universally observed by all countries. Many countries find it impossible to implement all the main principles, largely because their economic circumstances do not permit it. In other cases countries have opted for different approaches mainly because their perception – in many cases a mistaken perception – is that implementation of the Standards is not to their economic advantage. And in other cases conflict between different groups and classes of society leads them to adopt other regimes. The reader who comes to the end of the book will be fully aware of these divergencies and the ILO's attitude to them. But it is both useful and important to provide some brief statement at the start.

Two main problems are at the heart of the issues facing pension schemes in almost all countries of the world (the exceptions relate entirely to developed countries). These are questions of coverage and governance. Universal coverage of pension schemes is the first and most important of the normative principles, but many countries find it impossible to apply because of the large informal sectors of their labour force: the rural self-employed, the urban self-employed and the many who are employed, in one way or another, by informal sector enterprises. For these social groups earnings cannot easily be monitored or contributions collected and, frequently, the state does not possess the fiscal means to pay even basic pensions from general revenues. Participation in the pension scheme on a voluntary basis breaks another of the central principles (that of compulsory participation) and if an attempt is made to make participation mandatory it opens the way to large-scale evasion of contributions by groups of people who are too poor to contribute much anyway. Even where workers are employed by small enterprises with, say, fewer than five or ten employees, the social security pension scheme may find it too difficult, or the administrative costs too high, to enforce compliance.

There does not appear to be any easy answer to this problem, although two approaches are worth trying. The most obvious approach is for the pension agency to enforce compliance by all firms of any size, even if doing so makes the cost of collecting contributions from small firms greater than the benefits which will ultimately need to be paid. The social benefits from greater coverage far outweigh the additional administrative cost and reduce the social assistance which the state may ultimately need to pay to the poor. An alternative approach is to rely on institutions built up within the informal sector itself – savings clubs, cooperatives and other informal organizations – and to offer such organizations assistance in forming their own retirement anti-poverty protection schemes. This has implications for the design of such schemes: they would need to be self-controlling; they would be voluntary; they are likely to cover a range of social contingencies – health care, unemployment, family needs, food shortages and crop failures, education and business needs – as well as strictly retirement income; they would also need to operate on the basis of individual retirement savings accounts and could not benefit from the collective force of large-scale pension schemes. Nevertheless they would bring a degree of protection to large numbers of people who would otherwise be excluded. The problem is recognized in the International Labour Standards, which originally (Convention No. 102) accepted less than universal coverage but have subsequently increased the stipulated level of coverage. But many countries, especially those in Africa, have great difficulty in complying with these requirements and the problem is far from being solved.

The other major problem of pension schemes in developing countries is that of governance. Many schemes, or their beneficiaries, are in financial difficulties simply because of an inability to collect all the revenues due to them, to invest any reserves wisely, or to pay benefits promptly and in full. Administrative costs may be excessively high. In some cases the origin of these difficulties may lie with the government, which may appropriate the reserves of the pension fund for other purposes, or which may impose financial requirements, such as investment of the pension funds in government bonds at unrealistically low or negative real rates of interest, which effectively transfer resources back to the state. But the shortfall in contributions, or equally the non-payment of benefits, may also arise from general deficiencies in management and administration and from large-scale contribution evasion on the part of employers and their workers. Staff of the pension agencies may be too numerous, their salaries too high, and they may lack the necessary skills and training. And auditing and control techniques may be too weak. The remedy would seem to lie in improving the performance of pension agencies in all these areas. But the process is likely to be a long one and is likely to rely on general improvements in a country's governance, both public and private, and a greater degree of autonomy on the part of the pension agency itself. In some countries the difficulties may arise because of fundamental actuarial imbalances: the government has given over-generous promises of the benefits it can deliver on the basis of the contributions it expects to collect, but may be unwilling to increase contribution rates, reduce benefits or meet the deficit from general revenues. Or retirement ages may be set unrealistically low. In this case the problem of governance becomes a political one.

In these two cases – coverage and governance – the problems of pension schemes in a large part of the world do not permit easy or simple answers. Ultimately much depends on the economic growth of the country concerned, the transformation of its labour force into one largely incorporated into the formal sector of the economy, and a greater maturity in its political and corporate governance. This will all take time. For the moment, the situation of pension schemes, and social security generally, in many developing countries resembles the situation in the developed countries a hundred years ago.

However there are also major issues, affecting developed countries especially, which are more amenable to an analytical resolution. These are issues concerning the prospective ageing of population structures and whether or not to move from pay-as-you-go public social security schemes to schemes based on fully funded, defined contribution structures, based on individual accounts and possibly managed by private sector agencies.

As is well known, the population structure of the advanced OECD countries is likely to age dramatically over coming decades, both as a consequence of earlier declines in fertility and as a result of increases in life expectancy. As a result, the proportion of total national income which must be transferred to retired persons – provided their relative incomes are to be maintained and provided their actual age of retirement is to remain unchanged – will need to be increased almost at the same rate. OECD countries currently allocate about 10 per cent of national income to the 18 per cent of their population over the age of 60. By the year 2030 the proportion of the population over the age of 60 will have increased to nearly 31 per cent and will require a comparable increase in benefit expenditures. Together with other social charges, especially on health care, social assistance and unemployment, the contribution rate required to support these public expenditures is thought likely to become too high and politically unacceptable. At the same time, the social basis of public social security schemes is being questioned, quite apart from the necessity to support ageing populations. The public transfers to retired persons are thought to be too generous and to result in distortions in labour and capital markets (lowering the participation rates of older workers and reducing the national savings rate) which in turn affect the level and growth of GDP. One answer to both these perceived problems, ageing and overly expensive public sector involvement, which has been widely proposed is to convert public pay-as-you-go social security pension schemes into defined contribution ones, possibly managed by private sector pension funds. It is claimed that the pre-funding of pension schemes would avert the major increase in pay-as-you-go contribution rates to be expected as the population ages, would improve labour force participation by older workers, increase national savings, improve national competitiveness, reduce the financial obligations of the state and generally create a much more specific link between contributions and benefits. Such a scheme would need to be mandatory and to be supplemented by a basic anti-poverty pension financed from general revenues. The pension itself would need to be determined from an actuarially calculated annuity based on the lump sum accumulated at retirement.

Analysis of such proposals and their comparison with existing structures is complicated. The reader is directed to the relevant chapters for an account of the analytical details. For the purposes of this introduction, however, there are two main points to be made. In the first place, some of the perceptions about the operation of such a scheme are factually and analytically wrong. It would not reduce the burden (on the national economy and the population at large) of supporting an ageing population unless pension benefits were reduced relative to income in work, or unless it resulted in a significant increase in the actual age of retirement. But both these changes could also be achieved under a public social security scheme of the pay-as-you-go type. The reason is fairly straightforward. The standard of living of retirees can only be provided from the real incomes of those in work, whether this transfer takes place through a public mechanism or through market-based savings. If it is the former, contribution rates must be increased. If it is the latter, then the accumulated financial assets of pensioners must be sold to contributors in order to provide the pensioners with money for consumption. In the two cases the amounts of money involved (contributions or mandatory savings) are equivalent. They must react in the same way to increases in the proportion of pensioners to the active population.

More importantly the introduction of a mandatory retirement savings scheme (MRS) clashes with some of the normative principles established for social security schemes. There are a number of divergencies. In the first place, one of the most important fundamentals of the International Labour Standards is that the retirement income of workers should be predictable and guaranteed. Defined contribution schemes cannot meet this requirement. The lump sum accumulated at retirement relies on the income from the (market) rate of interest accumulated on a lifetime of contributions to the scheme. This can be very uncertain: simulations presented suggest that it might vary by 30 per cent or more, depending on the course of interest and wage rates over the previous 40 years. In addition the current interest rate at the actual point of retirement has a strong influence on the value of the annuity which can be derived from the lump sum. There can be major differences in the pension received, according to whether interest rates are high or low at the point of retirement and negotiation of an annuity.

Other principles are engaged, although perhaps less importantly than the question of the guaranteed income. One is the question of indexing benefits to prices and, at least to some extent, to wages. To achieve this the institutions providing annuities must have access to some form of indexed bonds in order to fix their benefit rates, or must provide their own indexing calculating the annuity on the basis of expected real rates. Another is the question of the responsibility of the state. If defined contribution schemes are to be operated by private agencies, they must be carefully regulated and monitored by the state and subject to a range of prudential regulation. Finally there is the question of democratic management, by which is meant that contributors and beneficiaries must have a voice in their management. This is difficult under a system of privately managed funded schemes. But it could be replaced by providing workers with a transparent choice of scheme, and the right to switch from one to the other without loss of assets.

Two alternative pension designs are currently being proposed, which would attempt to avoid this conflict between the normative principles and the wish to develop more direct links between contributions and benefits, and the desire to split risks more evenly between contributors and pensioners. The first design consists of financing retirement incomes from a range of different sources, in particular a mixture of defined benefit and defined contribution schemes. One such design would comprise a number of tiers:

- a bottom anti-poverty tier, means tested, and financed from general revenues, which would provide income support for those without other means;

- a second pay-as-you-go defined benefit tier, mandatory and publicly managed, which would provide a moderate replacement rate (say around 40 or 50 per cent of lifetime average earnings) for all those who had contributed to it, and which would be fully indexed;

- a third tier which would be defined contribution based, mandatory up to a determined ceiling, possibly managed by private pension agencies, and which would provide a pension by means of annuities;

- a fourth tier which would be defined contribution based, voluntary, without ceiling and also managed by private pension agencies.

Such a structure would have the merit of splitting the risks inherent in pension schemes – the risks associated with public management of defined benefit schemes and the market-based risks associated with defined contribution schemes – and would at the same time provide a basic guaranteed retirement income for the large majority of workers in the middle bands of income.

A second alternative is a notional defined contribution (NDC) scheme. The structure of such a scheme is very similar to a defined contribution (DC) scheme: a notional account is accumulated during the working life based on contributions and the (notional) interest obtained on them which, at retirement, can be converted into a pension by means of an annuity. The main difference is that the interest rate applied is not the market rate of interest but some other indicator, such as the rate of growth of GDP, or the rate of growth of wages. The scheme would be mandatory and it would need to be managed by the state. Both the interest and the capital sums to which it contributes are notional ones. Although pension entitlements are built up in terms of individual contributions, these are accounting ones without any equivalence in terms of real money. It would provide a more direct link between contributions and entitlements, but at retirement the risk of increasing longevity would be borne by the individual contributors/beneficiaries since the value of the annuity would be calculated over the then expected lifetime of the pensioners. Other risks, such as those related to economic progress, or those demographic risks arising from previous increases in birth rates, would be borne by contributors and involve some adjustment of contribution rates as the scheme progressed. It would also be necessary to incorporate a bottom tier of income protection in old age for those whose lifetime earnings were insufficient to provide a basic, anti-poverty income in old age.

But the future of pension schemes is evolving very rapidly. Obviously there is no single design which fits all circumstances, and the question of what is the most appropriate design has to be weighed against the other factors, in particular the need to provide universal coverage and good governance, which will determine where the most desirable balance lies.

PUBLIC AND NON-PUBLIC PENSION SCHEMES

2

Traditionally, the elderly in all countries have been supported by family, extended family and charity, and, for the fortunate few, by personal savings and wealth. That continues to be the case in many developing countries for a large percentage of the elderly. Starting at the end of the nineteenth century, and expanding through most of the twentieth century, government has played a role in supporting the elderly population in developed countries.

The gradually changing role of government has raised the question of the appropriate mix of public and private provision of retirement income. Interest in the appropriate mix also arises from an effort, in some countries, to reduce the role of government and privatize the provision of retirement income.

This chapter first examines the public-private mix in retirement income in developing countries. It then discusses the historical development and mix in developed countries. It concludes by examining policy issues, including ways in which the public sector affects the private sector provision of retirement income and possible reasons for privatizing retirement income.

The discussion of social security pensions is placed within the broader framework of the overall retirement income system. The remainder of the book focuses on social security pension schemes, retirement benefits, survivors' benefits, invalidity benefits and social assistance benefits. It generally does not consider the broader framework. In particular, it does not consider pension schemes that are voluntarily provided by employers. The broader framework is revisited in Chapter 19, on designing pluralistic retirement income schemes.

THE PUBLIC-PRIVATE MIX IN DEVELOPING COUNTRIES

In a few developing countries, such as Lesotho and Thailand (until 1995), there is no national social security retirement pension scheme. In most developing countries, the government provides social security retirement pension benefits, but coverage is limited to workers in the formal sector and relatively few workers are covered. There is no public-private mix in these countries for most workers; provision is entirely private. Income in old age comes typically from one or more of four sources. First, it comes from income from work, including the in-kind earnings of the self-employed in subsistence agriculture. Many people continue to work until they are no longer able to do so. Second, it comes from the family and extended family, including income in-kind, such as through co-residence with children. Third, it comes from membership of cooperative groups such as self-help groups, credit associations and cultural groups. Fourth, it comes from non-governmental assistance organizations, including charities and non-profit organizations, religious groups and trade unions.

In these countries the social security scheme typically provides retirement income only for upper-income urban workers and the coverage of the security pension scheme is low outside urban areas. The benefits provided in some countries for public sector employees are an important aspect of the role of the public sector in retirement income (see Technical Brief 3, on pensions for public sector employees).

By contrast, in many of the countries making the transition from planned economies to market economies, the provision of retirement income remains largely a governmental responsibility. This situation is also in transition in some of these countries as they are preparing and enacting reforms to shift responsibility to the private sector.

THE PUBLIC-PRIVATE MIX IN DEVELOPED AND MIDDLE-INCOME COUNTRIES

In most developed countries, the largest component of the provision of retirement benefits is the social security retirement benefits scheme. This programme is generally a defined benefit pay-as-you-go scheme providing monthly or biweekly benefits. In some lower- and middle-income countries, it is a provident fund, a funded defined contribution scheme managed by the government. Provident funds generally provide benefits as a single lump-sum payment at retirement. In a small but growing number of countries, social security pension benefits are provided through defined contribution schemes managed by private sector pension fund managers. Other governmental components included as social security pension benefits in this book are benefits for disabled workers and survivors of deceased workers, and social assistance for the low-income elderly.[1]

Private sector sources of retirement income include private savings, income from work, private transfers from other family members (including in-kind transfers), charity, life insurance, occupational pensions, occupational disability benefits, severance pay and individual account pensions.

OVERVIEW OF THE HISTORICAL DEVELOPMENT OF THE PUBLIC-PRIVATE MIX IN DEVELOPED COUNTRIES

A stylized narrative concerning the development of income sources in old age in developed countries highlights a gradual evolution from the family, to the state, to the employer, and, most recently, to an emphasis in some countries on personal individualized savings. Historically the aged continued to work until they were no longer able to maintain themselves in an independent household. At that point, co-residence was established where the working adult child moved into the home of the aged parent, or the reverse. Gradually the state came to play a larger role: through the traditional local Poor Laws schemes, through pensions for government employees, and then through the introduction of a national scheme of social insurance or its equivalent, such as a non-contributory pension. Bismarck's pension insurance in 1899 in Germany, the 1913 non-contributory old-age pension in the Netherlands and the 1905 one in Great Britain, and old-age pensions at the turn of the century in the United States are all examples of state-sponsored insurance schemes (Rein and Turner, 1999).

During the middle of the twentieth century, the role of the state in providing retirement income expanded in many countries. Some countries adopted retirement benefits for the first time, while other countries increased the level of their benefits, and others added new types of benefits. A natural process occurs in the development of the public sector role, with the state initially offering a relatively small scheme. Subsequently its coverage is extended until eventually it covers most workers. Its benefit level is raised and new categories of benefits may be added.

In most countries occupational pensions provided by employers play little part in providing retirement income. They have an important role in only about a dozen high-income countries, being particularly important in the Netherlands, the United Kingdom and the United States. In those countries, occupational pensions provided by large employers generally predated national social security pensions. Their role grew in the second half of the twentieth century, and some countries that have had a high percentage of the labour force covered by voluntary occupational pensions, such as Switzerland, have made them mandatory.

More recently there has been a trend in some countries towards reliance on individual account defined contribution schemes. These schemes have been adopted as the primary mandatory scheme in some countries of Latin America, with Chile being the leader of this trend. Some countries, such as Sweden, have made defined contribution schemes mandatory as secondary schemes. They have grown in importance as voluntary schemes in some countries, where occupational pension schemes play an important role, with Canada and the United States being examples.

EFFECTS OF THE PUBLIC SECTOR ON THE SIZE OF THE PRIVATE SECTOR

The public sector may affect private sector provision of retirement income in several ways. The public sector may "crowd out" the private sector, especially when the public sector provides generous benefits. However, to the extent that the social security pension encourages workers to retire earlier, that increases their total savings needs, which may encourage or "crowd in" the development of private sector provision of retirement income. In some countries these relationships between the private and public sectors are formalized in the way benefits are determined. First, it may occur through the integration of benefits. When benefits are integrated, the value of a worker's occupational pension benefits is reduced to take into account his or her social security benefits. Second, sometimes occupational pension schemes provide bridging benefits, which are supplemental benefits received during early retirement up to the point when the worker qualifies for retirement benefits.

Six public sector policies have a direct effect on the private sector: subsidies, mandates, contracting out, regulation, insurance and guaranteed minimum benefits.

Subsidy

The government can encourage the voluntary private provision of retirement income through the use of subsidies. This can be a direct subsidy or it can be a subsidy through favourable tax treatment, called a tax expenditure, as seen in Canada, Ireland and the United Kingdom (see Chapter 19). The government may also subsidize mandated schemes (the Czech Republic and Mexico) or contracted-out schemes (the United Kingdom).

Mandate

The government can increase private provision of retirement income by mandating that the private sector provide retirement income. This mandate can take the form of the government requiring that private sector employers provide their employees with pension benefits. It can also take the form of employees being required to contract with a private sector pension provider.

Contracting out

The government may increase the role of the private sector and permit voluntary privatization of social security retirement benefits by allowing employers to provide retirement benefits that replace benefits provided by the social security pension. Alternatively contracting out may occur on an individual basis, with private sector pension companies providing a replacement for part, or all, of state-provided pensions. The private sector role may be encouraged by the government allowing favourable terms for this type of arrangement, or by directly subsidizing it.

Regulation

The government may reduce the risk associated with private sector provision by regulating the provision of retirement income. Regulations may require that coverage be extended to all employees meeting certain qualifications if an employer provides any employees with pensions receiving favourable tax treatment. Regulation generally adds to the cost of providing retirement benefits in the private sector.

Insurance

The government may encourage the private sector role by reducing the risk associated with private sector provision by providing various types of insurance or guarantees. For example, it may provide insurance for pension funds or annuities. These types of insurance create a contingent liability for the state. The issue of these contingent liabilities is discussed in Chapter 14, on the consequences of social security pension financing for public financing.

Guaranteed minimum benefits

A form of insurance that may reduce the private sector role is government-provided guaranteed minimum benefits. Such benefits may discourage low-income workers from making private sector provision. Policy issues arise concerning the six ways the state affects the size of private provision of retirement income. First, the question arises as to whether the state should subsidize, either explicitly or through favourable tax treatment, occupational pensions or individual account schemes. The case in favour of doing so is that these forms of savings should be encouraged, and if they are not encouraged they will not develop into a major source of retirement income. The case against it is that such a subsidy is likely to benefit the higher-income groups and that it erodes the tax base by excluding employee pay in the form of employer pension contributions from the tax base.

Second, when employers are mandated to provide coverage, care needs to be taken to protect the retirement income of workers against the risk of employer bankruptcy. Compliance with employer mandates may be more expensive for small employers than for large employers because of scale economies, creating a cost disadvantage to small employers.

Because it is thought that many people will not save adequately on their own for retirement, in all developed countries the state mandates a minimum level of retirement saving. The mandate can require either public or private provision. The social welfare or income distribution function of the state, however, is not being privatized in any country. In nearly all countries, the state maintains a scheme of social assistance for the poorest elderly.

Third, with contracting out, there is the potential problem of adverse selection. Employers or employees for whom the social security scheme is not a particularly good deal will be more likely to contract out. The cost of the scheme per beneficiary will increase because it will be left with beneficiaries for whom it is relatively expensive to provide benefits.

Fourth, regulation of private provision of retirement income is necessary to protect the interests of workers and beneficiaries and to reduce the risks they face. Issues concerning regulation are discussed in Chapter 7.

Fifth, insurance provided by the state creates an uncertain role for it. The potential cost of these schemes is generally difficult to evaluate. The insurance can be explicitly provided or it may be an understanding that, if benefits fall below a certain level, or if institutions fail, the state will step in and provide benefits.

Sixth, generous minimum benefits for low-income workers may create an adverse incentive. However the government may find it necessary to supplement guaranteed minimum benefits with social assistance benefits for low-income retirees who do not qualify for the guaranteed minimum benefits (see Chapter 5).

The actual range of policy instruments the government has is wider than indicated by the options discussed here. For example, Australian occupational pensions are, strictly speaking, not mandatory, although they are often considered to be mandatory. It is legal for an employer not to provide a pension. If the employer fails to do so, however, the government levies an extra tax on that employer equal to the contribution the employer would have paid to provide a pension for its employees. Thus the Australian government has introduced a strong incentive to employers to provide pensions for their employees.

Some countries have mandated private provision of pensions to reduce the government role in retirement income. The government, however, retains a large role even in these types of systems, with that role shifting to regulating the private providers.

The relative size of the public and private sectors in different countries

The relative size of the public and private sectors varies between the developed and developing countries, as well as within regions according to national traditions. Most countries have a small government-provided safety net of anti-poverty benefits. Some countries, such as Canada, Denmark, Finland, Ireland, Japan, Norway and the United Kingdom, provide flat-rate benefits. Pay-as-you-go social security schemes have been established in most countries. They do not require capital markets but need the ability of government to collect contributions in labour markets.

A number of European countries have large government retirement benefits schemes. These include France, Germany and the countries of southern Europe: Greece, Italy, Portugal and Spain. Large government benefits schemes leave little room for private provision of retirement income. Canada, Japan, the United Kingdom and the United States have much smaller government-provided benefits and, in comparison to other countries, rely relatively heavily on employer-provided benefits. Even for these countries, the government-provided benefits are more important for most retirees than are private sources of retirement income.

An increasing number of countries have mandatory funded benefits. These benefits can be managed either in the public sector by provident funds or in the private sector by pension fund management companies or employers. In some countries, such as Argentina and Kazakhstan, the government competes with private pension fund management companies by offering a public sector pension fund management company. Countries with mandatory benefits managed by government include Indonesia, Malaysia and Singapore. In these countries the public sector is the dominant source of benefits. Countries with mandatory benefits managed by private pension fund management companies include Bolivia, Chile and Peru. In these countries the private sector is the dominant source of benefits. Countries with mandatory funded benefits managed by employers include Australia and Switzerland. When the Australian scheme is fully mature, the private sector will be the dominant source of benefits. In Switzerland, the public sector is the dominant source of benefits and the benefits provided by the private sector are supplementary.

The structure of a retirement income scheme can also be considered at the micro or personal level. At this level it is the percentage of retirement income the worker receives from different sources. The relative importance of different sources varies across families within a country, depending on the level of family income. In all developed countries, the bottom 40 per cent of the income distribution among retirees relies almost exclusively on government-provided retirement benefits, while the top 60 per cent also receive retirement income from employer-provided occupational pensions and private savings (Rein and Turner, 1999).

THE CHOICE BETWEEN PUBLIC AND PRIVATE

The choice between public and private is affected by political philosophies and by the relative governance capabilities of the two sectors. Some political philosophies favour individual reliance and, as a back-up, reliance on families and charity. Other political philosophies favour the social insurance that governments can provide to reduce social risks and increase security in society.

The choice between public and private provision also depends in some countries on the relative reliability of different institutions. In some countries the government may not be trusted, while in others there may be relatively little trust in the private sector institutions. These issues are discussed further in Chapter 19, on developing pluralistic designs and flexible structures.

REASONS FOR PRIVATIZATION

In choosing to reduce the role of government in providing retirement income, countries have indicated a number of reasons for privatizing their social security schemes, many of which are similar to the reasons for privatizing other government enterprises (Van der Hoeven and Sziraczki, 1997). Nonetheless controversy exists over the validity of some of the reasons, and they are discussed further in various places in this book.

In many countries the current social security scheme relies on large subsidies by the state because contributions are insufficient to finance outlays. Privatization has occurred to reduce the government deficit and the size of government. In the short run, however, in countries with a sizeable existing system, the cash flow of the government is worsened because of the cost of financing the transition. In the United Kingdom, because of incentives provided for workers to opt out of social security, privatization has been a sizeable net expense for the government.

Some governments have been unable to manage adequately public defined benefit schemes and believe that management of private defined contribution schemes would be easier, both politically and financially. Privatization has been motivated by the poor quality of services provided by government social security institutions. Competition in private sector management is thought to be more efficient and to lead to better services than monopolistic management by government. Experience has shown, however, that the administrative costs of government schemes are often less than for private sector management.

Some public pay-as-you-go schemes are inequitable in their distribution of benefits. For example, since most Latin American countries rely heavily on indirect taxation, the poor contribute disproportionately to the funding of benefits they probably will not receive (Lacey, 1996). Another aspect is inequity across generations in taxes paid and benefits received. As discussed in Chapter 11 on redistribution, privatized schemes tend to be regressive, however, in part because of the way fixed costs arise in managing accounts.

Countries see social security pension reform as a possible means of raising domestic savings, correcting economic distortions in labour markets presumably caused by traditional pay-as-you-go schemes and reducing contribution evasion. Chapter 13, on the economic implications of pension schemes, discusses these issues.

Demographic changes raising the retirement system dependency rate (the ratio of beneficiaries to covered workers) are making pay-as-you-go social security schemes more expensive. The declines in the population growth rate and the growth rate of real wages have reduced the implicit rate of return on pay-as-you-go social security, making market rates of return relatively more attractive. Chapter 11, on redistribution, discusses the effect of demographic change on unfunded and funded schemes.

Some people favour privatization as a way of increasing the range of individual choice and a move towards greater private sector reliance as an aspect of economic liberalization. Privatization is desired because it gives individuals greater responsibility for their retirement income and is seen as a way of developing private sector enterprises – money managers and insurance companies. It helps in creating a competitive market economy. In practice, however, restrictions on allowable portfolios and other regulations limit the range of choice.

For some social security policy analysts, the desire for privatization is due to a distrust of government as a financial institution. Experience with private management of pension funds has shown, however, that regulatory safeguards are needed as protection against private sector theft of funds.

Privatization is sometimes seen as a way of encouraging the development of capital markets in countries with poorly developed capital markets. Similarly privatization may be seen to be feasible in countries that formerly had poorly developed capital markets but whose capital markets have developed to the point where they could provide adequate investment opportunities. However there is a lack of transparency in many capital markets in developing countries.

In some countries privatization's popularity may depend on the recent history of financial markets. During periods when financial markets are providing stable high real rates of return, privatization may appear more appealing than it does in periods when financial markets are turbulent and declining in value.

The privatization of social security may be used to assist in the privatization of state assets. State assets can be sold or given to the privatized social security scheme.

The ease with which a country can establish a privatized system depends on aspects of the existing system. The greater the relative size of the group currently receiving benefits, the more costly it is to continue paying for those benefits while starting a new system. In general the greater the unfunded liability of the existing system, the harder it is the to make the transition to a privatized system.

The role of the public and private sectors in providing retirement income differs greatly across countries. In many developing countries the majority of workers are not covered by social security retirement benefits and the public sector plays little or no role in the retirement income of those workers. The role of the public sector in those countries is often largely confined to employees working in urban areas.

In developed countries the role of the public sector has grown increasingly complex over the course of the twentieth century. It subsidizes, mandates, regulates and insures benefits. The relative size of its role has grown as coverage has extended to more of the workforce, the generosity of benefits has increased and new schemes have been added.

At the end of the twentieth century, in many developing countries there is a need to extend the role of the public sector so that retirement benefit coverage is provided for a greater proportion of the workforce.

Note

[1] Invalidity and survivors' benefits are discussed in Chapter 4, and social assistance benefits in Chapter 5. Government provision, or financing of health care in old age, is an important benefit in some countries. Often, in countries with a personal income tax, the elderly receive a government subsidy through preferential income tax treatment, which is discussed in Chapter 19.

DEVELOPMENT: THE STRUCTURE OF PENSION SCHEMES AND THEIR PROBLEMS

This first part of the book covers social security pension systems around the world and the problems they have encountered. It is largely descriptive and can be viewed as a handbook on the structure of social security schemes. It is designed to be useful for policy analysts considering major changes in social security policy.

Part I begins by discussing benefits. The first three chapters look at the major types of retirement pension benefits. Chapter 3 describes the retirement benefits provided by social security defined benefit and defined contribution systems. These benefits are the main focus of the book. The chapter analyses entitlement conditions and the determination of the level of benefits. It also discusses questions concerning the annuitization of benefits in defined contribution systems. Chapter 4 describes ways that invalidity and survivors' benefits are provided. Invalidity benefits in some countries are an important source of benefits for older workers before they reach the minimum age for retirement benefits. Survivor benefits also have an important influence on the well-being of older widows. Chapter 5 studies social assistance benefits for low-income retirees. Social assistance benefits are important for some retirees who would receive low, or no, benefits through the retirement benefits programme because of low wages, or not having had substantial periods of work. These benefits are generally means tested. While invalidity benefits, survivor benefits and social assistance benefits are presented elsewhere in the book, they receive less attention than do retirement benefits.

The next two chapters discuss the financing and financial management of social security pensions. Chapter 6 considers the sources of financing for benefits, in both defined benefit and defined contribution schemes. In most countries social security retirement benefits are financed through contributions by workers and employers, but there are many variations on how that is done. Also in many countries the government provides financing out of general tax revenues. This can be determined by a formula, or can be a back-up source to cover deficits. Chapter 7 explains the financial management of funded benefits. Because most countries do not provide funded benefits, this chapter deals with issues faced by a more limited number of countries. The investments of funded benefits may be managed by employers, workers, financial institutions or the government.

The following three chapters discuss who ultimately receives benefits: the question of coverage, and the broad topic of governance, as well as how well social security systems are managed. In many developing countries, coverage and governance are the key social security issues. Chapter 8 deals with the problem of low coverage in most countries. For most workers in the world, the primary problem concerning social security is not how benefits are determined or financed, but that they are not covered. Chapter 9 looks at the problems of administering social security systems. Poor governance in some countries results in high administrative costs and poor service. These two chapters are primarily relevant for developing countries because developed countries generally have high coverage and are fairly well governed. Chapter 10 considers contribution evasion, which is the non-payment of required contributions by employers and workers. In most cases employers are legally liable for making contributions and collecting them from workers. Contribution evasion leads to reduced coverage when workers and employers evade payments altogether, and to reduced benefits when covered earnings are understated. Contribution evasion is a problem of governance, as it arises only if government is unable or unwilling to enforce the required contributions. It is a serious problem in many developing countries, but is also a problem, to a lesser extent, in developed countries.

The last four chapters of Part I study the effects of social security systems on workers, capital markets and government finances. Chapter 11 covers effects on income distribution. One of the primary goals of social security social insurance systems is to reduce poverty among the elderly. These systems often have features designed to reduce the inequality of income, although in practice features that increase income inequality by benefiting privileged groups may also be present. Social security systems in some circumstances may have as a goal the redistribution of income from younger to older generations, especially when the younger generation has considerably higher expected lifetime wealth than the older generation. Chapter 12 deals with the risks of social security systems, comparing the risks of pay-as-you-go, funded defined contribution and unfunded notional account systems. This chapter indicates that risks concerning replacement rates provided by defined contribution schemes are affected both by unexpected changes in capital markets and unexpected changes in the rate of growth of wages. Chapter 13 illustrates the economic effects of social security pensions on capital and labour markets. In capital markets pension schemes may affect savings and the development of the market. In labour markets they may affect hours worked and age at retirement. Chapter 14 analyses the consequences of social security pensions for public finances. It discusses problems with common accounting methods used to measure the effects of social security pensions on public finances. It also comments on the issue of the measurement of pension debt.

Part I ends with some brief conclusions.

RETIREMENT BENEFITS

3

This chapter discusses the determinants of the amount of benefits to be received under social security pension schemes, the age at which they become available and other conditions which affect the payment of pensions. Related issues presented elsewhere in the book include invalidity benefits (Chapter 4), social assistance benefits (Chapter 5), the redistribution of income (Chapter 11) and questions affecting the age of retirement (Chapter 18).

Countries determine social retirement benefits in a wide variety of ways. In all cases, however, they need to determine the entitlement conditions under which these benefits will be paid, and the factors that affect their level.

ENTITLEMENT CONDITIONS

Social security schemes must establish requirements for eligibility to receive benefits. These requirements usually include minimum age and minimum years of contributions; a brief summary is given in table 3.1. They sometimes include a retirement condition or an earnings test requiring that workers retire from their employment or receive less than a maximum level of earnings.

Minimum and normal pensionable ages

Social security retirement benefit provisions generally stipulate an age called the "normal" retirement age. At that age the retiree becomes entitled to an unreduced pension if other conditions (covered years and retirement conditions) are satisfied. This term in pension jargon can be confusing because it is not necessarily the age either at which or by which most workers retire. Workers may retire before the normal retirement age if they are willing to accept a reduced pension. Late retirement age may also be specified when the other entitlement conditions are relaxed or become ineffective.

The most common normal retirement age in countries outside the OECD is 60, although several countries in Africa, Asia and the Arab states have a lower

Table 3.1 Factors affecting individuals' retirement benefits from an earnings-related defined benefit scheme

Benefit determination factors	Age	Service	Earnings
Eligibility conditions	Minimum age	Minimum service	Maximum earnings
Worker's attributes affecting benefit level at first receipt	Age at first receipt	Years of service	Past earnings history
Benefit formula	Penalty or reward for early or late retirement	Benefit accrual rate	Earnings averaging period

Source: Compiled by the ILO.

normal retirement age (commonly 55). In the OECD countries, the most common normal retirement age is 65. Denmark, Iceland and Norway have a normal retirement age which is higher, at 67. (See figure 3.1. More detailed information is provided in the statistical annex at the end of the book.) Many countries have a lower minimum retirement age for women than for men

Figure 3.1 Distribution of normal retirement age by region

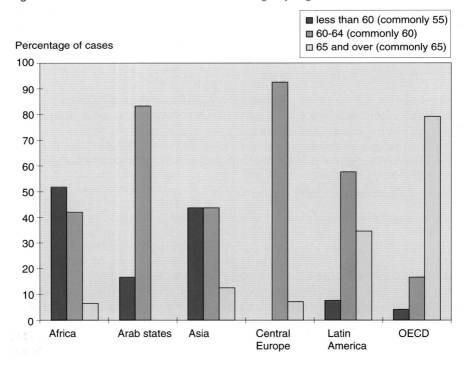

(typically five years less), but steps have been taken in recent years, especially in OECD countries, to gradually raise the age for women to that for men.

Many countries in the OECD and elsewhere have made retirement more flexible by allowing workers to retire with a reduced pension up to five years before the normal retirement age. The corresponding reduction of benefits is commonly around 6 per cent per year, but is less in a number of countries. Countries of Latin America that introduced defined contribution schemes also opted for flexible retirement, but often by fixing the minimum pension age on the basis of a minimum replacement rate or in relation to the minimum pension. For instance, in Chile early retirement is allowed when the pension is equal to at least 50 per cent of the average wage over the last few years and 110 per cent of the minimum retirement pension.

In some regions early retirement is generally allowed under specific conditions. In most countries of Central and Eastern Europe workers in hazardous or arduous conditions, and women who raise large families, are entitled to earlier retirement. In Africa workers considered prematurely aged because of disability or arduous working conditions are also entitled to early retirement. Some of the Arab states allow retirement at an early age (as early as 45) for workers with sufficient years of coverage.

Workers in developed countries, with their longer life expectancies, tend to have longer average retirement periods than workers in developing countries, though this occurs with a higher minimum retirement age. The minority covered by social security in many developing countries, however, tend to be upper-income workers with life expectancies similar to those in developed countries. When considering retirement age, life expectancies at the start of working life and at older ages, rather than at birth, are relevant for evaluating the minimum pensionable age – the minimum age at which retirement benefits can be received – as they indicate a worker's chances of reaching pensionable age and the number of years then spent in retirement.

For workers postponing retirement past the normal retirement age, defined benefit schemes typically increase their benefits. They do so because the benefits will be received later and for a shorter period. Some countries have made this adjustment sufficiently large for the increase in annual benefits with postponement of retirement to maintain the expected lifetime value of benefits when workers postpone receipt.

Minimum number of years of contributions

As an eligibility condition for the receipt of retirement benefits, social security schemes may require that the worker has been credited with a minimum number of years of contributions.[1] (Information on national requirements is shown in the statistical annex, table 5.) Defined benefit schemes usually require a minimum number of years of coverage in the scheme to receive pension benefits, with those working more years than the minimum receiving greater benefits. Workers who do not satisfy the minimum number of years of coverage often become entitled to a lump-sum payment, but there are countries, such as Japan, Morocco and the United States, where people who do not satisfy the minimum number of years are not entitled to any benefit. Some countries have a low limit on required years of contributions, with the benefits paid being proportionally reduced. In Canada there is no minimum and in Switzerland it is one year.

Some countries require a minimum number of years of contributions to receive benefits at the pensionable age, but with a lower minimum number of years to qualify to receive benefits at an older age. In Iraq, men and women can retire at any age with 30 and 25 years of contributions, respectively. Men can retire at age 60 and women at 55 with 20 years of contributions. In Jordan benefits can be received at age 46 with 15 years of contributions and at age 60 for men and 55 for women with ten years of contributions.

Defined contribution schemes usually do not have such a requirement because workers with few years of contributions simply receive smaller benefits. Nevertheless the regulations may allow for distinct modes of payment (lump-sum payment rather than annuity benefit) for people with limited benefit entitlement. Defined contribution schemes, as well as defined benefit schemes, may require a minimum number of years of contributions to qualify for a guaranteed level of minimum benefit. In Chile that requirement is 20 years.

A moderate requirement as to minimum years of contributions may encourage greater years of work among people who otherwise would not participate in paid work for long periods. However a long requirement may disadvantage people with intermittent labour force participation if they contribute to the scheme but receive no benefits in return. In particular the requirement of many years of work for receipt of a benefit is disadvantageous for women because they tend to work fewer years in the formal labour force than men. It may also encourage contribution evasion by people who know they will not be entitled to a regular benefit, even if they contribute for all their working years. Argentina requires 30 years of contributions to receive the guaranteed minimum benefit. A worker could contribute for 29 years and fail to receive the guaranteed minimum pension, but would receive a lower pension based on actual contributions.

Earnings test

Many countries with defined benefit schemes apply a retirement condition (retirement from gainful activity) or an earnings test to limit the receipt at the same time of both earnings and pensions. When there is an earnings test, workers who continue working past the minimum age for benefit receipt lose some or all of their benefits. The reduction is frequently one currency unit of benefits less for every two currency units earned above a minimum amount. The earnings test applies for increases in earnings until the worker's entire benefits have been taxed away. This is done in Japan. Generally the earnings test applies for work past the minimum retirement age. It may be less restrictive at older ages and generally ceases to apply for work past a maximum age – 65 in Canada.

The earnings test has the advantage of target efficiency. Benefits are only paid to workers or retirees with moderate or no labour earnings, reducing total benefit expense. The earnings test may distort labour market decisions, however, inducing some workers to retire who would otherwise continue working. The earnings test can be adjusted by having a high level of earnings that are exempt from it, so that it only applies to high-earning workers. Many of the countries of Central and Eastern Europe allow workers to receive their benefits and continue working, having no earnings test.

Some countries in western Europe have partial retirement programmes specifically designed to allow a mix of earnings and pension. People work part time and receive proportionally reduced benefits. This option allows workers to move gradually from full-time work to full-time retirement. Some workers may prefer a gradual transition to retirement rather than an abrupt one.

There also may be a means test to receive benefits. A means test could include all types of income rather than only earnings. A means test could be set so that most people qualify for it, in which case it could be considered to be an affluence test. It could be limited to exclude all types of income except other pension income, or limited further to include only occupational pension benefits. It could be expanded to include asset holdings. A test of asset holdings could be structured to exclude some assets, such as the value of owner-occupied housing.

BENEFIT AMOUNT

Determination of benefits in defined contribution schemes

The administrative simplicity of defined contribution schemes arises in large part because the participant's rights are defined solely in terms of the account balance. The simplest way this is done is to credit the worker's account for his or her contributions to the account, and then to credit the account with the investment earnings based on the market rate of return received on the balance in the account. Not all countries, however, use this approach. In Indonesia the investment earnings credited to the account of individual workers are not the earnings received by the provident fund but a lower rate of return fixed by the fund. Thus workers do not directly bear the risk of the investments in the provident fund and do not receive the full benefit of the investment earnings. In Malaysia workers receive a rate of return fixed by the provident fund that is changed infrequently and can be higher or lower than the rate actually received in a period.

In Chile, if the worker's pension fund earns a rate of return higher than a certain level in comparison to other pension funds, the excess amount is kept in reserve by the pension fund. Similarly, for a rate of return below a certain level in comparison to that earned by the other pension funds, the pension fund must credit the worker's account with the difference. Defined contribution schemes can to some extent smooth benefit fluctuations over time through a rate-of-return stabilization fund. Thus the worker's account generally bears the risk of market fluctuations but does not do so when those fluctuations are due to the fund's manager (rather than the market) when the monetary authorities put the rate of return outside a band determined by the rates of return earned by the other pension funds.

Notional defined contribution schemes are financed on a pay-as-you-go or partial funding basis. Each participant has an account, the same as for defined contribution schemes, but the funds in the account, if any, are less than the value of the account. Accordingly contributions are not credited with a rate of return on investments, but rather with the rate of growth of earnings or the rate of growth of GDP. To ensure the financial soundness of these schemes, it is necessary to have a link between the rate of development of the contribution base and the rate of return credited on contributions.

Benefit formulas in defined benefit schemes

In defined benefit schemes, the benefit formula determines the level of benefits the individual receives and the link between contributions and benefits. Benefit formulas might provide either flat-rate benefits which are not tied to earnings or earnings-related benefits. With flat-rate benefits, the level of benefit does not vary with the level of earnings, but may vary according to the number of years of contribution. Developing countries may find it desirable to have a scheme that provides a flat minimum benefit to all participants that increases with years of contributions. A minimal earnings-related benefit might be added for incentive effects. The minimum benefit should be sufficiently large to warrant the administrative costs of distribution. The ILO Social Security (Minimum Standards) Convention, 1952 (No. 102), indicates that the minimum benefit should provide a replacement of at least 40 per cent for middle income workers after 30 years of work. (See Technical Brief 2 and Chapter 15 for a discussion of ILO Conventions.) Few countries in Africa, Asia and Latin America have contributory schemes providing flat-rate benefits.

In the OECD countries where those schemes exist they are usually one part of the pension scheme, with social security or mandatory private earnings-related pensions as a second part. This is the case in Finland, Japan, the Netherlands[2] and the United Kingdom. Flat-rate benefits may also be non-contributory and paid to all citizens who satisfy residence requirements. Canada and Iceland have such flat-rate non-contributory benefits: a universal basic pension and an income-tested supplement.

Three important parameters of the earnings-related defined benefit formulas are length of the period used to calculate pension reference earnings, the benefit accrual rate and the penalty or reward for early or late retirement. These elements of the benefit formula interact with the worker's earnings history, years of service and age at first receipt to determine benefits (see table 3.1). Many countries base benefits on the average of earnings in the final five to ten years of the worker's career. This type of formula is commonly used in developing countries with defined benefit social insurance schemes. In this type of formula earnings are often unindexed when the averaging period is short. This type of formula has been used in Central and Eastern Europe, Africa and the Middle East. In Saudi Arabia the earnings base is the final two years of employment. In Brazil and Iraq the final three years are used. In Burundi and the Central African Republic the average over the final three or five years is used, whichever is higher. In Slovakia the base is the average of the highest five of the final ten years and in Slovenia the average over the highest ten paid consecutive years of employment is used.

The primary problem with this type of formula is that it redistributes income from those with flat (and hence, low) age-earnings profiles to those whose incomes increase with age (and who are consequently richer). It may also disadvantage workers who become sick during their final years of work and have low final earnings. Use of a short period has the further disadvantage that it may be subject to manipulation by workers and employers. Workers and employers have the incentive to collude in reporting high earnings for the worker in his or her last few years of work. In this way the worker is able to obtain relatively high benefits, but the claim is fraudulent. In Jordan some employees in the final two years before retirement have illegally arranged with their employers that they would pay the entire social security contribution (employer and employee share) in return for the employer greatly overstating their wage in reporting to the Jordanian Social Security Corporation.

A third problem with this type of benefit formula is that it provides an incentive to underreport earnings in all years that earnings do not affect benefits. The underreporting of earnings causes a financing problem for social security because it causes an underpayment of social security contributions.

The problem of overstating wages and, to a lesser extent, the problem of regressivity due to upward growth in wages during the career for higher-income workers, have been reduced in Jordan by a regulation that does not allow workers to claim a final wage that has increased or decreased more than 40 per cent during the final five years of earnings. Exceptions are granted to workers in labour unions or in the government where wages may grow by more than 40 per cent if the growth is due to an increase that applies for a group of workers. Egypt has a similar rule.

Many countries, especially in the OECD, have changed their benefit formulas to increase the number of years in the earnings base. As the averaging period is lengthened, the benefit formula approaches a career average benefit formula. In this type of formula, social security benefits are based on a worker's entire career and are not unduly affected by the worker's final earnings. Past earnings may be indexed to prices or to the growth of earnings in the economy to reflect an increase in the average standard of living during the worker's career. If not indexed, earnings when young would have little effect on benefits paid at retirement because inflation over a 30- or 40-year period greatly erodes their real value. This type of benefit formula, which is used in Japan and the United Kingdom, requires good record-keeping because the records are needed for monthly earnings received over 30 or more years. In order to reduce errors, it may be advisable to inform participants periodically of their earnings records as maintained by the social security institution, so that participants have the opportunity to correct errors.

Many countries with defined benefit schemes that use career average benefit formulas provide "drop-out" years. While most years of the worker's career are used in computing career average earnings, a few low-income years can be dropped. The drop-out years are an insurance feature against the effect of temporary low earnings, perhaps due to unemployment in some years. However, if a worker knows a particular year of work will be a drop-out year, he or she has no incentive to contribute to social security that year. Schemes with many drop-out years tend to have a problem with contribution evasion.

Earnings-related benefit formulas are also characterized by the benefit accrual rate. Generally a fixed benefit accrual rate applies to all contribution years (up to a maximum) and at all levels of earnings (up to the contributory ceiling), but the rate of benefit accrual may vary according to the number of credited years, months or even days (as in Morocco). In some countries years additional to the minimum number of years required for entitlement to a pension are credited at a reduced rate. Countries need to determine what is required of workers to receive credit for a given period.

Many countries with defined benefit schemes provide benefit credits for non-work periods – disability, unemployment, pregnancy, child rearing and education – to guarantee an adequate pension benefit for people with limited contribution records. These features can also be incorporated in defined contribution schemes by the government subsidizing contributions during those periods, but in practice that has not been done. Providing credits for many forms of activity outside the labour force moves a social security scheme away from being employment-based and towards being a universal system covering all residents.

Social security retirement benefit formulas are often based on worker earnings but never on income from other sources. While they are generally designed to replace earnings from work, it is presumed that there is no need to replace income from other sources. The formulas typically increase benefits for retirement postponed beyond the earliest age at which benefits can be received. The extent of the adjustment may affect the age at which workers retire, as discussed in Chapter 18, on influencing the retirement age.

Minimum pension

A minimum benefit is usually provided for workers who satisfy the entitlement conditions but whose benefits would otherwise fall short of an acceptable living standard. The minimum benefit can be a guaranteed benefit to qualifying workers in defined contribution schemes, as in Chile. In that case, the minimum benefit is financed by the balance in the worker's account plus a subsidy by the government sufficient to raise the benefit to the minimum level. The minimum benefit can also be a feature of the structure of defined benefit earnings-related schemes.

The level of the minimum benefit in OECD countries is usually based on societal standards of a minimally adequate level of income. Thus the minimum benefit should be determined relative to the subsistence level of living. In many countries data to determine the expenditures required to achieve a subsistence level of living have not been gathered and the subsistence standard established is based on an informal survey of the purchase prices of food and housing.

If the minimum benefit is the only benefit for which people with low incomes qualify, it should represent at least a subsistence level of income, taking into account other sources of income. If other poverty benefits are available, they should be taken into account. In developing countries, however, with limited resources and large populations of poor people, more limited goals must be set. A high minimum benefit provides relatively generous treatment of low-wage workers. However it provides low-wage workers with an incentive not to report and pay contributions on all their earnings because they receive the minimum benefit whether or not they accurately report all their earnings. In Norway the minimum and maximum benefits have converged over time (see box 3.1).

In countries where social security coverage is not universal or where social security contribution evasion is widespread, the problem of determination of standards for eligibility for the minimum benefit can be complex. Workers may work most of their lives outside the social security scheme and only work the amount within the system that is sufficient for qualifying for the minimum benefit.

The minimum benefit is not typically related to the worker's earnings but may increase with years of work. Having the benefit increase with years of work provides an incentive for work and turns the minimum benefit into a minimum band of benefits. In Ireland the minimum benefit also increases with the average number of weeks worked per year.

Hybrid benefit formulas

While most types of pension schemes can be conveniently categorized as defined benefit or defined contribution, some contain features of both types. The French industry-wide mandatory schemes have been characterized as pay-as-you-go defined contribution schemes. The Swedish notional account scheme, while

Box 3.1 Convergence of social security old-age benefits in Norway

The social security National Insurance Scheme (IS) in Norway was established in 1967 and replaced a flat benefit for retirement and invalidity pensioners. An important aspect of the IS was to provide all old and disabled with both a minimum benefit and a supplementary benefit related to the retiree's previous labour market earnings. The ratio between the maximum and minimum benefit (before taxes) was originally 4,2. Over time, however, that ratio has fallen, so that in 1997 the ratio was 2,4. Thus the Norwegian pension scheme is approaching a situation where again all pensioners will receive an almost equal benefit.

Social security pension benefits under the National Insurance Scheme

The minimum benefit. Both the minimum and maximum benefits in Norway (table 3.2) have two parts. Single pensioners and pensioners supporting their spouse receive a basic pension of 1 basic pension unit (BPU), while other pensioners receive 0.75 basic pension units. In 1998 a basic pension unit was approximately one-sixth of average earnings. Pensioners also receive a supplementary benefit that is based on previous labour market earnings. If the supplementary benefit is less than a benefit called the special supplement, the special supplement is received. The special supplement was introduced in 1969 as compensation for the introduction of a value added tax (VAT) in that year. From 1 May 1998 the special supplement is expected to be 0.85 basic pension units for single pensioners. It is higher for pensioners who are supporting children or a spouse. The basic pension plus the special supplement constitute the minimum benefit.

The maximum benefit. The maximum benefit is the sum of the basic benefit plus the maximum supplementary benefit. Originally the maximum earnings used in calculating the supplementary benefit were equal to 8 basic pension units. In 1971 this was raised to 12 basic pension units, with income between 8 and 12 basic pension units affecting benefits at a reduced rate.

Table 3.2 **Minimum and maximum pension benefits in Norway, 1967–97 (amounts in kroner deflated by the expected wage level in 1998)**

Year	Basic pension unit	Minimum benefit	Maximum benefit	Max./Min.
1967	56	56	233	4.2
1971	55	62	261	4.2
1976	48	59	227	3.8
1981	49	72	232	3.2
1991	45	72	215	3.0
1992	45	72	177	2.5
1997	43	71	171	2.4

Note: These are the pension benefits a 17-year-old can expect to receive under current parameters.

Source: Calculations by the author and the ILO using figures from Norwegian social security legislation.

Changeover time in the minimum and maximum benefit
The basic pension unit has fallen in real value over time, which would normally cause both the minimum and maximum benefits to decline in real value. The real value of the minimum benefit has grown over time, however, owing to the increase in the real value of the special supplement. The special supplement has increased in real value nearly every year.

Since 1971 the maximum benefit has declined in real value owing to the decline in the real value of the basic pension unit. During the 1970s several of the premises underlying the level of benefits changed. The total fertility rate fell from 2.8 in the late 1960s to 1.7 a decade later. Life expectancy, rather than stabilizing, continued to increase. These changes led to a reduction in the number of workers relative to the number of pensioners. A fall in the average retirement age also contributed to that reduction. In addition to the general decline in the maximum benefit since 1971, and because of the budgetary pressures these demographic changes caused, the formula for calculating the maximum benefit was changed in 1992, reducing the maximum benefit by 16 per cent. With increasing budgetary pressures, the retirement benefits in Norway have increasingly focused on providing adequate benefits for low-income workers, with a decreased emphasis on providing an adequate replacement rate for higher-income workers.

usually characterized as a defined contribution scheme, can also be considered to be a pay-as-you-go career-average defined benefit scheme. Cash balance schemes, popular among large US employers, are funded schemes that determine benefits similarly to notional account schemes but are regulated as defined benefit schemes under US pension law. These three types of schemes are discussed more fully in boxes 3.2, 3.3 and 3.4.

FORM IN WHICH BENEFITS ARE RECEIVED

Social security retirement benefits can be received as single payment lump sums, as annuities or pensions (paying periodic benefits to death) or from a defined contribution account as periodic phased withdrawals. With defined benefit schemes, retirees who satisfy the qualifying conditions usually become entitled to a lifetime benefit. The practice of lump-sum payments, either partial or full single payment of the account balance, is common in the Anglophone countries of Africa, such as Kenya and Uganda, and in some Asian countries where provident funds are used, such as Indonesia and Malaysia. It was once common in the former British colonies in the Caribbean but now no Caribbean islands have provident funds. Jamaica, however, provides part of its retirement benefit as a lump-sum payment. Ghana permits this as an option for 25 per cent of the benefit. Countries such as Chile, which introduced mandatory privately managed defined contribution schemes, do not normally allow for the full payment of retirement benefits as lump-sum payments. However, they provide

Box 3.2 Virtual defined contribution schemes: The example of France
Employees in the private sector in France are all covered by national supplementary pensions, ARRCO and AGIRC.[3] AGIRC was established in 1947 for managerial staff and ARRCO in 1962 for all other employees. These schemes provide a good example of what is now labelled "virtual" or "notional" defined contribution schemes.

These schemes are operated on a pay-as-you-go basis, but in a different way than traditional defined benefit schemes. They do not have a fixed target in terms of benefits. They set up a system of contribution which enables members to build up credits. When the pension is calculated, these credits are assigned a value based on the scheme's financial resources, which depend upon the flow of contributions collected. The total amount of contributions calculated under the scheme's rules is distributed to the beneficiaries in proportion to the credits they have acquired. Whereas in defined benefit pay-as-you-go schemes the amount of benefits to be paid determines the level of contributions, in these schemes the amount of contributions to be apportioned determines the level of benefits.

The contribution scheme of ARRCO and AGIRC consists of taking a given percentage of gross earnings. Contributions are then turned into value units called "pension points", which are entered into individual accounts. The number of points accrued during the year is calculated by dividing the amount of contributions by the point's purchase price for the year. Points accumulate in the member's account, irrespective of the company he or she is working for. At retirement, the annual pension is determined by the number of points in the account. It equals the total of points accrued multiplied by the value of the point when the pension is calculated. Subsequently the pension is adjusted according to the point's value.

In this financing method, managing the scheme's financial equilibrium means achieving equality each year between the available resources and the outlays or between annual contributions minus administrative costs and annual benefits. This is achieved by the administrators of the scheme through fixing the purchase price of the point and the point's value. On the whole the sums to be distributed are equal to the total of contributions collected, and this total is proportional to the total earnings on which these contributions are levied. Thus the level of benefits paid is directly linked to economic activity as reflected in changes in total salaries and wages in the private sector. (This can be contrasted to funded defined contribution schemes where the level of benefits depends on the changes in investment returns.)

The two basic parameters used to maintain a balance between benefits and contributions – the purchase price of the point and the point's value – are determined through negotiation between employers' and employees' representatives. ARRCO and AGIRC were set up through national collective agreements and are run by the main national employers' organizations and the trade union confederations. Since the late 1970s and the early 1980s, to adapt to socioeconomic and demographic shifts, the administrators of the schemes have implemented a policy of gradual reduction of the schemes' "yield", that is, a reduction of the ratio between the value of the point in a given year and its purchase price. This implies a trade-off between the interests involved:

those of contributors (for example, members and employers) and those of pensioners. Increases in the point's value have been less favourable than in the previous period, but increases in the point's purchase price have been higher than the rise in members' average earnings.

To limit the consequences of the reduction in yield on the benefit level, a third parameter has been introduced, the contribution collection rate or "call-up rate". It enables contributions to be collected, or called up, at a higher rate than the contractual contribution rate without interfering in the mechanism for accruing pension points. An extra contribution which does not build up pension credits is paid to support the rise of the point's value and ensure the scheme's financial equilibrium.

The ability to constantly adjust the parameters of the scheme is a major feature of ARRCO and AGIRC. It can be contrasted to the situation that prevails in traditional defined benefit pay-as-you-go schemes. Whereas the former involves a flexible method of adaptation in which overall contributions and benefit levels are determined regularly and concomitantly with a view to maintaining the scheme's financial equilibrium, the latter involves a much more abrupt method of adaptation: when the level of contribution cannot be raised further, the benefit calculation formula has to be modified, thereby calling into question the original commitment and establishing the terms of a new one. On the other hand, in virtual defined contribution schemes like ARRCO and AGIRC, the amount of the pension to be received is not known in advance. Furthermore their mode of adaptation totally depends on collective bargaining procedures and, thus, on the capacity of employers' organizations and trade union confederations to negotiate on pension issues and to reach an agreement.

Concerning benefits, the way in which credits accrue is similar to that used by defined benefit schemes in which the pension is based on the average salary earned during the full working life. Since the contributions are proportional to earnings, the pension replicates movements in earnings over the member's entire career, rather than the level of earnings at the career's end.

Another important feature of these schemes is that they pay full benefits from the moment they are first set up. The first pensioners will receive a full pension without paying the corresponding amount of contributions. The fact that pay-as-you-go financing allows benefits to be paid immediately to individuals who have never made contributions is a major characteristic of this method of financing. Defined benefit pay-as-you-go schemes seldom systematically take into account periods of employment prior to the setting up of the scheme. In defined contribution schemes like ARRCO and AGIRC the inclusion of past period is more than a possibility, it is a technical necessity, given the way these schemes are financed. To the extent that the total amount of contributions is what determines the level of benefits, as soon as the contribution scheme is in place, the benefits corresponding to a full career must be paid. If the scheme fails to distribute available funds, it departs from the pay-as-you-go model: it either accumulates reserves to pay future benefits or uses the funds for purposes other than to finance the pensions of its members.

Box 3.3 The Swedish pension scheme

Social security covers all Swedish residents. It was established in 1913, when a flat-rate benefit was introduced to ensure income security in old age. A supplementary retirement pension was introduced in 1960 to provide earnings-related benefits for all workers.[4] A further pension reform occurred in Sweden in the late 1990s. This box describes the pension scheme before the reform and outlines the new scheme.

The pre-reform pension scheme

Benefits. The pre-reform social security scheme is a defined benefit scheme consisting of two parts: a flat-rate benefit paid to all residents independently of previous labour market experience, and a supplementary retirement pension which is an earnings-related benefit paid to individuals with at least three years of labour market experience.

The flat-rate benefit provides basic support during retirement. It is approximately 20 per cent of the average wage for an unskilled blue-collar worker. The supplementary retirement pension benefit builds on the principle of replacement of loss of income. The benefit is based on an individual's 15 years of highest earnings and 30 years of labour force participation is required for a full pension. For retirees the supplementary retirement pension replaces 60 per cent of income up to a ceiling (15 per cent of working men and 2 per cent of working women have incomes above the ceiling). For less than 20 years of work the pension is reduced proportionately. For individuals with no or low supplementary retirement pension an additional benefit, the pension supplement, is about 50 per cent of the flat-rate benefit. Benefits, as well as wages on which pension rights are computed, are indexed for inflation in consumer prices. Benefits are taxed as regular income, although there is an extra deduction for individuals with low pension income.

The normal retirement age is 65; withdrawal of benefits can be postponed until age 70 or withdrawn early from age 60 with an actuarial reduction. Partial retirement is a separate mode of retirement. It allows workers to reduce the number of hours worked and receive pension benefits in place of lost earnings.

In addition to social security, most working individuals are covered by negotiated pensions, based on collective bargaining contracts between employers and employees.[5] Separately from the social security scheme there is also a means-tested supplementary housing allowance provided by municipalities.

Survivor benefits within the social security scheme cover spouses and children. The benefit is paid to spouses for 12 months, after which they are expected to support themselves through work, or they will receive benefits from their own retirement scheme. Children are covered until the age of 18 (age 20 if in school).[6]

Financing. The flat-rate benefit and supplementary retirement pension benefits are financed through payroll taxes levied on the employer. The contribution rate for the flat-rate benefit is 5.68 per cent and, for the supplementary retirement pension benefits, 13 per cent. The financing for the flat-rate benefit is supplemented from general tax revenues. Although pension rights are earned only up to a ceiling, the payroll tax is levied on the full income.

The supplementary retirement pension scheme is partially funded. When it was established, contributions were set higher than needed to cover benefits. The purpose of this was twofold: first, to act as a buffer against shifts in the contribution rate and, second, to offset the decrease in private saving expected to follow the introduction of the scheme. The surplus is funded by the National Pension Funds. The balance in these funds is about 40 per cent of GDP, equivalent to approximately five times the annual supplementary retirement pension payments. Most of the funds are invested in low-risk assets, mainly government and housing bonds. Beginning in 1974, the National Pension Funds were allowed to invest in equities and new funds were established for this purpose. These funds are mainly invested in domestic equities, and foreign investments cannot exceed 10 per cent of the assets.

The pension reform
At the time of writing the pension reform was scheduled to go into effect in 1999, with the first benefit payments in 2001. The reform was motivated by the ageing of the population and the sensitivity of the previous system to economic growth.

The new pension scheme
The objective for policy makers was to design a pension scheme that is fiscally sustainable, linked to economic growth and has a clear link between contributions and benefits. The new scheme will continue to be public and mandatory. It will be pay-as-you-go with a funded component.[7] The new scheme will have two components: the guaranteed pension and the income pension.

The guaranteed pension. The current flat-rate benefit will be replaced by a guaranteed pension. It will continue to be a flat-rate benefit providing basic income security. In contrast to the current flat-rate benefit, it will be means-tested and offset by other pension income. The guaranteed pension is payable from age 65. As in the current scheme, the guaranteed pension is indexed to consumer prices. It will be financed from general tax revenues.

The income pension. In order to create a close link between contributions and benefits, the earnings-related pension replacing the supplementary retirement pension benefit will be a defined contribution benefit. Contributions will be 18.5 per cent of earnings and levied equally on the employee and employer.[8] The scheme will continue to be financed mostly on a pay-as-you-go basis but with a funded component. Two accounts will be established for each worker.

In the pay-as-you-go-component, 16 per cent of annual earnings will be credited to a notional account.[9] The earned pension rights are indexed to wages, hence the rate of return on the accounts is the real wage growth. The retirement age is flexible and an individual can choose to retire any time after age 61. At retirement the account is converted to an annuity by dividing the balance by a "division number", which is based on average life expectancy at the retirement age for the given cohort, which means that benefits are indexed to follow life expectancy. The pension benefit will be determined by lifetime earnings, instead of depending on the 15 years of highest earnings. The indexation of pension benefits will be tied to economic growth.

In the funded component, 2.5 per cent of earnings will be paid into a personal defined contribution account. The individual can choose how the funds in this account are invested, but there will be a default option managed by the government if no choice is made. At any time after age 61, the worker can convert the account balance to an annuity with a survivor option.

Transition

The transition will be gradual. Starting with the cohorts born in 1938, every cohort until those born in 1953 will participate both in the old and the new scheme, with the share from the new scheme gradually increasing. Cohorts born in 1954 will only participate in the new scheme. The transition period is long, life tables suggest that there will still be people in the year 2040 who will receive pension benefits from the old scheme.

To summarize, the reform addresses problems of the current retirement pension scheme while keeping it mostly a pay-as-you-go scheme. The new scheme will be closely tied to economic growth, robust to demographic changes and will closely link contributions and benefits.

an alternative to the annuitization of benefits. It takes the form of phased withdrawals where benefits from the individual's account are gradually withdrawn during the remainder of his or her expected lifetime.

Private annuity markets and the provision of benefits from individual accounts

A number of arguments favour social security schemes providing retirement benefits as mandatory annuities or pensions, rather than as voluntary annuities, phased withdrawals or lump-sum payments. First, there is a moral hazard problem which is that, in the absence of mandatory annuities, some people will not manage their money wisely, will ultimately become destitute and will need public anti-poverty benefits. A related problem is that some individuals will underestimate their life expectancy or will be shortsighted in their financial planning during retirement and will spend their assets too quickly, again ultimately relying on public benefits. A mandatory annuity avoids these problems.

A second problem a mandatory annuity solves is adverse selection. Adverse selection arises because individuals who know they have higher than average mortality risk avoid buying annuities because they do not expect to live sufficiently long to recoup the cost of the purchase. If it is impossible for insurance companies to sell low-priced annuities to individuals with low life expectancy, and these individuals otherwise generally avoid the purchase of annuities, insurance companies will raise the price of annuities, realizing that their market is only people with longer than average life expectancy. Increasing the price of annuities limits further the number of people for whom annuities are attractive.

Box 3.4 Cash balance schemes

Although the last decade has witnessed a general decline in the number of defined benefit pension schemes in the United States, a new scheme has emerged to partially offset this trend. Since its inception in 1985, the cash balance scheme has been adopted by more than a hundred major employers with more than a million total employees. This type of scheme provides a defined benefit alternative that may be appealing to people attracted by defined contribution schemes.

The cash balance scheme is a defined benefit scheme that appeals to both employers and employees in many respects because of its perceived similarity to a defined contribution scheme. Thus, while the underlying vesting, accrual and participation rules apply to these schemes, as they would to a traditional defined benefit scheme in the United States, cash balance schemes are often presented to employees as being similar to individual account defined contribution schemes, where each participant's benefit is expressed in terms of an account balance that increases annually with employee contributions and earnings.

Although variations abound, the most popular design for a cash balance scheme is one that mimics a typical profit-sharing scheme. In this type of scheme a hypothetical account balance exists in the name of each participant in the scheme. Hypothetical "contributions" in the form of pay credits and hypothetical "earnings" in the form of interest credits are added to this. For example, each participant's account might receive an annual credit of 5 per cent of pay, and the account would grow at a guaranteed interest rate, which might be either a specified flat rate of interest such as 4 per cent, or a rate that matches an outside variable index, such as the yield on one-year US Treasury bills. The account balance is the benefit promised to the participant upon retirement. Statements are periodically sent to participants, charting the account's growth in contributions and earnings. Under most cash balance schemes, the participant is entitled to receive this account balance, with all pay and interest credits to date, as a lump sum upon retirement. Owing to US rules governing defined benefit schemes, participants in all cash balance schemes are also entitled to receive the actuarial equivalent of the account balance as an annuity.

From an employer's perspective, however, these accounts (which exist only on paper, although they denote the benefits guaranteed to participants) are mere record keeping and employee communication mechanisms that do not necessarily reflect the underlying operation of the scheme. For instance, although the scheme might specify certain pay credits and guarantee interest at a predetermined rate, what the employer actually contributes to the scheme will depend on the funding methodology followed, including actuarial assumptions with respect to interest, workers' job turnover and mortality.

Another hallmark of cash balance scheme design is that all participants earning the same compensation are treated equally; that is, they receive the same pay credits, regardless of age or service. This contrasts with a traditional defined benefit scheme, such as a final average pay scheme, which generally favours older, long-service employees. Where complete neutrality with respect to contributions is not considered appropriate, however, employers may weight the cash balance allocations to reflect another factor such as participant age or years of service, or both. Cash balance schemes may also be integrated so that the benefits paid take into account the employer's contributions towards social security, on behalf of the participant.

From an employee's perspective, cash balance schemes are easy to understand, and thus are often better appreciated than traditional pension schemes, whose benefits are expressed in terms of complicated formulas involving percentages of compensation and number of years worked, payable at a distant point in time. This appreciation is reinforced by the periodic statements sent to participants, emphasizing the increase in benefits and earnings in the individual's account balance. The ability to receive the account balance as a lump sum, or to convert it to an annuity benefit, is another element viewed favourably by many employees.

While the cash balance scheme is attractive to many employees in comparison to a traditional defined benefit scheme, many employers also find these schemes more appealing than defined contribution schemes. For instance, funding a defined contribution scheme, such as a money purchase pension scheme, requires an employer to contribute a set percentage of contribution every year. Because a cash balance scheme is funded as a defined benefit scheme however, the employer has some flexibility with respect to scheme contributions and may vary these amounts yearly, provided that statutory minimum and maximum funding constraints are satisfied. In addition, many cash balance schemes yield a favourable investment differential; where the scheme's long-term investment experience exceeds the rate of interest promised under the scheme, the employer may achieve significant savings in the cost of the scheme, compared to a traditional defined contribution scheme. The opposite could also be true: if investment experience falls short of the guaranteed earnings, the employer, as in any defined benefit scheme must assume the investment risk of paying the promised benefit.

Adverse selection causes the price of annuities to be higher than it would be if all retirees were required to purchase an annuity.

A third problem, which is a general problem when insurance and financial products are marketed to individuals, is marketing costs. This includes advertising and commissions for brokers and agents. They may be largely socially wasteful expenditures. Waste occurs when little useful information and few services are provided. Instead, corporate or product images, such as images of security, are created that may distract and confuse individuals into making poor choices and are used to attract them away from competitors. These problems can be limited by the regulation of advertising and sales practices, but are absent when government provides mandatory annuities.

A fourth problem for individual annuity markets relates to a lack of financial security for individuals. Insurance companies in most countries have a good record of financial solvency. Nevertheless they face a risk of bankruptcy and are generally not as secure a provider of benefits as the government. This problem can be alleviated through mandatory insurance protection of insurance companies.

Types of individual annuities

When an unfunded social security defined benefit scheme provides retirement benefits, it is difficult to use the private annuity market to pay the benefits because workers do not have access to a lump-sum amount with which to purchase an annuity. When funded defined contribution schemes are used to finance social security retirement benefits, however, the private annuity market often provides benefits once the worker reaches retirement. Annuity markets are typically better developed in OECD countries than in other countries. Issues concerning annuity markets in developing countries are discussed in box 3.5.

In the private market, individual annuities can be purchased with a single payment. Alternatively the workers may make premium payments or contributions over a period of time, as is typical of social security retirement benefits contributions.

Annuities with different payout features differ in the amount of risk workers bear. The simplest option is the fixed non-participating annuity, where a monthly fixed payment is guaranteed until the death of the recipient. This type of annuity subjects the worker to interest rate risk: the lower the interest rate when the worker retires, the lower the monthly benefits the worker receives. However all losses from adverse investment experience during retirement, longer than expected lifetimes, or from higher than expected expenses, are borne by the insurance company. Similarly all positive experiences with respect to rates of return or costs accrue to the company and presumably eventually to its shareholders. Because mortality trend risks are not easily diversified, insurance companies tend to price non-participating annuities conservatively, meaning that they tend to charge a relatively high price (provide low benefits relative to the account balance) to ensure that they cover their costs.

In contrast, participating fixed annuities offer a level guaranteed minimum benefit but supplement this with dividends paid to the beneficiary that depend on the investment and cost experience of the insurance company. Because of a lower guarantee, they have a lessened need to maintain large contingency reserves to cover various risks and the insurer is able to offer higher payouts on average than if it issued non-participating contracts. Another option, variable annuities, also fluctuates with the value of the underlying assets but lacks the feature of a guaranteed minimum benefit.

Annuities may also make standard or graded payments. The standard method is designed to pay a constant or slightly increasing amount during the lifetime of the annuitant. The graded method starts at a lower level than under the standard method but increases significantly from year to year when the rate of return on investments exceeds a minimum level. This option enables

> **Box 3.5 Annuities in developing countries**
>
> The provision of annuities through life insurance companies is well-developed in OECD countries but is subject to particular difficulties in most of the rest of the world. First, the survival in their existing form of the insurance companies themselves may be uncertain in a country where the climate of opinion, which once may have favoured national ownership of such institutions, has changed in recent years towards privatization. Even when this is not overtly an issue, governments generally wish to exercise close control over their countries' major financial institutions, which often leads to severe constraints on the freedom of funds to manage their investments efficiently.
>
> Second, the basis of an annuity fund depends on the pooling of the risk of longevity. The fund from which pensions are paid may run out while the beneficiaries are still alive to draw their entitlements. If the numbers of members are small, or the statistical data used to evaluate the risk are unreliable, the insurance company may be unable to provide a satisfactory level of guarantee that it will meet its commitments in the long term. This problem may be exacerbated if the national system for supervising the operations of the insurance companies is weak, as is often the case in developing countries.
>
> Third, because of the long-term nature of an annuity fund, it is important that the money in the fund be invested safely and effectively. This can present considerable difficulties even in countries with long-established insurance companies run on modern lines (such as Zimbabwe), as many countries have experienced unstable economic conditions, particularly in financial markets.

annuitants to receive during their lifetime a stream of increasing payments that roughly matches inflation, particularly if the inflation rate is fairly steady.

Insurance companies also offer annuity payout options that provide survivors with benefits. A joint-and-survivor annuity pays benefits until the death of both the participant and the spouse. The death of either the participant or the spouse may affect the level of the benefits paid to the surviving person. There are different varieties of these two-life annuities, such as a full benefit to the survivor, where income does not change at the death of the first person, or a half or two-thirds benefit to the surviving person. Survivors' benefits are discussed more fully in Chapter 4. Another possible feature is a guaranteed payment period, such as ten or 20 years, so that, if the annuitant dies before the end of the period, payouts continue to named beneficiaries for the remainder of the period.

Periodic or phased withdrawals

Periodic withdrawals are an alternative to benefit payments through an annuity. The retiree withdraws from his or her account an amount each month that is determined so that the amount remaining in the account is sufficient to provide benefits for the remaining life expectancy. There are many possible paths of periodic withdrawals from a defined contribution scheme. Under the recalculation method, the actual age-appropriate life expectancy is used each year to recalculate the value of the periodic withdrawals. With each year of survival, the person's expected age at death increases because he or she has survived the mortality risks of another year. Thus the recalculated benefit is reduced to reflect the higher expected age at death.

The recalculation period method works poorly when death occurs unexpectedly early or late. If the participant or the spouse dies early in the retirement period, payments to the survivor increase considerably, providing benefits that are relatively too generous in comparison to the payments received while both were alive. If the participant or spouse dies later than expected, the benefit level is gradually reduced.

To the extent that investment returns on the assets in the individual account keep pace with inflation, it is possible to provide some protection against inflation through a phased withdrawal. With a phased withdrawal and revaluation based on a modest but constant real interest rate, real benefits will increase for a few years. Eventually, however, the decline in benefits caused by the increasing expected age at death outweighs the growth in benefits caused by real investment earnings, and benefits decline in real value.

Costs of annuities

The transactions costs in annuity markets can be sizeable, even in well-developed annuity markets. During the period 1941 to 1984, for the typical retiree purchasing a single premium (single contribution) annuity with payouts starting immediately, US commercial insurance companies charged on average 22 per cent of premiums to cover marketing costs, corporate overheads, income taxes, additions to company contingency reserves, profits and the cost of adverse selection (Warshawsky, 1988). This compares with total administrative costs (including contribution collection costs) of 1 per cent of contributions for the US social security scheme. The costs varied significantly over time, rising when interest rates were high or rising and falling when interest rates were low or stable. The explanation for this pattern may be that when interest rates are relatively high insurance companies are unwilling to price annuities, which have long durations, assuming that interest rates will remain elevated.

Most countries that provide mandatory defined contribution schemes do not make choice of an annuity mandatory. The cost of adverse selection that occurs when annuity choice is not mandatory is the increase in price (compared to an annuity that was mandatory) that results from only relatively long-lived workers purchasing annuities. The cost of adverse selection in US annuity markets during the period 1941 to 1984 was 13 per cent of the contributions (ibid.). This indicates that there is a large difference between the mortality experience of the general population and annuity purchasers and that the difference imposes a significant cost on individual annuities.

A more recent study of US annuity markets has found a substantial dispersion of annuity prices: some companies offer good deals while other companies offer poor value (Mitchell et al., 1998). For 65-year old men, an 8 per cent difference exists between the lowest quartile of benefits by cost and the third quartile.

In Chile insurance companies converting defined contributions account balances to annuities charge fees of 3.5 to 4 per cent of the amount invested (Diamond and Valdes-Prieto, 1994). No study in Chile has been done, comparable to the studies for the United States, to determine by how much the level of annuity benefits is reduced as a result of adverse selection. The annuity markets in developing countries are subject to a lack of transparency and represent a considerable cost for countries wishing to establish defined contribution schemes.

Cost-of-living adjustments

As well as insuring against the risk of outliving one's resources, defined benefit social security schemes in OECD countries often provide insurance against inflation risk during retirement. This is not often provided in developing countries. This risk is insured against by the social security scheme providing indexed benefits. Benefits can be either indexed to changes in consumer prices (as is done in the United Kingdom) or wage indexed, or the indexing can be a combination of wage and price indexing, as in Japan and Switzerland.[10] If benefits are wage indexed, they can be indexed to gross wages, as was done in Germany until recently, or to net (after tax) wages, as done currently in Germany. Net wages grow more slowly than gross wages during periods when mandatory social security contributions are increasing. The Netherlands indexes its flat benefit against changes in the net minimum wage. Indexing benefits for changes in consumer prices (inflation) allows pensioners to maintain the purchasing power of their pension benefits as it was at the time of retirement. Indexing benefits for changes in wages allows pensioners to share in improvements (or decline) in labour productivity.

Indexing can be automatic or can be done irregularly. In some countries in Central and Eastern Europe retirement benefits are raised irregularly in line with increases in the minimum wage. Automatic indexing, tied to wages or prices, is preferable because it reduces the uncertainty that workers face and reduces the political aspect of benefit increases. The period of time between indexing adjustments should depend on the inflation rate. When inflation is low, adjusting benefits annually for inflation is sufficient. When it is high, more frequent adjustment is needed because of the erosion in the real value of benefits that occurs between adjustments.

In countries experiencing real wage growth, wage indexing results in more generous benefits than does price indexing. Thus a move from wage indexing to price indexing is a way of reducing benefits. In Poland pensioners have contended that benefits should be wage indexed. They argue that, because they bore the hardships of economic life under the communist regime during the Soviet era, they should be rewarded by being able to share in the benefits of economic transition to a market economy. The burden of paying for pensions, however, may foreclose increased spending on other social programmes, such as the health care scheme, that also affect their living standards. Tying benefits to wages also suffers from the problem that average wages may rise in downturns as low-wage workers are laid off, and fall in upturns as they are hired.

Some countries in Central and Eastern Europe have only indexed the minimum benefit. This type of indexing is less expensive to provide than indexing of all benefits. When inflation is high, this indexing has the effect of ending the earnings-related benefit. Inflation erodes all higher benefits so that, after a few years of retirement, depending on how high inflation is, all retirees receive the minimum benefit.

While indexing benefits is a common feature in defined benefit social security schemes (at least for developed countries), it is uncommon in defined contribution schemes. In defined contribution schemes, indexing benefits cannot be guaranteed unless the government provides indexed bonds in which the pension funds can invest. Lacking indexed bonds, where a real rate of return is guaranteed and the principal is adjusted for changes in the price level, it is impossible for a private sector institution to guarantee the payment of the promised indexed benefit. The Chilean government does provide indexed bonds, but most other countries do not. This situation could be remedied by other countries providing indexed bonds that could be used to provide pension benefit indexing.

Indexation of pensions in payment may affect the decisions that workers make about when to retire. For a given level of contributions, pension schemes may provide either a relatively high initial pension which is poorly indexed or a more modest initial pension which is well indexed. There is a strong tendency in Asian countries, as in most parts of the developing world, not to provide adequate indexation. This means that the initial pension may be misleadingly high and that workers who think that they can afford to retire at a relatively early age will find out later they were wrong. Their problems tend to be compounded by the fact that as they get older they are no longer likely to have any earnings to supplement their pension, their savings are likely to have been eroded or even exhausted, and their greater dependence and, possibly, ill health may require higher expenditure on personal and health services. Offering poorly indexed pensions may mislead ignorant and shortsighted workers. However lack of indexation is a secondary problem in some African countries where, owing to bad financing policies, it is difficult even to meet existing pension obligations.

What constitutes adequate indexation? Opinions on this question differ. Some think that it is enough to adjust pensions in line with the consumer price index, thereby ensuring – at least in principle – that pensions maintain

Table 3.3   Fall in the relative value of pensions with indexation to prices only

Period since retirement	Pension as a proportion of average earnings if real earnings increase at:		
Years	0% p.a. (per cent)	2% p.a. (per cent)	4% p.a. (per cent)
0	50	50	50
10	50	41	34
20	50	34	23
30	50	28	15

Note: p.a. = per year.

Source: Author's calculations.

their real value. Others point out that people's well-being depends not just on their absolute real income, but on their income in relation to what is normal in the society in which they live. This distinction is particularly relevant in countries where living standards are rising rapidly. In that case, wage indexing may be desirable.

Table 3.3 shows how the relative value of a pension, as a proportion of average earnings, falls if it is indexed in line with consumer prices only. The pension was set equal to 50 per cent of average earnings at the time of retirement. For rapidly emerging economies, the relevant figures are to be found in the last column which shows what happens if real earnings are rising at an annual rate of 4 per cent. For most OECD countries, on the other hand, the average has been closer to 2 per cent. After 20 years in retirement, the relative value of the pension is less than half of its initial level; for the minority of pensioners who survive for 30 years or more, it is well under a third. In virtually all societies an income of 15 per cent of average earnings is regarded as well below the poverty level, yet this can result if an initially good pension is indexed in line with prices only.

A consequence of indexing to prices only is that older pensioners will have much lower pensions than those who have recently retired, even if they have as many years in covered employment and worked in similar jobs. Women will be affected more than men, as they tend on average to have substantially longer life expectancy at retirement (especially where they have a lower pension age). The effect on invalidity pensioners may be catastrophic, as in some cases they may draw a pension for over 40 years.

In deciding on the appropriate system of indexation, adequacy is not the only criterion. Financial affordability must also be considered. For example, tying pensions to consumer prices can expose a pension scheme to financial imbalance if during a recession earnings rise more slowly than prices. The reason is that the scheme's revenue will rise only in line with the earnings on which contributions are levied (or even more slowly, if employment declines). If, instead, pensions are adjusted in line with earnings, pensioners will share in real growth, but they will also share in any general decline in living standards. In reality, even if pensions are normally indexed to prices, pensioners will still be exposed to the latter risk, as governments commonly suspend or reduce indexation when it leads to financial problems.

There may be circumstances when indexation in line with prices is the right solution. For example, if it is decided that the income replacement rates in a pension scheme are too high to be financially sustainable, these may be reduced for future pensions, but it would be unreasonable to reduce the value of pensions already in payment. One solution would be to freeze them in real terms, by indexing them in line with prices, until they have been brought into line with the new, lower rates of income replacement. However this would be a temporary measure, designed to effect a smooth transition to lower benefits.

PROGRESSIVITY

Progressivity can be measured by the extent to which lower-income workers receive more generous lifetime benefits relative to their contributions or earnings than do higher-income workers. Several aspects of the structure of benefit financing and benefit formulas affect the progressivity of a defined benefit social security scheme.

The taxation of benefits is generally a progressive feature of the retirement income scheme. Most countries treat social security benefits as taxable income. In countries with a progressive income tax structure, meaning that higher-income workers pay a higher marginal tax rate, the taxation of benefits reduces benefits relatively more for higher-income workers.

Progressivity can occur through the benefit formula, which can be structured so that more generous benefits relative to pre-retirement earnings are provided to lower-income workers. Flat benefits also add an element of progressivity since they replace a higher fraction of pre-retirement income for low-income workers than for high-income workers.

Cutting benefits

While the financial viability of a retirement benefits scheme can be assured by raising the pensionable age, increasing the required number of years of contributions or increasing the contribution rate, there is a tendency for countries to cut benefits to ensure the financial viability of their retirement benefits schemes. Benefits can be reduced either by an equal percentage for all beneficiaries or as a selective cut. An equal percentage cut could occur as a reduction in benefits at retirement or as a reduction in the indexation of benefits for inflation. An equal percentage cut may appear to affect all retirees equally, but in fact affects low-income workers most because they depend most on social security benefits as a source of retirement income. Thus an equal percentage cut would tend to affect adversely the distribution of income among the elderly.

Some defined benefit social security schemes have been criticized for adversely affecting income distribution, favouring high-income groups over lower-income ones. When considering cuts in social security benefits or other reforms of social security, this criticism can be addressed. Selective cuts may be made in numerous ways. Cuts could be aimed at beneficiaries with higher benefits (see box 3.1). A tax could be levied on benefits that hit larger benefits more heavily.

Other forms of benefit cuts affect particular individuals differently but are not as directly tied to income. The number of years used in calculating the income average in a defined benefit scheme could be increased, bringing lower-income years into the average. The age at which "full" benefits are received could be moved to an older age, resulting in a reduction in benefits if taken at earlier ages. Instead of using gross earnings in calculating the earnings used in benefit calculations, net earnings (after tax) could be used.

A worker's entitlement to social security retirement benefits, and the level of these benefits, are generally affected by the worker's age and years of work or contributions. Sometimes an earnings test affects eligibility to receive benefits, requiring workers to reduce their hours of work substantially or altogether. In some defined contribution schemes, workers are eligible for early receipt of benefits only if they have accumulated a sufficiently large account balance. In some flat-benefit schemes, eligibility is based on years of residence in the country, rather than years of work or contributions.

Two important aspects of benefit payments are whether they are provided as an annuity and whether their nominal value is adjusted upward so that their real value does not decline with inflation. Annuities, which are periodic payments that continue until the death of the recipient, or of the recipient and spouse, are the only form of payout that guarantees benefits will be paid over the worker's remaining lifetime. With lump-sum benefits (which are the form in which workers receive benefits from provident funds) and phased withdrawal of benefits (which are a commonly used form of benefit payment in some individual account defined contribution schemes) long-lived workers who had moderate earnings face the risk of poverty at the end of their lives.

Even moderate inflation can greatly erode the real value of benefit payments over the course of retirement. Protection against inflation can generally be provided through pay-as-you-go schemes because the wage base, used to finance those schemes, tends to keep pace with inflation. Nearly all funded defined contribution schemes, however, fail to provide automatic cost-of-living adjustments. Except in the handful of countries where the government provides cost-of-living indexed bonds, private sector pension fund managers cannot provide full indexing against inflation because no assets are available to finance such a guarantee.

When countries consider cutting future retirement benefits, cuts can be an equal percentage reduction for all retirees or they can be selective. Often cuts are aimed to reduce the benefits of higher-income retirees proportionally more than those of lower-income retirees. Norway, for example, has reduced the real value of maximum benefits while raising the real value of minimum benefits. A number of countries have cut benefits in defined benefit schemes by legislating changes that are not directly related to the generosity of the benefit formula. These changes include increasing the number of years used in calculating the earnings base for benefit computation, using earnings net of taxes and mandatory contributions rather than gross earnings to calculate benefits, indexing earnings used in computing benefits, or in setting earnings ceilings by prices rather than wages, increasing the penalty for early retirement, increasing the number of years of contributions required for benefit eligibility, reducing the generosity of indexing of benefits in payment or increasing the taxation of benefits.

While benefits from defined contribution schemes may be directly tied to the rate of return earned on the fund, often that is not the case. Instead benefits may be determined by minimum benefit guarantees or minimum rate of return guarantees. Alternatively benefits may be based on a rate of return that is less than is generally received by the fund, but that seldom fluctuates.

Notes

[1] Workers may be credited with years where they do not contribute for reasons such as education, child rearing, disability or unemployment.

[2] In the Netherlands, private pensions are mandatory in several branches of industry but they do not cover the whole workforce.

[3] Respectively, Association of Supplementary Pension Schemes and General Association of Pension Institutions for Managerial Staff.

[4] Before this, local and state employees had been covered by earnings-related pensions, but there was no universal coverage.

[5] There are four main negotiated schemes: for national government workers, for local government workers, for salaried (white-collar) workers in the private sector, and for hourly-wage (blue-collar) workers in the private sector. Generally they replace an additional 10–15 per cent of income but most of these schemes also have provisions to cover income above the ceiling. The negotiated pensions are financed through payroll taxes and, in the case of the schemes for government workers, through general tax revenues.

[6] The survivors' benefit was changed in 1990. Until then only children and women were eligible to receive benefits. The widow's benefit was paid for the remainder of her life. Survivors' benefits are also paid from most of the negotiated schemes.

[7] A fully funded scheme was also discussed, but the main argument against such a system was the cost of the transition.

[8] The employer part will be levied on total gross wage, while the employee part will only be levied on wages below the ceiling.

[9] The employer contribution above the ceiling will not be attributed to the individual account. Wage income, unemployment, sick leave, disability and parental leave insurance will earn pension

rights. For individuals in college or at home rearing children, assumed income will earn pension rights. Spouses have the option to share pension rights between them.

[10] Care needs to be taken in establishing the price or wage indexes used. In the United States, some analysts argue that the consumer price index has not adequately taken into account the addition of new products and the improvement in product quality, and that as a result it has overstated inflation.

INVALIDITY AND SURVIVORS' BENEFITS

4

This chapter deals with invalidity pensions and pensions provided for the survivors of a deceased insured person – mainly spouses and children. It discusses both qualifying conditions and levels and duration of benefits. Related issues discussed elsewhere in the book are mainly found in Chapter 18, which deals with early retirement.

Social protection schemes which include provision for old-age or retirement benefits invariably also provide similar protection in the event of invalidity or death. In both cases, benefit is payable to provide income security as a consequence of a contingency which has anticipated retirement. Depending on the rules of the scheme, invalidity may, in effect, be regarded as early retirement on the grounds of permanent incapacity or, sometimes, as a long-term incapacity which continues following exhaustion of entitlement to short-term sickness benefit. In the case of survivors' benefit, entitlement is derived from the benefit entitlement of a deceased person who was a member of the scheme, and thus a potential pensioner, or who was already receiving a retirement or invalidity pension. Payment of the benefit is usually conditional on the claimant being a member of the deceased's household and financially dependent on him or her.

In most countries there are separate and often more favourable provisions in respect of those who are injured, disabled or who die as a consequence of employment-related accident or disease.

INVALIDITY PENSIONS

Definition

Schemes have adopted different definitions of invalidity or disability depending on the desired scope of eligibility under the scheme. There are four broad situations covered by the following definitions.

- *Loss of faculty*: a total or partial loss of any part of the body or of any physical or mental faculty regardless of the economic or occupational consequences (this approach is more common in employment injury schemes or in compensation for war injuries).
- *Occupational disability*: a loss of earnings capacity arising from the inability to work in the previous occupation or to have the same earnings capacity in that occupation (this approach is common in special disability schemes for occupational groups).
- *General disability or invalidity*: a permanent loss of earnings capacity resulting from an inability to take up any opportunities in the labour market which would otherwise be within the scope of the person concerned; this implies the need to take account of other job opportunities.
- *Long-term incapacity*: similar to the previous category but without the necessity to establish that the loss of earnings capacity will be permanent, and with the objective of providing income support during incapacity which extends beyond entitlement to short-term sickness benefit.[1]

It should be noted, however, that the distinctions drawn in the above categorization may be blurred in specific national legislation, and some schemes contain elements of both occupational and general disability. The definitions chosen in different legislation reflect various considerations including, in particular, the desired scope of the scheme and its relationship with other social security schemes.

Qualifying conditions

Although all invalidity schemes link entitlement with a medical examination, there are generally additional qualifying conditions depending on the type of scheme. There are several possible approaches to the structure of invalidity benefit schemes:

- *social insurance*: a defined benefit scheme based on contributions paid by employers and individuals; a monthly pension paid generally until retirement age when it is replaced by a retirement pension;
- *provident fund*: a defined contribution scheme based on contributions, plus interest in individual account; a lump-sum payment;
- *employment injury*: social insurance defined benefit, but with no contribution conditions, and based on the conclusion that invalidity (disability) was caused by an injury or disease related to the employment;
- *workers' compensation*: social insurance as for employment injury but also, and more commonly, employer liability supported by private insurance arranged by the employer;
- *universal*: based on contingency and, often, a residence test; tax financed; a monthly pension until retirement age when replaced by a retirement pension;

- *means tested (social assistance)*: the same as for universal, but subject to a means test: the pension is subject to a review of financial circumstances;
- *private insurance*: based on premiums paid by employers or individuals; an annuity or lump sum.

Under a social insurance scheme, the eligibility tests generally base entitlement on an overall minimum period of membership, often supplemented by an additional test of recent insurable employment. Membership conditions need to be consistent with those under which entitlement to retirement pension is determined since, at the onset of insurability, there will be a potential entitlement to either benefit. But they must also take into account that invalidity can arise at any time. Thus a typical qualifying period would base entitlement on a maximum period of 15 years' contributions or insurable employment, with a reduced rate available after five years. The scheme in Costa Rica provides for the qualifying period to vary with the age of the insured person, within a minimum of 12 contributions for those up to age 24 and a maximum of 120 contributions for those aged between 52 and 65. A few schemes do not impose a qualifying period (for example Sudan) and the membership test is regarded as satisfied if the person was in insurable employment when the incapacity which resulted in invalidity commenced. Other countries require, in addition to the overall qualifying test based on contributions paid, the satisfaction of a minimum period of coverage immediately preceding the onset of the incapacity. Gabon requires five years of insurable employment, with at least 30 paid monthly contributions during the last five years.

Members of provident funds who cease work because of invalidity may claim a lump-sum benefit based on the accumulated contributions in their individual account, plus interest. Entitlement depends on medical evidence of invalidity, usually defined as being permanently incapable of further employment, although the process of establishing this typically may not be as strict as under social insurance schemes since the benefit is determined on a defined contribution basis. Thus the Employees Provident Fund in Sri Lanka requires evidence that the claimant is permanently and totally incapable of work.

A few countries (Iceland and Mauritius, for example) provide an invalidity pension under a non-contributory universal pension scheme subject to the satisfaction of a residence or citizenship test. The flat-rate universal pension in Mauritius is subject, for non-nationals, to a residence test of five years in the ten years preceding the claim: there is no residence test for nationals. Other countries prefer to link non-contributory entitlement to an invalidity pension to a means test. This may be done by specific provision for persons who are disabled (as in Australia, where there is also a residence test of ten years, or South Africa where entitlement is limited to citizenship). Alternatively it can be achieved through the application of a general social assistance programme under which all persons unable to support themselves to a prescribed minimum level may be entitled to income support.

Where social insurance pension schemes have been wholly or partially replaced by private pension funds under which benefit is determined in accordance with defined contribution principles (as in Argentina, Bolivia, Chile, Columbia, Peru and Uruguay), special arrangements have been made to provide income support protection as a consequence of invalidity. Although there are variations between the different countries, the approved pension fund selected by the contributor, in general, also arranges life or invalidity insurance with a private insurance company. This is financed by the worker through a combination of the funds in the individual pension account, and by a specified part of his or her pension contribution, for example 3.5 per cent of the worker's earnings in Argentina. This provides the basis for the purchase of an annuity. A minimum pension is guaranteed by the government.

Assessment of invalidity

As has been seen above, determining entitlement to invalidity benefit depends on the type of scheme. If it is a contributory scheme there will usually be a test of membership based on contributions paid. But, in addition, entitlement will also depend on a medical assessment to determine if invalidity exists, whether the condition which gives rise to the invalidity has stabilized, the extent of the invalidity, the need for further treatment and the scope for rehabilitation. Additionally, in the case of claims under an employment injury or workers' compensation scheme, it will be necessary to establish that the disability was caused by an employment-related injury or disease. The approach to these questions will depend on the definitions and conditions of entitlement prescribed in the law. The intention is for the medical assessment to be based on a full knowledge of the statutory provisions, and to provide the social security scheme with a clear and independent view on the medical aspects which affect entitlement. This is not always easy to achieve.

Invariably among the key issues to be resolved by the medical assessment are the extent, if any, of the disability and whether or not this is permanent. Many schemes set a threshold of entitlement based on a minimum degree of disability which is often prescribed as a percentage; for example, 66.7 per cent in France and in French-speaking Africa. Another approach, which aims to restrict eligibility to cases with a more significant level of disability, puts emphasis on the earnings capacity of the person, and an earnings capacity of one-third of the earnings of a person of a similar age, experience and qualifications is regarded as the threshold of entitlement. Raising the question of permanence is also significant, and generally implies that entitlement depends on a medical assessment that the disability or loss of earnings capacity will continue at least until retirement. Stability in the medical condition is generally presumed, but determining whether a condition is permanent as well as whether it is within the scope of the limits set out in the legislation, is often difficult. The loss of faculty or earnings capacity may change either way over time, and invalidity pensioners are often required to notify any change in their condition which may affect their entitlement.

Employment injury and workers' compensation schemes invariably provide for benefit to be paid in respect of partial disability. This is determined by medical assessment by reference to a schedule in the legislation which specifies the percentage degree of disablement for the loss of use of a part of the body or a loss of faculty. Where the disability does not correspond exactly to the schedule, the assessment uses the schedule as a guide.

Benefit rates

Most social insurance invalidity schemes calculate the rate of benefit in accordance with the same principles as retirement pension, that is, the rate of benefit is based on average earnings and length of insurable employment or number of contributions paid. However, in order to avoid penalizing the insured person who becomes disabled at a relatively early age, there is often provision in the legislation for special modification. This may be done through setting a minimum pension which represents a percentage of the insured person's average earnings and taking into account the period between the date of commencement of invalidity and pensionable áge when determining the length of insurable employment.

Some countries provide for benefit to be paid for partial invalidity, with the medical assessment being required to determine the percentage degree of disability, or percentage loss of earning capacity. Thus the Norwegian scheme provides partial invalidity pensions based on the percentage loss of earnings capacity. The social insurance scheme in Greece provides for entitlement to invalidity pension at the full rate of the retirement pension for those who suffer serious disability (loss of 80 per cent of earnings capacity) and 50 per cent of a full pension for those whose disability is assessed as between 50 and 66 per cent. But most countries opt for a scheme which simplifies, as far as possible, the difficulties of the medical assessment, and do not therefore apply the more precise determination of degree of disability which is a general feature of employment injury disablement schemes. This may also reflect the existence within the national social protection scheme of other means of income support which are potentially available to persons who are no longer able to work. At the other end of the disability spectrum, however, many countries provide special supplements to invalidity pensions for those persons who are so seriously disabled that they need the care and attention of another person. This may take the form of an additional benefit, such as the Attendance Allowance in the United Kingdom, or as a constant attendance supplement representing an additional percentage of the disability pension (40 per cent in Algeria, 50 per cent in Barbados).

INVALIDITY SCHEMES WITHIN NATIONAL SOCIAL PROTECTION SCHEMES

All developed countries, and many others, have established invalidity benefit schemes, but the level of protection and the role that invalidity policy plays in the general social protection scheme varies considerably. The invalidity benefit beneficiaries per thousand active labour force participants in five OECD countries (Germany, the Netherlands, Sweden, the United Kingdom and the United States) also vary dramatically across and within these countries, in ways that cannot be explained by differences in the underlying health conditions of these populations (see table 4.1). Rather the diversities in social policies appear to explain these differences (Aarts et al., 1996). Thus the response of a worker following the onset of an incapacity can be as much affected by the

Table 4.1 Invalidity beneficiaries per thousand active labour force participants, by age, in five OECD countries, 1970–94

Age	1970	1975	1980	1985	1990	1994
Total population 15 to 64 years						
Germany[1]	51	54	59	72	55	54[2]
Netherlands	55	84	138	142	152	151
Sweden	49	67	68	74	78	97
United Kingdom	29[3]	28	31	56	68[4]	–
United States	27	42	41	41	43	62
15–44 years						
Germany[1]	7	6	7	8	5	5[2]
Netherlands	17	32	57	58	62	66
Sweden	18	20	19	20	21	27
United Kingdom	8	9	11	20	23[4]	–
United States	11	17	16	20	23	38
45–59 years						
Germany[1]	75	64	84	103	75	80[2]
Netherlands	113	179	294	305	339	289
Sweden	66	95	99	108	116	143
United Kingdom	46	46	51	97	119	–
United States	33	68	83	71	72	96
60–64 years						
Germany[1]	419	688	1 348	1 291	1 109	1 064[2]
Netherlands	299	437	1 033	1 283	1 987	1 191
Sweden	229	382	382	512	577	658
United Kingdom	219	195	209	357	413	–
United States	154	265	285	254	250	294

Notes: – = not available. [1] German data refer to the former Federal Republic. [2] Figure refers to 1993. [3] United Kingdom age-specific data are derived from Lonsdale (1993) and *Employment Gazette* (several issues); United Kingdom disability beneficiary data for 1993 or 1994 were not available. [4] Figure refers to 1991.

Source: Aarts et al. (1996).

labour market opportunities, and the social environment he or she faces, as by the health condition responsible for the person's disability.

The social protection policy of a country may influence whether such workers remain in the labour force or shift to some form of benefit programme. Following the onset of a disability, workers may take any of five paths.

- *The early retirement path* encompasses public and private provisions that allow workers to retire before traditional retirement ages. Since the end of the 1970s, these provisions have become immensely popular in OECD countries and, together with invalidity benefit, account for a substantial part of the decrease in male labour force participation at older ages.

- *The work path* includes public programmes that provide or encourage rehabilitation (either publicly or privately provided) to overcome the work limitations caused by a disability. It also includes more direct labour market intervention through the creation of specific government jobs for people with disabilities, subsidies to those who employ such workers or to the workers themselves, job quotas and job protection legislation – dismissal rules, for example, or general anti-discrimination legislation requiring accommodation for workers with disabilities. These policies attempt to maintain those with disabilities on the job and in the labour market, either through the incentive of subsidies or through the disincentive of mandates.

- *The health path* encompasses traditional benefit programmes for temporary incapacity and invalidity. This may include short-term programmes that require employers to replace lost wages during the first few weeks of sickness, or to provide such replacement directly through short-term social insurance. In all European countries, this includes providing health care at no marginal expense to the worker. After some point, workers are then eligible to move to a long-term invalidity benefit scheme, which often requires the satisfaction of both health and employment criteria. This path eventually merges with the retirement benefit programme.

- *The unemployment path* encompasses short-term unemployment benefits to replace wage earnings lost as a result of cyclical economic downturns. At some point, longer-term unemployment insurance is made available, often at a lower replacement rate. Eventually this path also merges with the retirement benefit programme. Because the unemployment rate is often seen as a marker for a country's economic success, there is also the added problem that government policymakers will use the disability path to reduce the long-term unemployment rate/figures (Aarts et al., 1996, provide evidence of this in the Netherlands, compared to other countries).

- *The social assistance path* encompasses the set of means-tested programmes which serve as a safety net for those workers without jobs who are not eligible for health- or unemployment-based social insurance programmes. Social assistance programmes can be universal, subject only to a means test and linked to an inability to work, either because of poor health, poor job skills, or child-rearing responsibilities. This may continue past retirement age for those few individuals who are not eligible for social security retirement benefits. In the United States, which has no universal means-tested programmes, Supplemental Security Income provides such a floor for those aged 65 and over, and for disabled adults and the families of disabled children. Much of the growth in the invalidity benefit population aged 15 to 45 for the United States (shown in table 4.1) comes from this programme. In the European countries in table 4.1, more universal social assistance offers alternative sources of income for both adults and children, unrelated to their health status.

HOW INVALIDITY BENEFIT SCHEMES INFLUENCE BEHAVIOUR

In countries where social assistance is low or difficult to obtain compared to invalidity benefits, unemployment benefits are of short duration and little is available in terms of rehabilitation and job protection, it is likely that the number of claimants for incapacity and invalidity benefits will be relatively large. The number of claimants will increase as the replacement rate increases, and as the period over which benefits can be received lengthens. In such countries, for example the Netherlands and the United States, increases in benefit claims have put tremendous pressure on the invalidity benefit schemes in times of serious economic downturns. Alternatively, when the protection offered by unemployment provisions is similar to that offered by invalidity benefits, or there is a universal benefit payable to those unable to work, the administrative authority responsible for determining invalidity benefit entitlement will be under much less pressure. In Sweden, where incapacity and invalidity benefits are even more generous than in the Netherlands, the level of claims is lower because all those suffering from a disability are required to receive rehabilitation. Following rehabilitation, it is government policy to provide jobs in the public sector if private sector jobs are unavailable. In Germany, not only are the invalidity benefits lower than in the Netherlands or Sweden, but a combination of mandatory rehabilitation and a quota system also deflects much of the economic-induced pressure away from the invalidity benefit scheme. In many of the transition economies of Central and Eastern Europe, unemployment benefit programmes have not been fully developed, and unemployed workers may seek opportunities to claim invalidity benefit (see box 4.1).

The notion of the five paths discussed above can be used both as a framework for discussing how the incentive structure inherent in a country's social security scheme influences the supply of potential invalidity benefit claimants and as a means to control the demand for such claimants. To enter any of

Box 4.1 Invalidity pensions in transition economies

Many of the transition countries of Central and Eastern Europe have a problem due to the relatively large numbers of people receiving invalidity benefits. In Hungary, for example, the ratio of invalidity benefit pensioners to retirement pensioners is almost one to two, while in Poland it is 1.6 to two.[2]

In the United States, by comparison, where entitlement to invalidity benefit is more strictly controlled, the ratio of invalidity to retirement pensioners is about 0.3 to two.

The transition economies have a problem with excessive invalidity entitlement, due in part to a liberal eligibility standard. Invalidity pensions are paid to three categories of workers: (1) those who are unable to work at all, (2) those with a stable disability, and (3) those who are disabled but can continue to work. All three categories of pensioners are typically allowed to work. Workers disabled as a result of an employment-related illness or injury constitute yet another category of beneficiaries, but are paid separately from the pension scheme.

The explanation is sometimes offered that, in many transition economies, high invalidity benefit eligibility rates are due to poor public and occupational health conditions. While public and occupational health is, indeed, poor in many transition economies, invalidity pensions typically increased greatly when large state-run enterprises began to close. The many mid- and late-career workers who became unemployed were too young for retirement pensions, and unemployment insurance was unknown in most transition economies when economic restructuring began. Invalidity pensions thus served as income support for the workers rendered redundant. The large proportion of invalidity pensioners who continue to work further suggests that the problem is not one of public or occupational health, but rather one of lenient entitlement requirements.

Invalidity pensions are a fiscal problem because they go to younger people (those too young for retirement benefits) and, to the extent that their disabilities are minimal, to people who are likely to live a long time. Discouraging them from working is counterproductive since employment, and hence GDP, declines as a result, and because unused skills and work habits erode over time. Furthermore, since many transition economies still have poor controls over the private, or informal, employment sector, prohibitions against overt work by pensioners may simply drive their employment underground.

But paying invalidity benefits to people able to work is also counterproductive since it overburdens the contribution rate – already too high in many countries – for a dubious entitlement. A further fiscal problem is that, in many countries, people who continue to work while receiving an invalidity pension can accumulate pension credits that increase their ultimate retirement pension, while sometimes not even being required to pay contributions based on their earnings.

There are several possible solutions to this problem. Countries without unemployment insurance need to establish schemes that provide income support for those between jobs, while at the same time encouraging aggressive job search and a timely return to work. Invalidity benefit entitlement needs to be tightened, with elimination (or significant reduction) of partial invalidity cases. People who are recognized as disabled need to be provided with medical and occupational rehabilitation aimed at regaining employability. Earnings tests should be imposed on beneficiaries so that, while the search for work is encouraged, the budget recoups some of the cost of benefits. Thus those who are employed and in receipt of a pension should not be exempt from the payment of contributions. Finally both laws and cultural changes that prohibit discrimination against disabled workers need to be promoted. Disabled workers should be encouraged and assisted to do the work they are qualified and able to do. Resources that would otherwise go to paying invalidity pensions should be used for assistance that facilitates employment.

Most transition economies are unlikely to be able to reduce substantially the number of current beneficiaries: the rehabilitation of all those currently receiving benefits would be too expensive and time-consuming. Furthermore people who have been out of the workforce for a long time would present a formidable job-training or retraining challenge. But the policy actions outlined above could restrict the increase in the number of beneficiaries, while at the same time removing some of the incentives for workers who belong in the workforce to claim benefit.

the five paths, a worker must satisfy entry requirements. The entry rules for entitlement to an early retirement pension are usually straightforward. A worker must have worked in covered employment for a given time, or have performed other easily measured activities (for example, attended school, raised children) and must be a prescribed age. Such eligibility criteria are easy to administer, since they are relatively objective and leave little room for individual interpretation. The overall size of the population in receipt of retirement benefits will change if a higher benefit is paid, or the age of eligibility is lowered, but administrative discretion will not enter into this change. Determining eligibility for the various paths open to those who have a health condition that begins to affect their work, but who are below early retirement age, is not as clear-cut. The medical assessment associated with determining entitlement to invalidity benefit will often be difficult, and is thus open to different interpretation and conclusions, particularly as regards the question as to whether, or to what extent, the person is incapable of work and likely to remain so. Doctors can evaluate health conditions as they relate to a norm, but there is no unambiguous way to relate a health condition to an ability to work. Hence much of the problem with the administration of an invalidity benefit scheme is in establishing criteria for eligibility and developing procedures that will ensure consistency in its use. Here bureaucratic discretion in carrying out established criteria is much greater than it is for retirement.

Access to the work path and the health path may be closely coordinated, as in Germany and Sweden, where a centralized administration determines who is provided with rehabilitation services and who is entitled to receive a benefit.

These paths, however, may also be administered in quite independent ways. In the United States, rehabilitation services are administered with little or no connection to the administration of benefits. In the Netherlands, the policy emphasis on income protection and the use of the invalidity benefit scheme as an exit route from the labour market has discouraged the use of rehabilitation services (see box 4.2).

All of these factors affect the way in which the social security administration which determines eligibility for invalidity benefit responds to changes in supply, and to the voices of those at higher levels of administrative responsibility who are attempting to control the overall flow of people into the system. In periods of economic downturn, the number of workers who leave their jobs rises, and benefit claims increase. In the Netherlands and the United States – two countries with generous invalidity benefits relative to other alternatives – great pressure has been put on their invalidity benefit system over the past 25 years to provide income for those unemployed workers and their families. That same pressure has been seen in Sweden since 1990. Such pressure may lead to a specific easing of the rules, or simply a change in the interpretation of them. In this way demand may shift to accommodate supply. In Germany such pressures have also led to special invalidity-related entitlement, but they have been confined to workers aged 60 and above.

When a health condition begins to affect one's ability to work, important job-related decisions must be made, both by the worker and by his or her employer. These decisions will be influenced by the social institutions of the country. The relative rewards of continued movement along the work path, as compared with those of taking an alternative path, will be considered by the worker. In like manner, an employer's willingness to accommodate the worker will also be influenced by the social institutions and legal mandates within which the employer must operate.

This is not to suggest that all workers can, or will, transform themselves into invalidity benefit claimants. Rather it recognizes that those with some work limitations who are having difficulty with their current job, or who are no longer working, will be influenced by the relative rewards provided by the invalidity benefit, unemployment insurance or social assistance paths, in deciding whether to try to remain in the labour force or to apply for social security benefits.

Nor does it suggest that all people with disabilities have the ability to continue to work. Some have work limitations so severe that continued employment is impossible, and reliance on benefit is inevitable. But for those who suffer from a condition which affects their ability to work, the length of time they stay on the job depends on the social institutions that are in place as well as their specific pathology, particular job and employer. It is this section of the disabled that public policy can influence either to stay at work, or to become benefit claimants.

In the United States, where welfare (social assistance) benefits are low and difficult to obtain for households without children, unemployment benefits

Box 4.2 The experience of the Netherlands on invalidity benefits
The ageing baby boomers give a major long-term dimension to the growing public debate on the need to make existing social security schemes more sustainable. In the Netherlands, changes in invalidity benefit policy have been at the centre of this debate.

The Netherlands social insurance scheme
In the Netherlands all employees are insured against the risks of wage loss due to unemployment or ill-health. Moreover every citizen has access to partly privatized health insurance schemes. As an insurance of last resort, the Netherlands has a means-tested safety net, and a statutory minimum wage, to prevent anyone from falling below the social minimum.

Sickness benefits. A worker unable to perform his or her job because of illness or injury, irrespective of its cause, is entitled to sickness benefits. These benefits replace 70 per cent of gross wage earnings, but collective bargaining agreements between employers and employees stipulate that sickness benefits must be supplemented to the level of net earnings. Sickness benefits end after 12 months. They are not means-tested.

Until 1994 sickness benefits were financed by contribution rates that were pooled by sector. In 1994 employers with more than 15 employees were obliged to cover the first six weeks of sick pay themselves, and to contract with a private provider of occupational health services. These services monitor periods of sickness and advise employers on the nature and extent of the health risks to which their staff are exposed, as well as on how to reduce these risks.

In 1996 the Sickness Benefit Act was abolished and employers' responsibility for coverage of sick pay was extended to 12 months, after which invalidity benefit takes over. Under civil law, employers are obliged to replace 70 per cent of earnings lost to sickness. They may choose whether they want to bear their sick pay risk themselves, or to have all or part of it covered by a private insurer.

Thus a fully regulated public monopoly market to which private insurers had no access has been transformed into a deregulated one in which private insurers freely bid for contracts with employers that seek to insure their sick-pay liabilities.

Invalidity benefits. Any illness or injury entitles an insured person to an invalidity benefit after a mandatory waiting period of 12 months. While other countries distinguish people with disability according to whether the impairment occurred on the job or elsewhere, only the consequence of impairment is relevant for the Dutch disability insurance programme.

Since 1993 benefits have been based on age and wage earnings. Previously coverage did not depend on age or on insurance coverage years. When a person was found to be totally disabled (80 to 100 per cent), the statutory replacement rate was equal to that of sickness benefits, for example 70 per cent of before-tax earnings. As part of the reforms of 1993, the amount of earnings-related disability benefits now depends on age, to simulate a requirement for contribution years, with the previously prevailing 70 per cent replacement rate as a maximum.

The Dutch disability programme is unique in that it distinguishes seven disability categories ranging from less than 15 per cent, 15 to 25 per cent disabled, and so on to 80 to 100 per cent disabled. The minimum degree of disability yielding entitlement to benefits is 15 per cent. The degree of disablement is assessed by consideration of the worker's residual earning capacity. As of 1993 capacity is defined by the earnings flowing from any job commensurate with one's residual capabilities as a percentage of usual pre-disability earnings. The degree of disablement, then, is the complement of the residual earning capacity and defines the benefit level. Previously only jobs that were compatible with one's training and work history could be taken into consideration. Since 1987 the actual availability of jobs is not taken into consideration.

Not only has the definition of suitable work been broadened, the medical definition of disability has also been tightened. The causal relationship between impairment and disablement has to be objectively assessable. Finally, while reviews of the disability status of recipients used to be rare, the amendments of 1993 make regular reviews – a minimum of once ever three years – compulsory.

Until 1998 invalidity benefits were funded by nationally uniform pay-as-you-go contribution rates. As from 1998 new awards are financed by premium rates that differ by employer according to its disability record over the past five years. These experience-rated premiums are used to finance the first five years of benefits. Longer-lasting disability risks are pooled at the national level, as before. Employers may also leave the public insurance scheme and themselves insure the first five years of disability benefits of their personnel.

Statistics

The above reforms aim at reducing sickness and invalidity benefit dependency by confronting employers and employees more directly with the financial consequences of using the health path to shed redundant workers. Cross-national data on sickness and disability prevalence rates show that the Netherlands was an outlier. A study (Einerhand et al., 1994) compared work incapacity rates across six European countries. These rates indicate days lost to sickness and disability, as a percentage of the work force (in days). In 1990 the Dutch incapacity rate was about twice that in Belgium, Denmark and Germany, 67 per cent higher than in Sweden and almost triple that in the United Kingdom.

Another study (Aarts and de Jong, 1997) focused on invalidity benefit claims in international comparison. The number of Dutch disability benefit recipients per 1,000 workers grew from 55 in 1970 to 138 in 1980, and to 152 in 1990. The comparable figures for the United States are 27 in 1970, 41 in 1980 and 43 in 1990. After 1990 the Dutch rate decreased, to 142 in 1995, whereas the United States grew to 64 over the same period.

are of relatively short duration and little is available in terms of rehabilitation and job protection or accommodation, the number of invalidity benefit claimants has been sensitive to the business cycle (see Rupp and Stapleton, 1998, for evidence of the importance of economic variables on applicants and receipt of benefits for the United States). As market conditions worsen, those workers with disabilities who lose their jobs are more likely to apply for benefits.

EMPLOYMENT-RELATED SCHEMES

The first social insurance programmes established in developed countries to provide protection against the onset of a disability offered protection only for employment-related injuries. Replacement rates for employment-related injuries are generally lower than for temporary sickness benefits, but are often paid over a longer period and, in some cases, up to the age of commencement of eligibility for retirement benefits. They may provide entitlement for either total or partial loss of earning capacity. These schemes are financed by a contribution levied on the employer, sometimes at a uniform rate and sometimes rated according to risk or experience, but benefit entitlement does not depend on the satisfaction of any contribution conditions. Hence there is a potential for such schemes to attract claimants rather than non-employment related schemes.

Replacement rates

The replacement rates for invalidity benefit schemes vary considerably across family types, earnings levels and countries. In general the larger the share of earnings replaced, the greater the incentive for workers to claim benefits. The level of invalidity benefit relative to other potentially alternative benefits – for example, unemployment or social assistance welfare – should also increase benefit claims. Replacement rates for higher-paid workers tend to be lower, but schemes which provide a large part of the wage earnings of low-skilled or marginal workers are likely to offer a relatively good financial alternative for those workers who experience the onset of a disability, or workers with a disability who become unemployed during economic downturns. Employers may also view, during periods of job cuts or economic recession, the invalidity benefit scheme as an alternative to special early retirement offers. Hence it will be in the interest both of employers and of their employees to overuse the invalidity benefit scheme. Policy consideration must therefore seek to balance two goals: mitigating the consequences of earnings lost because of the onset of a disability, while minimizing the disincentives to work that such protection inevitably provides.

It is relevant to note, in contrast, that these factors do not, in general, apply to developing countries where there are different problems which affect the scope and operation of invalidity benefit schemes. In some African countries, such as Namibia and Zambia (and even South Africa where the principal scheme is means tested), pensions in respect of invalidity are only payable under an employment injury scheme in respect of disability which is due to an employment injury or occupational disease. In other African countries, such as Ghana and Nigeria, where the provident fund has been converted into a social insurance pension scheme, the reverse situation applies, and pensions are only payable in respect of non-employment related invalidity (since employment-related disability is covered under the Workers' Compensation Scheme which only requires employers to make lump-sum payments). In other countries in Africa such as Swaziland, or in Asia (for example, Indonesia, Papua New Guinea, Sri Lanka), where provident funds continue alongside employment injury schemes, lump-sum payments are payable under both systems, although on a different basis. The provident fund scheme provides a lump sum based on the member's contributions plus interest, whereas the employment injury scheme determines the lump sum through a formula based on the assessed degree of disability and the average level of pre-accident earnings.

The impact of invalidity schemes in developing countries is also inhibited by the limited coverage of such schemes. In the case of employment injury schemes, employers may also seek to persuade workers not to claim, since this would have financial implications for the employer and, furthermore, the standards of safety are generally lower in developing countries and thus workers are more at risk. On the other hand, weaknesses in the medical assessment process and the scope for corruption may result in a greater incidence of doubtful claims which may be compounded by the opportunities open for all beneficiaries to find work in the informal sector whilst in receipt of benefit (see box 4.3).

ENCOURAGING EMPLOYMENT

Once a person is in receipt of invalidity benefit, entitlement may cease because of recovery or increased work activity. The number of such cases has always been low, but this is not surprising since entitlement to an invalidity benefit is generally conditional on the existence of a severe disability, and often follows a long period of incapacity. In general disabilities worsen over time, just as labour market skills deteriorate if not used, so it is not surprising that benefit cessation is low. Programme incentives, however, can influence a return to work and they may have a carrot (positive) or stick (negative) component. Most long-term invalidity benefit schemes in developed countries offer a carrot (a trial work period) to allow beneficiaries the opportunity of re-entering the workforce without loss of benefits. In addition most schemes monitor beneficiaries to see if they still satisfy the eligibility criteria.

It is important to recognize, however, that trial work periods, or other incentives to make a return to employment more attractive, will also influence the number of new claimants. For instance in the United States, the criterion for entitlement is an inability to perform any substantial gainful activity. As a result of allowing beneficiaries the option of a trial work period, especially if it is prolonged for a significant period of time or allows a significant level of earnings, there may be an increase in the number of claimants, because many

Box 4.3 Invalidity and survivors' benefits in China

In China persons who are either physically or mentally disabled are estimated to number about 60 million[3], or nearly 5 per cent of the entire national population, and 12 per cent of the world's disabled people, which numbered about 500 million in the late 1990s.

Assistance, including income security, health care and rehabilitation, education and occupational training, and employment are provided for these people in China mainly through a national welfare network, in which the Ministry of Labour and Social Security, the Ministry of Civil Affairs and the Ministry of Public Health, as well as the China Disabled People's Association, are the major institutions. In addition traditional support by families and communities still assumes an essential role in the daily life of disabled people, particularly in the rural areas. NGOs and charities also contribute increasingly to improving the welfare of this group.

In 1998 it was announced at the 3rd National Assembly of the China Disabled People's Association that over the last decade the State has adopted a series of programmes to protect disabled people's rights and interests, which include the establishment and enactment of a Disability Act, setting out and executing three Five-Year Plans for Disability, establishing government institutions for coordination, instituting a unified national association for handicapped people, promoting social morality and practices to care for and help this disadvantaged group, and encouraging disabled people to be self-confident and economically self-sufficient, if possible. The progress in this regard has been significant: China has eliminated poliomyelitis; essentially limited the threat of lack of iodine to the health of a large part of the population; by adopting prevention methods, largely reduced the incidence of disability among the population, especially that rooted in hereditary diseases; rehabilitated four million disabled persons; increased the school enrollment rate of disabled children from 6 per cent to 64 per cent; increased the employment rate of disabled adults from less than 50 per cent to 73 per cent; and lifted 14 million people who were poor and disabled out of poverty.

Despite this progress, it is recognized that the living, working and education conditions of those 60 million disabled people are still generally lower than for other groups in the community.

Relevant social insurance provisions

The invalidity benefit scheme in China is designed and implemented within the framework of the Old-Age Insurance scheme, which is administered by the new Ministry of Labour and Social Security. In line with this and related laws, workers aged 50 in the case of men and 45 in the case of women, employed for at least ten years and certified by the Labour Verifying Committee as having a 100 per cent incapacity for work as a result of disability or illness, are allowed to retire before the normal retirement age. The monthly pensions to which they are entitled depend on their individual work history. Those who joined the revolutionary forces in the period of the Second World War and the Civil War, which took place before the founding of the People's Republic of China, receive an amount of pension equal to 90 per cent and 80 per cent, respectively, of their personal basic salaries, payable immediately prior to retirement; those who were employed after the founding of the People's Republic of China, receive a pension at a rate of 75 per cent, 70 per cent, or 60 per cent for a total length of employment of more than 20 years, 15–20 years, or 10–15 years, respectively. A minimum monthly pension is set at 25 yuan. These criteria are exactly the same as are applied to normal retirement. Workers who do not meet the above qualifying conditions are also allowed to resign from the workforce, provided their incapacity for work is endorsed by the Labour Verifying Committee. The pension amount payable for these people is less than that for the first category of disabled people. It is fixed at a uniform rate of 40 per cent of the pre-resignation basic salary of the person concerned. The minimum monthly pension for them should not be less than 20 yuan.

Two sets of standards are adopted and applied to senior civil servants and ordinary public employees, respectively. The qualifying conditions and pension rates for the latter are the same as those for the category of retired disabled workers mentioned above. For the former, the pensions payable equal their pre-retirement basic salaries, and there is no requirement for the verification and approval of their incapacity for work by the Labour Verifying Committee.

Main features of invalidity benefit provisions

The above arrangements for invalidity benefits available within the framework of the social insurance scheme in China are characterized by the following features.

- Only those who hold standard employment contracts in the urban areas are insured, and other urban disabled persons and the entire rural disabled population are helped through a range of welfare measures.

- Personal coverage of the social insurance invalidity insurance has been gradually extended from employees of the public sector, who used to represent more than 90 per cent of the urban workforce in the pre-reform period, to non-public sector workers in urban areas.

- The initial calculation base (basic salary), the benefit rates and the minimum pensions have been gradually increased in order to keep pace with the rapid evolution of the normal retirement pensions, and to maintain the purchasing power of the disability pensions. The actual benefit rates are determined by responsible employers, or local government authorities, and vary considerably across the country.

- As invalidity insurance is a part of the retirement social security scheme, the series of ongoing retirement insurance reforms over the last one and half decades, particularly the current one involving the setting up of a multi-tier scheme including a component of individual savings accounts, will have important effects on the development of this branch of social insurance.

people who meet the criteria for entitlement to benefit do not meet the work requirements. If current beneficiaries are encouraged to work more by easing the work standards, there is a risk that this will also increase the scope of potential claimants.

Box 4.4 Problems in the invalidity benefits programme in the Philippines

The invalidity benefit programme in the Philippines has weaknesses, both in allocation and in administration, and benefits are paid to several categories of beneficiaries who probably should not be receiving them. Invalidity pensions in the Philippines only require 36 months of contributions for eligibility, while retirement pensions require 120 months. For this reason elderly people who do not qualify for retirement benefits on the basis of their contributions can often qualify for invalidity benefits. Furthermore entitlement to invalidity benefit does not depend on a test of recent insurable employment, showing that the person was an active member of the scheme at the time that he or she became an invalid. Thus the linkage with employment is weak and many claims are made by people who last worked many years ago and who are clearly not in the labour force. In addition there is no age limit on claims and many people claim invalidity when they are already over 60.

The invalidity pension includes a supplementary allowance for extra needs, called a carer's allowance. Older people applying for disability benefits receive about 25 per cent higher benefits than those who have earned their entitlement to a retirement benefit through their contributions. As a result, even those workers with sufficient contribution months to qualify for a retirement pension prefer to receive disability pension benefits.

Among younger workers, a large number of disability pensions are granted after an insured person has had surgery, without termination of employment and functional disability. This results from the practice of considering some types of surgery as qualifying the individual for disability benefits regardless of the person's ability to continue working. Often a partial invalidity benefit is granted in the form of a lump-sum payment. The surgical procedures involved include hysterectomy, cataract, mastectomy, thyroidectomy and Caesarean section.

Invalidity benefits are paid without subsequent review of eligibility. A recent survey indicated that a significant number of invalidity beneficiaries had been deceased for as long as six years. Because no claim for a funeral grant had been made, the government continued paying the disability benefit.

A significant number of invalidity beneficiaries also receive a benefit from the Employment Compensation programme. Invalidity benefits are granted to those who have received compensation for work-related injuries, even though the Social Security Law provides that the invalidity benefit is only for non-work related claims.

Monitoring entitlement to invalidity benefit after award is an important aspect of the governance of the programmes in some countries. It may prove difficult to establish whether claimants have in fact started work, particularly in the case of self-employment or work in the informal sector. A combination of this problem with the difficulties in determining whether and to what extent a person is disabled may cause significant problems for the administration. (See box 4.4 on the experience in the Philippines.)

CONCLUSIONS ON INVALIDITY PENSIONS

The concept of an invalidity benefit evolved from the need to recognize that among those contributing throughout their working lives for a retirement pension, there will be a proportion who have no choice but to cease work before pensionable age because of invalidity. In order to provide these persons with what is effectively an early retirement pension, schemes were designed which were based on risk pooling. Such schemes have been modified to take account of national circumstances, social and economic pressures and apparent anomalies in relation to other disabled persons who cannot work, such as those who were not insured under the scheme, or those who were disabled as a consequence of an employment-related injury.

The number of invalidity pensioners may be significantly affected by social protection policies which have the effect of influencing the reactions of employers and workers. Administrative difficulties associated with identifying and measuring invalidity, and its consequences in relation to capacity for work, are also an important factor. Policy choices may encourage or discourage claims to what is essentially a long-term benefit, and careful consideration therefore needs to be given to the potential interaction between invalidity benefit schemes and other social protection provisions, particularly those covering the contingencies of retirement, unemployment or low income (see box 4.5).

There is clearly a need to provide long-term periodic payments for those who are unable to support themselves because of invalidity, and it is reasonable to distinguish between those who have been able to contribute to a reasonable extent to some form of risk pooling arrangements and those who have not. In the case of the former, the objective of this benefit should be, as a minimum, to prevent poverty and, beyond that, to provide an income which takes account of the level of earnings lost. In the case of those outside the scope of such a contributory scheme, the preferable policy option would be for some form of tax-financed universal benefit based on residence. In countries where resources are limited, principles used for targeting benefits are based on means testing.

SURVIVORS' BENEFITS

Entitlement to survivors' benefits is often linked with insurability for retirement or disability (invalidity) benefit and thus it is the death of the insured person which provides the basis for the payment of a continuing benefit to those who were dependent on him or her prior to death. In the social insurance context, therefore, this entitlement is not based on the contribution record or insurability of the dependant, but on that of the deceased. If the deceased was in insurable employment at the time of death, or had a record of such employment, entitlement to survivors' benefit would depend, in the first instance, on whether or not this period of insurable employment was sufficient to satisfy the

Box 4.5 Proposals in the United Kingdom for the reform of incapacity benefit
In the United Kingdom, insured persons are entitled to an incapacity benefit after 52 weeks of incapacity. In November 1998 the government announced that more people were claiming benefit on the basis of incapacity than on the basis of unemployment, that of the 1.75 million incapacity beneficiaries about 50 per cent came to incapacity benefit from unemployment rather than work, and that about 25 per cent of all men over 60 are receiving incapacity benefit. On this basis, proposals for reform were announced which would include the following:

- identification of the most severely disabled persons, and the improvement of their benefit entitlement;
- establishment of a single gateway for all people of working age to gain access to the social security scheme through a system of personal advisers, who would provide information on access to benefits, work and so on;
- requirement for all persons of working age (other than those who are seriously disabled) to undergo an employability test which would shift the emphasis from what claimants cannot do to what they can do;
- payment of incapacity benefit only to those who satisfy a test of recent insurable employment during which they paid contributions.

prescribed qualifying conditions. If, on the other hand, the deceased was already in receipt of a retirement or invalidity pension at the time of death, these qualifying conditions were already clearly satisfied.

The linkage with a deceased insured person will not, however, be relevant where survivors' benefits are paid under a universal or means-tested scheme. In such circumstances, entitlement will depend on the personal status of the claimant and on evidence of residence or of low means.

Survivors' benefits were originally conceived to fit a pattern of family life in which the husband was the breadwinner while the wife looked after the home and children. Typically, therefore, this resulted in provision being made in social security schemes for the payment of a pension to the widow, with increases or separate pensions paid to children for as long as they remained under school-leaving age. There were always exceptions to this situation (both husband and wife working, only the wife working, the death of a working wife, separated families, unmarried partners, and so on) and to a varying extent schemes attempted to address these variations where this was thought to be merited. But more general changes in society, and in patterns of dependency, have become common and established provisions which seek to determine dependency for the purpose of social security benefits may no longer seem appropriate.

These developments have introduced new dimensions to what was already a difficult aspect of social security provision. There are several issues to be considered which many social insurance schemes have sought to address in a variety of ways. These are discussed in the following paragraphs.

Qualifying conditions

Qualifying conditions are reasonably straightforward since they relate back to the deceased and, in general, schemes apply, on grounds of consistency, the same requirements for survivors' benefits as for invalidity benefits. As noted above, if the deceased was receiving a retirement pension or a disability pension at the time of death the qualifying conditions are automatically satisfied.

Determining the survivors

All schemes identify the widow as a principal surviving dependant, but the definition of widow is open to wide interpretation. It may often be restricted to a woman who was legally married to the deceased but may even then exclude so-called "deathbed marriages", that is to say, those which took place within a prescribed period prior to death. (Thus, in France, entitlement is restricted to a widow who is aged at least 55 years and who was married to the deceased for at least two years, or had a child of the marriage; in Greece the marriage must have lasted for at least six months or two years in the case of a pensioner, although the requirement is waived in the case of death by accident or if there was a child of the marriage.) On the other hand, it may extend to marriages by custom or even to common law marriages which were of a prescribed duration and which were continuing at the time of death. In Ecuador, for example, a common law wife of at least two years, or the mother of the deceased's child, is accepted. Most European countries do not, however, recognize common law spouses (although Hungary, Lithuania and Slovenia are exceptions).

Surviving dependants may include a widow who was separated from the deceased but whom he was maintaining or obliged to maintain. They may include several wives where polygamy is practised, or where there was a legal wife from whom the deceased was separated and a common law wife. (In Cameroon all non-divorced spouses are included.) Generally, if the wife was living with the deceased or maintained by him at the time of death, she is assumed to have been dependent on him. If, by the application of these provisions, there is more than one widow, pension entitlement is split.

Many schemes have provided for survivors' benefits to be payable to the widower of a deceased insured woman. While the same rules as for a widow generally apply, some schemes introduce tighter restrictions for widowers and seek to restrict entitlement to dependent widowers, often defined as those who were not employed at the time of their wife's death and who are incapable of further employment (as in Cyprus, the Islamic Republic of Iran and Turkey).

As regards children, there are similar difficulties in definition, with provision often extending to adopted or illegitimate children, and brothers and sisters of the deceased, subject to restrictions on dependency. Generally entitlement would extend to those children living in the household of the deceased at the time of death and/or to those others whom he or she financially supported.

Children would generally be defined as under school-leaving age at the date of death of the deceased, although some schemes include invalid children who are older and even unmarried daughters and sisters. Some schemes extend entitlement to a posthumous child born within ten months of the death of the deceased.

In recognition of the fact that in some societies there is often a close relationship between generations, with sons supporting elderly parents and so on, survivors' benefit provisions may take account of this by including – within the scope of surviving dependants – parents, or even grandparents, who were financially dependent on the deceased.

Under the provident fund schemes, the member is required, at the commencement of membership, to nominate from among his or her family those whom he or she wishes to receive the balance in the account in the event of death. In some schemes such as the one in Kenya, the nomination is restricted to spouses and children. In Ghana the social security scheme covers the contingencies of retirement, invalidity and death, and was established in January 1991 following the conversion of the national provident fund. It was decided that the nominee system of the provident fund would be retained, at least during a transition period, partly for reasons of continuity and partly because of difficulties in identifying surviving dependants and in determining whether they were dependent on the deceased. In addition, and again for reasons of administrative simplicity, the benefit payable to surviving dependants remained as a lump sum based on the actuarial present value of the deceased person's pension entitlement; the lump sum is divided according to the allocation specified in the nomination.

Establishing dependency

Most schemes seek to establish a dependency link between the survivor and the deceased. Rather than applying a case-by-case approach it is usual, however, for provisions to be devised in the legislation which will provide a framework for determining entitlement. But the issues to be covered by this framework may be complex and the relevant facts may be difficult to apply, particularly where they concern family relationships and finances. These issues relate to the desire to link entitlement to dependency, both at the time of the death of the deceased and subsequently. The approach taken varies considerably and equity, societal values, customs and administrative simplicity may all be relevant factors. Thus some schemes provide for the payment of a widow's pension without any conditions relating to age, incapacity or responsibility for dependent children. Other schemes might take into account the ability of the widow (and other surviving dependants) to find work. Thus some schemes might exclude from entitlement surviving relatives who were gainfully employed at the time of death of the deceased, but they also only provide benefit for a limited period to a widow who has no dependent children and is under a prescribed age, and thus presumed to have good prospects of supporting herself. If the widow was not working when her husband died, and has small children to care for or is over age 50, the scheme is likely to provide for her to receive a pension without limited duration. Pensions for widowers and parents tend to be more restrictive, and are often subject to suspension or cessation in the event of commencement of gainful employment. In the event of a change of marital status (or on the commencement of cohabitation), most schemes provide for the pension to cease, sometimes with a lump-sum payment (see box 4.6).

Benefit rates

In order to achieve consistency with the retirement pension and invalidity benefit schemes on which entitlement is based, the rate of pension available to surviving dependants is often related to the amount of pension that the deceased was receiving prior to death, or the amount that the deceased would have been receiving if he or she was an invalid. This provides the maximum amount available to be allocated between the surviving dependants, and it is common for their notional entitlement to be prescribed and applied to this maximum amount, although the prescribed allocation varies considerably between countries. Thus the widow's pension might vary between 40 and 100 per cent of the deceased's entitlement and each child might receive anything between 10 and 30 per cent. Where, on this basis, the aggregate of these entitlements exceeds 100 per cent it is usual for a pro rata reduction to be made. Where there is no widow, orphan children commonly receive up to twice the normal child allocation. Many schemes rank surviving dependants, with widows and children taking priority over dependants, parents, grandparents and other family members.

EQUITY AND COVERAGE PROBLEMS

It can be seen from the above that social insurance schemes have, in general, tried to adapt to cover a wide variety of situations, and to do so by prescribing rules which provide a substantial measure of uniformity and predictability for beneficiaries. Nevertheless there are a number of issues relating to entitlement to survivors' benefits which have been under consideration in various countries, including the provision and conditions for widowers and divorced people.

Treatment of widowers

It has been noted above that in many schemes there are significant differences in the treatment of widows and widowers, with the latter even being excluded from entitlement in some cases. This is largely attributable to past custom in family responsibility, but it is now more common for women to make a significant

Box 4.6 Survivors' pension in Egypt

According to Egyptian law, the state provides social security and health insurance services as well as retirement, disability and death benefits for all citizens. Four social security schemes cover all manpower in Egypt:

- The Social Insurance Scheme, Law No. 79/1975, covers all workers in the government sector, as well as the public and private sectors, in the following branches:
    - retirement, invalidity and survivors' pensions;
    - occupational injury and diseases;
    - sickness and maternity insurance;
    - unemployment insurance;
    - pensioners' social welfare insurance.
- The Social Insurance Scheme for Employers and Self-employed Persons, Law No. 108/1976, only provides insurance against old age, invalidity and death of the breadwinner, as well as occupational injury in the case of termination of service owing to total invalidity or death.
- The Social Insurance for Egyptian Workers Abroad, Law No. 50/1978, only provides insurance against old age, invalidity and death of the breadwinner, as well as occupational injury which causes termination of service owing to total invalidity or death.
- The Social Insurance Scheme for all manpower in casual employment not covered by the above pensions and social insurance laws, Law No. 112/1980, provides social protection against old age, invalidity and death of the breadwinner.

Survivors' pensions according to Laws Nos. 79/1975, 50/1978, 108/1976

This insurance scheme is intended to guarantee continuance after the death of the breadwinner of the income of the deceased person's family or persons who had been dependent upon him, regardless of any difference of religion among them. Survivors of the insured person or pensioner who are entitled to a survivor's pension shall be classed in four categories, as follows:

- widow/widower/divorcee of the insured person or pensioner,
- sons and daughters,
- parents,
- brothers and sisters.

Eligibility is subject to the following conditions.

Widow

- The widow (or widower) must be incapable of self-support;
- the marriage must have been concluded by an authenticated contract and proved by a court statement issued in response to an application submitted while the husband was alive;
- if the marriage was illegal, or unofficial, or concluded through an unauthenticated contract, or not ratified, it may be proved by police investigation or

witnesses' affidavit to the effect that the couple were living in marital cohabitation before the deceased had reached the age of 60; also by obtaining
from the court a statement of legitimate inheritance including her among
the heirs of the deceased. The widow shall then be entitled to all the corresponding benefits provided the other conditions are fulfilled;

- the disqualification of the widow for a pension shall not debar her children
from entitlement to a pension;

- the age of the husband at the time of the marriage must have been less than
60 years.

Exceptions to the age limit

- The pensioner's divorcee whom he married after attaining the age of 60
years and with whom he had lived in marital cohabitation before reaching
that age;

- the widow whose age was 40 years at least at the time of marriage, provided
that the pensioner had no other wife or divorcee entitled to a pension still
living after he had reached the age of 60 years.

Divorcee

- The divorcee whose marriage lasted 20 years at least and who has no
income whatsoever shall have the right to combine income and pension
with a maximum limit of L.E. 30, subject to the following conditions and rules:

- the marriage must have been concluded by an authenticated contract and
proved by a court statement issued in response to an application submitted
while the husband was alive;

- the divorcee was divorced against her will;

- the marriage lasted 20 years;

- the divorcee is not married to a person other than the deceased;

- the divorcee has no income of any kind in an amount equivalent to, or exceeding, the amount of the pension.

Exceptionally, the divorcee may obtain the income as well as the pension
provided the sum of both does not exceed L.E. 30.

- The marriage may be established by a birth certificate or official extract from
the birth register for one of her children from the former husband.

Sons

- Sons are eligible if they were not more than 21 years of age at the time of the
father's death, with the following exceptions:

- the dependant is incapable of self-support;

- the dependant is a student at an educational establishment not above university level, and is under age 26;

- the dependant has graduated but is not gainfully employed or practising
a profession, and has not reached the age of 26 (in the case of university
graduates) or 24 (for those with lesser qualifications).

Daughters
Must be unmarried.

Parents
No special conditions.

Brothers and sisters
The same as for sons and daughters. They must be eligible for pension and have been supported by the deceased insured person:

- sons and brothers over 21 years of age if incapable of self-support, which means any person suffering disability that renders him incapable of gainful activity or reduces his capacity for work by at least 50 per cent, provided the disability is congenital or due to injury or disease contracted before the age of 60.

In addition:
- proof of the legator's support by administrative certificate;
- when there are no sons or daughters eligible for the pension at the time of the death of the insured person or pensioner.

Source: ISSA Studies and Research No. 31, *Survivors' Benefits in a Changing World*, monograph printed in 1992 by the Social Insurance Organization of Egypt.

or even dominant contribution to the financial support of the family. The considerations which lie behind survivors' benefit for widows (dependency, inability to provide self-support, absence of social security rights) apply equally to widowers, and in principle there is no justification for distinguishing between widows and widowers. The application of this principle, however, is not straightforward where the existing provisions of the scheme provide a favourable presumption of dependency for widows and a phased revision of this would be necessary to achieve equality of treatment for widows and widowers.

Survivors' pensions for divorced people

Pension rights for divorced spouses is a major issue in several countries in western Europe where there are high levels of divorce and remarriage. Problems arise in social insurance pension schemes because of potential rights to survivor's benefit derived from marriage which disappear on divorce and remarriage. Special arrangements have been made in some schemes to provide rights to divorced spouses in western Europe (in Belgium, France and Luxembourg) but, more commonly, in Central and Eastern Europe (for example, in Estonia, Hungary, Slovakia and Slovenia) and the solutions adopted vary according to the national family law. One approach is to link entitlement to a survivor's pension with the receipt of maintenance from the deceased insured person at the time of death, but some schemes maintain the dependency linkage between the insured deceased and a divorced spouse provided that the latter satisfies the required conditions imposed by the scheme as to age, disability or responsibility for dependent children.

CONCLUSIONS ON SURVIVORS' BENEFITS

It is difficult for survivors' benefits to follow the principles of equality of treatment, since the basis for entitlement is derived from an insured person who, in most cases, is a man. Furthermore the provisions of entitlement are inevitably based on what are perceived as the most common circumstances, it being considered impracticable to determine entitlement on a case by case basis. But it is also difficult to devise general provisions which take account of a wide range of different considerations. Some of these considerations are based on different values which conflict with each other. Thus many married people are separated from each other and many people live together without being married. Dependency does not only exist between married couples: it exists between unmarried couples, between family members and between persons of the same sex. It would be easier if social security rights of an individual insured person were to be based solely on his or her contribution record, but those who have been unable to work include many who have not done so because they have assumed a position of dependency on another person. People of the same sex are often financially dependent on each other. In many families, the income of both the mother and the father is essential for family support.

These issues are more complex in developed, rather than developing, countries since it is here that there have been major changes in family roles and in social values. In developing countries wives are less likely to be the breadwinners, although many will have some source of gainful employment and complexities are more likely to arise with identifying patterns of dependency given the role of the extended family.

The difficulties described are attributable to the general reliance of social insurance schemes on established gender roles in which the man is the head of the family and works to provide income to meet the needs of his wife and family. In this context, social protection needs were focused on the man as the breadwinner and the wife only enjoyed social protection rights derived from her husband by virtue of his membership in a social insurance scheme. Although changes in family structures and in the role of women have led to acceptance of the principle of equality of treatment, this has proved difficult to implement in practice since it implies, at least progressively, a modification of derived rights and greater reliance on the individualization of benefit entitlement. Social protection schemes have been modified to provide gender equality but the characteristics of employment for many women, and the related limitation in the levels of benefit entitlement that they are able to build up, still place them at a disadvantage compared with men and thus make it difficult to remove entitlement based on derived rights. This problem is particularly acute where benefit levels are based on the value of contributions paid, since here there is no scope for modification, as under defined benefit social insurance schemes or under universal schemes, where special provision can be made to take account of periods of inactivity caused by, for example, child care.

The individualization of benefit rights could in theory lead to the abolition of benefit for surviving dependants, but this would imply the need for special provisions to credit women (home carers) with periods of insured pensionable service in respect of periods when they are unable to work because of domestic responsibilities. And this would need to be supplemented by an income/support system based on a means test for those living alone who had no other means of support and, on this basis, no distinction would be drawn between those deprived of financial support, whether through death, desertion, divorce, unemployment or incapacity.

Benefit schemes for surviving dependants based on derived rights thus remain very important, particularly in developing countries. Where the principle is retained, the trend is towards the equality of treatment for widows and widowers, with perhaps a stricter application of dependency tests in relation to incapacity for work and child care responsibilities, and even through the application of a means test. In this context, consideration could be given to the following approaches.

- Widows and widowers should be treated equally, with both subject to a dependency test which restricts the entitlement element to those surviving dependants who are incapable of self-support because they have young children to look after, or because they are disabled or unemployable. Conditions related to age or duration of marriage would seem less relevant to entitlement.

- A person who was cohabiting with the deceased in a long-term relationship should have similar rights to those of a legal spouse (although cohabitation would have to be closely defined and would undoubtedly give rise to difficulties in implementation).

- Divorced spouses should also have equal rights without reference to fault, provided that the deceased was obliged to provide maintenance.

- Under the above, multiple entitlements would become more common and overall benefit entitlement would need to be divided, perhaps on the basis of duration of the marriage or period of cohabitation.

- Where there was no entitlement to a long-term pension because of the failure to satisfy a more rigorous dependency test, an interim benefit could be payable, either as a lump sum or as a periodic payment for a short duration.

Notes

[1] Different schemes use different terms to describe what are essentially identical contingencies; thus the terms "invalidity", "disability", "disablement" and "incapacity" are often almost

interchangeable. In the context of this chapter, invalidity is generally, but not exclusively, preferred and denotes a condition which is expected to be permanent whereas incapacity implies a more temporary, though often long-term, condition.

[2] 1996 data provided by the World Bank.

[3] According to the *People's Daily* of 17 October 1998, reporting the opening ceremony of the Third National Assembly of the China Disabled People's Association.

PENSIONERS AND SOCIAL ASSISTANCE BENEFITS

5

This chapter concentrates on two elements of social assistance: the structure and principles of social assistance for pensioners, and the level of social assistance. It also focuses on benefits aimed at guaranteeing minimum incomes. Other parts of the book relevant to a discussion of social assistance address: retirement benefits (Chapter 3), the redistribution of income (Chapter 11), the normative basis for policy (Chapter 15) and problems of coverage and governance (Chapters 8 and 9).

In all OECD countries, except Australia and New Zealand, there is a social security pension paid on the basis of contributions from employers or employees or the state without a means or asset test. This may be supplemented by a private or occupational scheme, also based on contributions, personal savings or employment income, to determine living standards in retirement. Pensioners in most countries do not have to rely on means-tested social assistance for their income in old age. However in all countries there are some who do rely on social assistance. The reasons for this vary from country to country. In Australia and New Zealand the whole social security system is income- and asset-tested. In other countries residents may not have contributed – or not contributed enough – to a pension, perhaps because they have not been in employment long enough, or have never worked. They may have recently arrived in the country, or have exhausted entitlement to a pension that was payable for a fixed period. Because of inadequate inflation proofing, the level of the pension may have fallen over time, and may be too low to cover essential needs such as housing, medical expenses or the costs of residential care. For any of these reasons, a pensioner may be receiving social assistance. Therefore it is important to take account of social assistance in any appraisal of social security pension schemes.

A TAXONOMY OF SOCIAL ASSISTANCE

There are three basic mechanisms by which the state can directly allocate income or services to individuals or households:

- universal or contingency benefits, not related to income or employment status, allocated to all citizens within a certain social category;
- social insurance, where the benefit is related to employment status and contributions paid;
- means-tested or income-related benefits, where eligibility is dependent upon the current or recent resources of the beneficiary.

Within resource-tested programmes, there are three distinctions to be made between the following:

- poverty-tested benefits and general means or income-tested benefits; the latter may go to people well above any poverty line;
- cash and tied benefits; the latter cover reductions in costs for specific services, the most important of which is housing;
- schemes open to all people within a certain income group and those for specific categories, such as older or disabled people.

The structure of benefits in countries such as Australia and New Zealand, which extend beyond the poverty line, also requires the inclusion of benefits performing similar functions in the United States, the United Kingdom and some other European countries. Social assistance in this chapter therefore includes:

- *general assistance* – providing cash benefits for all or most people below a specified minimum income level;
- *categorical assistance* – providing cash benefits for specific groups (sometimes at a level above the minimum);
- *tied assistance* – providing free or subsidized access to specific goods or services, either in kind or in cash; this can be further divided into housing assistance and other tied assistance.

THE SIZE OF SOCIAL ASSISTANCE

To obtain an overall picture of the size of social assistance schemes, table 5.1 provides estimates of spending on social assistance as a proportion of GDP. Looking first at general, non-categorical assistance programmes, the United Kingdom stands out, spending 2.4 per cent of GDP on Income Support in 1995, followed by Canada and Denmark. When categorical schemes are considered, the distinctive patterns of Australia, Ireland and New Zealand are clearly revealed. Putting the two non-categorical and categorical schemes together, we find the English-speaking countries in the lead in spending, with the notable exception of the United States. In most continental European Union member countries, categorical assistance for specific groups is more important than general programmes. Among those countries for which we have data, the United Kingdom also leads the world in spending on specific means-tested

Table 5.1 Social assistance expenditure as a percentage of GDP, OECD countries, 1995

Country	General assistance [1]	Categorical assistance [2]	Cash assistance [1 + 2]	Housing assistance [3]	Cash plus housing assistance [1 + 2 + 3]
Australia	0.4	9.4	9.5 ·	0.5	9.1
Austria	–	0.2	0.2	n/a	0.2
Belgium[a]	0.1	0.6	0.7	–	0.7
Canada	1.8	0	1.8	n/a	1.8
Denmark[a]	1.4	n/a	1.4	n/a	1.4
Finland	0.5	–	0.5	0.6	1.1
France	0.3	0.8	1.1	0.9	2.0
Germany	0.5	1.6	2.1	0.1	2.3
Greece[b]	–	0.1	0.1	n/a	0.1
Iceland[a]	0.1	0.1	0.2	n/a	0.2
Ireland[a]	0.3	4.8	5.1	–	5.1
Italy	0.2	1.1	1.3	–	1.3
Japan	0.2	–	0.2	–	0.2
Luxembourg	0.4	0.2	0.5	n/a	0.5
Netherlands[a]	0.8	1.4	2.2	n/a	2.2
New Zealand[a]	0.1	13.0	13.0	–	13.0
Norway[a]	0.5	0.2	0.7	0.2	0.9
Portugal	n/a	0.5	0.5	n/a	0.5
Spain	0.03	1.1	1.1	–	1.1
Sweden	0.63	–	0.6	0.6	1.2
Switzerland	0.88	0	0.9	–	0.9
Turkey[c]	0.5	n/a	0.5	–	0.5
United Kingdom	2.4	0.2	2.7	1.6	4.2
United States[a]	0.4	0.9	1.3	0.3	1.6

Notes: Numbers may not add up as a result of rounding.
– indicates that there are no substantial forms of expenditure within the particular category, whereas n/a indicates that information is not available.
[a] 1992 figures. [b] 1988. [c] 1993.

Source: Numerators: data supplied by national official or academic respondents.

housing benefits (which go to people other than just those with incomes at the assistance level), followed by two very different countries: France and Finland.

The expenditure figures in table 5.1 are for all recipients of social assistance and not just pensioners. It is difficult to obtain comparable data on the categories of assistance recipients, but table 5.2 presents whatever information it has been possible to gather on older people. The numbers in the first column are expressed as a proportion of the total population, not the population of pensioners, since comparable information of this kind is not available for many of the countries. For some countries it has been possible to obtain an estimate of pensioners in receipt of social assistance as a proportion of the aged population (in column 2) and, for more countries, pensioner social assistance recipients as a

Table 5.2   Aged social assistance recipients as a proportion of total population, total aged population and total numbers claiming social assistance, OECD countries, 1995

Country	% total population	% total aged population	% total social assistance claimants
Australia	8.8		46.9
Austria	3.4 (1993)		–
Belgium	1.1	6.7 (1994)	30.0 (1994)
Canada	0.2		2.3
Denmark[a]	–	0.2	–
Finland	0.3	2.6	4.8
France[a]	2.2		21.7
Germany	0.6		18.3
Greece	0.3 (1993)		4.1 (1992)
Iceland[a]	6.8[b] (1992)	1.7	8.0 (1992)
Ireland	3.2 (1993)		24.0 (1993)
Italy	1.3 (1994)	8.7 (1993)	33.6 (1993)[c]
Japan	2.3		43.3 (1993)
Luxembourg	0.4		22.5
Netherlands	0.2 (1991)		–
New Zealand	14.8 (1993)		58.0 (1993)[d]
Norway	0.2 (1992)	1.1	5.3 (1992)
Portugal[a]	1.2		45.7
Spain	0.4		11.4
Sweden[a]	0.3	1.6	3.3
Switzerland	2.3 (1994)		–
Turkey	n/a		–
United Kingdom (60+)	3.0		27.0
United States	0.6 (1993)		

Notes: Total number of social assistance claimants may include some double counting.
[a] Total beneficiaries including partners and children (NOSOSCO, *Social Protection in Nordic Countries 1995*, Copenhagen, 1997). [b] Including recipients of supplemental pension. [c] Number of claimants of local social assistance not known. [d] Total New Zealand superannuation. This pension is conversely means-tested: that is, available to all over the age of 65 but subject to income tax and tax surcharge on other income over a certain limit.

Sources: OECD population numbers: national informants provided estimates of claimants receiving aged social assistance from their national accounts.

proportion of all social assistance recipients (in column 3). Older recipients of means-tested benefits are, not surprisingly, numerous in Australia and New Zealand – which have no social insurance schemes – but also in the United Kingdom and Ireland, where assistance benefits supplement relatively low basic pensions. In the United Kingdom, for example, 18 per cent of pensioners were receiving Income Support in 1995 and represented 27 per cent of all recipients aged 60 or over. Older recipients of social assistance are relatively insignificant in the majority of other countries. Apart from the countries mentioned above, pensioners on social assistance represent more than 1.5 per cent of the whole population (or roughly 10 per cent of the retired population) in Austria,

France, Japan and Switzerland. The composition of social assistance recipients in a country is a function of various factors, but pensioners represent less than a fifth of all social assistance recipients in all countries except Australia, Austria (probably), Belgium, France, Ireland, Italy, Japan, Luxembourg, New Zealand, Portugal and the United Kingdom.

Although older people receiving assistance represent only a small proportion of all assistance recipients in most countries, they are often single women. The feminization of poverty, while varying among the countries studied, is a significant feature of social assistance provision in the OECD countries.

Eardley et al. (1996) collected data on trends in the proportion of the population who were aged recipients of social assistance between 1980 and 1992. Among these, Australia, Austria, Canada, Germany, Greece, Japan, the Netherlands, the United Kingdom and the United States exhibited a decline and Norway showed no change – only in New Zealand was there a significant growth. In Iceland changes in the structure of pensions brought a large number of older people into receipt of means-tested supplements. Belgium, Portugal and Switzerland also experienced small increases. However old age is, generally speaking, a diminishing reason for people to claim means-tested benefits, in absolute as well as relative terms.

THE STRUCTURE OF SOCIAL ASSISTANCE

Government respondents in the Eardley et al. (1996) study were asked for a statement of policy aims for social assistance. Those provided, which included both statements enshrined in laws and constitutions and expressions of policy by officials, were fairly similar across the whole range of countries. They basically encompassed three main principles.

1. The schemes are there to guarantee a minimum standard of living for people whose incomes are insufficient.

2. To be eligible to receive them, people must lack the ability to support themselves adequately by other means or by access to other resources.

3. Schemes are not meant to encourage dependency but should incorporate measures to promote self-sufficiency and independence.

The relative emphasis placed on these three principles, as well as the term "minimum", varies between countries. In some countries, including Austria, Germany and Luxembourg, reference is made to decent standards or those in keeping with human dignity: others refer to reasonable or adequate resources. The basis for the establishment of the reference minimum for assistance schemes differs widely between countries. Several, especially the Northern European and Nordic countries, place a particular, expressed emphasis on the principle of subsidiarity, or the necessity of drawing upon all other available help or resources before being entitled to public assistance. However the practical application of this principle again varies considerably, both in terms of the range and level of personal resources which are exempted from means testing and in the extent to which it is expected that the resources of other people should be called upon before an individual has a right to public assistance.

Table 5.3 provides a broad, comparative outline of some of the main characteristics of the resource-tested benefits in the countries studied. The picture provided is inevitably oversimplified and partial. However this form of presentation helps to illuminate patterns of similarity and difference. It is concentrated here on income-related or means-tested benefits providing either general or group-specific cash help, and excludes the separate tied benefits, such as housing support. The table differentiates between general and categorical social assistance schemes for pensioners (where they exist). In most countries where there is a categorical scheme for the elderly the general scheme will be of limited or no importance for the elderly, and this factor has been noted on the table. The table includes information on the target group, the minimum age of eligibility, use of a nationality test and whether the main general minimum income benefit available is organized predominantly on a national or subnational basis, and is primarily rights-based or discretionary.

The policy of guaranteeing minimum incomes through one generalized, all-encompassing means-tested benefit is still fairly unusual, and confined mainly to the Nordic states (Bradshaw and Terum, 1997). Canada has one broad national assistance framework, but the provincial autonomy of regulation and administration has the effect of creating a set of regional subsystems of assistance. Japan is a marginal case, since the assistance scheme there has a unified structure, but is divided into a number of functional elements. It could be argued that Austria and Switzerland also belong to the unitary group, since they share with some of the Scandinavian countries a high level of regional or local discretion and their main assistance benefits are general. However the categorical schemes outside the main assistance benefits are payable to pensioners.

The majority preference is still for separate coverage by population category, but here a number of approaches must be distinguished. One group, comprising principally the southern European or Mediterranean countries, including Greece, Italy, Portugal, Spain and Turkey, organizes limited minimum income protection, principally in relation to specific groups such as older or disabled people. In some of these countries there is then a discretionary local assistance back-up. Although the scale of assistance provision in the United States is much greater than in any of these countries, it may be argued that the structure is not dissimilar.

Another group, including the United Kingdom and other northern European countries, has one primary and inclusive national assistance benefit, together with a varying number of other categorical benefits which serve somewhat different functions. The various categorical minima in Belgium and Luxembourg allow less restrictive rules to apply to groups such as the elderly, who might be seen as more deserving, and have different sources of finance. In the Netherlands the different schemes relate primarily to claimants' labour market status. France and Ireland may be seen as fitting into this group, although the extent of their coverage derives more from the range of group-specific benefits rather than from one overarching one. Finally Australia and New Zealand have to be seen jointly as a separate case, where comprehensive coverage derives from their fully resource-tested categorical benefit systems. None of these divisions, however, can be seen as absolute. All countries have developed individual approaches based on national history and policy traditions, and it is not possible to understand how widely income protection is offered through different systems simply from the clusters of population groups named as the target beneficiaries.

The treatment of resources

The principle of means-testing implies a series of administrative decisions about what constitutes the private resources of a benefit applicant, with whom these resources are assumed to be shared, who in a family or household should be expected to contribute personal resources to the upkeep of other individuals, and how much of the available private resources should be consumed before there is a call on public assistance. The decisions different countries take on these questions may reflect wider attitudes concerning the balance of responsibilities between the state and the individual/family.

Table 5.3 below lays out, in a schematic and abbreviated way, some of the main elements of the assessment process for entitlement to assistance benefits in the countries in our study. It relates primarily to the main, generalized assistance benefits where they exist. One difficulty involves making comparative sense of all the many and varying ways in which assets are treated and the forms and levels of income which are disregarded in the test of resources. As a way of classifying the treatment of earned income, countries are divided into four categories: those applying (a) no disregard, (b) a minimal earnings disregard (up to 15 per cent of the standard single person rate), (c) a medium disregard (between 16 and 40 per cent), and (d) a higher disregard (over 40 per cent). It should be noted that these are approximate calculations, since disregards are often made up in different ways, apply only to earned or unearned income, or vary for different family types. Sometimes they are only available for limited periods or are reduced over time, and this is indicated in the table.

Looking at the treatment of earnings, it is first of all the group of Latin and Mediterranean countries, along with Austria and Switzerland, which operate the most stringent tests and allow the least amount of extra earnings to be retained. In the same group are the Nordic countries of Iceland, Sweden and, in effect, Finland, since it is reported that discretionary disregards are not often applied. The same applies to Denmark, even though the guideline earnings disregard is rather higher. Ireland comes into this group for Supplementary

Table 5.3 Main conditions of eligibility for income-related and means-tested benefits for pensioners in the OECD countries

Country	General benefits	Categorical benefits	Target group	Minimum (max.) age	Residence/nationality	Other/comment
Australia	Special Benefit K		People who have no other income support payment and are in hardship	16 years	Resident in Australia, newly arrived migrants in need etc.	Safety net benefit National aministration
		Age Pension	Older people	61 or 65 (Age of retirement for women to be raised to 65 by 2014)	Australian resident and living in Australia	National administration
		Wife Pension	Partners of age or disability pensioners	21, unless claimant or partner has child		No new claims since July 1995
Austria	General Assistance (Sozialhilfe) K		People with insufficient resources to maintain a minimum standard of living	19	Residence in relevant province; some provinces also require Austrian citizenship; but EU nationals and recognized refugees also covered	Discretionary local administration
		Supplementary Pensions (Ausgleichszulage)	Older people whose insurance pensions are below the minimum	Retirement age	As above	National insurance societies administration
Belgium	Minimex (Revenu Minimum de Moyens d'Existence et de l'Intégration) K		All citizens in need	18	Anyone registered in Belgium; some restrictions on foreigners	Local by Public Centres for Social Welfare
		Guaranteed Income: Older People (Revenu Garanti pour Personnes Agées)	Older people with insufficient income for a minimum standard of living	60 (women) 65 (men)	Belgium citizenship (or EU citizens), plus residence for 5 years in Belgium before claim or 10 during lifetime	National by Insurance Office

(continued)

Table 5.3 Main conditions of eligibility for income-related and means-tested benefits for pensioners in the OECD countries (continued)

Country	General benefits	Categorical benefits	Target group	Minimum (max.) age	Residence/nationality	Other/comment
Canada	Social Assistance		General	18	No minimum period of residency; refugees are eligible when status decided; benefits not portable between provinces	Provincial by local offices
Denmark	Basic Maintenance Allowance (Social Bistand) K	Non-contributory Supplementary Pensions Scheme	People with low pension rights to guaranteed minimum level	Older people	Residence in Denmark; non-Danish citizens given temporary help until resident for a three-year period; recognized refugees and EU citizens; foreign claimants, with the exception of Nordic citizens, can be sent back to their country of origin	
Finland	Living Allowance		All who have exhausted all other forms of obtaining income	18	Legal resident and registered by municipality	'Safety net provision', local
France	General Social Assistance (Revenu minimum d'insertion) K		People ineligible for other social minima who satisfy residence/ nationality test	25	French nationals and EU nationals legally recognized	Local Family Allowance Office
		Benefits for the Elderly (Minimum Vieillesse) 7-8 benefits according to past activity plus supplements to guarantee minimum level of income	Older people	65	As above	National from Pension Funds

Country	Benefit	Coverage	Age	Residence/eligibility	Notes
Germany	General Social Assistance (Sozialhilfe)	Those who have insufficient income to meet needs. Supplements for old age	Irrespective of age	Residence in Germany; restrictions for non-German citizens, including refugees	'Safety net provision'
Greece	Older people without insurance: 1. Medical care, 2. Minimum pension	Older people without adequate social insurance cover	65	Greek citizenship and permanent residence; refugees and asylum seekers eligible if they have permit to stay	Subject to decision by local caseworker
	Social protection of those economically weak – lump sum K	Those in need with no social security cover		As above	
Iceland	Financial Assistance K	All whose income is insufficient to meet needs	16	Legal residence; reciprocal agreements with Nordic countries.	
	Supplements for pensioners; minimum income guaranteed	In receipt of basic Old Age Pension	Pension age (67)	As above	
Ireland	Old Age Non-Contributory Pension	Older people	66	Residence in Ireland; some restrictions for refugees and asylum seekers until residence determined	
	Supplementary Welfare Allowance K	People with exceptional needs			Exceptional/urgent need
Italy	Social Assistance (Minimo Vitale)	All, including the elderly to bring them up to the minimum pension level	All including minor living independently	Residence in municipality and legal residence in Italy, including EU citizens	Local and discretionary
	Social Pension (Pensione Sociale)	Older people	65	As above	No new claimants since 1996
	Social Allowance (Assegno Sociale)	Older people not entitled to supplementary pension	65	As above	Replaced Social Pension in 1996 for new claimants
Japan	Social Assistance	Those unable to maintain minimum living standards	No specific limits	Japanese nationals and others with long-term residence licence	Administered by caseworkers

(continued)

Table 5.3 Main conditions of eligibility for income-related and means-tested benefits for pensioners in the OECD countries (continued)

Country	General benefits	Categorical benefits	Target group	Minimum (max.) age	Residence/nationality	Other/comment
Luxembourg	Income Support Benefit (Revenu Minimum Garanti)		All	30	Resident for 10 out of previous 20 years and registered with local authority	
Netherlands	General Assistance (Algemene Bistand)	'Safety net' benefit to cover all expenses including limited housing costs		18	Residence in Netherlands; non-Dutch citizens only if covered by agreements	Baseline system of income support
New Zealand	Special Benefit K		All who have no other means of support, 'safety net' provision	16, self-employed not eligible	Resident in New Zealand, including refugees and asylum seekers	
		New Zealand Superannuation	Retired people	60; by year 2006: 65	Residence for at least 10 years since age of 16, including last 5 years prior to claiming	
Norway	Social Economic Assistance		General local provision where no other means of provision exists	18	Legal residents, plus other Nordic citizens	
Portugal	Guaranteed Minimum Income K		Person or household in serious economic need	18	Legal residence in Portugal	Introduced pilot scheme in 1996; national scheme 1997; administered by Regional Social Security Centres
		Social Old Age Pension	Older people not covered by other social security schemes, for example insurance-based retirement pension	65	Nationals and EU citizens; six months residency period for political refugees and stateless persons	Came into effect January 1994
		Social Supplement to the Pension	Pensioners whose social insurance contributions are insufficient to generate a minimum level of pension	65	As above	

Country	Scheme	Eligibility	Age	Nationality/residence	Administration
Spain	Minimum Income Scheme K	Low-income, working age households	25 (65)	No nationality conditions but a minimum of one year residence in the region 10 years residency in Spain, including two preceding the claim	Varies between regions
	Social Pension	Older people without insurance pensions	65		Centrally administered
Sweden	Social Welfare Allowance	People who have no other means of support; and as a supplement to people claiming social security benefits	18	Legal residence in Sweden; EU rules apply	Administered by Local Welfare Boards; discretionary
Switzerland	Social Assistance (Soziale Fuersorge, Sozialhilfe, Aide Sociale, Assistenza Sociale)	Individuals or households without other sources of support; to ensure a minimum standard of living	Not defined	Legal residence in Switzerland; minimum period of residency varies across cantons and communes	Considered a temporary benefit; discretionary
Turkey	Social Assistance and Solidarity Scheme K	Nationals and aliens in need who would become independent with minimum assistance	18	Turkish nationals, immigrants, refugees and other non-nationals	
	Old Age Assistance	Low-income elderly people with no other source of income	65	Turkish national.	Administered through the Civil Service Pension Fund
United Kingdom	Income Support	All excluding unemployed	Normally 18, unless parent or in hardship	'Habitually resident' in United Kingdom, unless 'worker' under EU regulations or accepted refugee; restrictions relating to immigration status	October 1996 Job Seekers' Allowance replaced Unemployment Benefit

(continued)

Table 5.3 Main conditions of eligibility for income-related and means-tested benefits for pensioners in the OECD countries (continued)

Country	General benefits	Categorical benefits	Target group	Minimum (max.) age	Residence/nationality	Other/comment
United States	General Assistance K		Serves as a 'safety net' benefit for those not eligible for other assistance	Not stated	Resident within the state of application; period of residency varies between states; most restrict applicants to US citizens or legal aliens;	1996: 42 States (including District of Columbia) run schemes; in 33 states schemes operate throughout the entire state
		Supplemental Security Income	Eligible older people to guarantee a minimum income level	65	US citizens only; 1996 law denies participation to legal immigrants	

Notes: K. These general assistance benefits have no impact on categorical benefits for pensioners in particular countries. Service/veteran benefits not included; lump sum benefits: grants or loans not included.

Source: National informants to Eardley et al. (1996) updated by national informants to Ditch et al. (1998).

Welfare Allowance. The United Kingdom falls into a small group, including Norway and the Netherlands, with relatively low disregards.

Among the countries with higher levels of disregards, which includes Australia, New Zealand and the United States, these vary between client groups and some are only available for a specific period. It is noticeable, however, that Australia and New Zealand – the two countries with entirely selective benefit systems – have means tests for most of their basic benefits which cut in at a considerably higher level in proportion to benefit rates than do many of those in Europe. This effect is accentuated by the tapered withdrawal rates of benefit, which is unusual outside the English-speaking countries.

The treatment of assets is also very complex. A basic comparison is presented in two parts. First, countries are divided into two groups: those which take all liquid assets into account, applying only a small disregard or none at all, and those applying a higher disregard to capital. Second, they are divided according to whether, when they determine eligibility, they disregard the value of a private dwelling or might expect claimants to sell their homes before drawing on assistance. There is also variety in the range of other income, including social security benefits, which are counted or disregarded in the means test.

In the group which takes more capital and assets into account, we first of all find Austria and Switzerland, with their highly discretionary and locally based systems. They are also among those countries which pursue family financial obligations further than most. But this group also includes several of the Scandinavian countries, normally regarded as the most socially liberal. It is among these countries that the principle of family financial obligation appears to be weakest in relation to the resource unit for social assistance. Yet in Sweden, for example, it is regarded as reasonable that, before having recourse to social assistance, people might well be expected to sell their house, and a car if they have one, unless there are no public transport alternatives for essential travel. A number of other countries, including the Netherlands, can insist on a home being sold if the value is above prescribed limits, while in Austria and some states of the United States (for general assistance only) the authorities can claim part of the equity of a claimant's house to recover benefit if the house is sold.

Benefit and resource units

Although many countries describe entitlement to benefit as individual, that is, claimants can be assessed for benefit on the basis of their individual entitlement, the actual unit for whom benefit is payable is still normally the claimant, plus spouse. Only Austria, Japan and Luxembourg count other non-dependent adults in the household as part of the benefit unit (and thus include their needs in the calculation of benefit due) and in Luxembourg there are many exceptions to this rule.

The differences become more marked, however, when we look at the resource unit: that is, whose resources must be taken into account when applying the test of a claimant's means. Again the majority of countries take into account only the resources of the claimant and the spouse, if there is one. In the United Kingdom non-dependent deductions from housing costs imply an assumption of resource sharing within the wider household, but the expectation of intra-family support does not extend beyond this point. But there are a number of countries where expectations of family support extend further. In Austria, Germany, Japan and Switzerland social assistance claimants may be expected to seek support from children and grandchildren – even, in Switzerland, potentially from siblings – before having recourse to public assistance. It is also of interest in this respect to note that in Switzerland there are no standardized means tests: benefits are assessed according to a detailed and individual investigation of both resources and needs, using standard household budgets as a template. In France local *Aide sociale* for older people is subject to a prior test of their (future) inheritors' means: monies paid can be reclaimed from these family members or by first claim on any assets left on death. In Belgium, too, regulations were recently introduced which oblige local authorities to seek to recover assistance payments from parents or adult children of claimants. How these rules work in practice varies considerably and social welfare workers often have the discretion not to apply them, but what these countries have in common is a strong tradition of family responsibility and obligation, backed up in several countries by laws which specify duties of intra-family maintenance which go beyond that of spouses or of parent and child.

At the other end of the spectrum is a small group of countries (Denmark, Iceland, the Netherlands and Norway) which do not place a maintenance or resource-sharing obligation even on spouses unless they are legally married. Although no countries have gone as far as general individualization of means-tested benefits, several, including the Netherlands and Ireland, have introduced the possibility of splitting payments between partners.

Housing costs

Housing costs are often a crucial element of the income requirements of low-income households, and many countries either include all or part of the costs of accommodation within the assessment of needs for social assistance, or provide some form of separate income-related or means-tested housing allowance to people on low incomes. The relationship between housing needs and low income in a comparative perspective is, however, a matter of considerable complexity. To do justice to this area of assistance, a separate, comprehensive study would be needed (see, for example, Kemp, 1997) and for present purposes only the key elements of housing assistance are examined here. Table 5.4 summarizes the main forms of help with housing costs in the countries in the study. The table shows that only three countries (Italy, Spain and Turkey) do not have either a generalized scheme for housing assistance or an element within social assistance payments to meet housing costs. However there are also differences between countries as to whether the housing element of social assistance is paid as a specific supplement or is meant to be met out of the standard assistance payment. Belgium and the Netherlands are the two main examples of the latter approach, although where claimants face particularly high housing costs any extra help available is purely discretionary in Belgium, whereas there is access to a regulated housing benefit scheme in the Netherlands. As with other elements of assistance in Switzerland, help with housing costs is largely discretionary and varies according to the canton or municipality.

Countries which operate general housing benefit schemes available to all those on low incomes, as well as assistance recipients, include Denmark, France, Germany, Sweden and the United Kingdom. Portugal also has a time-limited general scheme, while Finland and Greece both have limited schemes for certain categories of people.

One important aspect of housing support is whether it can cover mortgage payments for owner-occupiers as well as rents. The picture is somewhat more complicated than it appears from table 5.4, because there are often other forms of subsidies outside benefit systems for both tenants and owner-occupiers, including public house building, tax reliefs, rent controls and special loan arrangements. However it is clear that the predominant pattern among the OECD countries which have housing allowances is for means-tested help to be available directly through social assistance to house buyers and tenants alike. The exceptions are Australia, Austria (normally), Greece, Japan, Luxembourg and Portugal. Within this broad pattern, however, there are differences as to whether support is available to owner-occupiers in the same way as for tenants. Some countries, for example, meet only the interest element of mortgage payments, whereas others meet capital repayments too. As indicated earlier, some countries, including Austria and some states of the United States, for general assistance, have the power to claim part of the equity of claimants' housing property. The United Kingdom has recently introduced limits on the level of mortgage for which interest payments can be made through Income Support. There have also been calls in the United Kingdom for a form of housing benefit to be extended to owner-occupiers because of a perceived imbalance in the support available to Income Support recipients compared with others on low incomes.

The costs which can be covered often include heating and other services, as well as rent or mortgage interest, but what is more difficult to judge from the information gathered for this study is how far, in practice, assistance recipients' full housing costs are met in different circumstances, and how much has to be met out of the main benefit payments. The model family approach taken in the next section provides some further information on this question for a number of family types living in rented accommodation (see table 5.4).

Table 5.4. Means-tested help with housing costs, OECD countries

Country	Help available?	Form of housing assistance	Tenures covered	Extent of housing costs covered
Australia	Yes	Separate rent assistance for pensioners and beneficiaries in private rented housing Public sector tenants have rents subsidized through Commonwealth State Housing Agreement	Renters only	For private tenants, up to 75% of rent over specified thresholds Public sector tenants pay 20-25% of their incomes in rent
Austria	Yes, but varies by province	Payment as addition to social assistance	Usually renters only To prevent homelessness authorities can take over mortgage payments	Varies according to province; can meet full costs or fixed amounts
Belgium	Only on a local discretionary basis	Social assistance payments (Revenu Minimum Garanti: RMG) are meant to cover housing costs. No generalized housing benefit system Subsidies mainly in 'bricks and mortar'	At discretion of local welfare centre	
Canada	Yes, from provincial governments	Shelter costs included in assistance payments, up to maximum levels set by province Social housing tenants pay rents according to their incomes	Both private renters and owner-occupiers, but some provinces require reimbursement of increased equity	Actual housing costs up to provincial maximum
Denmark	Yes	Separate housing benefit scheme open to all those on low incomes	Both renters and owner-occupiers	Full costs over a threshold graduated according to household composition and size
Finland	Yes	Supplementary payments of social assistance can be made to meet housing costs Also three other income-related housing allowance schemes: general, for older people, for students	Both renters and owner-occupiers	Up to 80% of housing costs covered; social assistance recipients can receive help with remaining 20%
France	Yes	Separate housing benefit scheme	Both renters and owner-occupiers	Generally only part of costs met, depending on household composition and size

Country	Scheme	Details	Tenure	Payment
Germany	Yes	Supplementary payments to meet 'reasonable' housing costs can be made to social assistance recipients, at the discretion of local authorities (but within guidelines) / Separate income-related housing benefit scheme (Wohngeld) for low-income households	Both renters and owner-occupiers	Social assistance recipients can receive full housing costs, including heating / Payments of mortgage interest only, up to local maxima
Greece	Yes, but only for the elderly	Income-related housing benefit scheme for older people without full insurance-based pensions / Various other loans/subsidies and tax exemption schemes for building homes	Private tenants only	Rent paid direct to landlords
Iceland	Yes	Housing policy tends to favour owner-occupation; means-tested loans are available for up to 90% of cost / Financial assistance includes component for rent, but since January 1995 local authorities have the power to operate separate housing allowance schemes	Both renters and owner-occupiers	For house buyers, interest rate for loans set according to income, household size and family type / For renters on social assistance, only about a third of average rents likely to be met within financial assistance
Ireland	Yes	Rent and mortgage supplements available through Supplementary Welfare Allowance / Local authority tenants have rents related to their incomes, according to rules set by each local authority	Private and housing association tenants and owner-occupiers / Public tenants	Mortgage assistance limited to interest only; otherwise full costs met minus £IR 5 per week
Italy	No housing allowance scheme	Small number of public housing places for those on low incomes		
Japan	Yes	Housing Aid	Renters only	Can cover housing deposits, rent and necessary repair costs, up to locally determined maxima
Luxembourg	Yes	Rent allowances payable only as part of Revenu Minimum Garanti (RMG)	Renters only	Difference between gross rent and 10% of RMG payment to household, up to specified maximum

(continued)

Table 5.4 Means-tested help with housing costs, OECD countries (continued)

Country	Help available?	Form of housing assistance	Tenures covered	Extent of housing costs covered
Netherlands	Yes	Social assistance payments meant to cover housing, but separate housing benefit available to meet particularly high costs; administered separately from social assistance Where costs exceed specified ceiling, temporary supplement available through social assistance; recipient supposed to seek cheaper dwelling	Renters and owner-occupiers in flats or houses (single-room tenants not covered)	Cost met above specified level and below set limit
New Zealand	Yes	Accommodation Supplement	Renters, boarders and owner-occupiers	Supplement meets 65% of costs over threshold (25% of 'base benefit rate' for renters and 30% for home owners), up to specified regional limits For owner-occupiers, both interest and capital payable
Norway	Yes	Payable as supplement to social assistance payments	Renters and owner-occupiers	Full rent and both interest and capital payments met if 'reasonable'; capital element may be limited
Portugal	Yes	Means-tested housing allowance administered by Ministry of Public Works; recipients must have suffered 30% reduction in monthly income or have income at level of the non-contributory social pension	Renters only	Fixed amounts, limited to 12 months' duration
Spain	No general scheme			
Sweden	Yes	Social assistance recipients can have housing paid as supplement to assistance standard if 'reasonable' Also general, income-related housing benefit scheme administered by regional social insurance office Pensioners can also receive income-related municipal housing supplement	Renters and owner-occupiers	For assistance recipients, full costs met if reasonable. Interest payments only on mortgages

Country				
Switzerland	Yes	Assistance payments can include housing costs Help also through social housing aimed at low-income groups	Renters and owner-occupiers	Discretionary
Turkey	No housing assistance scheme			
United Kingdom	Yes	Housing Benefit scheme open to all tenants; administered by local authorities; rules of eligibility, entitlement and means test aligned with Income Support (except for double capital limit)	Private and public tenants	Income Support recipients can have full rent met if reasonable; for those with incomes above this level, maximum benefit is reduced by 65p for each £1 of extra income
		Owner-occupiers can receive help with mortgage interest payments as supplement to Income Support (but not Family Credit) Council Tax Benefit Scheme open to all householders; means-tested help with local Council Tax; Council Tax is based on house valuation bands	Owner-occupiers	Mortgage interest only, subject to maximum level of mortgage. If claimant under 60 years, only 50% of interest met for first 16 weeks Additional non-means-tested reduction of 25% for a household with one adult
United States	No national housing assistance	Various state and local schemes for rental and mortgage assistance, based on reducing housing payments to fixed percentage of income; rental schemes mainly through low-cost housing projects or vouchers Also Low-Income Energy Assistance Program (LIHEAP) permits states to provide assistance to low-income households with heating, air conditioning and weatherproofing of homes	Renters and owner-occupiers	Provision of assistance geographically uneven and limited

Source: National informants to Eardley et al. (1996) updated by national informants to Ditch et al. (1998).

Take-up

It has long been a criticism of means-tested benefits that the proportion of eligible people claiming benefits is often low compared to that for other types of benefit. Van Oorschot, who has carried out perhaps the most extensive studies to date of take-up in a comparative context (1991 and 1995; van Oorschot and Schell, 1991), has suggested that, with the exception of the United Kingdom, the proportion of eligible people not claiming social security benefits has been a particularly neglected topic in the welfare state literature. This observation was supported in the information provided by national informants for the Eardley et al. (1996) study. Less than a quarter of the countries were able to provide any recent estimates of the percentage of eligible people claiming benefits, and the basis of these was not always clear and tended to provide more information of take-up among groups other than pensioners eligible for social assistance.

Non-take-up is influenced by factors at three levels: first the way benefits are designed, second the way benefits are administered and third the way potential claimants respond (van Oorschot, 1995). Non-take-up is more likely to be a problem in means-tested benefit schemes, in schemes that have a density of complex rules, have vague criteria for entitlement, are aimed at social groups which are the subject of prejudice, supplement other sources of income and leave the initiative in taking up benefits to the claimant. These characteristics exist in many of the social assistance schemes in this study.

Many of the national informants also suggested that claiming social assistance continued to be stigmatized to some degree, even where the existence of the benefits had wide levels of support and legitimacy. Stigma, of course, is hard to measure and the information available is impressive, but examples were given, particularly from countries where local and discretionary systems combine with small numbers of claimants. In these circumstances it is possible for individuals, or particular groups, to be singled out as welfare recipients, and for them to become the subject of prejudicial public attitudes. By contrast, receipt of benefits in countries like Australia and New Zealand seems relatively lacking in stigma, although even in these countries being able-bodied and unemployed can attract residual prejudice.

Official estimates of the percentage of eligible people claiming benefits in Australia suggest a relatively high level of take-up for most benefits. However most of the estimates provided are of coverage of the known population group and take no account of those who might be ineligible because of excess resources. In this light, the Australian estimates look even higher, a fact which may be partly explained by virtually all benefits being resource-tested in some way. In Germany it was suggested that take-up was controversial. Studies in the mid-1980s pointed to an increase for *Sozialhilfe* from an estimated 50 per cent in the 1970s to around 70 per cent. Japan appears to have had a low take-up rate, at least in the early 1980s, but there are no more recent estimates and the present situation is unknown. An official estimate from Luxembourg put take-up for the *Revenu minimum garanti* (RMG) at only around 50 per cent – surprising, perhaps, given the relatively high level of benefits. However the RMG is generally received as a supplement to some other source of income and it may be that small entitlements are less commonly taken up. This is a feature of take-up which has been observed in the extensive research carried out in the United Kingdom, both by government and non-government researchers (see, for example, Kerr, 1983; Fry and Stark, 1987; Craig, 1991; Marsh and McKay, 1993; Department of Social Security, 1994; Corden, 1995). Official estimates put take-up of Income Support in 1992 at 77–87 per cent of expenditure and 65–77 per cent of caseload, depending on household type, and most of the amounts not claimed are estimated to be fairly small.

Informants from a number of other countries, including Austria, Belgium, France, the Netherlands and the Nordic countries, all suggested that there were likely to be some take-up problems with the minimum benefits in their countries, but that the question had not been extensively researched. The Nordic social assistance schemes present particular difficulties in discussing take-up, partly because of local variations in benefit levels in some of the countries, but also because of certain specific features of the conditions of entitlement. Take-up is also particularly difficult to assess in other countries with highly discretionary systems, such as Austria and Switzerland.

LEVEL AND STRUCTURE OF SOCIAL ASSISTANCE FOR PENSIONERS

Analysis of the level and structure of social assistance payments in the countries in the study is based on data provided by the national informants on the impact of different benefit packages on a series of model pensioners in specified, near-identical circumstances. National informants were asked to produce estimates of the package of income for pensioners in two different circumstances (see table 5.5).

Social assistance

Social assistance comprised the package of benefits that would be received by pensioners on social assistance. The package was estimated for two pensioner households: a single retired person aged 68 and a retired couple both aged 68. It was assumed that they were out of the workforce and did not have contributory records sufficient for any insurance-based pension. Even where minimum, income-tested pensions were available they were not counted if they required a record of insurance contribution.

Table 5.5 Structure of social assistance package, for a couple aged 68. Amounts per month in dollars at purchasing price parities (after housing costs), of 1992. OECD countries

	Social assistance	Income tax	Employee contributions	Housing	Health costs	Other	Total
Australia	825			−165	−8		652
Austria	458						458
Belgium	647			−259	−5		383
Canada	1 188			−485	−5	73	771
Denmark	1 038	−21		−146	3		874
Finland	124				−32	631	723
France	831			16	−47		800
Germany	491						491
Greece	121			−175			−54
Iceland	1 005			−266	−19		720
Ireland	588			−92		52	548
Italy	660			−51			609
Japan	593			−149			444
Luxembourg	890		16	−243	−8		655
Netherlands	831			−146	−25		660
New Zealand	941	−141		−273	−17		510
Norway	865			−326	−11		528
Portugal	248			−213			35
Spain	362			−95	−8		259
Sweden	739			−40	−19		680
Switzerland	1 440			−612	−167		662
United Kingdom	612			−12			600
United States							
New York	736			−560		79	255
Pennsylvania	682				−16	97	763
Texas	633			−170	−15	111	559
Florida	633			−402		111	342

Note: For non-pensioner households, the Italian figures should be regarded with particular caution. They represent optimistic assumptions about the likelihood and the level of awards to these households.

Source: National informants to Eardley et al. (1996).

Social security retirement benefits

For comparison purposes the social assistance benefits were compared with a social security retirement benefit. It was assumed that none of the social security retirement pensioners had any income from earnings. They were assumed to be receiving the social security retirement pension payable to a person who had worked since the age of 21, with a full record of contributions based on national average earnings throughout his or her working life. This is a simplification of real experience in many countries where pension entitlements have changed in the last 40 years and does not reflect the real earnings trajectory of most workers. Occupational pensions were not included unless they were compulsory and underwritten by the state. Again this assumption leads to the underestimation of pensioners' incomes in those countries (such as the United Kingdom) where occupational pensions are commonly payable on top of the state schemes. In the case of couples, it was assumed that the female partner had not been employed (again an unlikely assumption in some countries).

The calculations of cash benefits received, and tax and social security contributions payable, were relatively straightforward, given the model pensioners' circumstances. However, the calculation of other elements of the package called for the establishment of a common context and framework for the analysis. One of the most problematic areas is that of housing costs.

Housing costs

Housing costs are especially difficult to take into account. Costs vary within countries and between countries according to tenure and the size, age and location of the dwellings. In some countries rents may be controlled for those persons occupying dwellings before a certain date. For owner-occupiers, loan structures and interest rates vary between countries, often according to the stage in the economic cycle, while the level of mortgage interest is also affected by the stage of a purchaser's life cycle. There are also significant differences between countries in tenure distribution at different income levels. Nevertheless housing costs cannot be ignored. In many countries help with housing costs is a critical element in the benefit package and, even where such support does not exist, variations in housing costs mean that real income levels differ substantially before and after taking account of housing. For this exercise, the pensioners were assumed to be living in rented dwellings: rented from a public authority, housing cooperative or housing association, if they were common forms of tenure in the country, or from a private landlord if that was the most common tenure pattern. In those countries with high levels of owner-occupation, this assumption is less representative. However, leaving aside the difficulties of making assumptions about owner-occupiers' costs, pensioners receiving social assistance are more likely than others in most countries to be living in rented dwellings.

National informants were asked to fix typical or representative rent levels for such dwellings in a given town in their country. There is an argument for using national average rents rather than local estimates, but previous experience has suggested that up-to-date information on average rents is often not available. Locating the families in a given commune, town or city helps to structure the comparisons where benefits vary locally, but it can be difficult in some countries to nominate a typical or average location. The size of the dwellings was specified and varied with the model families, so that single pensioners were assumed to be living in one-bedroom dwellings and pensioner couples in two-bedroom dwellings. Again this is an artificial assumption, as families on constrained incomes will in practice make different choices in response to local housing markets. The national informants were left to determine whether the dwelling was a house or an apartment on the basis of what was the most likely accommodation type in their country.

Informants were also asked to provide the gross rent. One defect of this method is that it does not take account of the value of any "bricks-and-mortar subsidy" on the dwelling: the difference between the market rent and the gross rent. If certain pensioners are benefiting more than other households from living in houses with a bricks-and-mortar subsidy, and therefore have lower rents for the same dwelling, the support package for such pensioners will be underestimated. It is also anomalous that the rents assumed in some countries are those subject to rent control. In these cases the rent is being subsidized by the landlord.

National informants were then asked to give the net rent: that is, the rent actually payable by the pensioners. The difference between the gross rent and the net rent was then treated as part of the package of support. There is no denying that these assumptions are both arbitrary and unsatisfactory in many respects. However to ignore altogether the impact of housing costs and housing subsidies would have been misleading.

Housing costs are not only a problem at the design stage of comparative projects, they are also difficult to handle at the analysis stage, particularly in a study comparing the level of social assistance payments. The problem arises because in some countries housing costs, or a proportion of them, are paid together with social assistance. Thus the basic benefit takes account of some, or all, housing costs. In other countries, housing costs are subsidized either by a reduction in rent payable or by a housing benefit or allowance scheme which is administered separately from social assistance. If comparisons are made of the level of social assistance before housing costs, the first group of countries – those that pay the housing subsidy in with social assistance – will appear to have higher levels than the others. The answer to this is to avoid making comparisons of social assistance before housing costs and to concentrate on comparisons after housing costs, when income net of housing represents the income people have left to spend on living costs other than their housing.

There is no simple solution to these problems. It would be wrong to compare social assistance only before housing, yet it would also be misleading in certain circumstances to compare social assistance incomes only after housing. The answer is to present the results in most circumstances both before and after housing costs, but also to bear in mind that results after housing costs are strongly affected by the assumptions made.

The implied equivalence scale in social assistance

Table 5.6 provides a representation of the implied equivalence scales in each country's social assistance scheme, before housing costs. In this table, the assistance paid to a couple without children is set at 100 for each country: thus it

Table 5.6 Implied equivalence scale of social assistance (before housing costs), couple (35) = 100, OECD countries, 1992

	Couple (35)	Single (68)	Couple (68)
Australia	100	60	100
Austria	100	86	117
Belgium	100	76	101
Canada	100	104	170
Denmark	100	57	115
Finland	100	59	134
France	100	118	210
Germany	100	66	120
Greece	100	127	253
Iceland	100	80	100
Ireland	100	78	112
Italy	100	55	93
Japan	100	62	94
Luxembourg	100	75	101
Netherlands	100	71	100
New Zealand	100	87	133
Norway	100	60	87
Portugal	100	50	99
Spain	100	58	99
Sweden	100	46	80
Switzerland	100	69	100
United Kingdom	100	86	133
United States New York	100	88	120
Pennsylvania	100	136	200
Texas	100	261	384
Florida	100	249	367

Source: National informants to Eardley et al. (1996).

is possible to compare the relative treatment of pensioners and of childless couples.

Most countries provide relatively larger assistance benefits to people over retirement age: Canada, France, Greece and the United States are notably more generous to people above pension age than to childless couples below pension age. Other countries – including Belgium, Luxembourg, the Netherlands, Portugal, Spain and Switzerland – do not vary their social assistance payments between those below and above pension age. There are a few countries that appear to pay higher benefits to working-age couples than to pensioners. These include Italy, Japan, Norway and Sweden, although in Japan higher benefits are paid to people over 70. On the face of it, these differences in payments to younger and older people without children do not appear to follow any obvious pattern, though they may be related to the level of benefits available from retirement insurance pensions.

There is also little consistency in the ratio of social assistance paid to single pensioners compared with couples. In Finland single pensioners receive only 44 per cent of that received by pensioner couples, whereas at the other end of the scale, in Iceland, it is 80 per cent. There certainly appears to be little consistency in the valuation that countries make of the relative needs of younger and older childless people dependent on social assistance, or single pensioners and pensioner couples (see table 5.6).

Replacement rates

Table 5.7 presents a comparison of net incomes of pensioners on social assistance with the net income they would have received if they had been working

Table 5.7 Pensioners' replacement ratio (net disposable income on social assistance as percentage of net disposable income on average earnings), OECD countries, 1992

	Before housing costs		After housing costs	
	Single person %	Couple %	Single pensioner %	Pensioner couple %
Australia	34	54	36	57
Austria	30	40	46	80
Belgium	39	47	28	35
Canada	45	69	23	57
Denmark	47	81	55	100
Finland	23	54	42	109
France	42	71	48	83
Germany	21	34	28	46
Greece	7	12	−7	−8
Ireland	37	47	38	53
Italy	42	52	43	54
Japan	24	33	23	24
Luxembourg	43	52	36	44
Netherlands	58	77	53	78
New Zealand	39	61	32	58
Norway	45	62	34	54
Portugal	22	43	−1	10
Spain	17	28	19	22
Sweden	40	70	53	110
Switzerland	62	89	51	91
United Kingdom	28	42	31	49
United States				
New York	33	50	10	26
Pennsylvania	32	49	32	49
Texas	29	47	25	50
Florida	32	53	9	34

Source: National informants to Eardley et al. (1996).

for average earnings (one earner only in the case of the couple). It is in effect a measure of the extent to which social assistance in retirement replaces net income in work. The ratio is also a relative measure of the living standards of pensioners on social assistance: the higher the ratio, the closer the incomes of pensioners on social assistance are to those of similar people in work.

Before housing costs, the ratios vary for a single pensioner from 62 per cent in Switzerland (the Canton of Fribourg) to 7 per cent in Greece and, for a couple, from 89 per cent in Switzerland to 12 per cent in Greece. The United Kingdom, at 28 per cent for a single person and 42 per cent for a couple, comes well down in the ranking. After housing costs, in most countries, pensioners' replacement ratios improve because housing benefits are of more help to social assistance recipients; the United Kingdom, for example, moves up the table for this reason.

It appears that in most OECD countries spending on social assistance for older people represents a declining share of an already small proportion of the total expenditure on social assistance as a proportion of all social security. The income of older people in many countries has increased, partly because of the maturation and improvement of pension schemes, and in a number of countries even poorer older people are protected from having to claim general social assistance by the presence of minimum, non-contributory citizens' pensions.

Older people are more likely to be receiving assistance in the English-speaking countries, where social assistance covers larger proportions of the population. However the population structures of Australia, Canada, Ireland, New Zealand and the United States are relatively youthful, whereas the United Kingdom has already effectively undergone much of the ageing process. In Australia there has been some increase in the selectivity of pensions. In New Zealand, a more concerted attempt to restrain expenditure has been made, including the taxation of benefits. Yet even here demographic pressures do not in themselves appear to be significant causes.

FINANCING PENSION SYSTEMS

6

This chapter discusses the conceptual techniques and some of the problems of financing pension systems, including especially the way in which the degree of funding affects the financial equilibrium of pension schemes and determines contribution rates. Other relevant sections of the book include the discussion of investment policy (Chapter 7), the consequences for public finances (Chapter 14) and the design of pluralistic structures (Chapter 19). Technical Brief 1 places some of the issues in the framework of a formal model, and Technical Brief 4 discusses the impact of demography.

The rules of the pension scheme determine the total amount of expenditure which a society spends on pensions and the distribution of that amount among beneficiaries. These rules determine who is eligible for a pension and the size of his or her pension. Which, and how many, people, will receive a pension will depend on the age distribution of the population, the rules governing the age of retirement, and who within the population is to be covered by the pension scheme. How much they will receive is often a complicated function of the number of years of contribution and the size of the contribution, and the latter is often, in turn, related to the insurable earnings, which is rarely the same thing as total earnings. To provide for pensioners' needs the financing of pensions must ensure that sufficient amounts of money are available when benefit obligations fall due. But since both the length of the contribution period and the length of retirement are long and uncertain, and because many things may change during this period – earnings, demography and the pension rules themselves – estimates of total pension outlays are difficult to forecast. And although they do not generally change rapidly from year to year, they may change by large amounts over the span of a 40-year working life and a 20-year retirement. For these reasons the financing of pensions is one of the most complex tasks in social security, and one which involves long-term projections as well as current concerns. Failure to get the estimates at least broadly correct may lead to broken promises to the retired generation, unanticipated increases in contribution rates or unwelcome calls on public sector finances.

THE DEVELOPMENT OF PENSION EXPENDITURES

Two definitions

Two definitions are useful in the analysis of this kind of situation, both of which provide an overall measure of the relative cost of the pension scheme. The first is the *pay-as-you-go cost rate*. This is the ratio of pension expenditures to total insurable earnings, which is itself a function, not only of the proportion of total earnings which are taken into account for calculating pension contributions, but also of the number of people covered by the pension scheme. Few countries cover all their workers for purposes of contributions, and in some cases the proportion of uncovered workers can be a very large proportion of the total labour force. It should be observed that the pay-as-you-go cost measure is equal to the product of (a) the system old-age dependency ratio, which is equal to the ratio of the number of pensioners to the number of active contributors, and (b) the financial ratio, which is defined as the ratio of the average pension to average insurable earnings.

The second measure is the *national pension cost*. This is simply total public expenditure on pensions as a proportion of GDP. In this formulation the system old-age dependency ratio is different from the population old-age dependency ratio in that it includes only those contributors and pensioners who are actually covered by the scheme, rather than the population-wide ratio of the total number of people over the age of retirement to the total labour force. But if the share of total insurable earnings in the total remuneration of employees remains constant, and if the share of total remuneration of employees also maintains a constant share of GDP, the two measures are proportional and the curves of the two indicators have the same shape over time. The mathematical formulation of the two measures in shown in box 6.1.

The pension life cycle

As a starting point it is useful to consider the likely growth of expenditure for a pension scheme from its date of inception, on the assumption that earnings, demography and the rules of the scheme do not change, and also assuming that pensions are paid only to those who have contributed and in proportion to their contributions.

In the first few years pension expenditures are small, mainly reflecting invalidity pensions. This is because only a few individuals will have passed from work to retirement and because they have contributed for only a very few years and receive only small benefits. But as time goes on more workers will retire, adding to the total number of retirees who will receive pensions. And each new generation of retirees will have contributed for a longer period and will receive a larger pension. Expenditure will increase rapidly.[1] Eventually, however, this rate of growth will slow down and come to a halt. This will occur when all new retirees have made contributions to the pension scheme

Box 6.1 Two basic indicators for the development of pension cost
The pay-as-you-go cost (PAYG) measure is defined in year t as:

$$PAYG_t = P_t/A_t * AP_t/AIW_t$$

where, for any year t,

$PAYG_t$ *is the pay-as-you-go cost measure,*
P_t/A_t is the system old-age dependency ratio,
AP_t/AIW_t is the financial ratio,

and

A_t is the number of active contributors,
P_t is the number of pensioners,
AP_t is the average amount of pensions,
AIW_t is the average amount of insured wages or income.

The National Pension Cost (NPC_t) measure is defined as:

$$NPC_t = (P_t * AP_t)/GDP_t$$
$$= PAYG_t * W_t * WS_t$$

where, for any year t,

NPC_t is the National Pension Cost measure,
P_t is the number of pensioners,
AP_t is the average amount of pensions,
W_t is the share of insurable wages in total gross remuneration of employees,
WS_t is the share of total remuneration in GDP.

If the share of insurable earnings in total remuneration of employees (W_t) remains constant, and if the share of total remuneration in GDP remains constant, then $PAYG_t$ and NPC_t are proportional.

over the full span of their working lives (and so will be entitled to a full pension), when all existing pensioners are also entitled to a full pension, and when the number of pensioners who die each year exactly matches the number of workers who retire to become new pensioners. At this point, and in this idealistic world, expenditure on the pension scheme will have reached a stationary state. A picture of this growth pattern is shown in figure 6.1.

Two points need to be noted about this stylized development. In the first place, it applies to all forms of financing method: pay-as-you-go, fully or partially funded. The key requirement is that pension payments are related to both years and level of contribution, and that no pensions are paid in respect of years for which the individual did not make a contribution.

Second, it is very rarely that conditions remain unchanged for such a long period. Real earnings grow over time; the demography changes, in particular the age structure of the population covered and expected longevity; and the rules of benefit entitlements may also change, usually in the direction of

Figure 6.1 Typical expenditure development in a social security pension scheme

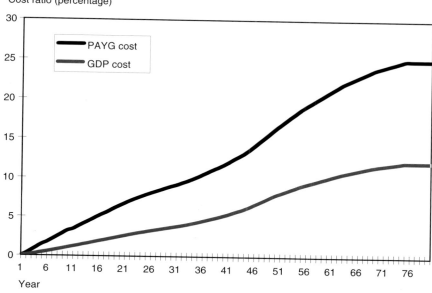

Cost ratio (percentage)

Source: ILO estimates.

improved entitlements or extended coverage, and sometimes with retrospective effect on the calculation of benefits. This latter effect means that the growth path of pension expenditures comprises several S-shaped curves imposed one upon the other and that the outcome is simply one of very rapid growth spread over a long period of time. Even without a subsequent change in rules, it may take a long time for the scheme to reach maturity – some 70 or 80 years from its beginning – to the extent that some analysts claim that no existing social security pension scheme has ever reached a fully stationary (that is, mature) state.

Trends in pension expenditure

In these circumstances it is readily understandable that most public pension schemes throughout the world have, over the second half of the twentieth century, faced (in some cases rapidly) increasing levels of expenditure. Almost everywhere pension expenditures now absorb the major share of total national social expenditures, although the actual levels and share of pension expenditures vary greatly between countries. Not only have levels of earnings and income increased greatly, but the demographic structure of the population has aged (and is continuing to age rapidly), life expectancy has increased, the

Table 6.1 Total expenditure by major functions as a percentage of GDP, selected countries

Country	Year	Special schemes				
		Total social expenditure	Pension	Health care	Other social security functions	For government employees and war victims
Africa						
Benin	1996	0.40	0.30	0.00	0.10	0.00
Niger	1992	0.66	0.10	0.07	0.22	0.00
Tanzania	1989	1.74	0.09	0.00	0.01	0.06
Togo	1996	1.09	0.62	0.05	0.42	0.00
Arab states						
Bahrain	1992	1.60	0.43	0.01	0.11	0.00
Kuwait	1996	5.00	4.70	0.00	0.30	0.00
Saudi Arabia	1996	0.18	0.17	0.00	0.01	0.00
Asia						
India	1992	0.85	0.29	0.03	0.03	0.48
Malaysia	1996	0.10	0.04	0.00	0.06	0.00
Philippines	1996	1.31	1.01	0.24	0.062	0.00
Singapore	1996	1.70	1.42	0.26	0.02	0.00
Latin America						
Colombia	1992	2.49	1.38	0.98	0.13	0.00
Chile	1992	10.64	5.57	1.69	1.45	0.00
Mexico	1996	1.17	0.70	0.26	0.21	0.00
Uruguay	1992	14.11	11.15	1.21	1.05	0.00
Central and Eastern Europe						
Bulgaria	1996	9.17	7.37	0.42	1.38	0.00
Poland	1992	21.35	13.11	3.20	5.45	1.29
Romania	1992	13.18	5.52	0.53	5.20	1.64
OECD						
Japan	1992	11.65	3.81	3.7	1.43	1.94
Sweden	1992	39.86	18.67	7.33	11.86	0.01
United Kingdom	1992	21.19	5.80	5.52	6.61	2.16
United States	1992	13.89	4.81	2.03	4.35	2.19

Source: ILO. *International inquiry into the cost of social security* (various issues); see ILO 1996a.

coverage of pension schemes has expanded, the insured population has increased (in large part because of greater employment of women, and because the rules of the pension systems themselves have been enhanced, providing better pensions).

Table 6.1 describes the current and past levels of pension and social expenditure for selected countries in six regions,[2,3] measured as a percentage of GDP, figure 6.2 displays this information in graphical form, and figure 6.3 shows the

Figure 6.2 Relation between pension expenditure as percentage of GDP and GDP per capita

Pension expenditure as percentage of GDP

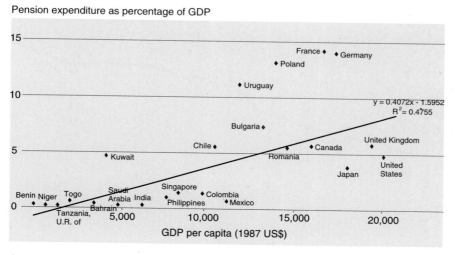

GDP per capita (1987 US$)

Source: ILO. *International inquiry into the cost of social security* (various issues).

growth of expenditure on public old-age benefits as a percentage of GDP for the OECD countries. In the OECD countries, expenditure estimates now stand at around 10 to 12 per cent of GDP. This is the most affluent region of the world, one whose pension schemes are the most mature. In many developing countries of Africa and Asia expenditure on formal sector pension schemes does not exceed 1 per cent of GDP. Latin America shows a wide range of expenditure figures, with some countries spending similar proportions of GDP to those in OECD countries, and other countries with very low expenditures. Pension schemes in Central and Eastern Europe appear to absorb proportions of GDP similar to those in OECD countries. But in all countries, and at all levels of expenditure, there is strong evidence of rapid growth. As already discussed, much of this growth was due to the maturation of the public pension schemes, but a significant proportion was also due to demographic factors, in particular the ageing of population structures, to the growth of earnings and incomes, and to an enhancement of the pension provisions themselves, especially the coverage of the schemes and the level of benefits. For the OECD countries as a whole it seems likely that between 1960 and the early 1980s roughly one-third of the growth was accounted for by demographic factors, the remainder being attributable to extensions of coverage and improvement of benefits. Pensions as a share of GDP have also clearly been influenced by economic conditions in general and, in the case of the OECD countries, reflect the slower growth which occurred in the mid-1980s.

Figure 6.3 Public social expenditure on old age as a percentage of GDP, 1960–93

Percentage of GDP

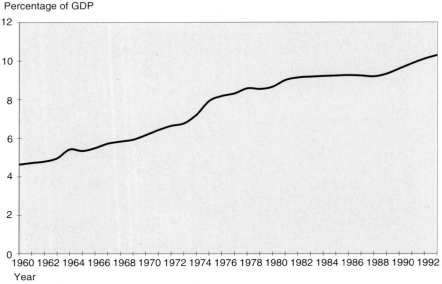

Year

Source: OECD estimates of social expenditure.

FINANCING SOCIAL SECURITY PENSIONS

The level of annual expenditure determines the amount of financial resources required to finance a pension scheme, but it does not determine how this income is generated. The actual choice of a pension-financing system requires separate policy decisions, and there are various types of financing systems among which to choose.

Objectives and definitions

Financing systems are defined as a set of legal provisions which aim at ensuring that, in every year, the amount of expenditure obligations will be matched by sufficient financial resources to meet them. It should be noted that this does not mean that revenue and expenditure need exactly match each year: reserves may be built up or drawn down, and borrowing may be allowed, provided access to borrowing (or state finance) is assured. Financing systems are fully described by the following parameters: (a) the *financial rules* under which they operate, (b) the *financing method*, that is, the definition of the level of funding pursued by the system, and (c) the *type of resources* which are used to finance pensions.

The ultimate objective of any pension financing system is to keep a pension scheme in financial equilibrium. A scheme is in short-term equilibrium if revenue equals expenditure in the current year. A pension scheme is in long-term financial equilibrium at a given point in time if the present value of all future expenditure is equal to the present value of all future revenue of the scheme plus reserves held in the base year. This can be translated into a fundamental (simplified) equation for the general financial equilibrium of a pension scheme:

$$R_{t0} + \sum \prod_t * AIW_t * r_t = \sum TEX_t * r_t$$

where R_{t0} is the reserve in year t_0,

$\prod_t$ is the contribution rate charged in year t,
r_t is the discount rate $(1/(1+i))^t$,
TEX_t is the total expenditure in year t,
AIW_t is the total amount of insurable wages or earnings in year t,
and t runs from 0 to infinity.

This equation must hold at any point in time for a theoretically unlimited future period of time. The indefinite time frame is justified by the fact that the existence of social security schemes is guaranteed by law for unlimited periods.

All pay-as-you-go schemes are (or should be) in short-term equilibrium, but may not be in long-term equilibrium unless changes are made to bring future revenues and expenditures into line. Conversely all fully funded schemes are in long-term equilibrium (or should be) but may not be in short-term equilibrium. This does not mean, however, that they are not viable provided short-term deficits (or surpluses) can justifiably be covered by borrowing or lending.

The financial equilibrium of a pension scheme is influenced by three sets of determinants: demographic development, the economic environment and the governance of the scheme. Box 6.2 lists the main factors influencing the financial equilibrium of a pension scheme.

The above equation applies to pay-as-you-go financing systems, as well as to systems which are financed on a fully funded basis,[4] or all forms of intermediate funding, but general long-term equilibrium does not automatically guarantee liquidity at each specific point in time. In the case of pay-as-you-go systems, the scheme is by definition in equilibrium on an annual basis, that is, revenue and expenditure must equal each other each year, whereas under other options temporary negative balances are theoretically possible (which would have to be financed by borrowing) provided they would be covered by later annual surpluses. Annual liquidity has to be ascertained by a further set of rules.

The specific provisions of the financing system must translate the financial equilibrium and the annual liquidity requirement into a legal definition of actuarial equilibrium. The actuarial equilibrium is defined by the social security law which stipulates the size of the reserve which a pension scheme has to have at any given point in time.

Box 6.2 Summary of factors affecting the financial equilibrium of a pension scheme

	Impact on the income side	Impact on the expenditure side
Economic factors		
(1) Growth	Insured persons and wages	Entitlements and numbers of beneficiaries
(2) Employment (most likely depends on (1))	Number of insured persons	Number of beneficiaries (invalidity immediately, old-age in the long run)
(3) Wage share and wages (might depend on (1))	Insurable earnings	Benefit amounts (after time lag)
(4) Wages/inflation	Insurable earnings	Benefit amounts
(5) Interest rates increase	Investment income	
Demographic factors		
(1) Initial population age structure	Relationship of actives to beneficiaries	Relationship of actives to beneficiaries
(2) Mortality changes	Change in potential number of contributors	Change in the number of beneficiaries and average length of service
(3) Fertility increase	Number of contributors (long run) if economic development permits	Number of beneficiaries (long run)
Governance factors		
(1) Design	Contribution provisions	Pension formula and entitlement conditions determining the number and amounts of benefits
(2) Maintenance (adjustment)	Ceiling on insurable earnings	Benefit levels
(3) Administration cost		Total expenditure
(4) Registration compliance	(Short-term) insurable earnings	(Long-term) number of beneficiaries
(5) Wage compliance	(Short-term) insurable earnings	(Potentially long-term) level of benefits

A private pension scheme is in actuarial equilibrium if, at each point in time, the amount of reserves is equal to the present value of all liabilities of the scheme, including the present value of all pensions in payment as well as the present value of all pension rights accumulated by active contributors. If this condition is met, the scheme is fully funded. The respective reserve level is called the terminal funding level, since the reserves are sufficient to finance all present benefit obligations if the scheme were to be terminated at some later date. With the exception of very few social insurance schemes, such as the Social Insurance Fund in Kuwait, no major social security pension scheme pursues a funding strategy of this type.

In social security pension schemes the actuarial equilibrium is a discretionary concept.[5] It translates the somewhat abstract formula of the long-term financial equilibrium into concrete practice. Technically it is usually stated in the form of a provision in the social security law which stipulates that the scheme must maintain a certain level of funding, say k times the annual expenditure, and that this ratio must be maintained over a certain number of years x (the period of equilibrium). The periodical actuarial reviews of many national social security pension schemes try to establish whether the present, and likely future, financial status of the schemes complies with the legally defined actuarial equilibrium. If this is not the case then the valuation will make recommendations as to how the actual equilibrium can be reinstated. Such an evaluation clearly involves a number of uncertainties about the future course of events, and how they are likely to affect pension obligations, and is itself clearly open to considerable uncertainty.

Financial rules

Statutory public social security schemes operate on the basis of financial rules, or principles, which are fundamentally different from private arrangements for income security. Private insurance companies, for example, finance pensions on the basis of a single financial rule of individual equivalence, which stipulates that the present value of the contributions of each individual contributor entering the scheme must, on average, equal the present value of all benefits expected by him or her. In the case of defined benefit schemes, in practice this generally leads to pension insurance contribution rates which are calculated for cohorts defined by the age of entry into the insurance. Individual premiums might be charged for persons with certain handicaps. In principle, there are no transfers between generations or income groups, the only risks insured being longevity, premature death or invalidity (in case the latter two contingencies are included in the insurance contract). In the case of defined contribution schemes, the principle of individual equivalence is automatically fulfilled if each participant's account balance is determined solely by his or her contribution and the associated investment earnings.

The rules governing social security financing systems are more discretionary than those dictated by private sector financial requirements, but can be deduced from the general principles governing social security. One may identify three main rules of social security financing, although in practice all three are hardly ever fulfilled at the same time and, in reality, political compromises are inevitably made.

Financial solidarity[6]

Required contributions or taxes for pension purposes are charged on the basis of the individual's ability to pay and regardless of his or her personal risks or circumstances (for example, existing health impairments or the existence of eligible dependants). In social insurance schemes this principle is generally embodied in uniform contribution rates across the insured population charged as a fixed percentage of insurable earnings. This might even be modified to provide lower contribution rates for low-income earners. Generally, in the case of pension financing from direct taxation, this rule automatically applies owing to the usual progressiveness of tax rates.

Collective financial equivalence

Collective financial equivalence requires that, at any point in time, the total present value of all expected future expenditure of the pension scheme is equal to the present value of all future income of the scheme (plus the initial reserve at the respective point in time, if existing). This has three implications. First, it simply demands that the scheme be in long-term financial equilibrium (which is equivalent to the principle of individual equivalence in the private sector). Second, it permits the redistribution of income between groups as long as the long-term financial equilibrium is secured. It also stipulates that, over the long run, income must cover expenditure regardless of whether reserves are built up or whether the scheme runs on a pure pay-as-you-go basis. Third, it implies that social security resources should not be used to finance non-social security expenditure, which may happen if governments borrow resources and either do not return them or return them at a value substantially lower than market rates of interest would require. Nor should there be an external subsidy to the scheme. The latter can occur if a scheme does not cover the full population but is subsidized from general revenues. Both situations raise serious equity questions with respect to whether one specific group of the society should be asked to pay extra taxes (which occurs if social security contributions are used for purposes other than social security requirements) or whether the general public can be forced to subsidize the standard of living of a specific group (which occurs when a scheme is subsidized from general revenues).

Intergenerational equity

The principle of intergenerational equity requires that members of all generations pay roughly the same share of their disposable income during their active life in order to earn equal benefit entitlements (in terms of replacement rates). This principle is the most contentious one, the least clear and the most open to diverse interpretations. In pay-as-you-go or partially funded systems, early generations normally pay lower contribution rates than the generation at, or near, the maturity stage of the scheme, while often earning similar pensions. This might be called a windfall profit when a new pension scheme is started in an economy with a roughly constant high standard of living. For developing economies one might argue that a lower contribution rate for early generations is justified on the grounds that their living standard is normally only a fraction of that of the following generations and it is thus only equitable to transfer some of the benefits of the growth backwards to early generations. If one were to finance a pension scheme on a theoretical constant contribution rate, most of the contributions of the early generation would go into the building up of reserves. At the maturity stage of the scheme, the income from investments would help to finance the scheme and keep the contribution rate at its permanent level. If the early generations had not contributed to the building up of reserves, the missing investment income in the later stages would be equivalent to the redistribution of income from later (normally richer) to earlier (normally poorer) generations. Such an income redistribution might still be regarded as socially equitable even if it is not, in a strict sense, actuarially equitable.

In most cases these rules are not applied in their pure form. Often there are tax subsidies for pension schemes which do not cover the total population or, on the contrary, pension reserves are borrowed and consequently written off. Both cases violate the rule of collective equivalence. In the case of defined contribution schemes, survivors' benefits might depend to a crucial extent on the time the breadwinner dies, which would violate the financial solidarity rule. The concept of intergenerational equity is much debated, but not often clearly defined. It may even be in conflict with reality, if there are no capital markets which could absorb the initially high reserves under constant contribution rates, or if the scheme lacks access to experienced investment management skills. The extent to which societies adhere to the different rules, and their priorities between the principles, are a matter of political preference. The choice of a specific financing system implicitly reflects these preferences.

Financing methods and funding levels

Actuaries commonly distinguish three financing methods creating different levels of reserves in a pension scheme: virtually no funding (that is, pay-as-you-go), full funding and partial funding. The level of benefit protection provided and the financing of the scheme are, in theory, mathematically independent areas. This can be demonstrated by table 6.2, which shows that both major types of pension benefits, that is pensions calculated on the basis of the defined benefit method and pensions calculated on the basis of the defined contribution method, can be financed by each of the three main financing methods.

Private sector pension schemes are usually fully funded; that is, they have to dispose of sufficient resources to honour their obligations should the insurance company, or the occupational pension scheme, be dissolved. Public pension schemes, which are backed by a societal promise guaranteeing their liquidity

Table 6.2   The independence of financing methods and benefit calculations

Type of calculation	Financing method		
	Pay-as-you-go	Partial funding	Full funding
Defined contribution	Notional defined benefit schemes in Poland, Latvia, Sweden	Could be achieved in notional defined contribution schemes with minimum funding requirement	Mandatory savings schemes in Latin America (e.g. Chile, Peru, Mexico)
Defined benefit formula	Tax-financed first-tier system (e.g. in Denmark and the Netherlands), contribution-financed system (e.g. in France and Germany)	All social security schemes with higher than pay-as-you-go funding level (e.g. Japan, Cyprus, the United States)	Occupational pension schemes (e.g. in the United Kingdom), some social security schemes (e.g. Kuwait)

and indefinite existence, do not require the same level of funding. The level of funding in social security schemes is determined by objectives other than the exclusive financial safeguarding of pension promises, and by the legal definition of the actuarial equilibrium of the scheme.

If, in the legal definition of the actuarial equilibrium, the funding ratio k is smaller than one (that is, the scheme holds less than the equivalent of one year's expenditure as reserves) and x equals 1, then the scheme is financed on a pay-as-you-go basis with a small contingency reserve. A bigger k indicates that the scheme is at least partially funded. A wide variety of rules are applied internationally. In the United States, for example, k is relatively high and x equals 75 years, whereas in Germany k is smaller than 1 and x is only 15 years. A full terminal funding level of reserves would lead to a much bigger k, which in each case would depend on the mortality rates of the population, the interest rates and the benefit provisions of the scheme (for example, the retirement age). Recent ILO calculations for the social security scheme in Trinidad and Tobago, for example, indicated that the terminal funding level of k would be in the order of ten times the annual expenditure.

Complex and pluralistic national systems composed of pay-as-you-go tiers and fully funded tiers are, from an aggregate point of view, no more than a partially funded pension scheme. Hence fully funded national pension schemes are a rare exception rather than the rule, but a national pension scheme may well have fully funded components.

SOURCES OF FINANCING

Public pension schemes have four types of revenues:

1. taxes in the form of allocations from general revenues, or in the form of earmarked taxes;

2. social security contributions paid by employers and/or workers;

3. investment income; and

4. a range of other revenues, which generally only play a marginal role (such as, for example, administrative fines or transfers from other social security schemes).

Social security pension schemes are generally categorized as predominantly contribution-financed or tax-financed. Yet fully tax-financed or fully contribution-financed schemes are rare. Most social security pension schemes are financed by a mix of sources.[7] Even many predominantly contribution-financed pension schemes are subsidized to some extent from general revenues. Social security benefits can, in practice, be financed using any source of government revenue. The source of financing is normally related to the characteristics of the benefit. Universal benefits are generally funded from general tax revenues. Universal basic pensions in Denmark, for example, are paid from general revenues. Means-tested social assistance benefits (such as, for example, the public pensions in South Africa) are also usually funded from general tax revenues.

Provident funds and individual account defined contribution plans are financed from workers' contributions withheld from wages, sometimes without a match by employers' contributions. Social insurance schemes are usually financed by both employers' and workers' contributions, sometimes complemented by government contributions. To the extent that schemes are funded, investment earnings also help finance benefits.

In Africa, where coverage is low, social insurance schemes are usually financed entirely from employers' and workers' contributions and investment income. General tax subsidies for schemes with low population coverage cannot be justified on equity grounds. In countries where coverage is low but the government contributes to the social security system from general revenues, if the source of the general revenues includes taxes from low-income people, this type of financing is regressive since low-income workers tend not to be covered in countries with low coverage. Primarily tax-financed social protection systems are generally progressive (and are thus often more efficient at alleviating poverty than social insurance schemes). They usually provide flat-rate benefits, paid also to people who have little or no attachment to the labour force, or who have a limited capacity to contribute.

General revenue is used to finance a third of the earnings-related social security benefits in Japan. In Cyprus the government contributes 3.5 per cent of the total payroll (out of a total contribution of 16.5 per cent) to the financing of the pension scheme. Because there is virtually complete population coverage in both countries, this poses no equity problems. In many countries, general revenue is used to pay for any deficit in social security, notably in the Middle

East (for example, in Jordan) and in countries such as Bulgaria, the Russian Federation and the Ukraine.

Financing can also come from earmarked taxes, which are reserved specifically for social security financing. For instance, social security benefits for agricultural workers could be financed through a tax on agricultural products rather than a tax directly on the workers. This approach has been used in France. Revenue from income taxation of social security benefits of high-income beneficiaries is used to help finance benefits in the United States. Part of the government contributions to social security in Panama comes from a tax on alcohol.

Proceeds from the privatization of government enterprises can also be employed to finance public pensions, or the transition from one pension scheme to another. Part of the financing of the Bolivian defined contribution scheme, for example, came from the privatization of several state-owned industrial enterprises. The proceeds of privatization were deposited in individual accounts and will be used to pay an annual benefit for life to all citizens who were aged 21 or older on 31 December 1995, regardless of their income or their insured status under social security.

The source of financing also bears some relationship to the level of funding. Predominantly tax-financed social security schemes are generally financed on a pay-as-you-go basis, whereas contribution-financed schemes can operate at any level of funding.

CONTRIBUTION SCHEMES

Contribution schemes are characterized by the incidence of contributions, the contribution base and type and the desired funding level.

The incidence of contributions

The relative level of employers' and workers' contributions varies considerably across countries, although in most the employer pays half or more of the total contribution. In the former planned economy countries of Central and Eastern Europe the contribution was paid almost entirely by the employer. More recently, in countries of Latin America such as Bolivia, Chile and Peru – which opted for radical reforms using defined contribution schemes – social security contributions are being paid entirely by the employee. El Salvador, however, has established a mandatory defined contribution scheme to which the employer contributes at a higher rate than employees. The split between the employers and workers might not affect total labour cost at all. Many social security analysts argue that workers – regardless of the formal sharing of the contribution payments – bear the full contribution burden through forgone wages. An advantage, however, of having employers and workers pay at least part of the social security contribution is that it makes both

Figure 6.4   Pension contribution rates, 1997

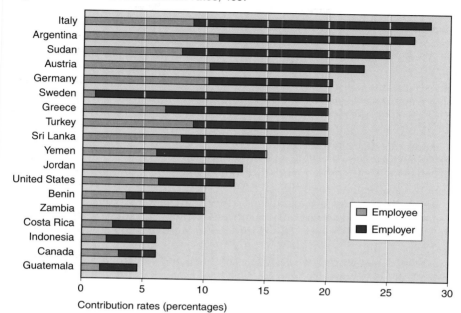

parties aware of the cost of the scheme and achieves some sense of ownership of the scheme. Contribution rates for selected countries are shown in
figure 6.4.

In some countries, the contribution rate varies according to the worker's age
and gender. It may also vary by occupation, especially when special provisions,
or special schemes, apply to some occupational groups. In Switzerland the contribution rate to the mandatory employer-provided pension is higher for older
workers and increases at earlier ages for females than for males because women
can retire at an earlier age. In Bulgaria the contribution rate varies according to
occupation. In Norway it is reduced in certain geographic areas to encourage
employment in those areas and is lower for workers under age 16 and over
69. In Finland the contribution rate is reduced for workers starting up a business. In a few countries the employers' mandatory contribution rate varies
according to the perceived ability of the employer, and perhaps ultimately the
workers, to pay. In Iraq the contribution rate of oil company employers is considerably higher than for other employers (25 per cent, against 12 per cent). In
Australia and Finland large companies must contribute at a higher rate than
small companies.

While contributions to social security pension schemes are usually mandatory, in a number of countries some categories of workers may contribute on

a voluntary basis. In Argentina, for example, housewives may make voluntary social security contributions. Some countries allow self-employed workers to be covered on a voluntary basis. This is the case in Chile and Panama, where self-employed workers who fall within a certain income band and have no employees may make voluntary contributions. In several countries, including India and Indonesia, establishments with fewer than five or ten employees, respectively, may voluntarily cover their workers. In a few countries workers meeting qualifying conditions can reduce their social security contribution payments so long as they participate in an individual or occupational pension scheme with a sufficient level of protection. This arrangement, called contracting out, is possible in Japan and the United Kingdom. Some schemes allow for the payment of supplementary contributions on a voluntary basis, as in Chile, where a 10 per cent contribution rate is mandatory but workers can voluntarily contribute more to their defined contribution plan.

In most countries the mandatory contribution rate is constant across all income levels. However in some countries the rate is progressive, being higher for higher-income workers. This is the case in Haiti and the United Kingdom. In Egypt a higher contribution rate applies for earnings above a certain threshold. Two features of social security financing contribute to the progressiveness of social security pension schemes. First, countries can establish an earnings deduction. For all workers, earnings below a fixed level are not subject to contributions but the earnings deduction does not affect the earnings used in calculating future benefits. Because the earnings deduction is a fixed amount, it is relatively more important to low-income workers than to upper-income workers. This feature is used in Canada.

A second feature is to charge progressively higher social security contribution rates on higher-income workers but base benefits on earnings rather than contributions. This feature is used in the United Kingdom in its defined benefit scheme. The defined contribution scheme in Colombia requires all members who earn more than four times the minimum wage to contribute an additional 1 per cent of their income as a solidarity tax. The revenue is matched by budget transfers and used to subsidize the contributions of specific poor groups in an attempt to extend the coverage of the formal social security scheme.

The financing of pension benefits for the self-employed under social security is a critical topic in many national schemes. Compliance is a notorious problem. Defining contribution obligations in such a way as to not be a deterrent to self-employment, while at the same time maintaining a meaningful level of protection, is a major challenge and national approaches vary greatly. In many pension schemes self-employed workers pay a contribution rate equal to the sum of the employers' and workers' contributions, as in the United States. In the United Kingdom low-income self-employed are exempt from the requirement to contribute but may voluntarily do so. Self-employed workers earning above a minimum amount pay a flat weekly contribution, while higher-income self-employed workers also pay an earnings-related contribution. To encourage self-employment, the contribution rate charged to higher-income self-employed workers is less than half the combined employers' and workers' rate. In Egypt self-employed workers can choose the level of earnings on which their contributions are based, while taxi drivers pay a flat rate, which is paid when they renew their drivers' licence.

In Panama self-employed workers may be covered voluntarily, and in Chile self-employed workers earning above the minimum wage may participate if they choose, but nearly all choose not to participate. Those who do participate pay the same rate as employed workers.

Contribution base

Most contributions are levied on wages and individual earnings. Rather than using actual earnings as a contribution base, some countries use a series of wage bands, where all workers whose earnings fall within a particular band pay the same amount. This system is currently used, for example, in some countries of Central America, the Caribbean, and in Japan and Turkey. In Jordan employers submit to the Social Security Corporation a statement of the earnings for each employee as of 1 January. For employees who remain with the same employer, those earnings form the contribution base for the entire year, even though the employee's earnings may increase or decrease during the year. These systems of basing contributions on a single earnings figure for an entire year, or on the mid-point within an earnings band, are assumed to simplify record-keeping and the calculation of benefits.

Restrictions are often placed on the earnings subject to mandatory contributions. As mentioned earlier, many countries have a ceiling on insurable earnings, with no social security contributions required on higher earnings. Most countries believe it is desirable to allow room for high-income workers to establish occupational pension plans and to have private savings. Alternatively, if there is no ceiling on insurable earnings, but there is a ceiling on benefits, high-income workers receive no additional benefit for contributions made on earnings above those necessary to receive the maximum benefit.

A minority of countries, such as Ecuador and Guatemala, have no ceiling on employers' and workers' contributions. Brazil and the United Kingdom have no ceiling on employers' contributions, whereas a ceiling exists on employees' contributions. Not to apply the ceiling on contributions while maintaining a ceiling on benefits makes the scheme more progressive, but contributions above a ceiling not relevant for benefits are effectively a tax. Most OECD countries have a ceiling on covered earnings and it generally lies between 100 per cent and 200 per cent of the average wage. In the other regions, there are wider variations in the level of a ceiling when expressed as a percentage of average wage.

The non-indexation of the ceiling is a major problem in some developing countries. Often ceilings are not adjusted in line with wages or inflation, hence the proportion of the total earnings subject to contributions of the total wage bill of the countries is declining rapidly. As long as benefits are more or less related to covered earnings, this may not pose a big problem for the financial equilibrium of the scheme but may make benefit levels, calculated on the basis of a declining proportion of the total wages in the country, irrelevant from a social point of view. The ILO has observed these phenomena, for instance, in some Caribbean countries and Turkey.

Earnings ceilings should generally be indexed in line with the growth of earnings in order to maintain the level of protection over time, otherwise the level of protection will gradually erode and could ultimately lead to the payment of flat-rate or minimum pensions to all participants.

Many countries have a floor on income subject to mandatory social security contributions, not requiring workers with low earnings, or who work only a few hours, to contribute. If workers with earnings under a certain floor are not covered by social security then this might create perverse incentives for employers to create low-income no social security jobs (as is apparently the case in Germany). Low-income earners either have no benefit entitlements or enjoy only reduced benefit entitlements, as for example in Japan. Also workers below a minimum age are often not required to contribute. This age is 16 in Jordan. Some countries do not require workers above a maximum age to contribute.

The contribution base is the measure of worker earnings subject to mandatory contributions. In some developed countries, the growth of non-wage benefits, such as special compensations and fringe benefits, has eroded the contribution base (and tax base) by reducing the percentage of total compensation that is subject to mandatory contributions. To deal with this issue in the United States, employee contributions to a popular type of employer-provided defined contribution plan, called the 401(k) plan (after the section of the tax code that created it), are taxable under the social security payroll tax.

Total contributions can be increased by raising the contribution rate or extending the contribution base. When governments need to increase pension contribution income, they often do both. The contribution base could be extended by raising the ceiling or lowering the floor on earnings subject to contributions, or by making additional aspects of non-wage earnings subject to social security contributions. However this may result in only a temporary relief of financial pressures, as it may lead to a corresponding increase in the future benefit level, in schemes providing earnings-related benefits.

Types of contribution

The type of contribution that a pension scheme charges reflects two things: the policy choice a country has made concerning its preference with respect to the different financial rules and principles of social security; and the level of funding it has accepted or aimed at. A summary of the different types of contribution methods and their major characteristics is provided in table 6.3, and more details are provided in Technical Brief 1 on modelling tools.

Table 6.3 Types of contribution

Financing method/ contribution types	Characteristics of the contribution rate	Funding level
Pay-as-you-go	Contributions collected year by year should exactly balance the expected expenditure for the year	Does not lead to the accumulation of funds except for a modest contingency reserve maintained to avoid liquidity problems
Partial funding (I) (scaled premium)	The contribution rate is fixed over a defined period (called "equilibrium period") so that income and expenditure should be in actuarial balance over this period, taking into account the funding objective at the end of the equilibrium period	The size of the reserve normally goes along with the length of the equilibrium period, and a funding objective at the end of the equilibrium period is fixed, either to avoid liquidity problems or to pre-fund part of the liabilities
Partial funding (II) (general average premium)	Premium balances the present value of total expected future benefits minus initial reserves and contribution income, stays constant in theory ad infinitum	Accumulates similar level of reserves to full funding but higher during initial phases of a scheme and lower towards the final years (if calculated over a defined period)
Full funding (I) (mandatory savings)	Earnings-related constant rate throughout the life cycle of the scheme, scheme is in automatic equilibrium	Terminal funding level of reserve automatic
Full funding (II) (terminal funding)	Contributions collected over a defined period should be equal to the discounted value of the benefits accrued during this period, subject to adjustments for accumulated surpluses or past unfunded liabilities	A reserve equal to the value of all accrued benefit entitlements is accumulated. The value of accrued benefit entitlements includes the value of current pensions and the value of benefit entitlements earned to date by active and inactive members
Full funding (III) (constituent capitals)	Contribution rate calculated so as to cover each year the total present value of all newly awarded pensions during that year; generally only applied to disability benefits under employment injury insurance schemes	Terminal level of funding, but, owing to absence of acquired rights of contributors, lower level than under (I), (II)

Source: Author's compilations.

Most occupational schemes (defined benefit or defined contribution) and virtually all social security schemes charge an earnings-related contribution in the form of a fixed percentage of insurable earnings (that is, a contribution rate). This approach is an effort to charge contributions according to the ability to pay (based on the financial solidarity rule). Benefit levels may, but do not necessarily, depend on the amount of contributions paid or on earnings during active age.

Most social security schemes are scaled premium systems. Even systems which started out as fully funded schemes, or schemes financed on the basis of a general average premium (the term is defined in table 6.3: a general average premium can be interpreted as an "average" pay-as-you-go premium constant over a very long period), were often turned into scaled premium systems when the real financial development of the scheme, often the deterioration of the reserves as a result of inflation, was not in line with original expectations, and contribution rates had to be increased successively (the more than 100-year history of the German social security pension scheme is an example).

The typical development of the most important alternative contribution rates – such as the pay-as-you-go rate, the terminal funding rate (or the full-funding rate), a scaled premium rate, or the general average premium – for a social security pension scheme experiencing a typical expenditure development, as described in figure 6.1, is displayed in figure 6.5. It should be noted that the contribution rate developments show an actuarially idealized picture of reality. They assume that all assumptions made on the demographic, economic and governance environment of the scheme hold true in reality. This will not be the case. Thus the height and the width of the steps in the staircase of the scaled premium system might vary over time and the general average premium will not remain perfectly constant.

Determining the level of contributions

Even if benefit levels and eligibility criteria (and thus the level of total expenditure, as well as the basic type of contribution financing) are fixed, the actual setting of the contribution rate remains to some extent discretionary and a matter of political choice. The level of the contribution rate in social security pension schemes chosen by governments varies according to the following:

- the political need to maintain the stability of the contribution rate over extended periods for reasons of political acceptability and the maintenance of the public confidence in the system;

- the necessity to adapt the contribution level (and hence non-wage labour cost) of the scheme to the present economic situation and expected future developments;

- the capacity to invest and manage the accumulated reserves effectively without undue risk of mismanagement or asset depreciation;

Figure 6.5   Typical development of alternative contribution types

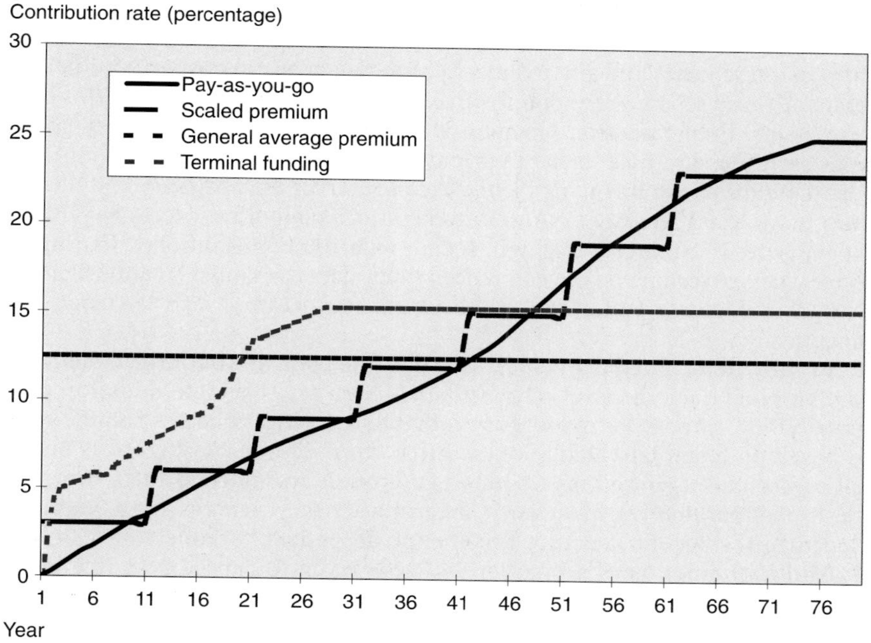

Contribution rate (percentage)

Year

Source: ILO estimates.

- the need for a contingency reserve to cope with unexpected income shortfalls or increases of expenditure.

Rate setting in fully funded and highly funded schemes

The least room for manoeuvre, with respect to the level of the contribution rates, occurs if countries decide on a high level of funding, or even full funding of a pension scheme. Some countries have decided to operate their schemes on a high level of funding in the belief that this would increase their national savings rate, although research results on the issue provide an inconclusive answer, as discussed in Chapter 13, on the economic implications of social security. Other countries follow a full funding regime for other purposes. An example is Kuwait, which simply turned to full funding since it wanted to exploit the positive economic situation, which was backed by abundant oil supplies, in an effort to achieve some security for its long-term pension promises even for the time when the oil supplies will have been exhausted. However there is no guarantee that future generations will honour this effort to hedge the entitlements of former supposedly richer generations. In any case the present economic situation makes high initial contribution rates, determined on a terminal funding basis, possible.

India and Jordan have a relatively high level of funding of their defined benefit pension schemes and aim to have full funding of their pension liabilities. The assets of those schemes are mainly invested in either public securities or short-term assets. Public pension schemes which are funded by investing in government securities are little more than pay-as-you-go financing in the context of overall public sector financing. While excess reserves are invested in public securities, non-social security tax rates are kept artificially low, excess government expenditure is financed through social security contributions. During the phase when governments have to redeem their debt, this must be done from current government revenues; that is, government must raise taxes or forgo other expenditure.

In fully funded defined benefit schemes, the contribution rate is the dependent variable once the level of benefits has been set. The determination of the contribution rate under mandatory retirement savings schemes should ideally be based on a similar calculation, starting from desired benefit levels under a full career and assumptions about wage growth and interest rates. But, once the broad parameters have been determined, they remain fixed and other aspects of the benefit structure become the dependent variables.

The accumulation of a high level of reserve funds can be desirable to promote the stability of the contribution rate in the context of an ageing population or a maturing scheme. Nevertheless stability of the contribution rate is not synonymous with full funding of pension liabilities. Maintaining a high level of funding makes the contribution rate sensitive to the unavoidable deviations of experience from the actuarial assumptions underlying contribution and benefit projections. These deviations generate surpluses, or deficits, that necessitate periodic changes of the contribution rate to maintain the funding objective of the scheme.[8] The risks of pension funding are more important for countries with unstable macroeconomic conditions or limited capital markets. History has shown that pension assets may be depleted by high inflation, bad investment policies (that is, bad management) or government abuse of pension reserves.

In any case, if a country decides to accumulate a substantial reserve for economic purposes, it must do this during the early stages of a scheme's existence while expenditure is low and contribution rates substantially higher than necessary by pay-as-you-go standards. One way of doing this is to aim at a constant contribution rate from the inception of the scheme. This is theoretically possible with a general average premium system. While this contribution level is not needed to cover current expenditure in the early years of the scheme, it can be considered fair to the early contributing generations as they acquire the same title to future benefits in exchange for their contributions as future generations. The stability of the contribution rate may enhance the sustainability of the scheme by strengthening fiscal discipline via an early recognition of the long-term cost of the scheme and the cost implications of benefit amendments.

If a scheme was operated on a scaled premium, or a pay-as-you-go system, from its inception, the first generations of insured persons would inevitably benefit from the scheme as their return on investment, compared to that of subsequent generations, would be positive. The general average premium can be calculated on the basis of the formula for the general financial equilibrium. The resulting reserve level is a dependent variable which will reach a maximum around the mid-point of the period over which it is calculated (which is usually a long period used as a proxy for the theoretically infinite period over which the concept of the general average premium is based).

Rate setting under pay-as-you-go or scaled premium regimes

Even after the reforms instituting first- or second-tier defined contribution schemes in eight Latin American and three Eastern European countries, most national social security schemes are still financed on a pay-as-you-go, or scaled premium, system. The borderline between the two systems is a matter of definition. Whether a scheme is financed on a pay-as-you-go basis with a necessary contingency reserve, or by the scaled premium method with a relatively small technical reserve, is a matter of judgement. Still the process of fixing the level of contribution rates under both systems deserves some reflection.

There is no fixed rule as to the level of the contingency reserve that a pay-as-you-go scheme has to maintain. The most rational procedure would be to simulate, through a combined analysis of economic and actuarial risks, the financial development under a most pessimistic economic scenario, and then calculate a contingency reserve which would cover income shortfalls during the period in which policy makers would need to adjust either the contribution rate or the benefit provisions to the different economic circumstances. The level of reserves depends on the volatility of the economy and the state of maturity of the scheme, but a contingency reserve of one to two times the annual expenditure should be sufficient in most cases.[9]

Frequent revisions of the contribution rate under a pay-as-you-go or scaled premium would be preferable to avoid an excessive accumulation of reserve funds, and to gradually adjust the contribution rate, or alternatively to keep the contribution rate at a low level in a period of economic difficulties or in the early stages of economic development.

The decision of countries to opt for partial funding rather than pay-as-you-go financing is generally motivated either by the intention to limit contribution rate increases during the first years of the scheme or by an interest in receiving investment income to finance part of future pension expenditure. Some OECD countries (Canada, Sweden) have recently decided, or are discussing, the possibility of raising the funding level of their social insurance schemes as a way of reducing future contribution rates during periods of high pension expenditure associated with the ageing of their population.

However experience has shown that the phased increase of contribution rates under a pure pay-as-you-go or a scaled premium approach has substantial political risks. It is tempting to introduce a pension scheme with a generous pension formula and an initially low contribution rate, since the scheme has only a few pensioners during the first one or two decades. But when expenditures increase, as they will normally do with full force during later years of the maturation phase (figures 6.1 and 6.2), contribution rates will have to be increased. The rule of thumb which generally applies in this situation is that, the longer the period of contribution stability under a scaled premium system, the higher the necessary increase in contribution rates between the different periods of stability, provided that a defined level of funding (that is, a defined capitalization ratio of k) is to be maintained.

The political problem is that governments often wait too long before a contribution rate is increased, as each contribution hike, even if perfectly normal and foreseeable financially, is politically unpopular. Waiting too long means either running the scheme into liquidity problems or having to ask for a large rise in contributions. Political managers often react by using consolidation measures, which imply the reduction of benefit levels or the tightening of eligibility conditions. To some extent these might be justified, as beneficiaries in young schemes generally have only limited entitlements and generous pension formulas help boost their standard of living. Later on, as the average careers of beneficiaries lengthen, tighter eligibility conditions and benefit entitlements earned per year of service might be justified. However maintaining the financial equilibrium by adjusting benefits has become common practice, often necessary but certainly not always good governance. Reductions in benefits are generally detrimental to the public credibility of the scheme, which is its most important asset. In order to avoid ad hoc manipulations as much as possible, all schemes and particularly new ones, need three provisions.

1. A clear definition of the actuarial equilibrium (that is, stipulating the period of equilibrium x and the funding ratio k) combined with a rule as to when the contribution rate must be increased.

2. A benefit formula which can be maintained at the stationary state (not only during the early years or decades of the scheme), possibly combined with transparent transitional benefit provisions for the early pensioner generations (the so-called "grandfather clauses").

3. A set of demographic and financial stabilizers which stipulate how the financial consequences of adverse future demographic and financial developments will be allocated between contributors and beneficiaries.

Without such a clear set of rules, the financial equilibrium of a partially funded scheme, or even a pay-as-you-go scheme, cannot be maintained. When partially funded schemes have failed in the past, failure can often be traced back to political opportunism which has failed to define or adhere to rules similar to these.

This reasoning also shows that the independence of pension expenditure and pension financing is a theoretical concept which might hold true for the initial determination of the financing system, but that the political realities of later financial management of a scheme clearly abolish that independence. In political practice, benefit levels will be challenged whenever contribution rates are under pressure.

CONCLUSIONS: POLICY CHOICES

From a social security point of view it is of secondary importance whether the necessary cash flow is generated entirely by current revenues financed on the basis of wages or entirely from the returns on invested reserves or some mixed sources. What is important is that it covers the costs set by the benefit provisions, and the administrative costs. Once the sources of cash are decided then the determination of a financing method for social security schemes is entirely a matter of social and economic policy choice. But there are constraints, opportunity costs and risks involved in the choice of any financing system.

The choice of a financing system and method is equivalent to fixing two of the following four parameters:

- the target or benchmark benefit levels (either absolute amounts or in terms of a replacement rate),
- the degree of actuarial equity between generations,[10]
- the desired level of reserves,
- the desired level of the contribution (or tax) rate.

But out of the numerically possible six combinations only three make sense.[11]

1. If one were to determine the desired benchmark replacement rate and a specific level of reserves for a number of years, one would select the pay-as-you-go or a partially funded method of financing. One advantage lies in the low burden on the early generations and the fact that the level of reserves can be adapted to the absorptive capacity of the capital market. The opportunity cost is embodied in the loss of actuarial equity. The risk is that increasing contribution rates (driven in part by demographic developments) during the maturing phase might not remain politically acceptable in the future. Non-acceptance might lead to a political downward correction of the replacement rates.

2. To aim for an equal distribution of the burden between all generations, thus pursuing actuarial equity, and to fix a desired contribution rate, the replacement rate would have to become the dependent variable. This would be the case under a defined contribution scheme where the level of overall reserves, and hence the replacement rate, would be dependent variables. These variables

would depend, to a substantial extent, on the performance of the capital market. If the government were to guarantee a certain minimum replacement rate, there would be the risk that future generations might be required to subsidize the system on a pay-as-you-go basis and hence compliance with the rule of intergenerational equity could not be guaranteed.

3. To fix a benchmark replacement rate and pursue the principle of actuarial equity, the level of the contribution rate would be the dependent variable. Most likely substantial reserves would be built up, but the level of reserves would also be a dependent variable. The build-up of reserves could be of the same order of magnitude as those under the defined contribution scheme, and the degree of risk with respect to operations of the capital market would be similar. Future shortfalls in investment income (for example, owing to the fact that capital markets do not have sufficient absorptive capacity) would need to be compensated by additional contributions from future generations. Hence the principle of intergenerational equity might not always be guaranteed.

The above reasoning shows once more that the theoretical independence of benefit levels and financing systems is little more than academic theory. If countries pursue multiple social, economic, financial and fiscal objectives in their pension schemes, which all of them do, then the level of benefit expenditure and hence benefit levels and the financing systems are interdependent in both political and economic terms. Pension financing must take account of this interdependence.

Notes

[1] If the growth of the pension cohort in the early years – after the first pensioners become eligible for benefits – exceeds the growth of the active population in the same years, the pay-as-you-go cost increases. This is a normal phenomenon since the growth of the first pensioner cohorts during the maturation phase also reflects the growth of coverage of the scheme in its early years, which normally slows down after the first one or two decades of the scheme's existence.

[2] Technical Brief 4 shows a comparable pattern of expenditure growth.

[3] The estimates are drawn from an ILO enquiry into the cost of social security which contains data furnished by national authorities. See ILO (1996a) and various editions.

[4] "Fully funded" in this context means that the scheme holds at each point t in time an amount of reserves equivalent to the present value of all future pension payments, and all future financial liabilities which would arise from accrued entitlements of the insured population. This would theoretically permit termination of the scheme at point t while the scheme would still be able to honour all its liabilities to the insured persons.

[5] For a discussion of the concept of the actuarial equilibrium, see also ILO (1997h, p. 39).

[6] It should be noted that this solidarity rule, or principle, refers to the financing side of a pension scheme only; the expenditure side, embodied in a pension formula, might have more solidarity elements.

[7] See also Chapter 14.

[8] The great difficulty of guaranteeing pension indexation with funded schemes illustrates this point.

[9] Until recently the Quebec pension plan estimated that, to face an economic downturn, a contingency reserve of twice the annual expenditure was sufficient. However, in order to provide for

some smoothing of future contribution rates through returns on the investment of technical reserves, it will in future gradually increase the level of funding to four to five times the annual expenditure.

[10] Actuarial equity is used here as a replacement for the somewhat loose concept of actuarial fairness, since fairness cannot be defined in objective quantitative terms. Actuarial equity implies either that contributions and benefits are equivalent for all consecutive generations of contributors in the sense of the principle of equivalence or that a possible imbalance between benefits and contribution rates is equal for all consecutive generations.

[11] Other combinations would lead either to socially unacceptable results (such as fixing the contribution rate and the desired level of reserves, or the reserve level in combination with perfect actuarial equity, which would make the replacement rate entirely unpredictable) or to financially unacceptable outcomes (such as fixing the contribution rate and the benefit level, which would put the financial equilibrium at permanent risk).

THE MANAGEMENT OF INVESTMENT

7

This chapter sets out principles and issues for the appropriate investment of assets by mandatory funded pension schemes, drawing on relevant country experience as well as theory. It makes particular, but not exclusive, reference to the situation of developing countries, and notably to the Latin American model of pension funding pioneered by Chile. The chapter is structured as follows. It first outlines four real-world models of mandatory funded pension provision, of which the Chilean is one; the others are national provident funds (such as Singapore and Malaysia), mandatory occupational pension schemes (as in Australia and Switzerland) and social security trust funds, which provide a back-up for social security pay-as-you-go pensions (as in Sweden). It goes on to examine the financial and economic preconditions for funding, covering the general pattern of financial development and focusing on the point in this process at which funding becomes feasible. It examines management issues, including general themes regarding investment, and politicization of investment that may be a risk for publicly managed funds. It then focuses on regulatory concerns for pension funds. The regulatory capability for developing countries is also considered. The chapter considers the performance of existing schemes, viewed in the light of the various regulatory and structural factors outlined above, and compares them to various benchmarks. Related issues in other parts of the book include the operation of public and non-public pension schemes (Chapter 2), the financing of pension schemes (Chapter 6), the risks to individuals (Chapter 12), the normative basis for policy (Chapter 15), the development of pluralistic designs (Chapter 19); see also Regional Brief 3 on Latin America.

The difficulties facing pay-as-you-go social security pension schemes in both developing and OECD countries are leading to growing interest in the advance funding of pensions as a complement or even a substitute. Given the belief that individuals may not voluntarily save sufficiently for old age, and in order to reduce future government liabilities durably, mandatory schemes which involve the investment of pension fund assets are sometimes favoured. A crucial issue in this regard is the investment of assets by mandatory funded retirement pension schemes. If investment provides an inadequate rate of return, pensions may be insufficient to ensure satisfactory living standards for retirees. Low rates of return may arise owing to investment in low-yielding assets or to excessive administrative costs. Meanwhile, if investments are too risky, pensioners risk poverty if they retire in unfavourable market circumstances, even if the mean rate of return over time is high. Excessive risks may arise if assets are inadequately diversified. A poorly designed funded scheme may indeed be worse than the pay-as-you-go scheme it replaces.

Whether potential rates of return on financial assets are actually realized by a funded pension system depends on the efficiency of the investment process. Retirement benefits actually obtained also depend on whether assets may be used for other non-retirement purposes, such as education or housing. Moreover the risk of investment in financial assets may also play an important role in retirement income security. This is because it influences both the value of assets and the potential for the cost of annuities to be prohibitive at the time of retirement.

INVESTMENT IN THE CONTEXT OF FOUR MODELS OF FUNDED MANDATORY RETIREMENT PENSION SCHEMES

Mandatory funded retirement pension schemes tend to be of four types:

1. personal defined contribution accounts managed on a decentralized basis by investment management companies;

2. personal defined contribution funds invested centrally by public institutions (provident funds);

3. mandatory occupational funds, which are usually defined contribution accounts as a minimum requirement; and

4. social security trust funds, which are basically an adjunct to defined benefit pay-as-you-go pension schemes.

With the exception of social security trust funds, such mandatory retirement saving schemes are an intermediate form between pay-as-you-go social security and voluntary occupational pension funds in that, like the former, they are compulsory and rights are freely transferable between jobs, but, like the latter, they are funded.

Personal defined contribution accounts invested by management companies

The main features of personal defined contribution funds for retirement are that they are held in individual accounts and managed by private (or public), competing asset management companies selected by the individual. Chile is a case in point: this is the longest-established such system, although others have been introduced in Argentina, Colombia, Peru and Uruguay.

The Chilean system, set up in 1981, is a decentralized mandatory retirement scheme. The system is based on defined contribution schemes. The system replaces pay-as-you-go social security retirement benefits for most workers, with no intentional redistribution, but the government guarantees a minimum pension of about 22 per cent of average earnings to those retiring after 20 years' contributions, and is thus obliged to make up the difference when the pension fund falls short.

Pension assets are invested by private investment management companies on the basis of one account per worker. Workers are allowed to transfer if they are dissatisfied with the manager's performance. On retirement, workers are obliged either to buy an indexed annuity with the bulk of their accumulated funds – a system facilitated by long-standing and credible use of indexed debt in Chile – or to carry out programmed withdrawals, again to seek protection against the risk of longevity. A complex regulatory structure protects workers – and the government, given its minimum pension guarantee.

Personal defined contribution funds invested by public institutions (provident funds)

The main feature of provident funds for retirement is that they are accumulated and invested solely by the government. The examples chosen for illustration are Malaysia and Singapore.

The Malaysian fund (see Bateman and Piggott, 1997) was set up in 1951 in response to the challenge of providing a system of retirement income provision from scratch. Whereas Malaysia was well provided with banking facilities, it lacked long-term domestic private investment sources and, owing to political instability in the region, it could not rely on foreign capital inflows. Only lump-sum benefits are provided; early withdrawal for house purchase is also permitted. Historically most assets have been held in the form of government securities, which are lent for development purposes by the Employees' Provident Fund Board, under the direction of the Minister of Finance. More recently the government's need for financing has declined and the Employees' Provident Fund has diversified.

The pension fund in Singapore (Asher, 1998a) is a compulsory, defined contribution fund, set up in 1955. The fund is administered by the government investment agency, the Central Provident Fund, although the actual investment of the accumulated monies is carried out by the Government of Singapore Investment Corporation and the Monetary Authority of Singapore. The Central Provident Fund invests in non-tradable government bonds and liquid bank deposits with the Monetary Authority of Singapore. The latter then invests the assets as foreign exchange reserves, and the Government of Singapore Investment Corporation invests in foreign equities. Since 1987 workers have been required on retirement to purchase life annuities providing 25 per cent of average earnings; the rest may be withdrawn as a lump sum. A certain proportion may also be used for housing and education. Withdrawals are also allowed for personal investment in approved securities once a minimum sum is in the account. Redistribution within the system is avoided, and there is some inequality, since only high earners are able to accumulate a sufficient amount to invest in higher-yielding instruments.

Mandatory occupational defined contribution funds

A number of OECD countries require companies to provide defined contribution pensions for their employees, and select managers to invest the monies. Defined benefit funds also often continue to exist under such regimes. Self-employed individuals are obliged to contract with life insurance companies for their pension savings. Two examples are Australia and Switzerland.

The retirement income system in Australia (covered by Bateman and Piggott, 1997 in a comparison with Malaysia) was shaped by a series of reforms culminating in the introduction of a superannuation guarantee charge (SGC) in 1992, which makes membership in a defined contribution private pension scheme a right and condition of employment.[1] Related reforms reduced tax concessions and the attractiveness of lump sums relative to annuities,[2] and improved vesting and portability conditions. Well-developed financial markets were an important precondition for the reforms. As a consequence of these reforms, since 1983 – when overall coverage stood at 40 per cent – both coverage and assets have increased dramatically; in 1993 an estimated 92 per cent of full-time workers were covered and national saving is thought to have increased. Some concerns remain about the structure of provision; for example, annuities are not paid from the funds themselves, leaving pensioners vulnerable to fluctuations in private annuity rates. Workers are not able to lock in an interest rate in advance for converting their account balance to an annuity. Thus the value of their monthly benefit depends on the interest rate prevailing at the time they retire. Most pensioners still take lump sums, thus putting their retirement income security at risk, and this option increases adverse selection for those choosing annuities. Those taking annuities tend to have long life expectancies, and thus life insurance companies price annuities so that they are only attractive to people with long life expectancies. Also the imposition of compulsory pension funds on small companies has prompted them to cut employment, lower wages and employ more casual workers.

The Swiss pension system (Hepp, 1990) consists of the social security scheme (AHV-IV/AVS-AI) and the compulsory occupational pensions (BVG/LPP). The BVG requires companies to set up a defined contribution scheme, invested either internally by foundations set up for that purpose or externally by banks or insurance companies. When instituted in 1985, the BVG scheme was grafted onto existing private pension schemes, which already covered 85 per cent of the workforce. Many individual company funds offer defined benefits, which may aim for a higher replacement ratio than that required. The BVG system is complemented by a large personal pension sector for the self-employed.

Funded defined benefit social security pensions

The rationale for a social security trust or buffer fund is typically to cover the period when the pay-as-you-go social security pension scheme would require increased contributions or lower benefits, as the demographic transition to an older population takes place. Trust funds are often intended to be temporary, to run out once this period ends. Whereas a number of countries (including the United States) have trust funds to cover social security obligations, Sweden invests in a range of private sector securities and not merely in government bonds. The Swedish system is therefore particularly appropriate for study. The funded social security scheme is known as the National Supplementary Pension Scheme (ATP Scheme), set up in 1960. This is effectively a form of funded, earnings-related social security, which complements a basic, flat rate, pay-as-you-go social security scheme. It covers 90 per cent of the workforce. The aim is to accumulate significant funds to provide future benefits, thus offering an occupational pension that is indexed and equal to a sizeable proportion (60 per cent) of the best years of earnings.[3] The fund is administered independently of the government in a series of sub-funds, which invest monies from different sectors of the economy (public sector, large companies, small companies/self-employed) in a variety of both public and private financial assets.[4] In 1995 assets were over 30 per cent of GDP. The Canadian province of Quebec provides another example of a funded defined benefit social security scheme (see box 7.1).

FINANCIAL AND ECONOMIC PRECONDITIONS FOR DEVELOPING FUNDED PENSION SCHEMES

There are a number of preconditions that developing countries which wish to adopt funded pension schemes must fulfil before introducing them. Financial market development is the main focus of this section. That, however, may not be the only criterion. Any form of mandatory retirement savings requires a certain level of income and wealth in the population, as poor households cannot afford to put aside large sums for their future needs. The issue addressed is whether a higher-income developing country, which has sufficient income and wealth to justify a funded social security scheme, can do so given its financial market and macroeconomic environment.

The pattern of financial development

A well-functioning funded pension scheme requires a stable and efficient financial market infrastructure. The financial infrastructure consists of the legal

Box 7.1 A success story of public funds management: The case of the Quebec Pension Plan

While government management of pension funds has often resulted in high expenses and low returns, there are also examples of successful management. Canada has two social security retirement benefit plans: the Quebec Pension Plan for the Province of Quebec and the Canada Pension Plan for the other provinces. Since the introduction of the scheme in 1966, the funds of the Quebec Pension Plan have been invested in much the same way as private funds. The funds are managed by a public institution which operates independently from the Quebec government: the *Caisse de dépôt et placement du Québec*. The funds of the Canada Pension Plan, by comparison, have been invested in long-term non-marketable government bonds at the rates prevailing when the bonds were purchased.[5] An Act passed in 1997 created the Canada Pension Plan Investment Board, whose mandate is "to invest its assets with a view to achieving a maximum rate of return, without undue risk of loss, having regard to the factors that may affect the funding of the Canada Pension Plan and the ability of the Canada Pension Plan to meet its financial obligations".

The main features of the experience and investment rules of the Quebec Pension Plan funds are summarized below, following a brief review of historical rates of return. The rates of return earned on the Quebec Pension Plan funds since its beginnings are similar to the median returns obtained by Canadian private pension plans. The slight difference in favour of the Quebec Pension Plan funds is possibly due to the lower level of administrative costs. By comparison, rates of return on the Canada Pension Plan funds are somewhat lower.

Stocks and bonds both account for about 45 per cent of the total Quebec Pension Plan funds. The remaining 10 per cent is invested in the money market, mortgages and real estate. The proportion of bonds is slightly higher than is found in private schemes and a large share of the bond portfolio is invested in Province of Quebec bonds (including state-owned enterprises such as the electricity company).

Legal regulations and internal rules governing the management of the Quebec Pension Plan funds may be summarized as follows.

- Persons or organizations given investment responsibilities have a fiduciary duty with respect to the interests of the Quebec Pension Plan contributors, and investment decisions must be made independently of political influences or social pressures.
- The *Caisse* is administered by a board of directors named by the Government. About half of the seats are earmarked for representatives of the Government, the pension board, the workers and the business community.
- Several funds are managed by the *Caisse* (for example, social security pensions, workers' compensation, an occupational scheme for public sector employees) and each fund has an investment committee composed of both government representatives and employer and employee representatives, who are responsible for the definition and monitoring of investment policy.
- The decision on the mix of investments made periodically by the investment committees is subject to restrictions specified by law. These restrictions aim

to ensure the diversification of the portfolio and to limit risk. The asset mix has evolved over time, as market expertise developed, the institution became well-established and profitable investment opportunities in equities emerged. As a consequence, the proportion of total funds invested in government bonds has gradually decreased.

- Assets bought must meet quality conditions, and limits on the amount of assets that can be invested in a legal entity are prescribed to ensure diversification and make it impossible for the *Caisse* to hold a majority of the ownership shares of a company (maximum of 30 per cent).

- Active management of funds by managers is allowed, but subject to limits approved by the investment committees.

- Most of the asset management is carried out in-house, but managers may call upon external managers, subject to the investment committee's approval and subject to the same restrictions on the choice of financial instruments.

- In addition, to obtain the best possible return while ensuring the safety of the capital under its management, the *Caisse* must contribute to a dynamic Quebec economy. Most of the regulations and internal rules are similar to those applicable to private schemes and those that will be applicable to the new Canada Pension Plan Investment Board.

framework, the financial accounting system, the regulatory and supervisory framework, clearing and settlement systems, and an institutional structure for trading securities.

An overview of the financial development process can provide a menu of situations in which a switch to funding might be considered. The processes whereby an economy develops from an informal financial system through banking to securities markets can be analysed using theories of corporate finance. Whereas an entrepreneur can start up a firm by relying on personal savings and retained earnings, rapid growth of the enterprise requires access to external finance. The simplest form of this is money from the entrepreneur's family, who will be able to monitor the firm closely and hence protect their own interests. Beyond this, banks tend to be the first to offer funds, as they have a comparative advantage in monitoring and control of entrepreneurs lacking a track record, for example in terms of access to information, ability to take security and to exert control via short maturities. They are also able to offer benefits to depositors in terms of pooling across investments and liquidity insurance; that is, ability to offer access to deposited funds at any time, at a positive interest rate. This may then dominate the alternatives of extremely undiversified finance of enterprises or hoarding.

Share issuance becomes important when companies' bank debts become sizeable in relation to funds invested by the owners, because this situation gives rise to conflicts of interest between debt and equity holders, such as for example the fact that owner-managers have the incentive to carry out high-risk investments. Banks may also protect themselves by means of covenants or even the acceptance of equity stakes, which internalizes the associated agency costs. Apart from banks, at the initial stages of development of share markets, securities are typically held by wealthy individuals as an alternative – diversifiable and liquid – investment with higher returns, albeit one which is riskier than bank deposits. Insurance companies may also develop. Corporate bond markets are only viable when companies have a high reputation, as this then constitutes a capital asset that would depreciate if the companies engaged in opportunistic behaviour. High credit quality is needed because bond market investors are likely to have less influence and control over management than equity holders or banks. Rating agencies help to alleviate associated information problems, but do not thereby open the bond market for companies with poor reputations or volatile profitability.

Evidence from history suggests that the progress of an economy through these stages depends on a number of preconditions. Partly these relate to macroeconomic and structural factors. Notably, high and volatile inflation hinders financial development. However, without a satisfactory framework for enforcing property rights and financial contracts, as well as for providing public information, securities markets cannot develop. A variety of forms of relationship banking, with equity stakes in borrowers held mainly by banks, are likely to be the limits of financial development. The institution of limited liability for equity claims, a structure for collateralizing debt, satisfactory accounting standards and appropriate protection against securities fraud (listing requirements and insider trading rules, for example) are also important for public securities markets (Stiglitz, 1993). The development and satisfactory regulation of the banking system may be a precondition for the growth of securities markets, given the role of banks in providing credit to underwriters and market makers, even when they do not take on security positions themselves.

Preconditions for developing funded pension schemes

The issue arises as to whether securities markets are preconditions for the development of funded pension schemes or whether funded schemes may emerge first, and then stimulate capital market development. Although funded schemes could develop on the basis of loans or property investment, their greatest comparative advantage is in the capital market. Loans require monitoring, so the customer relationship may give banks a comparative advantage there. Trading and risk pooling are more efficiently undertaken in the capital markets, where transaction costs are lower. Hence capital markets facilitate development of funded pensions, at least those managed on a decentralized basis. One could go further and say that countries must have at least fairly well-established financial markets before funded pensions can be put in place, as well as considerable regulation and supervision to avoid fraud and excessive risk taking (IMF, 1998).

Table 7.1   Share index behaviour of selected emerging and OECD equity markets: Monthly percentage changes, 1980–96

	Republic of Korea	Mexico	Chile	India	Switzerland	Australia	United States	United Kingdom
Mean	1.1	5.7	2.1	1.2	0.9	0.9	1.0	1.1
Standard deviation	5.5	15.8	8.8	7.0	4.2	5.1	3.3	3.9
Kurtosis	0.5	12.8	26.9	6.5	4.2	8.4	3.0	6.6
Skewness	0.6	1.6	−2.9	0.0	−1.0	−1.5	−0.6	−1.3

Source: IMF, "International Financial Statistics", CD-ROM, 1997.

Many developing and transition economies have fledgling stock markets which have only a few securities traded, few regulatory safeguards, inadequate information disclosure and a patchwork of government subsidies and financial instability, which make the value of securities and companies difficult to evaluate. In transition economies, even basic legal systems protecting property rights, and ensuring legal rights in bankruptcy, may not be established. Regulatory protection is needed for minority shareholders and against insider trading. Inflation can be high and volatile, which renders financial assets vulnerable to real losses. Share and bond prices are typically volatile and vulnerable to the effects of purchases and sales by foreign investors, as well as insider manipulation. This is indicated by the data in table 7.1, which compares equity price movements in developing and advanced countries. For developing countries with emerging markets, it indicates higher volatility and a tendency for extreme movements to be relatively common. The data cannot show certain additional difficulties, such as wide spreads between buy and sell prices and low liquidity, which also characterize emerging markets. (Additional data concerning capital markets can be found in the statistical annex.)

In such situations pension funds may risk being used as a captive source for financing government deficits, to bail out state enterprises or, if they are free to invest in non-government assets, may be channelled into speculative or risky assets (like real estate, loans to related parties – such as the owners of the management companies – and equity stakes in related companies; see Vittas and Michelitsch, 1994). Countries without securities markets may also lack technically trained personnel and the regulatory capacity needed to run a funded pension system.

It can be argued, however, that a dynamic link of decentralized funding and securities market development may permit funding to be introduced at an early stage in financial development. Even if they initially invest largely in government bonds and bank assets, pension funds may in due course, and given appropriate easing of regulations, spur further growth of capital markets.

This growth may occur in terms of market structure, the role of fund management strategies, liquidity and volatility of markets and demand for capital market instruments.

It is important to consider the fundamental differences between pay-as-you-go and funding. Unlike pay-as-you-go social security pension schemes, where there can be an immediate transfer of income to those who have not contributed (that is, who are old at the outset), in funded pensions the assets are built up while they are maturing, and this may stimulate investment and the development of securities markets. Individuals are forced to start saving at an earlier age; aggregate saving may increase. Saving tends to become more long-term; and, given their focus on real returns, institutions should be particularly beneficial to the development of equity markets, including privatization. In OECD countries, equity market capitalization and the size of institutional investors seem to be correlated. Equally, funded schemes are ready customers for long-term corporate bonds and securities debt instruments. A further benefit may be increased allocative efficiency in the economy as a whole.

However further preconditions may need to be fulfilled for pension funds to have these beneficial effects (Vittas, 1994). Local personnel skilled in asset management (as well as support staff such as actuaries, accountants, auditors, financial management experts, lawyers and computer specialists) may be scarce, implying a need for joint ventures with foreign companies. Pension funds may only be attractive when other financial assets such as deposits and bonds are (effectively) taxed, which is not often the case. Erratic changes by government in fiscal treatment are damaging. Laws governing financial prudence, self-dealing and other aspects of fiduciary behaviour and concerning settlement of property disputes and bankruptcies are necessary prior to introducing funding to prevent excessive financial risks (Turner and Rajnes, 1995b). To be effective, social security and pension reform requires a streamlining of the regulatory framework, including not only pension providers themselves but also providers of other financial services such as insurance, payment services, the securities markets, as well as in the legal, accounting and auditing fields.

A sound banking sector is an essential precondition for pension reform, as funded pensions typically hold some bank assets. Thus weak banks and weak bank regulation threaten retirement income security. Banks are also necessary (as providers of collateral, clearing and settlement services) for security markets to grow and provide alternative pension fund investments. On the regulatory side, such a stable banking sector requires a system of licensing, supervision, closure and a lender of last resort facility. Efficient and liquid government bond markets are also essential, given the role such bonds have as pension fund investments at an early stage in financial sector development.

Also a strong insurance sector – and a profession of actuaries – are needed to provide a competitive annuity market which is an essential counterpart to defined contribution pension funds if individuals are to be protected against longevity risks. A problem, even for well-run schemes in countries where capital markets are moderately developed, is a lack of annuities.

International investment and financial development

Difficulties relating to domestic capital market development may to some extent be overcome by allowing pension funds to invest offshore. International investment may also have external benefits such as helping funds to take advantage of modern accounting, regulatory and risk pricing techniques (Mitchell, 1997). In developed countries some of the benefits of international investing can be obtained by investing in domestic companies that have sales and production facilities in other countries.

International investment may be seen as cutting down the potential to develop domestic capital markets. It may, however, be beneficial to pension funds because the volatility of returns could be reduced. There may also be some benefit at the national level if national income is subject to frequent terms-of-trade shocks owing to the position of being largely dependent on commodities for export earnings, while export earnings account for a large proportion of GDP, as is common in developing countries. Hence holdings of assets offshore can contribute to greater stability of national income (Fontaine, 1997).

Holding a diversified portfolio of assets in a domestic market can eliminate risks resulting from the different performance of individual companies and industries, but not the risks resulting from the performance of the economy as a whole. In an efficient and integrated world capital market, that risk would be minimized by holding the global market portfolio, where assets are held in all national stock markets in proportion to their current value (Solnik, 1988). In effect the improvement in the risk/return position from diversification more than compensates for the additional element of volatility arising from currency movements.

Whereas a large developed country such as the United States can provide a reasonable range of instruments and securities to permit a purely domestic portfolio to provide a reasonable degree of diversification, a small developing country is much less able to do so and hence international investment may be essential to avoid exposing pensioners to unnecessary risks.

Many countries are reluctant to allow foreign investment by pension funds. Particularly in developing countries, governments often want to keep the funds within the domestic economy. However pension fund managers also have a home bias in their investments even when restrictions do not prevent them from investing abroad. Investment overseas involves higher transaction costs and foreign exchange risk. Often fund managers are not sufficiently familiar with foreign financial markets and tax laws and thus the information costs of foreign investments are high. In addition, there may be a language barrier in making foreign investments.

How the requirements for financial development differ between the models of mandatory funding

For personal defined contribution schemes managed by competing investment management companies, the general arguments presented above may apply most directly. Whereas a certain level of financial development is required (for example, a banking sector and a rudimentary securities market), feedback effects from the growth of funds may aid capital market development. While these funds may initially focus investment on government bonds, they may diversify over time, thus enhancing the development of markets for corporate bonds and equities. The population, however, must be educated well enough to make sensible investments, and the need for skilled personnel and regulatory capabilities is acute.

For provident funds, because the government directs and invests the funds itself, there may be no need for a pre-existing securities market or even a banking sector. However the difficulty for financial development is that such a system may also inhibit the development of securities markets, leaving a country in a state of financial underdevelopment.

Mandatory occupational funds are typically introduced late in the process of financial development in countries with a widespread pre-existing system of voluntary occupational pension funds (Davis, 1998b). Such a system requires well-developed securities markets, although feedback effects on domestic capital markets are also likely to arise as the system develops. Social security buffer funds also require a degree of financial market development if they are not to be invested solely in government bonds.

MANAGEMENT ISSUES FOR MANDATORY RETIREMENT BENEFIT FUNDS

Issues in investment

This section outlines the main investment issues for different types of funded pension schemes (see also Davis, 1995c, 1996a). Such information is important background for an evaluation of actual or planned schemes. In a basic sense, institutions active in investment in mandatory funded schemes face the same problem in investment as other investors in the economy, whether they be households, companies, banks or the government. This is to achieve an optimal trade-off of risk and return by allocation of the portfolio to appropriately diversified combinations of assets.

Implicitly, defined benefit pension liabilities are typically determined in real terms because of the link of liabilities to workers' earnings. This link points to a crucial difference from insurance companies as well as households, in that pension funds face the risk of increasing nominal liabilities (for example, as a result of wage increases), as well as the risk of holding assets, and hence they need to trade volatility with return. In effect their liabilities are typically denominated in real terms and hence their assets should be similar. This implies focus on equities and property, although bonds or liquidity are also useful for short maturity liabilities such as pensions in payment.

In this context the ratio of active to retired members is a key underlying factor for deciding portfolio distributions of both defined benefit and defined contribution funds. Given the varying duration of liabilities due to varying lengths of time until benefits must be paid, it may be rational for immature funds to invest mainly in equities (long duration), for mature funds to invest in a mix of equities and bonds, and funds which are winding up mainly in bonds (short duration) (see Blake, 1994). Moreover, for both defined benefit and defined contribution funds, there is a fiscal incentive to maximize the tax advantage of pension funds by investing in assets with the highest possible spread between pre-tax and post-tax returns. In many countries this tax effect gives an incentive to hold bonds (Blake, 1998). Portfolio considerations are important because small differences in the rate of return compounded over a working life lead to large differences in retirement income (see box 7.2).

Investment decisions

The portfolio distribution may be chosen by the sponsor and its investment managers (for occupational funds) or employees may choose their own asset manager, or they may even decide the asset allocation themselves (for personal funds). Whatever the approach, it may be desirable for older workers to shift to lower-risk assets as they approach retirement, to reduce the risk that market volatility shortly before their retirement might sharply reduce their pensions (see box 7.3). The superior returns on equities, despite higher volatility, will probably ensure that a significant share of the portfolio is accounted for by them, while risks – notably in developing countries – may be minimized by international diversification.

Unlike defined contribution funds, defined benefit funds are public or occupational but not personal (given the need for a sponsor or guarantor against shortfalls). For defined benefit funds, appropriate investment strategies will first depend on the nature of the obligation incurred, whether it is indexed or nominal, and the demographic structure of the workforce. In all cases, the liabilities will be influenced by interest rates, real earnings and inflation. Second, investment strategies will be influenced by the minimum funding rules imposed by the regulating authorities. Third, there is an incentive for profitable companies to overfund to maximize the tax benefits, as well as to provide a larger contingency fund.[6] Corporate sponsors are likely to focus closely on investment management performance given their direct liability for any shortfalls. Minimum funding levels and limits on overfunding provide tolerance limits to the variation of assets around the value of liabilities (Blake, 1997).

Box 7.2 Rate of return affects retirement income

Studies have shown that individuals tend to be more risk averse in their investment allocation decisions than professional portfolio managers. Furthermore
women may be more conservative investors than men (Bajtelsmit, 1996). If individuals are allowed to make their own investment allocation decisions and they
are conservative in their investment choices, this will usually result in lower
retirement income.

This box explores the impact of investment conservatism on retirement
income. Bajtelsmit (1996) examined the related question of stock versus
bond investing and found that, even after accounting for risk, the much
higher long-term returns on stocks than on bonds produced extremely divergent retirement income levels. The question that remains is whether small differences in portfolio return have much effect. This issue is a relevant concern
for self-directed accounts in both private and social security pension schemes.
It is also a way of estimating the impact on retirement income of small differences in administrative expenses between scheme alternatives.

Empirical methodology

To illustrate the impact of small differences in the rate of return on individual
retirement income, the following fact pattern is used as the basis for the forecast. An employee begins work at age 18 with a salary of $20,000. Her wages
grow at a nominal rate of 3 per cent per year and she makes an annual end-
of-year contribution to a pension equal to 5 per cent of her gross income
throughout her career. In the initial example, it is assumed that the pension
investment earns a constant rate of return each year, the employee retires at
age 60 and lives to age 80.

There are many possible variations on this fact pattern (differential wage
growth, lower starting salary, cyclical investment returns). A more complex
fact pattern does not, however, significantly change the results with respect
to the impact of differences in rates of return.

Investment returns

The average return on an American stock portfolio for the period 1926–96 was
12.3 per cent (Ibbotson Associates, 1997). Although returns in the last five years
were substantially higher, the 40-year investment period in this example makes
it more appropriate to consider long-run averages. Since many individuals will
not choose to invest 100 per cent of their portfolio in stocks, this level of return is
the maximum for the analysis.

Wealth at retirement is forecast assuming that contributions are made to the
retirement plan until retirement, at which time the lump sum is converted to a
life annuity of constant value. Thus two values that can be used for comparison
of investment results are the total wealth at retirement and the retirement annuity relative to final salary. The annuity estimate as a measure of retirement
income is not perfectly realistic in several respects. First, life expectancy is
based on current mortality estimates for people aged 60. If life expectancy continues to improve over time, this is probably a conservative estimate for years
in retirement. The annuity is assumed to be fairly priced, meaning that the price
is based on actuarial life expectancy, which is not currently the case because of

adverse selection in annuity markets. Lastly, in the presence of inflation, a constant annual payment in retirement would not be particularly desirable. Despite these errors in measurement, it is still critical to consider the annuity measure in addition to total retirement wealth, since the effects of inflation make nominal values difficult to interpret in today's terms. This model is estimated under a variety of return assumptions.

Results

On the basis of this analysis, the "cost" of investing more conservatively can be estimated. For this hypothetical individual, a 50-basis point (0.5 per cent) decline in annual average long-term investment yield, from 12.3 per cent to 11.8 per cent, results in a 13.2 per cent decline in retirement accumulation, which translates into a comparably lower retirement annuity. This indicates that what appears to be a small difference in rate of return translates into a much larger difference in retirement income.

Another way of expressing this difference is in terms of the increase in wealth that can be attained by taking more risk. Under the assumptions of this hypothesis, an individual with an average risk investment portfolio earning 7.3 per cent nominal return will have approximately one-quarter of the accumulation from the 12.3 per cent return portfolio. An increase of only 50 basis points in return (to 7.8 per cent) will result in a 13.7 per cent increase in the retirement annuity. A 100-basis point (1 per cent) increase in portfolio return will boost retirement income by almost 30 per cent (see table 7.2).

Table 7.2   The effect of investment returns on pension wealth, retirement income and replacement rates

Annual investment return	Accumulated pension at age 60 (dollars)	Retirement annuity (20 years, dollars)	Percentage of pre-retirement income
7.30	394 837	32 475	47
7.80	448 739	36 909	53
8.30	511 050	42 034	61
8.80	583 141	47 963	69
9.30	666 612	54 829	79
9.80	763 323	62 783	91
10.30	875 446	72 005	104
10.80	1 005 507	82 703	119
11.30	1 156 450	95 118	137
11.80	1 331 705	109 532	158
12.30	1 535 265	126 275	182

Source: Calculations by Vickie Bajtelsmit.

Performance measurement

The development of performance measurement is a prerequisite for effective investment. Performance measurement entails a precise calculation of the returns on a pension fund over a given period, followed by further assessments

Box 7.3 The effect of rebalancing retirement portfolios as retirement nears
Investment professionals commonly recommend that workers in defined contribution schemes should periodically rebalance their portfolios to maintain their desired asset mix, and that they should shift to lower risk securities as they near retirement. Doing so would reduce their possibility of a large fall in the value of pension assets just before retirement. It would, however, also cut the expected rate of return on pension fund assets. This raises the question of how large is the fall in expected rate of return. Generally, when the proponents of defined contribution plans calculate expected rates of return for those plans, they do not take into account the effect of portfolio rebalancing.

There is little disagreement that stock portfolios will, on average, result in greater retirement wealth accumulation than lower-risk portfolios.[7] Shifting investment strategies as retirement nears allows individuals to capture the long-term gains of stocks while attempting to avoid shocks to retirement wealth from late declines in the risky asset portfolio. However portfolio rebalancing can be expected to reduce retirement wealth as well, so investment allocation strategies must be evaluated by considering whether the reduced wealth is associated with a sufficient reduction in risk. Since risk aversion is not uniform across individuals, differences in risk aversion will imply that no "one size fits all" investment strategy will be optimal for all investors.

This box compares the wealth and risk implications of only allocating contributions to different asset classes and that of annual rebalancing of assets to maintain a particular portfolio allocation. Because stocks tend to have a higher rate of return than bonds, if contributions are allocated in a fixed proportion between stocks and bonds, over time the allocation of the portfolio will become increasingly weighted towards stocks. The box also considers the effect of shifting investment strategies as retirement approaches.

Simulation model and results
The hypothetical individual is assumed to begin work at age 18 at a salary of $20,000 per year, and that salary will increase at a rate of 3 per cent per year. The contribution to savings is 5 per cent of salary per year, of which 60 per cent is allocated to a diversified stock fund and 40 per cent to a diversified intermediate-term government bond fund. The returns for these asset classes are estimated on the basis of American historical returns from 1926 to 1996 as calculated by Ibbotson Associates (1997). During that period, the average return on stocks was 12.3 per cent and the average return on intermediate term government bonds was 4.9 per cent.

Retirement wealth in the absence of risk
Forecasts of retirement wealth and income commonly make the assumption that average return levels for a particular asset class will be achieved in every year of the forecast. While this makes the calculation much easier, it is inferior to forecasts that incorporate security risk. Owing to time diversification, the results of these static forecasts will be similar to the average results of a simulated risky distribution of retirement wealth. However the forecast will fail to provide the decision maker with an adequate basis for making allocation

decisions, since the asset class with the highest returns will, by definition, result in the highest retirement wealth.

To illustrate this, assume that average returns on each portfolio are achieved each year. If the allocation percentages are applied to new contributions but the portfolio balances are not rebalanced each year, the individual's portfolio allocation to stocks gradually increases over the working career as a result of the higher average returns on the stock portfolio. At the time of retirement, the total portfolio allocation to stocks is 91.26 per cent, which presumably exposes the individual to considerably more risk than originally intended. If the portfolio is rebalanced each year to maintain the 60/40 mix, the "cost" of rebalancing is approximately a 33 per cent decline in retirement income.

Another possible way to reduce the risk of the portfolio is to shift the allocation to less risky securities a few years prior to retirement. The logic of this strategy is that the investor can take advantage of the generally higher returns on risky securities for a longer period, but still reduce the likelihood of drastic portfolio declines close to retirement. In this hypothetical situation, it is assumed that contributions are allocated 60/40 as above but, at age 55, the entire pension wealth is shifted to the government bond portfolio. In a static model, assuming no intermediate rebalancing, this causes a 30.4 per cent decline in retirement wealth compared to the base case above.

The risk effects of rebalancing

How much risk reduction is achieved for the "cost" of such large percentage declines in retirement wealth and income? To answer this question, risk is incorporated in the calculation by means of a dynamic simulation model in which annual stock and bond returns are assumed to be drawn from risky distributions based on historical distributions of returns on those asset classes.[8] Using the Ibbotson Associates accumulated data, the stock portfolio is assumed to have a standard deviation of 20.64 per cent, and the government bond portfolio is assumed to have a standard deviation of 8.46 per cent. Both return distributions are assumed to be log normally distributed.

The static and dynamic models for forecasting retirement wealth are compared in table 7.3. The simulation results show that, while there is significant reduction in mean retirement wealth as a result of annual rebalancing (−38 per cent), there is also substantial reduction in risk. The worst case retirement wealth outcome with rebalancing is only slightly lower than the worst case outcome without rebalancing. The coefficient of variation (standard deviation/mean) is 23 per cent lower when the portfolio is rebalanced annually.

In contrast the retirement wealth reduction due to switching to low-risk assets at age 55 is comparable to the annual rebalancing case, but does not have a corresponding effect on risk. The worst case outcome is slightly lower than in the other two cases, but the coefficient of variation is approximately the same as without rebalancing.

These simulations suggest that portfolio allocation strategies for defined contribution plans can have a significant effect on retirement wealth and risk, and that rebalancing can be an important component of the optimal risk/return mix. Although there are many different ways that a portfolio can be allocated over time, the three scenarios considered above illustrate the potential

Table 7.3   Forecasts of retirement wealth at age 60: Three scenarios

	Static model			Dynamic simulation model		
	60/40 allocation	Annual rebalancing	Switch to bonds at 55	60/40 allocation	Annual rebalancing	Switch to bonds at 55
Mean	1 009 417	673 835	702 163	1 080 529	672 463	685 994
Standard deviation	n/a	n/a	n/a	941 887	408 064	589 631
Minimum	n/a	n/a	n/a	235 405	222 715	212 113
Maximum	n/a	n/a	n/a	14 701 265	4 865 836	7 864 566
Coefficient of variation	0	0	0	0.87	0.61	0.86

Source: Calculations by Vickie Bajtelsmit.

magnitude of seemingly small differences in investment strategy. Rebalancing the portfolio annually to be consistent with contribution allocations will result in lower retirement wealth but also reduces the risk of the retirement wealth distribution. Shifting allocations to low-risk securities as retirement nears will lead to a similar reduction in wealth but without substantial reduction in risk.

A portfolio strategy that combines annual rebalancing and shifting to low-risk assets as retirement nears is arguably a good strategy for workers with defined contribution pension plans. It may also be argued, however, that most workers are not sufficiently financially sophisticated to pursue such a strategy. If that is the case, then the requirement of financial knowledge of workers is a weakness of defined contribution schemes.

which may include calculations of risk, of performance relative to other pension funds and of performance relative to the market. Performance measurement is valuable in ensuring that investment is efficient relative to the opportunities available. The uses of such information vary between the various models of mandatory funding.

In personal defined contribution funds managed on a decentralized basis by investment management companies, performance measurement is essential to enable individuals to assess whether their funds are being well managed. When they conclude this not to be the case, their option to shift to another company ensures competitive pressure is enforced on managers to perform well, lest they lose their customers. Regulators also require performance measurement in the case of a system such as that in Chile, as there is regulation of returns.

As regards provident funds and social security buffer funds, the issue of performance measurement applies first to parliamentary oversight of the overall performance of such funds. Second, if part of the portfolio is delegated to independent managers, there is a concern to ensure that they are investing efficiently. Social security buffer funds are in a similar situation. The results of performance measurement in the cases of Malaysia and Singapore in practice rarely reach the public domain (Asher, 1998a).

Politicization of investment

A mandatory pension scheme may face political problems in investment, particularly if it is centralized (Thompson, 1992). This has occurred in some African countries. In some cases the effects of politicization may be so severe that the benefits of funding are not realized. Notably its management could be subject to political interference. Funds which are accumulated may simply be used to finance government consumption, thus leaving no assets to pay pensions. Even if used to fund investment, finance may be diverted to unprofitable projects for political reasons. Government bonds which are not indexed are vulnerable to erosion in value by inflation. Lack of international investment, which is typical of social security trust funds, leaves them dependent on the performance of the domestic economy. Also at a macro level, a large provident or trust fund, being a ready source of cheap government borrowing, may induce fiscal laxity, thus actually reducing national saving.

Although its investment is believed to be relatively efficient, political risk manifests itself in the Singaporean Central Provident Fund: first, in terms of a total lack of transparency in actual investments, extent of diversification and the returns realized; and second, in terms of the preemption of a significant proportion of the realized rate of return on the (foreign) investments of the Central Provident Fund by the government. In Malaysia funds of the Employees' Provident Fund have been used to finance government-sponsored privatization and infrastructure projects, mainly via corporate bonds, which may entail inefficient resource allocation (Asher, 1998b).

The schemes in Malaysia and Singapore, as well as Fiji and other Asian and Pacific countries, are examples of how such schemes may succeed, despite direct or indirect government control – even though real returns remain low. The vast majority of other such schemes have invested mainly in public bonds (issued by governments or nationalized industries) at low interest rates, which during periods of inflation turned sharply negative (World Bank, 1994). Low or negative real rates of return have been recorded in Egypt, Ghana, Nigeria and Zambia. In Africa high operating costs reduced returns further. The use of funds to finance government consumption or wasteful investment meant the funds may have reduced economic growth, and hence income security of pensioners; they may also have favoured privileged groups able to lobby for government expenditures that benefit them.

Funding through private occupational pension funds or individual defined contribution schemes avoids some of these political difficulties, but even in the case of decentralized funds political difficulties may not be entirely avoided. One aspect may be that regulatory authorities impose strict minimum portfolio holdings of government bonds, that in effect, force pension funds to subsidize

government finances, which in developing countries often implies sharply negative rates of return in real terms. More overt influence cannot be ruled out,
although the structure of the Chilean system, for example, gives a political constituency to those who oppose it. Political pressure may also come from other
interest groups or institutions besides the government, as different groups
may attempt to influence investment decisions to advance social goals.

REQUIRED REGULATION AND NECESSARY REGULATORY CAPABILITIES

Whereas politicization is a key issue for centralized funds, regulation is crucial
for decentralized ones. Without adequate regulation, the benefits of funding
may not be realized. Regulation is of particular importance, given the compulsory and long-term nature of mandatory funding.

Necessary regulatory capabilities

Developing countries often lack the pre-existing capacity to regulate financial
markets and institutions. A country which is unable to manage an unfunded,
or funded, public pension scheme well – because of administrative inefficiency,
shortage of skilled personnel or political interference – will probably be unable
to regulate and supervise a private pension system, be it mandatory or voluntary
(Vittas, 1993). In developing countries, however, the private sector is often
better managed than the public sector in that it benefits from competent personnel, many of whom come from the public sector, often having benefited from
experience in particular fields, such as finance or data processing.

In the government, because of weakness in governance capabilities, ability
to enact clear rules and penalize malfeasance in a predictable way may be lacking (James and Vittas, 1995). It may be added that pension regulators typically
rely on other regulators such as those of securities markets (for example, to prevent insider trading in equity markets) and financial institutions (notably of
banks) and pension regulation can thus not be seen in isolation. In addition efficient oversight of contributions is needed via computerization and secure
record-keeping (Mitchell, 1997). A further complement for regulation is use
of a sound accounting methodology such as the FASB (Financial Accounting
Standards Board) of the United States, including a requirement to value
assets at market prices. The importance of valuing assets at market prices is
seen in the case of Japan (see box 7.4).

Specific aspects of the regulatory structure are needed in order to introduce
an effective mandatory funded pension scheme (Vittas, 1994). In particular, it
may be necessary to create or reorganize insurance regulatory agencies, which
have traditionally been concerned with the verification of compliance with
arbitrary price and product controls, to shift their emphasis towards market
discipline, solvency monitoring and consumer protection, and to employ

Box 7.4 Funding Japanese social security pensions
Adequate management of social security funding requires adequate accounting rules, a flexible discount rate, efficient investments, fiduciary responsibility
for management and investments, limited political risks and sound pension
governance. This box considers these issues as they apply to Japan.

Accounting rules
Pension assets should be valued at market value because that is the best
measure of their economic value. The pension assets for Japanese social
security are valued at book value, which overstates the market worth of the
assets in the late 1990s because of bad loans made to inefficient government
units and due to the decline in the Japanese stock market in the 1990s. Because
assets are listed at book value, participants do not know the true worth of social
security assets.

Discount rate
The discount rate for valuing pension liabilities should be related to interest
rates in financial markets. The Japanese Government, however, has fixed
the discount rate for valuing social security liabilities at 5.5 per cent for several
decades, even though there have been great changes in financial markets. The
official discount rate of the Bank of Japan was at its historical lowest level of 0.5
per cent in September 1995. The yield rate on the benchmark No. 182 Japanese
government bond, which carries a 3.0 per cent coupon and is due in 2005, was
below 2.0 per cent between September 1997 and September 1998. The investment earnings on the Social Security Employees' Pension Insurance and the
National Pension have been at 5.0 per cent or lower in recent years, not
taking into account capital losses, which would cause the true rates of return
to be even lower. Because a high discount rate produces a relatively low present value for future benefit payments, the discount rate of 5.5 per cent under-
states the value of liabilities for Japanese social security.

Fiduciary responsibility
With population ageing in Japan, the financing method for social security pensions has been changing from partial funding towards pay-as-you-go. But even
at the end of fiscal year 1996 (March 1997), the National Pension fund had
assets of 2.3 times the annual benefits and the larger Employees' Pension
Insurance fund had assets that were 5.4 times as large as annual benefits.
   These large pension funds have been invested by Zaito, the Japanese Government's investment and loan programme. Zaito is the largest investment
bank in the world. However, it has lent money to inefficient government programmes at below market interest rates. The Pension Welfare Institution,
which is a government agency, has borrowed over 23.7 trillion yen from
Zaito and has invested it in financial markets. Because of the weakness of
Japanese financial markets during the 1990s, it has lost 1.3 trillion yen. Much
of this money was spent in a futile attempt to prevent the Nikkei Dow Jones
index from falling, not realizing that the value of the stock market was decided
by the fundamental strength of the economy. It has also spent 141 billion yen to
build and manage a number of large and unprofitable hotels in resort areas.

The Japanese Government has decided to stop new investments by Zaito and to abolish the Pension Welfare Institution. It intends to establish new institutions to manage the investment of Japanese social security funds. To avoid the problems of the past, strict fiduciary responsibility needs to be established for the government agency that manages the investment of social security funds. The goal of the investment of social security funds should be solely to pay benefits to participants.

Political risks

Every five years the Department of Health and Welfare of the Japanese Government re-evaluates the social security programmes in light of current and projected economic and demographic developments. Following this re-evaluation, it proposes amendments to the social security programmes. To best determine the need for new amendments, the Government needs to use reasonable values for future economic and demographic variables. In recent projections, however, relatively high values have been used for the total fertility rate and the expected rate of economic growth, resulting in lower social security contribution rates than would have been obtained with more reasonable values used in the projections. The main reason for this is not the poor ability of the demographic and actuarial sections of the Department of Health and Welfare, but the political pressures they have faced to use unrealistic assumptions in their projections. This suggests that the governance of the Japanese social security scheme might be improved if its actuarial projections were carried out by an agency with greater independence from the Government.

Pension governance and the rule of law

The Pension Insurance Agency within the Department of Health and Welfare is responsible for managing social security. Advisory Committees of the Department have frequently not been truly independent and democratically chosen. They often have not made their own proposals, but rather ratified ones made previously by the Department. Important subjects such as investment regulations and the discount rate for valuing social security liabilities have not been regulated by laws enacted by the Diet (the Japanese Parliament), but instead governed by rules and regulations determined by the Government. Important decisions concerning social security governance have been made by Directors or Managers of the Department of Health and Welfare rather than by the Diet.

experienced professionals. They may need extensive training, perhaps aided by close links with agencies in OECD countries and international financial organizations or Latin American countries experienced in this type of regulation, and also consultation and cooperation with market professionals. Such training should be given to regulators and professional staff, as well as fund managers, actuaries, accountants and auditors.

Furthermore developing countries need to strengthen the supervision and intervention powers of regulators. Regulators must be independent of the regulated institutions, but this may be difficult to achieve. To ensure systemic stability and compliance with solvency, investment and consumer protection rules, regulators must exercise effective supervision via off-site surveillance and on-site inspections. They need effective intervention powers to enforce corrective measures. They must establish objective criteria for entry and exit, setting out authorization criteria for insurance companies and pension fund managers, establishing rules for the exit of insolvent fund managers and opening the market for new entry from domestic and foreign fund managers. Market dominance by a small number of government-controlled insurance companies is a recipe for low returns. Openness to new entry,[9] while ensuring stability, may require moderate but not excessive capital requirements.

One possible model for the structure of regulation is Chile. The supervisory structure for pension funds in Chile is simple in that divisions of a single agency, the superintendency of pension fund administrators (AFPs), carry out all relevant tasks, including on-site inspections. It employs 100 professionals (lawyers, auditors and examiners). Investment transactions are reported daily, while monthly reports are made of financial positions and performance. Although three pension fund management companies have failed, workers have suffered no losses in relation to their associated pension funds. Another model is the Netherlands, where regulation of pension funds is carried out by a single statutory authority, the Insurance Supervisory Board, and pension funds are legally obliged to provide the board with detailed information annually on the benefit payments and investments of the fund. It ensures that the commitments of the pension funds are sufficiently covered by their assets. It also involves itself in more general structural issues. If the board finds procedures or regulations unsatisfactory, it can apply social pressure by making a public complaint. In practice this is rarely necessary.

Regulation of pension fund managers

Placing responsibility for managing the considerable sums of money in mandatory defined contribution pension accounts in the hands of private pension fund managers requires some mechanism to ensure that those funds are not stolen or otherwise misused. Experience with the management of private pension funds in OECD countries suggests that the regulation of pension managers requires considerable care. Pension fund management presents notable and perhaps obvious opportunities for self-dealing whereby the managers improperly benefit themselves. In addition, managers may mismanage their funds either through laziness or excessively zealous pursuit of profit, to the detriment of beneficiaries who will often find it difficult to evaluate accurately the performance of the managers in whose funds they participate. There must be realistic and effective legal means of addressing these potential problems.

While most are undoubtedly honest, managers of private pension funds in developed countries have found many ways to redirect fund money to their own uses or to the benefit of their friends or business partners. Pension fund managers have at various times withdrawn money from the pension funds they manage, in their own or in fictitious names; made loans from the fund to their associates without realistic expectation of repayment; fraudulently paid for non-existent goods and services; paid money to ineligible beneficiaries; steered contracts for benefit plan services to companies paying kickbacks; and assigned loss-making trades to pension fund accounts while profitable trades have gone to the accounts of private clients, friends, relatives or business associates. There is no obvious reason to expect that managers working in a privatized social security pension scheme will be either less ambitious or less self-interested. Indeed, given the size of the funds, the temptations to engage in inappropriate transactions may be greater, and the ability and incentive of beneficiaries to keep track of managerial performance may be less than is true of traditional private pensions.

Regulatory requirements

Ensuring that investment managers behave in a responsible manner requires at least three elements. First, there must be some ability to oversee the activities of the manager. There must be accounting rules that result in useful information being provided about businesses, an independent auditing process to verify the information and regular reporting of solvency and financial performance data to some party with the necessary incentives and capacity to evaluate those data. Second, there must be some assurance that managers' incentives are reasonably aligned with those of the system. This requires a clear expression to the manager of the expectations and requirements upon him or her, a compensation system designed to give the manager the incentive to perform managerial tasks adequately, meaningful sanctions which can be applied against the manager in the event those requirements are violated, and some party with the incentive and ability to enforce those sanctions. Third, there must be legal institutions capable of enforcing these obligations. Courts or regulatory agencies must be reasonably honest and effective, there must be an administrative mechanism capable of working effectively to seize assets or otherwise enforce judgments or administrative rulings and, assuming at least some reliance on financial sanctions in the event of managerial misbehaviour, some pool of assets owned by the manager which can be seized, and which is adequate in size to deter misbehaviour and to compensate injured parties.

Accounting system

A preliminary requirement for preventing financial misfeasance in any investment management arrangement is a system of accounting sufficient to allow an outsider to understand what the manager is doing on behalf of the account, and a system of reporting in which those accounting records are made available to some supervisory agency. A pay-as-you-go scheme in which investment is made exclusively in government securities needs this, as do privatized systems of defined contribution schemes, but the latter may impose greater difficulties: such schemes require that the manager have substantially greater discretion than is necessary in the former, making the accounting and reporting rules more important yet also more open to manipulation.

While accounting rules in the developed economies differ somewhat, most are sufficient to permit an understanding of the pension fund's activities and financial status. That is not, however, always the case in transition or developing economies. In the Russian Federation and the other former Soviet states, for example, accounting figures are notoriously unreliable. Whether or not the pension fund accounting is accurate in itself, the equity transactions in which the fund manager engages are likely to be quite opaque, and both the reported cost and the reported value of the acquired assets may be difficult to determine. Most Russian enterprises apply accounting standards which date back to the Soviet era and which give notoriously distorted impressions of profit and loss. Furthermore the rules change regularly, with new laws, decrees and instructions; needless to say, it is extremely difficult for enterprise managers to keep up with this frequent change of accounting regulations. Despite the apparently strict (though constantly changing) specification of accounting rules, many managers reportedly fail to apply even the official rules on a regular basis. The central government's effort to promote the adoption of International Accounting Standards, the global benchmark for bookkeeping, is largely stalled. As a result, the assets and financial condition of many companies are all but impossible to determine, which makes the value of fund assets, and thus the size of an individual participant's account, difficult to determine. This environment would seem to present unusual opportunities for the fund managers to misstate the funds' financial position, as well as the funds' liabilities to individual participants.

Furthermore stock markets and other asset markets may not work as experts from OECD countries assume they do. The vast majority of enterprises in Central and Eastern Europe are not traded on open stock markets. Those relatively few enterprises that do trade on stock markets do not trade there exclusively, and many transactions are not simple cash transactions in which shares are bought for a simple determinate price. Rather, many transactions, including those which occur through the facilities of the formal stock exchanges, are in kind or involve swaps of assets which are themselves difficult to value. Valuing a fund's assets, and thus the fund's liabilities to individual participants, can be quite difficult under these circumstances. These problems also affect the auditing and reporting of fund balances.

The government's role

Accounting problems may present serious conflicts of interest for the government, which could easily reduce its willingness to monitor fund status. As the description of accounting problems in the former Soviet states suggests, the government is often responsible to a considerable degree for the confusion and misorientation of accounting rules. Effective fund regulation requires obtaining a clear picture of a fund's transactions and net assets, yet the government's own rules make this difficult. Governments may be unwilling to challenge the opaque accounting practices of a fund, because a realistic auditing process would require exposing and challenging the government's own mandated accounting rules. The rules which the government mandates, however, may be confusing or unclear specifically to avoid problems the government would otherwise have to face, such as the functional bankruptcy of government enterprises. Governments may have other reasons as well to prefer opaque or unrealistic accounting practices. For example, forcing more rational accounting rules could expose the actual insolvency of many private enterprises. It has proved politically difficult to implement bankruptcy laws in many former communist countries, because bankrupt enterprises risk being closed or forced to lay off employees, to the political detriment of the government. Furthermore, making a realistic examination of an asset's value might require the government to reveal an insolvency when a court has refused to find the enterprise bankrupt. Indeed some former communist states have structured their new bankruptcy laws specifically to allow courts to avoid a determination of bankruptcy. If the government in its pension regulation role was to find an enterprise insolvent when the courts had refused to find bankruptcy, creditors would have legitimate cause to complain that their assets were being taken for the benefit of the owners of the insolvent employer, including fund participants. What is more the finding of insolvency or bankruptcy might accelerate a financial crisis for the employer because creditors would refuse to extend further credit or call in their loans, a result the government is normally trying to avoid and thus might be unwilling to risk. Finally the government may have interests more important (or at least more immediate) than protecting the pension funds of its citizens. Meaningful accounting rules that reduce the reported level of profitability are also likely to reduce tax liabilities for those enterprises. This has been a particularly significant problem for foreign enterprises in the former Soviet states: to the extent that they rely on OECD-style accounting practices, they risk criminal prosecution for failure to adhere to the nuances of local accounting rules. All of this suggests that governments may have good reasons to do a poor job of monitoring the activities of a privatized social security pension fund, further expanding the opportunities for managerial malfeasance. Thus the central government may be incapable of objectively evaluating pension fund reporting because it may have a variety of vested interests in distorted enterprise accounting. The real value of assets held by privatized pension funds may be difficult if not impossible to determine and the government may have little interest in doing so. Most fund participants will, however, be far less capable of evaluating the financial position of funds than is the government. There may therefore be relatively little willingness, much less ability, to monitor the investment success of particular funds. This goes to the core of the case for privatization. The market process of choosing between funds is likely to be ineffective because it will be based on meaningless signals, and the size of the pensions to which fund participants are entitled may also be quite difficult to calculate.

Enforcement

In addition to these basic problems of monitoring, there is also the question of ensuring that the manager actually performs the tasks the pension fund manager is expected to perform. Pension fund law in the United States makes fund managers fiduciaries, imposes duties on them as such, and subjects them to liability in suit for violations of those duties. It follows the traditional common law of trusts in imposing two central legal duties on pension fund managers: a duty of prudence and a duty of loyalty. The first, a duty of prudence, requires that the manager make investments in the manner that would be employed by a prudent person of professional skill. This usually involves, at a minimum, avoidance of excessively risky investments and maintaining a reasonable level of diversification. The second legal requirement, a duty of loyalty, is intended to punish conflicts of interest; investment must be solely in the interests of the workers whose money is in the plan. In addition to these two requirements, American pension fund law imposes a further duty to comply with plan documents, essentially an accuracy-in-advertising requirement. It seems likely that any social security pension fund would require essentially these same duties.

There is an additional responsibility on the manager, though one that is not legally enforceable: the task of achieving reasonable investment returns. Incentive to achieve reasonable returns is normally provided by tying the amount of managerial compensation either to the size of the investment fund or to the returns achieved. The terms of compensation normally would be determined by market processes. Yet in determining the fees for managing social security pension funds, there is a clear agency problem. With respect to purely private investment contracts, the manager would like fees to be entirely unrelated to investment performance, while the client would like fees to be determined solely by performance; typical contracts seem to represent a compromise between these positions. However, with public investment contracts, the party negotiating the contract (typically a government agency or employee, and rarely a plan beneficiary) will have incentives different from those of the pension beneficiaries. The government negotiator's welfare is not necessarily tied in any way to the investment returns achieved, and thus that individual may be willing to devote less energy to insisting on the deal most favourable to plan beneficiaries; indeed the agency or individual involved in compensation negotiations may receive kickbacks or other illicit compensation from the manager. In general, then, there may be less-than-optimal incentives facing the investment manager to achieve maximum returns given a level of risk, since the negotiation process may not be entirely unbiased. It is not clear that there is any effective way to solve this problem in order to make compensation and plan management more favourable to plan beneficiaries.

The duties imposed by law on managers must be effectively enforced to be meaningful. One critical issue for the effectiveness of a regulatory agency is the degree to which its interests are aligned with those of the parties they are charged with protecting. In other words, does the regulatory agency have the incentive and ability to defend the interests of plan beneficiaries? A problem sometimes occurring with such agencies is an identification between the interests of the regulated party and those of the regulator. This problem arises through shared professional focus on a single set of problems; overlapping career opportunities for fund managers and regulators, and the greater ability of a small group of people with focused long-term interests to lobby the regulatory agency, as compared to a diffuse, large group composed of individuals with small interests in the agency's decisions.

However, in the developing or transition economies, these problems are likely to be more severe than in developed countries, where the legislature normally has oversight responsibility for regulatory agencies, and the electoral concerns of legislators impose a democratic constraint on the special interest-oriented behaviour of the agency. That constraint is likely not to be present in a government with a relatively weak democratic structure or tradition. Furthermore any tradition of citizen or consumer service may be completely absent in the bureaucracy. For example, in many former communist states, the governmental bureaucracy has traditionally viewed itself in a rather adversarial position with respect to individual citizens, with essentially no responsibility to protect their interests; the bureaucracy has instead been far more likely to view its task as that of serving the state's interests. It cannot be assumed, therefore, that a governmental agency with responsibility to regulate a fund management industry in the interests of its beneficiaries would actually do so.

It is also possible that the state would not view social security pension funds as sacrosanct. The large amounts of money that can build up in them will inevitably be a temptation to a government short of operating funds; indeed those funds are likely to tempt the politicians running the government. Politicians in some former communist states and developing countries have demonstrated a willingness on occasion to view public resources as presenting opportunities for self-enrichment, and these impulses are hardly unknown among politicians in developed democracies. The tendency of bureaucracies to respond to the agendas of the political leaders to whom they are immediately responsible suggests those ambitions may be realistic. In short it is plausible that the fund managers, the governmental agencies with responsibility to regulate them, and the political leadership may share an agenda which is not in the best interests of fund participants.

Juridical systems

When the regulatory agency under some circumstances has independent responsibility to impose sanctions and in other cases must seek legal sanction in a court, this raises the question of the impartiality of the courts themselves. While judicial corruption is often difficult to measure and opinions differ on the extent of the problem in most countries, in some countries it is a significant problem.

There are at least two ways in which judicial corruption might affect cases relating to the behaviour of managers of privatized pension funds. First, bribery is always a possibility, and seems in fact to be a continuing problem in many developing, as well as developed, countries. Judicial salaries in many developing countries are extremely low by OECD standards, and many judges live and work in conditions of near destitution. Even relatively minor bribes or gifts to judges have effectively decided all kinds of cases, from contested elections to minor commercial matters. The potentially significant sums of money involved in pension funds create the opportunity for bribery. Second, judges in most civil law countries (including almost all of the former communist states, and many developing countries in other regions) are employees of the government, and are vulnerable to pressure from governmental officials relating to salaries, assignments or even job tenure. Even when the judge is theoretically not an employee of the Ministry of Justice or some other government agency and thus putatively independent, there is often significant opportunity for this kind of pressure to be placed on judges. The problem of so-called "telephone justice", in which the apparent outcome of cases is changed as the result of a well-placed telephone call or other pressure from a high official, is regarded as commonplace in many countries. To the extent that a regulatory agency or political official may be illicitly financially involved with a pension fund, part of the service the official may render to earn his kickback or fee is the ability to influence judges through this relatively inexpensive form of manipulation of judges.

There is always the possibility that the appropriate agency may identify a case of misfeasance by the pension fund manager and impose a sanction or successfully bring legal action against the fund or the manager. The concern, whatever sanction is imposed, is that the sanction must be effective to have any impact on the behaviour of the manager. The problem with administrative or criminal penalties is that they may be difficult to tailor to the size of the sanction to the offence – small cases of corruption or mismanagement are likely either to evoke no sanction at all, or a sanction no different from that which would apply in a larger case.

Monetary penalties can be tailored quite exactly, but have one significant drawback: the pension fund management institution may not have sufficient corporate funds to pay the sanction. If the management institution is judgment-proof because it is incapable of paying the appropriate fine or penalty, it is effectively immune from the behavioural standards the sanction is intended to enforce. In the United States, banks are required to maintain a minimum ratio between their reserves and their loans to ensure solvency if some borrowers default on their loans. The conventional wisdom, however, is that investment firms do not require capital adequacy ratios, as do banks, as long as there is mandatory segregation of client accounts. Segregation implies clients' assets are protected from the claims of general creditors against the employer. Without some capital at stake, however, there is nothing to deter managerial misfeasance. Pension fund management institutions could be required to post a bond or maintain a minimum ratio between their own capital and the size of the fund they manage. There is the problem of ensuring that management institutions adequately segregate their own funds from the pension funds they are managing, to ensure that it is truly the institution that pays the sanctions, and not the pension beneficiaries. There is also a problem with the relationship between the individual manager and the management institution: if sanctions are paid out of the institution's assets, the individual managers may in effect be allowed to gamble, say, for their own benefit while risking only the assets of the institutions for whom they work, so that the personal assets of managers ought to be at risk. Those assets will probably be minuscule relative to the size of the injury a manager may do. Thus it is likely that administrative or criminal penalties almost certainly would have to be employed along with monetary sanctions against managers.

In order for enforcement of sanctions against management institutions to be effective, one more element must be in place: there must be some administrative mechanism to seize the assets which constitute the sanction imposed on the institution. The effectiveness of law enforcement agencies should not be assumed automatically. In some developing and transition economies, judgments are simply not enforceable because the enforcement office has been so deprived of resources, and procedures are so ineffective, that it cannot effectively undertake the apparently simple task it has been assigned. At least some former communist states have claimed to address this problem by incorporating the enforcement office directly into the Ministry of Justice, a measure which may or may not increase its effectiveness, but which brings the enforcement of judgments directly under the control of the political branch of government. To the extent that the accumulation of funds in pension accounts provokes the interest of members of the government, that misbehaviour is facilitated and the ability of independent courts to interfere has been reduced. Requiring that fund managers post bonds in amounts sufficient to pay some predictable level of sanctions will not necessarily avoid this problem, since one responsibility of the enforcement office is often to seize posted bonds.

Portfolio regulations

Portfolio regulations can take two forms. Under the prudent man (or prudent person) approach, portfolios must be judged to be prudent under generally accepted financial market standards. Under the quantitative approach, maximums are set as to the percentage of the portfolio that can be held in different asset classes. Quantitative regulation of portfolio distributions seeks ostensibly to protect pension fund beneficiaries against "imprudent" investments. Limits are often imposed on holdings of assets with relatively volatile nominal returns, such as equities and property, as well as foreign assets, even if their mean return is relatively high. For occupational funds, limits are often set on investing in the sponsoring employer (self-investment),[10] to protect against the risk of insolvency of the sponsor.

For advanced countries, apart from the control of employers sponsoring pension schemes using the pension funds to invest in their own companies, the degree to which such regulations actually contribute to benefit security is open to doubt since pension funds, unlike insurance companies, may face the risk of increasing liabilities as workers' wages increase as well as the risk of holding assets and hence the need to trade volatility for return. Moreover diversification of assets can thus minimize the increase in risk. Motives such as ensuring a steady demand for government bonds, or protection of benefit insurers, may also play a part. Restrictions will also limit the benefits to the capital markets from the development of pension funds. And, in the case of restrictions which explicitly or implicitly[11] oblige pension funds to invest in government bonds, which must themselves be repaid from taxation, there may be no benefit to capital formation and the "funded" plans may – at a macroeconomic level – be equivalent to pay-as-you-go.

Even for defined contribution schemes it is hard to argue a sound case for such rules, given the superior alternative of prudent man rules. There seems to be little evidence that defined contribution investors need "protecting from themselves", that is prevented from taking high risks. Indeed experience suggests that workers with individual defined contribution funds tend to be too cautious to develop adequate funds at retirement, while companies running defined contribution funds may invest excessively cautiously to avoid lawsuits.

Some possible exceptions may be made to this argument in developing countries with emerging securities markets. There could be a rationale for portfolio regulations initially if fund managers as well as regulators are inexperienced and the markets are volatile and open to manipulation by insiders. Risk may easily become excessive in such cases. Also compliance with portfolio limits is more readily verified and monitored than for prudent man rules. One key aspect may be that such regulations should not impose minimum requirements on holdings of certain assets, which may lead pension reserves to be used as a captive source of government financing. Regulation should become more liberal as financial markets become more sophisticated and mature.

A major point of discussion in developing countries is whether minimum rate of return guarantees, as in Chile, promote herding behaviour by pension fund managers and restrict pension funds in their investment policies, to the disadvantage of members. Herding behaviour occurs when all pension funds have similar investment portfolios. Such behaviour may be encouraged by regulations that require pension funds to earn a rate of return that is within a certain band of the average of rates of return earned by all pension funds. Another hypothesis for the herding that is observed is that pension fund managers all seek the same portfolios, so as not to be distinct from one another when the risk of losing clients in the case of underperformance is greater than the chance of gain from superior performance (Davis, 1995d).

As regards national experience, in Chile investment rules set by the government seek to ensure adequate diversification by setting maximum limits on different assets, and not a prudent man rule. There is, however, no direction of investment to priority areas. Up to the early 1990s these rules set maximums of 50 per cent for government bonds, 30 per cent for equities and only 3 per cent for foreign assets in the form of AAA-rated bank debt. Equities and corporate bonds held had to meet stringent rating requirements. Rules also limit the fractions of funds invested in individual companies, in terms both of the companies' market capitalization and of the funds' own assets.[12] Following the idea of sequencing as a pension system develops, an easing took place in the late 1990s. Foreign investment was allowed to expand from 3 per cent to 20 per cent,[13] funds were allowed to invest in foreign bonds and equities and not merely bank deposits, and the maximum for domestic government bonds was set at 45 per cent. AFPs can invest in a much wider range of companies, and in venture capital, a move which it is hoped will raise interest in flotation of family-owned companies in Chile.[14] The reforms are also expected to introduce new instruments such as mortgage-backed securities, convertible bonds and revenue bonds, the last aimed at facilitating institutional investment in infrastructure projects. Scope for AFPs to use derivatives will be increased.

In Singapore there are no formal portfolio restrictions, as the government takes the bulk of Central Provident Fund contributions to invest in government instruments. Both the Monetary Authority of Singapore and Government of Singapore Investment Corporation invest assets at their discretion. Interest rates paid to members are linked to those on bank deposits. In Malaysia there is a requirement that at least 70 per cent of the total and 50 per cent of additional Employees' Provident Fund assets should be invested in Malaysian government bonds, funds from which are used for development purposes. Recent legal amendments have allowed investment by the Employees' Provident Fund in other securities, joint ventures, real estate and foreign securities.

Minimum funding rules and regulation of returns

Regulation of the funding of benefits and associated accounting rules[15] is a key aspect of the regulatory framework for defined benefit pension funds, which may strongly influence portfolio distributions, notably by influencing the degree of volatility in asset prices that fund managers are willing to accept.

Minimum funding requirements set by regulation seek to protect the security of benefits against default risk by the company, given that unfunded benefits are liabilities on the books of the employer, and therefore risk is concentrated and pensioners (or pension insurers) may have no better claim in case of bankruptcy than any other creditor.

In Switzerland companies must pay in for defined contribution plans if returns fall short of 4 per cent. This may be particularly constraining, forcing companies to adopt a one-year horizon despite 30-year liabilities. Moreover, in Switzerland, accounting conventions also affect funding decisions, as short-falls of defined benefit pension funds assets relative to liabilities (with assets valued at the lower of cost and market value) are included in the company accounts (Hepp, 1990). This may help to account for conservative investment strategies based on bond holdings, independent of portfolio regulations discussed above, despite the fact that funding of projected "real" obligations should make equities attractive. There are also minimum contributions. In Australia, companies are obliged to contribute on behalf of workers to a complying pension fund, otherwise the government levies a charge – the Superannuation Guarantee Charge – on the employer to enforce the contribution.

Information disclosure

Given the length of pension commitments, possibly covering 30 or more years of work and 20 or more years of retirement, detailed reporting and information disclosure are essential. Accordingly standards of information for members are a crucial complement to regulation. Defined contribution pension schemes may require even better information for members than defined benefit schemes, given the direct dependence of pensions on the performance of the portfolio. Members need to be able to judge whether contributions are adequate and investments too risky: a difficulty for individuals in advanced societies, let alone developing countries. Information disclosure is also important for defined benefit schemes. In developing countries there is generally no information on contributions given to participants. They often do not know if their employer has correctly reported their earnings, or reported them at all, until they submit a claim.

In Chile information to members is essential to enable the competitive mechanism of transfers to operate. Funds are publicly valued daily at market prices. Funds are required to provide statements to members three times a year showing the last four contributions, financial performance of the fund, accumulated balances and returns on the account. Malaysia and Singapore disclose the value of individual accounts, but little other information. Notably in Singapore there is no information about ultimate investments, and policies and performance relating to them. Accounts of the Central Provident Fund are not publicly audited. In Australia and Switzerland audited annual accounts and an individual benefit statement must be made available to members.

Other types of regulation

In Chile, the inferior financial information of workers as compared with fund management companies is aggravated by lack of familiarity of workers with capital market investment, as well as the thinness and lack of credibility of capital markets. As a consequence (albeit also to protect the government's guarantee), regulation focuses particularly on consumer protection. For example, regulation of the AFPs seeks to ensure solvency of funds, both by separating funds from the management companies (funds belong to the members and are not affected by losses by the AFP) and by imposing minimum capital requirements on them. An additional safeguard is that managers must invest a sum equal to 1 per cent of funds under management on their own books, and in the same way as the client funds, bearing in mind that each AFP may only have one fund, so they will share the losses from bad investment.

INVESTMENT PERFORMANCE OF MANDATORY FUNDED SCHEMES

It is important to assess the overall performance of the various schemes outlined above, in that they illustrate the effects of the various factors and indicate the overall effectiveness of the different approaches to mandatory funded pensions.

In Chile the funds initially invested largely in government bonds, but later shifted to equities, via purchases of existing shares in the secondary market and of new shares created by the sale of privatized companies. Corporate bonds became popular investments as more companies met the government's rating targets: offering an attractive alternative to short-term bank credit, which was the only form of corporate debt available until the late 1980s. In 1994 AFP portfolios were invested 39 per cent in public bonds, 33 per cent in equities, 6 per cent in deposits, 6 per cent in corporate bonds and 13 per cent in mortgage bonds (see table 7.4). Their influence on the capital market may be gauged by the fact that they hold 55 per cent of Chilean corporate and mortgage bonds, 10 per cent of all equities and no less than 95 per cent of privatization issues.

Performance of the funds in terms of investment returns has shown an average real return in Chile of 13 per cent per year over the period 1970–95 (see table 7.5) and 10.5 per cent even allowing for the high level of administration costs. However low-income workers' returns have been much lower (7.5 per cent) owing to a flat-rate element in the administrative costs (this element was later eliminated: see Vittas, 1993). The good returns – well in excess of average earnings growth and above returns in international markets – have been linked to the overall performance of the Chilean economy, and in particular a sharp fall in the real interest rate. Poorer returns in the 1990s have led to questioning of investment policies and restrictions, especially on foreign investment, for increasing risk unnecessarily.

Table 7.4   Portfolio distributions of mandatory funded pension schemes in selected countries, mid-1990s (percentages)

Country	Bonds	of which public	of which private	Shares	Property	Loans and mortgages	Short-term assets	Foreign assets
Chile (1994)	45	39	6	33	2	13	6	1
Singapore (1996)	70	70	0	0	0	0	28	0
Malaysia (1996)	55	34	21	16	1	0	30	0
Switzerland (1994)	28	–	–	14	16	41	2	0
Australia (1995)	15	13	2	41	9	0	20	14
Sweden (1995)	83	37	46	1	3	7	2	0

Sources: Chile: Mitchell and Barreto (1997); Singapore and Malaysia: Asher (1998b); Switzerland: OECD (1997); Australia and Sweden: Central Bank Bulletins.

In Singapore, 90 per cent of assets are invested in government bonds. The returns credited to accounts have been around 2 per cent in real terms on average since the 1960s (Vittas, 1993), although over the period 1987–96, the real return was lower, at 0.33 per cent, with negative real returns for half these years (Asher, 1998a). Calculations (table 7.5) suggest that real returns were 1.3 per cent over 1970–95 and 2.3 per cent over 1980–95. Since 1986 the return has been set according to the deposit rates for short-term funds (up to 12 months) with four domestic banks, subject to a nominal minimum of 2.5 per cent. The return compares unfavourably with those realized in many of the OECD countries (Davis, 1995a), as well as in Chile, and with real wages growing at 4 per cent or more. The real rate of return may be insufficient to secure a high replacement ratio, despite the high contribution rate (especially as some of the assets are used for non-pension purposes). Asher (1998b) noted an actuarial study that suggested that sizeable additional contributions on top of the existing 40 per cent would be needed to attain a replacement ratio of 66 per cent. Low interest rates on housing loans from the fund are one underlying reason for its low returns. The availability of cheap housing loans has also reportedly driven the price of housing to high levels. But the main reason for low returns to investors is that a sizeable proportion of (reportedly high) returns on foreign investments are accumulated as hidden reserves for the future needs of the economy.

On the other hand, the investments of those individuals allowed to allocate their own excess balances with the Central Provident Fund as they desired have been even more disappointing (Asher, 1998b). Over 1994–97, only 20 per cent of investors achieved returns in excess of those available from leaving the money in the Central Provident Fund, and aggregate losses in nominal terms of those investing exceeded gains; and this was before the financial crisis in southeast Asia began. This is a sobering illustration of the capabilities of individuals to manage long-term investments.

Table 7.5 Estimated real total returns for mandatory funded pension schemes, 1970–95 (percentages per annum, standard deviations in brackets)

Country	Real return	Average earnings	Global portfolio	Domestic balanced portfolio	Return less average earnings	Return less global portfolio	Return less domestic balanced
1970–97							
Chile	—	2.1 (6.3)	—	—	—	—	—
Singapore	1.3 (2.0)	6.9 (3.3)	5.1 (18.4)	—	-5.6	-3.8	—
Malaysia	3.0 (3.9)	4.4 (2.9)	6.7 (17.2)	—	-1.4	-3.7	—
Switzerland	1.7 (7.5)	1.5 (2.1)	3.7 (17.0)	2.4 (18.1)	+0.2	-2.0	-0.7
Australia	1.8 (11.4)	1.0 (3.4)	6.1 (18.2)	3.5 (17.5)	+0.8	-4.3	-1.7
Sweden	2.0 (13.1)	1.4 (3.5)	6.3 (14.8)	8.0 (20.1)	+0.6	-4.3	-6.0
Netherlands	*4.6 (6.0)*	*1.4 (2.6)*	*4.8 (14.7)*	*5.5 (18.3)*	*+3.2*	*-0.2*	*-0.9*
United Kingdom	*5.9 (12.8)*	*2.8 (2.3)*	*5.9 (15.0)*	*4.7 (15.4)*	*+3.1*	*0.0*	*+1.2*
1980–95							
Chile	13.0 (9.5)	3.2 (5.7)	9.1 (19.1)	—	+9.8	+4.1	—
Singapore	2.3 (2.0)	6.4 (3.5)	9.2 (15.3)	—	-4.1	-6.9	—
Malaysia	4.3 (2.6)	4.1 (3.0)	11.7 (14.0)	—	+0.2	-7.4	—
Switzerland	1.8 (7.7)	0.8 (1.3)	9.2 (15.8)	3.4 (18.6)	+1.0	-7.4	-1.6
Australia	6.1 (8.6)	-0.1 (2.2)	10.2 (17.8)	8.8 (15.8)	+6.2	-4.1	-2.7
Sweden	4.9 (15.9)	0.3 (2.4)	10.4 (15.3)	10.3 (21.7)	+4.6	-5.5	-5.4

Notes: For Chile, Singapore and Malaysia, average earnings growth is proxied by growth in GDP per head. Global portfolio returns are estimated by using total returns on G-7 bonds and equities (50 per cent each), weighted by approximate GDP weights and translated into domestic currency using the effective exchange rate index. The domestic balanced portfolio column shows real returns on 50 per cent domestic bonds and 50 per cent domestic shares.

Data for the Netherlands and the United Kingdom are shown for comparison. Neither country has mandatory funded pension schemes.
Sources: For Singapore and Malaysia: Asher (1998b) and Vittas (1993); for Chile: Holzmann (1997a); for Switzerland, Australia and Sweden: own calculations.

Box 7.5 How government agencies can invest pension funds well

Two federal agencies of the United States government are responsible for managing the investment of retirement funds. One of the smallest federal agencies, with approximately 100 employees, established in 1986, invests over $60 billion in assets, with the amount growing rapidly. The Federal Retirement Trust Investment Board administers the Thrift Savings Plan, which allows federal employees to supplement their defined benefit plans with contributions to a tax-deferred defined contribution plan. The Thrift Savings Plan is particularly interesting because it has been viewed as a possible model for privatizing social security in the United States.

The Thrift Savings Plan is one of the three parts of the Federal Employees' Retirement System. Participants choose between three Thrift Savings Plan investment funds. The government securities fund has slightly underperformed relative to its benchmark of related securities. The common stock fund is an indexed fund managed by Barclays Bank, and it charges only 9 basis points (0.09 per cent) for administration, which is lower than the 15 or more basis points charged to individuals and other funds. The stock fund charges ten basis points for administration, and it has met or exceeded its benchmark.

The president appoints the five-member board that oversees the investments. The board is governed by similar rules for auditing, reporting and prudence that cover the private sector. The Thrift Savings Plan pays out annuities and has complete responsibility for participant communication.

The second major agency, the Pension Benefit Guaranty Corporation, manages a $16 billion portfolio. It functions partly as an insurance company and partly as an investment fund. It was established in 1974 to collect premiums from companies that sponsor defined benefit pension funds to insure the pensions of companies who may default as a result of bankruptcy.

The Pension Benefit Guaranty Corporation board of directors is political: three cabinet secretaries sit on the board of directors and the advisory board is made up of seven presidential appointees. The staff, like those of the Thrift Savings Plan, are hired under the formal rules and restrictions of civil service law. The Pension Benefit Guaranty Corporation also faces investment constraints that do not fetter private managers or for-profit private insurance companies. The Pension Benefit Guaranty Corporation must invest its premium income (about half of its revenues) in bonds and its other income in a broad portfolio. The Corporation's political nature inhibits investing in real estate or overseas.

Malaysian investments have until recently been wholly domestic. For many years, funds were invested solely in domestic government bonds. The share was 89 per cent in 1987, but fell sharply thereafter to 34 per cent in 1996, reflecting an improvement in the fiscal position. Corporate bonds increased from 11 per cent in 1991 to 20 per cent in 1996, and equities from 2 per cent to 16 per cent. In terms of investment returns, the Malaysian provident fund has done considerably better than the Singaporean, with real returns of 3 per cent on average over 1970–95, and 4.3 per cent over 1980–95. This performance was achieved despite the focus on domestic assets, and illustrates the success of the related economic growth policies, which have been reinforced by the availability of pension fund assets. It may nonetheless involve an element of taxation, possibly of around 2 per cent;[16] it also falls slightly short of estimated real average earnings growth, and is well below potential returns on international investment. Other provident funds have done much worse than Malaysia or Singapore, with Zambia achieving minus 25 per cent real returns in the 1980s (World Bank, 1994).

The Pension Benefit Guaranty Corporation and the Thrift Savings Board in the United States are two examples of successful government management of pension assets (see box 7.5). In the case of bonds issued by the Thrift Savings Board, government employees choose from a limited set of investment funds managed in the private sector. In both cases, however, these programmes involve assets that are a small fraction of what a national programme would be and do not encounter some of the problems that a national programme would, such as the capital market effects of a national programme and the problem of dealing with a large number of low-wage earners who would have small accounts.

The mandatory funded pension scheme is becoming a more popular means of providing retirement income for individuals both in developing and developed countries. A number of different types operate in the world today. Notably one can distinguish schemes where asset management is decentralized and pensions are provided on an individual basis, schemes where asset management is wholly centralized and schemes where asset management is decentralized on an occupational basis. Trust funds of social security schemes are another variant. Behavioural differences arising from such differences in the structure of schemes have been shown to affect the performance of funds, although the influence on performance from the regulation and politicization of investment can also be traced. Returns accruing to members are also influenced by widely differing levels of administrative costs. Meanwhile, although developing countries need not wait until capital market development is complete before introducing funded mandatory pensions, some preconditions exist nonetheless, in respect of capital market structure and regulatory capacity.

Notes

[1] Existing defined benefit funds did not have to be switched to defined contribution.

[2] Bateman and Piggott (1997) cast doubt on the efficacy of these incentives.

[3] However, the ceiling up to which pensions replace wages at this rate is only indexed to price inflation, thus leading in future to declines in average replacement ratios as incomes of more workers exceed the ceiling.

[4] There are also supplementary private schemes in Sweden arranged through collective bargaining, and which cover virtually the entire labour force, one for white-collar workers (the ITP system) and one for blue-collar workers (the STP system). The ITP system is funded either through book reserves, through insurance contracts or through contracts with a special pension company, while the STP scheme is provided solely through a mutual insurance organization (AMF).

[5] In practice, loans are made to provincial governments, and the interest rates charged are those of federal long-term bonds. This means that the rates of return are lower than market rates since rates on federal bonds are generally slightly lower than those on provincial bonds.

[6] The importance of pension liabilities as a cost to employers, and hence the benefit from higher asset returns, is underlined by estimates from the European Federation for Retirement Provision that a 1 per cent improvement in asset returns may reduce companies' labour costs by 2–3 per cent, where there is a fully funded, mature, defined benefit pension plan.

[7] For example, Bajtelsmit (1996) shows that a simulated risky stock portfolio (based on historical performance) will, on average, produce ten times the retirement wealth of a simulated government bond portfolio over a 42-year pension contribution and investment period.

[8] The Monte Carlo simulations were conducted using @RISK, an add-on statistical package for use with Microsoft Excel. This software allows each annual return to be drawn from a specified distribution of returns. For each simulation reported, 1,000 iterations were performed. Repetitions of the simulations produced results consistent with those reported.

[9] This openness may help to create a contestable market, wherein a seeming oligopoly may be characterized by competitive behaviour on the part of existing companies, because of the potential for new companies to enter in a "hit and run" manner in response to excess profits.

[10] These limits do not apply to reserve funding schemes such as those common in Germany, Japan, Luxembourg and Sweden, where 100 per cent of assets are invested in the sponsor.

[11] For example, by closing down all alternative investment strategies such as international diversification.

[12] This tends to reduce the returns of large funds, which are unable to invest as much of their portfolios in equities with good prospects as smaller ones may.

[13] In 1988 about 3 per cent was held internationally.

[14] Ceilings are higher for employers willing to submit to limits on their managerial independence.

[15] Regulation of funding is typically carried out by periodic submission of accounts and actuarial reports to the authorities.

[16] The comparison made is between real returns over the 1971–96 period of 2.74 per cent per year, equity yields of 5.61 per cent and a yield on bank assets/liabilities of 4.26 per cent.

COVERAGE AND ITS SHORTFALLS

8

This chapter discusses the level of coverage of pension schemes in all regions of the world in terms of the proportion of the population who are insured for pensions under social security schemes. It also discusses the main reasons for the level of coverage being low in many countries. Related issues discussed elsewhere in the book are questions of governance and administration (Chapter 9), contribution evasion (Chapter 10) and problems relating to the extension of coverage (Chapter 16).

In 1944 the International Labour Conference recognized in the Declaration of Philadelphia that economic security should be a right for all people and that the nations of the world should develop programmes "which will achieve . . . the extension of social security measures to provide a basic income to all in need of such protection and comprehensive medical care". More than 50 years later, however, that right is still denied to the vast majority of people, among them retired and disabled people, widows and orphans throughout the world. For them the key issue concerning social protection in old age and disability is their lack of entitlement to any pension, and not the basis for its determination.

In the case of pensions, as with other branches of social security, social protection coverage has three dimensions:

- *the range of protection provided* – the social security system may provide protection against some contingencies, such as employment injury, but not against others, such as old age;

- *the level of protection provided* – while there may be provision to meet a contingency, the benefit level may be low and insufficient to prevent hardship;

- *the categories of people covered* – the social security system may cover some categories of workers but not others.

TRENDS IN POPULATION COVERAGE

Population coverage

According to the US Social Security Administration (1997), 166 countries have

Table 8.1 Types of social security programmes providing cash benefits to the aged, disabled and/or survivors, 175 countries worldwide, 1997

Continent/region	No. of schemes	Contributory		Non-contributory		Mandatory	Mandatory savings		
		Flat-rate	Earnings-related	Means-tested	Flat-rate universal	Private pensions	Public	Private	Total
Africa	5	1	34	3	3	1	6	–	
Asia	3	2	29	2	1	–	7	–	
Latin America and the Caribbean	1	1	34	6	–	–	–	5	
Europe	–	14	31	12	2	3	–	–	
North America	–	–	2	1	1	–	–	–	
Oceania	–	–	3	–	–	1	6	–	
Total	9	18	133	24	7	5	19	5	220

Note: The inclusion of five Latin American countries in the private mandatory savings category requires some clarification. Private systems exist in Bolivia, Chile, El Salvador and Peru, but in Argentina, Colombia, Mexico and Uruguay schemes can also be managed by public institutions, the social security institute, family allowance programmes and cooperatives.

Source: US Social Security Administration, 1997, updated from ILO sources.

one or more social security schemes which cover the contingencies of old age, disability (invalidity) and survivors while nine have none (see table 8.1). But, in spite of this, more than half the world labour force and their dependants are not covered by such schemes. The problem is particularly acute in sub-Saharan Africa and South Asia where formal social security coverage is estimated at 5 to 10 per cent of the labour force, but it is also of great significance in East and South-East Asia and in Latin America. Although the scale of exclusion is not so great in Central and Eastern Europe and Central Asia, the process of economic and political transition has led to a significant increase in the informalization of employment and thus to a fall in coverage. This has also been echoed in middle-income and even industrialized economies through the reaction to the competitive pressures of globalization.

Most countries rely on a social insurance scheme providing earnings-related benefits (although most OECD countries which follow this system also underpin it with a social assistance safety net which provides general anti-poverty coverage on a means-tested basis). The development of social security indicates that, typically, priority was first accorded to ensuring that the scheme provided income replacement in respect of the long-term contingencies of old age, disability and survivors. Such schemes were invariably aimed, however, at the circumstances of formal sector workers who worked for an employer and the linkage between social insurance and formal sector employment has remained central to the issue of coverage.

In some countries special schemes were devised for certain occupational groups, but the tendency has been for these to be gradually incorporated in one scheme which covers virtually all formal sector workers at least in the private sector. Public servants and members of the armed forces, together with special categories such as judges and politicians, are still often covered by special provisions which are administered separately by government (see Technical Brief 3).

The extent of population coverage for social security pensions depends on many factors, of which the following are particularly significant.

1. *The method of financing.* Universal or social assistance schemes are typically financed from general taxes rather than social security contributions. Provided that the tax base is broad and yields sufficient resources, coverage may be extensive and not depend directly on individualized financing.

2. *The age of the scheme.* Generally the more established the scheme, the broader the coverage.

3. *The level of economic development.* There is a close link between the level of coverage and the level of social protection resources available to finance it, with more developed countries generally having a higher level of coverage.

4. *The size of the formal sector.* It is easier to collect contributions and taxes from those in formal sector employment than from the informal sector.

5. *The capacity of the social security administration.* This affects both the credibility and viability of the scheme and has implications for existing coverage in that many schemes experience difficulty in ensuring compliance, but it also limits the extension of coverage to excluded groups and contingencies.

6. *Government policy.* The extent to which the government gives priority to extending coverage for social protection varies according to national priorities and may be sufficient to counteract other factors. Thus, for example, Costa Rica is less developed than Mexico but has considerably higher coverage owing to government initiatives in the 1970s. Although most workers and their families in developed countries, where levels of formal sector employment are high, are covered under social security schemes, it often proves difficult to cover effectively the self-employed, contractors, agricultural workers, domestic workers and casual workers. Where this is attempted, difficulties arise in identifying and in registering such persons, and then in the collection of the appropriate contributions. If the scheme is contributions-based, it will be difficult to identify the correct level of earnings and if it is tax-based there will be similar problems in identifying the taxable income.

Those countries which formerly functioned with centrally planned economies generally have well established social insurance schemes which cover employees and, in some cases, the self-employed. In these countries the process of transition to market economies has led to a shift from public to private sector employment within the formal sector, as well as to a significant growth in self-employment and the informal sector. The schemes in the transition countries have not, in general, come to terms with the administrative obligations related to ensuring compliance by private sector employers and the self-employed.

Social security coverage is low in many sub-Saharan African countries (only 1 per cent of the labour force in Chad, Gambia and Niger), and only reaches moderate levels in North Africa (22 per cent in Egypt and 24 per cent in Tunisia). Even there the figures reflect coverage under the law rather than compliance, which is low, particularly among the self-employed. Similar conditions exist in Latin America: less than one-third coverage in Colombia, Ecuador, Guatemala and Peru and less than 15 per cent in Bolivia, El Salvador, Honduras and Paraguay. Coverage levels are higher in many of the Caribbean countries (at least 80 per cent in the Bahamas, Barbados and Jamaica) where the self-employed and informal sector workers represent a smaller proportion of the labour force.[1]

Coverage rates are also low in much of Asia (for example, 8 per cent of the labour force in India). The rapid growth of the economies of some countries in East and South-East Asia from the late 1980s up to the late 1990s illustrates the connection between high growth, increases in formal sector employment and low rates of unemployment, but this has not necessarily been reflected in significant increases in social security coverage for the labour force. Coverage under the social security scheme is only 10 per cent in Thailand (prior to the scheme's expansion in 1995) and 12 per cent in Indonesia. In Indonesia, Malaysia, Singapore and Thailand retirement pension schemes have yet to be established for private sector workers, and none of these countries has a social assistance system for the poor. Reliance is placed instead on the provident fund system, although Malaysia has a social insurance pension scheme covering the contingencies of invalidity and survivors' dependency. The financial crisis in Asia in 1997/8 exposed the weaknesses of the social protection schemes, and in particular the low level of protection and coverage.

Pension schemes, based on social insurance principles covering public and private sector workers, have been established in countries such as the Philippines, the Republic of Korea and Viet Nam, and one is envisaged in Thailand, but among both the pension schemes and the provident funds population coverage is low, restricted to formal sector employment and diminished by substantial evasion. It would seem likely that competitive forces have tended to persuade employers to seek lower labour costs either through direct evasion of social security liability or through an informal workforce (for example, with reliance placed on homeworkers or contractors).

Those Asian countries in transition from centrally planned economies tend to have higher levels of coverage. In China, out of an estimated labour force of 592 million in 1992, there were 277 million workers in wage and salaried employment, of whom 3.2 million were employed in the private sector. Social security coverage is estimated at 100 million or 18 per cent of the labour force, but is declining as a result of the privatization of state-owned enterprises.

Categories of people excluded from coverage

The trends in personal coverage, particularly in developing countries, are inconsistent with classical development theory which assumes that, as economies grow, most workers will eventually be employed in regular wage employment in the formal sector. In addition development has often not improved the position of the most vulnerable groups outside the labour force, such as the disabled and old people who cannot count on family support, are not covered under other social policies and have not been able to make provision for their own support.

Many categories of people are excluded from coverage because their employment conditions differ from those in the formal sector. Most social insurance schemes have been established to suit the circumstances of people in regular employment in the formal sector, so that, over a working life, a pattern of rights will be built up that enables the pension, on termination of employment, to relate to the length of this period, and to the level of earnings. Furthermore, since such people work for an employer, that justifies a system of financing which includes an employer's contribution. The structure of such schemes has also been governed by reference to pre-existing public sector, or special group, schemes which, whether contributory or not, have tended to provide a high benchmark in terms of the benefit structure, and set goals for private sector workers to attain.

Formal sector workers were seen as the priority for social security protection, first, because their dependence on a regular wage income rendered them vulnerable when this income was interrupted and, second, because administration through employers was seen as feasible. In addition they were also the most organized and the most similar to public servants who had already been covered for some time. Those employed outside the formal sector were more likely to be, at least partially, dependent on agriculture which, together with family support, provided a basis for subsistence in times of adversity.

In addition the workers excluded from coverage are a heterogeneous group. Professional self-employed people who have an established business might be prepared to participate in the national social security scheme, but may feel capable of making their own arrangements to finance provision for retirement from business income. They may be reluctant to participate in the social security scheme if this involves a contribution equivalent to both the employers' and the employees' contributions.

Many workers outside the formal sector, such as the lower paid self-employed, casual workers and agricultural workers, are likely to be obliged, by the irregularity of their incomes and the uncertainty of their circumstances, to live on a day-to-day basis and thus tend to give lower priority to saving for old age, particularly in a scheme which requires a high contribution rate. For those with casual and intermittent employment, it is difficult to meet the conditions of entitlement for a retirement pension, which require the satisfaction of a long qualifying period of work and thus imply a stability of employment beyond their reach. In addition they may give priority to more immediate contingencies such as health care.

Domestic household workers are often a particularly difficult group to cover. Since their employer is a private individual and they work in his or her home, compliance is difficult to enforce. Furthermore their wages are generally low and may be provided substantially in kind, so that it will be difficult to determine the basis for a meaningful social security contribution. However, many work for their employers for long periods and their need for income security on termination of employment is apparent.

Finally many of those excluded are in fact formal sector employees. These may be broadly divided into three groups:

- those excluded by statute because, for example, of their conditions of service, or because they work for small employers not within the scope of the scheme;
- those who are insurable under the scheme but for whom contributions are not being paid by their employers (either through default, through evasion or through ignorance) – this may even apply to public sector workers;
- those whose conditions of service have been so arranged, or are portrayed as such, to avoid liability (contract labourers, part-time workers, people supplied through a third party).

REASONS FOR EXCLUSION FROM COVERAGE

Various studies[2] have been undertaken to analyse and overcome the reasons for exclusion from coverage. A common conclusion, particularly in developing countries, is that many workers outside the formal sector are not able or willing to contribute a relatively high percentage of their incomes to finance social security benefits that do not meet their immediate priority needs. In addition they may not be familiar with, or may distrust, the way the formal social security scheme is managed. As a result, some groups of workers outside the formal sector have set up schemes that better meet their priority needs and contributory capacity.

Similar considerations even apply to those who work for employers in small enterprises, or who are employed on a casual, temporary or contractual basis, except that here the employer is also likely to resist contributing to the social security scheme. There are also a range of factors, such as legal restrictions and administrative bottlenecks, which effectively restrict access to formal social security schemes.

Social security priorities and contributory capacity

Most developed and some developing countries have set up social assistance schemes that are aimed at people in financial need who cannot be reached by policies for employment and who cannot – and/or have not been able to – contribute to self-financed social insurance schemes (see Chapter 5). Social assistance schemes provide benefits in cash or in kind, and may either apply to wide social groups such as children, disabled and retired people, or be limited to certain occupational groups. The advantage of social assistance benefits is that they can be directed to those most in need, but they require a sophisticated administration to determine who is really deserving, and to make sure that the benefits reach the target population effectively. Therefore the cost of delivering the benefits is often high: without a tight benefit administration there are likely to be leakages or corruption. The feasibility and effectiveness of these schemes depends on the resources, administrative capacity and priorities of the country. Where a significant proportion of the population is poor (as in many developing countries), a general social assistance scheme may be both inappropriate and impracticable, but it may be possible to aim assistance at defined vulnerable groups such as the old, the seriously disabled, widows and orphans.

An alternative approach is to provide a universal pension for specific categories of people subject to satisfying a residence test, but without any contribution liability or means testing. Such schemes, which have been established in Botswana, Brunei Darussalam, Canada, Namibia and the Seychelles, are financed from taxes and are thus more likely to be found in countries where the number of potential beneficiaries is relatively small and tax revenue collection is ample and efficient.

Workers outside the formal sector are generally employed in small, often family-based, enterprises. If they own their business, they are often not, or only partly, integrated into the formal economy. If they are wage workers, they usually have informal labour relations with their employers, probably with no written labour contracts. Such informality affects not only wage earners and other groups, such as homeworkers in the informal sector, but also casual labourers who work – directly or indirectly – for formal sector enterprises. A considerable proportion of these informal sector workers and their families live in poverty, and many of them are women.

Most formal sector workers can contribute regularly to social insurance. Given their regular earnings, they can provide for their retirement. This is not the case for most informal sector workers, especially in developing countries, who are 'psychologically engrossed in their problems of immediate survival to such an extent that any concern or motivation to provide for a distant eventuality gets almost obliterated' (Singh, 1994). They often live from one day to the next and face risks that can throw them into permanent indebtedness. These risks could be grouped into the following four categories:

- calamities (flood, fire, civil unrest and famine);
- loss of earning power (disability, ill health, loss of assets);
- life cycle crises (death and marital breakdown);
- sudden and large expenditures (hospital).

It is difficult for institutionalized social security schemes to protect informal sector workers against all these risks. Most informal sector households already spend a considerable part of their budget on vital life areas, such as health and education, and as a priority they feel they need protection against loss of earnings capacity (particularly attributable to disability or death) and to short-term concerns such as health care. This perception may be inspired by the belief that, if they reach retirement age at all, they would be looked after by family or relatives, and by the recognition that their limited resources must be allocated first to immediate and short-term needs. The concept of retirement cannot be readily applied, either to the self-employed or to those working on a casual basis in the informal sector, since the former are likely to be involved in income-generating activities beyond normal retirement age and the latter to seek work as long as there is a chance that it will be available to them and they are capable of doing it. However, many of them will reach an age when they are unable to work and, if they cannot find family support, will face destitution in the absence of any form of social safety net. The same is true of orphans and widows who cannot be reached with employment and labour market policies.

Legal restrictions

Most social insurance schemes in developing countries have adopted a cautious approach to the extension of coverage beyond the formal sector. Not only does this often result in the exclusion of the self-employed, agricultural workers, family workers, domestic employees and casual workers, but it has also meant that restrictions have often been imposed on coverage for those in regular employment. Here the considerations are principally administrative. It has long been the practice for new social insurance schemes to adopt a policy of gradually extending coverage, so that account is taken of the limited administrative capacity of the system and of employers. The view is taken that it is better that the scheme operates satisfactorily on a restricted basis before gradually widening its coverage. Thus coverage may be restricted by the size of the employer on the understanding that larger employers are more likely to comply with the obligations of the scheme.

An alternative approach adopted in some developing countries is to restrict the scheme on a geographical basis (in Mozambique and the least developed countries in Latin America coverage was initially limited to the capital city) or with regard to certain occupational groups. In some countries (as in the case of the Employees' Old-Age Benefit Institution scheme in Pakistan), social security was at least initially focused on the lower-paid or manual work-ers, while higher-paid workers or management were specifically excluded from coverage in the belief that such people could make their own arrangements, or were likely to be adequately covered by their employers' arrangements. Similar provisions apply to the Malaysian social insurance scheme. The Employees' Provident Fund in India applies a combination of provisions to restrict membership. First, employment must fall within the scope of 177 prescribed occupations; second, the establishment must have at least 20 workers; and third, until 1997, the establishment must have been operating for at least three years (termed an "infancy period").

Administrative bottlenecks

Only limited progress has been made in the extension of coverage to those sections of the formal sector labour force which were initially excluded on administrative grounds. Indonesia introduced its scheme in 1977 and has progressively extended its coverage from employers with a minimum of 100 employees to those with at least 25 in 1983 and to those with ten or more in 1990. After 21 years' experience, the Malaysian scheme was finally extended to employers with one employee in 1992. There are two reasons for this slow progress. First, amendment of the legislation is a slow process, which often has to be negotiated (see Chapter 20). Second, many social insurance schemes continue to have difficulty coping with the administrative obligations relating to the existing insured population and liable employers.

Those currently excluded would, in general, be even more difficult to administer and are likely to pose considerable problems of compliance and records processing. The view might be taken that the contribution income derived from their coverage may not be worth the administrative cost. This is short-sighted, however, because these people are more likely to require social protection, and because it creates disparity of treatment within the labour force, in relation both to contribution liability and to access to social protection.

The extension of coverage and administrative capacity are closely con-nected. In developing countries it has often proved difficult to cope with the volume of administrative tasks associated with the operation of a social insur-ance scheme, or a national provident fund, that requires the maintenance of accurate lifetime records for insured people. These problems are intensified by the dependence of the administration on the cooperation of employers and insured people in providing the necessary data accurately and regularly.

Other factors affecting the extension of coverage are a general lack of aware-ness among the excluded groups, or reluctance where the scheme is perceived to be either inefficient or not in their best interests. Some people (both employers and workers) feel overwhelmed by the bureaucratic obligations associated with registration under the social security scheme or may fear that entry into the public system will have other implications, in that it might bring them within the scope of the tax system or of the obligations of labour legislation.

Non-compliance

Often the number of people who are insurable under the social security scheme by virtue of the legislation is significantly greater than those who are actually registered members and active contributors. This may apply to employees and self-employed people, and to the public and private sector. The gap represents the level of non-compliance and those to whom it applies can be distinguished from those who are excluded by virtue of arranging conditions of service to avoid liability (see Chapter 10). This can prove to be a major difficulty for a social insurance scheme. Solidarity and redistributive principles of the programme can be undermined by some employers and workers effectively opting out of a scheme, in spite of the fact that their circumstances and needs may be similar to those of employers and workers who remain active participants.

Some middle- and lower-income countries (for example, Turkey) and countries in transition have sought to extend coverage to some of the self-employed and even to employees such as domestic workers. The Philippines has accorded high priority to providing the whole working population with access to membership of the social security scheme, and the legislation obliges virtually all self-employed people, farmers, fishermen and domestic workers to be insured. However the Philippines also provides an example of the gap which exists in many countries between coverage under the law and coverage in practice. There is a close linkage between the problem of extending coverage and the problem of compliance or evasion, and this is particularly acute in developing countries (and some countries in transition). Non-compliance takes several forms; employers may:

- fail to register under the scheme;
- fail to register all of their employees;
- treat some of their employees as self-employed contractors or as casual workers;
- understate the earnings on which social security contributions are payable;
- register their workers but not pay the contributions;
- take advantage of loopholes in the legislation.

All or some of these situations may arise with the collaboration or agreement of the workers, who may prefer to give priority to short-term income rather than to contributing to a long-term objective, such as a retirement pension. Most countries are not able to assess the extent of non-compliance. Such statistics as are available generally relate to outstanding contributions which have been calculated, but the problem of identifying and enforcing liability is significant for most social insurance schemes.

APPROACHES TO THE EXTENSION OF COVERAGE

In principle the most effective way of ensuring general coverage under a social protection programme for the elderly and the disabled is through a universal pension scheme which provides entitlement subject to satisfaction of a basic contingency test, such as attainment of age 65, supplemented, generally, by a residence test. Under such schemes, individual contribution records do not need to be maintained and entitlement is easily determined in countries with good birth records. But because such schemes are universal and uniform, the level of social protection provided is generally low and unlikely to provide more than anti-poverty protection. Furthermore, since such benefits are neither aimed at need, nor related to contributory employment, they require a considerable commitment of tax resources to finance them. Thus only a few countries have felt able to provide pensions on this basis. Canada, Denmark, Japan, Mauritius, Namibia, the Netherlands, the Seychelles and Switzerland are examples. Botswana has introduced a universal flat-rate pension scheme for all residents aged 65 and over. Other countries provide means-tested pensions for the elderly and disabled (Australia and South Africa) and others – particularly the United States and most European countries – have a broad-based social assistance system which includes the elderly and the disabled poor. Approaches to the extension of pension coverage to those outside the core labour force are examined in box 8.1.

Beyond universal coverage, in most developing countries efforts to extend coverage have been patchy, and three approaches have been taken.

- Concentrate on coverage for formal sector workers and presume that economic development will gradually lead to an expansion of coverage as the formal sector grows.

- Gradually extend coverage to include all employed people and devise special arrangements for some of the self-employed within the limits of administrative capacity.

- Provide (almost) universal coverage under the law, but recognize that for the foreseeable future compliance levels will be low.

An increasing number of countries, particularly in Africa and Asia, have recognized that full social security coverage cannot be attained through the extension or adaptation of existing formal systems. China and India have adopted policies that take into account the specific circumstances of workers outside the formal sector, and they support schemes adapted to the specific needs and contributory capacities of such workers. The specific problems of coverage of the agricultural sector are discussed in greater detail in box 8.2.

Covering the self-employed

In countries outside western Europe and North America, four different approaches have been applied to cover self-employed workers: inclusion, at

Box 8.1 Extending pension coverage to groups outside the core labour force: The experience of OECD countries

Most pension schemes are formally contribution-based or eligibility is tied to previous activity in the labour market. Certain subgroups in the population, however, have difficulty acquiring sufficient pension rights in contribution-based schemes to be eligible for invalidity or retirement benefits. These groups include the born or young disabled; the long-term unemployed and workers who have lost their job and left the labour force; part-time, seasonal and temporary workers; abandoned or divorced homeworkers; refugees and migrant workers.

Three strategies are available to provide income protection for such individuals:

- social protection systems financed from general revenues;
- social security systems which incorporate groups that make few or no contributions or tilt benefit formulas to the benefit of such groups;
- laws mandating responsibility of family members to care for their poor and disabled.

Social protection financed from general revenues
The first public pension schemes of Denmark (1891), New Zealand (1898), Australia (1908), the United Kingdom (1908), Sweden (1913), Canada (1927) and Norway (1936) were means-tested minimum protection systems financed from general revenues. The United Kingdom later shifted to a formally contribution-based minimum approach, while the others still regard tax-financed minimum pensions as the first tier of their public pension schemes. These initially meagre and means-tested minimum protection systems have evolved into basic security schemes which are usually tied to criteria of residency. New Zealand has no means test, while Denmark only has an earnings test for its universal flat benefit. Finland, Norway and Sweden provide a guaranteed minimum pension only, tested against public superannuation. Australia and Canada use income tests, but they are in effect affluence tests since a majority of the elderly are at least eligible for a partial benefit.

Unlike the Scandinavian and most Anglo-American countries, other OECD countries chose a version of the German (1881) contribution principle when introducing their first public pension scheme. However, many countries which initially focused on contribution-based schemes have subsequently set up a subsidiary system of "social pensions" for individuals with limited contribution periods. This is the case in Belgium, France, Italy, Portugal and Spain. Germany, which initiated the contribution-based approach to public pensions, has not set up a separate minimum protection system financed from general revenues. Instead it maintains a standardized and rights-based social assistance system to provide protection for the poorest pensioners.

Social security systems which incorporate groups with few or no contributions
Many countries which initially established a contribution-based approach to public pensions have gradually extended the contribution requirement to

encompass groups outside the core labour force. This has been achieved also in some of the public systems set up in countries which initially focused on tax-financed minimum protection only (such as Sweden and Norway). These extensions come in many forms. Periods of registered unemployment are often regarded as contribution periods (in countries where unemployment benefits represent taxable income, the unemployed may also contribute). In Austria, Germany, Norway and Sweden periods of child rearing count as contribution periods. Those caring for frail or disabled close relatives earn contributory pension rights in Norway. Such rules grant homeworkers at least a partial earnings-related pension in their own right. Some countries, such as Germany and Switzerland, split the rights to contribution-based social security in the event of divorce. This further strengthens the pension entitlement of divorced homeworkers.

The position of vulnerable groups within contribution-based social security systems can be further enhanced by minimum guarantees granted to those with short contribution records. Moreover the pension rights of part-time and seasonal workers, as well as workers with interrupted careers, can be enhanced through liberal inclusion criteria, and linking deferred rights either to a wage index or a capital market index.

To soften, or in effect disregard, the contribution requirement in order to extend coverage to groups outside the core labour force is possible in defined contributions as well, but this may require members to cross-subsidize one another. The new Swedish superannuation system grants pension points to homeworkers looking after pre-school children, although it is designed formally as a defined contribution scheme.

Laws mandating responsibility on behalf of other family members to care for their poor and disabled

Before the advent of social security, the family was the major risk-pooling institution in society. Some OECD countries still require family members to provide financial support for each other. Thus, in Spain, spouses, parents and children must provide "broad support" for each other (help maintain an accustomed standard of living), while siblings or half-siblings must provide more "restricted" (minimum) support. Other countries, among them Austria, Belgium, France, Germany and Luxembourg, have legislation which gives the state the power to reclaim social assistance benefits from adult children, but do not extend legal obligations beyond the child-parent relationship.

Relying on one or several strategies

Some countries use these strategies jointly, while others focus primarily on one. By combining several approaches to cater for groups outside the core labour force, a country might "spread the risk" of poverty due to disability or old age among these groups. If one set of institutional devices should for some reason fail to deliver, other systems will serve as back-up devices to secure at least minimum protection. However, if one strategy is well-developed, there may be less need to introduce several strategies jointly to protect those at risk.

Box 8.2 Expanding coverage to the agricultural sector

Coverage rates in countries with large, particularly rural, agricultural sectors are generally low. In Latin America, for example, only 38 per cent of the economically active population make contributions, and only 31 per cent of people over age 60 receive pensions. High rates of social insurance coverage, particularly in less developed countries, may be difficult for several reasons.

The nature of the agricultural labour market

Many agricultural workers are family members, migratory or employed for short periods of time by several employers; such workers in general do not appear in an employment registry. A number of factors complicate the evaluation of the contributory capacity and collection of contributions.

Administrative factors. Traditional tax formulas often rely on shares of cash income for calculating and collecting contributions. However, much of the income received by farmers, or agricultural workers in general, is non-cash or in-kind; that is, received in the form of goods or services. Calculating, collecting and investing the appropriate contribution from, for example, a herder whose flock increased by five sheep, or a farm worker who received housing and a share of the harvest, is more complex than for a salaried worker.

Infrastructure. Many rural areas have no adequate public services, roads, education or health care. This makes any social insurance distribution or collection mechanism costly.

Socio-economic factors. Rural agricultural populations generally have lower living standards than urban dwellers. A social insurance scheme designed for urban workers may not be best for rural workers, as they generally live shorter lives and have different insurance needs and labour market experience from urban workers.

Costs of compliance. Owing to the nature of the agricultural labour market, as noted above, the costs of compliance with pension legislation to either the workers or the employers may be prohibitively high. Regardless of whether the worker or employer is liable for the social insurance contribution, the burden of setting aside funds – as well as understanding and fulfilling the administrative requirements for coverage – may be prohibitive for individuals or small employers with low levels of education or minimal resources.

Options to increase coverage through changes in the contribution system

Many of these problems relate to difficulties in collecting appropriate contributions for agricultural workers. Even if a flat-rate contribution amount was imposed on all agricultural workers, thereby removing the necessity to calculate an individual worker's income or to keep employment registries, there are problems of equity and hardship. There are wide variations in income, both across workers and across time. For example, farmers with small or unproductive lots may, in many years, receive only subsistence from their land. In addition all farmers face financial variations due to bad weather, insect pests or changes in the market price of goods. This variation makes imposing flat contribution rates burdensome for some and leads to inadequate coverage for others. Policies will therefore need to be designed with care to promote both equity across different types of agricultural workers and efficiency in programme administration. As opposed to the traditional mechanism of financing social security through contributions based on earnings, one may have to think differently when designing the financing mechanism for the rural agricultural sector. Contributions could come from shares of agricultural produce, or through the donation of labour by contributors to government development projects. Similarly benefits may be provided in the form of food, housing or other in-kind assistance to the elderly, as opposed to cash benefits.

Because of these difficulties, many countries exclude agricultural workers, family labour or other casual labour from full social insurance coverage. El Salvador, Iraq and Yemen all exclude agricultural and casual workers, while other countries base agricultural coverage on the size of the employer (Honduras and Taiwan, China) or the length of service (Panama and Saudi Arabia). Other countries, such as Austria, Croatia, Finland, France, Germany, Greece, Italy, Japan, Poland, Spain and Turkey, have developed special alternative systems for coverage of the agricultural sector. Several countries (such as Ecuador and Tunisia) have a single social security scheme that includes coverage of the agricultural sector, but have instituted different contribution formulas for agricultural workers than for non-agricultural workers.

The example of Poland
Poland has attempted to include the agricultural sector in its public pension scheme. Roughly 12 per cent of the Polish population list farming as the primary activity of their head of household. Both the benefit and contribution formulas for farmers are different from those of other workers. The contribution amount for all farmers is not connected to their earnings level, and is set quarterly at 30 per cent of the base pension (the minimum monthly pension for employees). Benefits are a function of the base pension and the individual's number of contributory years. This system allows farmers not to contribute in years in which harvests may be low, and to contribute small amounts when farm income is higher. The formula is highly regressive, however, as those with small farms are more likely not to be able to contribute in some years, and will therefore have fewer contributory years than individuals with larger or more successful farms. Furthermore, as the contributions are set at a flat amount for all farmers, those with large farms contribute the same as those with small farms.

Several initiatives to reform the Polish social security pension scheme have been set forth, with the most comprehensive system developed by the Office of the Government Plenipotentiary for Social Security Reform. This proposal would base contribution rates on the level of capitalization of the farm, with workers at smaller farms paying lump-sum amounts and larger farms' contributions based on the farm's average income. The benefit structure would also change. Farmers with pension rights below a defined minimum could choose to receive a subsidy to reach the minimum. However the subsidies would not be a pure transfer. Rather they would be given as loans on the basis of secured assets (land, buildings, machinery) and function as reverse mortgages, with the size of the deduction at the time of death dependent on the total paid in the form of subsidies.[3]

least in principle, of all self-employed in the main social insurance scheme; selective coverage under the general scheme; coverage under a special scheme; and voluntary coverage.

Inclusion of all self-employed in the main social insurance scheme

Countries following this approach include Argentina, Brazil, Bulgaria, Estonia, Hungary, the Philippines, the Russian Federation and Slovakia. Experience suggests that this is difficult to achieve in practice, particularly in a developing country where there is a high incidence of self-employment and also where the contribution structure of the scheme obliges the self-employed to contribute a relatively high percentage of their earnings. The Social Security System scheme in the Philippines is mandatory for virtually all the self-employed (although this implies some evidence of status). Contribution liability is based on a minimum of 1000 pesos per month (about one-third of the minimum wage) and this provides entitlement to a broad range of benefits, including loans which are effectively subsidized by the contributions of employees and their employers. In spite of this, coverage is low among the self-employed (estimated at less than 10 per cent) and the Social Security Scheme does not have the resources to monitor compliance.

Selective coverage under the general scheme

Examples are the Islamic Republic of Iran, the Republic of Korea, Latvia, Poland and Tunisia. Under this approach an attempt is made to distinguish certain categories of the self-employed who are earning above a prescribed amount, are formally registered or licensed, or who are engaged in certain occupations or professions (box 8.3 provides the example of the Republic of Korea). This recognizes the fact that such people are the most likely both to be able to contribute on a similar basis as employees and to be within the scope of reasonable compliance controls.

Coverage under a special scheme

Examples are Poland (farmers), Romania (professional self-employed) and Turkey. This approach seeks to segregate the self-employed from the principal scheme for employees, based on the presumption that their circumstances, their needs and their financial capacity are different. In Turkey the Bag-Kur scheme applies to all self-employed people who are either taxpayers or registered with a professional, craft or artisans' association. The contribution rate is 20 per cent of earnings for pensions, plus 12 per cent for health care. Earnings are determined by the contributor on the basis of 24 income levels, but if an income level below the sixth level is chosen then the earnings level increases each year at least to the sixth level. In 1994, 61 per cent of the active insured people contributed at the sixth level. Non-compliance is a major problem: only 4 per cent contribute regularly.

Box 8.3 Progress on extending coverage in the Republic of Korea
In the Republic of Korea, the National Pension Scheme was implemented in 1988, with compulsory coverage for all private sector employees working for employers with ten or more employees. In January 1992 coverage was extended to employers with five or more employees. The scheme was also open to the voluntary participation of the self-employed, farmers, fishermen and housewives but, with effect from July 1995, participation of the rural self-employed, farmers and fishermen has been mandatory. All those insured are covered for the same range of earnings-related benefits under the defined benefit pension scheme and, in principle, all contribute at the same rate (9 per cent in 1998). The voluntarily insured contribution is based on the median income of all those insured on a mandatory basis.

To encourage participation of the rural self-employed, farmers and fishermen, the Government, as a transitional measure, is subsidizing their contributions, with only 3 per cent being paid by the contributors; however there is provision for a phased increase to 9 per cent with effect from 2006. As of October 1996 the self-employed covered on a mandatory basis accounted for 1,900,000 out of 7,470,000 insured people. Extension of coverage to all self-employed people is envisaged for the first decade of the twenty-first century.

Voluntary coverage

Countries using this approach include Chile, Costa Rica, the Islamic Republic of Iran, the Republic of Korea (urban self-employed) and Romania (farmers). Under this approach the self-employed are allowed to choose whether to insure themselves under the principal scheme. Difficulties arise where the scheme is financed on a social insurance basis, because of the need to ensure that the arrangement is equitable both to the self-employed contributor and to the other contributors. Voluntary insurance therefore implies a contribution level equivalent to that paid by employees and employers, and this may be prohibitive to participation. It certainly causes self-employed people to weigh the potential risks of membership and thus to make decisions based on adverse selection. It is also necessary to take account of the lengthy qualifying periods for entitlement to benefit, and to ensure that the level of contributions is maintained in real terms. For these reasons, many schemes limit voluntary insurance to those people who have left insurable employment but who wish, within a reasonable period of time, to opt to maintain their record for pension purposes. In these circumstances the contribution can be related to the average earnings immediately prior to the termination of insurable employment.

In summary, the extension of coverage to the self-employed is easier to achieve for those people who have a well-established business or profession that is readily identifiable and produces a level of income that leaves scope for contributing to future social protection. Even for this group it may be difficult to be incorporated within a scheme dominated by the circumstances of employees and in respect of which contributions are also paid by employers. This tends to result in a basic design choice in the financing, between employers and employees (and/or government) subsidizing the self-employed through the payment of a higher combined contribution, or the self-employed paying a contribution which equates with the combined contribution paid for employees. Both courses are prone to dispute and dissatisfaction.

Unless it is attractive to them, either through a cross-subsidy or because it reflects their circumstances and needs, many of the self-employed will not join, or will subsequently evade payment or underdeclare their insurable income. (In some countries, for example in Eastern Europe, Egypt and Turkey, the self-employed are obliged to pay a contribution rate equal to the combined employer/employee contribution but are able, to some extent, to choose their level of participation in the scheme by selecting an earnings band.) Special schemes may be designed to better suit their circumstances. Voluntary insurance may help in some cases, but is not a solution to the problem of extending coverage. Such an arrangement has been established on a voluntary basis for the self-employed in Chile but neither there nor in other countries where provident funds are open to the self-employed do many self-employed people find such arrangements attractive. Attitudes to mandatory schemes based on defined contribution principles will depend in part on investment performance and on the presence of incentives, such as tax concessions for the social security contributions.

The self-employed may prefer to invest in their own business as a form of future social protection, or may see better opportunities for investing any spare resources. If the scheme is based on social insurance principles, there is a risk that, even if it is mandatory, many self-employed will effectively practise adverse selection and the level of opting out may harm its financing.

SCHEMES FOR INFORMAL SECTOR WORKERS

The limited possibilities for extending statutory social insurance schemes have contributed to the development of many varied schemes for informal sector workers, since such workers have different employment conditions which directly affect their social security priorities and the way they can organize social security for themselves. The following typology recognizes this heterogeneity (van Ginneken, 1996b).

* *Urban/rural.* Urban informal workers tend to be more heterogeneous than rural informal workers, so that they have greater difficulty in establishing associations for social security purposes. Urban workers tend to be more interested in housing than workers in rural areas, where there is more space and directly available building material.

- *Self-employed/wage earner.* Self-employed workers with established businesses (such as shopkeepers, farmers or taxi drivers), with special skills (such as electricians or mechanics), as well as those following professions (such as doctors and lawyers) are generally richer and better organized than wage earners, with the result that they are better candidates for successfully organizing social protection for themselves in cooperatives or other associations.

- *Resident/transient.* Where people are working and living in a fixed place, they are more likely to build up the necessary trust for setting up a social security scheme among themselves. Therefore people working in the street economy of the urban areas, or circular migrants in the rural areas, are unlikely to be covered by social security.

- *Regular/casual.* Most regular workers in the formal sector are covered by compulsory social insurance schemes but, because of non-compliance, a sizeable proportion of regular workers is not effectively covered by them. Except in developed countries, casual workers have little chance to be protected by compulsory or voluntary social insurance schemes.

A broad distinction can be made between schemes that are self-financed and those that function with government support in financing or management. The first group of schemes is usually run by the self-employed, whereas the second group tends to benefit casual wage earners.

Self-financed schemes

The mechanism used for self-financed schemes is generally one of providing mutual support through pooling of resources, based on the principles of insurance, help being extended to those in need within the overall framework of certain basic regulatory conditions. In this system the group itself decides on the size and the source of contributions that members are obliged to make. The collection and management of contributions as well as the disbursement of benefits are matters for the group to consider and arrange.

There are two fundamental requirements for the establishment of a self-financed social insurance schemes (van Ginneken, 1996b): the existence of an association based on trust, and an administration that is capable of collecting contributions and administering benefits. Various types of groups organize informal sector workers. Some associations or organizations could be directly governed by the informal sector workers themselves (examples include producer and employer organizations, cooperatives and credit associations) or they could use some intermediate agencies such as trade unions, non-governmental organizations (NGOs) and private insurance companies.

The activities organized by, and for, informal sector workers are generally based on a comprehensive concept of development and social security. Organizations such as NGOs and cooperatives have a good understanding of the particular needs and priorities of their client groups, and have developed institutions and policies with them that are quite different from what the government is used to and/or can cope with. This broader concept of social security includes not only the nine contingencies traditionally defined by the ILO (see Technical Brief 2), but also preventive steps both in the social and economic field. In the social field, NGO action integrates the traditional social security measures with complementary measures in the fields of (primary) health care, child care, housing and selective social action. In the economic field, more security can be achieved through self-help and self-employment, resulting in an enhancement of income and a creation of productive assets. The schemes usually operate within the context of a credit scheme which already has experience collecting and administering benefits.

In some countries (Colombia, Indonesia, the Philippines and the United Republic of Tanzania) a wide range of self-help schemes have been developed to provide mutual support within either a district or an occupation. Groups of workers such as rickshaw drivers, shoemakers, textile workers or fishermen establish cooperatives with mechanisms to pool resources both to support business activities and to provide social protection. Often these arrangements are preferred to membership of social security schemes and include people who should be insured under such schemes but who have chosen not to participate.

Thus, while these schemes do provide some assistance for their members, it usually takes the form of a lump-sum payment. One example of a self-financed scheme in India is the Cooperative Development Foundation, an institute which aims at strengthening cooperatives and is mainly working with thrift and credit groups. Its groups are mostly in Andhra Pradesh, with similar structures existing in Tamil Nadu, Karnataka and Kerala. For social security a death relief fund has been constituted by Cooperative Development Foundation covering about 25,000 members. The scheme covers the risk of death (natural or accidental injury up to the age of 60), the assured amount being a multiple of the deposit, ranging between five and 20 times, depending on the age of the member. Besides life insurance the other benefit under the schemes is security for the thrift cooperatives loans, which gives total debt relief for the surviving family and the guarantors. On a person reaching age 60 or withdrawing from the scheme, the deposit amount is returned with a 2 per cent bonus (Gupta, 1994).

Government-supported schemes

Examples of specific programmes for informal sector workers with government support are the labour welfare schemes in India, financed from resources derived from a tax on the produce of about five million workers in the cigarette and cinema industries as well as in certain mines. A similar scheme operates in the Philippines for sugar workers. In general, however, the level of resources generated is low, and only limited social protection is provided.

In many developing countries a majority of workers – although working for an employer in the strict sense of the law – are employed under circumstances which are casual, seasonal, part-time or illegal or where, as in the case of contractors or workers supplied through a third party, the existence of an employer–employee relationship is not clear or is disputed. Family employment and employment of a spouse are examples, but similar problems relate to domestic and casual workers. Some countries have sought to clarify liability for such workers by special definition in the schemes, which either excludes them from coverage or specifically includes them within the definition of the insured worker.

Legislative action does not necessarily solve the problem. In the Philippines homeworkers have been categorized as employed people for social security purposes, and the person who supplies the homeworker with the raw material and then makes the payment is specified as the employer. However, although the law is clear, it is difficult to apply and to enforce in a situation where there is a network of relationships, and where the homeworker often works for different employers. Similar problems arise in relation to legislative attempts (in the Philippines and elsewhere) to prescribe liability for people who are supplied through a third party. Further, although some schemes attempt to combat evasion of casual workers by providing a legislative definition linked either to hours worked or earnings paid, compliance and enforcement remain formidable problems.

Certain trades and industries are particularly difficult to bring within the effective scope of social security pension legislation. Employment in the construction industry in many countries is notoriously insecure and workers are employed in a variety of casual, seasonal and contractual relationships which, regardless of their status, are effectively outside the scope of social security coverage. Some countries have made special arrangements to provide social protection for construction workers (for example in Uruguay, where a levy is imposed on the main contractor to provide resources to ensure the coverage of construction workers on the site).

Those working in agriculture in developing countries are one of the largest groups of workers excluded from social security coverage; this includes people working on their own account and those working as labourers, often in a casual or seasonal capacity. Some countries have attempted to include such people within the scope of social security pension schemes. The principal social security programme in Turkey – the SSK – covers seasonal agricultural workers on a voluntary basis. The contribution payable by the worker is set at 20 per cent of the lowest earnings level, and need only be paid for 15 days a month, or 180 days a year. Entitlement to retirement benefit may arise on retirement after 15 years of insured membership, during which contributions must have been paid for at least 3,600 days.

Self-employed farmers in Turkey are within the scope of the pension schemes for self-employed people (Bag-Kur). They are required to contribute

15 per cent of their chosen income level and earn entitlement to a pension on retirement of up to 70 per cent of this earnings level, depending on the length of insured membership. In Turkey there is only limited cross-subsidization of these provisions by other sections of the insured population and compliance/participation rates in these programmes are low. In Ecuador and the Republic of Korea, however, the government subsidizes pension provision for agricultural workers (also fishermen in the Republic of Korea).

Social assistance

In most developed countries social assistance has become important, mainly because higher unemployment as well as changing employment and family patterns have resulted in some people not having accumulated enough social insurance entitlement. In Central and Eastern Europe the large-scale provision of social assistance is a relatively new phenomenon. In addition, the non-governmental sector is beginning to be recognized as a partner in granting financial support to the needy (Bagdy, 1996; Topinska, 1996). Both groups of countries have a system of generalized income-dependent social assistance.

In the developing countries social assistance programmes play a less important role because government resources are much lower. They are predominantly contingency-based as they limit means-tested support in cash or in kind to specific needy groups, such as widows, orphans and elderly people without income and family support. In many developing countries the role of the non-governmental sector is important, as it can play a leading part in protecting and integrating marginalized groups in urban and rural areas. These organizations are involved in health, education and nutrition, as well as financial and material help.

With regard to government social assistance programmes, the example of India is worth mentioning. In mid-1995 the government of India announced the introduction of a National Social Assistance Programme consisting of three cash benefits: a flat benefit pension for people older than 65 years with low incomes and generally without relatives; a lump-sum payment for families whose prime income earner dies before the age of 60 years; and a lump-sum payment per pregnancy for the first two live births. This programme was intended to standardize, on a national basis, measures which had already been operating in most states.

In Mongolia local Assistance Councils provide free lunches as well as discount rents and fuel costs for the disabled and elderly who either have no family support or have not been able to insure themselves during their working life.

In its transition to a market economy, China, in the late 1990s, modernized its social relief system. The minimum livelihood protection scheme for urban residents is a scheme in which poor people in urban households, whose average per capita income is lower than the minimum livelihood protection line, can receive subsidies from the government. In rural areas the government has started to experiment with a minimum livelihood protection system that provides a combination of benefits in cash and in kind.

In the debate on the structure of social security pension schemes, insufficient attention has been paid, at both the national and the international levels, to the fact that workers in most countries are excluded from social protection in respect of the loss of income when they are no longer able to work because they are old or disabled, or when they are deprived of support by the death of a relative on whom they were dependent. The degree of exclusion from coverage is low in developed countries but varies among developing countries; it is high especially in sub-Saharan Africa and south Asia where it is more than 90 per cent of the labour force. But it is a growing problem almost everywhere as a consequence of the informalization of employment. Those excluded are most likely to be the self-employed, casual workers, agricultural workers and domestic servants but also migrant workers and a significant, but unknown, number who work in a variety of relationships and circumstances in what has been termed the informal sector.

There are many reasons for the failure to provide coverage under a social protection scheme and these vary between countries. Probably the most common and fundamental reason for such exclusion is that the public schemes do not correspond to the perceived social protection needs and the circumstances of those not covered. Many workers outside the formal sector are not able or willing to contribute a relatively high percentage of their incomes (which are often both low and irregular) to finance social security benefits which they do not see as relevant to their priority needs. In addition they may not be familiar with, or may distrust, the way in which the social security scheme is administered. In general they are likely to give more priority to immediate needs, such as health care, particularly if the public health care scheme is ineffective. Within the range of pension benefits, the consequences of disability or death may be seen as more important than old age which, especially in developing countries, is seen as the least likely of risks. This negative reaction to membership of a formal social security scheme may also be compounded by what are seen as bureaucratic obstacles to membership.

The state, acting in the best interests of all its citizens, has an obligation to provide social protection consistent with needs. Also compulsory insurability is a fundamental principle of social security schemes and thus membership should not be a matter for individual choice. But the solidarity base implicit in this principle must be derived from a broad consensus among the insurable and this does not exist among the labour force in many developing countries where there are marked differences as regards social protection needs and capacity to contribute. In addition the difficulty in enforcing liability urges the necessity of a different approach. Possible solutions are discussed in Chapter 16.

Notes

[1] Social security statistics relating to coverage in developing countries are subject to inaccuracy and difficulties of interpretation. For example, (*a*) they often reveal the number of registered insured people without indicating how many of these are active participants, and (*b*) the number of people who are economically active or employed in the labour force is often difficult to determine. Latin American statistics relate to the percentage of economically active covered and are derived from Mesa Lago (1991a and b).

[2] Mathew (1973); Wadhawan (1989); Guhan (1994); Bailey (1994); Jenkins (1994); van Ginneken (1996b); Midgley and Tracy (1996); Gruat (1997) and Thompson (1997) and technical cooperation projects, ILO (1989b and 1990), ILO-SAAT (1996d).

[3] For a discussion of the larger issue regarding obstacles to the extension of social security in the agricultural sector, see Jenkins (1992).

GOVERNANCE AND ADMINISTRATION

9

This chapter deals with many of the issues discussed elsewhere in the book. It deals with issues regarding the structure of benefits, discussed in Chapters 3, 4 and 5, and with the design and management of financing, discussed in Chapters 6 and 7. The institutions governing social security are the focus of Chapter 17.

Except in the most developed countries, the overall performance of social security pension schemes in many countries has been disappointing. This is attributable to a broad range of problems, some of which are outside the control of the social security administration. Some, however, reflect mismanagement or are due to weaknesses in the design of the scheme. Good governance is the key to an effective social security scheme. It is essential to be clear as to what this term means. In this book, the definition is broad and embraces the processes of consultation and decision making which determine the structure of the scheme, the institutional arrangements responsible for its administration, and the managerial and administrative functions which relate to the implementation and supervision of social security schemes. It is also concerned with the interrelationship between national policy, national management and scheme management.

OBJECTIVES OF GOOD GOVERNANCE

In the context of this definition, the following objectives for good governance are put forward, grouped according to whether they relate to strategic or macro policy issues, institutional arrangements or administrative obligations at the operational level.

Strategic and macro policy objectives

Determining the social protection structure

Here we are concerned with the choices which determine the overall structure of the social protection, the respective roles of public and private provision, and the type of schemes to be introduced.

217

1. Establish a process of policy formulation which balances the full range of social protection needs against national resources.

2. Create a balance within national policy between public social security schemes and individual private provision which ensures widespread coverage and adequate benefits, and achieves the desired level of income redistribution.

3. Create a mechanism for the enactment of legislation to give effect to the policy decisions and subsequent changes.

Institutional arrangements

Deciding how the structure is going to be implemented

4. Establish institutional arrangements which are accountable for the implementation of social security programmes.

5. Ensure that contributors and beneficiaries have an opportunity to influence the decision-making process and to monitor the administration of social security schemes.

6. Establish financial control mechanisms to monitor the allocation and management of resources.

Administrative obligations

Making the structure work

7. Ensure that contributions are collected and accounted for and that benefits are paid promptly and accurately and with appropriate explanation.

8. Minimize the cost of administration within the desired level of service.

9. Ensure that contributors and beneficiaries are aware of their rights and their obligations.

10. Establish a mechanism for monitoring and reviewing administrative performance.

These ten objectives for good governance provide the framework for the conception, development and monitoring of a sound and viable social security. The governance of social security has received increasing attention in recent years as part of a growing awareness that schemes are only as effective as their administration. There has been a tendency in the debate on the reform of social security, however, to fail to distinguish governance issues from conceptual ones. This has led to criticism of social insurance principles when, often, the focus should have been on weaknesses in the way such schemes were designed and then administered.

When policy makers develop a strategy to provide effective income replacement in respect of the contingencies of old age, invalidity and death, it is essential to look beyond the structure of the scheme. In the context of the above objectives, the policy process should address three fundamental questions.

1. What is the most appropriate scheme for the country ?

2. What are the most suitable institutional arrangements for the administration of the scheme?

3. How can efficiency at the operational level be maximized?

These questions are, however, interrelated. Thus the scheme may have been carefully designed to provide an effective benefit formula in return for a contributory structure which is equitable and sustainable, but if the scheme does not work in the way envisaged by its planners these basic objectives will not be attained. It is important to be realistic about expectations. The effectiveness of governance of social security schemes will inevitably reflect the level of development, with particular regard to the political situation, the quality of the infrastructure and the level of education. Many developing countries have administrative and management weaknesses, both in the public and private sectors. Related to this is the advisability of taking such limitations into account in designing the structure and administration of the social security scheme.

As a starting point, it is advisable to look at the respective roles and responsibilities of those involved in the governance of social security: the stakeholders. The relationship between them is likely to be complex, but it also has an important bearing on the achievement of good governance.

THE STAKEHOLDERS

The following groups have an interest in social security and thus should be involved to some extent in the governance of that system:

- the state,
- social security institutions (both public and private),
- employers and workers as contributors and beneficiaries,
- beneficiaries.

The roles and responsibilities of these groups in the development, management, supervision and regulation of social security schemes are crucial, and weaknesses and inconsistencies in their involvement lie at the heart of many governance problems. The following paragraphs look at the role of each.

The state

The structure of the scheme will reflect decisions which have already been taken, based on a national consensus as to the respective division of responsibility for meeting social protection needs and thus the extent to which the state will determine and ensure the level and scope of protection and the extent to which individuals and their employers will themselves be responsible. But the state, through its government, will, regardless of the structure of the scheme, also have a key role in the governance of social security. This will either be directly, through the discharge of its responsibilities, or indirectly, through creating the environment and the framework to enable employers, employees and beneficiaries to carry out their roles and responsibilities. The Social Security (Minimum Standards) Convention, 1952 (No. 102), makes it clear that overall responsibility for the proper administration of the scheme and its institutions lies with the state (see Technical Brief 2). Social security is an essential component of a government's programme and represents its obligation to provide adequate living standards for its citizens. This overriding responsibility cannot be delegated. Furthermore government involvement reflects the fact that in many countries the resources provided to finance social security account for a considerable proportion of national GDP.

Within this overall responsibility, the primary roles of the state are in relation to the development and finalization of policy, the drafting and enactment of legislation, the creation of a sound financial and monetary framework, the supervision of public and private institutions, the establishment of transparent and accountable organizational structures and the establishment of consultative bodies. But the division between direct and indirect responsibility is significant and varies considerably between countries. It is also an evolving process, with some countries adopting policies which seek to limit the role of the state to fundamental tasks and objectives and then to create a framework supported by regulation within which individual responsibility and private sector competition can develop.

The role of the state will also reflect the interaction of the respective roles of the executive and the legislature. A democratically elected parliament may be able to influence government policy, determine the legislation and monitor the financial performance of the scheme, and generally operate as a moderating influence on government policy and on the authority of the responsible minister. In a country where democratic principles are well established, with freedom of the press, a sensitive and educated electorate and active pressure groups, society will have mechanisms to influence government policy and to expose weaknesses in policy and administration. In such countries, typically those which are fully developed economically, social security policy and its implementation will thus be generally responsive to these democratic signals even where the government directly administers the scheme.

Responsibility for policy formulation entails a means of reviewing the operation of the system. It also implies the need for a mechanism for weighing the merits and priorities of possible reforms, both within the overall social protection context and in relation to public expenditure commitments. In this context, actuarial studies will be useful (see box 9.1). Governments are also responsible for managing the process of reform and the speed and success of this is largely in their hands.

Box 9.1 Actuarial valuations and good governance

An actuarial valuation is a tool of financial governance and planning to assist governments and the management of social security schemes to ensure their long-term viability. Actuarial valuations are undertaken:

- to inform about the present financial status and likely future financial development of a scheme;

- to assess the financial sustainability of a social security scheme in relation to the benefit provisions and the financing arrangement of the scheme under present law; and

- to advise and make recommendations on possible amendments to the scheme's provisions and financial arrangements.

The primary focus of an actuarial valuation is not the short-term financial management of a scheme but rather its long-term financial viability. The actuarial projections must therefore be extended over many years to assess the cost of the scheme once it reaches maturity and beneficiaries are entitled to full benefits. Long-term projections are also necessary properly to reflect expected changes in the environment or to test how the system reacts to changing economic and demographic conditions (population ageing, for instance). Actuarial projections may be carried out under status quo conditions as well as for alternative reform options.

On the basis of those projections of contributory earnings and pension expenditure, it is possible to estimate whether the income compared to benefit payments and expenses will balance in the future under the financial system (including the contribution rate) which has been established. It is also possible to test alternative schedules of contribution rates and their effect on the funding level of the scheme.

To be an effective tool of financial governance and planning, actuarial valuations must be conducted in proper circumstances. There are five conditions necessary to make actuarial valuations relevant and useful. These conditions are normally specified in the legislation.

1. The legislation must specify that no amendment may become effective without an actuarial study assessing the financial implications of the proposed changes. The actuarial study is needed to ensure that no decision is taken without a proper knowledge of the long-term financial implications. It can also be used to draw the attention of employers, employees and beneficiaries to potential financial problems and proposed solutions, and to help build a consensus on needed changes.

2. Statutory actuarial valuations should be conducted periodically to monitor the development of the financial situation of the scheme. These valuations allow for an early detection of emerging financial problems and the implementation at an early stage of measures to maintain financial stability. Although some schemes are subject to annual valuations, legislation normally requires a scheme to be evaluated once every three or five years.

3. The legislation can also specify the conditions under which the scheme is considered in actuarial equilibrium as well as the authority responsible for

amending the financial system (either by legislative or by administrative action) when those conditions are not met. The actuarial equilibrium specifies the minimum (and sometimes the maximum) funding level to be maintained over the projection period. The sustainability of the current financial system can be assessed with reference to this target funding level.

4. The actuary must be mandated to discuss in the report any matter which affects the financial status of a social security scheme. These include deficiencies in the design and operation of a pension scheme, the adequacy of the financial system applied, effectiveness and cost of its administration, the investment policy and performance.

5. Actuarial valuations of social security schemes need to be conducted by independent actuaries, or actuaries who are obliged to adhere to strict rules of professional conduct developed by institutions or professional corporations to which they belong. The law will normally give indications on the necessary qualifications of the actuary.

In many countries, the enactment of legislation takes a considerable time and this negative effect is compounded by the failure to delegate legislative powers to ministerial authority. A typical example of this relates to changes in the earnings ceiling for contributions liability or the level of the minimum pension: these should be reviewed regularly to keep in line with earnings levels. There is a delicate balance here between the need for democratic control and efficiency. Thus government ministers may be inexperienced in social security issues and there may be a risk that decisions will be taken for short-term political considerations which are against the long-term interests of the scheme. There is also generally a hierarchy among government departments which can have a significant bearing both on the policy-making process and on the management of the scheme. Thus the Ministry of Labour might have technical responsibility for social security matters but, in view of the funding and economic implications, it is usual for the Ministry of Finance and the Ministry of Planning (or the government institution with that function) to occupy a dominant role and for the central bank also to be very influential.

The role of government in the management of social security is closely linked to the financial basis of this system. Thus, where a scheme is financed directly from tax revenues or the government pays a contribution to the fund, or where there is a continuing public subsidy to the scheme, whether envisaged or not, government will inevitably be closely involved in the management of the scheme. Generally tax-based schemes are in fact administered directly by a government department or agency.

Social security institutions

If the scheme is financed only by the contributions of employers and workers there is a greater potential for autonomous administration by a public institution.

Figure 9.1   Governance of social security: Institutional division of responsibility

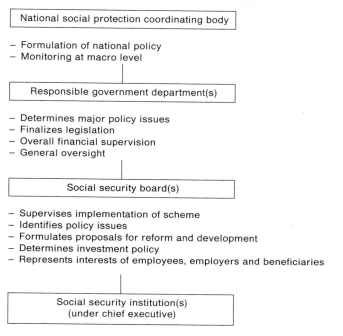

| National social protection coordinating body |

– Formulation of national policy
– Monitoring at macro level

| Responsible government department(s) |

– Determines major policy issues
– Finalizes legislation
– Overall financial supervision
– General oversight

| Social security board(s) |

– Supervises implementation of scheme
– Identifies policy issues
– Formulates proposals for reform and development
– Determines investment policy
– Represents interests of employees, employers and beneficiaries

| Social security institution(s)
(under chief executive) |

– Administers scheme

Source: ILO compilation.

In such situations the social security institution, with a board of directors or trustees, will be responsible for the administration of the scheme, with the government occupying a more distant position as guarantor but with direct responsibility for major policy and legislative aspects. In many countries it has proved difficult to define and then apply the limits of government involvement in the governance of social security with financial considerations at the heart of the problem. No matter what type of scheme exists, however, the political and fiscal implications of providing effective and affordable social protection benefits, particularly pensions, are such that governments will inevitably be involved in monitoring the progress of the scheme and will seek to intervene. Figure 9.1 illustrates a typical division of responsibility where a social security institution has been established to administer the scheme.

There is a wide variety of institutions but their status and powers are generally prescribed in legislation and include the establishment of a governing body (a management board or a board of trustees or a commission), which represents the interests of those affected by the scheme, such as the government, employers and workers and sometimes special interest groups. Some boards include representatives of the banking industry or the medical profession, as well as pensioners.

The intention is not for the board to become directly involved in the daily administration of the scheme: this is entrusted, again by statute, to a chief executive. The board is thus charged with the overall supervision of the scheme to ensure that it complies with the legislative and policy requirements. This task will inevitably lead to the identification of legislative weaknesses or to the consideration of policy issues. Such aspects lie at the margins of responsibility between the institution and its parental government department, and there is often some uncertainty in this area. But the institution has the responsibility to identify the issues, to consider solutions and to bring to the attention of the responsible minister issues which seem to have a significant policy element, which could impinge adversely on the performance or perception of the scheme, or which could require legislative change. It should be given the power to exercise this responsibility.

In general, however, the responsibility of the social security institutions is related to the basic tasks associated with the identification of insured persons and employers; the collection, recording and enforcement of contributions; the processing, award and payment of benefits; and the management of funds. Their capacity to perform these tasks lies at the heart of perceptions as to their effectiveness, but the chief executive is responsible for ensuring that the board is aware of any significant problems with regard to these matters. Training for the board and chief executive and their staff may be needed to ensure that they have adequate skills to perform their tasks. (The Social Security Technical Programme of the International Training Centre of the ILO in Turin, Italy, provides training for personnel of social security institutions, government ministries and employers' and workers' organizations.)

Social security benefits may also be provided through private institutions rather than public bodies. There are two basic examples of this, although many variants:

- occupational pension schemes provided by employers as part of the conditions of service: such schemes may be voluntary (as in Canada) or mandatory (as in Australia or Switzerland) and may be provided directly by employers or through private pension companies under contract to employers;
- private pension schemes provided directly for individuals on either a voluntary basis (as in the United Kingdom) or on a mandatory basis (as in Argentina, Chile, Peru and several other Latin American countries).

Figures 9.2 and 9.3 illustrate the institutional arrangements relating to the supervision of the mandatory private pension schemes in Argentina and in Peru.

The social partners: Employers' and workers' organizations

Employers have responsibilities under most social security schemes for the payment of contributions on behalf of their workers, and for the submission of

Figure 9.2 Institutional division of responsibility (Argentina)

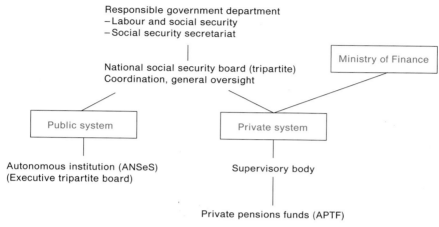

Source: ILO compilation.

Figure 9.3 Institutional division of responsibility (Peru)

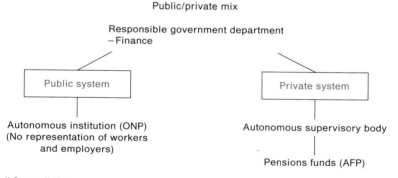

Source: ILO compilation.

information relating to their workers to provide an eventual basis for determining entitlement to benefit. These responsibilities are invariably turned into statutory obligations. Workers are generally obliged to provide their employers, and/or the scheme, with information to enable themselves to be identified and registered, are required to pay contributions and, when in receipt of benefit, to follow prescribed rules relating to continuing entitlement in order to avoid abuse.

But in addition to, and partly because of, these obligations – and because a social security scheme is effectively a mechanism to provide social protection on the basis of mutual support – there is a strong case for the representatives of the contributors and the beneficiaries to play a role in determining the development of the scheme and in monitoring its performance. This is typically provided in two ways: in the case of schemes administered by an institution, through the employees and employers being represented on the management board or, in the case of schemes administered by a government department, through a social security consultative or advisory body. But in some countries, such as Belgium, the employees and employers acting together also have a dominant role in the day-to-day administration of the social security scheme.

Participation of the employees and employers in the administration of the schemes can be justified on several grounds: (a) in recognition of their financial contribution to the scheme, (b) to support the financial and administrative autonomy of the scheme, and (c) by virtue of the legitimacy of employers' and workers' organizations.

Should the state limit its role to legislative and regulatory functions, and should government representatives restrict themselves to the role of observers, supervisors or arbitrators of schemes administered on a bipartite basis? To some extent this may depend on the competence and experience of the institution and its governing body. Participation by the employees and employers should ensure a better understanding and acceptance of contribution liability and this should help make undertakings more accountable and encourage them to fulfil their obligations.

Direct participation by the social partners in the supervision of the scheme may not be seen as necessary in certain countries (United Kingdom and United States are examples). This is attributable to a number of factors. Where the scheme is very comprehensive and provides a wide range of benefits for the vast majority of the population, it may be difficult to present employers' organizations and labour unions as speaking on behalf of the entire insured population. Also, as in the United Kingdom, the nature of the scheme, which was a flat rate for many years, presumed that separate arrangements would be made by employers in consultation with their workforce. Finally, as has already been noted, in such countries the operation of the democratic system is highly developed and effectively results in the application of a supervisory system which exposes issues and weaknesses for political debate and public scrutiny.

Beneficiaries

Beneficiaries may be identified separately on the basis that, although they have a direct interest in the structure and management of the scheme, to the extent that they are retired from employment or are surviving dependants they have no connection with the labour force and thus with workers' representatives. In recognition of this and their vulnerability, such persons, in particular pensioners

– as in Uruguay – have formed themselves into well-organized and influential groups for the purpose of protecting their interests and are represented on the management boards.

The excluded

Similarly, in some developing countries associations have been established by informal sector or self-employed workers who are excluded, whether in law or in practice, from coverage under the social security scheme, but who seek access to social protection through the presentation of their needs from the strength of a group (examples of such groups which have had a measure of success are the homeworkers in the Philippines and Indonesia and the Self-Employed Women's Association (SEWA) in India).

THE FUNDAMENTAL GOVERNANCE QUESTIONS

The fundamental governance questions are (a) what is the most appropriate social security pension scheme for the country, (b) what problems are typically experienced in strategic planning, and (c) what are the most suitable institutional arrangements for the administration of social security?

What is the most appropriate social security pension scheme for the country?

Governance at the strategic or macro policy level

The design and implementation of a social security pension scheme is a major step in the socioeconomic development of any country and the process requires careful planning. There will inevitably be both short-term and long-term implications for economic and fiscal performance as well as for the labour market and, more directly, for the overall level of social protection and living standards. The related policy studies should therefore be macroeconomic in structure, supported by quantitative analysis, and should enable policy options to be weighed from a broad socioeconomic perspective. Even within the social protection sector careful judgments need to be made about relative priorities in benefits and their financing and with regard to the extent to which public systems should seek to meet social protection needs.

What problems are typically experienced in strategic planning?

Fragmented development

In many countries social protection schemes have developed on a piecemeal basis, often in response to particular issues or problems, rather than as part of a national long-term strategy. While gradual development was often unavoidable, progress being determined by the pace of economic development, the resolution of political differences and emerging priorities, it has become apparent that there is now, in many countries, a patchwork quilt of social protection provisions which address particular needs but which cannot readily be seen as components of a national strategy. It is not uncommon to find that responsibility for social protection issues is spread among several government departments so that, for example, the Ministry of Labour may be responsible for the direct administration of a workers' compensation scheme and for the supervision of a social security board which administers a social insurance pension scheme for private sector employees, the Ministry of Health may supervise a health insurance scheme, the Ministry of Defence may administer a pension scheme for members of the armed forces and the Civil Service Department may administer a pension scheme for public servants. There may be separate schemes for other public servants and there may be many occupational or private pension arrangements which may be supervised by the Ministry of Finance or a regulatory body. All these public bodies will have responsibilities relating to one of these schemes, but no overall responsibility for social protection in general. Achieving policy coherence and consistency in this situation will be difficult. Schemes will tend to be reformed but on an individual and isolated basis and structural reform across the social protection will be inhibited by the fragmentation of responsibility.

While it may be inevitable for responsibility of social protection to be shared among several government departments and public agencies, given the structure of government in the country and the way that social protection schemes have evolved there are several adverse implications:

- there may be an overall lack of policy cohesion resulting in inconsistencies between the different provisions;
- it may be difficult to determine the respective roles of the employees, employers and beneficiaries in the financing and provision of social protection;
- there may be overlaps at the operational level between the various sub-systems.

Lack of coordination

The absence of a national mechanism for monitoring the overall performance of the social protection and for examining problems and proposals for reform in the broader context is also common. Once authority has been allocated to a particular department or agency it is often difficult to overlay that authority with a structure which seeks to coordinate policy development at the macro level. The problems of fragmentation and lack of coordination have been evident from ILO technical cooperation activities in many countries, for example in India, Indonesia, Malaysia and the Philippines in Asia, and Nigeria, Tanzania and Zambia in Africa.

Inadequate planning

Whether or not responsibility for social protection planning is fragmented, it is common for insufficient time, research and analysis to be given to the design and reform of a social protection. This may be due in some cases to a desire to give early effect to political decisions, or to react quickly to a particular problem. But although the consequences of hasty policy making may not be apparent for some years, particularly in the case of pension schemes, when they emerge they are likely to be significant and difficult to correct. An example would be a decision to lower retirement age in order to reduce the number of public servants or to increase job opportunities for the unemployed, but the impact on the financing of the pension scheme could be dramatic.

In the planning process, time and resources need to be allocated to economic and labour market studies, and to an analysis of the consequence of alternative policy scenarios. Increased levels of social protection may be desirable, but can they be sustained, and who will bear the burden? Policy making often takes place under pressure without adequate consultation or preliminary study and evaluation. The process of reform is difficult to manage, particularly in developing countries and countries in transition, where knowledge of the issues tends to be concentrated among a few specialist officials but where the decision-making process is often determined by political considerations without adequate regard to the technical implications. Decision makers are often unaware of the implications of decisions on issues which directly affect the financial status of the scheme, such as the level of the minimum wage, the contribution rate, the level of pensions and pension age. There is a tendency for popular decisions to be taken and unpopular decisions to be deferred, with serious adverse consequences for the scheme. An example can be found among the defined benefit pension schemes of Latin America and French-speaking Africa. Although most of these schemes were established with a financial system based on partial funding, with provision for periodic reviews and increases in contributions, subsequent governments were either reluctant to apply the system or did not fully understand it, and many of these schemes became underfinanced and effectively reverted to a pay-as-you-go scheme with no reserves.

Many countries do not have the data or the technical capacity to assess the effect of alternative courses of action, either on overall social expenditure or on household incomes and living standards, and consequently decisions are taken without it being possible to forecast the consequences.

Rigidity in the legislative process

The social security legislation often represents a major obstacle to efforts to ensure that social security provisions remain valid in changing circumstances. If the principal legislation specifies such aspects as coverage, contribution rates, contribution and benefit ceilings and the minimum benefit, it may prove difficult to ensure that these remain valid if the process for legislative change is cumbersome and the system is overburdened. The effectiveness of the protection provided by many schemes and their financial viability have suffered from this rigidity in their legislation. Similarly the process for adjusting benefits is often slow and ineffective, resulting in a reduction in benefits in real terms. Examples are to be found in India where the process for the extension of coverage is cumbersome in that each additional sector of the labour force to be covered has to be specifically mentioned in the legislation, in Zambia where the provident fund contribution was effectively reduced to a flat-rate contribution in the early 1990s by the failure to increase the ceiling for contribution liability, and in Kenya where the contribution ceiling under the provident fund has never been increased.

Conceptual rigidity

The development of most social security schemes is influenced by experience elsewhere. This may be based on the emergence of new concepts or reactions to new problems, or it may reflect political or economic influence. Most of the countries which were formerly part of colonial empires either have schemes which represented a standard model considered appropriate for such countries (as in the case of former British colonies) or adopted as far as was possible social security schemes which were similar to those of the colonial power (as in the case of France). The countries which were formerly part of the Soviet Union, or under its control, also have similar schemes. Many of these countries have found that, as they have developed, the social security they inherited does not correspond to their social and economic circumstances. Experience thus illustrates the need for each country to develop a social protection which reflects its particular national circumstances and to take advantage of foreign experience and expertise with caution.

What are the most suitable institutional arrangements for the administration of social security?

International review of institutional arrangements

A wide variety of institutional arrangements has been introduced throughout the world to provide a framework for the governance of social security. These often have a direct bearing on the effectiveness of that governance, but what works in one country does not necessarily do so in another. Just as the scheme must be designed to suit the circumstances of the people, the institutional arrangements will reflect the level of development and, in particular, the political situation in the country. In many countries these institutional arrangements were devised to administer a scheme for a particular occupational group, such as civil servants, the armed forces, teachers and lawyers. The subsequent development of social security and the extension of coverage has sometimes been built around these initial schemes (Argentina and Uruguay), others have remained outside the system (Zambia) and in some cases they have set a precedent for the development of other schemes (Germany).

In Central and Eastern Europe and countries of the former Soviet Union the collapse of the political system linked with the centrally planned economy and the adoption of market-based economies resulted in the need for a complementary restructuring of the social security schemes, but it also created a climate of reform which extended not only to the design of the schemes but also the way they were administered. This led, in many countries, to a new division of responsibility under which authority shifted from a central government department to social security institutions with varying degrees of autonomy and to the introduction of tripartite consultation and supervision. It has been found, however, that while the enactment of legislation creates, in principle, the basis for the development of schemes which are more democratic, both in their outlook and in their system of governance, it takes time for these new roles and responsibilities to be taken up. Furthermore the scale of the inherited obligations to pensioners and future pensioners, and the resultant dependence on central government funds, restrict the opportunity for the new range of social security managers to take advantage of their new authority.

There is one other aspect of relevance to Central and Eastern Europe. Participation in governance is linked to entitlement: the acquired rights to benefits arising from the contributions paid. In most countries in the region, contribution rates paid by workers remain low with the bulk of the contribution being paid by employers. This affects responsibility for the administration of the scheme, inhibits the workers' participation in its management and tends to hold back the development of tripartite authority.[1]

In western Europe, there are essentially three different models for the governance of social security. In Ireland and the United Kingdom responsibility lies, in general, with a single government department and there is little opportunity for the employees and employers to influence policy or control the management of the system. In Ireland, however, social security reform has been included in various Social Partnership accords and the latest accord refers to a National Pensions Policy Initiative which, following broad consultation, will produce recommendations on the future development of a national pensions policy. In the United Kingdom, a Social Security Advisory Committee exists to advise the Secretary of State on social security matters but, of its between eight and 11 members, only one is appointed after consultation with employers' organizations and one after consultation with the Trades Union Congress.

In the Scandinavian countries there are also unitary systems, but the administration is more decentralized and the employees and employers have a greater involvement in governance. Thus in Finland the pension reform in 1995 was negotiated directly by the employees and employers. In Sweden, however, neither the trade unions nor the employers' associations have a significant role in the administration of pension benefits and they have only limited participation in policy making, this being achieved by consensus among the political parties.

Elsewhere in western Europe the tendency is for the administration of social security to be fragmented among several autonomous institutions (as in Germany and the Netherlands) although the structure and scope of these vary considerably and the employees and employers generally have a significant role. In Germany and Austria major decisions on pension reform are considered to require consensus not merely among the political parties but also among social groups including unions and employer organizations.

Within this general classification, and as a reaction against what is seen as the increasing burden of social security obligations, two separate trends in the development of the institutional arrangements can be discerned. First, in the United Kingdom, a social security scheme administered by a monolithic government department has been broken into different units, partly through privatization and the establishment of semi-autonomous executive agencies, each charged with the responsibility for the administration of one aspect of the scheme. This is underpinned by steps to reduce the scope of the public system in favour of employer-based and personal arrangements and a series of measures to introduce more cost controls into the system. The executive agencies were introduced in the late 1980s as part of a large-scale restructuring of the civil service which opened the door to the adoption of private sector management practices. This broke, to some extent, the traditional reliance on a centralized and unified bureaucracy. Six agencies were established to perform prescribed functions and meet targets under the supervision of the Department of Social Security. They are answerable to a Cabinet minister and not to a tripartite board, and they represent an attempt to provide more effective performance within the constraints imposed by public expenditure limits. The establishment of these agencies has, however, institutionalized the separation between operational and policy-making functions and they have not been accompanied by increased participation of the employees and employers. The governance of social security in the United States is discussed in box 9.2.

In other countries the trend has been towards a greater degree of centralization. In Belgium and France, the employees and employers have traditionally, through social insurance institutions, had considerable responsibility for the administration of social security schemes, with the parliament only being able to discuss the programme and its costs and not control it. Recent concerns in France over the cost of social security led to changes in the division of responsibility, with parliament now able to determine on an annual basis the general financial parameters and to set expenditure limits. The government will also conclude multi-year agreements with the social security funds to cover expenditure objectives and standards of service, with such agreements to be supervised by an independent supervisory committee. In the Netherlands provision has been made for the establishment of a new organizational structure for the

Box 9.2 The institutional framework for the governance of social security pensions in the United States

Public pensions in the United States are provided almost exclusively through the Old Age, Survivor and Disability Insurance programme which is operated directly by federal government agencies. Contributions are collected by the Internal Revenue Service as a fully integrated part of its procedures to collect federal income tax, and benefit payments are made by the Treasury Department. Most of the other functions of the pension programme are the responsibility of the Social Security Administration, an independent agency whose head reports directly to the President.

Under the Constitution, laws must be passed by majority vote of each of the two houses of Congress and approved by the President. Legislation affecting the Old Age, Survivor and Disability Insurance programme must first be considered and recommended by the Committee of Ways and Means in the House of Representatives. The Senate is an equal partner in the legislative process and here matters concerning the programme are considered by the Committee on Finance.

Two different kinds of institutions share responsibility for monitoring developments in the plan: the boards of trustees of the programme's trust funds and periodic social security advisory councils and commissions. Financial oversight of the programme rests primarily with the boards of trustees of the various social security trust funds. The programme has six trustees. Four are the heads of executive agencies in the government: the Secretaries of the Treasury, Labor and Health and Human Services, and the Commissioner of Social Security. Each is a presidential appointee. The other two are private citizens appointed to a four-year term by the President: one must come from the opposition party. The trustees' work is assisted by the periodic advisory social security councils and by the establishment of a committee of economists and actuaries.

Virtually every major policy change in the programme is finalized only after consideration and recommendation by some form of broad-based, officially established advisory group or committee. Until 1995 the Secretary of Health and Human Services was required to appoint a new advisory council every four years to review all aspects of the programme and report through the Secretary to the Congress. These councils consisted of 13 members with equal representation of employers' and workers' organizations and at least one representative of the self-employed. However the law requiring the regular appointment of advisory councils was repealed when the Social Security Administration was established as an independent agency in 1996. Instead provision was made for the establishment of a new permanent advisory board consisting of members appointed by the President, and by minority and majority leaders in both houses of Congress.

Source: Adapted from Lawrence H. Thompson, "The public pension system of the United States", in E. Reynaud (ed.). Social dialogue and pension reform (Geneva, ILO 2000).

employers' schemes with a central board composed of employers' and workers' representatives which will seek to provide a greater degree of coordination between the various schemes. Box 9.3 discusses how the governance of social security pensions may affect their design.

Turkey provides an example of a country where, although the legislation established social security institutions as autonomous organizations, this does not apply in practice. There are three social security institutions: the SSK covering mostly private sector employees, Emekli Sandigi covering public servants and the Bag-Kur covering the self-employed. All three have an autonomous status under their respective statutes. In practice there is considerable control and supervision by central government over many aspects relating to the administration of the schemes. The schemes are all in deficit, principally because of policy decisions by previous governments which have undermined their viability and, as a result of their consequential reliance on government subsidies, their status.

Africa is probably the continent which can provide the most striking examples of the failure to meet social security objectives. This is partly attributable to a range of economic and political factors – some external – which have seriously inhibited the development of many countries, but is also due to weaknesses in almost every aspect from the design of the schemes to their day-to-day administration. The African experience illustrates the linkage between the efficient governance of social security, a sound infrastructure and a favourable economic and political environment. If there is hyperinflation, political unrest, poor human resource development, insufficient resources to meet basic needs and ineffective communications, it is not surprising that the social security does not work as it should. But even given these significant factors, there is much which could have been done to provide more effective governance, and recognition of this as a basis for sustainable reform is now noticeable in many countries throughout the continent.

In most of the African countries where there are social insurance schemes, responsibility for their administration is entrusted by statute to a social security institution, generally with a board constituted on a tripartite basis and under the supervision of a central government department. The objective was to separate the financing of social security from the government budget, but the practice has not always corresponded with the intention of the legislation. It has often happened that government, as the political authority, controls the appointment of the board and its chief executive, and also determines a whole range of administrative issues including the flow of funds, which one would ordinarily expect to be delegated to the board or its administrators. This continuing direct involvement is fostered in some countries by the legislation, which fails to create a truly tripartite structure for the board, neglects to define roles and responsibilities and limits the power of appointment to the minister. It is also relevant to note the relative weakness both of the trade unions in many African countries and of tripartite structures.

Box 9.3 The effect of different governance traditions on the design and financing of pension systems

The governance of pension schemes varies considerably between different countries, even where the underlying structure of provision might be similar. For example, funded defined contribution schemes are offered by commercial organizations in the United Kingdom, by joint employer and employee organizations in Australia and by the state in Singapore. The question that arises, therefore, regards how far this variation in the form of governance affects the design and financing of the respective schemes.

There are typically four potential participants in the governance of a pension scheme: the state, employers, employees and commercial organizations. Each of these could operate a scheme on its own, or two or more can combine to run a scheme together. Further variation arises from the possibility that a particular scheme might cover a single employer or a group of employers, and the possibility that employees might be involved directly or through their collective organizations, for example trade unions.

The number of possible combinations of participants in the task of pension scheme governance is therefore substantial. In practice, however, within this range of possibilities, the main structures that are typically adopted in OECD countries can usefully be characterized as follows:

- direct state control,
- control by a commercial provider (for example, an insurance company),
- control by a single employer, as a scheme sponsor,
- joint control by a single employer and its employees, as co-sponsors of a scheme, and
- joint control by a group of employers and their employees.

In most countries two or more of these structures exist alongside each other, with some countries, such as the United States, where all five perform a significant role.

The path that has led each country to adopt its particular combination of structures has depended on a variety of factors, including its legal framework, industrial relations structure, historic attitude to supplementary pension provision (including the level and form of compulsion), political climate, and cultural and political values.

The result in some countries is a greater stress on achieving a consensus between the social partners, for example in Denmark and France, leading to the greater use of jointly run pension schemes, both in the public and private sectors. At the other end of the spectrum there are countries where there is little employee involvement, for example the United Kingdom, where provision is governed largely by the government, as with the National Insurance Scheme, or by individual employers, even following recent legislation that required some employee involvement in employer-sponsored schemes.

Distinguishing the effect of these different traditions of governance on the structure and outcome of the respective pension schemes is clouded by the effect of other variables in pension provision. It is also difficult to decide what constitutes cause and effect. However it is possible to identify some general tendencies, in particular the following:

- Collective arrangements, with or without the involvement of members, lead to a lowest common denominator result in terms of benefits, unless there is some form of state-backed compulsion setting standards of provision.
- Collective arrangements are in most cases established on a defined contribution basis as this is thought to minimize cross-subsidies between members and, hence, employers.
- Single employer-sponsored schemes can lead to some groups getting a relatively high level of total benefits, but only in those sections of the labour market that generally enjoy good employment conditions.
- Public schemes operating on a tripartite basis, for example with state, employer and employee all involved, are associated with a relatively high level of benefits and greater autonomy from the government's general finances.
- Collective schemes in the private sector, for example those covering more than one employer, are associated with a high level of member involvement, either directly or through their trade unions, with the members often in practice having more influence than the employers.

The form that has been adopted for the governance of pension schemes varies significantly from country to country. It appears to be determined by a number of factors which are quite specific to individual countries. It is certainly not the case, therefore, that the adoption of a particular governance structure in one country will, of itself, automatically lead to similar results in another country, in terms of the level or form of pension provision.

There have been significant improvements in the last decade, however, with a trend towards greater real autonomy for social security institutions supported by the general adoption in some countries of democratic principles of government. The Côte d'Ivoire, Gabon, Ghana, Nigeria, Senegal, Tanzania, Uganda and Zimbabwe all provide examples where autonomy is well developed, while in other countries, such as Benin, the Central African Republic, Ethiopia, Togo and Zambia, it is developing. Direct responsibility for the administration of the scheme still lies with the responsible government department where the scheme is universal or means tested, as in Mauritius and South Africa, where it is based on employer liability principles as in Malawi and Sierra Leone and where it relates only to public servants, as in Kenya, the United Republic of Tanzania and Uganda. Autonomy is not the sole requirement for good governance, and in Africa it is often associated with high administrative costs and excessive staffing levels, but it helps to create an environment where accountability, participation and motivation can be developed and different interests can be balanced.

South Africa provides an example of a country where responsibility for social security is fragmented and thus where, in the new political framework, it is difficult to plan comprehensive reform. Social protection for old age, for example, is provided on a means-tested basis through a scheme administered by the Department of Social Welfare, while the development of occupational pension schemes is regulated by the Ministry of Finance. The Department of Labour is responsible for a Workers' Compensation Fund and an Unemployment Insurance Fund.

There are a wide range of institutional arrangements in Asia which include several countries where the government is directly responsible for the administration of the social security scheme (for example, Australia and New Zealand). The countries in transition – China, the Central Asian republics, Laos and Viet Nam – generally have systems still administered by central or provincial governments. In China the size of the country and wide variation in economic development, together with an established reliance on state-owned enterprises for the provision of social protection, have combined to present considerable difficulties to the central government in instituting even a partially uniform system. However the problem is being vigorously addressed and a new national Ministry of Labour and Social Security has been formed. In Viet Nam, responsibility for the administration of the system is gradually shifting away from central government in the case of long-term benefits and from the trade unions in the case of short-term benefits to an autonomous social security organization, Viet Nam Social Insurance (VSI), but this is a gradual process which depends on the capacity of the VSI to take on new responsibilities and, in particular, to cover private sector workers effectively.

Although schemes have been established with their own identity in many Asian countries, their status and degree of autonomy vary considerably. Examination of the variety of arrangements indicates that this is not necessarily based on definitions of status or responsibility in the law but on the practice and working relationships in the country and this in turn sometimes depends on the personality and experience of the key officials and perhaps on the general administrative approach taken by the government. In some countries autonomy and decentralization are fostered and have developed; in other countries there is a greater tendency for central control of all public sector activities.

In some countries, notably in East and South-East Asia, tripartite structures are not yet fully established and in 1997 the ILO *World Labour Report* concluded that, in Asia, the mechanisms which facilitate social dialogue are, on the whole, still undeveloped. It was further noted in the same report that the proportion of employees covered by collective agreement rarely exceeds 4 per cent in most countries of the region. Membership of trade unions is still at a low level (2.6 per cent of the non-agricultural labour force in Indonesia, 3.1 per cent in Thailand, 11.7 per cent in Malaysia, 22.8 per cent in the Philippines). A tendency to authoritarian leadership, and to limitations in democratic activity and restrictions in some countries on trade union activities, has resulted in the limited development of social security and an absence of opportunities for workers' representatives to participate in social protection planning and administration.

Responsibility for financial resources and, in particular, control of the investment of reserve funds and the determination of recruitment and conditions of service of personnel are also key considerations. At one end of the spectrum are to be found the Employees' Provident Fund and the Employees' Trust Fund in Sri Lanka, and the Social Security Organization in Thailand, which are administered by divisions of the Ministry of Labour. The Employees' Provident Fund Organization in India is semi-autonomous, with a Central Board of Trustees established as a body corporate, but it is subject, in practice, to considerable control by the government. A similar situation applies to the Employees' State Insurance Corporation which is responsible for the administration of the health care and short-term cash benefits scheme. In Pakistan, where there are similar divisions of responsibility between central government and the states, both the federal Employees' Old Age Benefit Institution and the provincial social security schemes enjoy a greater degree of autonomy within their relationship with the Ministry of Labour.

In South-East Asia, however, some of the social security institutions have established considerable autonomy, both in law and in practice: in particular the Central Provident Fund in Singapore, the Employees' Provident Fund, the Employees' Social Security Organization in Malaysia and ASTEK in Indonesia. In the Philippines there are several autonomous social security institutions responsible either for certain sections of the population or for different benefits. Each has its own supervisory board which is responsible for policy issues which, in other countries, are dealt with in government departments. Thus the Secretary of Labour and Employment is only a member of the Social Security Commission which is responsible for the policy of the social security system. The chief executives who are appointed by the President are also influential. Although enjoying considerable autonomy, these institutions are subject to public sector budgetary constraints and are unable to determine their own conditions of service or recruitment policy.

In Indonesia, although the principal social security organization JAMSOS-TEK has autonomous status and is established in statute as a profit-making public enterprise, it has become apparent that there was considerable political interference by the government in its administration and, in particular, in the management of its investment programme. Allegations of corruption and mismanagement have resulted in calls for the removal of the monopoly accorded to JAMSOSTEK, and for employers and workers to be permitted to choose from a range of public and private social protection providers.

The provident fund system is still strong in Asia and the Pacific and the schemes here have generally not suffered the adverse effects of inflation to the same extent as in Africa (except recently in Indonesia). This has beneficial implications for compliance and record-keeping, although both aspects represent major problems for provident funds in India, Indonesia and Sri

Lanka, and for social insurance schemes in the Philippines, Pakistan and Viet Nam.

In South America are to be found some of the oldest social security schemes in the world: in particular in what are regarded as the pioneer countries of Argentina, Brazil, Chile and Uruguay. Initially these schemes were administered directly by government and, even when subsequently autonomous social security institutions were established, government involvement was evident. The model of a social insurance scheme administered by an autonomous institution with a tripartite board was also widely adopted in Central America and the Andean countries. Although they are still prevalent in many countries, dissatisfaction with the performance of these well-established social insurance schemes has led to radical reforms. The structural reforms can be categorized as those where:

- the public scheme has been closed and replaced by a privately administered scheme based on fully funded defined contribution principles (Chile, Bolivia and Mexico are examples);
- a defined contribution element has been integrated with a restructured defined benefit scheme as part of a mixed system and where public and private institutions have prescribed roles (Argentina and Uruguay);
- separate defined contribution schemes operated by private approved pension funds have been established as an alternative to the public scheme (Colombia and Peru).

Although the reform was largely driven by the inability of the schemes to provide adequate levels of protection, there was also considerable dissatisfaction with what were seen as inefficient and corrupt institutions which were subject to considerable political influence. Many of the bad practices had a direct effect on the financing of the scheme and thus on the benefit structure. Typical examples of malpractice by governments were:

- not fulfilling their obligations as employers: delaying or not paying contributions in respect of their own employees or in accordance with their commitment to contribute to the fund;
- obliging the social security scheme to invest in public securities which yielded little or no return;
- requiring reserve funds to be deposited with a government bank with no interest or with a negative real rate of return.

PROBLEMS AT THE INSTITUTIONAL LEVEL

Most countries have chosen to adopt a system in which a public autonomous institution has been established to take responsibility for administering the scheme. What problems arise from this arrangement?

Determining and implementing roles and responsibilities

The basic model of the autonomous public institution seeks to take account of the interests of all the principal actors: government, employers, workers and beneficiaries. It recognizes that the scheme is financed by employers and workers and thus that their representatives should be involved with the administration of the scheme. It also recognizes, however, that the state has an overall responsibility, both as regards the level of social protection and the economic implications, and as guarantor for the social security fund. The difficulty arises in the translation of these considerations into legislation and then into practice. First, it may be very difficult to identify organizations and/or individuals who can satisfactorily represent the contributors and beneficiaries of the scheme. The scheme may be broad-based in scope and coverage, and there may be several organizations representing employers and workers, while some insured people may not have any identifiable point of representation. Then there is a risk that the issues considered are those which are the concern of only those groups who are represented and who then effectively seek to capture the consensus in their own relatively narrow interests. The level of unionization of those covered by the scheme may be low, and both workers and their representatives may not fully understand the concept and practice of social security administrations. Second, the conceptual basis for the sharing of responsibility implies the need for a delicate balance of power, first between central government and the board, then within the board between the different representatives, and finally between the board and the chief executive. In this context it would be surprising if the desired objective was not distorted by political considerations, or by the effect of the human relationships which lie behind the structure. In some countries problems start with the legislation, in that the board may be dominated by representatives of the government with the position of chair perhaps reserved for the most senior official of the responsible ministry (or even of the Ministry of Finance). Several countries also require that all appointments are made by the responsible minister, even those representing the employees and employers. Often the chief executive and other senior administrators are also appointed by the minister rather than by the board. This type of arrangement ensures that government retains a close control over the administration of the scheme, with the board being accorded limited autonomy yet in a position where it can be held accountable for the scheme's performance.

Establishing autonomous institutions

The status and powers of the institution should determine the parameters of its autonomy. If it is to be truly autonomous it should have a legal status of its own and be fully accountable for its own actions. Two types of situation seem to have limited the powers in practice. First, a newly established institution will often commence its responsibilities with a close relationship with the parent department which retains substantial control during what might be seen as a probationary period; but a pattern of working develops and the probationary period never ends, particularly when there are frequent changes of key personnel. Second, the scheme may run into financial difficulties resulting in reference to government subsidies and then to a position of dependence.

Limitations on autonomy

In many cases limitations are imposed on the degree of autonomy of the institution. This may be a reflection of anxiety on the part of government which realizes that it will be held responsible in the eyes of the public if the scheme fails to meet expectations in benefit provision, or it may stem from government's desire to control the resources of the fund. But it seems that it is also difficult to draw a distinction in some countries between government departments and public agencies. All are within the scope of the government auditor, accountable before the parliament and part of the public sector. This is reflected in problems relating to the financial responsibility of the institution. It can be argued that a social security institution has the capacity to be self-supporting financially and therefore to determine its own budget, including expenditure on accommodation, equipment and staff. The nature of the task of administering a social security scheme is such that specialist skills are needed in occupations such as computerization, accountancy and investment management which command high salaries in the private sector. In developing countries there is often concern, however, about establishing precedents which can be exploited by other public agencies, and many public social security institutions are obliged to follow public sector conditions of service as regards the recruitment and payment of staff – in fact in some countries staff are recruited by the central government. This leads to difficulty in recruiting and retaining staff consistent with the expectations of the autonomous status. The placement of staff is also often associated with political patronage and this, together with similar obstacles in the application of personnel policies, has had grave consequences both for administrative expenditure and for quality of performance.

Representation of the social partners

It has already been noted that the effect of representation of the employees and employers may be diluted by their appointment by government. In developing countries it may also be judged that the employers' and workers' representatives do not have the experience and capacity to take important decisions on the administration of the social security scheme. Furthermore, if there were genuinely equal representation from each of the three groups the government could always be outvoted. So a lack of faith in the application of the concept may result in an imbalance of the governmental representation or the introduction of experts, for example on banking or investment. In some countries the number of representatives on supervisory boards or commissions is large, perhaps owing to a desire to ensure participation of all interested organizations. Thus the Central Board of Trustees of the Employees' Provident Fund of India has 43 members with representatives of employers, workers and both central and state government. A similar approach is adopted by the EOBI in Pakistan, which has 19 members, and by the Employees' Provident Fund in Malaysia with 20 members. In the case of the Employees' Provident Fund organization in India, there is provision for the establishment of an executive committee of 12 members, but it is questionable whether boards with large numbers of members can reasonably be expected to carry out the functions with which they are charged and whether many of the individual members will have the experience or the knowledge to play a meaningful part in the process.

Relationship between the board and the chief executive

The relationship between the board and the chief executive can also lead to difficulties. In theory the board should supervise the operation of the scheme and leave the day-to-day administration to the chief executive. This arrangement may, however, be distorted by political relationships and patronage and by the relative inexperience of the individuals. The chief executive is generally a member of the board or attends the meetings and may, by virtue of his greater knowledge and experience, be obliged to direct the board on policy initiatives. Where the chief executive is appointed by the government, as is often the case, there is a risk that not only is the appointment of a political nature but the person appointed will not be familiar with social security administration. While this may be overcome when the appointee is capable and committed, in some countries the chief executives of public institutions are rotated or replaced regularly. This, together with the frequent change of board members, tends to inhibit the management of the scheme and in particular the development of initiatives for reform.

The division of responsibility between the board and the chief executive may also be unclear in some situations and difficulties may arise. Much will depend on the personalities and experience of the individuals. An experienced and dominant chief executive may heavily influence the decisions of a board whose members may only meet infrequently and who may have little knowledge of social security issues. This is more likely to occur where the chief executive is appointed by the minister or President rather than by the board or with the board's approval. There are situations, however, where the reverse has occurred and the board has wielded executive power over the administration of the scheme. Figure 9.4 illustrates the effect of the interaction between the government, the board and the chief executive.

Figure 9.4   The operation of social security boards

A. Tripartism

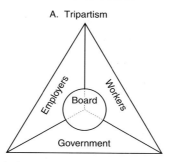

All three partners have broader interests and responsibilities which they represent but within the board and subject to the legislative division of responsibility, they are all equal.

B. The role of chief executive

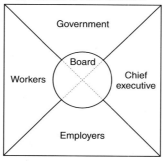

The chief executive may be appointed by the board and thus responsible to the board, but may also be appointed by government and by virtue of this and his technical knowledge and experience may be very influential within the board.

C. Government influence

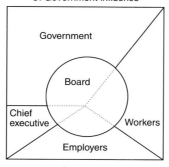

Government may dominate the board either by controlling the appointment of its members or by loading its representation.

Source: ILO compilation.

Direct administration by government

Where the scheme is administered directly by a government department, there is a need to ensure that mechanisms exist for public scrutiny and consultation. These controls are more likely to be found in developed countries since they invariably depend on the political situation and on the opportunities for democratic process such as freedom of the press and the establishment of pressure groups. Problems may also arise with regard to the financial basis for the scheme. First, it may prove difficult in practice to separate the financing of the scheme, even if based on contributions from employers and workers, from central government revenue and public expenditure. This may have adverse implications for real benefit levels and for investment. It may also inhibit the administrative performance of the scheme. Thus, in spite of the fact that the scheme has its own source of income, the integration of this with government revenue and expenditure may result in the staffing and operation of the scheme being subject to national budgetary constraints.

PROBLEMS WITH ADMINISTRATION AT THE OPERATIONAL LEVEL

It has already been noted that in many countries the degree of autonomy accorded to the social security institution in the legislation does not exist in practice and that this reflects a lack of confidence in the management of the institution in a situation where the government has overall responsibility. This lack of confidence has proved to be well founded in some countries, although it is sometimes hard to tell where the adverse effects of inappropriate interference by central government end and unsatisfactory management by the institution begins.

Given the basic objectives of a social security scheme, it is at this level that its success or failure is perceived by those it is seeking to serve. A system which is compulsory, obliges the payment of contributions (taxes), provides for redistribution and determines needs and priorities on a global basis and then applies them uniformly to individuals is not going to be popular with all its contributors and beneficiaries. But both the structure and the performance of the scheme should reflect a broad consensus in favour of its objectives and in support of the way that it is administered. In this context, where do problems arise?

Lack of transparency

There is often a lack of transparency in the administration of social security provisions. This weakness applies to the failure to explain adequately the broad concepts and objectives of the scheme, and to the failure to advise the insured persons how their pension records are progressing or what is happening to the contributions that they have paid. Many schemes do not issue regular pension or contribution statements. Often the legislation is complex and difficult to understand for insured persons, employers and even administrators. The problem applies across the whole spectrum of social security provisions, but is particularly acute in the case of pensions since, first, the contribution rates are the highest and, second, benefit may not be payable for 30 years – on retirement. People inevitably wonder what is happening to their contributions.

Schemes may not be accessible

Many schemes are also too inaccessible to their contributors and beneficiaries. This may be because the organization is highly centralized or because it has not yet been possible to establish a network of branch offices. This feeling may be compounded both by the attitude of the staff to the public and by the lack of facilities for public reception. Whatever the reason, the effect is the same: a gap is created between the institution and its clients which is eventually reflected in a poor public perception and in reduced levels of cooperation and compliance.

Limited coverage

Limited coverage, which is discussed in Chapter 8, is an important problem which all social security schemes need to address. The coverage of many schemes is very limited, with often only a minority of the labour force being insured. Even when the legislation prescribes coverage, problems arise in achieving this. Many schemes experience difficulty in identifying and registering both employers and insured persons. To an extent, this is an aspect of evasion, which may in turn be attributable to a poor public image of the scheme, but many schemes experience great difficulty in processing the registration of insured persons, in allocating a social security number and in ensuring that this number is applied to that individual regardless of change of employment. This is a fundamental prerequisite if an accurate lifetime record of insurable employment is to be obtained.

Maintaining accurate records

Most social insurance schemes require employers to regularly submit details as to the employment and earnings of insured persons in order to provide the basis for eventually determining entitlement to a pension: this is linked to the registration process. This requirement depends on the continuous cooperation of employers and workers and on efficiency within the social security administration. Delays, omissions and mistakes in the information create bottlenecks, often compounded by administrative problems such as the shortage or breakdown of computer processing. In some countries there are backlogs of data processing covering several years.

Delays in processing benefit claims

Difficulties over registration and data processing lead inevitably to delays in dealing with benefit claims which are compounded by irritating enquiries to both employers and insured persons seeking information which has already been provided but which has not been recorded or cannot be found.

Evasion[2]

One of the biggest problems experienced by social security schemes seeking to administer a mandatory scheme is evasion. This takes many forms but it generally focuses on employers who, sometimes with the collusion of their workers, either do not register with the scheme or register but do not pay regularly or underdeclare insurable earnings. The problem is particularly severe among smaller employers in developing countries but is to be found throughout the labour market in every country, with many employers seeking to informalize their workforce in order to reduce costs and with some workers prepared to cooperate in order to find work or to maximize their take-home pay. Levels of non-compliance are difficult to measure and depend on where the lines are drawn in the legislation between the covered and the non-covered, but typically in developing countries between 30 and 40 per cent of those who should be covered are not, in one form or another.

Many schemes do not have effective measures either for identifying evasion or for taking enforcement action. There are a wide range of weaknesses:

- the legislation may prescribe a level of coverage which it is unrealistic to enforce, it may contain loopholes which facilitate evasion, the enforcement penalties may be weak and there may be inadequate powers granted to the institution to take enforcement action or to its inspectors to investigate non-compliance;

- there may be a lack of political support for strong enforcement action where economic circumstances are not favourable or where unemployment rates are high;

- there may be a poorly defined compliance policy and thus no integrated programme for ensuring regular compliance checks on new and established businesses;

- inspection teams may be poorly staffed and organized, or may lack training and support services such as transport.

Bureaucratic procedures

Some of the administrative mechanisms may represent an obstacle to the attainment of the overall objectives because they involve the double handling of papers, excessive checking and limited delegation. A study in 1966 of the procedures of the Employees' Provident Fund Organization in India revealed that the processing of a benefit claim took 37 handling stages during an average processing period of one month. There is a tendency in some schemes to develop procedures which are designed to reduce all risk of error, abuse or internal fraud to the point where the overall level of service suffers and even the introduction of computerization may only serve to provide another layer of bureaucracy in which records and procedures are duplicated.

Inefficiency in the use of resources

The quality, training and personnel management of social security staff are often a weakness, with poor conditions of service and an unsatisfactory working environment. In addition many public social security institutions are over-staffed, often as a consequence of political interference, and this is reflected in the high levels of administrative expenditure which still exist in some countries, particularly Africa. The following list illustrates the administrative expenditure of the social security pension scheme or provident fund of selected developing countries as a percentage of contribution income:

Barbados	1993	4%
Indonesia	1992	18%
Swaziland	1990	29%
Tanzania	1994/5	25%
Uganda	1994	34%
Zambia	1995	102%

It should be noted that the level of the contribution rate and the scale of evasion will have a significant bearing on these figures. Thus in Zambia the contribution ceiling had not been increased for several years in spite of high levels of inflation, although even in 1991 administrative costs represented 72 per cent of contribution income. In Uganda in 1985/6, the National Social Security Fund (a provident fund) had, during its first year of reconstruction, administrative expenditure of 4.9 million shillings, compared with an income of only 1.7 million from contributions: administrative expenditure was 284 per cent of contribution income.

Autonomy may sometimes lead to excessive administrative expenditure if the board of directors is unable or unwilling to exercise control. In some cases excessive expenditure may even be encouraged by a parent ministry with limited resources since it may be able to benefit from its connection with an institution which has its own source of funding and which has some freedom from central government budgetary restrictions. (Table 9.1 below illustrates administrative expenditure for pensions and provident funds for a range of countries compared with both benefit expenditure and contribution income.)

Table 9.1 Administrative expenditure expressed in percentage of the benefit expenditures and the contribution income (all numbers are in millions of local currency)

| Country | Currency | Fiscal year | Contribution | | | | Total contribution | Benefits | Admin. expenditure | Admin. benefits | Admin. contrib. | Index human development | Continent |
			Insured persons	Employers	State participation	Participation of other public authorities	(1)	(2)	(3)	(3)/(2)	(3)/(1)	1995	
Austria	Schillings	1993	83 276	90 818	57 486	0	231 581	225 648	4 954	2.20%	2.14%	high	Europe
Canada	Dollars	1/4/93–31/3/94	5 850	5 850	0	0	11 699	18 536	268	1.44%	2.29%	high	N.America
Chile	Pesos	1993	681 536	0	923 274	0	1 604 810	1 072 177	129 760	12.10%	8.09%	high	S.America
China	Yuan	1992	886	34 292	0	0	35 178	93 198	823	0.88%	2.34%	medium	Asia
Denmark	Kroner	1993	2 823	1 393	71 290	2 672	78 178	75 836	90	0.12%	0.12%	high	Europe
Fiji[a]	Dollars	1/7/91–30/6/92	49	49	0	0	98	65	4	6.08%	4.05%	high	Oceania
Germany	Deutsche Mark	1993	126 734	111 830	69 811	0	308 375	310 374	4 880	1.57%	1.58%	high	Europe
Ghana	Cedis	1993	24 600	61 500	0	0	86 100	2 618	9 933	379.43%	11.54%	low	Africa
Grenada	EC$	1993	6	6	0	0	12	3	2	54.25%	13.16%	medium	C.Amer/Car.
Guatemala	Quetzales	1993	81	155	0	0	236	151	29	19.15%	12.30%	medium	C.Amer/Car.
Guinea equ.	Franc CFA	1992	52	247	0	0	299	108	104	96.30%	34.78%	low	Africa
Italy	Lire	1993	39 025 633	51 750 618	29 490 681	10 762 028	131 028 960	154 697 753	2 912 888	1.88%	2.22%	high	Europe
Malaysia	Ringgit	1993	111	388	0	0	499	174	33	18.71%	6.52%	high	Asia
Mauritius	Rupees	1993	0	0	1 066	0	1 066	1 050	14	1.33%	1.31%	high	Africa
Morocco	Dirham	1992	271	541	0	0	812	1 037	167	16.10%	20.57%	medium	Africa
Niger	Francs CFA	1992	441	677	0	0	1 118	713	369	51.83%	33.04%	low	Africa
Philippines[b]	Pesos	1993	4 355	6 631	0	0	10 987	11 861	881	7.43%	8.02%	medium	Asia
Togo	Francs CFA	1993	544	817	0	0	1 361	2 872	766	26.67%	56.28%	low	Africa
Yemen	Kwachas	1994	137	205	0	0	342	96	27	27.75%	7.75%	low	Asia

Notes: [a] Includes pension scheme and provident fund. [b] Includes sickness/maternity cash benefits.

Source: ILOffice, *Cost of social security 1990–1993*, published on Internet only.

Inappropriate investment policies[3]

Many social security schemes have failed to meet their objectives to manage the social security pensions fund in the best interests of the contributors and beneficiaries. The schemes based on social insurance principles have either adopted a pure pay-as-you-go approach or a partially funded system which implies the establishment of reserves and the adoption of an investment policy. Provident funds are fully funded and the real value of the benefit depends entirely on the effectiveness of the investment of the contributions. It is generally considered that social security pension funds not required for immediate expenditure on benefits and administration should be invested to achieve a balance between considerations of safety, yield and liquidity. It is sometimes argued that they should also be invested with regard to social considerations, or to assist economic development on the basis that this will also benefit the standard of living of those insured under the scheme, but this has dangers and, in many countries, the funds have been invested in accordance with the instructions of the government: sometimes in bonds, sometimes in property, sometimes to support ailing public enterprises or prestige projects, sometimes for political motives, but not often with regard to the best interests of the contributors and beneficiaries of the scheme.

The adverse effect of inappropriate investment policies has been compounded by unfavourable economic circumstances, particularly during the 1980s and especially in the case of sub-Saharan Africa and Latin America, where the rates of inflation were such as to make it impossible to protect the value of social security pension funds. There is an obvious linkage between this fundamental problem and the relationship between the scheme and central government.

The social security administrations in countries in transition are facing some of these administrative and operational problems for the first time. The changes both in attitude and in obligations for employers, workers and administrators alike are just as significant as those relating to the reformed structure of the schemes. Formerly contributions were collected directly from public enterprises in which workers tended to be employed for most of their working lives. Political and economic changes have resulted in a rapid growth in the private sector and an increase in labour mobility. This in turn has resulted in the introduction of new obligations for employers and workers relating to registration and the payment of contributions and, for the administration, with regard to the recording of contributions, the maintenance of financial accounts and ensuring compliance. Devising and implementing these procedures have proved to be formidable tasks for the restructured schemes in Central and Eastern Europe and the countries of the former Soviet Union; China and Viet Nam are also experiencing similar problems. Furthermore changes in the political system inevitably result in an increase both in public expectations as to the quality of service provided by the social security scheme and in a tendency to "opt out" if those expectations are not met.

Choosing the design of a social security scheme to suit the national circumstances, establishing the institutional arrangements for its administration and making the scheme work so that its objectives are met, are fundamental issues which all fall within the scope of good governance. Many schemes have fallen short of the desired level of effectiveness and this has encouraged calls for radical reform, such as the privatization of the social security scheme in some countries. Elsewhere the focus of reform has been placed not on the structure of the system, but on making it work better. (Policy options for improving governance will be reviewed in Chapter 17.)

Notes

[1] A similar situation is found in Pakistan where workers do not contribute to the Employees' Old Age Benefit Scheme but in this case workers are represented on the same basis as employers on the tripartite board.

[2] See also Chapter 10.

[3] See also Chapter 7.

CONTRIBUTION EVASION

10

This chapter discusses the evasion of contributions and its consequence for the management and administration of pension schemes, as well as for their financing. Related issues in other parts of the book include issues of coverage (Chapter 8), governance (Chapter 9), and policies to improve both (Chapter 17).

Non-compliance, or contribution evasion, is a critical issue in the design and operation of contributory social security pension schemes. It influences the adequacy of benefit payments to participants as well as both the financial status and the political legitimacy of the entire programme. Contribution evasion occurs when employers, employees and the self-employed do not pay required social security contributions. It is a critical problem in much of Central and Eastern Europe, Latin America, Africa and Asia. It has seriously undermined the social security system in some countries, with revenue falling far short of that needed to pay benefits. This shortfall has resulted in social security schemes failing to pay benefits, paying low benefits and in their receiving subsidies from general revenue. Even in OECD countries, many schemes lose considerable revenue as a result of this phenomenon.

Contribution evasion is a consequence of social security schemes having been made mandatory: some workers will not voluntarily save enough on their own to fund their retirement. The problem is compounded because employers generally act as a collection agent, and they may have even less interest in collecting contributions than some workers have in making them. Contribution evasion is thus a problem in all types of retirement income schemes.

THE PROBLEM OF EVASION

In most countries social security law imposes a liability on employers to contribute for themselves and their employees. Thus evasion results from employers:

- failing to register themselves and some or all of their employees;

- portraying their workers as contractors, as family members or belonging to other categories for which the employer is not required to contribute;
- failing to contribute, or paying late, for registered employees;
- underdeclaring earnings in order to reduce contribution liability.

Similar situations occur where the self-employed are liable to contribute under the scheme. Governments and other public sector employers may also fail to pay or may underpay contributions for their employees. In some transition countries in Central and Eastern Europe, as well as many countries in Africa, public enterprises are the worst offenders.

Contribution avoidance is a closely related phenomenon and occurs when:

- workers take jobs not covered by social security by becoming self-employed (or working in the informal sector) to avoid making social security contributions (see box 10.1 on contribution evasion in Japan);
- employers organize work conditions and payment so that the people who work for them will not be classified as employees;
- employers are not required by national legislation to cover their workers if they employ less than a fixed number; consequently small enterprises may hire fewer employees for more hours to avoid being required to make social security contributions;
- employers organize wages so as to reduce that part covered by social security (for example, by paying compensation in the form of contributions to occupational pensions).

Contribution evasion has several undesirable effects.

- It may undermine the solidarity consensus on which the scheme is based. Widespread evasion undermines the credibility and legitimacy of the entire system.
- It causes inequities in effective contribution rates between contributors and non-contributors, with resulting effects on income distribution.
- In defined benefit schemes where there is not a tight link between contributions and benefits, it may result in underfinancing of benefits, eventually causing contribution rates to be higher than they would need to be, although the increase in the mandatory contribution rate may occur with a long time lag and an intervening period of revenue shortfall.
- Contribution avoidance and contribution evasion may distort labour market activity, affecting where workers work, which has attendant welfare costs. The informal sector has grown considerably in Africa, Asia and South America, and is reaching significant proportions in some of the countries in transition in Central and Eastern Europe and Central Asia. This may be seen in part as an attempt to avoid paying taxes and mandatory contributions.

Box 10.1 Contribution evasion in Japan

The Japanese social security scheme is divided into two programmes. The Employees' Pension Insurance Programme is compulsory for all employers with one or more regular employees. Each employer has the duty to collect taxes and social security contributions from employees from their monthly earnings. The employer must pay the employees' contributions along with his or her own contributions on behalf of the employees to the Social Insurance Agency. In 1996, 98.6 per cent of all employers who were required to pay contributions to the Agency did so.

Participation in the Employees' Pension Insurance Programme is not compulsory for part-time employees, temporary employees and daily employees. When these employees work more than three-quarters of the working hours of regular employees, however, they are required to contribute to this programme. There are no statistics on evasion by this group of workers, but there is the possibility that many employees and employers who were required to contribute did not.

The second social security programme in Japan is the National Pension Insurance Programme. Participants are composed of three groups: employees, spouses of workers who themselves had no earnings and the self-employed and unemployed. The non-working spouses of workers are not required to contribute. Among the self-employed and unemployed, in 1997, 7.5 per cent who were required to contribute had failed to register for the programme and were not contributing, and an additional 8.2 per cent had registered but had made no contributions in the past two years. Of all those required to contribute, these two groups together accounted for 4.6 per cent.

These statistics thus suggest that most contribution evaders in Japan are either self-employed or unemployed. The government can collect contributions for employees with the help of employers, but it must collect the contributions of the self-employed and unemployed itself. While the Tax Agency of the government has attached the assets of tax evaders, the Social Insurance Agency, which also has that power with respect to contribution evaders, has never done so.

Contribution evaders are more likely to be in large cities than small ones and are more likely to be in younger age groups (particularly those aged 20–29) than middle age groups. The income levels of non-participants were almost the same as those of participants. In 1996, 91.7 per cent of non-participants and 80.4 per cent of non-contributors were participants in the compulsory state medical insurance programmes, and 56.7 per cent of non-participants and 66.3 per cent of non-contributors purchased contracts of life insurance or annuities from financial institutions. In a survey, 53.8 per cent of non-participants and 76.2 per cent of non-contributors indicated that they did not want to be participants or make contributions because they considered social security to be unreliable or because of its high required contributions.

- When evasion occurs as a result of underreporting of earnings, it causes the replacement rate relative to actual earnings to be reduced and tends to flatten the benefit structure (for example, in Egypt, Pakistan and Turkey, where the majority of workers contribute at the lowest level in schemes designed to provide relatively high replacement rates).

Since liability is almost always imposed on the employer, many schemes recognize that the benefit rights of an employee who was unaware of the non-payment of contributions should not suffer. Provision may therefore exist for the social security scheme to pay benefits as if the contributions due had been paid, with obvious adverse implications for the fund.

THE PREVALENCE OF EVASION

Because evasion is illegal by definition, it is often concealed, and thus accurate data concerning it are difficult to obtain. Nonetheless crude estimates can be made using data on the size of the labour force and average wages, by comparing the estimated aggregate contribution liability with the payment actually made. In some Latin American countries, estimates suggest that as much as 50 to 60 per cent of the liability for social security contributions to social security is unpaid (table 10.1). For example, contribution evasion was an estimated 60 per cent in the defined benefit social security scheme in Brazil in the 1980s (Mesa-Lago, 1991a). Late payment of contributions by employers has been estimated to occur for 44 per cent of contributions in Barbados and Jamaica (ILO, 1992). ILO technical assistance teams estimated that in Central and Eastern Europe during the mid-1990s the non-collection of contributions due amounted to between 20 and 30 per cent of total contribution income.

Even in OECD countries evasion may be a significant problem. The United States Internal Revenue Service estimated that, in 1987, non-payment of individual and corporate income tax was about 20 per cent of the total tax liability (Slemrod, 1992). This figure provides a rough estimate of the non-payment of social security contributions.

Employees being misclassified as contractors represent an important aspect of contribution evasion in OECD countries. The United States Internal Revenue Service moved 500,000 workers from contractor status to employee status between 1988 and 1995, and assessed about $1 billion in taxes, penalties and interest (de Jong and Jakabin, 1997).

Some analysts have considered contribution evasion to be primarily a problem of defined benefit schemes, with their replacement by defined contribution

Table 10.1 Estimated contribution evasion in selected countries

Country	Evasion rate (%)	Time period	Source
Argentina	49	early 1990s	Cottani and Demarco (1996)
Brazil	60	1980s	Mesa-Lago (1991a)
Peru	33	early 1990s	Nitsch and Schwarzer (1996)

Note: Because contribution evasion is illegal, all estimates are imprecise.

schemes solving the problem since contributions and benefits would be clearly linked (World Bank, 1994). In Chile's defined contribution scheme, however, funds that catered to lower-paid employees had contribution evasion of 45 to 55 per cent in 1990 (Gillion and Bonilla García, 1992). Experience in Colombia and Uruguay also indicates that switching from a defined benefit to a defined contribution scheme does not solve the problem of contribution evasion. In all these countries only around half of the labour force participates in the mandatory defined contribution scheme.

CONTRIBUTION EVASION COMPARED TO TAX EVASION

Mandatory payments by employers and workers to finance social security benefits are called "taxes" by some American social security analysts but otherwise are generally referred to as "contributions". Throughout this book the term "contributions" is used to refer to a specific payment which directly provides some basis for entitlement to benefits. Thus contributions imply a right to a future benefit. A tax, by contrast, finances the general functioning of government, but the government-provided benefits the individual receives do not depend on the amount of taxes the individual pays.[1]

The analysis of tax evasion compares the expected gains workers or employers receive from evasion with compliance. This involves an assessment of the probability of being caught, the expected financial loss if caught, and the risk aversion of the employer or worker. It involves the financial loss due to paying the tax. The analysis of contribution evasion is more complex because it also involves the worker's assessment of the gain in expected future benefit payments from contributing to the social security scheme.

Understanding the causes of evasion is important for structuring social security reform. A partial understanding could lead to an overstatement of the reduction in evasion due to reform and thus an overstatement in the increased revenues caused by a change in social security schemes. Most reasons for evasion occurring apply equally to defined contribution and defined benefit schemes. One system does not have a clear advantage over the other in managing evasion.

REASONS FOR CONTRIBUTION EVASION

Contribution evasion involves employers, employees and the government. Its prevalence depends on the attitudes of each and on the cost and reward structure they face. While both employers and employees have incentives to contribute or evade – the incentives for each group are examined separately – the actual prevalence of contribution evasion depends on interactions between incentives of employers and those of employees, and the interaction of both with government enforcement.

Because, in most social security schemes, the legal burden of contributions is placed on employers, opportunities for workers to evade are limited and depend on collusion with employers. Alternatively workers may change their employment to become self-employed, casual or contract workers, where contributions may not be required, or where required contributions are more easily evaded.

When an employer has deducted the contributions from an employee's pay but not paid these to the social security scheme, the employee will often be unaware of the non-payment. If payment is made later, he may never know and will only become aware if he receives a statement of account or claims benefit. If deductions for contribution are not made, however, the worker will probably be aware of the situation as these deductions will not be made from his wages. This may reflect voluntary collusion because of the desire of the worker to avoid paying contributions to the scheme or it may be that he is given little choice by the employer. Where the supply of labour to the formal sector exceeds the demand at current wage rates, the worker may be forced to accept terms of service which exclude social protection rights and may be obliged to collude with the employer.

The reasons for contribution evasion can be divided into those affecting employees' willingness to pay or reluctance to report non-payment to authorities and those affecting employers' motivations. A further factor is the government's attitude towards this practice.

Contribution evasion can only occur if three conditions coincide:

- employers wish to evade, or place a low priority on making, social security contributions relative to other expenses;
- employees prefer non-payment of contributions, are reluctant to report non-payment to authorities or are unaware of the non-payment;
- government enforcement tolerates evasion or is inadequate to prevent it.

Issues relating to the effect of a worker's contributions on his or her future benefits were analysed by Burkhauser and Turner (1985), among others. The relationship between contributions and benefits, however, is only one aspect of evasion. This relationship depends on the structure of the defined benefit scheme, but the following aspects are relevant:

- Under many defined benefit schemes, the benefit depends on the period of insurable employment, which is based on the number of contributions paid, and on the earnings used as the basis for contributions liability.
- Both under long-established national provident funds and more recently under mandatory retirement savings schemes, experience suggests that evasion is still a significant problem.

The amount of evasion may be related to the level of mandatory contribution rates. As noted in box 10.2, however, effective contribution rates are generally lower than legislated ones.

Box 10.2 Effective contribution rates are lower than legislated ones
Mandatory social security contribution rates are relatively high in some countries. For three reasons, however, effective contribution rates are generally lower than legislated rates. Because the strength of these effects varies across countries, a comparison of legislated rates can be misleading.

First, when the employer pays part of the contribution rate, the effective rate is lower than the legislated rate because the base of the effective rate includes the value of the employer contribution. In most countries the employer contributes a portion of the mandatory social security contribution. To take the case of a high mandatory contribution rate to clarify the magnitude of the effect, if the employer contributes an amount equal to 20 per cent of pay and the employee contributes an equal amount, the traditional measure of the contribution rate is 40 per cent ($= 20 + 20$). However the effective rate is 33 per cent ($= (20 + 20)/(100 + 20)$). As another example, when the employer contributes the full amount, as was basically the case in some Central and Eastern European countries, and the contribution rate is 25 per cent, the effective contribution rate is 20 per cent ($= 25/125$).

Second, in most cases the effective contribution rate is also lower than the legislated rate because not all aspects of compensation are taxed. For example, pension contributions made by the employer, contributions for health insurance, housing and transport allowances and other benefits are often not treated as insurable earnings and some countries exclude overtime payments, bonuses and commission payments. If only 80 per cent of compensation is subject to mandatory social security contributions, the effective contribution rate in the first instance where 20 per cent is paid by both employer and employee falls from the 40 per cent legislated rate to 27 per cent ($= 40/(100 + 25 + 25)$). (Related to this, and of particular relevance to evasion, is the practice common in some countries of underdeclaring insurable earnings. This may be done by manipulation of the earnings so as to exclude some from the scope of liability or merely by providing false information as to actual earnings.)

Third, it is common in defined benefit schemes to impose a contributions ceiling which limits liability and which is often intended to provide scope for employers and workers to make their own supplementary pension arrangements.

Evasion by, or instigated by, workers

For self-employed workers, the workers' motivations for evasion are most important. For employees, the workers' demand for evasion is a factor that employers must consider in deciding whether to evade. The temptation to evade is present in all social security pension schemes. There are a number of reasons why that is so.

Myopia

Social security contributions around the world are mandatory because some workers would not adequately save for retirement on their own. Some workers have difficulty planning for distant needs such as for retirement. They place a low value on future consumption, sometimes because of current needs. For this reason the value of future benefits to workers is low so they attempt to evade contributions. A tendency for workers to evade is a natural consequence of the basic premise for state intervention in providing mandatory social security.

High income tax rates and contribution rates for other social programmes

When social security contributions are collected with income taxes, contribution evasion may be an aspect of tax evasion. When the overall tax rate is high, contribution evasion may occur even if the contribution rate for social security is moderate. Even if income taxes are collected separately from social security contributions, the payment of social security contributions may provide public information concerning a worker's income tax liability. It is often difficult for a worker to evade high income taxes and other mandatory contributions and at the same time contribute to social security. In some countries, such as Jordan, however, income tax payments are confidential information and the social security agency cannot gain access to tax records to compare declared earnings for tax purposes with declared earnings for social security purposes (or vice versa).

Poverty or temporary financial hardship

Poor workers may feel that they cannot save because their immediate needs are so pressing. Because the contributions are mandatory savings, they may seek to avoid contributing.

Low expectation of benefit receipt

Young workers may wish to evade because benefits would not be received for many years and their discounted value is low or their probability of receipt is low. Some workers may not expect to live until retirement.

Low rate of return compared to alternative uses of funds

When workers receive a lower rate of return on their defined contribution account than on other investments, they are motivated to evade because of the better rate of return elsewhere. A low rate of return on a defined contribution scheme in comparison to what the worker could have earned acts as a hidden tax that workers seek to evade. Defined contribution schemes may have unattractive rates of return for a number of reasons. This could occur for a low-wage worker because of the fixed expenses charged against individual accounts, or for workers generally because high expenses of the scheme manager cause the rate of return to be low. It could occur because tight regulation of the allowable investments keeps the rate of return low. Self-employed workers may prefer to invest in their own businesses rather than make social security contributions. Evasion may also occur if the mandatory contribution rate is high and the worker does not want to save that much for retirement. Workers may lack confidence that their defined contribution scheme will provide adequate benefits.

Defined benefit schemes do not have an account earning an explicit rate of return, but when benefits are linked to contributions the worker's contributions earn an implicit rate of return in terms of accrued future benefits. The future benefits can be considered to equal the accumulated contributions plus the implicit rate of return. If the social security scheme provides a low implicit rate of return, evasion may occur. Defined benefit social security schemes typically provide a high rate of return at the start of the scheme, but the rate of return declines over time.

In many defined benefit social security schemes, benefits are based on the highest few years of earnings and, for workers with a long period of insurable employment, earnings in a substantial number of years have no effect on benefits. When that type of benefit formula is combined with high contribution rates, workers have a substantial incentive to evade contributing in years not counted in computing benefits.

Schemes which impose an earnings-related contribution in return for a flat-rate benefit, or which apply a ceiling to benefits but not to contribution liability, risk evasion by workers who realize that there is no benefit entitlement flowing from part of their contribution liability. Where social assistance benefits or a guaranteed minimum pension are available under the scheme, this may also act as a disincentive to contribute for low-wage workers.

Inflation

High inflation makes it financially advantageous to postpone contributions because their real value quickly falls. For workers disinclined to contribute, high inflation increases the value of postponing contributions. In some countries high inflation is probably the major cause of contribution evasion.

Exploiting

Exploiting the system refers to workers rationally calculating the pattern of contributions that maximizes their gain. Some pension schemes are structured so that workers can avoid contributing in some years with little or no effect on their future pension benefits. Some workers will determine how much in benefits is lost by not contributing and decide whether to contribute. Exploiting occurs for low-income workers when they become eligible for alternative benefits by reducing their contributions to social security.

Compliance cost

All workers and employers bear a compliance cost in time, expense, inconvenience and frustration in obtaining necessary forms, completing them and otherwise complying with contribution requirements. These costs may be particularly high for self-employed workers and workers in the informal sector. Workers in rural areas may need to travel long distances to reach a government office that can assist them with compliance. The compliance cost increases with the complexity of the contribution and tax laws and the frequency with which they are changed (US General Accounting Office, 1996b). It is less costly for employed workers to comply than for the self-employed because the administrative burden of compliance is borne by the employer, who generally can bear it more efficiently.

Lax administration of benefit qualification regulations

Evasion may occur when workers realize they need not make required contributions to receive benefits.

Legitimacy and fairness

Workers are more likely to evade contributions when they feel that the system is unfair or that it lacks legitimacy. In some countries, workers view the social security scheme as a way for the government to raise revenue for other purposes, thus viewing the mandatory contributions as a tax. Evasion may be a form of economic protest. Workers may rightly mistrust government to handle their money properly.

Attitude towards evasion

In some countries evasion is viewed as an acceptable practice. Workers' attitudes towards evasion are affected by their perception of how common it is. When workers believe that evasion is common, they tend to feel that it is acceptable. Similarly, if they believe or know that the government as an employer, high government officials, wealthy people, professionals, sophisticated people or other influential or powerful people evade, other workers will tend to view it as acceptable.

Illegal activities

Workers engaged in illegal occupations generally attempt to conceal the income derived from them and do not pay social security contributions.

Factors causing workers to be reluctant to report evading employers

Workers may wish to participate in the social security scheme but be reluctant to report their employer who is not making required contributions on their behalf.

Anonymity and negative repercussions

The willingness to report their employer depends in part on the worker being able to remain anonymous. Employees may fear that if they report their employer, they will lose their jobs and become unemployed. Employees may not report evasion because they feel powerless or intimidated in dealing with employers.

Unreliability of the government

Employees may feel that the government will take no action. They may believe that the judicial institutions are slow and unpredictable.

Factors affecting the scope for evasion by workers

Inadequate penalties or enforcement

Evasion could occur because the penalties are low or because of the small probability of their being imposed. Contributions may be routinely paid in arrears when the interest penalty for late payment is low. Whatever the reasons for evasion, ineffective enforcement makes it more likely.

Easy access to the informal sector

Evasion is greater when a large informal sector makes it easy for workers to find employment comparable to that in the formal sector. The US Internal Revenue Service has estimated that self-employed individuals (such as street vendors) who informally supply goods and services report less than 20 per cent of their business income. Other self-employed individuals who operate more formally, such as gas station owners, reported less than 70 per cent (US General Accounting Office, 1996a).

Self-employment

In some social security schemes, self-employed workers are not required to contribute but may do so voluntarily. For part-time or temporary workers it may be difficult to determine whether they are self-employed and this provides an opportunity for evasion. In schemes where self-employed workers are required to contribute, they frequently have high evasion rates because of the difficulties in enforcing contributions. It is generally difficult to determine the insurable earnings of self-employed workers because they are often paid on a cash basis, they have legitimate costs that reduce their income and their record-keeping is generally less developed than for large enterprises. The US Internal Revenue Service has found that independent contractors have much lower income tax compliance than employees (US General Accounting Office, 1996a). In some countries self-employed workers form self-help associations that develop social protection mechanisms more attuned to their needs than the national social security scheme.

No income tax

While high income tax rates may encourage evasion, lack of an income tax makes it more difficult for the government to obtain information about the earnings of workers in order to enforce contributions. Thus lack of an income tax, as in the Bahamas, facilitates social security contribution evasion.

Minimum employers' size requirement

In countries where employers with fewer than a minimum number of employees are not required to provide social security coverage it may be easy for small employers exceeding that level to evade coverage. It may be difficult for social security and labour inspectors to determine the number of employees working in a small enterprise. Labour inspectors, for example in Jordan, have reported cases where people who appear to be employees leave the establishment when they arrive, or where employers claim that people who appear to be employees are actually customers or friends visiting for the day.

Payment in cash

When payment is made in cash, it is more difficult for social security inspectors to determine the full amount of the payment. In this regard, underreporting of income is much more difficult to detect than complete evasion.

Evasion by employers

Employers presumably have less motivation than the workers to contribute towards the workers' future social security benefits. When workers wish to evade social security contributions, there may be collusion with employers and thus the employment offer that requires no social security contributions may be more attractive to workers than an offer at a higher wage that also requires contributions. The factors of lax enforcement and low penalties, compliance costs, inflation and financial distress discussed for workers also apply as motivations for evasion by employers and will not be repeated here. Employers may evade, however, even if their workers value the future benefits gained by contributions. In this situation evasion by employers makes their offer of employment less attractive to workers.

Factors leading employers to evade

Cost savings

Financially weak employers may evade contributions because they place a low priority on those expenditures. Paying salaries would be a higher priority than paying social security contributions. Among benefits, providing health benefits is often a higher priority expenditure than providing retirement benefits.

Financially healthy employers may evade contributing to reduce their expenses. Doing so may give an employer a cost advantage over his competitors. Cost savings arise from the non-payment of contributions and the avoidance of administration costs. Compliance may require additional record keeping and calculations. Imprecise and ambiguous language in laws can add to compliance cost by creating uncertainty as to what is required. Costs may be incurred by employers in bribing social security inspectors or in other efforts to evade enforcement.

Employers are more likely to postpone contributions in periods of high inflation, when interest and penalties for late payments are lower than the interest on bank loans that would otherwise be needed for operating capital, or when it is more profitable to invest the funds in financial markets than to make payments on time.

Fraud

Evasion may occur as a result of employers collecting social security contributions from their employees but keeping the contributions. This is the worst form of evasion since it involves defrauding workers of their own contributions. Fraud occurs in a more subtle form when employers delay transmitting employee contributions to the appropriate authorities. Such a practice benefits employers because of the interest gained while holding the employees' contributions.

Corruption

Employers may not comply because it is cheaper to bribe the labour inspector.

Low reputational cost

Evasion may occur because the cost in terms of the employer's reputation may be low. If evasion is widespread, tolerated by the government, considered an acceptable business practice, widely accepted because the government is unpopular, or if government agencies and enterprises do it, then individual employers are more likely to do it too.

Alternative arrangements

Employers may have developed their own retirement arrangements for their workers and see no advantage in participating in the social security scheme.

Small-scale production

Evasion is more easily accomplished by small enterprises or by employers with no fixed place of business. It is easier for the government to control evasion where large employers are concerned. The larger the workforce of an employer the greater the number of employees that the employer must induce or force to collude with evasion. Thus, in many circumstances, it is more difficult for a large employer to evade contributions. Evasion is more difficult when a business is publicly traded and must disclose its labour costs. However, if evasion is due to macroeconomic causes such as high inflation and declining national output, large employers as well as small ones may be contribution evaders. Also large employers may be able to evade because of their political power.

Poor records

Some employers in the informal sector may have difficulty making social security contributions because they have poor records and do not know the amount of insurable earnings they have paid to different workers. It is more difficult for the government to enforce compliance when employers have poor records. It is difficult for employers to evade when they are required to have good records and certification of their record-keeping by outside accountants, as is generally the case for large publicly owned companies in OECD countries.

Non-compliance with other government regulations

Employers that do not comply with minimum wage laws are unlikely to report their wage payments and make social security contributions on those payments.

Weak legal system

Contribution evasion by employers may be a manifestation of a weak legal system. Laws may exist only on paper and may not be known or respected by the public and enforced by the state.

In summary, a number of factors cause workers and employers to evade contributions, or make it easier for them to do so. In both defined contribution and defined benefit schemes, non-contributors tend to be self-employed, young, domestic employees, short-term, low-paid or part-time workers; or tend to work in the informal sector or underground economy, for small enterprises, or for employers in financial distress. Evasion tends to be higher in poor countries that attempt to provide broad coverage and by doing so include workers in categories where evasion tends to be high. In some countries evasion occurs in large enterprises, government enterprises and within the government. Evasion is also associated with macroeconomic distress, such as high inflation, high unemployment and declining gross national product.

REASONS WHY GOVERNMENTS TOLERATE EVASION OR ARE UNABLE TO PREVENT IT

The government also has a role in contribution evasion. Some countries do not enforce compliance, levying no penalties but relying instead on persuasive techniques. The reasons why governments do not fully enforce compliance can be divided into attitudes, resources and costs.

Attitudes towards compliance policy

Mandatory contributions are effectively voluntary

Some social security administrations do not take evasion seriously. They perceive their objective as helping people who are their clients rather than being law enforcers. They prefer to act through education, persuasion and incentives, rather than through enforcement, inspectors and penalties. The government has the attitude that contributions are for the benefit of the workers and their families, and if the workers feel that they cannot or do not want to contribute it should not force them to do so. The government treats contributions as being voluntary. Similarly it may be reluctant to take strong action against employers in case this has adverse implications for the economy or for employment. In some countries, such as Guatemala and Nicaragua, failure to pay social security contributions is not illegal.

Reluctance to levy penalties

Because in some countries workers and employers who evade tend to have lower income, some social security administrations are reluctant to levy penalties against these groups that are already in a poor financial situation. Levying penalties or forcing compliance might force a poor enterprise into bankruptcy. Government officials often believe that it is better for an employer to provide employment without social security contributions than not to provide employment. The extent to which this trade-off is valid is an empirical issue that should be addressed rather than taken on faith. Reluctance to levy penalties may also arise when evasion is widespread because it is felt that it is unfair to penalize a few while most evaders are not punished. If the minimum penalties are viewed as excessive, they may not be levied because the enforcement office believes that the offence does not warrant the penalty.

Political considerations

The administration, either nationally or regionally, may be reluctant for political reasons to act against employers, particularly if they are influential or in an adverse economic situation.

Bribery

In some countries bribery and corruption are widespread. In this situation, the social security institution may tolerate bribery of enforcement agents and corruption of employers.

Division of responsibility

In individual account defined contribution schemes, enforcement of contribution evasion may be more difficult because of the division of responsibility between the government regulatory agency and the administrators of pension funds. It is the responsibility of the pension fund management companies in some countries, such as Chile, to collect contributions, but responsibility for ensuring compliance rests with the regulatory agency, which needs to collaborate with the pension funds to determine if contribution evasion has occurred. Enforcement of compliance is not normally a function of pension funds and thus they may be poorly designed to carry out this costly function. In addition they have little or no incentive to encourage compliance among low-income workers because the expense of managing small accounts may exceed their fees from such accounts.

Adequate resources are collected

In a pay-as-you-go system when there are few retirees, the level of contributions needed to pay benefits will be relatively small. In this situation the government may only make an effort to collect revenues sufficient to pay benefits and not pursue non-compliance beyond that point. In Kazakhstan, where contributions and benefits are collected regionally, less effort is made to collect contributions in the regions with few retirees (see box 10.3).

Resources and costs

Collection costs play an important role in the level of compliance enforced by a social security institution. The higher the collection costs, the less will be the revenue collected relative to the total revenue that workers and employers are legally required to pay the government.[2] Collection costs tend to be higher in developing countries because the informal sector is larger and record-keeping by businesses is not as well developed. Well-designed enforcement programmes first attempt to collect revenue from sources where collection costs are low. Attempts to further reduce contribution evasion will involve extending enforcement to areas where collection costs are higher.

The government may have inadequate resources to enforce a high level of compliance. It may have too few enforcement officers or inspectors. They may be inadequately trained and paid or may lack support services such as transport or funds to reimburse travel costs. Because it is not possible to enforce complete compliance, the level of compliance will be affected by the amount of

Box 10.3 Contribution evasion in Kazakhstan: The whole and its parts
A difficult problem in managing national retirement schemes in transition economies – and in many developing countries as well – is achieving adequate revenue performance. Many observers assume that employers do not pay because they do not have the money or because enforcement is lax. These factors are undoubtedly important, but a recent study of the pension system in Kazakhstan suggests that contribution evasion may also reflect problems in governance.[3]

Background
Kazakhstan has had problems with pension payment arrears for some time, but the scope of the problem varies by *oblast* (region). Some *oblasts* have high arrears; others have never missed a pension payment. All *oblasts* have similar pension obligations relative to the size of their populations, but widely differing financing capacities. In 1995, for example, average household income in the highest-income *oblast* was 2.7 times higher than that of the lowest-income *oblast*.

Who pays, who does not
Conventional wisdom would indicate that collection efficiency (the ratio of actual collections to accrued obligations) should be lowest where incomes are low. But collection efficiency is consistently lower in the higher-income *oblasts*. In 1995, for example, the seven highest-income *oblasts* collected 69.8 per cent of the amount they should have, while the seven lowest-income *oblasts* collected 83.1 per cent. For the first half of 1996 collection efficiency in the high-income *oblasts* was 84.8 per cent, compared with 99.3 per cent in the low-income *oblasts*.

These collection patterns have predictable effects on pension payments. High-income *oblasts* collect more than enough revenues to pay benefits to their own pensioners, while low-income *oblasts* cannot. In short, an *oblast*'s own benefit obligations, not accrued contribution liability, appear to be the collection target in the high-income *oblasts*. But collecting even one-quarter of the revenue arrears pending as of the middle of 1996 would have allowed the pension fund as a whole to eliminate all pension payment arrears.

Options for reform
Several options for increasing revenue compliance are available. Some are inherently regional in scope, while others are national.

Regional strategies. Revenue enhancement initiatives that are regionally differentiated could be especially productive. The same percentage compliance increase will yield more revenue in a high-income *oblast* than in a low-income one. Regional strategies could focus on pilot projects promoting improved record-keeping, personnel training and other strategies.

National strategies. Strategies that are national in scope can strengthen the pension fund system by creating the shared belief that everyone must pay to receive benefits. This concept is not necessarily taken for granted in many transition economies, as many retirement pension recipients have had few contributions withheld on their behalf.

Pension fund collection rates are especially low among the self-employed, in agriculture and in the retail sector. Strategies could be designed for the specific characteristics of these sectors. Kazakhstan – and probably many countries in the same situation – could also profit from improved coordination among the various social insurance funds that collect payroll tax contributions. Amnesties for interest penalties on contribution arrears have also been effective in the past, though recurrent amnesties could create the belief that contributions can be delayed with impunity.

But improving revenue enforcement may not be enough. The regional and local departments of social protection are not fully under the direct control of the central government (Ministry of Social Protection). Unless the subnational departments are willing to cooperate with the central government it might not be possible to achieve much improvement in collection efficiency. A promising long-term policy option might thus be restructuring the ministry to achieve a truly integrated national programme.

resources the government devotes to enforcement. The government needs to weigh the use of resources for compliance against the use of resources for other purposes.

Furthermore the courts may be ineffective. Thus enforcement action is time consuming, subject to considerable delays and weak in collecting outstanding contributions or in imposing penalties.

In some countries the government provides matching contributions to the social security scheme. If the government is having financial problems, it may not pursue contribution evasion because reducing contribution evasion would increase the matching contributions it needed to pay.

Contribution evasion occurs when the three following conditions coincide.

1. Employees either prefer non-payment of contributions or are reluctant to report non-payment to authorities.

2. Employers wish to evade or place a low priority on making social security contributions relative to other expenses.

3. Government enforcement tolerates, or is inadequate to prevent, evasion. Evasion of social security contributions is a common problem in both defined benefit and defined contribution social schemes. A number of different factors may cause it, with some factors being the primary cause in some countries but having little effect in others.

Notes

[1] The extension has been analysed by Cowell (1990), Slemrod (1992), Tanzi and Shome (1993) and others, and the literature has been surveyed by Alm (1996). Manchester (1997) discusses economic effects of social security contribution.

[2] The role of collection costs in determining the rate of mandatory contributions and taxes is discussed in Kenny and Toma (1997).

[3] This analysis is based on Vroman (1996), but not all conclusions reached here should be attributed to that study.

PENSION TRANSFERS AND THE
REDISTRIBUTION OF INCOME

11

This chapter examines redistribution under different types of pension schemes and discusses how their design and financing can be adapted to achieve the desired allocation of incomes. Related issues elsewhere in the book include the redistributional effects of contribution evasion (Chapter 10), progressivity as an issue in the design of retirement benefits (Chapter 3), other economic effects of pension schemes (Chapter 13) and policies to avoid the regressive effects of fixed costs of mandatory defined contribution schemes (Chapter 19).

All pension schemes have redistributive elements: they receive contributions from the active members of the workforce during the earning part of their lives, pay benefits to pensioners when they are retired and no longer working and, as a consequence, the distribution of income between the young and the old is different from what it would otherwise have been. These transfers between generations make up by far the greatest part of the redistributive functions of pension schemes.

But governments design pension systems to be redistributive for a number of other reasons. Income is redistributed towards those who die later than other people and away from those who die early. Transfers are greater to those who retire early because of disabilities. In many cases there are ceilings and floors to pension contributions and benefits which alter both the revenue collected from some individuals and the benefits received by others. Governments may design the pension scheme in order to guarantee adequate retirement incomes for retirees who were in low-paid employment while working, or whose accrual of pension benefits was reduced because they were temporarily out of work for reasons such as sickness, unemployment or family responsibilities.[1]

Redistribution between generations may also be desired to share the benefits of economic growth, or to provide decent pensions for people who had low lifetime incomes due to an economic depression or war. And in some circumstances the redistribution may be fortuitous, arising from unforeseen changes in earnings, interest rates, the longevity of retirees, the old-age dependency ratio, or the gender balance of workers and those entitled to a pension. Redistribution from upper-income to lower-income workers is generally seen as an essential feature of a pension system, but opinions differ as to how much is appropriate and the desire of governments to shift income distribution also raises questions about how this can be done equitably, both for those who contribute and for those entitled to benefits. On occasions the schemes may act in an adverse direction, either because of the way they are designed or because of political pressure which favours the benefits received by powerful groups, such as the military or public servants. Such redistribution may occur either through the social security scheme itself, through exclusion from the social security scheme (for example, for the self-employed or those in the informal sector) or through membership in a special system for a particular occupation or employer.

All the effects mentioned above clearly result in a distribution of income which is different from what it might otherwise have been, as between the retired and the active, high-income earners and low-income earners, and various other categories of workers, such as the disabled, those who retire early and those who die prematurely. But it is extremely difficult to assess what would happen if such redistribution did not occur. In the absence of the pension scheme individuals will have made alternative arrangements (through their own savings or by relying on their families, for example) and there may also have existed other public programmes, especially social assistance and anti-poverty allowances, which would have influenced the distribution of income in the absence of an articulated pension scheme. Thus there is no clear-cut benchmark against which to measure the redistributive effects of a pension scheme. Although the general direction of the redistribution seems relatively clear, it is not possible to put an estimate on its magnitude.

Distinguishing between the distribution of wealth and the distribution of income is vital. In some pension schemes, such as defined contribution schemes operated on an individual basis, individuals accumulate wealth during their working lifetimes and this wealth is held by the scheme as their individual property. In other schemes, notably public social security defined benefit schemes, individuals do not accumulate wealth but instead accumulate promises of future income, and no specific value is placed on the capital value of the promise.[2] Thus the distribution of wealth may differ from one type of scheme to another, although the distribution of actual income may remain unchanged.

Distinctions also need to be made between insurable and non-insurable risks and current income and lifetime income. For an individual, if part of his or her contribution is set aside to cover unforeseeable and insurable contingencies, such as invalidity, he or she will have received some value from this insurance, even if the need to claim its benefits never arises. In this case the redistribution of income has only a limited meaning. Equally, if the present value of the pension which he or she receives up to the time of death exactly matches the present value of the contributions made during his or her working life, there is no transfer from the individual to anyone else in society over the course of his or her lifetime, although clearly the pension scheme has enabled him or her to transfer income from work to retirement.

These issues leave the topic of this chapter on rather murky ground, and what follows can provide only a broad review of some of the main issues. In particular, it does not address the broader (and more difficult) question of whether redistribution would have occurred in the absence of a social security scheme.

INTERGENERATIONAL REDISTRIBUTION

There are two main sources of intergenerational redistribution commonly associated with pay-as-you-go schemes: the maturation of the scheme and population ageing. There are also intergenerational effects of funded schemes.

Maturation of the scheme

Intergenerational redistribution occurs when a defined benefit scheme is created and the first generations of participants receive benefits that exceed the value of their contributions. This occurs especially when the scheme is financed on a pay-as-you-go basis.[3] Similar redistribution may also take place, but to a lesser extent, when a scheme is modified, either to improve or to curtail the benefit structure. Governments may wish to make new provisions fully effective quickly, considering the needs of the beneficiary population. Early generations of participants in defined benefit schemes normally become entitled to a fraction of the regular benefit or to a minimum pension once they have accumulated a few years of credit. The state earnings-related pension scheme (SERPS), established in the United Kingdom in 1978, started to pay full pensions in 1998 and will become fully mature in 2027 (Davies, 1996). The determination of benefits paid to early generations of retirees is highly flexible. Those benefits are financed from current contributions (on a pay-as-you-go or partial funding basis).

Notional defined contribution schemes are well adapted to situations of conversion, where credits accumulated in a previous scheme entitle the first generation of pensioners to a high pension. This explains, at least partly, the interest in those schemes for countries like Latvia, Poland and Sweden, which are reforming their pension systems.

With fully funded schemes the first generations of contributors do not gain from intergenerational redistribution if the amount of benefit is based strictly on the contributions they had paid. Early generations of retirees could be entitled to anti-poverty benefits that would take the form of an income-tested benefit or a minimum benefit. In the context of a conversion from a pay-as-you-go system to a funded system, the benefits paid to workers retiring in the years following the introduction of the new scheme are based on the entitlements in the old one.

With fully funded schemes, if full benefits are paid to the early generations of retirees, they must be financed from extra revenues such as state revenues or state borrowing, or special contributions used as a solidarity tax. The question of the double burden borne by the working generation during the transition from an unfunded to a funded scheme is discussed in box 11.1.

Population ageing

A key factor which drives pension costs is the old-age dependency ratio, defined as the ratio of the population over a certain age (commonly age 60 or 65) to the population of working age (often set as age groups 15–59 or 20–64). These ratios have been rising in most countries for a half-century or more. Further increases are projected in the next few decades. Unless people retire later or become entitled to a lower benefit, a growth in the old-age dependency ratio leads to an increase in the total level of pension expenditure, and hence contribution or savings rates, since pensions are paid out of current GDP. Nevertheless the redistribution implications of this increase in the level of transfers for different individuals, or successive generations of participants, may vary, depending on the type of pension scheme and the way it is financed.

Both a reduction in birth rates and an increase in life expectancy, especially post-retirement life expectancy, increase the old-age dependency ratio. The redistribution implications of those changes differ, however, and they are discussed below. At this stage it is assumed that the demographic changes are fully anticipated.

Regardless of the type of pension scheme, an increase in the length of time that workers expect to live in retirement raises the lifetime cost of providing them a given monthly income. When this occurs, the choices facing workers are the same under all types of pension schemes. They must make higher contributions during their working years, extend their working lives or accept lower retirement incomes. Successive generations of participants will pay higher contributions if life expectancy at retirement increases, but the age of entitlement and the benefit level remain unchanged. Figure 11.1 shows the necessary progression of the contribution rate to provide a fixed replacement rate for successive generations of participants in the context of a rapid increase in life expectancy. It corresponds roughly to the development of life expectancy in Japan over the last four decades. Life expectancy at age 60 has increased by about one-third in Japan since 1950. In 1994 it was 20.4 years for males and 25.3 years for females, compared with 15 years for males and 17 years for females in 1950.

The effect of an increase in life expectancy on contribution rates is shown for a traditional defined benefit pay-as-you-go (PAYG) scheme and for a defined contribution (DC) scheme.[4] The contribution rate of a funded scheme has to be raised at an earlier stage to achieve the target replacement rate, and to avoid transferring part of the contribution burden to the following generations.[5] With pay-as-you-go defined benefit schemes, the contribution rate is only increased when the increase in the duration of retirement becomes effective.

Box 11.1 Funding pensions: The individual and the economy
It is frequently thought that pensions can be funded in advance by saving and building up financial assets from which pensions can later be paid upon. In addition it is thought that the process of saving will enable higher levels of investment to be achieved, which in turn will increase future GDP and permit higher pensions to be paid. If this view is correct, it clearly opens possibilities for coping with the consequences of ageing populations. Pension funds can be accumulated when the population structure is relatively young. When the population structure becomes older, the funds can be reduced to pay for the growing numbers of pensioners without increasing the burden of support required from younger workers. This scenario is one of the arguments put forward by proponents of funded pension schemes.

For individuals the way this works is the following. People who wish to save for their own retirement may do so, either as individuals or as part of some group arrangement, often in a funded occupational scheme to which their employer also contributes. The mechanism is a simple one. During the individual's working life, contributions are paid into an account which accumulates interest and builds up capital. On retirement, when there are no more earnings, this account is run down to provide for current consumption: either directly or through the purchase of an annuity which will provide a regular stream of income until the individual dies. Obviously the higher the rate of interest, the larger the contributions; or the longer the working life, the larger will be the capital on retirement and the higher the ultimate pension. There are risks. The rate of return is not known in advance, and the individual may end up saving more or less than he or she needs. The individual may die earlier or later than expected, but on average, and over a lifetime, the individual accounts can be expected to be in balance, with withdrawals in retirement matching savings during active life.

Collectively, however, and at the level of the whole economy, things do not work this way. Even if funds of financial assets have been established in advance, it is not possible – except on a limited scale – to carry over consumption goods from one year to another, or to ensure that they are directed uniquely at pensioners. The point is illustrated in table 11.1, which shows how the annual national accounts might look for a hypothetical population of 100 (25 retired, 75 active) and a total gross domestic product of 10,000. In this highly simplified example, the economy is pictured as running a small balance of payments deficit which is funded by an equal volume of transfers from abroad. The income of active persons is set at 91 per cent of national income and includes both earnings and profits. The income of retired persons is therefore 9 per cent of national income, includes no earnings and on a per capita basis is only one-quarter of that received by active persons. However the per capita consumption of retirees is nearly three-quarters of the per capita consumption of active persons. It must be financed by dissavings on the part of retirees, something they are able to do by selling their stock of financial assets to active persons. Active persons must save 24 per cent of GDP, which is sufficient to provide not only for investment in fixed assets and stocks (here pictured as 15 per cent of GDP) but also to purchase the financial assets sold by retired persons (an additional 9 per cent of GDP).

The balance is clearly a fragile one. If the proportion of retirees in the population increases (from, say, 25 to 30 per cent), or if their consumption relative to that of active persons increases (because interest rates increase), something has to give. The number of options is limited:

- stock building might be reduced, but this option provides very limited resources;
- gross fixed investment might be reduced, but this will reduce future GDP and economic growth;
- government consumption might be reduced, but this may result in reduced services such as education, health or defence;
- the current external balance may be widened, but this is not a long-term option;
- the per capita consumption of retirees – and the implied replacement rate – might be reduced, but this would break the implicit contract between retirees and active workers.

None of these options appears particularly palatable, optimal in terms of economic development or feasible in terms of the economic and political instruments which might be brought to bear.

Three features of this framework are important. First, the level of GDP is fixed. It is a consequence of the total productive capacity of the economy, which in turn will have been influenced by past levels of investment. But it is not influenced by

Table 11.1   Annual expenditure on GDP and annual national income (hypothetical example)

Expenditure on GDP		Incomes generated by GDP	
Personal consumption expenditure by retirees	1 600	Wages and salaries of active persons	7 800
Personal consumption expenditure by actives	6 700	Profits received by active persons	1 300
Total personal consumption expenditure	8 300	Total income of active persons	9 100
Government consumption expenditure	400	Wages and salaries received by retired persons	0
Gross fixed investment	1 400	Profits received by retired persons	700
Increase in stocks	100	Total income of retired persons	700
Exports minus imports	−200	Transfers from abroad	200
Gross domestic product	10 000	Gross national income	10 000
Population of retirees	25	Savings by actives	2 400
Population of actives	75	Dissaving by retirees	−900
Total population	100	Total net savings	1 500
Per capita consumption of retirees	64	Per capita income of retirees	28
Per capita consumption of actives	89	Per capita income of actives	121
Ratio of per capita consumption	0.72	Ratio of per capita incomes	0.23

Source: ILO estimates.

what happens in the current year. Second, the ability of retirees to dissave will be made easier if they have previously built up financial assets, which they can later sell to active persons. But this sale of financial assets does not in itself result in additional new resources in the current year. Third, it is not possible to make room for more retirees without either reducing other components of GDP or reducing the implied per capita replacement rate.

Thus for all practical purposes, and at an aggregate level, funded pension schemes operate as pay-as-you-go schemes under which the consumption of today's pensioners is drawn from the consumption of today's workers. There is a conflict between the perception of individuals and the macroeconomic constraint just described. How are the two to be reconciled, and what happens to the money which individuals save for their retirement? There are at least two possibilities, depending on whether or not the additional savings result in increased gross fixed investment.

If the retirement savings of individuals do not result in higher fixed investment, an inflation of asset prices will occur. The volume of money seeking a financial investment will increase relative to the (unchanged) level of real fixed assets, with the result that asset prices will increase. There will be no increase in GDP resulting from an increase in real fixed capital, but instead the real rate of return on financial investments will decline. Pensioners and active persons will end up sharing the same total level of consumption, and if one group is to increase its level of consumption that will mean a reduction in the level of consumption of the other.

If the retirement savings of individuals result in higher real investment, it can be expected that the capital stock, and hence future GDP, will be increased. Both profits and wages will rise. If they grow in the same proportion, there will be no change in the capacity of the economy to provide for a higher replacement rate for the same number of pensioners or to provide for more pensioners at the same replacement rate. If the profits received by pensioners increase proportionately more than the profits plus earnings received by active workers, pensioners may be able to increase their share of total consumption, but only by reducing the share received by active workers. What matters here is not the size of GDP and total consumption, but the share of GDP and consumption flowing respectively to pensioners and active workers (that is, the overall replacement rate). To increase the share flowing to pensioners means that the share flowing to active persons must be reduced.

Of course the pension funds might invest abroad, with the implication that the country would operate a deficit on capital account and a surplus on current account. These flows would be reversed when the funds were drawn down and the country began to import more than it exported. This transfers the problem from a national to a global scale and would clearly be most advantageous if the pension funds from ageing populations were invested in countries whose populations were younger. But the problem does not go away simply by being globalized.

Another possibility is that the process of increasing asset prices would lead to financial speculation about their further increases, and hence fuel additional increases in asset prices. This might alter the share of profits – especially in the form of capital gains – flowing to pensioners, but ultimately the bubble would burst, especially when pensioners wished to cash in their assets in return for pensions, and the consequent reversal of asset prices would be correspondingly more abrupt.

Much also depends on the circumstances in which funded defined contribution schemes are being introduced. If the funded scheme is being introduced in a situation where no previous pension scheme exists, the scenario will follow the one described above. There will be a period during which the financial assets of funded pension schemes grow rapidly. This corresponds to times when there are few individuals with entitlements to a pension but there are many contributors. Eventually the number of pensioners will increase and, provided the demographics are stable, equilibrium will be reached in which withdrawals for pensions will equal savings by contributors and net savings will be zero. However if the demographics are not stable, that is, if the population structure is ageing, the number of pensioners will increase relative to the number of contributors, the number of people in the dissaving part of their lives will increase relative to the number in the saving part, and the scheme as a whole will result in a net reduction of savings.

In many cases, however, funded schemes are likely to be introduced as a replacement for a public, pay-as-you-go social insurance scheme which will continue to be responsible for providing pensions for those who have contributed to it, at the same time that contributors will also be setting aside savings as part of their funded scheme. There will be a transition period under which some pensions, or part of them, will continue to be paid by the old pay-as-you-go scheme, while the new funded scheme and its pension payments are expanded. How is the transition to be financed?

One popular impression is that, in such circumstances, the transitional generation will be required to contribute twice: once in the form of savings for its own pensions, and again in the form of contributions to the pay-as-you-go scheme for the pensions of the current generation of retirees. However this impression is also incorrect. There are many ways in which the transition can be financed without calling for double contributions.

If a country decides to change its pension regime from a pay-as-you-go to an individual-funded system, there are a number of courses it can adopt to ensure that entitlements built up under the existing pay-as-you-go scheme are honoured, while at the same time ensuring that individual contributions are collected under the funded scheme. First, it may require the active population to contribute, both to the existing pay-as-you-go scheme and to the new funded scheme. Alternatively the government may borrow from the financial markets amounts sufficient to pay its obligations under pay-as-you-go, leaving workers to make their full contributions under the new individual-funded scheme, but not the old pay-as-you-go one. Or it may allow individuals to borrow in order to meet their double contributions. Finally the government may simply pay its obligations from general finances, raising taxes to do so. For some time after the reform date, workers will be retiring with mixed pensions, partly acquired under the old pay-as-you-go scheme, partly saved under the new funded one, but as time passes, payments for pay-as-you-go entitlements and the need for pay-as-you-go revenue will diminish until the pay-as-you-go component eventually disappears.

If the two schemes are intended to be equivalent, in the sense that the income of retirees does not change, the question arises of what happens to the financial flows which ensure this income. The answer depends on how the transition is financed. If the government covers the pay-as-you-go component by borrowing, it will simply be borrowing part of the savings under the funded scheme being placed on the financial market which are not yet needed for pensions. If contributors are asked to contribute twice, once to pay-as-you-go and once to the individual-funded scheme, they may either borrow back the unused money themselves or the government will borrow it and make a corresponding reduction in taxes. If governments increase taxes to pay the pay-as-you-go component, contributors may borrow back their savings to pay their additional taxes. Or they may make countervailing reductions in other savings. Clearly any method or mixture of methods of financing the transition is likely to cause considerable turbulence in financial markets, together with increased transaction costs, and may result in a national economy which in aggregate saves more or less than it did previously. What it will not do – by definition – is to alter either the flow of money to retirees or the net contributions and savings set aside by active workers.

Whatever way is chosen, it is clear that, in aggregate terms, no generation is required to pay twice. Indeed, if the active generation were required to pay simultaneously its old pay-as-you-go contributions in addition to its savings under a new funded scheme, what would happen to the money? As indicated earlier, it would either result in a very large macroeconomic imbalance between savings and investment, or very large and self-defeating increases in asset prices – either way would prevent funded schemes behaving at an aggregate level in the same way as pay-as-you-go schemes.

Differences in the timing of the increase in the contribution rate resulting from anticipated changes in post-retirement mortality should have limited redistributive implications. The illustration above refers to rapid increases in life expectancy that were fully anticipated. In most countries, life expectancy does not increase so rapidly, and a significant increase in the expected duration of retirement could well lead to a mixture of increased contributions and reduced benefits that would limit the degree of redistribution. Moreover episodes of high growth of life expectancy generally follow rapid economic development that makes providing a given level of pensions more affordable, while limiting the adverse consequences on pension costs of those demographic changes.

Following a reduction in birth rates, the number of people entering the labour market will eventually grow at a reduced rate or even decline. This means that the number of workers available to support each retired person will decline. With a defined benefit pay-as-you-go scheme, successive generations of contributors will therefore have to a pay a higher contribution rate if the benefit provisions are unchanged and successive generations of beneficiaries become entitled to the same benefit value at retirement. This has clear redistributive implications. The impact of changes in birth rates may be illustrated by

Figure 11.1   Contribution rates and duration of retirement

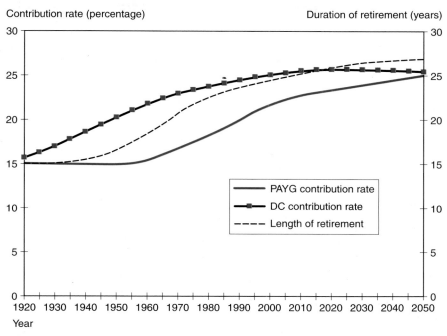

Source: ILO estimates.

looking at a hypothetical scheme that covers a constant percentage of the working-age population of a country and pays benefits to the same percentage of older persons. Figure 11.2 shows the development of such a scheme for the Japanese population. It is assumed that people start to contribute at age 20 and become entitled to a benefit equal to 40 per cent of final earnings (and indexed in line with wages) at retirement. People are first assumed to retire at 60 (constant retirement age) and in a second scenario retirement age is assumed to increase along with changes in life expectancy, in order to maintain constant the proportion of adult life spent in retirement. From an initial level of 60 in 1950, retirement age increases to 67 by 2020.

Assuming a constant retirement age, the pay-as-you-go contribution rate increases from 7 per cent of wages to reach a maximum of 33 per cent around 2050. It increases partly because of the greater number of people reaching retirement age (population structure) and partly because of the greater number of retirement years. Under the scenario of a gradual increase of retirement age, successive generations are entitled to the same benefit value at retirement and the increase in the contribution rate is then due entirely to changes in the population structure. Under these conditions the contribution rate is stable

Figure 11.2 PAYG contribution rates with constant and variable retirement age

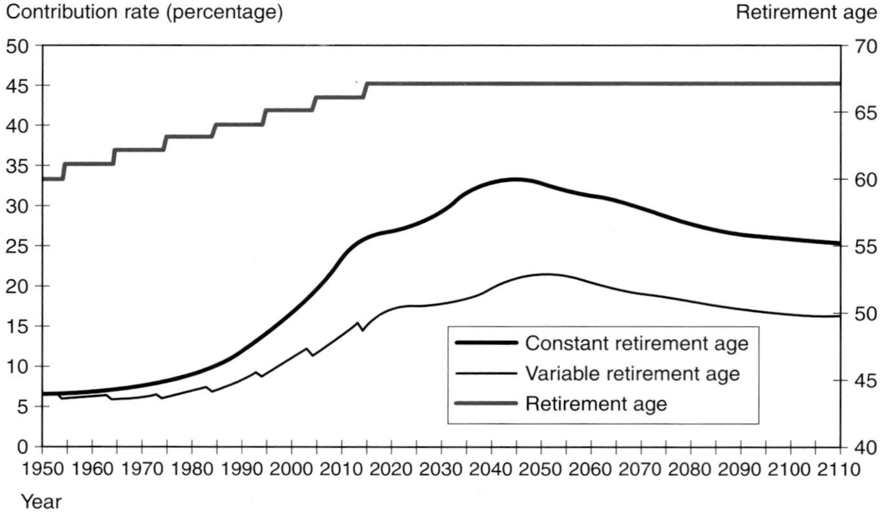

Source: ILO estimates.

to the year 2000, but it increases thereafter when the number of people reaching retirement age exceeds the number of people joining the labour market. The generations contributing in those years will have to pay a higher contribution rate to become entitled to the same benefit value.

Pre-funding pensions is commonly regarded as a way to limit the redistributive implications of a change in birth rates. A defined benefit scheme can be pre-funded (either partially or totally) by increasing the contribution rate to build a trust fund. The investment income earned on those assets – and ultimately the sale of assets – can be used to finance the pension expenditure at a later date. The same logic applies to funded defined contribution schemes where participants save during their working years and use the money accumulated to finance their individual pension once they have retired.

Figure 11.3 shows simulations of the development of the contribution rate for the hypothetical scheme discussed above, and for different financing options, as well as the effect of having the scheme either partially funded or fully funded.[6] It shows that increasing the funding level of the scheme reduces the sensitivity of the contribution rate to changes in birth rates, assuming that the rate of return is immune to those demographic changes. The annual rate of return credited on accumulated contributions was assumed to exceed the rate of wage growth by a constant 2 per cent throughout the projection period.[7]

Along with changes of population structure, the relative number of people wishing either to buy or to sell financial assets will change. A large number of people willing to buy financial assets to fund their pension could inflate asset

Figure 11.3   Contribution rates for PAYG, partial and full funding: Constant retirement age

Contribution rate (percentage)

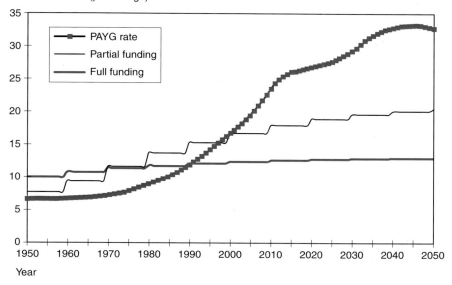

Year

Source: ILO estimates.

prices, and asset prices could fall when a large number of retirees try to sell their assets to the younger generation of workers. Such changes in asset prices affect the rate of return earned by successive generations of participants.

An increase in the proportion of the population in the older age groups should also increase the level of capital stock available per worker. This could reduce the rate of return and contribute to the devaluation of the capital owned in pension funds. The effect of population ageing on the relative size of the labour force and stock of capital is discussed in box 11.2.

Thus funded schemes are not necessarily immune from demographic changes. This important point is often overlooked. In a country where capital markets are highly sensitive to demographic changes, population ageing could have redistributive implications for funded schemes similar to those of pay-as-you-go schemes. Transactions taking place within the retirement system, however, are only a subset of all capital market transactions. Asset prices are determined not just by what is happening within the retirement income system, but by the aggregate of all sales and purchases in the capital markets. The effect of demographic changes would then be spread across the whole capital market, and would not be borne entirely by pension contributors and beneficiaries. Other factors could also affect the total level of savings and

Box 11.2 Simulation of the impact of population ageing on the labour and capital markets

Neither the labour market nor the capital market is totally immune from changes in the population structure associated with population ageing. The proportion of the population of working age groups varies over time, along with the changes in the population structure. This should also affect the total stock of savings, or at least retirement savings, considering that people save during their working years and dissave during their old age.

This box illustrates potential effects of population ageing. It provides a simple example where both men and women are assumed to enter the labour market at age 20 and to retire at age 65. It is further assumed that active people save a fixed percentage of their earnings throughout their career and deplete those savings uniformly over their retirement years. The savings rate, which may be viewed as a contribution rate of a pension scheme, is assumed constant over time; it does not vary by age and it is fixed throughout the projection period.

The Japanese population is used as the reference population. Fertility rates are currently low in Japan (1.5 children per woman on average) and life expectancy has increased considerably over the last 50 years. Consequently the Japanese population will age rapidly over the next decades. On the basis of these assumptions, the total population would grow until approximately 2010, when it would reach close to 130 million people; it would then decrease gradually to 110 million in 2050.[8] According to the assumptions used for the period 2050–2100, the size of the total population is relatively stable then. Details are shown in figure 11.4.

Figure 11.4   Japan: Population by age groups

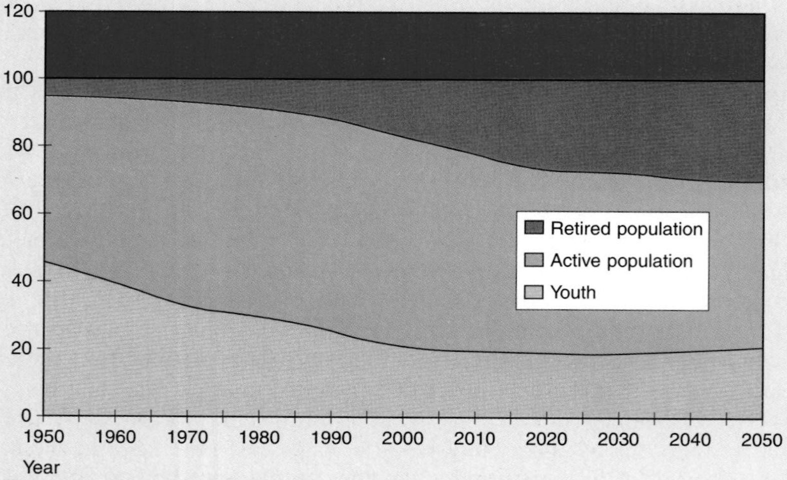

Source: UN population estimates.

investments. Foreign transactions can provide another source of offsetting flows.

Pension specialists are just beginning to analyse the effects on the economy of a major liquidation of pension assets.[9] It cannot be predicted at this time what effect a change in the old-age dependency ratio – produced by a decline in the birth rate – would have on the ability of an advance-funded system to pay promised retirement benefits.

Intergenerational effects of funded schemes

Population ageing will cause future generations of participants in defined benefit pay-as-you-go schemes to receive a lower rate of return on their contributions. Contribution rates shown in figures 11.2 and 11.3 clearly highlighted the fact that the pay-as-you-go rate has to be increased substantially over time in order to maintain the scheme in actuarial balance and, as a result, the implicit rate of return earned decreases.

Successive generations of participants in a fully funded scheme cannot expect to earn a constant rate of return on their contributions either. They will have to pay a different contribution rate or accept a different benefit level because of the variations in the average rate of return earned over their period of participation in the scheme (both as a contributor and a beneficiary). Individual fully funded defined contribution schemes do not redistribute between generations because the value of the benefits paid to an individual has to equal the value of accumulated contributions. Nonetheless the outcome is similar in some respects to defined benefit pay-as-you-go schemes: the rates of return earned on contributions vary from one generation to the next and, therefore, successive generations either have to pay a different contribution rate or receive a different benefit level.

This can be demonstrated by looking at the economic experience of major industrial countries over the last 40 years. Table 11.2 shows average figures of wage growth and interest rates for the period 1953–95 in Germany, Japan, the United Kingdom and the United States.[10] Figures are shown in real terms. Over the first two decades of the period, wages grew relatively rapidly everywhere except in the United States, and real interest rates were fairly low. In all these countries the rate of wage growth exceeded the interest rate over the period 1953–72. In the last two decades, wage growth was slower and real interest rates rose in all four countries. Since 1973 the real interest rate has been consistently higher than the rate of growth of real wages in three of the four countries, while in Japan it was higher at least until 1993.

Table 11.2 also shows the contribution rate required to produce a target pension of 50 per cent of the average wage, using the average rate of wage growth and of investment returns for each period.[11] These data make it clear that the contribution rates required to produce the target pension replacement rate are extraordinarily sensitive to the economic environment. Actual experience

Table 11.2 Real wage growth, interest rates and implied defined contribution rates in four OECD countries, 1953–95

Periods	Germany			Japan			United Kingdom			United States		
	Wage growth rate	Interest rate	Contribution rate	Wage growth rate	Interest rate	Contribution rate	Wage growth rate	Interest rate	Contribution rate	Wage growth rate	Interest rate	Contribution rate
1st 10 yrs (1953–62)	8.36	3.79	64.19	9.5	5.32	57.68	5.84	0.98	70.51	2.71	1.42	28.61
2nd 10 yrs (1963–72)	6.06	3.87	35.98	7.67	4.32	47.81	5.22	2.49	41.66	1.84	-0.56	39.04
3rd 10 yrs (1973–82)	3.43	2.99	22.43	2.24	2.84	16.58	1.32	-1.23	40.7	-1.21	2.92	5.2
4th 10 yrs (1983–92)	2.66	4.96	9.84	1.26	3.5	9.93	2.68	4.06	13.09	1.02	4.96	5.72
First 21 yrs (1953–74)	7.13	3.75	48.51	8.48	4.6	54.21	5.43	1.71	53.51	2.17	0.33	33.42
Next 22 yrs (1974–95)	2.57	3.99	12.93	1.82	2.98	13.95	1.78	1.92	18.95	-0.13	4.12	5.09
Full 43 yrs (1953–95)	4.77	3.87	25.5	5.02	3.77	28.07	3.55	1.82	32.16	0.99	2.25	13.5

Source: Thompson (1998).

at several points in the history of these countries saw wage growth so high relative to real interest rates that the contribution rate required to produce the target replacement rate under the simple model exceeded 50 per cent (for example, the 1950s in Japan, Germany and the United Kingdom and the 1960s in Japan). At other times, wage growth was so slow relative to the level of interest rates that the target pension could have been produced with a contribution rate of less than 10 per cent (for example, the 1970s and 1980s in the United States and the 1980s in Germany and Japan).[12]

Variations in the level of contributions and benefits across generations could be reduced, not by substituting a defined contribution for a defined benefit scheme, but rather by designing pension schemes that include both defined benefit and defined contribution components. The questions of diversification and mixed systems are particularly important because of risks and uncertainties about future changes (discussed in depth in Chapter 12). Nevertheless greater stability in the contribution rate and the benefit level of successive generations of participants could be achieved by a proper mix of different pension components, even in a hypothetical context of total certainty where all changes are properly anticipated.

A mixed system (either a partially funded system or the combination of a pay-as-you-go scheme and a fully funded defined contribution scheme) limits the variability of the contribution rate compared to what is achieved with a pure pay-as-you-go system or a fully funded system. It is possible to limit the sensitivity of a pension system to economic and demographic changes by a combination of components that react differently to different types of changes.

Intergenerational transfers as a whole

Transfers taking place via the pension system are a subset of all the transfers being made between the economically active population and the retirees. Moreover there are also transfers to children and inactive or unemployed persons of working age. These consist of transfers in cash or in kind, and they can be achieved through different formal and informal transfer mechanisms. Assessing the redistributive implications of pension systems without looking at other forms of transfers gives a partial and biased view.

Important transfers between workers and pensioners occur outside the pension system. Each generation passes on to the next the stock of public wealth, net of public debt. Private wealth transfers follow or anticipate death. Informal transfers take place in the family or the community. Most transfers in the informal sector are in kind or informal cash transfers, such as providing shelter and food for children, older persons, disabled or unemployed members of the family, the clan or the village. In the formal sector many of these transfers have largely been commissioned by societies to the formal social protection schemes. This is the case in most OECD and Central and Eastern European countries.

Table 11.3 Estimated percentage of total income transferred to inactives worldwide, by region, 1950–2050

Regions	Transfers to retirees only			Transfers to all inactives		
	1950	1995	2050	1950	1995	2050
I Constant replacement rates, retirement age and labour force participation rates						
OECD: Europe	20.7	26.7	40.6	45.2	42.3	49.3
OECD: others	15.4	19.8	32.3	41.3	36.3	42.9
ECEU	13.3	22.7	34.7	35.1	39.6	43.4
Central Asia	15.5	12.9	25.0	39.5	34.1	36.9
Asia	9.0	10.1	24.6	34.5	31.8	37.8
Arab states	13.3	9.5	20.0	51.3	47.2	44.3
Africa	7.6	8.1	13.0	37.8	39.5	31.1
Latin America + Caribbean	11.8	12.1	28.4	47.9	39.9	44.1
All regions	11.7	13.0	23.9	37.4	34.4	38.0
II Increasing labour force participation rates for women						
OECD: Europe	20.7	26.7	37.6	45.2	42.3	45.0
OECD: others	15.4	19.8	30.1	41.3	36.3	39.3
ECEU	13.3	22.7	33.5	35.1	39.6	41.8
Central Asia	15.5	12.9	23.1	39.5	34.1	33.5
Asia	9.0	10.1	20.9	34.5	31.8	30.7
Arab states	13.3	9.5	13.2	51.3	47.2	26.7
Africa	7.6	8.1	11.0	37.8	39.5	24.8
Latin America + Caribbean	11.8	12.1	22.3	47.9	39.9	32.8
All regions	11.7	13.0	20.4	37.4	34.4	31.0
III Gradual increase of retirement age						
OECD: Europe	20.7	26.7	32.6	45.2	42.3	43.0
OECD: others	15.4	19.8	29.9	41.3	36.3	40.5
ECEU	13.3	22.7	31.3	35.1	39.6	40.4
Central Asia	15.5	12.9	22.1	39.5	34.1	34.0
Asia	9.0	10.1	22.3	34.5	31.8	35.7
Arab states	13.3	9.5	18.4	51.3	47.2	43.2
Africa	7.6	8.1	12.0	37.8	39.5	30.0
Latin America + Caribbean	11.8	12.1	26.2	47.9	39.9	42.3
All regions	11.7	13.0	21.9	37.4	34.4	36.1
IV Reduced benefits (from 75% in 2000 to 60% in 2050)						
OECD: Europe	20.7	26.7	35.3	45.2	42.3	45.5
OECD: others	15.4	19.8	27.7	41.3	36.3	39.6
ECEU	13.3	22.7	29.8	35.1	39.6	39.8
Central Asia	15.5	12.9	21.0	39.5	34.1	34.2
Asia	9.0	10.1	20.7	34.5	31.8	35.2
Arab states	13.3	9.5	16.7	51.3	47.2	42.7
Africa	7.6	8.1	10.7	37.8	39.5	29.6
Latin America + Caribbean	11.8	12.1	24.1	47.9	39.9	41.5
All regions	11.7	13.0	20.1	37.4	34.4	35.5
V All of the above (II, III, IV)						
OECD: Europe	20.7	26.7	26.2	45.2	42.3	36.8
OECD: others	15.4	19.8	25.2	41.3	36.3	37.6
ECEU	13.3	22.7	25.8	35.1	39.6	35.3
Central Asia	15.5	12.9	17.2	39.5	34.1	28.3
Asia	9.0	10.1	15.9	34.5	31.8	26.2
Arab states	13.3	9.5	10.0	51.3	47.2	23.8
Africa	7.6	8.1	8.4	37.8	39.5	22.5
Latin America + Caribbean	11.8	12.1	17.2	47.9	39.9	28.4
All regions	11.7	13.0	15.7	37.4	34.4	27.0

Source: ILO calculations.

The transfers taking place via the retirement pension scheme may make more sense when analysed in this more global context. In particular the payment of generous benefits to the first generation of pensioners of a pension scheme takes the place of family responsibilities of workers towards their old parents. In this context the capacity to adapt the pension scheme to reflect social and economic changes can be seen as a positive feature of pay-as-you-go schemes.

On the basis of normal consumption levels, policy analysts can establish a level of total social transfers society must make if it wants to provide a socially agreed-upon level of consumption for all individuals. Table 11.3 shows the results of estimates of the normal levels of transfers in the regions used as geographical aggregates throughout this book. The estimates refer to the period 1950 to 2050. They are based on a simple model which assumes that employed persons earn all the income in society (wages plus profits). The employed population shares its income with children, non-employed persons in the working-age group and retired older persons. The ratio of consumption of a child to an employed person is 0.25 to one, of a non-employed working age person to an employed person is 0.50 to one, and of a retired person to an employed person is 0.75 to one. The model produces the ratios of the three types of transfers to total earned annual income in the country and their sum, which describes the total amount of social transfers.[13]

The results permit three main observations.

1. The level of transfers to retirees will increase in all regions over the coming decades. The increase will be particularly large in Asia and Latin America, which are undergoing rapid demographic transformations. Between 1995 and 2050 the transfers to retirees will more than double relative to earned income. By then, under status quo conditions, those regions will have transfer to retirees ratios comparable to the current European ratio.

2. In no region (except perhaps Africa) will the total transfer rate change dramatically during the next five decades (figure 11.5). Within the umbrella of total transfers there will be a marked shift away from child and non-employed working-age transfers to old-age transfers.

3. For an unchanged level of income for the inactive old, the increase in transfers from the active to the inactive section of the population would be greatly reduced by either an increased retirement age or an increased female labour force participation rate.

The increased transfers benefiting retirees will be offset by reduced transfers to other groups. This result indicates the necessity of substantial shifts of resources between transfers benefiting the different clientele. It may also alter the balance between the portion of those transfers occurring through public programmes versus individual or informal arrangements (see figure 11.6).

As the population is ageing, a higher proportion of total transfers takes place through public mechanisms, since pensions and health care are often

Figure 11.5 Transfers to retirees

Percentage GDP

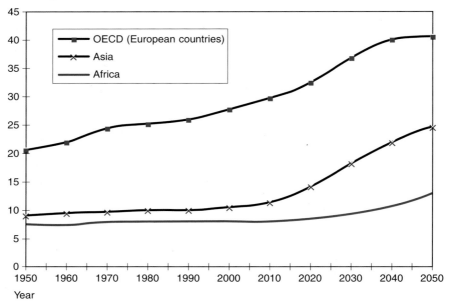

Source: ILO estimates.

publicly financed while expenditures benefiting children occur primarily through private transfers. The effect of future demographic changes on the public-private mix should vary significantly from country to country. It should be less important or even have the opposite effect in countries of French-speaking Africa, which currently have a high proportion of total population at a young age and where family benefits are an important component of the social protection scheme. In most OECD countries, where the coverage of the social security scheme is more extensive, a change of population structure should have a more limited effect on the balance between transfers occurring between public and private schemes (Cichon et al., 1999).

INTRAGENERATIONAL REDISTRIBUTION

Social security retirement pension schemes redistribute within generations of contributors and beneficiaries. Redistribution is needed to prevent poverty among retirees and to guarantee an adequate replacement rate among people with different characteristics or experiences. Social security may redistribute between high- and low-income people, males and females, and single and married people.

Figure 11.6 Transfers to all inactives

Percentage GDP

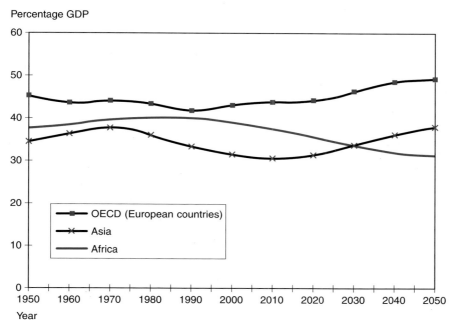

Year

Source: ILO estimates.

While some redistribution may be intended and explicitly pursued when implementing social security, some may be unintended and regressive.[14] A pension scheme can be either progressive or regressive depending on its provisions and how it is financed, including how administration costs are shared among participants. Characteristics differentiating groups of participants, such as mortality profiles and earnings and employment profiles, may also cause redistribution.

Design issues

Since defined benefit schemes are financed collectively, the equilibrium between inflows (contribution and investment income) and outflows (benefits and administrative costs) must be maintained for the scheme, but not necessarily for each individual. There is therefore flexibility in the design to allow for intra-generational redistribution.

With defined contribution schemes (either funded or notional), the amount of benefit paid to each contributor is established on the basis of the individual account balance. Progressive features can be added through subsidization of the

289

accounts of low-income workers. For example, they can be structured to provide guaranteed minimum benefits, as is done in Chile. Part of the contribution paid by high-income people could also be used as a "solidarity tax" and transferred to low-income people, as in Colombia. The government can make a periodic flat-rate contribution to the accounts of all contributors, as in Mexico. They can be structured so that the government pays matching contributions that are phased out at higher income levels, or ceilings can be set on the maximum amount of matching contributions.

Defined benefit schemes in some OECD countries allow workers to exclude years of low earnings to calculate the pension. This limits the reduction in the level of pension payments to people who have suffered periods of sickness, unemployment or temporary low earnings. Defined contribution schemes may allow governments to pay special contributions under such circumstances, but in practice virtually none does. Temporary periods of low earnings are generally not covered by specific provisions in defined contribution schemes, but general provisions designed to support low-income earners, such as a minimum pension, provide some form of a guarantee.

The way benefits are calculated under defined benefit schemes may perversely redistribute in favour of high-income earners. This occurs when only the earnings in the years preceding retirement (or the best earnings of the career) are taken into account to calculate the pension.[15] This is the case in many countries in Africa and in Central and Eastern Europe (see the statistical annex for more details). High-income earners generally have a steeper age-earnings profile and, therefore, limiting the reference period for calculating benefits to only a few years to calculate the pension will be more advantageous for them than for people with a more modest growth of earnings over time.

The way redistribution operates will also vary according to whether a unified scheme covers the whole population or special schemes apply to special groups. Social security law often explicitly excludes the civil service or the military. Special schemes exist in many countries, mainly because of the development at an early stage of schemes covering specific groups. Contracting out may be allowed for employers or individuals covered by at least equivalent pension provisions, although it is unusual; however it is a prominent feature of the British and Japanese systems. Redistribution is more easily achieved (although it is not necessarily more progressive) in a unified scheme covering different participants. Special schemes normally cover people earning higher salaries and enjoying greater employment security, as they are less likely to benefit from the redistributive provisions of the social security scheme.[16] Participants in the special schemes may still be covered by a basic tier that covers larger segments of the population and is designed to be highly redistributive, as in Australia or the United Kingdom. The development of special schemes could help to maintain a low benefit level of the base scheme. In such systems, the base scheme is more likely to rely on general revenue financing as a way to ensure redistribution between different groups.

The problem of partial coverage is fundamental when considering redistribution. If a scheme does not offer universal coverage, there is a real danger that schemes with a low level of coverage may be internally redistributive, but have a regressive effect overall through being supported by budgetary subsidies that are partly funded by consumption taxes paid by non-participants. In designing retirement benefit schemes, countries need to address this issue. If the slow extension of formal social security means an indefinite period of regressive net impact, the public policy justification for such extension may be weak.

Finally, qualifying conditions may redistribute under both defined benefit and defined contribution schemes. For instance, the minimum number of years required to qualify for a pension, or a minimum pension, limits the possibilities of redistribution in favour of people with limited entitlements. Provisions of defined benefit schemes that allow people who have accumulated many years of credit to retire early with an unreduced pension may have a redistributive effect if not compensated by the lower life expectancy of the people who started to contribute early.

Financing issues

Both defined benefit and defined contribution schemes may be subsidized by the state in a period of financial difficulty. Typically this would happen with defined benefit schemes in periods of high expenditure where an increase in the contribution rate is not considered acceptable. With defined contribution schemes, state subsidies would be needed if low rates of return on investments lead to pensions that are considered insufficient.

Pension schemes financed by payroll contributions are usually subsidized by governments through the tax system. Pension contributions and investment income of pension funds normally have preferential tax treatment. This is regressive since it primarily benefits middle- and upper-income workers.

Mortality and morbidity differentials

Defined benefit schemes may be regressive because wealthier people live longer and therefore receive benefits for longer periods (World Bank, 1994). The same argument applies for defined contribution schemes that provide annuities benefits. For people of the same sex, in most countries wealthier people tend to have higher life expectancy. However, when considering both men and women, women have longer life expectancy than males and tend to have lower incomes. In many countries poverty in old age is more prevalent among women than among men. Thus the effect of life expectancy on regressivity is more complex when considering both men and women.

Furthermore, while retirement benefits may be regressively distributed, the pension system may be progressive when taking into account other types of benefits. Higher morbidity rates among low-income people may increase the cost of providing disability benefits to them, and higher mortality might increase the cost of providing survivors' benefits.

Finally, practical ways to deal with this question of different mortality rates at each earnings level also raise concerns. Providing people with lump-sum benefits as a way of avoiding redistribution to higher-income workers does not ensure retirement income security. Opting for phased withdrawal will not allow people with shorter life expectancy to raise their pension level; it will simply modify the amount of savings left as a bequest. In other words, people who die early will have accumulated too much and those who live longer than was originally forecast might have to adjust their standard of living gradually downwards.

Insurance companies might offer better rates for annuities to men (because of their lower life expectancy on average) than to women and to people in a significantly worse health condition at the time of retirement, but it is not common practice to reduce the price of an annuity for people with limited savings. This is justified by the fixed cost incurred by insurance companies in issuing contracts and by the variations in mortality within each income group being greater than variations between income groups. Moreover the cost of providing disability and survivors' insurance could be made more expensive for low-income people because of the higher incidence of claims.

Individual management of retirement savings accounts and administrative costs

In comparison to traditional social security defined benefit schemes, defined contribution schemes may penalize low-income workers because of the lower rate of return those workers may receive and because of charges levied to cover administrative and transaction costs.

The individual management of retirement savings accounts can cause defined contribution schemes to be regressive, as lower-income workers tend to be less sophisticated in managing their financial accounts and are apt to receive a lower rate of return. In plans where the individual is responsible for managing the investment of the funds, low-income workers tend to invest in low-risk, low-expected return portfolios. In most mandatory defined contribution schemes the government bears part of the risk by providing different types of guarantees, but individuals still bear considerable financial market risk. Individuals differ in both their capacity and their preferences for bearing risk. It is sometimes argued that a benefit of the individualistic approach is that individuals can choose the amount of risk that matches their preference for risk. However individual preferences are to some extent dictated by earnings capacity, wealth level and financial knowledge and information. Lower-income workers tend to have less financial knowledge (Hinz et al., 1997). In comparison to traditional defined benefit plans, defined contribution plans have a regressive effect because of the preference of low-income workers for low-risk assets.

Table 11.4 Rates of return in individual account plans with portfolio choice, United States, 1990

Annual salary (US$)	Rate of return (per cent)
less than 20 000	11.3
20 000–29 999	11.9
30 000–39 999	12.0
40 000–49 999	11.8
50 000–59 999	12.3
60 000–69 999	12.3
70 000 or more	12.4

Source: US Thrift Savings Plan data for 1990.

Data from the Thrift Savings Plan for federal government workers in the United States, shown in table 11.4, indicate that lower-income workers tend to pick more conservative portfolios. These workers had a choice between a stock index fund, a mixed corporate bond and government bond fund, or a government bond fund. Chapter 6 indicates that even apparently small differences in the rate of return, as indicated in table 11.4, cause important differences in retirement income. This problem can be partially overcome by having pension savings managed by professional fund managers, and ultimately by having each fund manager offering one fund only. This is the case in Chile. Nonetheless contributors still have to choose between different fund managers, and one fund may not be appropriate for all contributors.

Transaction costs of investment trading and annuitization of benefits are largely fixed costs. The administrative costs of receiving contributions, paying benefits and maintaining a pension account are also primarily fixed costs, not varying by the amount in the account or the size of the transaction. This tends to make defined contribution schemes regressive, for three reasons. First, the charges levied by service providers for an account tend to follow the pattern of costs. Some defined contribution plans, as in Australia and the United Kingdom, charge a fixed entrance fee for opening an account. Defined contribution plans frequently charge both fixed and variable costs for maintaining individual accounts. In some accounts charges are waived for large account balances, or the fee diminishes as a percentage of the account balance as it grows. Because the primary costs to financial institutions of maintaining an individual account are fixed costs, low-income workers with small accounts generally bear the higher charges relative to their account balances than high-income workers. This causes a tendency for the net rate of return on individual accounts to be higher for large accounts, even when the gross rate of return does not vary by account size. While it could be argued that each worker should bear the cost of maintaining his or her account, this feature of defined contribution plans causes them to provide a lower rate of return to low-income workers who have small accounts, and thus causes these accounts to be regressive.

The importance of the effect of administrative charges depends on the level of the charges. If the charges are low, the effect is unimportant. Evidence from some countries, however, indicates that the charges as a percentage of contributions have been sizeable for workers with average contribution levels. In the United Kingdom women have lost up to a third of their savings in personal pensions in flat-rate administrative charges, while men have lost up to a quarter. The disadvantages women face are due to fixed charges, as few women earn throughout their working life and they generally earn less than men when they do work.

This source of regressiveness can be superficially eliminated by prohibiting pension management companies from charging fixed fees. If this is done, however, pension management companies may refuse to accept small accounts, or might seek subtler ways to avoid having low-income workers as clients, such as by locating offices where they would not be convenient for such workers.

Second, low-income workers tend to contribute intermittently to defined contribution plans, while expenses are often charged in each period, an additional factor which is causing defined contribution plans to be regressive. Low-income workers tend to contribute sporadically because they try to evade contributing while in the labour force, are apt to be in the labour force intermittently and are more likely to be unemployed.

Third, annuity prices vary across insurance companies. If low-income workers are less sophisticated in purchasing annuities than higher-income workers, they will receive a less favourable price. In the United Kingdom financial advisers are available to help workers choose annuities. The fixed-cost element in the pricing of financial advisers' services may also add to the regressiveness of defined contribution plans.

Available data support the argument that low-income workers receive lower net rates of return than higher-income workers in defined contributions plans. In the United Kingdom a study has found that, in contracted-out plans, smaller defined contribution plans that were subject to flat-rate charges either diminished in value or failed to grow, but this was not the case for plans with larger account balances (Legal & General Insurance plc, 1997; see also table 11.4).

Over the period 1981–90, the average net rate of return for a worker participating in one of the funds in the Chilean pension system with the maximum eligible earnings was 10.4 per cent, and for a worker with minimum eligible earnings the rate was 9.2 per cent (Habitat, 1991). Vittas and Iglesias (1991) showed that, over that period, low-income workers on average only received 7.5 per cent, in comparison with 10 per cent for a high-income worker. This is a substantial difference when compounded over the career of a worker, as it would cut the amount accumulated at retirement by about 40 per cent.

THE STRUCTURE OF PENSION SCHEMES

A pension scheme may be structured in different ways to achieve redistribution. A highly redistributive basic benefit, such as a flat-rate or an income-tested pension, could be introduced to guarantee a minimum level of benefit to all contributors or ultimately, to all older people in a country. A second scheme would then be primarily designed to achieve an objective of income replacement, but it could allow for some redistribution. Redistribution would be intended to achieve a higher degree of equity between people at comparable levels of income but with different characteristics (males v. females, single v. married) or facing different situations (unemployment or child rearing).

Pension schemes can also be designed to achieve the two objectives of poverty alleviation and income replacement in one single scheme. They can take the form of a defined benefit scheme that guarantees a higher replacement rate for low-income people. Alternatively they can be a defined contribution scheme that incorporates minimum guarantees or redistribution provisions such as those discussed in the section on design issues.

The decision to opt for a combined, or split, approach may be motivated by several factors. First, it could be decided to opt for a split approach because the anti-poverty component and the income-replacement component would cover different segments of the population. Canada, Denmark and Norway have a universal non-contributory benefit payable to all citizens on the basis of age and residence, while their employment-related pension schemes cover only the active part of the population.[17] Other developed countries have income-tested pensions that guarantee a minimum pension to all senior citizens. Participation in an earnings-related scheme (either public or private) may then be made compulsory or voluntary. Australia and New Zealand introduced a guaranteed minimum income in old age many years ago. More recently Australia made participation in private-funded schemes compulsory.

The coverage level of the anti-poverty and income-replacement component may also differ in developing countries. There could be a basic contributory pension that would reach a larger segment of the active population than the traditional earnings-related component. Earmarked anti-poverty programmes could also be introduced. (These questions are discussed in more detail in Chapter 19.)

A distinct anti-poverty scheme could also be introduced in countries where different groups of the active population are covered by distinct schemes. For instance, in the United Kingdom it is possible to contract out from the state earnings-related pension scheme, but all employees are covered by the basic state retirement pension (a flat-rate pension). In France, where there are special schemes covering different occupational groups, the anti-poverty provisions are organized differently. All schemes must guarantee the same level of minimum pension, but the state provides variable levels of subsidies for the different schemes.

Although designed to redistribute in favour of low-income workers, distinct anti-poverty mechanisms could prove to be regressive (or of limited progressivity) if they are financed from state revenues and if only a limited portion of the workforce is covered and eligible for minimum benefits. For instance, in Argentina a minimum pension is guaranteed to people with limited accumulated contributions and at least 30 years' coverage. In that country a significant proportion of the workforce (especially among low-income workers) does not contribute to a pension scheme on a regular basis and therefore will not be eligible for the minimum benefit financed by the state. Combining the components in one single scheme could make it easier to ensure that the scheme was self-financing and avoid the negative consequences of state financing in a context of limited coverage.

Conversely, in countries with extensive coverage, social security pensions can be made more progressive by financing at least part of pension expenditure with state revenues, and by providing higher benefits relative to income to low-income people. This can be achieved either in a single scheme or with two distinct components.

A redistributive mechanism should also be structured to make participation in a mandatory income replacement component more attractive and to encourage the development of complementary occupational pension schemes or voluntary retirement savings. Stand-alone income and asset-tested programmes may have the opposite effect (World Bank, 1994).

To have a distinct scheme designed to be highly redistributive makes the role of the different schemes more transparent and easier to understand by the population. In some countries a distinct anti-poverty component designed explicitly to redistribute might gain little political support. This argument has been made in the United States. In others, such as in Scandinavian countries, it could make the use of public money to finance pensions more acceptable because it is efficiently aimed at a needy population.

Having the anti-poverty and the income-replacement components combined in one scheme may ensure a greater stability of the redistribution provisions over time if they are considered as part of the pension entitlement. This would require pensions to be financed at least partially from contributions (rather than from state revenues), since people often feel that they have a stronger entitlement to a pension if they have paid pension contributions. In other countries, however, there may be a strong feeling of the poor being entitled to anti-poverty benefits simply because they are fellow citizens who are in need. This appears to be the case in Norway.

The way redistributive provisions are structured may also affect the level of administrative costs. Means-tested benefits are more expensive to administer than other benefits, although a statutory guaranteed minimum income scheme based strictly on the income level is less expensive to administer than a social assistance scheme taking into account other factors such as wealth or the family situation to determine the amount of benefits. Finally social security retirement benefits are but one aspect of benefits provided, or subsidized, by the government. A full analysis of the progressivity of government policy towards the aged would also need to consider disability benefits, survivors' benefits, the subsidization of occupational pensions through preferential tax treatment, and other government benefits directed towards the aged.

Redistribution takes place in all social security pension schemes properly designed to provide income security in retirement. Redistribution within generations is necessary to ensure a decent level of income to people who earned low levels of income during their working years (vertical equity). Redistribution may also take place between people at comparable levels of income but with different characteristics (men v. women, single v. married), and redistributive measures designed to grant pension credits during periods of temporary withdrawal from the labour force (for reasons such as child rearing, sickness or unemployment) may be considered desirable in some countries as well (horizontal equity).

Redistribution makes it necessary to have some form of collective financing that is more easily achieved with defined benefit schemes. Nevertheless, it can also be achieved with defined contribution schemes, using state guarantees, state subsidies or part of the individual contribution to finance redistribution provisions. This helps to make redistribution more transparent. The pension system may also be structured to have a distinct scheme that is highly redistributive, in a context where the income-replacement function can be fulfilled by either a defined benefit or a defined contribution scheme. In practice, pension systems with defined contribution schemes are most often designed to ensure a degree of vertical equity, whereas pension systems with defined benefit schemes are also meant to guarantee a measure of horizontal equity.

Unintended forms of redistribution or effects on income distribution also take place with all types of pension schemes. This may sometimes be corrected by amending the specific provisions that generate the perverse redistribution effects. For instance, extending the length of the period used to calculate reference earnings could eliminate the redistribution from poor to rich that results from differences in age-earnings profiles. More generally a scheme may be made progressive without eliminating all elements of unintended redistribution. For instance, subsidizing individual accounts of low-income workers could compensate for the lower rates of return or the higher administrative costs they face. With defined benefit schemes, the contribution formula, or the benefit formula – or both – may be adjusted to achieve the desired level of redistribution.

Redistribution also takes place between generations, especially when changes affect societies as a whole (rather than only individuals). Social transformations leading to the disruption of traditional/informal systems of old-age support and the introduction of formal pension schemes make redistribution necessary in favour of the first generations of pensioners. This can be more easily achieved with pay-as-you-go schemes, since benefits are financed from current contributions.

Demographic changes may also be a source of intergenerational redistribution. In a context of population ageing, the increased level of pension expenditure will have to be paid out of current GDP, no matter how the pension is financed. Nevertheless redistributive implications for the contributors to a pension scheme are more transparent and important in the context of pay-as-you-go schemes since the increased level of transfers has a direct effect on the contribution rate. With funded schemes, transfers and redistribution occur through profits and the capital market, and the implications of an increase in old-age dependency are unclear, unpredictable and possibly less important for the participants in a pension scheme, because retirement savings are only a subset of the capital markets (both nationally and internationally).

On the other hand, the contribution rate, or the benefit level, of funded pensions is more sensitive to economic changes. Even in a theoretical context where economic developments are fully anticipated and there is no risk, successive generations of participants in funded schemes either have to pay a different contribution rate or accept a different benefit level because of variations in the rate of return over time. Individually funded schemes do not redistribute between generations, but the effect of changes in the net rate of return for funded pensions is similar to the redistribution caused by demographic changes for pay-as-you-go pensions.

Finally one cannot look at transfers or redistribution taking place within pension systems without questioning their political acceptability. Redistribution, occurring both within and between generations, may express a deliberate social policy designed to ensure an appropriate level of income to retirees. However societies have limits to the politically acceptable level of resources that can be transferred through public programmes. With respect to their political acceptability, it may make a big difference whether pension transfers occur through public mechanisms, or whether the same amount of resources is moved on the basis of individualized entitlements. The redistributive implications of pension systems must also be assessed, looking at the interactions between the pension system and the other components of the national social protection scheme. Pensions are a major component of those systems, but redistribution benefiting retirees or other groups also occurs through different programmes.

Notes

[1] Although not necessarily intended, redistribution might also take place in a pension system for the following reasons:

- redistribution so as to accommodate changing needs or to ease changes in pension provisions, most commonly to accelerate the payment of full benefits by a new system;
- redistribution that is accepted as a trade-off against provisions that achieve other desirable objectives, such as smoothing of lifetime income, low cost, comprehensibility and acceptability to members, a typical example being rules that base benefits on a member's final earnings;

- redistribution arising from chance or from eventualities outside the control of the pension system that might or might not be foreseen, for example cyclical movements in the return on investments (Davies, 1996).

[2] The promises are in fact not tradable, and consequently have no market value which can be used to determine their price.

[3] See Chapter 6 for a description of the cost increases for pay-as-you-go defined benefit schemes.

[4] The assumptions were defined to make the two schemes differ only in the way they react to changes in the duration of retirement: the pension of the defined benefit scheme is calculated on the basis of the indexed average earnings earned over the full career; the rate of return on the account balances of the defined contribution scheme is assumed to be equal to the rate of growth of average earnings per worker; the number of contributors is assumed to be stable.

[5] Those figures also show that a scheme is less sensitive to an increase in the duration of retirement (either the contribution rate or the replacement rate) if it is funded and the rate of return on the account balance exceeds the rate of earnings growth. The discounted value of payments made in the last years of life then represents a lower proportion of the total value of the pension.

[6] With partial funding, the funding objective is set initially at a level equivalent to two years of expenditure. The funding level is gradually increased to five years of expenditure in 2030 (and maintained constant at that level thereafter) to avoid a more substantial increase in the contribution rate during the demographic transition, when large generations of baby-boomers are in retirement. The funding level ranges between 20 per cent and 50 per cent. It varies over the years and according to the economic assumptions used.

[7] The relevance of using 2 per cent is debatable; Davis found that, on average, in ten developed countries between 1967 and 1990, the excess in the rate of return over the rate of earnings growth has been only 0.75 per cent, excluding administration costs (Davis, 1995c). On the other hand, rates earned on pension funds since 1990 have exceeded 2 per cent in most countries.

[8] The assumptions used up to 2050 are consistent with those used by the United Nations (medium-variant projections) to project the population up to 2050 (United Nations, 1996): fertility rates below the replacement rate of 2.1 up to 2050; increase of life expectancy at birth from 76.4 years in 1990–5 to 80.7 in 2045–50. The parameters are assumed to remain constant over the ultimate period 2050–2100.

[9] One of the first papers to look explicitly at this issue is Schieber and Shoven (1997).

[10] Wage data tending to reflect increases in manufacturing wages and interest rates are for ten-year government bonds.

[11] It was assumed that contributors entered the labour force at age 22 and were employed consistently at the economy-wide average wage for the following 43 years. All workers then retired at age 65, and they all died on their 82nd birthday. The target pension for each worker was equal to one-half of the average wage, indexed after retirement to reflect changes in prevailing wage levels.

[12] One could expect that fluctuations over periods of ten or 20 years will level off over time and that variations in the rates of interest and the rate of wage growth will be smaller when looking at longer periods such as the full career of an individual. This would help to limit the variability in the contribution rate or the pension replacement rate, but it would not eliminate it. This point is discussed in more detail in Chapter 16.

[13] Since the consumption differentials between the payers and recipients of transfers are kept constant throughout the projection period, the estimates of the normal rates of transfer basically reflect changes in the demographic environment. In industrial countries they also reflect the progression of unemployment rates. Reduced rates of growth of total employment are assumed for those countries for future years compared to what was observed between 1950 and 1995. For the other regions, where benefits paid to unemployed people are limited, it was assumed that all active people pursue some form of gainful employment (either in the formal or the informal sector). Future activity rates were kept constant for each age group in the base scenario, and alternative scenarios with a gradual increase of the retirement age and a gradual increase of female labour force participation to the labour market were also tested: (a) an increase in the retirement age by five years between 2000 and 2010 (increase of one year every two years) and (b) female participation

rates at least equal to 80 per cent of male participation rates in 2050 and for each age group. The income share of GDP is assumed to remain constant throughout the projection period, and incomes increase in line with real GDP growth. As long as the differential between GDP growth and productivity does not change, and the assumption of a constant profit and wage share at GDP is maintained, variations of the real rate of growth do not affect the relative transfer ratios. The projections are thus relatively robust with respect to the economic assumptions.

[14] A pension scheme is regressive when the rate of return received by contributors increases as incomes rise. In those circumstances, there is redistribution from poor to rich. A scheme is progressive when the rate of return decreases as income increases. Progressivity is determined by comparing the contributions paid and the benefits received over a lifetime by people at different income levels.

[15] Different reasons explain why pension schemes calculate the pension based on the salary in the years preceding retirement. First, the pension is more in line with the standard of living of the participant at the time of retirement, and therefore it ensures a more adequate level of income replacement. Final salary plans were also introduced to simplify the provisions and the administration of the scheme. Using a reference period of a few years limits the necessary record-keeping and avoids the necessity of indexing the salary earned in the early years of a career to calculate the pension. The calculation of a wage index is a problem in countries where there are limited official statistics on wages. The problem of regressive redistribution may be avoided by extending the reference period used to calculate the pension. Amendments that gradually extend the reference period have been introduced in recent years, for example in France.

[16] In a context of segmented defined benefit schemes, redistribution may also take place because of limited transferability of pension entitlements. People changing jobs and being covered by different schemes during their career will end up with a lower pension in cases of limited transferability of pension entitlements. Pension entitlements are more easily transferable with defined contribution schemes and it is easier to achieve more uniformity of pension provisions because of the simplicity of that type of scheme. Nevertheless participants in those schemes could end up with a low residual pension if they are allowed a withdrawal benefit (such as the refund of their contributions) every time they leave a scheme.

[17] In Denmark the contributory pension is a flat-rate pension and the self-employed are not covered.

THE RISKS TO INDIVIDUALS

12

This chapter examines how the main sources of risk interact with the three major types of pension arrangements: defined contribution, notional defined contribution and defined benefit. It considers the three major types of financing mechanism: pay as you go, partial funding and full funding. It also reviews the different institutional arrangements, centrally managed or privately managed. Related issues discussed elsewhere in the book include managing the investments of funded schemes to reduce risks (Chapter 7), the effects of foreseeable demographic changes (Chapter 11), the design of retirement schemes so as to reduce risks to retirement income (Chapter 19) and some of the economic effects of pension schemes (Chapter 13).

The primary purposes of a social security pension scheme are to provide a stable, predictable and adequate source of retirement income for each participant. These should not be the only goals that a society has for its pension scheme, and such aims should not be pursued without due consideration for other social, political and economic effects, but a social security pension scheme that does not do an adequate job of producing low risk retirement income must surely be judged a failure.

The challenge in delivering stable and predictable retirement income is that the world is changing and is inherently unpredictable. Pension schemes are subject to a variety of risks: the economy may not behave as expected, demographic trends may alter, political systems may change, and private and public sector institutions important to the pension scheme may fail to execute the responsibilities they have been assigned. Moreover, at the beginning of a working career, the worker's own fortunes are not entirely predictable. He or she may experience prolonged unemployment, or have a promising career disrupted or prematurely ended by industrial restructuring. Conversely the individual may experience a more rapid growth in earnings than expected, and will require a larger pension to maintain his or her replacement rate. Each of these possibilities introduces risks that expected pension benefits may not be received.

No pension scheme in an unpredictable world can completely succeed in providing a predictable source of retirement income. Some threats to a predictable retirement income, however, have more serious consequences under one approach to pension provision than another. This chapter examines the major risks which can affect pension benefits, and assesses their effects under the different approaches to organizing a social security pension scheme. The analysis focuses on the following categories of risk:

- *demographic risk* arising from unexpected changes in birth rates or mortality rates;[1]
- *economic risk* arising from unexpected changes in the rate of growth of wages or prices, or from unexpected changes in the rate of return earned in financial markets over the course of the worker's career;
- *political risk* arising from a breakdown in governmental decision processes that allow politicians to make benefit promises in excess of what society can afford to pay, which cause benefits to be reduced on short notice owing to political changes, or lead to other flaws in system design, or prevent the political system from making timely adjustments to meet changing economic and demographic trends;
- *institutional risk* arising from the possible failure of private financial institutions or their government regulators, or from the inability to obtain retirement benefits because of inadequate record keeping or other kinds of incompetence on the part of pension administrators; and
- *individual risk* arising out of uncertainties about the individual's future work career.

DEMOGRAPHIC RISKS

Unanticipated demographic changes may be important for workers who have accumulated entitlements or people who are in retirement at the time those changes occur. Unanticipated changes in birth rates and post-retirement mortality are considered separately.

Changes in birth rates

The effect of changes in birth rates on the cost of defined benefit pay-as-you-go schemes can be substantial.[2] However the changes in the retirement dependency ratio caused by such movements in fertility occur only gradually. The annual number of births generally changes gradually over a period of several decades, and change in the number of births has no direct effect on pension finances for at least 15 or 20 years, after which it begins to influence the size of the labour force. The effect on pension finances is then phased in gradually as less or more numerous generations enter the labour market. It is therefore possible to adapt the scheme by phasing in new provisions to limit future changes in contribution rates without significantly altering the promises made to participants.

The possible magnitude of such a change can be illustrated by one particularly dramatic historical example. Between the early 1950s and the early 1990s, a time span which represents roughly the working career of someone born in 1930, the crude birth rate in Japan fell by half.[3] The decline in the birth rate, taken by itself, would eventually cause that country's retirement dependency ratio to double. In a pay-as-you-go pension programme, this will eventually require that the average benefit fall to one-half its previous level, the contribution rate double, or some intermediate combination of the benefit cut and contribution increase.

The decline in the number of workers relative to the number of retirees causes worker contributions to fall short of the amount needed to finance retirement benefits. Either the contribution rate must be increased or retirement benefits must be curtailed. The adjustment will be decided through the political process and is likely to involve some mixture of benefit reductions and contribution increases. This would limit the risk for individual participants, since the risk would be shared across generations.

In designing notional accounts, the way of measuring economic growth used to determine the (nominal) interest credited to each account must be established. The effect of changes in birth rates on pay-as-you-go notional defined contribution schemes is the same as for defined benefit schemes if notional account balances are increased by average earnings per worker. The size of the annual update will not be affected by changes in the number of workers, and contribution income will fall short of the amount needed to meet benefit payments. The political process must produce an adjustment in one or the other, or both.

The sensitivity of notional defined contribution schemes to changes in birth rates can be reduced by increasing notional account balances by the growth rate of aggregate wages (or aggregate GDP) rather than by average earnings per worker. Under this variant a slowing in the growth rate of aggregate employment will automatically reduce the increase in the value of individual accounts. In turn this will slow the growth rate in the amount of benefit that future retirees can expect to receive. Future retirees then face a higher level of risk, because the adjustment to a lower birth rate occurs virtually entirely in the initial benefits of future retirees, with little change in contribution rates.[4]

Funded schemes (either partially or totally funded) are not immune from demographic changes, but the effect is substantially more complicated, and therefore much more difficult to predict. The question of the effect of population ageing on funded schemes is discussed in the preceding chapter. Once a defined contribution scheme has reached maturity, older people support themselves by drawing down their accounts (selling assets) at the same time as the working-age population saves for retirement by adding to their accounts (buying assets). Considering only the transactions that occur within the retirement system, if the number of workers who are buying assets falls relative to the number of retirees who are selling assets, as with any market, the price of the item being sold can be expected to decline.

Retirement savings transactions, however, are only a subset of a larger set of capital market transactions. The effect of retirement dissavings on the price of assets would then be spread in a larger pool, which would lessen its effect. Box 12.1 discusses steps taken by the Canada Pension Plan and the Quebec Pension Plan to reduce the effects of demographic change on contribution rates (in comparison with pay-as-you-go) by partial funding.

Changes in post-retirement mortality

A second risk involves general mortality trends. Life expectancies at age 65 have increased substantially in many parts of the world since the Second World War, causing populations to age and pension costs to rise. Japan provides a particularly dramatic example. Between 1953 and 1990 life expectancy at age 65 for Japanese men increased by 40 per cent, from 11.8 to 16.7 years. A young Japanese worker initiating his retirement savings programme in 1953 could find by 1990 that he had accumulated only 70 to 75 per cent of what was needed to finance his target retirement income, simply because life expectancies for him and his colleagues had increased so dramatically.[5] Defined benefit pension schemes would face cost pressures of similar magnitude owing to the dramatic drop in mortality.

Regardless of the type of pension scheme, an increase in the expected duration of retirement increases the cost of providing pensioners with a given monthly income. Successive generations of participants must either make higher contributions during their working years, extend their working lives or accept a lower retirement income. The different types of pension schemes differ, however, in their effects on contributions and benefits of those who are currently in mid-career, or who are in retirement at a time of unanticipated increase in life expectancies.

Under both the funded defined contribution and unfunded notional accounts schemes, the promise to mid-career workers is limited to the monthly benefit that will be purchased at the time of retirement by the balance in the worker's account. Under these approaches mid-career workers face the risk of an unanticipated increase in life spans. It takes the form of a lower than expected monthly benefit.

With notional accounts, the pension is calculated at the time of retirement and is payable until death. Financial implications of deviations between forecast mortality at retirement and real post-retirement mortality are then a source of financial imbalance for the scheme. In this respect notional account schemes are similar to defined benefit pay-as-you-go schemes.

With funded defined contribution schemes, the risk of unanticipated increases in life spans following retirement may either be borne by the pensioner, if he or

Box 12.1 Immunizing defined benefit schemes against demographic change: The Canadian case[6]

The Canadian population will age rapidly in the early decades of the twenty-first century. In this context a moderate increase in the funding level of the social insurance pension schemes was decided in order to stabilize the contribution rate over a long period. Canada has a comprehensive pension scheme consisting of two types of public programmes plus tax-assisted savings for retirement. The fundamental objective of the Old-Age Security Programme is to ensure a basic level of income for all of Canada's elderly. The Canada Pension Plan and the Quebec Pension Plan are additional social insurance schemes that cover all employed and self-employed workers. They replace part of the income lost in the event of retirement, invalidity or death.

For a single person with pre-retirement earnings near the average wage, the public programmes ensure a pension income which is a little less than half of pre-retirement income. The replacement rate is significantly higher for low-income people, but it falls as incomes rise above the average. Consequently a significant proportion of people with above-average incomes contribute to either an occupational pension scheme, a retirement savings scheme, or both.

The Old-Age Security Programme is totally financed from general tax revenues on a pay-as-you-go basis. The Canada Pension Plan and the Quebec Pension Plan are financed from the contributions made by employees, employers and self-employed, and from investment income earned on the accumulated fund. So far the funding target of the Canada Pension Plan/Quebec Pension Plan has been to maintain a fund equal to two years of expenditure. This corresponds to a funded ratio of 6 per cent, or to an unfunded proportion of 94 per cent.

Maintaining a fund-expenditure ratio target of two years would require a gradually increasing contribution rate from a current level of 6 per cent to 14 per cent in 2030. A contribution rate of 14 per cent far exceeds the long-term rate of 5.5 per cent estimated at the start of the scheme in 1966. As shown in table 12.1, this substantial increase of the long-term rate is due to a combination of several factors.

The contribution rate of 14 per cent would come when the baby-boom generation had fully retired, and it would mean that following generations of workers would have to pay greater contributions than needed for their own eventual pensions. Therefore an alternative course of action was agreed upon: over a period of six years the contribution rate will be increased faster than under the current schedule so as to reach a steady-state rate much sooner. An agreement was also reached on other financing and benefit changes, so as to stabilize[7] the contribution rate at approximately 10 per cent.

The current fund/expenditure ratio of about two years is projected to increase gradually to a level of 4.9 around 2020 and then decrease gradually to 4.3 around 2040, after which time it would remain essentially stable until 2075.[8] Under the modified scheme, a long-term fund-expenditure ratio of 4.3 years corresponds to a funded ratio of 17 per cent.

Following these changes, the contribution rate of the Canada Pension Plan/Quebec Pension Plan is not totally immunized against changes due to future

Table 12.1   Projected costs of the Canada Pension Plan in the year 2030 (if no changes are made to contributions or benefits)

Cost projections	Costs as a percentage of covered earnings
Cost in 2030 as projected when the Plan began (1966)	5.5
Reasons for increased costs	
Changed demographics	2.6
Changed economics	2.2
Enrichment of benefits	2.4
Increased utilization of invalidity benefits	1.5
Costs in 2030 as projected in 1995	14.2

Source: Tamagno (1997).

demographic and economic developments. Nevertheless, with actuarial valuations being performed on a regular basis, it will be possible to react promptly to any substantial change in the economic and demographic environment, and to ensure the financial stability of the scheme. Moreover financing the schemes on a collective basis will ensure that no individuals or generations will suffer disproportionately from those changes.

she opts for phased withdrawal, or it can be transferred to an insurance company if the account balance is converted into an annuity. Insurance companies can easily manage the risk of variations in individual age at death, but the risk of unanticipated variations in the average life span for a population as a whole cannot be diversified. This reduces the attractiveness of the annuity market, causing insurance companies to provide annuities with conservative (low) benefits.

Under the defined benefit approach, the pension promise is a monthly amount. At least initially, the extra cost associated with an unanticipated increase in life spans must be borne by the sponsor of the pension scheme. This kind of cost increase will also eventually be offset, at least in part, through benefit reductions, or contribution rate increases, in pay-as-you-go pension schemes. The reductions may come either through lower monthly benefits or through increases in the programme's retirement age. Benefit changes tend to be phased in over a number of years, however, so that the risk to workers who are in the middle of their working lives should be significantly less than under either of the other two types of schemes.

ECONOMIC RISKS[9]

The contribution rate needed to finance a pay-as-you-go scheme is sensitive to changes in the number of contributors relative to beneficiaries, and unanticipated labour market developments may affect the size of the contributory population.

The contribution rate needed to finance a given replacement rate under funded schemes is not as sensitive to changes in the ratio of contributors to beneficiaries, but is sensitive to changes in the rate of return on investments and the rate of growth of wages. The accumulated amount available to finance the pension is highly dependent on the rate of return on investments, and the pension level has to be closely related to the wage level at the time of retirement (and consequently the rate of growth of wages over the full career).

Finally inflation is a source of risk once individuals have retired because of the necessity periodically to index pensions to avoid a gradual reduction in the standard of living.

Labour market developments

Economic factors, such as the unemployment rate and the degree of informalization of the labour market, affect the coverage level of pension schemes. Over the last decades other changes in the labour market – such as the increased participation of women, the reduction in the number of years between the date of entry and the time of retirement, and the more frequent movements in and out of the labour force – have also modified the coverage pattern of pension schemes.

Changes in the worker's coverage status affect the level of credits accumulated by the worker at retirement under all types of pension schemes. In this sense they can be seen as a source of individual risk, assuming they are not voluntary. (The question of individual risks is discussed in a later section.) Unanticipated changes in the coverage level are also a source of systemic risk for pay-as-you-go schemes since they may create a financial imbalance. Substantial variations in the number of covered workers are a source of risk for pay-as-you-go schemes because current benefits must be financed from current contributions, while it takes many years before a reduction in contribution leads to a proportional reduction in benefit.

Large variations in the coverage level of pension schemes in transitional and developing countries have occurred over the last few years. Some countries have let inflation erode benefits as a way to deal with the financial imbalance. Some (the Russian Federation and Tajikistan) have even failed to pay benefits. Normal fluctuations in the level of employment, however, can easily be accommodated in unfunded schemes by the creation of a contingency reserve to avoid liquidity problems. Funds accumulated in those reserves may be used in periods of economic slowdown to compensate for a reduction in the amount of contributions collected, without putting at risk the payment of benefits to current retirees.

The financial situation of funded schemes is less sensitive to changes in the labour market that affect coverage and contribution income, although it may affect the payouts of subsidized minimum benefits, while major economic changes almost inevitably affect the capital markets and the rate of return earned on investments.

Wage growth and investment rates of return

Funded schemes are a risky alternative, especially in a period of economic instability or high economic uncertainty. The real value of accumulated savings can be depressed sharply by inflation. Investments can rapidly become obsolete in a context of economic transformations or economic modernization.[10] Funded schemes are sensitive to economic risks, even in a context of relative economic stability characterized by normal variations in the rate of development of wages and the rate of return on investments.

Wage and investment returns cannot be expected to follow a regular and predictable path over the course of an individual's working life. Every time they increase or decrease, the contribution rate needed to finance a given retirement pension under a defined contribution scheme also changes, leading to changes either in the amount that workers must contribute for a given pension or in the replacement rate associated with a given level of contributions. Since the economic environment cannot be known in advance, the contribution rate must simply be established to reflect the best information currently available about future developments, and modified as new information becomes available. For individual pensions, however, this means that the contribution rate actually prevailing during working years may turn out to be either too high or too low to produce the target pension at the point that retirement age is reached. Alternatively stated, the resulting benefits will be either too high or too low. Mistaken estimates of the required contribution rates have serious implications under defined contribution schemes, because pension benefits are determined solely by the total amount contributed and the investment returns earned on it. Any difference between the contribution rate actually used and the rate that should have been used (regardless of the reason for the discrepancy) creates a gap between the actual asset accumulation and the amount necessary to produce the target pension benefit. The retiree either overshoots or undershoots the target. Those who overshoot will have saved too much. They will be able to enjoy higher than anticipated retirement incomes, but at the cost of having made greater sacrifices during their working years than were necessary. Retirees who undershoot will be forced to live in retirement with less than they had anticipated. The magnitude of the mistaken estimate may be substantial, since it results from the combination of three factors:

- *Long-term developments are unknown.* Forecasts of the differential between the average rate of growth of wages and the average rate of return on investments over the full career of an individual are uncertain, and the pension replacement rate at retirement is sensitive to this differential.

- *Timing is important.* Even if it were possible to forecast accurately the average wage-interest rate relationship over a full career, there could still be high variations in pensions because the timing of the variations has a significant effect on the amount accumulated at retirement.[11]
- *Short-term variations have an effect.* There can be a substantial appreciation or depreciation in the value of assets (both stocks and bonds) over a period of a few years, and the effect of such a variation is substantial when it happens in the years immediately preceding retirement.

To gain an appreciation of the possible magnitude of the risk to retirement benefits with funded defined contribution schemes, simulations were performed of the effect of economic variations that actually occurred in four major economies. The historical evidence used is from the period 1953–95 in Germany, Japan, the United Kingdom and the United States. The objective of the exercise is to apply plausible decision rules about how contribution rates would be set and to see how close people would come to achieving their target pension. Several different decision rules are used to set initial contribution rates and to adjust these rates in response to experience. The simulations lead to the conclusion that high sensitivity to the economic environment makes it difficult to achieve a target replacement rate at retirement with a defined contribution scheme. Even if the long-term trends were predicted perfectly, annual variations in the values that produce the average could make the effective replacement rate miss the target by 50 per cent. Instead of replacing 50 per cent of pre-retirement income, the simulations indicate it could provide a replacement rate anywhere between 37.5 per cent and 75 per cent. Simulations of economic variations were run using the wage rate-interest rate relationship that actually occurred and in exactly the opposite time pattern of the actual experience. The assumption is that changes of the magnitude actually observed historically can easily occur again, and that the trend could go in either direction. Details are shown in table 12.2. The 43-year average interest rate is used to convert the account balance to an annuity. Thus the analysis does not consider the risk arising from changes in interest rates on the value of annuities benefits (see box 12.2).

The simulation results show that the variations in the effective replacement rate at retirement are even greater when assuming that long-term trends are not known, and the contribution rate is adjusted periodically to reflect current economic conditions. The effective replacement rate at retirement then varies from 30 per cent up to more than 100 per cent.

It is highly desirable to diversify the portfolio to reduce risk. It is also desirable for risk-averse workers to modify the composition of the portfolio by selling stock and buying bonds to reduce the risk of asset depreciation in the years preceding retirement.[14] Nonetheless the possibilities of reducing the risk of variations in pension replacement rates at retirement by proper investment portfolio management are not great. The simulations were performed on the basis of the annual current rate of interest on ten-year government bonds. In

Table 12.2   Simulated actual asset balance as a percentage of the balance required to produce the target pension (100 per cent bonds: all values in per cent except where indicated)

	Germany	Japan	United Kingdom	United States
Simulation 1:				
contribution rate set at level appropriate for long-term (43-year) trend				
Actual sequence	137	132	140	138
Reverse sequence	88	80	73	80
Simulation 2:				
contribution rate set at level appropriate for first half of period				
Actual sequence	261	255	233	342
Reverse sequence	41	40	43	30
Simulation 3:				
contribution rate adjusted every 10 years in line with economic conditions of previous 10 years				
Actual sequence	163	153	165	181
Reverse sequence	66	68	64	58
Basic data				
43-year average wage increase	4.8	5.0	3.6	1.0
43-year average interest rate	3.9	3.8	1.8	2.3
Ratio of target accumulation to average wage	9.2	9.5	9.9	7.6

Source: Thompson (1998).

other words, they reflect the evolution of interest rates over time, but do not incorporate additional risks associated with possible appreciations and depreciations of asset prices over short periods. Most types of assets, including stocks and bonds, are subject to such variations. No account is taken of the risk of default (assuming the default risk was negligible in those countries during this period).

In conclusion, defined contribution schemes are quite sensitive to economic conditions over an individual's working life. In a pure defined contribution scheme, all of the risk associated with this source of variation is borne by the individual participant. The history of the last half-century suggests that uncertainties about future economic developments can easily cause asset accumulations in defined contribution schemes to fall one-third short of the initial target, and just as easily to become twice as high as the target. In either case the amount by which the initial target was missed will be translated directly into retirement benefits that are higher or lower than expected.

Inflation

Pensions being paid out should be adjusted periodically to guarantee retirees a standard of living in line with either what they enjoyed at retirement (price

Box 12.2 Interest rates and the conversion of capital into an annuity
Under a defined contribution pension scheme, the normal practice is to convert the accumulated capital into an annuity when the participant reaches retirement age. But the periodic amount of pension resulting from this conversion depends on the level of interest rates at that time. Sudden changes in the level of interest rates just before retirement may thus significantly affect the periodic income a participant will receive.

The present value concept
If a person invests $1 at an interest rate of 5 per cent over one year, this dollar will accumulate at the end of the year to a value of $1.05. Inversely the amount that a person has to invest today in order to obtain $1 at the end of the year, with the same interest rate of 5 per cent is:

$$\$1/(1.05) = \$0.952$$

The amount of $0.952 is called the present value at the beginning of the year of $1 payable at the end of the year. In order to receive $1 at the end of two years, the present value using the same interest rate of 5 per cent will be:

$$\$1/(1.05)^2 = \$0.907$$

The value of an annuity
An annuity is a series of periodic payments all separated by the same interval of time. It may be payable for a fixed period. This type of annuity is called an annuity-certain. It may also be payable as long as a person lives. It is then called a life annuity.

To compute the present value of an annuity, it is necessary to compute the present value of each individual periodic payment, and to sum these values. For example, to compute the value of an annuity-certain of $1 per year payable for ten years, with the first payment due at the end of the first year, and using the same 5 per cent interest rate, the present value is:

$$1/(1.05) + 1/(1.05)^2 + 1/(1.05)^3 + \ldots + 1/(1.05)^{10} = 7.7217$$

So if a person has a capital of $100,000 to convert into an annuity, at this 5 per cent interest rate, the resulting annual payment over ten years will be $12,951 (=$100,000/7.7217). If the interest rate is higher, for example 10 per cent, the annual payment resulting from the same capital of $100,000 will be $16,274 (=$100,000/6.1446, which is calculated the same way as above, but assessing a 10 per cent interest rate).

As regards the level of the interest rate, the same conclusion applies to a life annuity: for a given amount of capital, an increase in the interest rate leads to an increase in the periodic amount of the annuity payment.

The value of a bond
A bond is a type of investment promising the payment of regular periodic coupons during a determined period, plus a redemption value which is paid at the end of that period. As with an annuity, the value of a bond is equal to the present value of future cash flows generated by that investment, and thus

depends on the interest rate used to calculate the present value of these future incomes. Consider the example of a simple ten-year bond under which is paid an annual coupon of $50 and a redemption value of $1,000 at the end of ten years.

Time	1	2	3	4	....	8	9	10
Income	$50	$50	$50	$50	....	$50	$50	$1 050

If the investor has paid $1,000 for this bond, he or she will receive 5 per cent of his or her initial investment each year, and will recover his or her initial investment of $1,000 at the end of the period. The present value of these cash flows, using an interest rate of 5 per cent, is thus $1,000.

When interest rates rise, investors will be more attracted by the good return offered on new bonds issued at these new higher coupon rates. If you want to sell an old bond promising interest payments lower than those offered on current issues, you will then have to offer a discount to attract buyers. So the market value of a bond decreases when interest rates increase.

For instance, you may have bought last year, for $1,000, this ten-year bond at a nominal rate of 5 per cent, under which you were to receive annual coupons of $50 plus a redemption value of $1,000 at the end of ten years. If interest rates do not change over the ten-year period you own your bond, the value of the bond will always remain at $1,000. But let us suppose that one year later, when you have just received your first coupon, the nominal interest rate on this type of bond has increased to 6 per cent. You then want to sell your bond to an investor who has the choice between your 5 per cent bond and the new 6 per cent bond issue. In this case you will have to sell it for $932 (instead of $1,000), being the present value of the remaining coupons of $50 plus the redemption value of $1,000, all discounted at a 6 per cent interest rate. With this price of $932, the buyer of your bond will be able to realize his or her expected return of 6 per cent.

The duration of a bond may be defined as the average amount of time that it takes to receive the coupons and the redemption value. The duration is calculated as the weighted average of the present value of all cash flows (coupons and redemption value) expected to be received from this investment, divided by the face value of the bond.

The conversion of capital into an annuity

Under a defined contribution pension scheme, the usual practice is for participants to convert the capital accumulated from past contributions into a life annuity. Once the amount of the accumulated capital to be converted is established, the resulting monthly pension will depend directly on the level of interest rates at the time of retirement. The returns may have been very high during the period of accumulation, but if interest rates drop sharply just before the retirement date of that person the resulting pension will decrease accordingly.

The level of interest rates has varied greatly in Canada during the 1990s. Table 12.3 shows, in column (1), the level of nominal interest rates on long-term federal bonds.[12]

Considering only the interest factor in the decision of a participant to delay retirement from 1996 to 1997, such a deferral of the retirement date would have

Table 12.3   Interest rates in Canada, 1990–97

Year	(1) Nominal interest rate %	(2) Inflation rate %	(3) Real interest rate %	(4) Return on common stocks %
1990	10.9	5.0	5.6	−14.8
1991	9.8	3.8	5.8	12.0
1992	8.8	2.1	6.6	−1.4
1993	7.9	1.7	6.1	32.6
1994	8.6	0.2	8.4	−0.2
1995	8.3	1.8	6.4	14.5
1996	7.5	2.2	5.2	28.4
1997	6.4	0.7	5.7	15.0

caused a reduction of 5 per cent in the annual payments under a ten-year annuity owing to the decrease in interest rates. This assumes that the accumulated capital to be converted would have been the same in 1996 and 1997.

But the amount of capital to be converted may also be affected by a change in interest rates. For example, if the funds of the participant were totally invested in bonds, a decrease in interest rates just before retirement would cause an increase in the value of investments, and thus in the capital available for conversion. The net effect of this interest rate change on the amount of the periodic annuity payment will depend on the average duration of the bonds included in the capital to be converted. The longer the duration of the portfolio, the greater the effect of an interest rate change in the value of a bond, because interest becomes an important factor in the present value calculation. For example, if the whole portfolio was invested nine years ago in ten-year bonds, the whole portfolio will mature next year and even a sharp change in the level of interest rates would not have a large effect on the capital to be converted, as compared to a situation where the same portfolio had been totally reinvested in a new bond issue last year. A person may decrease the risk of unexpected changes in the value of the capital just before retirement by appropriately choosing the maturity of investments.

If we modify the example by considering the case of a person having invested all his or her portfolio in common stocks, the value of the portfolio would have increased by 15 per cent between 1996 and 1997, thus increasing directly the capital available for conversion. On the other hand, the decrease in interest rates from 7.5 per cent to 6.4 per cent reduces the periodic payment by 5 per cent, as seen earlier. But this pensioner still benefits from the combined effect of a decrease in interest rates and a good return on his or her equity portfolio, with a net gain of 9 per cent on the amount of his or her periodic pension.

Real versus nominal interest rates

A person investing money generally expects to obtain, at the end of the investment period, a real gain. This means that he or she will want to recover his or her capital, plus a compensation for inflation, plus a real return for having been deprived of the use of that money during the investment period. In that case the nominal interest rate may be seen as having two components: a real interest rate and a compensation for inflation.

Indexed pensions

What happens to the investor approaching retirement at a time when nominal interest rates are comparable to those observed during the accumulation period, but with an inflation rate increasing sharply? If he or she chooses to convert his or her capital into an annuity with fixed periodic payments, there will be no effect on normal payments, but real payments will decline. In addition, if the totality of his or her capital is invested in bonds, the nominal or market value of his or her portfolio will not be affected by the change in the real rate of interest, as long as the nominal rate is unchanged, but the real value will decline. This was the situation for 1994 and 1995 in our Canadian example, where the nominal interest rates were comparable (8.6 per cent versus 8.3 per cent), but the inflation rate rose from 0.2 per cent to 1.8 per cent.

On the other hand, if that person chooses to purchase an indexed annuity, with the indexation rate trying to match the current inflation rate, the annuity payment must be computed using the real interest rate instead of the nominal rate. For example, consider the following figures:

	1994	1995
Nominal interest rate	8.6%	8.3%
Inflation rate	0.2%	1.8%
Real interest rate[13]	8.4%	6.4%

Returning to the example of a person having a capital of $100,000 to convert into an annuity at retirement, the initial annual payment under a ten-year annuity-certain, calculated with an interest rate of 8.4 per cent, would be equal to $15,172. With an interest rate of 6.4 per cent, the initial annual payment becomes $13,845. The level of the real interest rate then becomes determinant in the calculation of an indexed pension.

indexation) or what is enjoyed by the active population at the time the pension is paid (wage indexation) or some combination of the two.

In countries where indexed securities exist, these can provide protection against inflation under funded schemes. Indexed bonds are currently available only in a limited number of countries (Australia, Brazil, Canada, Chile, the United Kingdom and the United States) but for most of those countries the volume of such securities remains limited. In these circumstances, the inflation risk is transferred to the state.

Where indexed securities are unavailable, there are other ways, more risky for pensioners, to cope with pension indexation. Equities offer some protection against inflation, but they are characterized by a higher expected rate of return and greater volatility. Using a lower than market interest rate to calculate the annuity premium, or the amount of phased withdrawal, is also a way to cope with inflation. The interest rate margin plus any additional interest earnings are then used to supplement subsequent payments. While the correlation between market values and inflation is not perfect, variable annuities, where the periodic payment depends on the market value of a portfolio of securities, can provide some inflation protection.[15] Increasing annuities involving arrangements on the future indexation of pensions may also be used, but this may, or may not, reflect actual future inflation.

Pay-as-you-go schemes are less subject to inflation risk. This is especially true when pensions are indexed to wages. Contributory earnings and pensions develop at the same rate assuming that the ceiling on covered earnings is also indexed. In actual practice, however, earnings ceilings for pay-as-you-go schemes are sometimes adjusted on an ad hoc basis, and at times failure to make adjustments has resulted in pensions which, after a few years, are derisory.

In summary, inflation protection can be provided more easily with unfunded schemes than with funded ones in countries lacking indexed securities, although, as will now be discussed, in some countries those schemes may be more subject to political risks.

POLITICAL RISKS

An entirely different category of risks arises out of the political process. All public pension programmes are creatures of the government, whether the state's role is to manage the scheme directly or to establish and enforce the rules under which the scheme will operate. If the state adopts faulty policies, or fails to implement good policies effectively, its actions may cause pensions promised at the beginning of a worker's career to fail to materialize.

Pay-as-you-go defined benefit pension schemes have proved to be vulnerable to the problem of excessive promises, particularly in those countries where institutions and traditions do not force politicians to consider and acknowledge the future cost of current promises.[16] Where cost implications can easily be ignored, irresponsible politicians are able to use promises of higher future benefits as an apparently inexpensive way of securing the support of influential groups. Common recipients of such largesse are the military, the police, civil servants and workers in transport, mining and other key export or public utility industries. Newly established pay-as-you-go programmes can have this problem, since the low contribution rates associated with the early years can invite general benefit increases that push the costs of the mature scheme beyond a politically sustainable level. The problem arises as the pension scheme matures and the cost implications of prior promises become clearer. If it is decided that these costs exceed what society is willing to bear, promised benefits will be scaled back. Those caught in mid-career when such benefit reductions are implemented will have their retirement schemes upset, as the retirement benefits they had been told they could expect fail to materialize.

Defined benefit schemes (and, to a lesser degree, notional accounts) are also susceptible to the related risk that the political system will be unable to enact timely adjustments to meet unfavourable demographic trends of the country. As noted previously, a decline in either birth rates or mortality rates can cause a defined benefit scheme's pension promises to become inconsistent with its contribution rate. Where the political system is unable to come to a consensus about the adjustments to be made, the imbalance may develop into a source of social division and continuing fiscal difficulties for the government. A political stalemate about how to adjust the pension scheme introduces an additional risk for mid-career workers. Although they may understand that the current promises must be adjusted, they will not know what kind of adjustments they need to plan for. Moreover continued controversy is likely to eventually undermine public confidence in the pension programme, compromising its social value and increasing the odds of a major disruption of pension promises.

Privately managed defined contribution schemes are particularly attractive in countries that have experienced serious problems of excessive promises and political stalemate involving pay-as-you-go defined benefit schemes. Under the defined contribution alternative, the politicians' ability to use pension promises to reward favoured constituents loses its attractiveness since each such promise will require an immediate transfer of funds to the private pension manager. Nonetheless the contribution rate of defined contribution schemes is established (explicitly or implicitly) on the basis of expected future rates of return necessary to achieve an appropriate pension level at retirement. Defined contribution schemes could therefore lead to a certain form of overpromising if the contribution is set on the basis of overoptimistic expectations on the rate of return. For instance, introducing funded schemes is falsely attractive in a period of high interest rates if it is assumed that those conditions will prevail forever. Defined contribution schemes do not eliminate the potential for political stalemate in adjusting to unfavourable demographic developments either, since a revision of the contribution rate must go through the political process. If it does not happen the working-age contributors bear a higher risk themselves, particularly of unexpected lengthening in retiree life spans.

The financing of minimum pension provisions may also be a source of political risk, especially where there is a benefit financed from general taxation that provides some kind of a basic or minimum pension. Benefits are not paid on the basis of the past contribution record and they may be more easily modified in a context of reduced political support.

Finally it is difficult undertaking to shift from a pay-as-you-go defined benefit scheme to a funded defined contribution scheme in order to reduce the political risk leading to fiscal imbalance, since the implicit unfunded liabilities of the old system must somehow be paid off. Governments experiencing fiscal problems traceable, at least in part, to imbalances in their pay-as-you-go pension schemes may be tempted to try phasing out those schemes as part of a strategy for restoring general fiscal balance. They are likely to find, however, that phasing out a pay-as-you-go pension as a way to reduce the risk of overpromising is a greater fiscal challenge than fixing the system.[17] Government, trying to undo the effect of past excessive promises in its pay-as-you-go pension scheme, may end up making a new set of excessive promises in the form of future transition payments that it eventually finds it cannot afford.

The notional defined contribution approach is sometimes used as an attempt to secure some of the advantages of the traditional defined contribution approach without incurring the transition costs. The transition costs are those costs associated with switching from an unfunded to a funded scheme. With notional defined contribution schemes, benefits are calculated as if the system were being run as a funded set of defined contribution accounts, but it continues to be financed on a pay-as-you-go basis. It remains to be seen whether the change in the benefit calculation method proves to be a sufficient deterrent to irresponsible political interference, without the corresponding discipline of having to transfer resources to private pension management companies.

To summarize, defined benefit schemes may expose individuals to political risk owing to two sources of vulnerability: promises of future benefits do not need to be paid until later, and the adjustments to accommodate demographic changes require overt political action. Defined contribution schemes largely avoid both these sources of political risk, but introduce a new source of political risk if those schemes are developed on the basis of falsely high expectations about the rate of return. Shifting from pay-as-you-go schemes to fully funded schemes also introduces a risk in a context where the costs of the transition can be substantial and do not materialize fully for years. Notional account schemes avoid the transition costs and are less susceptible to (but not immune from) the other two vulnerabilities associated with defined benefit schemes. Because of limited experience with these schemes, it is not possible at this time to quantify the relative amount of political risk in each type of pension scheme, or to analyse how that risk might vary from one country to another.

INSTITUTIONAL RISKS

Pension schemes which are flawless in their conceptual design can still fail to deliver the benefits they have promised, as a result of weaknesses in the institutions charged with their management. At least three kinds of institutional failure have undermined the predictability of pension promises in the past, and must therefore be considered as risks to future pension promises. They are the loss of financial assets through fraud or mismanagement, the inability to collect pension contributions effectively, and inefficient or ineffective administrative arrangements.

Failure to preserve financial assets

An advantage of funded schemes is the ability to accumulate financial assets in advance to help pay for the pensions. The corresponding disadvantage, however, is that the value of the pension promise depends directly on the effectiveness of the management of these assets. The focus in the mid- to late 1990s was primarily on financial problems in some of the countries in Asia. Problems commonly materialize after a sharp increase in either real estate or stock market prices which turn out to be unsustainable. When the financial situation begins to unravel, large investment losses aggregating 10 per cent of a country's GDP can suddenly appear.[18] It is not clear whether the risk of major financial losses such as this should be treated as a risk to be assumed by individual participants or a risk that the state will end up assuming on behalf of all participants. In principle, in defined contribution schemes, the risk of investment losses is borne by the individual participant.[19] In practice, however, with respect to other financial institutions, governments have often stepped in to protect individuals from the consequences of major financial collapses, even when not legally required to do so.[20]

Collection problems

Non-compliance, or contribution evasion, will reduce future benefits and produce inadequate retirement incomes for people evading contributions. It can create financial problems, putting at risk promises made to covered workers and pensioners.[21]

Under pay-as-you-go schemes (either defined benefit or notional defined contribution), benefits of current beneficiaries must be financed from current contributions. A variation in the level of compliance could create short-term financial imbalance, and a significant reduction in compliance would force either an increase in the contribution rate or a cut-back on benefit to maintain the financial equilibrium of the scheme. This creates a risk that promises made to covered workers or pensioners will not be kept.

Non-compliance may also pose problems for defined contribution schemes, since there is usually a minimum pension, or a social safety net, that guarantees a minimum level of income at retirement.[22] This may create incentives, especially for low-income workers, to underdeclare earnings, or to not pay contributions. The financial consequences are generally borne by the state that guarantees the payment of the anti-poverty pension or safety net, therefore it does not directly put at risk the pension entitlements of other contributors, but it may undermine the political support for the pension scheme, or ultimately create problems for public finance.

Ineffective administration

A powerful motive for reform of a public pension programme can be the risk that benefits will be lost as a result of incompetent administration. If administrators are not able to maintain the records necessary to establish entitlement, the value of any pension promise will depend entirely on the ability of the individual participant, or some third party, to maintain records. Neither is an acceptable arrangement in a dynamic economy. Each increases the chances of fraudulent benefit awards while also raising the possibility that individuals will lack information needed to receive all the benefits to which they are entitled.

The public sector does not have a monopoly on incompetent administration. However, since social security pension programmes have traditionally been managed by public sector institutions, most of the egregious examples of incompetent public pension management involve these public sector institutions. The search for an alternative to an incompetent public sector institution naturally tends to focus on private alternatives.

Recent experience in the United Kingdom, however, illustrates the potential risk from fraud and mismanagement in privately managed, defined contribution schemes (see box 12.3 on misselling). Salesmen for personal pensions convinced several hundred thousand people to make financial decisions that benefited the salesmen but harmed the individuals. Whether this was the result of overzealousness, incompetence or fraud, the individuals affected have lost pension benefits to which they were otherwise entitled through the failure of private sector institutions.

In summary, each of these types of pension schemes functions only as effectively as the institution that operates it. Promised benefits may be lost because of administrative incompetence, financial mismanagement or fraud. Any of the three problems can arise in any administrative arrangement, although the first has probably been encountered more frequently in the public sector, the second is less of a problem under a pay-as-you-go scheme and the third is probably more likely to be a problem for privately managed pension schemes.

INDIVIDUAL RISKS

A final category of risks involves uncertainty about the working career of each individual. Projections of the pension that can be expected under different pension schemes typically assume that an individual is always employed and always earns some constant multiple of the average wage in the economy. While useful for illustrating the general characteristics of different pension approaches, these assumptions are not a realistic representation of working lives. Actual careers are substantially more varied, and are interrupted by periods of illness and spells of unemployment, which may be frequent and prolonged for some people, while infrequent and of short duration for others. Moreover some people enjoy earnings that generally rise more rapidly than the economy-wide average over the course of their careers, while others might find themselves displaced in mid-career and forced to accept employment at much lower pay rates than they had been used to. Defined benefit public pension schemes are often

Box 12.3 The misselling of personal pensions: The United Kingdom experience
Personal pensions were introduced in the United Kingdom in 1988 as a new form of individualized defined contribution pension scheme. How they have developed since then is a useful illustration of problems that can arise with this type of scheme. In particular, large numbers of these contracts were missold to people who, as a result, have been at risk of suffering a significant reduction in their prospective retirement income.

Fortunately the problem of missold personal pensions has been uncovered, and an extensive review is now under way to identify and compensate the individual holders who have been adversely affected. Unfortunately the review did not start until personal pensions had been running for six years and millions of contracts had been sold. As a result the Financial Services Authority – the supervisory authority concerned – estimates that the number of missold pensions exceeds two million and the total amount of compensation that will have to be paid by providers will be around £11 billion (about US$18 billion).

Background
Although contracts similar to personal pensions had been available in the United Kingdom prior to 1988, what was entirely new was the way in which they were popularized for a mass market, not just by the providers but also by the government. The main driving force at the time was the government's desire to promote greater use of individualized funded pension schemes particularly, but not exclusively, for people who were not already in an existing private pension scheme. The result of these efforts, including the financial support that was available in many cases from the government, was that a large number of personal pensions were taken out. Thus by 1993 there were over five million such contracts in existence, covering around 20 per cent of the workforce, although not all of these contracts were currently receiving contributions.

Judged simply by these numbers, personal pensions have to be viewed as a considerable success. What is not so clear, however, is whether they can be judged a success in terms of providing pensions. On this matter it is too early to reach a final conclusion, mainly because the great majority of contracts have yet to mature and start providing a pension. It appears that many people, particularly those on higher incomes but who do not have the opportunity to belong to an employer-sponsored scheme, have found personal pensions to be a valuable and cost-effective way of saving more for their retirement. It is also clear, however, that many of the people who took out these contracts were ill-advised to do so, the main reasons for this being the way in which these contracts were sold and their high cost.

The background to this problem of misselling is that employees are not generally permitted to have a personal pension and at the same time to belong to an employer-sponsored collective pension arrangement – known in the United Kingdom as an occupational pension scheme. Similarly it is possible to choose between a personal pension and the earnings-related part of the state pension. Given these choices, large numbers of people were persuaded to make the wrong choice and to leave an occupational pension scheme, or the state scheme, to have a personal pension instead.

The source of the problem

The main cause of the problem with personal pension misselling lies with the providers of personal pensions and, in particular, the primacy of their marketing function over any assessment of individual need. It was therefore unfortunate that a new system of regulating such financial products, which was introduced at virtually the same time as personal pensions, took some time to become effective. In the meantime there was a culture that approved of high-pressure selling, coupled with inadequate training of the salesforce and weak management by providers.

The United Kingdom's life insurance industry, with few exceptions, had developed an overemphasis on securing distribution channels. Too many companies were content to pay for the business they generated, without being fastidious as to how the sales had been made. This meant that the rules, intended to ensure that individuals only took out personal pensions when it was in their interests to do so, simply failed to work. In particular the principles of "know your customer" and "best advice" that were meant to apply to the practice of the salesforce were simply ignored by providers in a headlong rush to get more business.

Unfortunately the supervisory structure meant to be regulating this market was new and fragmented. It also failed to undertake any effective monitoring of what was going on. As a result, it was over six years before any systematic study was undertaken of what was happening. Once completed, the study's results caused considerable public concern. The study showed that, of those members who had taken the opportunity under the new legislation to transfer their accrued benefits from an occupational pension scheme to a personal pension, up to 90 per cent should not have done so. The doubts about the precise number arose because the providers did not have information in their files showing whether or not the recommendation to transfer to a personal pension had been right in the first place.

The review

When the scale of the problem became fully apparent in 1995, the main supervisory body at that time, the Securities and Investment Board, initiated a wide-ranging review of missold personal pensions. This required providers to review all contracts taken out since 1988 that involved either a transfer of benefits from an occupational scheme or a decision not to belong to an occupational scheme. Certain priority groups were identified to be dealt with in stage one of the process, involving those who were older, already retired or dead – totalling around 640,000 people – and in these cases an early review was mandatory.

The Securities and Investment Board laid down precise terms for the review. In particular the onus was placed on the providers, or their sales intermediaries, to demonstrate that the member's decision was the correct one to take under the rules and circumstances of the time at which it was taken. If they could not do so, they were required to offer the individual members redress for any loss they had suffered, under terms laid down by the Securities and Investment Board. The first aim was to see that the individuals were reinstated into their occupational scheme and provided with the benefits they would have received had they never left. If this was not possible, a payment then had to be made into their personal pension to provide benefits of an equivalent value.

Originally the review process was meant to be completed within two years. Regrettably it has now fallen well behind this timetable, with large numbers of individual reviews still to be completed. It is now estimated, however, that the average amount of compensation in these priority cases amounts to £8,000 which, given the number of cases, means compensation payments will total £4.5 billion.

Considerable regulatory and government pressure is being brought to bear to complete the first-stage review. Providers are then meant to move on to stage two and look at younger individuals. Although it is anticipated that the average compensation in these cases will be smaller than in the first stage, the numbers involved are larger, with up to 1.8 million people involved. On this basis, the Financial Services Authority, which has now replaced the Securities and Investment Board as the supervisory body, estimates that a further £6.5 billion will need to be paid as compensation, which would mean a total bill of £11 billion. It also means that the number of people who have been mis-sold a personal pension could be as high as 2.4 million, which is not far short of half the number of people who took one out in the period concerned.

In addition to the cost of the compensation payments, providers are having to meet their administrative costs in undertaking the review, which are considerable, with each amount having to be individually calculated. Some providers, who have not dealt with the review quickly enough, have also had to pay substantial fines levied by the Financial Services Authority. The overall cost to the industry could therefore be as much as £15 billion. Unfortunately most of this will end up being paid out of the general funds of the providers concerned − which would otherwise have been used for the benefit of policy holders − with an inevitable adverse effect on their ultimate benefits.

Contracted-out personal pensions

A particular feature of personal pensions in the United Kingdom is that they can be used to contract out of part of the state's National Insurance Pension Scheme. Such contracts are known technically as appropriate personal pensions, where the holders give up their right to accrue benefits year by year in the state earnings-related pension scheme (SERPS) and, in return, have part of their national insurance contributions for those years paid to the personal pension provider of their choice. They therefore receive this personal pension as a replacement for the SERPS benefit they have given up. No guarantees are offered, and it depends on the investment returns they receive on the personal pension as to whether or not the personal pension is greater than the lost SERPS benefit.

One of the main reasons for the initial popularity of personal pensions, the great majority of contracts being of this type, was that younger people were allowed to contract out in this way on terms that were financially attractive. In effect the terms were heavily subsidized by the state. As a result there has been a cost to the national finances considerably in excess of the putative savings, in terms of the present value of the reductions in future state benefits. Over the first six years the United Kingdom's National Audit Office estimated that the net cost was around £6 billion, meaning that the cost of the contributions paid over to personal pension providers exceeded the current value of the savings in future SERPS benefits by this amount. Since 1997, however, the terms for contracting out have been adjusted and are now much less generous.

Despite the generosity of the original terms for contracting out through appropriate personal pensions, it did not mean that it was always the right decision to have such a pension. In 1995 the Securities and Investment Board undertook a study of those which had been taken out, and found that there were up to 250,000 people who could expect to have worse pensions as a result. It also found that, of those who could expect to be no worse off with an appropriate personal pension, many only avoided a loss of expectations because of the generosity of the terms for contracting out. In other words, the subsidy paid by the government to promote the use of personal pensions has in many cases been swallowed up by the high level of the provider's expenses, and the individuals concerned were no better off.

The effect of expenses on personal pensions

While misselling is the main cause of the difficulties with personal pensions in the United Kingdom, the extent of the problem has been compounded by the effect of the high level of expense deducted by many providers. This has been a particular problem for employees on relatively low incomes, where low earnings have meant that the contributions paid into the personal pension have tended to be small as well. As a result, depending on the precise terms of the contract, a large proportion of the contributions can be swallowed up in the fixed expenses that are levied in many arrangements. Given this potential problem, it is therefore important to note that the main market for personal pensions in the United Kingdom is among lower earners, because the great majority of employees in the United Kingdom who are not in occupational schemes tend to have lower than average earnings. As a result they are more at risk of losing out owing to the effect of expenses.

The structure of the charges on personal pensions varies considerably from contract to contract. The main variables are the proportion of the expenses expressed in cash terms, as opposed to being a proportion of contributions of the fund, and the extent to which they are deducted as a lump sum when, or soon after, the contract is taken out, as compared to being spread over its whole term. This latter aspect, described as "front-end loading", is particularly significant for the large number of contracts where contributions are not maintained for the whole of their term. Unfortunately, because of the emphasis on selling and the wish of many providers to recoup their selling costs at an early stage of a contract's expected existence, proportionately large deductions for expenses are made from contracts at an early stage. The result is that, in the large number of cases where policy holders are unable to continue with their contributions for the full term of the contract, a very high proportion of their contributions is consumed in expenses.

What this can mean is that, in cases where fixed expenses are relatively high and the fund in the personal pension is low, the expenses can actually swallow up the entire fund. Such a situation might arise because the individual concerned has ceased to pay contributions through unemployment. Given that there is no control, statutory or voluntary, over the charges that are levied on personal pensions, the only protection for members is to ensure that they never get into such a contract in the first place. As explained above, this protection for members has, in too many cases, simply failed to work.

The record so far of personal pensions in the United Kingdom presents a sorry picture. For some individuals they have worked well, but in almost 50 per cent of cases they were missold and, as a result, threatened the individuals concerned with significantly worse retirement provision than they would have had otherwise. It is true that arrangements are now in place to provide them with compensation for these prospective losses, but the distress they suffered in the meantime, and the money that has been wasted in carrying out the compensation exercise – mainly at the cost of policy holders in general – still means that the episode must be regarded as a major disaster for this type of scheme.

There remains the question of how far the underlying causes of the disaster (for example, a failure by providers to offer proper advice, and high costs) are inherent in individualized defined contribution pension schemes. The United Kingdom's experience suggests that there is, at the very least, an inbuilt tendency for such problems to arise, that can only be avoided by specific and forceful action on the part of an effective regulatory regime.

constructed to help individuals with irregular work histories receive higher benefits than they would otherwise be entitled to. Although not done in practice in defined contribution schemes, this can also be incorporated in either funded defined contribution schemes or notional accounts. More relevant is whether there are intrinsic differences among the approaches in which people with a history of irregular earnings receive different treatment under one type of scheme than under another, in ways that were not designed or intended.

This question could be illustrated by examples similar to those used earlier in connection with the analysis of the effect of economic variation. The analysis consists of four simulations, each of which focuses on a worker with a different irregular variation on the previous regular earnings pattern. The first experienced prolonged unemployment at the beginning of his working life, the second was unemployed for some time at the end of her working life, the third enjoyed sharply-rising earnings over the course of his career and the fourth suffered a significant fall in relative earnings during the last third of her employment. The retirement benefits of each of these workers are calculated under a defined benefit pension scheme and under a defined contribution scheme, and the results are compared with the benefits that more typical workers would have received under each scheme.

When the defined benefit scheme links benefits directly to career average earnings, little difference is found between the two types of schemes in their treatment of workers with irregular work patterns. Although benefit entitlements are more variable under the defined contribution scheme, the average benefit awards are similar. The implication is that any systematic difference in the treatment of irregular workers between the different types of schemes is caused by features that were explicitly built into one scheme or the other, not characteristics intrinsic to the schemes themselves. However, defined benefit schemes frequently have the feature of drop-out years, which are years where the worker's earnings are not counted in the benefit calculation. This feature provides insurance against irregular earnings due to short-term unemployment or ill health. While technically feasible through the use of government subsidies, defined contribution schemes have not been designed to provide this type of insurance.

An important attribute of public pension programmes is their ability to produce predictable pensions. This chapter has focused on the kind of risks to which individual workers are exposed over the course of their careers, to see how each risk is handled in each of the three public pension schemes now being debated throughout the world. The risks include those associated with demographic and economic developments, political and institutional failures, and uncertainty about an individual's lifetime employment prospects. The different types of schemes are the traditional defined benefit scheme (either pay-as-you-go or partially funded), the defined contribution scheme and the pay-as-you-go notional account scheme.

The major types of schemes differ substantially in the way they adjust to different sources of risk. Some are far more sensitive to a particular risk than are others, but each is sensitive to one or more major sources of risk. No one type of scheme emerges as the least risky under all circumstances.

The benefit promises under defined benefit schemes are relatively insensitive to unexpected changes in the rate of growth of average earnings, or to changes in investment returns, but are exposed to the risk of unanticipated changes in either birth rates or retiree life spans. This type of scheme also requires a greater degree of overt political intervention to adjust benefits and contribution rates in response to these unanticipated demographic developments. The advantage of this political intervention is that it provides an opportunity to spread the effect of the demographic changes among the rest of the population, reducing the risk they pose to the benefit promises of an individual retiree. The disadvantage is that, where the political system is not strong enough to make the necessary decisions, the need for overt intervention can lead to policy impasse, social discord and perpetual government budget deficits.

Retirement benefits under defined contribution schemes are just as sensitive to changes in retiree life spans, but this type of scheme transfers the risk of this change completely to the individual retiree. Where the political system is not capable of making overt adjustments, this may in fact provide a more predictable result than is provided by defined benefit schemes. Where the political system is stronger, defined contribution schemes involve a greater risk that unanticipated changes in retiree life spans will upset benefit expectations.

Because of its closer linkage to the decision processes of the political system, the benefit promises under defined benefit schemes have been more exposed to the risk of irresponsible political behaviour. Such behaviour often takes the form of promises of future benefits that exceed the ability and willingness of society to pay. These promises must eventually be retracted, upsetting the expectations of people caught in the transition. Political risks of this sort appear to have been a much greater problem in some parts of the world than in others.

Where this kind of political risk is a serious problem, defined contribution schemes are attractive precisely because their benefits are more insulated from political interference. However the transition from pay-as-you-go schemes to advance-funded schemes is expensive. This can create a new source of political risk if a transition is attempted without facing its fiscal implications responsibly. Moreover the experience of misselling of individual pension schemes in the United Kingdom indicates that politicians are not the only people prone to promising more than they can deliver. Defined contribution schemes require sophisticated oversight and regulation to ensure that fraud or mismanagement in the private sector does not lead either to upsetting retiree benefit expectations or to expensive public sector bailouts of private financial institutions.

Individuals face the risk that they will experience prolonged periods of unemployment or that their job prospects will suddenly worsen partway through their careers. With defined benefit schemes, various features are commonly incorporated to offer a measure of protection against these risks.

A final difference is the substantial sensitivity of retirement benefits to unforeseeable year-to-year fluctuations in the economic environment with defined contribution schemes. If the defined benefit and defined contribution approaches were similar in their ability to handle all other important risks, this feature alone would argue against relying too heavily on defined contribution schemes as a basic source of retirement income.

Notional accounts schemes are hybrid and seek to capture some of the advantages of each of the other two types of scheme. They avoid the sensitivity to economic conditions found in the defined contribution model. Notional accounts schemes should be less susceptible to the problem of excessive political promises than are defined benefit schemes, but not as well insulated as defined contribution schemes. By the same token, they are less susceptible to the risks associated with private sector fraud and mismanagement. This type of scheme is so new, however, that generalizations are difficult and any assessment may prove premature.

None of the models is without risk, but the risks differ. This suggests that societies should seriously consider approaches which feature a mixture of types of schemes as a way of reducing the total risk in their pension schemes.

One way to achieve such a mixture is to mandate participation in two different types of scheme, as has been done in Argentina, Finland, Switzerland and Uruguay. Another way is to set up a pay-as-you-go state scheme and allow opting out of one part of that system, as is the current approach in Japan and the United Kingdom. A third way is to set up a defined benefit scheme which is not adequate by itself for the retirement income needs of middle- and upper-income individuals and to encourage private supplementation, the approach followed in Canada and the United States.

Societies can be expected to follow different approaches depending on tastes, traditions and their own institutional histories. Since political risk can be a major source of uncertainty, and often varies from one culture to another, one should expect that the relative importance of the different types of schemes would differ in countries with different political traditions and institutions. Whatever the decision a society makes, however, that decision should reflect appropriate concern for, and careful consideration of, the role that the pension scheme plays in providing participants with a predictable source of retirement income.

ANNEX: PENSION GUARANTEES

The most important distinction between defined benefit and defined contribution schemes is the allocation of risk and responsibility for the delivery of promised benefits. Defined benefit schemes are generally seen as placing the risk of benefit delivery on the sponsor: the employer in the case of occupational pension schemes, or the state in the case of social security[23] programmes. Defined contribution schemes, in contrast – at least in the United States – place the risk of investment performance on the participant. The participant bears economic and investment risks even if all required contributions are made on schedule.

But in many parts of the world, the distinction in risk bearing between defined benefit and defined contribution schemes is less clear. For reasons that may be political, economic or both, many countries establishing defined contribution schemes to provide part or all of benefits in their national social security programmes hedge these schemes with a complex system of guarantees.

Guarantees in defined benefit schemes

Defined benefit schemes offered in the context of social security programmes are typically pay-as-you-go funded, though many schemes, including the United States, Canadian and Japanese social security programmes, maintain cash reserves. Depending on the country, defined benefit schemes offered by employers, typically as supplements to a national social security programme, may be unfunded, or subject to statutory minimum funding rules to maintain participants' benefit security.

But, whether in a social security programme or an employer-sponsored scheme, benefits in a defined benefit scheme are payable at the promised level to workers who meet the scheme's service or participation criteria, whether or not money has been set aside to cover them. Benefits are secured by certain implicit or explicit guarantees. In a social security programme, benefits are guaranteed by the programme's ability to levy payroll taxes or compel contributions, by the government's ability to levy general taxes, or both. In an employer-sponsored scheme, benefits are guaranteed by assets accumulated in the pension fund, by the employer's ability to fund benefits out of its other income and, in some cases, by external guarantee funds or insurance, such as in Germany, Japan and the United States.

Guarantees in defined contribution schemes

Formal guarantees. Defined contribution schemes in transition and developing economies bear little resemblance to the United States model. As defined contribution schemes are emerging around the world, sometimes under the leadership of the World Bank, the International Monetary Fund or other donors, they represent a different balancing of the interests and risk-bearing ability of the government, the employer and the pension participant. In many countries a wide range of formal guarantees are available: minimum benefit guarantees, minimum investment return guarantees, either at absolute levels or relative to an index, and guarantees against fraud. Formal guarantees include those provided in laws or regulations. The effectiveness and affordability of such guarantees may depend critically on the stage of development of a country's financial system as well as its system of collecting pension contributions.

Social security schemes based on defined contribution individual accounts typically provide for a *guaranteed minimum benefit*. In Chile individuals with at least 20 years of contributions to the old (pre-1981) system and the new system combined are guaranteed a minimum benefit of 85 per cent of the legal minimum wage (90 per cent for those age 70 and over), an amount equal to what most people received under the old pension scheme (Myers, 1992).[24] The recently enacted three-pillar[25] Hungarian reform provides for a minimum benefit in the second (individual account) pillar of 25 per cent of the pension benefit calculated under the first (social security) pillar. One of the privatization options proposed by the 1994–96 United States Advisory Council on Social Security also included a flat minimum benefit of about 47 per cent of the benefit currently payable to an average earner (who receives about 43 per cent of his or her indexed pre-retirement wages). The Chilean minimum benefit is to be financed out of the government's general revenues if the participant's account is insufficient to do so, while in Hungary the shortfall is the responsibility of the Government Guarantee Fund.[26]

Minimum benefit guarantees tend to benefit low earners, people with short contribution histories and those whose investments perform poorly. In these respects they can perform an important distributional function, since defined contribution schemes do not otherwise easily lend themselves to redistributional policies. But minimum benefit guarantees may also reduce revenue compliance. The Chilean system has had problems with maintaining adequate compliance, as has the Hungarian system, along with many others in transition economies. The Chilean government has projected significant future liabilities as a result of contribution evasion (Campbell, 1994b). Since the Chilean system requires less than a full career of contributions for the minimum benefit, it could be rational for workers to attempt to exploit the system by spending as much of their working careers as possible in jobs where their employers do not contribute, or as self-employed workers, who are not required to contribute.

Participants in United States employer-sponsored defined contribution schemes are at the mercy of the market in the timing of their retirement. Those who retire at the wrong time (when financial markets are low) can do much worse, even given the same contribution amounts and investment performance, than those who retire at the right time (when financial markets are high). But some people have only limited control over the timing of their retirement. Some countries still have mandatory retirement ages. While the United States has largely eliminated such requirements[27], some people may be forced by family, job or health considerations to retire earlier or later than would be best for optimal investment performance.

In Chile participants in defined contribution social security accounts are *guaranteed a minimum investment return* relative to an index, which is the average return of all pension fund managers. In good years funds must contribute to profitability and investment reserves; in bad years they can draw on these reserves to make up shortfalls. A fund whose reserves are inadequate to make up a shortfall can be forced to liquidate. The state will then make up the shortfall in investment returns and transfer the balances of individual accounts to other funds.

Investment return guarantees put the government budget far more at risk than does a traditional defined benefit social security programme. In a traditional scheme the government bears demographic risk (pensioners may live longer than foreseen, workers may retire sooner than predicted, fewer new workers will enter the system than expected) and macroeconomic risk, especially if benefits are explicitly indexed for inflation.[28] These risks can be accommodated through policy changes, such as raising retirement ages or pension fund contribution rates. But if the government is insuring the performance of investment markets, as it does when it stands behind minimum investment return guarantees, it has no way to limit its exposure other than refusing to pay. It does limit its exposure, however, when it guarantees a return relative to an index.

Direct *guarantees against fraud* are not typically provided in either defined benefit or defined contribution schemes. Rather participants or others may have recourse to the courts if they have been harmed by fraudulent actions of scheme managers or sponsors. In the United States, for example, the Pension Benefit Guaranty Corporation, the government agency that insures many occupational defined benefit schemes, may file suit against certain sponsors of terminated defined benefit schemes if scheme assets are not adequate to cover liabilities. Managers of private defined contribution schemes may also be liable to participants for damages if they have violated fiduciary or other rules.

But the line between aggressive investment management and excessive risk taking or fraud can be difficult to draw and document. Consequently the existence of comprehensive benefit guarantees can create problems of moral hazard. Investment managers who know that their account holders will be protected in the event of an adverse investment decision could take undue risks, since success could mean higher management fees and greater marketability. Employers usually monitor investment practices and performance in schemes they sponsor, but pension funds in countries such as Chile, Argentina and Hungary have no employer affiliations, putting the guarantee fund directly at risk when a fund fails.

Informal guarantees. Informal guarantees provided by the government can go much further than formal ones. Such guarantees can be implicit, as in the "too big to fail" approach. If an institution is considered by the government to be too big – or too important economically or politically – to fail, it may be allowed to carry on (improper) operations or practices longer than would be optimal on the grounds that everyone knows it will be bailed out, usually by a government or government-sponsored entity. These types of guarantees can lead to excessive risk taking and eventually financial crashes as the government's implicit, or explicit, guarantees exceed its ability to pay.

Other guarantees can be implicit in a country's social, economic or political structure. In Switzerland, for example, the sponsor of a struggling defined contribution scheme may receive a discreet tap on the shoulder from government regulators, encouraging it to provide an infusion of cash into the scheme. Such informal guarantees may be strongest in a socially cohesive country with sponsors with adequate financing. They may function less well in countries such as the United States, where such a tap on the shoulder would be considered unwarranted government intrusion; in countries where the financial resources are unavailable, such as in many developing countries or transition economies; or in countries where, for various reasons – political, historical, religious, cultural or ethnic – a high degree of social cohesion and mutual responsibility cannot be assumed.

The United States has had experience of its own with implicit, and hence unfunded, guarantees. Deposits in federally insured savings and loan associations were, by law, only insured up to $100,000. Yet large depositors of failed associations were nevertheless reimbursed for the full value of their deposits, on the basis of the political calculation that widespread losses by uninsured depositors could lead to a loss of confidence in the banking system as a whole. But implicit and informal guarantees are inherently ad hoc, and hence fundamentally unreliable.

In many social security schemes using individual accounts participants have the right to move their entire accounts to a new fund periodically. The move may be to an entirely new fund manager, rather than simply an alternative investment vehicle offered by the same pension fund. Liberal provisions governing account switching can be considered a type of implicit guarantee. Employees with the freedom to change accounts can seek the combination of investment returns and service that best suits their own risk-return trade-off. Liberal switching provisions can also serve as an extra protection against poor management, or even fraud. Employees may be able to see signs of trouble in a fund (account statements are late, inquiries are not answered satisfactorily) before regulators, who will generally rely on audit reports.[29] Yet minimum benefit and investment return guarantees already serve to homogenize fund performance (and benefit levels) beyond what a system without these guarantees would yield. Consequently liberal switching provisions could be considered redundant with these guarantees.

Contribution guarantees

Despite elaborate guarantees, benefit security in many defined contribution schemes may still be inadequate. Many developing and transition economies face problems with pension fund payroll tax compliance.[30] Compliance problems span the entire range of types of employers, from government entities (in Hungary the police are one group with high payroll tax arrears), to cash-short state-sponsored enterprises, to emerging private (sometimes called "informal") businesses.

As long as pension funds are a government obligation, the participant has little concern during his or her working career about whether contributions are made. But when a defined contribution scheme accounts for part or all of retirement income provided by a national social security scheme, the visibility of this issue is raised dramatically, since participants whose employers are in arrears face the possibility of receiving account summaries stating that their account has nothing in it.

During the debate over the Hungarian pension reform, one Hungarian pension expert proposed that the government guarantee contributions by being essentially the contributor of first resort. Under this proposal the government would make pension contributions out of its general revenues, then recover these contributions from enterprises responsible for them. The idea behind this proposal was that the government, in its capacity as a tax collector, would be better able than the pension fund to collect pension contributions. While this proposal was not adopted, it represents a measure of the problems of public confidence defined contribution schemes can face.

How should guarantees be priced?

How any given country chooses to balance the potential fiscal costs of defined contribution scheme guarantees with the potential economic benefits of individual account schemes is a matter of politics and social choice. But responsible policy making and budgeting demand that the cost of making good on guarantees be projected and, where necessary and appropriate, provided for in a fiscally responsible way. In defined contribution schemes offering a minimum pension benefit, the proportion of pensioners likely to require a government subsidy to meet the minimum standard is, at least in concept, a quantifiable statistic. Likewise the proportion of pension funds likely to fail or be forced into liquidation should also be predictable.

But social security schemes based on defined contribution individual accounts are too new to have the track record to allow such predictions. For example, how many people will require a subsidized minimum benefit will depend not only on the contribution compliance rate a country is able to achieve, but also on employment and productivity growth. Likewise, whether and how many pension funds will fail will depend not only on the future course of financial markets, but also on the quality of pension fund regulation.

While individual behaviour is hard to predict, however, pension funds are typically registered entities that are subject to reporting requirements. Good – that is, effective, efficient and meaningful – reporting requirements are crucial to achieving a functioning regulatory regime that protects the interests of both the government and pension fund participants. All the information sought by regulators should give insight into the fund's riskiness, and information that does not serve this goal should not be collected. For example, voluntary (third-pillar) pension funds in Hungary must file quarterly investment schemes (including percentage asset distributions) with their regulatory agency and must be prepared to explain later deviations from these schemes. But market conditions can change far more often than quarterly, sometimes necessitating rapid adjustments in investment strategy. Likewise the funds must submit copies of all service contracts entered into with other entities, but it has never been made clear whether or how these contracts are used in the regulatory process.

But the dictum that information collected by regulators should be relevant may be easier to pronounce than to implement. Countries where social security schemes based on defined contribution accounts are riskiest also tend to be countries where financial markets do not easily provide reliable, accurate information. In many transition economies, for example, accounting is in the process of transformation from a method of economic control to an impartial source of financial information.

One way to shield the budgets of such countries from undue pension liability, while at the same time short-cutting the process of developing accurate and effective regulation, could be to sell the liability to investors, in much the same way as one might insure a building against fire. (Foreign investors could be preferable, since they might not be subject to the same macroeconomic influences as a country's own pension funds.) Pension fund regulators could find the task of collecting relevant information simplified, since investors would dictate the information needed to determine whether a given fund was insurable, and at what price. The central government budget could be protected, in turn, because its liability would be, not open-ended, but limited to premiums. A drawback of such a scheme could be that foreign investors might be seen as dictating a country's policy toward its pension funds.

Interest in defined contribution schemes is growing throughout the world. But these schemes are different in almost every country that has adopted them. In the United States' model, a defined contribution scheme is seen as a vehicle for allowing either employers, in the case of private schemes, or the government, in the case of social security, to shed the contingent liability that flows from guaranteeing a specified retirement benefit. In many other countries, however, this transfer of risk to the employee is not considered desirable. Consequently defined contribution schemes are hedged with a number of guarantees.

Worldwide, defined contribution schemes as a major source of retirement income are relatively new. Even in the United States, where this trend has exploded in recent years, it is limited to voluntary employer-provided schemes, most of which have not yet matured to the point where their retirement income performance can be conclusively assessed. The Chilean retirement scheme, the oldest prototype of a social security scheme based entirely on individual accounts, has operated only since 1981. Most countries that have had to adopt strong guarantees to ensure the political acceptability of social security schemes based on defined contribution schemes are reaping the benefits of their decisions (increased savings, reduction of a large future liability) and not yet the costs. But the demographic changes that can make defined contribution schemes appear attractive substitutes for pay-as-you-go defined benefit schemes may pale when policy makers are faced with making good on defined contribution scheme guarantees.

Notes

[1] A high migration rate could also be a source of demographic risk.

[2] This is calculated by comparing the steady-state population structure produced by using the crude birth rate at the beginning and end of the period, in combination with the actual 1950 Japanese mortality structure. It does not represent an actual projection, since it ignores a host of other factors that will also influence the development of Japan's old-age dependency ratio.

[3] The fertility rate dropped by a third over the same period.

[4] In this situation, the adjustment to benefits may occur more slowly than the decline in contribution income, causing a temporary imbalance which must be financed either through a contribution increase or from some other sources.

[5] The estimate of 70 to 75 per cent represents the difference between the value of an annuity that could be purchased with a specified sum, assuming the 1950 Japanese male life table and the annuity that could be purchased with the same sum, the 1990 male life table and a real interest rate of 0 per cent and 3.5 per cent, respectively.

[6] The sources used for this box were Canada Pension Plan (1997) and Tamagno (1997).

[7] Financing-related modifications were investment in a diversified portfolio rather than in government bonds (Canada Pension Plan only, since Quebec Pension Plan funds are already invested in a diversified portfolio) and freezing of the year's basic exemption (the lower limit below which employment earnings are not subject to contributions). Benefit-related modifications were an earnings index based on the average over five instead of three years, invalidity pension and death benefit.

[8] Figures for the Canada Pension Plan. For the Quebec Pension Plan, the value of the ratio for 2020 is 5.5.

[9] The analysis in this section is based on work originally done as part of the Stockholm Initiative of the International Social Security Association (see Thompson, 1998).

[10] Economic and financial preconditions necessary to the development of funded schemes are discussed in Chapter 14.

[11] The assets accumulated at retirement will be more substantial if wage increases take place in the early years of work and if the funds earn a high rate of return in the years preceding retirement. This is the situation that has prevailed for workers approaching retirement, or for those who have retired over the last few years.

[12] This interest rate serves as the basis for determining the transfer values in occupational pension schemes, and is used here to show the effect of a variation of interest rates on the periodic payments resulting from a conversion at retirement.

[13] A precise calculation of the real rate of interest involves the following multiplication of factors:

$$(1 + \text{real rate}) * (1 + \text{inflation rate}) = (1 + \text{nominal rate}).$$

[14] See Chapter 9.

[15] See Chapter 3.

[16] The use of quantitative modelling to avoid this problem is discussed in Technical Brief 1 at the end of the book.

[17] See the analysis in Chand and Jaeger (1996). The conclusion that costs are likely to be *permanently* higher would not necessarily apply, however, if major reductions in future benefit promises could be introduced at the time of the changeover.

[18] See, for example, "A survey of banking in emerging markets", *The Economist*, 12 April 1997.

[19] Subject to the state-guaranteed minimum pension floor.

[20] Thus, in the case of the financial collapse of the network of individual savings account institutions in the United States, the government eventually ended up assuming (and passing on to the general taxpaying public) losses equal to just under 20 per cent of the aggregate deposits in the institutions prior to their collapse, even though, technically, the government was not liable for any of the losses.

[21] The causes of non-compliance are examined in Chapter 10, and the policy options to deal with this problem are reviewed in Chapter 17.

[22] For a discussion of guarantees, see the annex to this chapter.

[23] The term "social security" is used here to refer solely to old-age, invalidity and survivors' benefits awarded on the basis of employment and earnings history.

[24] The minimum wage has, in the past, amounted to half the average wage (Myers, 1992).

[25] A pay-as-you-go defined benefit pillar, a funded individual account defined contribution pillar and a voluntary funded private pension pillar.

[26] This fund is financed by premiums to be paid by covered pension funds. But, since the

premiums will not be based on the risk assumed by covered funds, there is no reason to assume that premiums will be adequate to finance any losses that might occur.

[27] Exceptions for employees in key business decision-making positions remain allowed under law.

[28] Though, even without explicit statutory provisions for indexing, a government scheme may be under pressure to grant ad hoc benefit increases during inflationary periods.

[29] On the other hand, however, liberal switching provisions may reward funds waging aggressive sales campaigns at the expense of financially unsophisticated workers.

[30] In some countries pension fund revenues are considered contributions rather than payroll taxes, often because the pension fund is an off-budget entity. The two terms are considered as equivalent here.

ECONOMIC EFFECTS

13

This chapter analyses the behavioural consequences of defined benefit social security pension schemes and compares them with the behavioural consequences of mandatory defined contribution schemes that are fully funded. The chapter does not consider voluntary schemes. In addressing defined contribution schemes, it further limits its focus by examining only mandatory defined contribution schemes that are managed in the private sector by pension fund management companies. The World Bank (1994) has documented problems of the management of investments by many government-managed defined contribution schemes. First discussed are the desired economic effects of mandatory pension schemes. These effects are often overlooked. The chapter then studies undesired or distortionary effects of social security on labour and capital markets. The study by economists of economic implications of social security has focused largely on social security schemes in developed countries. While the basic issues of the effects of social security on labour supply and demand, and on savings, are similar in developing and developed countries, because the social security schemes and the structure of the economies differ, the economic effects presented in this chapter may be primarily of direct relevance in developed countries. This chapter considers the economic effects of social security on workers and retirees but not the effects of the economy on social security, which are presented in Chapter 6. The effects of defined contribution and defined benefit schemes on income distribution and on the distribution or risk bearing are examined in Chapters 11 and 12. Beliefs about the economic effects of different social security schemes have become important issues in the design of retirement income systems, which is discussed in Chapter 19.

Social security retirement pensions are determined by the political process in democratic countries, and in such countries their effects are to some extent desired outcomes of conscious decisions concerning design. Some effects of social security, however, may be undesired, owing to inherent trade-offs in the design of systems, consequences unanticipated when systems were designed, or failures of the political process.

Every society must have a way of determining what commodities are produced, how these goods and services are made and for whom. Of central concern are the effects which social security pension schemes may have on the scarcity of goods and the efficiency of their production, including questions of what, how and for whom. The investigation of effects on the production factors, labour and capital will play a prominent role.

Economists have extensively analysed the effects of defined benefit social security schemes. These schemes may affect hours employees work, their choice of work in the formal or informal sector and their decision as to the age of retirement. They may also affect savings decisions of workers and national aggregate savings. In most cases theory yields ambiguous predictions concerning these effects, empirical work has failed to resolve the issues and controversy remains.

Because of the apparent simplicity of defined contribution schemes, economists have not been greatly concerned to analyse them. These schemes collect contributions, make investments and disburse payments. Policy analysts generally treat them as savings schemes that do not affect the way workers behave. However a closer look at the provisions of mandatory defined contribution pension schemes indicates that they may affect retirement age and other worker labour supply decisions. These effects occur because the schemes are mandatory. Any mandatory scheme that causes people to change their behaviour, such as causing them to increase their savings, will cause distortions, as individuals act to minimize the consequences of the programme that are undesired by them. Defined contribution schemes also have behavioural effects because of their relationship to minimum benefit and poverty programmes, their sometimes high administrative expenses, and the effects of worker myopia and capital market risks on account balances and interest rate risks on monthly benefits when they are annuitized. Because they are imposed on workers, rather than being voluntarily chosen, the effects of mandatory defined contribution schemes differ from those of voluntary defined contribution schemes (such as the Registered Retirement Savings Schemes in Canada and personal pensions in the United Kingdom).

DESIRED ECONOMIC EFFECTS OF SOCIAL SECURITY RETIREMENT BENEFIT SCHEMES

Because much of the focus of economic analysis is on the undesired effects of social security retirement benefit schemes, this chapter begins by examining their desired economic effects. It compares the effects of social security schemes with the situation that would exist if these schemes had not been instituted.

The most obvious outcome of an existing pension scheme is that (part of) the older population of a society draws a regular cash income which can be spent on goods or saved. To the retiree, receiving regular cash income means to be continuously entitled to spend this income on desired goods and services. Freedom of choice about what to consume is maintained during retirement. The distinction between cash and non-cash (in-kind) income may be important because, if retirement income takes the form of in-kind transfers, this will normally mean a loss of choice about consumption while replacing individual choices with socially determined decisions. The better developed a country's social security pension scheme, and the higher the cash component of transfers, the more the older generation's freedom of choice will be preserved.

Cash, as well as in-kind retirement income, may have other important economic effects that depend on the share of the older generation in the total population and on the level of individual disposable income. The effect of retirement income on the rest of the economy can normally be expected to be small if the demand arising from pension payments is small in comparison to total demand. Economies supporting a relatively young population (small portion of older people) can be expected to experience only small demand effects of retirement income on the general economy. The situation is different in the case of countries with a relatively old population. If such countries have developed fully fledged social security pension schemes as, for example, in the OECD countries, the specific demand resulting from aggregate retirement income may have significant effects, not only on the overall level of demand, but also on the structure of both demand and production.

Pension programmes are established to allow people to retire with a secure source of retirement income. Thus it is plausible that facilitating retirement is a desired effect of these programmes. Because people are more likely to be forced to retire during periods of economic difficulty, social security retirement benefit programmes provide a source of retirement income during difficult economic times and thus help smooth variations in aggregate consumption over time, reducing macroeconomic swings in aggregate demand and employment. They presumably reduce unemployment among older workers by providing retirement as an alternative to unemployment. Yet the availability of this alternative to work may cause employers to be relatively more likely to lay off older workers than they would in the absence of social security. Thus they may help maintain flexibility in labour markets. Some policy analysts have argued that the availability of social security benefits for older workers reduces unemployment among younger workers by creating job vacancies. That point is unproven and is contested by other analysts who argue that there is not a fixed supply of jobs and that the labour earnings of older workers create increased aggregate demand.

Some analysts have argued that a positive effect of a funded defined contribution plan in a country with poorly developed capital markets is that it encourages the development of domestic capital markets. It encourages the development of regulation of the markets and provides greater liquidity for them, thus encouraging greater foreign investment. These issues are considered in more detail later in the chapter when the issue of the effects of pensions on savings is discussed.

Though examined more fully in Chapter 19, it should be noted that risk reduction through providing insurance against different risks is a positive effect of traditional defined benefit social security schemes. Redistribution of income, discussed in Chapter 11, is another desired outcome of traditional social security schemes.

As well as having positive economic effects, social security may have positive social effects. Social security provides a safety net that helps maintain political acceptability of economic restructuring during economic transformations, such as during the changes from a command to a market economy in Central and Eastern Europe, or from a state-controlled economy to a market economy in Africa. By providing a safety net, it lessens the negative effects of free markets and helps maintain support for those markets. When workers become owners of capital in funded systems, traditional conflicts between labour and capital may be reduced and they are more likely to support economic policies that are beneficial to capital. Because of the personal benefit to themselves, workers may be more willing to support policies that are adverse to other workers, such as corporate "downsizing" that involves firing workers.

The potential labour and capital market effects of introducing a social security pension plan[1]

The effect of a social security pension benefits scheme depends in part on how saving behaviour is changed as a result of its introduction. Economists assume that people will view their social security mandatory contributions as a substitute for at least a part of their own personal saving and the future benefit they expect to receive as a substitute for all, or a portion of, the retirement reductions in wealth that would otherwise occur.

If people actually behaved this way, logic would dictate that the introduction of the social security pension plan would have no effect on aggregate saving so long as all of the following conditions held:

- mandatory contributions were less than, or equal to, the amount each person would have saved in the absence of social security;
- the relationship between benefits paid to each individual and that individual's contributions (for example, the rate of return that can be expected) mirrors the relationship the individual would have experienced in the private market place;
- social security accumulates and invests assets in the same way as the individual would have done; and
- creation of the plan has no effect on the desirability of saving to deal with future uncertainties.

Of course no social security pension plan meets all four of these conditions. Indeed no purpose would be served by creating a plan that did. Such a plan would produce a result that would have been achieved anyway by the private market. Social security pension schemes are designed intentionally to depart from one or more of these conditions precisely because societies wish to alter the private market result. But what effect might these intentional departures have on national saving and labour supply?

Effect of higher mandatory contributions

Presumably a mandatory pension plan will require larger contributions than some in the working-age population would have set aside voluntarily. These higher contributions force the affected individuals to reduce current consumption and, in the absence of an offsetting effect, their reduced consumption would increase national saving.

One possible offset to the higher savings involves the workers' ability to borrow. If credit markets allow them to go deeper into debt, they can offset the effect that the national pension plan would otherwise have on their consumption levels. Workers can easily offset a mandatory contribution rate of only a few per cent by reducing other forms of savings and increasing debt. Increasing mandatory savings in some countries will likely reduce savings through occupational pension schemes. To the extent that workers are not able to easily offset the forced savings that occur through mandatory pension systems, they may seek to avoid participation in those schemes through choosing jobs where they are not required to participate, or where they are able to evade participation.

An additional possibility is that the forced participation in the social security pension system encourages people to retire earlier and with a higher total retirement income than otherwise. This encourages them to increase their private savings in order to supplement their pension benefit, thereby increasing national savings.[2]

Effect of the relationship between benefits and contributions

Most defined benefit social security pension schemes offer some individuals benefits that are higher than they would have been able to obtain in the private market with the same contributions. These individuals are typically lower earners and those already in the labour force at the time the schemes were established. They may also be workers in particular occupations or industries that have been afforded special treatment.

Others can expect to receive less from the social security pension scheme than they would have had they made the same contributions to individual savings accounts. Typically this would include higher earners who have spent most of their careers working under the pension plan. In many mature social security pension schemes the majority of newly joined workers can now expect to find themselves in this situation.[3]

Those who would otherwise have allocated their lifetime earnings according to the pattern implied by the life cycle theory will change that allocation if they find themselves in either of these two groups. The former group, those who foresee returns in excess of the private market rate, can be expected to increase their consumption and possibly reduce their hours worked during their working lives in recognition of the higher expected retirement benefit. Increased consumption implies reduced national saving. The latter group, those who foresee returns below the private market rate, can be expected to increase their savings during their working years in order to replace some portion of the retirement income they lost as a result of being forced to participate in the social security pension scheme.

The net effect of differences in the relationship between benefits and contributions depends on the relative strength of the offsetting reactions of these two groups. In countries with mature social security pension schemes, the net effect ought to be an increase in national savings owing to the larger size and higher income of the latter group. The net effect is apt to be a net reduction in savings where social security pension schemes are relatively new and are structured so that most current participants can expect above-market returns.

LABOUR MARKET EFFECTS

The main design elements of pension arrangements from which major labour market impacts might be expected are the minimum retirement age, the benefit formula and the method of financing. Account has to be taken of the fact that these elements are normally interdependent; for example, the minimum retirement age might depend on the benefit formula, which might depend on the method of financing.

The labour market effects of social security on prime age workers depend in part on whether social security contributions are viewed as a tax by workers.

Labour supply of prime age workers

If social security contributions are viewed as a tax, they distort labour markets when workers act to reduce their liability. Taxes have a distortionary effect because they drive a wedge between the amount that employers pay workers and the net after-tax wage workers receive, which is lower. Workers are thought to base their decisions on how much to work and in what jobs on the net after-tax amount that they receive.

One aspect of the question whether workers view mandatory social security contributions as a tax is the link between contributions and benefits. When workers voluntarily contribute to a retirement savings plan, their labour market behaviour is not distorted. Similarly, when a social security scheme redistributes income, upper-income workers will be less likely to view social security contributions as a tax if they support the government taking care of the less fortunate in society. If they contribute to a mandatory social security pension scheme because they believe that it is a good one, there is no distortion of their labour market behaviour.

Thus there are at least two aspects of social security pension schemes that cause workers to feel they are receiving something in return for their contributions. First, if their own benefits are linked to their own contributions, similarly to a savings scheme, they are more likely not to consider the contributions as a tax. Second, if they support the redistributive goals of the scheme, similarly to a private charity, they are also more likely not to consider the mandatory contributions as a tax.

Contributions and benefits can be linked by establishing a defined contribution plan. A worker's mandatory contribution increases his or her account balance and his or her future retirement benefits. Thus mandatory contributions are mandatory savings that increase future benefits. Mandatory contributions to a defined contribution plan do not act as a tax if the worker would have saved that amount anyway and received the same rate of return with the same risk. The first of these conditions, however, conflicts with the reason why governments mandate social security contributions, which is that some workers are myopic and do not save sufficiently for their own retirement. Workers for whom the mandatory contribution is greater than the amount they would have saved will attempt to maintain their consumption by reducing other savings. The higher the mandatory contribution and the lower the savings of the worker, the more likely the worker will be unable to maintain his or her desired consumption and will view the mandatory contribution as a tax. In this respect defined benefit and defined contribution schemes are similar. To the degree that mandatory savings in the two systems are greater than optimal from the workers' perspective, the systems will have the same problem of trying to induce workers to save through social security more than they view to be in their own self-interest.

Chapter 10 discusses reasons why workers may wish to evade or avoid social security contributions. These reasons may all lead to a distortion of labour market activity. For example, low-income workers may seek to avoid contributions by working in the informal sector because the benefits based on their own contributions do not sufficiently exceed the amount they could receive from guaranteed minimum benefits or means-tested anti-poverty benefits.

If a country switches from a defined benefit to a defined contribution scheme, labour supply may also be distorted by the income taxes imposed to finance the transition. The general government taxes to finance the transition are likely to be more distorting than the social security contributions they replace. If the social security contribution rate acts as a tax on labour earnings, it will reduce the net hourly wage. This may encourage low-income workers especially to work in the informal sector where they are able to avoid paying this tax. It may also encourage employers to offer informal employment arrangements. Alternatively, if the social security scheme is viewed as a desirable benefit, it may encourage workers in the informal sector to seek employment in the formal sector.

For workers in the formal sector the tax will reduce disposable income, which may cause them to work more, but its reduction of the net hourly wage may have the opposite effect. Thus the net effect is theoretically ambiguous and must be determined empirically.

The mandatory contribution for defined benefit social security schemes acts as a tax if there is no connection between the amount contributed and the expected future benefit. Contributions and benefits can be linked, however, through the benefit formula by directly tying benefits to contributions. Alternatively they can be linked by having both benefits and contributions increase with earnings. When benefits increase with increases in contributions or earnings, the extent to which the contributions act as a tax is reduced because the worker receives something directly in return for his or her contributions. If benefits increase by a sufficiently large amount, the net effect is a wage subsidy rather than a tax. Mandatory contributions act as a tax in periods when contributions have no effect on the ultimate benefit.

Often, defined benefit social security schemes treat different categories of workers differently. For example, married workers where one spouse does not work may receive a spousal benefit that would not be received by single workers or married workers where both spouses work. Thus, comparing the situation of workers, there appears to be little relationship between contributions and benefits. The pattern is irrelevant, however, for determining whether the mandatory contribution acts as a tax. The relevant issue is the effect of increased earnings on increased contributions and benefits for each worker. If the increased earnings of the worker increase his or her social security benefits, that effect offsets the mandatory contribution rate in determining whether the mandatory contributions act as a tax.

In social insurance defined benefit schemes, the insurance provided by the schemes weakens the link between the contribution paid and the benefit received. For example, defined benefit schemes often provide drop-out years as a form of insurance against unemployment reducing future retirement benefits. For workers not needing this insurance, the mandatory contributions during drop-out years may be a tax because they do not increase future benefits. Thus there is a trade-off in designing these schemes. The greater the insurance provided by the schemes, the weaker the link between contributions and benefits and the greater the possibility that incentives for workers will be distorted. The insurance provided by social security is one of its benefits and, if the value of the insurance increases with contributions, that also will reduce the likelihood of economic distortions. To some extent economic distortions are a necessary cost of social insurance. The distortions should not be viewed in isolation. Their cost must be balanced against the benefits provided by social insurance.

Defined contribution schemes can also be structured so that they provide the redistribution that occurs in traditional defined benefit schemes. This can be done, for example, by providing subsidies for the accounts of low-income workers. Achieving redistribution through defined contribution schemes would cause the same kinds of efficiency problems ascribed to traditional defined benefit schemes. Hence the issue is not traditional defined benefit schemes versus mandatory defined contribution schemes, but the optimal mix of redistribution and insurance components within those schemes.

Labour demand

The demand side effects of old-age security include the way the number and structure of work places offered by employers might be affected by pension provisions, and how the offerings might change depending on changes in the scheme design. In other words, while, with respect to labour supply, we have been looking at behavioural impacts of pension schemes on workers' behaviour, we now investigate employers' behaviour more closely.

Provision of social security may affect the demand for labour by employers. When social security contributions are not levied on small employers, those employers may have an incentive to hire fewer employees for more hours in order to stay below the minimum number of employees that exempts them from making social security contributions. A similar effect may occur when there is a ceiling on the earnings of workers that are subject to mandatory social security contributions.

The employer's costs of complying with social security may cause him or her to structure labour demand to avoid having to make social security contributions. In a defined contribution scheme with multiple service providers, an employer may have to send monthly cheques to 15 or more different service providers, keeping records of frequent changes in service providers made by employees.

Competitiveness

Defined benefit social security pension schemes have been accused of undermining international competitiveness and increasing unemployment by increasing labour costs. This argument is not valid to the extent that these costs are borne ultimately by workers through lower wages rather than shifted to employers through higher labour costs and to consumers through higher prices. For most workers it is thought that the supply of labour is inelastic, meaning that the number of hours worked does not change much in response to changes in net wages. Workers in this situation will accept a lower net wage in response to an increase in mandatory social security contributions. To the extent that real wages are inflexible downwards, in the short run the increase in labour costs may cause an increase in unemployment, which will put downward pressure on wages (Thompson, 1998). Thus it is not clear that higher social security contributions mean higher total labour costs.

Retirement

Retirement occurs when a worker no longer works a substantial number of hours in paid employment. When workers retire at relatively young ages, that reduces the GDP of a country as it is traditionally measured. That measure, however, does not incorporate the value of the added leisure time, which might more than offset the reduction in GDP if a full economic measure were used. We review here the effects of traditional defined benefit pension schemes on retirement age and compares them to effects caused by defined contribution schemes. A number of empirical studies, focusing primarily on OECD countries, have attempted to assess the empirical magnitude of the effect of social security on retirement.[4]

The level of employment of older workers in OECD countries has decreased significantly over the last few decades. In 1990 approximately 50 per cent of the men aged 60 to 64 in OECD countries were economically active, compared with 82 per cent in 1950. As shown in table 13.1, the effective retirement age, based on the cessation of economic activity, has decreased on average from 66.5 in 1950 to 61.8 in 1990 in the OECD countries (Latulippe, 1996).

Disability and unemployment benefits

In a number of OECD countries retirement benefits can be received through programmes for disability, unemployment or special early retirement benefits sooner than the earliest age at which benefits can be obtained through the social security retirement benefits scheme. In more than half the OECD countries workers may receive unemployment benefits from age 55 to the standard retirement age, either because benefits can be received for an unlimited time or because special rules apply to older workers. In some countries these programmes have become used as early retirement programmes. In OECD countries disability benefits are more commonly used than the other two types of benefits for financing early retirement. In Canada, Ireland and the United States the number of disability beneficiaries aged 55–64 is less than 10 per cent of the age cohort. However more than a third of the population aged 55–64 receives those benefits in Finland and Norway, and more than half in Austria (Blöndal and Scarpetta, 1998b).

The entitlement conditions for disability benefits are an important determinant of their use as a path to early retirement. Disability benefits were originally intended as an income support for persons who were incapacitated. There are strong indications that entitlement conditions have eased in disability systems throughout OECD countries even in the absence of formal changes in the requirements for entitlement.

Social security retirement benefits

The availability of other types of schemes lessens the importance of social security retirement benefits schemes as a determinant of retirement. Nonetheless social security retirement benefit schemes may distort the retirement decision,

Table 13.1 Effective retirement age

Region	Countries	1950	1970	1990
Asia	Japan	66.2	66.7	65.5
North America	Canada and United States	65.9	64.8	62.6
Oceania	Australia and New Zealand	65.3	63.2	60.0
Northern Europe	Denmark, Finland, Iceland, Ireland, Norway, Sweden, United Kingdom	67.2	64.5	61.9
Southern Europe	Greece, Italy, Portugal, Spain	69.0	63.6	60.1
Western Europe	Austria, Belgium, France, Germany (FRG), Luxembourg, Netherlands, Switzerland	65.7	63.3	59.3
Average		66.5	64.5	61.8

Note: The effective retirement age is obtained from the gradual reduction of activity rates with age. A retiree is then defined as a person who has withdrawn from the labour market and is no longer economically active. Regional effective retirement age is calculated as a simple average of national values of retirement age.

Source: Latulippe (1996).

causing some workers to retire earlier than they would otherwise. Most countries require that workers retire in order to receive social security old-age benefits.

In democratic countries the availability of government benefits facilitating early retirement presumably reflects views of the majority of workers concerning the age at which they wish to retire. Thus it can be argued that the age at which people wish to retire determines the age at which social security benefits can be received, rather than vice versa. The development of programmes for early retirement outside the social security retirement benefits schemes may be viewed as evidence supporting that contention. Nonetheless social security retirement benefits schemes may establish a minimum age at which benefits can be received, which causes workers to retire earlier than otherwise, and in many countries in Africa and elsewhere the political process does not result in the features of the social security plan reflecting the retirement age at which covered workers would otherwise retire. This may occur through a lack of understanding of the effect of the choice of retirement age in the programme, or be due to poor functioning of the process that determines minimum pensionable age, or to increasing life expectancy, with political difficulties in raising the minimum retirement age once it has been set. Even in a well-functioning democratic process, the structure of social security will not reflect the desires of all workers because of differences across workers.

Defined benefit schemes

Defined benefit social security retirement benefits schemes may affect retirement age through the minimum pensionable age, an earnings test for workers to receive retirement benefits, the generosity of the benefits and the adjustment of benefits when workers postpone receiving them.

Minimum pensionable age

The minimum pensionable age is the youngest age at which workers can receive retirement benefits. Generally, as well as meeting an age requirement, workers must have contributed for a minimum number of years. In many countries the majority of workers have accumulated few savings at the point of retirement and they rely largely on social security retirement benefits for retirement income. Because they have few savings, many cannot retire until they reach the minimum pensionable age. Thus the minimum pensionable age may have an important effect on the age at which workers retire, with an increase in the minimum raising the average age at retirement. For other workers, however, the availability of retirement benefits may cause them to retire at a younger age than if there were no social security scheme. In both cases the effect of social security will also depend on the labour market opportunities and other benefits programmes available to workers.

Though to a lesser extent than after the minimum pensionable age, social security retirement benefits schemes may encourage retirement before the minimum pensionable age. The increase, if any, in pension entitlements due to an extra year's work may be insufficient to offset an extra year of pension contributions. With pension contribution rates increasing in many countries and pension accrual rates declining as a result of cutbacks in pension generosity, this outcome becomes increasingly likely (Blöndal and Scarpetta, 1998b).

Earnings test

As well as minimum age and years of contribution requirements, social security schemes may have an earnings test requiring the worker to cease or reduce substantially paid employment as a qualifying condition to receiving benefits. An earnings test directs benefits towards those who need them most because they no longer receive labour earnings.

If the earnings test is structured so that workers receive the same income whether they are fully or partially retired, losing a dollar of benefits for every dollar of earnings, workers will retire altogether because their efforts from work produce no financial advantage. Even if workers lose half a dollar of benefits for every dollar of earnings, the earnings test acts as a 50 per cent tax on their earnings.

Often an earnings test allows workers to receive a minimum level of earnings and above that ceiling benefits reduce with additional earnings until they are zero. The requirement that workers retire, or reduce hours of work, to receive social security retirement benefits may cause some workers to retire at a younger age than they otherwise would. The partial loss of benefits for earnings above a minimum level may have the same effect. Both requirements act as a tax on the earnings from work.

In countries where the basic state pension is not means-tested but is low, as in the United Kingdom, those older people who have no other individual or occupational pension – and who are entitled to claim means-tested welfare benefits – are also effectively discouraged from working to supplement their incomes and are thus encouraged to retire.

The United Kingdom abolished its earnings test in 1989. Japan has raised the level of earnings before which the earnings test applies. The United States has reduced the rate at which benefits are lost with increased earnings, from $1 of benefits lost per $1 of additional earnings to $1 per $3 for work above normal retirement age, up to age 70, at which point the earnings test ends.

Generosity of benefits

For schemes requiring that workers retire in order to receive benefits, the greater the generosity of benefits the more likely it is that workers will retire to receive them. Even if retirement is not required, however, the availability of income not requiring work will cause some workers to retire. Studies indicate, however, that sizeable changes in the generosity of benefits only have modest effects on the age at retirement. Studies done by the OECD suggest that a 20 per cent reduction in benefits in Germany and Italy would cause male workers to postpone retirement by only a few months (Blöndal and Scarpetta, 1998b).

Adjustment of benefits with postponed retirement

Benefit formulas that give credit for only a limited number of years of earnings may provide little incentive for continued work. For example, if there is no increase in benefits with added years of work for workers with more than 20, or even 30, years of service, many older workers may find little inducement to continue work, especially if they must continue paying social security contributions. In most OECD countries social security pensions rights accrue only until the individual attains a maximum number of years of contributions, commonly 35 or 40 years. Social security benefit formulas should place no maximum on the number of years of service counted in computing benefits. Placing a maximum may be relatively unfavourable to low-income workers because they tend to begin work at younger ages than high-income workers.

Schemes in OECD countries that have an earnings test often increase benefits for workers who postpone retirement. The more generous the increase for postponed retirement, the more likely it is that workers will choose to do so because the increase in future benefits with postponed retirement acts as a wage supplement for continued work.

Pensions are long-term benefits and the stream of income associated with their receipt can be viewed as an asset or wealth. Social security wealth for a worker at a particular age is the present discounted value of social security benefits. If the increase in benefits is just sufficient for the benefits lost by post-ponement, plus the processed contributions paid, to be exactly offset by the wealth value of the increase in future benefits, the postponement of retirement will have no effect on the wealth value of social security benefits. In that case a worker's decision to retire is not affected by the postponement of retirement affecting the lifetime wealth value of social security benefits. If there is a positive accrual of wealth, that will encourage postponed retirement. In many OECD countries the accrual is negative for workers past the minimum pensionable age. There is an insufficient increase in future benefits to compensate for the shorter period over which benefits are received. This negative accrual is an implicit tax on work and encourages retirement. Even for an adjustment factor that is neutral for workers with the average life expectancy, it will be insufficient for workers with a short life expectancy and they may be induced to retire.

The adjustment of benefits with postponed retirement can alternatively be described as a reduction in value for early receipt. The reduction factor in the United States, where social security benefits can be received at age 62, is 6.67 per cent per year before age 65 that first receipt occurs. This reduction factor is at a level that maintains a constant wealth value of social security for people with life expectancy equal to the actuarial average, whether it is taken at age 62 or receipt is postponed to age 65. In France the penalty for early retire-ment is 5 per cent per year that retirement is earlier than the normal retirement age, and in Germany it is 3.6 per cent per year. Because these penalties are relatively low, they provide an incentive for workers to retire early.

Features of social security that encourage partial retirement

The reduction in the labour force participation of older workers in OECD countries has been coupled with a greater popularity of part-time work. Part-time work has increased as a percentage of employment for older workers, both men and women, in most OECD countries (OECD, 1995b). This in part reflects an increase in part-time work as a proportion of employment at all ages. In most countries the proportion of employed men aged 55–59 working part-time is no higher than for younger male workers, less than 10 per cent. However the proportion of 60–64 year-old male workers who work part-time is higher than for all male workers, and this is also true for women.

Partial retirement occurs when older workers markedly reduce their hours of work. Different countries have used three alternative policies to allow or encou-rage older workers to take partial retirement (see table 13.2). First, they have allowed partial retirement combined with an earnings test that provides a partial pension benefit. Second, they have allowed partial retirement with no earnings test for receipt of benefits, so that the worker would receive full social security benefits. Third, they have distinct provisions in their social secur-ity plan, or a separate plan that provides for the payment of partial pensions.

Table 13.2   Partial retirement provisions in selected countries

Country	Minimum age	Type of programme
Canada	60	Earnings disregarded
France	55	Special provisions
Germany	55	Special provisions
Japan	60	Earnings test
Netherlands	55	Employers may provide
Norway	67	Special provisions
Sweden	60	Special provisions
United States	62	Earnings test

Source: National legislation.

Partial retirement with an earnings test

Many countries with an earnings test for receipt of social security benefits allow workers earning below an exemption amount to receive full social security benefits. Over an intermediate range, increases in a worker's earnings reduce social security benefits until those benefits are reduced to zero.

The earnings exemption amount in the earnings test allows workers to partially retire and receive full social security benefits. This feature provides greater flexibility to low-wage than to high-wage workers because the fixed ceiling allows the former to work more hours. The application of an earnings test could even allow "career part-time" workers to draw a pension without reducing hours worked.

Often the earnings test provides greater incentives for partial retirement at older ages than at younger ages: the level of earnings disregarded is higher, and the percentage reduction factor is lower. In certain cases the earnings test does not apply at all for workers beyond a certain age. Workers can take partial retirement at an early age, but it is more attractive to opt for partial retirement at a later age. This could encourage workers who opted for partial retirement to continue part-time work at older ages.

In the United States, as in virtually all countries, a higher proportion of women work part-time and on average women earn lower wages than men. The earnings test is therefore less of a constraint for them, and they are entitled to lower benefits as they reach retirement age.

No earnings test

If a country does not have an earnings test, or for older ages where the earnings test does not apply, workers can choose to continue working or partially retire. In either case, they receive full social security benefits.

Partial pension

A partial pension is an alternative policy to an earnings test as a way of allowing for partial retirement with a partial benefit. Partial pension benefits are calculated using a different formula from that used for calculating regular pension benefits and, therefore, the distributional effects of the two approaches (earnings test and partial pension) may differ significantly.

The amount of a partial pension is based on the reduction in number of hours worked and on the worker's earnings during the years preceding partial retirement. In comparison, pension benefit formulas are generally based on the work history of participation in the scheme, taking into account the worker's job tenure and earnings. Comparing a partial pension with an earnings test, a partial pension is relatively more favourable for people with short tenure under the pension scheme. Depending on how they are designed, partial pensions would only be attractive to people with limited pension entitlements. Partial pensions based on reduced hours would be more favourable to high-wage workers than an earnings test that required them to work only a few hours in order to receive a pension.

In countries with high unemployment, early retirement of older workers is often thought to make room for younger workers having trouble finding jobs. Special programmes are sometimes instituted encouraging partial or full retirement. This argument is generally wrong. The argument assumes that older and younger workers are fully substitutable, which may not always be the case. Older workers may have accumulated job-specific skills that younger workers do not have, while younger workers may bring new skills to the workforce. More important, there is not a fixed supply of jobs. Wage earners create a demand for labour through their expenditures. Excessively young retirement ages will slow economic growth by reducing the supply of labour to the economy and raising the mandatory contribution rates necessary to provide the benefits to support the added retirees. This increase in mandatory contribution rates reduces the demand for younger workers.

Defined contribution schemes

Most analyses of retirement effects of pension schemes have focused on defined benefit schemes, assuming that defined contribution schemes would be neutral with respect to the retirement age of workers. This section discusses ways in which mandatory defined contribution schemes may affect retirement age.

Similarly to defined benefit schemes, the establishment of a minimum pensionable age, before which workers cannot enjoy their benefits, may affect retirement. Depending on what age limit is set, the minimum pensionable age could cause workers to retire earlier or later than they would in the absence of a social security plan. Also the generosity of benefits available from a defined contribution plan may affect the age at which workers retire. Thus the age at which a worker retires may be affected by the rate of return in capital markets near the age of expected retirement. If in his or her defined contribution account the worker has accumulated less than he or she had projected, this may cause him or her to retire later than expected.

By retiring at the earliest possible age with non-annuitized benefits by choosing the phased withdrawal option, low-income workers in Chile may be able to qualify later for government-subsidized minimum benefits after they have reduced their pension assets through withdrawals. A similar strategy may be used by low-income workers in Australia in order to qualify for government-provided benefits.

Defined contribution schemes may affect workers' retirement decisions because of the effect of changes in the interest rate on the level of monthly benefits provided by an annuity. Workers may postpone or advance their retirement date, depending on when they expect annuity markets to be more favourable in the future. Because interest rate changes affect the level of monthly benefits provided by a given account balance, workers in defined contribution schemes will randomly be induced to retire early or postpone retirement on the basis of their expectations concerning interest rate changes. Thus defined contribution schemes may affect retirement age through expected and unexpected changes in asset values, annuity markets and interactions with minimum benefit programmes. While these changes in asset values and annuity markets affect workers' decisions as to age at retirement, they do not cause distortions of behaviour, as arise when workers make strategic decisions based on parameters of government programmes.

Pre-retirement effect on labour supply

A social security earnings test may affect the hours a person works before retirement. Because an earnings test acts like a tax on work, it may cause workers to stop working and retire. It may also cause workers to work longer hours earlier in life when they are not affected by this tax. Some evidence indicates that this effect has increased the average working week in the United States by one to two hours (Burkhauser and Turner, 1978).

Savings and investments

One of the most hotly debated topics in retirement income policy concerning unfunded defined benefit versus funded defined contribution schemes is the effect of social security retirement benefits schemes on national savings. An adequate level of investment is crucial to improving living standards. Savings generate the resources that can finance investment.

The relationship between social security pension policy and savings is interesting for two distinct réasons. One is a concern that, while some social security schemes may have succeeded in ensuring adequate retirement incomes, they have distorted capital and labour markets. In particular, pay-as-you-go schemes are said to have reduced national savings below what would have prevailed

> **Box 13.1 Unfunded occupational pension schemes**
> In France, Germany and Japan the pension schemes provided in the private sector are to varying extents unfunded. In France the mandatory industry-wide pension schemes use pay-as-you-go financing. In Germany most occupational pension schemes are financed using book reserves, meaning that a separate fund is not established but the pension promises are backed by the assets of the company. Book reserve financing is used to a lesser extent in Japan.

without such schemes. The social gains from more adequate retirement income are supposedly being offset, at least partially, by the social losses associated with lower savings and thus slower growth. In this respect it is interesting to note that the occupational pensions in several countries are pay-as-you-go or partially funded (see box 13.1).

A second reason to focus on the relationship between social security pensions and savings is that society may decide it needs to generate additional savings for reasons apart from concern about retirement income. Societies may decide to adopt a particular social security pension policy to try to increase savings above levels that would have prevailed had governments never instituted a social security scheme. Those who advocate these kinds of policies, however, need to explain why the level of savings produced by the free market is inadequate, demonstrate that the changes in pension policies will increase savings rates, establish that such changes will not also introduce unacceptable distortions elsewhere in the economy and show that alternative policy tools, such as income tax policy, would be worse suited to accomplishing the goal.

Opinions differ about the possibility of structuring pension policies to encourage productive investment without sacrificing other important social objectives. Part of the dispute involves the strength of any connection between pension policy and investment. If the linkage is weak, social security policy may not be an effective way to encourage investment. Another part involves the compatibility between social security schemes that seem to encourage investment and those that help achieve other important social objectives. Defined contribution schemes that might encourage investment are less attractive if they require substantial sacrifice of social objectives of reducing risk through defined benefit social security schemes.

THE LINK BETWEEN NATIONAL SAVINGS AND ECONOMIC GROWTH

Economies grow because of increases in the amount of labour and capital employed and through increases in their productivity. Investment increases the amount of capital available for each worker to use and facilitates the introduction of new, more efficient production techniques.

For well-functioning economies operating near capacity an increase in the fraction of productive capacity devoted to investment goods is only possible if the fraction devoted to consumption goods is reduced. When there are no unemployed resources, a society cannot invest more unless somebody consumes less (saves more). But the link between individual saving and investment is complex and imperfect. Investment is only possible if the amount of resources used for domestic consumption is reduced, or if capital can be imported from abroad.[5] Saving is the process through which domestic consumption is reduced and provides the chief engine for investment.

First, national saving is the sum of the net saving of a country's households (usually called personal saving), its business and its governmental units. An increase in saving among households will translate into higher national saving only if it is not accompanied by an offsetting reduction in either business or government saving. For example, a particular change in a country's tax laws might encourage individuals to save more, which would increase national saving in the absence of any other changes. But the tax change may also cause a deficit in the government's budget. Unless the increase in household saving is larger than the increase in the government deficit, the net effect of the change in the tax law will be to reduce national saving.

Second, saving occurs only when the net effect of a set of transactions is a reduction in total consumption. A particular household may save for retirement by reducing its consumption and making a deposit in a financial institution. One cannot know whether this transaction translates into higher national saving, however, without knowing what use was made of the funds deposited in the financial institution. If these funds are lent to a business establishment to finance a new facility, they have added to national saving and helped finance new investment. The transaction will produce no increase in net saving or investment, however, if the funds are (a) loaned to another working-age household to finance the purchase of a new car or other consumer item, (b) loaned to the government to finance a budget deficit, or (c) paid to a retiree who is supporting himself by drawing down the balance he had accumulated in the same financial institution.

Third, economic growth can be enhanced only if any increase in national saving is translated into productive investment. In particular, macroeconomic conditions must encourage investment or else higher saving may cause a near-term economic contraction instead of the desired longer-term increase in economic capacity. In addition available investment funds must be allocated to productive uses. Political interference in investment decisions, imperfections in domestic capital markets or internal structural barriers cause investment funds in Africa to flow to less productive uses, limiting the effect of higher saving on future economic growth.

How pensions affect personal saving: Predictions from economic theory

Unfortunately it is not possible to predict the likely effect of pensions on the basis solely of our understanding of the general operation of the economy. Economic reasoning reveals that several forces may be at work. These forces push in conflicting directions and their relative magnitude cannot be known in advance.

The life cycle theory of consumption

Over the past four decades the starting point for most analyses has been the life cycle theory of consumption. According to this theory, individual saving behaviour is geared to closing gaps between the timing of expected income receipts and the timing of desired consumption expenses over the course of the life cycle. In particular savings are accumulated during the working years and drawn down during retirement years.

The life cycle theory predicts that, in the absence of government intervention, a nation's accumulated stock of savings (its aggregate wealth) at any given time will be determined largely by the age structure of its population, per capita income and its retirement patterns. Wealth increases as people save for retirement and declines as they draw down their retirement savings. The size of the wealth stock at any time depends on the relative size of the two flows. It will tend to grow if the working-age population is large relative to the retiree population, but will decline if the retiree population rises without a corresponding increase in the working-age population.

Increases in the rate of growth of the economy will also lead to increased saving rates. When they expect higher future earnings levels, workers will increase the amount they set aside for retirement to ensure a corresponding increase in their retirement income. Finally, if workers decide to increase the fraction of their lifetime spent in retirement by retiring earlier, they will increase their saving rate; if they decide to work longer, saving rates will fall.[6]

Other theories of consumer saving

The implications of the life cycle model are often adjusted to reflect the effect of several other theories. Two have particular importance for discussions of national pension policy. The first is that part of aggregate household savings may be motivated by the desire to bequeath wealth to one's heirs. A second is that an important motivation for saving is the uncertainty about consumption needs in the future, in particular about how long one will live and what extraordinary expenses (particularly medical and long-term care expenses in some countries) might arise near the end of one's life.[7]

Effect of differing asset accumulation patterns

One significant difference between most social security pension schemes and any private saving they have displaced is that the former tend to be operated more or less on a pay-as-you-go basis, whereas the latter are, by definition, advance-funded.

During the start-up phase of an advance-funded system, contributions are made but almost no benefits are paid. Instead, if prudently invested, the contributions finance the accumulation of wealth. Only after the system matures are most of the retirees able to receive full benefits by drawing down their accumulated retirement assets. However the retired population may be forced to liquidate its accumulated assets at reduced prices if it is a large generation selling to a small working generation. In contrast, under a classic pay-as-you-go system, early contributions are collected at a lower rate and used to finance higher benefit payments to the initial retirees. As the system matures, the pay-as-you-go contribution rate rises to approximate – or even exceed – the contribution rate necessary under advance funding for the same level of pension.

In principle the advance-funded approach should generate additional national savings during the start-up phase through two mechanisms: the higher initial contribution rate required of the employed and the lower benefits paid to retirees. Each reduces aggregate consumption relative to the situation under the pay-as-you-go approach. These effects are offset by the added taxes, or increased government deficit needed, to finance the benefits of current retirees.

Several theories have been advanced which might substantially narrow the differences between the effects of pay-as-you-go schemes and funded schemes. One involves possible offsets operating through bequests. If the working-age population reacts to the introduction of a pay-as-you-go scheme by increasing the volume of bequests, the greater savings needed to generate these bequests can partially offset the lower savings otherwise associated with starting a pay-as-you go scheme.[8] A second complication can arise if the alternatives to a government-sponsored pay-as-you go scheme are privately operated pay-as-you-go schemes, such as those produced through informal intra-family arrangements, or more formal systems associated with fraternal or occupation-based organizations.[9]

Effect on incentive to save for uncertainties

National social welfare programmes reduce many of the uncertainties people face in planning for retirement. Social security pension schemes normally pay benefits as life annuities, reducing the uncertainty associated with not knowing how long one's assets must last. In developed market economies these benefits are often indexed to reduce uncertainties associated with future inflation. Some countries offer the aged, if not the entire population, comprehensive assurance that needed health care will be provided, further reducing retirement uncertainties. And some countries have formal systems for handling the long-term care needs of a frail population. All of these policies enhance social welfare by increasing the security of the retired population. All also reduce the incentives that people might otherwise have to save in advance to cover these contingencies.

Effect on financial market development

These quantitative elements in turn lead to qualitative benefits including financial innovation and modernization of the infrastructure of securities markets which should help reduce the cost or increase the availability of capital market funds, and hence aid industrial development as well as facilitating privatization. There may be important indirect benefits in this context, as pension funds press for improvements in the "architecture of allocative mechanisms", including better accounting, auditing, brokerage and information disclosure (Greenwald and Stiglitz, 1990). Modern banking and insurance supervision, new securities and corporate laws, junior equity markets and credit rating agencies may also develop. In addition an increase in capital investment may raise labour productivity, which can raise the economic growth rate. This effect may be particularly powerful in developing countries if a switch from pay-as-you-go to funding induces workers to shift from the labour-intensive and low-productivity informal sector to the capital-intensive and high-productivity formal sector (Corsetti and Schmidt-Hebbel, 1994), but both the economic analysis and the empirical evidence supporting such an effect appear weak. Equity market development has been shown to enhance overall economic development (Demirguc-Kunt and Levine, 1996).

An often-quoted example of the beneficial effects of funding is that of Chile. The growth of pension funds accompanied an expansion of overall financial savings from 28 per cent of GDP in 1980 to 68 per cent in 1993 (Fontaine, 1997), with pension savings accounting for a third of this total. Initially funds invested mainly in debt securities, owing to regulatory prohibition of equity investment, but not solely those of the government: also bank certificates of deposit and mortgage bonds. Debt maturities increased as a consequence of the development of pension funds to 12–20 years by 1990. Equity investment was permitted in 1985 and holdings have grown to over 30 per cent of assets. This accompanied and encouraged a marked expansion of equity market capitalization from 32 per cent of GDP in 1988 to 90 per cent in 1993. In 1991 the Chilean pension fund managers (AFPs) held a third of public bonds, two-thirds of private bonds and 10 per cent of equities. Some econometric evidence suggests that the development of financial markets in Chile correlates with strong development of the real side of the economy, via rising total factor productivity and capital accumulation (Holzmann, 1997c).

Pension fund development may have facilitated internal resource transfers, enabling the Chilean government to service its international debts without extreme fiscal adjustment which was, in other countries, damaging to the real economy (Fontaine, 1997), by providing a domestic source of borrowing without requiring excessively high interest rates (in fact the debt was generally indexed to the consumer price index). Correspondingly public sector debt rose from 5 per cent of GDP in 1980 to 28 per cent in 1990. Later the demand for pension funds enabled debt conversion – by both private and public institutions – to occur smoothly. In addition the fact that pension funds were not permitted to invest internationally until 1989, and then only in a limited way, is considered to explain why the capital markets in Chile grew in size and depth so rapidly. Given the existence of domestic long-term institutions, Chile is probably better insulated from the shifting behaviour of international investors, as witness the lower financial market correction in 1992 than for other Latin American markets. Development of pension funds may have been a major factor behind Chile's bonds being rated investment-grade, the first bonds of a Latin American country to be so rated since the debt crisis (Hansell, 1992). Disclosure standards are reportedly higher than elsewhere in Latin America. Chile has been unsuccessful, however, at ownership dispersion, one reason being unwillingness of closely held companies to accept dilution of control. And the rating regulations for pension fund investment in the stock market have, until the late 1990s, prevented funds investing in start-up companies and venture capital.

Summary of possible effects

In summary, economic reasoning does not lead to a clear prediction about the effect of a social security pension scheme on personal saving. Introduction of a social security pension plan is likely to increase national saving to the extent that:

1. it forces people to make higher contributions for their retirement programmes than they would otherwise make,

2. it encourages people to retire earlier than they had intended, or

3. it offers people a lower return than they would receive on individual retirement savings.

When people are encouraged to retire earlier than planned they must save more for a longer retirement period, which is funded by a shorter working period. This increased saving is partially offset by an increased number of dissavers. Such introduction is likely to reduce national saving to the extent that:

1. it offers people higher returns than they would receive on individual retirement savings,

2. it replaces advance-funded retirement arrangements with pay-as-you-go arrangements, and

3. it effectively reduces the risks associated with not knowing how long one will live, or what future inflation rates might be.

Finally a social security pension plan might have little effect on saving to the extent that:

1. it codifies the arrangements that would have existed in its absence (including private, pay-as-you-go arrangements),

2. people are able to offset any forced saving that might otherwise occur by increasing their borrowing, or

3. any change in the liabilities of future generations is offset by changes in the volume of bequests from current generations.

How pensions affect personal saving: Statistical evidence

Attempts to measure the actual effect of pension schemes on saving behaviour face a number of challenges that analysts have so far not successfully overcome. Comparisons that focus on aggregate national saving look either at trends over time in one particular country or at differences at a point in time among different countries. In either case the available data are imperfect and the ability to adjust for the influence of other factors is seriously limited. A frustrating consequence is that two researchers can produce studies which convincingly convey contradictory findings. Slight variations in the particular way a statistical test is conducted, the particular ways that other influences are accounted for, or the particular set of years or sample of countries studied can mean the difference between finding that social security schemes increase saving, reduce saving or have no effect.[10] Studies that look at variations in saving behaviour among different individuals in a particular country suffer from other statistical limitations and are unable to generalize from the possible effects on one part of the population to the effect on total national saving. Simply comparing across countries to see a relationship between savings accumulated in the form of pension assets and national savings rates does not indicate any relationship (see table 13.3).

Studies of the effect of pay-as-you-go pension schemes

In many countries social security pension schemes now operate largely on a pay-as-you-go basis, regardless of whether they were originally designed with that approach in mind. By far the most common premise for statistical studies has been the examination of whether such approaches have had the unintended effect of reducing national saving.

Unfortunately efforts to establish the relationship between pay-as-you-go pension schemes and national saving rates have not been successful. After an exhaustive review of cross-country studies, and studies of the potential effect of the system in the United States, one noted American economist concluded:

> For a variety of reasons, ranging from introspection and personal experience to the analysis of statistics on saving, people have developed hunches about how social security affects saving. Economists, who are no more immune to hunches than anyone else, have applied the tools of their discipline to try to determine which of these hunches is correct.

Table 13.3 National savings rates and funding of pension systems

Country	National savings/GDP	Pension assets/GDP
Australia	18	39
Canada	15	3
Denmark	19	60
France	21	3
Germany	23	4
Ireland	20	37
Japan	34	8
Netherlands	25	76
Switzerland	30	70
United Kingdom	14	73
United States	15	66

Note: Savings rate is the total (private sector plus government) savings rate.

Sources: Hughes (1996) derived from World Bank (1994, table 5.1), OECD (1994b, table 2.1).

The evidence is conclusive that so far they have failed. Using the best that economic theory and statistical techniques have to offer, they have produced a series of studies that can be selectively cited by the true believers of conflicting hunches or by people with political agendas that they seek to advance.[11]

Reviewing the evidence a decade later, the World Bank reached much the same conclusion:

> numerous empirical investigations (most of them based on U.S. data) have been unable to prove conclusively that saving did, indeed, drop once pay-as-you-go programmes were established. ... Analyses of saving rates in other countries yield similar conflicting results. Studies of the saving effect of old-age security programmes in Canada, France, the Federal Republic of Germany, Japan, Sweden and the United Kingdom found no significant effect, except for a slightly positive aggregate effect in Sweden, where the pension programme is heavily funded.[12]

Studies of the effect of advance-funded schemes

Even if pay-as-you-go schemes have not reduced saving, switching to advance-funded schemes could increase saving. As noted previously, such a policy might be pursued because of a concern that, without government intervention, the free market would generate inadequate saving. Mandatory, advance-funded pensions are a form of government intervention that has the potential for altering this result.

Only a handful of studies have systematically explored the possible effect on national saving of advance-funded pension or retirement arrangements. One category of studies examines programmes that offer tax subsidies to encourage individual retirement saving. They explore the extent to which such policies cause people to save more, or simply cause people who had already saved to switch their assets into tax-favoured accounts. No clear conclusion emerges from the studies.[13]

Other studies have focused on whether the asset holdings of individual households vary systematically with variations in their prospective pension entitlements. They focus on the experience in the United States and Canada, where private pensions are often a part of the employment package but are not required by law. These may not represent the situation in other societies and under a universal, mandatory scheme.

The question being researched in these studies is whether households scheduled to receive higher pensions appear, relative to their income levels and holding other things constant, to have smaller holdings of other financial assets. To the extent that they do, the smaller holdings can be assumed to be offsetting some of the increased saving that would otherwise result from the asset accumulation occurring in pension funds. These studies tend to find evidence of partial offset. Perhaps 60 per cent (results commonly range between 40 per cent and 80 per cent) of the assets accumulated in pension funds are *not* offset directly by reduced asset accumulation among recipient households.[14] Since pensions in the United States and Canada are more common among higher-wage earners, the degree of asset offset under a universal pension plan may be even lower. Lower earners have less ability to make offsetting reductions in personal asset holdings.

Summary of statistical evidence

Despite numerous attempts to measure the effect statistically, no consistent evidence has emerged linking the creation of pay-as-you-go social security schemes with reductions in personal saving rates. This suggests that, if these schemes have had a negative effect on personal saving, it probably has been a modest one. At the same time studies also suggest that advance-funded schemes can lead to an increase in personal savings, though by less than the gross amount of the assets accumulated in them. Although pay-as-you-go pension schemes may not be responsible for depressing personal saving, relying instead on advance-funded approaches may nevertheless cause personal saving to rise.

THE LINK BETWEEN PERSONAL SAVING AND NATIONAL SAVING

Generalizations are even more difficult when the perspective is broadened to include potential links between pension policies and total national savings. On the one hand, limited evidence available suggests that the positive relationship between advance-funded pensions and personal saving rates may not carry over into a positive relationship between advance funding and the national saving rate. On the other hand, while pay-as-you-go pensions may themselves have had little effect on either personal or national saving, attempts to maintain the broader welfare state may have reduced national saving through their effect on government budgets.

The positive relationship between advance-funded pensions and personal saving will only translate into increased national saving if the funds flowing into pension schemes do not trigger offsetting changes in either the government budget or the economy's financial liabilities. Unfortunately both kinds of offsetting changes are possible. In most countries deferred pension income is taxed more lightly than ordinary saving. Thus any switch in the holding of assets away from individuals and towards pension schemes will reduce the government's tax revenue and lead, other things being equal, to an increase in government borrowing. Also increases in financial assets held by private pension funds need not necessarily lead to higher saving in the economy if they are used to finance additional consumption rather than additional investment. National saving does not rise if pension managers use their funds to finance credit card debt.

Data describing recent experience in several OECD countries show no clear relationship between the accumulation of assets in pension funds and national saving rates, suggesting that these types of offsets may have been occurring. OECD countries differ widely, both in the prevalence of advance-funded pensions and in levels of national saving. A comparison of saving rates over the decades of the 1970s and 1980s with the rates at which pension assets grew during each decade in each country essentially suggests no correlation between the two.[15]

In an extensive review of OECD saving patterns, Dean et al. (1990) analyse a number of factors that appear to account for some of the differences between the countries and time periods. They note the role that the growth of social security pensions may play, but they also present evidence of the effect of a number of other factors, including variations in demographic patterns and trends, increases in consumer credit due to financial market liberalizations, unanticipated inflation, changes in housing and equity prices, tax policies and real interest rates. Any differential effect from the growth of pension plan assets may simply be lost in the interaction of all these influences.

At the same time recent OECD data also suggest that government fiscal policies may play a major role in national saving trends. Although national saving rates declined substantially between the 1960s and 1980s in almost all OECD countries, in most of these countries virtually all of the decline is associated with deterioration in the fiscal conditions of government. The fiscal problems experienced by most OECD governments since the mid-1970s arose, at least in part, from pressures to maintain social welfare spending in the face of deteriorating economic conditions. To the extent that those pressures can be traced back either to challenges in meeting past pension promises or to the consequences of tax incentives to encourage retirement saving, part of the responsibility for the decline in government saving may appropriately be attributable to pension policies. Indeed it may be that pension policies affect national saving as much through their effect on the government budget as through any direct adjustments they trigger in private saving rates.

A similar story emerges in another study which focuses only on the experience in Sweden but carefully traces the interactions of personal, business and government behaviour after the introduction of a partially funded, earnings-related social security pension in 1960. The evidence suggests some reduction in both personal and business savings offset – at least in the initial years – by the increase in government savings. Problems developed, however, when the public sector began to find itself overcommitted in the late 1970s.[16]

Potential gains from higher savings

Several analysts have developed quantitative estimates of the potential economic gain from changing national pension programmes in a way which they believe would lead to increased national saving and investment. These estimates always find that the kind of offsetting adjustments just discussed will not occur in the future. They suggest that, under these circumstances, major changes in social security pension policy might have measurable but rather modest effects.

Feldstein (1996) calculates that changing the current pay-as-you-go social security scheme in the United States into one based on funded, defined contribution schemes would eventually increase the aggregate capital stock by about 25 per cent. But he further calculates that an increase of this size in the capital stock would only lead to a 5.7 per cent increase in GDP. Since the changeover would occur over a period of 50 years or more, the calculation implies an acceleration of about 0.1 per cent per year in the rate of growth of GDP.

Kotlikoff et al. (1996) assume that a similar change in the structure of the social security scheme of the United States would have an even larger effect. They find that, after 70 years, the change will have produced a 37 per cent increase in the capital stock which, they calculate, will generate an 11 per cent increase in GDP. In their simulation, however, all of this translates into an increase of only 3.7 per cent in real wage levels. Cifuentes and Valdés-Prieto (1996) simulated the effect of two proposed Hungarian pension reforms and found that the proposal involving greater reliance on advance funding might increase future GDP by some 8 per cent, whereas the proposal that relied on pay-as-you-go financing might produce an increase of only about 1.5 per cent of GDP.

Efficiency of financial markets

A related debate among financial economists involves the question whether altering pension institutions can have a positive effect on economic growth for reasons not directly related to their effect on national saving. The issue is the relative advantage of relying primarily on the banking sector as the source of outside capital for a nation's private business enterprises (the traditional practice in Japan and continental Europe) as opposed to relying on independent financial intermediaries and equity markets (the traditional practice in the United States and the United Kingdom). Independent financial intermediaries are said to be more receptive to financing new enterprises and imposing financial discipline on older, inefficient enterprises. They are also said, however, to impart an undesirable short-term bias to financial decision making.[17]

Those who believe that the use of independent intermediaries is more likely to foster economic growth may see in the creation of advance-funded pension accounts a means to facilitate the emergence of financial markets, especially in transition economies that did not previously have such markets. The argument would be that the form of the pension institution may affect economic growth indirectly through its effect on financial markets even if it has no direct effect on saving rates.[18] Research on this issue is fairly recent. The experience of those countries implementing reforms needs to be monitored for evidence of the existence and magnitude of these possible positive effects.

Summary of evidence concerning social security and savings

Economic reasoning cannot be relied upon to conclude that a social security pension scheme will have a particular effect on national saving. Systems that offer low implicit returns on contributions and systems which encourage people to retire earlier or to make higher contributions than they would otherwise prefer may increase saving. Systems that give people higher returns on their contributions encourage later retirement and reduce the risks associated with living in old age. Substituting pay-as-you-go arrangements for advance-funded arrangements may reduce saving.

Statistical studies have not resolved controversies about the relationship between saving rates and pension plan structure and finance. Those who have examined in detail the whole range of studies of the effect of pay-as-you-go schemes on saving seem to agree that these studies do not support the conclusion that national saving rates have declined as a result of the introduction of pay-as-you-go pensions.

An advance-funded social security pension scheme ought to have a more favourable effect on national saving rates than a pay-as-you-go system, at least during the start-up phase. Studies do suggest that the assets accumulated in such pension schemes are not entirely offset by the action of participating households. But the statistical evidence does not afford a clear picture of the net effect on the economy as a whole of advance-funded pensions.

Studies suggest that pension policy is only one of many factors influencing national saving rates. Policy changes designed to increase saving probably need to deal comprehensively with a variety of factors, including tax, fiscal and credit market policies. Such policies may also include changes in the way pensions are organized and financed, especially if pension policies can be adjusted to promote greater saving without unduly sacrificing other important retirement income objectives. The statistical evidence is not of sufficient quality, however, to justify adopting a particular pension approach deemed to be inferior on other grounds solely in the hope that it will increase national saving rates.

While considerable empirical work has been done on the economic effects of social security defined benefit schemes, little empirical work has been done on the effects of defined contribution schemes and thus much less is known about their effects. In general, social security schemes are mandatory, whether they are defined benefit or defined contribution, because of the desire by policy makers, or society generally, to change the behaviour of some workers. Thus some of the economic effects are desired because of the goals of the pro- grammes. Because they are mandatory, they may, however, have undesirable as well as desirable effects, as workers attempt to minimize the effects of the schemes.

Undesirable effects are reduced to the extent that workers support the goals of schemes that are redistributive or where benefits are linked to contributions. These two criteria are conflicting and workers may choose, through their poli- tical system, to have a programme that weakens the link between contributions and benefits in order to provide income redistribution.

Perhaps the most heavily researched, important and controversial issue is the question of the effect of social security schemes on savings. After years of research the question is unresolved. Most observers interpret the results as indicating that an unfunded social security scheme probably does not reduce savings, but that switching to a funded scheme might increase them. This result leaves open the more fundamental question of whether social security schemes should be used to increase savings if such schemes sacrifice other goals, such as the goal of providing low-risk retirement benefits. Furthermore, if society desires to increase its aggregate savings, it has other policies at its disposal, such as tax, private investment and infrastructure policies.

Notes

[1] National pension schemes contain provisions according to which either taxes or mandatory contributions are collected and benefits are paid. For ease of exposition, the discussion here assumes a model of earnings-related benefits financed entirely by earmarked social insurance contributions, although the results also apply to other models.

[2] The effect could only occur among those individuals (or in those countries) where the benefits under the social security pension scheme are insufficient to fully support retirees so that they need to supplement the public pension benefit if previous living standards are to be maintained (see, for example, Feldstein, 1974).

[3] See, for example, Steuerle and Bakija (1994) or World Bank (1994, pp. 297–302).

[4] Reviews of the empirical studies on retirement can be found in Leonesio (1996), Lumsdaine (1996) and Magnussen (1996).

[5] Foreign capital is imported whenever a country runs a deficit in its international trade accounts. In effect, foreigners have shipped more goods and services to the country than they have taken out of it, leaving the country able to utilize more goods and services that year than it produced domestically. Foreign capital flows will be ignored in the balance of this brief since it is concerned with the effect of pension policy on the ability of a country to finance its own investment.

[6] See Modigliani (1986). Note that the life cycle theory implies that it is higher growth that produces higher saving whereas popular discussions seem always to assume the reverse, that the higher savings are causing the higher growth. The more common assumption is that causation runs in the other direction. Perhaps both are true.

[7] See, for example, Kotlikoff (1988). These two supplemental theories may help explain why the aged appear to reduce their wealth less and wealth appears to be distributed less equally among the population than the life cycle theory would seem to imply.

[8] See, for example, Barco (1974).

[9] This point may have little relevance for today's developed economies but may still apply in parts of the developing world where family and informal arrangements remain important. After analysing the finances of then existing craft-based pension arrangements, Pigou concluded that introducing a social security pension insurance scheme in the United Kingdom was likely to have only a modest effect on capital formation for this reason. See Pigou (1920). See also the discussion of informal retirement income systems in The World Bank (1994, ch. 2).

[10] Leimer and Lesnoy (1982) demonstrate this point for time series studies in the United States.

[11] Aaron (1982, p. 51).

[12] The World Bank (1994, p. 307). Knut Magnussen of Statistics Norway has compiled what is probably the most thorough and careful current review of studies of the effect of social security on saving. (See Magnussen, 1996).

[13] These particular studies, along with others addressing more generally the relationship between social security and saving, are summarized in Hughes (1996).

[14] This literature is summarized in Munnell and Yohn (1992), Magnussen (1996) and Hughes (1996).

[15] This analysis follows the lead of Hughes (1996).

[16] Palmer (1987).

[17] See, for example, Singh (1997).

[18] For example, Holzmann finds that improvements in the financial markets in Chile added something over 1 per cent per year to the growth rate. Some portion of these improvements is probably attributable to the pension reform there. See Holzmann (1997c).

THE CONSEQUENCES FOR PUBLIC FINANCES

14

This chapter first sets out ways in which pension expenditure and financing are usually recorded in public budgets and accounts, and goes on to review how pension financing, directly and indirectly, affects the long-term financial positions of governments. There are shortcomings with respect to the full recording of actual public pension expenditure, as well as hidden government liabilities for the financing of pensions. The last section places the menu of national choices of pension financing methods in the wider context of public finance policies. Among related issues discussed elsewhere in the book are the fiscal problems arising from pension financing (Chapter 1), methods of pension financing (Chapter 6) and tax expenditures (Chapter 19). The appropriate accounting for pension costs is relevant to both developed and developing countries.

Public outlays on pension schemes can amount to as much as 15 per cent of GDP, depending on a country's state of development, the age structure of the population and other characteristics of its employment and social structure. Financing transfers of this magnitude inevitably affects the system of public finance in a country: either directly when governments pay benefits and finance them from general revenues or through contributions, or indirectly when private institutions pay benefits and finance them through contributions, which are part of the overall tax and contribution burden of citizens.

PENSIONS IN NATIONAL AND GOVERNMENT ACCOUNTS

Public pensions are pensions paid by government or public autonomous social security institutions. In standard national accounting they are subsumed under social security income and expenditure. In the system of United Nations standard national current accounts, the most frequently used account structure,[1] public social benefits – whether financed directly by government or by autonomous public bodies – are regarded as government expenditure and appear in the general government accounts. The general government accounts include all income and expenditure of the government sector. Thus they include income and expenditure of central, state or province (if existing) and local governments as well as some parastatal autonomous organizations such as social security institutions.

All, or a subset, of these accounts can be combined into one consolidated account. International Monetary Fund financial statistics, for example, provide consolidated accounts for central governments that combine the budgetary sphere of the central government with nationally operating social security schemes.[2] Consolidation does not simply imply the adding of all income and expenditure components of the various accounts for the different benefit levels, as the accounting levels (or levels of government) are often connected by a complex system of transfers. State governments might receive transfers from the central government while at the same time they subsidize local governments. Social security institutions might receive government transfers, or they might transfer excess contributions to the central government account. The different transfers between government levels cancel each other when a summary account is established for the overall government sector.

The balancing item of the consolidated (central) government account or general government account (which is technically called "net borrowing or net lending", or "cash balance", or "public sector borrowing requirement", in the terminology used in the United Kingdom), indicates whether the general government sector is in surplus or deficit. The component accounts within the different government levels, including the social security account, help trace where a deficit or a surplus stems from. This means implicitly that current deficits in social security institutions are part of the national deficit.

A surplus or deficit measures the difference between the current income and expenditure and, in the case of short-term cash benefits such as maternity and sickness, this approach might provide a full picture of the financial status of a social security programme. Short-term benefit schemes' income and expenditure are normally expected to balance within a year. Social security pension schemes whose accounts are in balance do not contribute to national deficits in terms of the consolidated general government account. However balanced annual accounts do not necessarily signal a sound financial status for the pension scheme which might still be underfunded in the long run. Thus, by implication, current national accounts also fail to provide a full picture of government financial obligations in respect of the financing of pension schemes. The focus on annual balances is a crucial deficiency of current national accounts for assessing government obligations for pension financing.

This standard international accounting practice indicates that, in the logic of the System of National Accounts and International Financial Statistics, social security benefits provided through public institutions, or lower-level government agencies, are regarded as government expenditure in the same way as benefits organized and financed directly by the central government. In effect the provision of benefits through autonomous social security schemes is, from an accounting perspective, considered as merely a different form of government organization or provision. The International Monetary Fund's and the United Nations' accounting methods subsume social security contributions under tax revenues.

However current national accounting usually does not cover the full national expenditure on pensions – both public and private – nor its financing. Incomplete accounting of liabilities and benefits is the second major shortcoming of standard national accounts with respect to pension and social security accounting. Not captured in government accounts is the provision of pensions by private entities, such as employers, private occupational pension schemes and life insurance companies. Most importantly this also includes pension provisions mandated by law but administered, as in Switzerland, by private insurance companies. This effect not only distorts international comparisons of national pension expenditure based solely on government accounts, but could also lead to an underestimation of total long-term potential government liabilities for the financing of pensions. Some of these liabilities are implicit and contingent: for example, government guarantees for private pension schemes, which only lead to concrete expenditure when private schemes fail. These are difficult to account for under any accounting system. Others are implicit and hidden: for example, tax subsidies for private pension schemes, which represent income forgone by the government (tax expenditures) but should in fact be counted as an implicit part of overall government pension or social security expenditure (see the annex to this chapter).

This does not mean that the revenue and outlay of non-public pension schemes is unaccounted for in the standard national accounts. (Individuals' contributions to funded private schemes, and the benefits they receive, are to be found in the accounts of household income and expenditure. Employers' contributions are to be found in the production accounts and in the savings accounts of the private sector.) What it does do is to underline the dangers of comparing pension provision solely on the basis of the government accounts, particularly between countries which may have very different proportions of pension income derived from public and private sources.

In principle the accounts for all identifiable pension expenditures and revenues can only be captured in national social expenditure accounts (social expenditure budgets) used in countries of the European Union. They are pivotal tools for the overall management of the social sector at a macroeconomic level.

Social budgets compile expenditure on all national social transfers, including the expenditure for benefits financed and administered by private entities, but mandated or promoted by law, or agreed upon in collective agreements between employers and workers. As well as pensions and other long-term benefits, these include health care and short-term cash benefits, as well as goods and services in kind. The accounts relate them to the totality of all sources of financing, which include mandatory social security and private insurance contributions, voluntary contributions, out-of-pocket contributions, employer liabilities and imputed contributions and financing through taxes. Only when such a comprehensive social accounting is established and projected under realistic economic and demographic assumptions can the long-term sustainability of the total national social protection system be assessed. Furthermore only then can one assess to what extent the government budget will be affected by the financing of social transfers.[3,4]

The annex to this chapter shows the accounting of pension expenditure within a hierarchy of government accounts for Turkey, as well as a summary of the overall social budget. Other countries include the estimated tax revenues forgone through tax allowances. In Germany, for example, indirect fiscal benefits accounted for 7.6 per cent of total social expenditure in 1993. In the case of Turkey, the government has covered the deficit of the social security institutions, while a fundamental reform of the system is negotiated and widely discussed in public. This budget link is more or less automatic. However it is not the only way to associate government budgets and social security budgets.

FINANCIAL LINKS BETWEEN PENSION SCHEMES AND GOVERNMENT ACCOUNTS

There are a number of ways in which social security pension expenditure and government accounts are explicitly (or implicitly) linked, and in which pension financing in particular affects the short-term and long-term financial positions of governments. There are three ways to organize pension benefits:

1. *government provision*, where pensions are provided through government agencies or departments;

2. *public institutional provision*, where pensions are provided by autonomous public institutions;

3. *private provision*, where pensions are provided by private entities (private insurance schemes, occupational pension schemes and employers).

There are also three sources of financing for pension schemes:

1. *taxes,* where benefits are financed simply by allocations from general revenues or earmarked taxes;

2. *social security contributions,* where benefits are paid by mandatory contributions collected from employers and workers (this includes mandatory contributions to private pension provisions which are charged as a percentage of insurable earnings);

3. *private sources,* such as private insurance contributions or imputed contributions attributed to an employer, or to employees, who finance pensions directly out of the current income of a company or through forgone wages paid on the basis of collective agreements or legal obligations (entirely voluntary individual financing is excluded here).

Table 14.1 Combinations of types of pension provisions and pension financing in selected national pension schemes

Dominant source of financing	Government provision	Public institutional provision	Private provision
Taxes	Denmark (first-tier schemes), Australia, South Africa (social assistance schemes)	Sweden (universal pension)	
Social security contributions	USA, Cyprus, Canada, UK, Ireland	France, Germany, Belgium, Spain, Portugal, Costa Rica, Poland, Bulgaria, Ghana (basic schemes), Sweden (second tier)	
Private sources			Switzerland, Australia (second-tier schemes), Germany, France (second-tier schemes)

Source: US Social Security Administration.

Table 14.1 shows some of the main cases of the possible combinations of benefit provisions and sources of financing. Apart from the case of government provision tax financing, the income of most national pension schemes comes from a mix of different sources. General tax revenues are a major source of income, even in systems that are not predominantly tax financed. In many cases government resources flow in the form of open or hidden subsidies to national social insurance schemes, and there are even cases where government resources flow to the accounts of private insurance companies, for example when governments contribute to privately managed pension schemes on behalf of their own employees or when they grant tax concessions to employers or workers contributing to a private pension scheme. At the same time, not all the current income of pension schemes might be used to finance concurrent pensions. Resources flow from pension schemes to the private sector or government accounts when social insurance or private insurance reserves are lent to governments or private companies.

As a result there are many explicit or implicit, conditional or unconditional recurrent or occasional transfers of financial resources between the government accounts and social security and pension schemes.

FINANCIAL FLOWS FROM PENSION SCHEMES TO GOVERNMENT ACCOUNTS

The debate about public deficits and high overall public spending on social protection may hide the fact that some government budgets have benefited from the existence of national pension schemes. Young pension schemes normally produce large surpluses in their early years, as that is a period when often substantial contributions are collected but no, or few, pensions are paid. In schemes with direct government provision and earmarked financing (for example, through payroll taxes), these surpluses might simply be absorbed into the general government budget. The social security pension schemes in many Central and Eastern European countries, for example, for many years transferred surpluses into the general government account, sometimes even without any formal accounting. The volume of money, collected through the high social security contributions levied on the wage funds of enterprises, bore no relationship to present or expected future benefit expenditures. Social security contributions were thus simply another form of tax.

Also young pension schemes, operating under the social insurance model of public provision, accumulate substantial reserves. These reserves must be invested. Many schemes are forced by law, or simply adopted the practice of investing in government bonds. In many countries these investments have been devalued by high inflation rates or have earned lower than market interest rates.[5] In other cases governments have simply forced the scheme to write off government debt. In all these cases, the social security pension schemes subsidized government budgets by accepting a low interest rate, write-offs or no inflation proofing of interest rates. In such cases social security contributions are simply another form of tax helping to finance current government expenditure. These types of implicit transfers from a social security scheme to the government budget are often not directly visible in government accounts.[6]

FLOWS AND LINKS BETWEEN GOVERNMENT ACCOUNTS AND PENSION SCHEMES

Direct flows

Direct government involvement in financing pensions is not limited to full financing of pension benefits as occurs, for example, in Denmark. Governments may also subsidize social security pension schemes through a general subsidy, as in Cyprus, where the government contributes four percentage points of the total insurable earnings to the social security pension scheme, which collects a total of 16.6 per cent from employers, employees and the government combined. In other countries, government subsidies transfer specific amounts or percentages of total benefit expenditure which compensate the scheme for specific tasks considered to be those of general government, as in Germany, where the Ministry of Finance transfers a fixed percentage of the benefit expenditure to social insurance pension schemes. Governments also often contribute to social security pension schemes or private pension schemes (as, for example, in Switzerland) through employer contributions for their own employees.[7]

The public financing of transition costs, which fall due when a country is changing its social security pension scheme from a pay-as-you-go or partially funded defined benefit scheme to a funded defined contribution scheme, is another form of explicit government financing of a national pension scheme. Government could finance these additional obligations through immediate tax increases, by using the proceeds from privatization, borrowing on the capital market, or even from the new pension scheme which is accumulating substantial reserves in its early years; or it could issue recognition bonds which are bonds that honour the pension rights of beneficiaries from the old pension scheme. These recognition bonds thus transform a government debt (which is equivalent to the current value of all pension rights of all present pensioners, as well as the acquired rights of all contributors at the time of the reform) into a series of annual transfers from the budget into the new pension scheme. The use of borrowing, or recognition bonds methods, spreads the financing of the transition over several decades, or even over a number of generations of insured persons. In this context it should be noted that the issuance of recognition bonds, or the promise to finance a defined transitional cost, transforms a conditional government liability into an unconditional one. Pension promises that are underwritten by governments, or even directly financed by them, are generally conditional as the related or contingent government liabilities are, in practice, often adjusted to fiscal and financial constraints. Bonds, or other forms of financing and defined debt, are unconditional liabilities. Such switches might be good policies for a variety of non-fiscal reasons, but they greatly reduce the flexibility that governments have in dealing with future financial situations. The limitation of future financial flexibility becomes even more severe when governments issue price-indexed bonds in order to permit the private insurance industry to issue price-indexed annuities.

Table 14.2 shows the degree of general revenue financing within the overall national public social protection scheme[8] in selected countries. The countries have been selected according to their system of providing and financing basic pension benefits, ranging from schemes which come under the system of government provision (Australia, Netherlands, United Kingdom) to those dominated by social security provision through autonomous public institutions (Austria, Bulgaria, Egypt) and to those dominated by the private provision model (Chile). All countries have some form of mixed financing system. Even in the United Kingdom, which is often quoted as the standard case for general revenue financing of social protection, social security contributions account for about one-third of the total social security financing. In Chile, however, with its emphasis on private financing, in the late 1990s current benefits were overwhelmingly financed from general revenues. The reason for this is that the government collected contributions only from those who decided to remain in the old system. These contributions were not sufficient to cover the benefits awarded on the basis of the old law and therefore those benefits were financed from general revenues.

Table 14.2   Simplified central government accounts for selected countries mid-
1990s (in percentage of GDP)

	Austria 1994	Australia 1995	Bulgaria 1995	Chile 1995	Egypt 1993	Netherlands 1995	United Kingdom 1995
Expenditure							
Social assistance and social security	18.8	9.2	10.5	6.4	3.0	18.8	13.0
Health	5.5	3.7	1.4	2.3	0.7	7.4	5.8
Other	16.2	14.5	29.6	10.5	23.7	24.6	23.0
Total	40.5	27.4	41.6	19.2	27.4	50.9	41.8
Revenues							
Taxes	18.8	22.2	20.3	16.5	14.2	23.8	27.3
Soc. Sec. Cons	14.1	0.0	7.7	1.3	2.6	19.2	6.2
Pensions	0.0	0.0	0.0	0.0	0.0	0.0	0.0
Other income	3.3	2.5	8.4	3.8	13.8	3.1	3.0
Total	36.2	24.6	36.4	21.5	30.6	46.1	36.5
Surplus/deficit	−4.2	−2.3	−5.2	2.3	3.2	−4.7	−5.3
General revenue share of financing of the social sector as % of total social expenditure	41.98	100.00	35.36	85.05	28.86	26.92	66.83

Source: International Monetary Fund.

The data in table 14.2, based on the International Monetary Fund government account data, are limited to measuring explicit financial flows into the
social sector, and hence into basic public pension schemes. Government
accounts generally do not display indirect or implicit government liabilities
for the financing of public and private pension schemes, which are discussed
below.

Indirect subsidies and contingent liabilities

In addition to direct financial costs, governments may bear indirect costs or be
liable for potential costs. When government agencies administer pension benefits directly, they often pay part of the administrative cost which might not be
clearly attributed to the administration of pension benefits. If pensions are
administered by the Ministry of Labour and Social Affairs (as in Cyprus),
part of the administrative cost of the ministry should normally also be financed
through social insurance contributions. If this is not the case, the government
supports the scheme through a further indirect transfer. If pension provision
is commissioned to private entities (as in the case of the Australian occupational
pension schemes, the pension fund administrators in Chile, or the mandatory
occupational pension scheme in Switzerland), the provision of pensions still

creates costs for the government, which must supervise and regulate these private bodies (for example through the superintendent of pension funds in Chile). The granting of tax concessions to persons or employers who join private occupational pension schemes is another form of indirect government cofinancing of national pension expenditure.

Yet another form of government participation in the financing of pensions which is becoming increasingly important, especially after reforms which mandated some of the national pension provision to private entities, is the role of the government as financial guarantor, or ultimate underwriter, of social security and private pension schemes. This contingent liability through underwriting of social security or private pension schemes can take several explicit and implicit forms. An explicit form occurs when the social insurance law stipulates that the government would cover potential deficits of a social security scheme. The latter are often linked to an obligation of the scheme to reduce the deficit, either through increasing contributions or through expenditure reductions. Guarantee payments of this type exist in several western and Central and Eastern European countries (for example, Bulgaria). In other cases of direct guarantees, governments might guarantee minimum pension levels by complementing social security or private pension benefits, which provides each beneficiary who meets certain conditions with a minimum benefit level (as is the case in the pension scheme in Chile). These benefit guarantees are sometimes called "conjectural liabilities".[9] They are affected by systemic declines in the price of assets of private savings schemes, or liabilities associated with market turmoil-induced drops in asset prices.

An implicit guarantee is given if, owing to public political pressure, the government simply must bail out non-performing private or social security schemes (as with, for example, Bag-Kur, the public system for the self-employed in Turkey). A form of indirect bailing out of failing public and private pension schemes is the increased payment of social assistance benefits in case pension systems are not in a financial position to pay benefits in full, or when benefits are provided at a low level.

Through financial guarantees, governments provide reinsurance for public and private social transfer systems. Thus, even if governments do not directly finance pension benefits, they underwrite multiple risks, including the following:

- unforeseen negative developments in system demographics and economics,
- insufficient returns on investments (lower than expected interest rates and falling asset prices),
- bad management,
- failing political support for the existing systems leading to changes in the regime.

These risks may be difficult to predict. However they embody substantial financial commitments by the government which, if it were a private sector financial management company, would have to be accounted for by recurrent reinsurance premium payments. It can be concluded that the direct amount of pension expenditure in government budgets to be financed from general revenues is higher under the government provision model (direct delivery) than under the other models. However, under the indirect delivery models, governments may face substantial hidden fiscal risks. Indirect delivery of benefits also means that the government's ability to manage the financial development of the main national pension benefit may be more limited than under the direct delivery pattern. Under the private delivery model, the government share in the financing of pension schemes could in theory be reduced to zero, but the implicit – and to an extent unpredictable – liabilities, some of them stemming from capital market risk that is to a large extent outside government managerial control, are bigger than under the public institutional delivery of pensions.

Standard government accounts and other commonly used ancillary accounts fail to record indirect subsidies and contingent liabilities. This might be largely due to the technical difficulties in quantifying these liabilities. Yet their quantification should be part of the design of a rational long-term overall public finance strategy incorporating a social security financing strategy.

THE EFFECT OF PENSION FINANCING ON PUBLIC DEFICITS AND DEBT

All types of explicit public expenditure, indirect subsidies and contingent government liabilities, including those for publicly guaranteed or financed pensions, can produce annual deficits in institutional or government accounts. Since annual deficits are components of debt, the discussion here focuses on the concept of public debt caused by pension expenditure. This discussion of necessity focuses on the effect of direct pension expenditure, as indirect subsidies and contingent liabilities are generally not, or not completely, recorded in government accounts. However it should suffice to clarify the principal nature of the impact of pension financing on public deficits and debt.

It has become common practice to distinguish between explicit and implicit pension debt, although both notions are fraught with definitional and methodological problems.

Explicit debt

The above analysis of the links between current government accounts and pension financing indicates that any explicitly recorded expenditure position in a negative consolidated government account contributes to a deficit and hence to public dissavings or the creation of public debt. In the same way, deficient tax collection, attributable either to a poor design of the tax revenue structure or to tax evasion (see Chapter 10), contributes to deficits, and hence also to public dissavings or debt.

If a social security pension scheme (whether government executed or administered by an autonomous public institution) has its earmarked resources in the form either of social security contributions or of earmarked taxes, annual positive or negative balances can be calculated, as demonstrated in the Turkish example in the annex to this chapter. Consequently explicit debt accumulated in the past can be calculated. The debt accumulation can be rapid if the revenue shortfall is large. The debt accumulation should include the interest that government must pay to lenders to finance the accumulating debt in case of an overall negative government budget, or the forgone interest income that the government would earn on the total accumulated amount of pension subsidies. In the latter case the government could have invested the resources elsewhere and would have earned interest on those investments had the pension scheme not required subsidies. In the case of Turkey, debt would accumulate within one decade from 1.7 per cent of GDP in 1995 to 23 per cent in 2005, provided that the present financing practice was not changed.

If a social security pension scheme is financed from general revenues, no annual deficit or surplus – and consequently no pension reserve or debt – can be calculated directly. The only way to introduce the notions of deficits and debt would be to fix a certain arbitrary level of maximum acceptable expenditure, codified, for example, in the form of explicit budget allocations, and to regard positive or negative past deviations from that benchmark as a (normative) deficit or surplus. In the same manner as in the case of schemes with earmarked revenues, these deficits can then be linked to the overall national public surplus and deficit and hence, in a longer-term view, to savings or debt.

But, even in the case of a scheme with earmarked resources and a negative balance, earmarked taxes or contributions might never have been designed to cover the full social security pension cost, as general revenue subsidies might always have been foreseen (as is the case in Cyprus or in the Farmers' Pension Scheme in Germany). This also applies to the provision of pensions through public institutions where, when the contribution rates were determined, government subsidies have always been envisaged. In this case, singling out explicit pension deficits as a unique or major source of general public debt is misleading.

In the case of private pension provisions, deficits and debt have a double meaning: there are the annual deficits, and the accumulating monetary debt, that a private insurance company can experience like any other private business; however there is also the notion of an actuarial deficit/surplus which is estimated as the difference between the assets of a scheme and the present value of all its accrued pension commitments. The actuarial balance sheet can be in a deficit without an insurance company facing any actual cash flow problem; it simply means that, if the company were to be liquidated at a given point in time, the total amount of assets would not, under a given set of assumptions, be sufficient to cover all pension obligations of the company towards present pensioners and contributors. This private insurance notion of pension debt is the root of the concept of the implicit pension debt of social security schemes.

Implicit debt

While explicit public debt is a retrospective concept summarizing real past deficits, implicit debt is a prospective concept. Implicit debt is the result of a summation of expected future deficits. Depending on the source, the term is often defined in two different ways: (1) implicit social security pension debt equals the present value of all future benefits to present pensioners and all accrued rights of current contributors/taxpayers, *minus* the amount of the initial reserve of the pension scheme; (2) implicit social security pension debt equals the present value of all future benefits to present and future pensioners, *minus* the amount of the initial reserve of the scheme, *minus* the present value of all expected future contribution payments of present and future insured persons at a constant initial contribution rate.

The first definition follows a strict private insurance concept, while the second is a modification of the concept which follows a public finance approach. The first definition has been used by the World Bank[10] in its publication *Averting the old-age crisis* and the second is preferred by the International Labour Office and the International Monetary Fund and is commonly used by the World Bank in its analysis of client countries.[11]

An amount is calculated in the first definition that (except for the initial reserve) is equal to the termination reserve, which is the reserve that one would need to have available in order to settle all financial obligations to present pensioners and present contributors with accrued rights according to the present rules of the scheme.[12] The level of the termination reserve can be regarded as the full funding level of the scheme. This amount thus also equals the resources that would be required to close down a social security scheme (in order to start a new one) while honouring all past commitments. No major social security scheme around the world has a termination level of reserves. For social security schemes, which are not secured by amounts of invested financial resources but rather by societal commitments and contracts between generations, this level of funding is unnecessary. This notion of debt may be useful for some intergenerational accounting, for example for determining the amount of contributions that would be required in the future to pay for already accrued pension liabilities, but it has little relevance as an indicator for the overall financial status of a social security pension scheme.

The second definition assumes that promises are made to all present and future generations of pensioners and contributors, which must be honoured and protected by law, and that present and future contributors will always have to pay their dues to finance the system. These assumptions have sometimes proved to be invalid, as countries have failed to honour their social security commitments. For countries with sound governance, however, this definition describes the gap between expected future expenditure and revenues, provided that present and future contributors continue to contribute at currently legislated contribution rates. In tax-financed systems the second definition can only be applied by proxy. It must be assumed that the present level of government resources used to finance pensions (measured in relative terms, for example, as a percentage of GDP) will stay constant throughout the foreseeable future, and rising pension expenditures (also in relative terms) will open up the potential pension deficit gap and thus implicit pension debt is accumulated. For the responsible ministry this potential financing gap is an indicator of its potential additional financial liability in the financing of the pension scheme.

It must be stressed that the term "implicit pension debt" (second definition) does not describe a real financial liability of the government. Owing to its prospective nature it only describes potential debt. The potential debt is only an indicator of a financial risk for the government rather than a real financial obligation. This debt might never occur if the government, as a consequence of good and pre-emptive governance, is always able to adjust the contribution rates or the tax allocation for the financing of pensions, or to reduce benefit expenditure. Sweden's pension reform in the 1990s, for example, will most likely reduce its potential debt substantially.

The concept of implicit pension or social security debt is frequently misused in pension reform debates. Frequently it is argued that a large implicit debt using the first definition is a problem that should be corrected by a change in social security financing. However that is only correct if there is a large debt under the second definition. If there is a large implicit debt under the first definition, but financing has been agreed upon by society and ratified in legislation so that there is no implicit debt under the second definition, there is no social security financing problem. It is thus questionable to offset transition costs triggered by a change of pension financing systems (for example, from pay-as-you-go defined benefit to funded defined contribution) against implicit pension debt (as is done in many national reform debates), since fiscal transition costs are real or unconditional, whereas implicit debt is only occurring if governance fails.

Figure 14.1 shows an estimate of the emerging financing gap between social security pension expenditure (measured as a percentage of GDP) and the present financing level for all OECD countries. OECD countries in 1990 spent an average of 8.5 per cent of GDP on pensions. An ILO model projects that this ratio will increase to 15.2 per cent of GDP by 2050.[13] The graph assumes that the present level of financing as a percentage of GDP would be maintained throughout the 60-year projection period.

On the basis of emerging annual social security pension financing gaps, the implicit pension debt (according to the second definition) can be calculated. Figure 14.2 shows the total implicit debt (assuming the present financing level) in 11 selected countries for which data could be obtained which permitted long-term projections. The figure shows that the implicit social security pension

379

Figure 14.1   Potential pension deficit, OECD, 1990–2020 (in percentage of GDP)

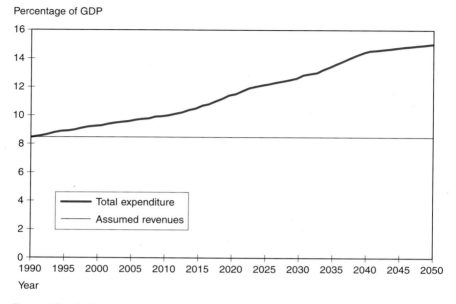

Percentage of GDP

Source: ILO projections.

debt under the second definition ranges from virtually zero in the United Kingdom to about 210 per cent of GDP in Turkey. The middle ground is covered by
countries like Denmark, Germany and Sweden, with implicit debts around 100
to 160 per cent of GDP.

Figure 14.3 demonstrates how a potential financing shortfall of a social
security pension scheme can be resolved. It is assumed that, for the OECD
countries, the retirement age will increase by, on average, 3.5 years combined
with an increase of the financing level of 20 per cent. The combination of
policy measures reduces the implicit debt over 60 years to zero. It implies
that, at first, the national schemes will be overfinanced for a number of years.
In later years, the return on investments on the accumulating reserves – and
ultimately phased dissavings, together with current tax and contribution allocations – would be sufficient to cover the expenditure.

PENSION FINANCING AND PUBLIC FINANCING STRATEGIES

The above analysis of the direct and indirect links between public finances and
pension financing shows that governments, representing society at large, always
remain the ultimate guarantor of national social security pension schemes. If
promises covering the lifetime of several generations can be made at all, they

Figure 14.2 Estimated potential implicit pension debt, selected countries, 1990 (in percentage of GDP)

Percentage of GDP

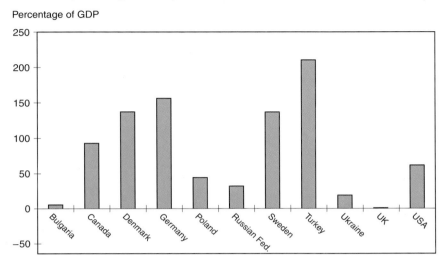

Source: ILO calculations.

can only be made by societies as a whole. Capital markets, private insurance companies or enterprises, as alternative providers of old-age security, cannot give long-term guarantees as to their proper functioning or even their mere survival over such long periods.

If one takes a global view of social security schemes and presupposes that the ultimate government responsibility is to ascertain at least a minimum level of transfer of resources for consumption to the elderly, the disabled and survivors, then national choices of public and private provision of pension benefits, or any specific public-private mix, are reduced to questions of social and income policies versus questions of public finance policies.

The public provision of the majority of all pension benefits means that the income distribution effects of these transfers can be designed to provide anti-poverty protection, and to achieve a certain reduction of income inequality through the pension scheme. Commissioning a part or even, as in the case of mandatory defined contribution schemes, the bulk of all pension provisions to the private sector will inevitably lead to greater income inequality among the beneficiaries, since private entities can hardly be expected to include redistributive elements in their benefit provisions. In these cases, the state usually maintains a redistributive pension programme, such as a guaranteed minimum benefit.

The fiscal policy angle of pension financing is explored here in more detail. The design of a national pension financing system also reflects the overall public finance strategy of the government. Fiscal policy makers must match the cost of

Figure 14.3 Consolidated potential pension deficit, OECD, 1990–2050 (percentage of GDP)

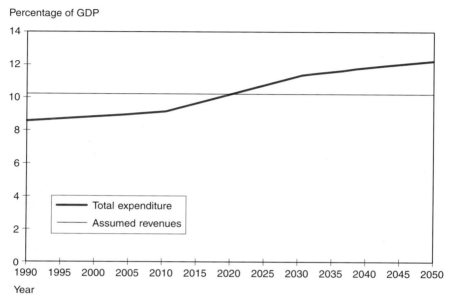

Percentage of GDP

Source: ILO calculations.

fulfilling a set of government obligations with the amount of scarce resources generally available. They have a limited range of income sources at their disposal, namely tariffs and excise duties, charges for government services, indirect and direct taxes and social security contributions. They basically have two options to discharge their obligations to society, either by direct provision or by commissioning services out to the private sector, or to parastatal institutions. They can also mandate private financing of services commissioned to the private sector, for example by requiring mandatory contributions to private pension schemes. However the different financing and delivery options are interconnected. If, for example, the level of pension expenditure, regardless of how it is financed, becomes too high, either it will begin to crowd out other national social expenditure or public expenditure, or fiscal pressure will result in a reduction of pension benefit levels in an effort to keep the overall tax and contribution burden for citizens at an acceptable order of magnitude.[14] Contributing and tax-paying citizens demand that governments provide, directly or indirectly, a certain range and quality of services, and they naturally want to minimize the cost of these services in terms of overall tax and contribution burden.

It should not be assumed that commissioning the financing and provision of pensions to the private sector has no effect on tax revenues, though these effects will normally be indirect. Apart from the above-mentioned implicit or explicit government obligations, as ultimate underwriter of national pension provisions, government budgets can indirectly be affected by private provision of social security. There is no rule as to what the acceptable limits of overall taxation and contribution payments are, but there are indications that societies in Europe, notably northern Europe, are accepting higher limits than in North America and elsewhere.[15] It is also unclear whether these limits generally depend on the actual mix of financing instruments (for example, taxes or contributions). However, with such limits, mandatory contributions to pension schemes, regardless of whether they are paid to parastatal social insurance schemes or mandatorily to private insurance carriers, potentially limit the government's general taxation capacity, or are restricting other government expenditure.

Thus, whether governments prefer to commission pension financing to parastatal authorities or to private insurance carriers, or prefer to administer all compulsory pension provisions themselves, it inevitably becomes a matter of overall national financial and fiscal planning. Leaving income policy considerations aside for a moment, a government would then prefer direct provision of all mandatory pension programmes over mandated private sector provision if its tax revenues, available for the coverage of non-pension benefits, are higher. Should it believe that the overall tax, plus contribution income, would be higher under mandated private sector provisions and that the earmarking of resources for pensions would leave it with a bigger amount of revenues to finance non-pension obligations, it would most likely prefer this type of financing mix. When comparing the different options, however, it should also take into consideration the hidden cost of the financial guarantee it offers with mandated private sector provision, as well as the loss of room for financial manoeuvre when overall uniform tax revenues are replaced by a system of earmarked taxes (or contributions). Considerations of this nature have led some representatives of the International Monetary Fund to prefer, in the case of some countries, direct public financing of public social transfer obligations through the government or, in other words, the promotion of the principle of unifying all public finance commitments under "one roof" in the interest of greatest possible manageability of the overall system of public finance.[16] The interests of citizens, however, might differ from those of fiscal policy planners. Citizens might prefer to have a certain share of their overall tax and contribution burden at least formally reserved for their old-age provisions. They might not be aware of the fact that they might have to pay for this earmarking in the form of a higher overall financial burden (for example as a result of higher administrative costs under indirect institutional or private provision of pensions) or they may be willing to accept these transaction costs to insulate resources for old age against rival uses of public resources, or they may try to shift "excess cost" to employers.

The design of the overall national public finance policy, including the choice of the pension financing system, is always the result of a long explicit – or

Table 14.3 Consolidated government account, Turkey, 1995–2005

Base case	Percentage of GDP						
	1995	1996	1997	1998	1999	2000	2005
Revenues	21.6	19.0	18.4	18.0	17.6	17.3	16.9
Direct taxes	6.4	6.5	6.6	6.7	6.7	6.8	7.2
Indirect taxes	7.6	6.3	5.8	5.6	5.4	5.2	4.9
Social security contributions	3.1	3.3	3.3	3.3	3.3	3.3	3.4
Other non-tax revenues	2.5	2.4	2.2	2.0	1.9	1.7	1.2
Grants	0.1	0.1	0.1	0.1	0.1	0.1	0.0
Annexed budget	0.1	0.1	0.1	0.1	0.1	0.1	0.0
Privatization revenues	1.2	0.0	0.0	0.0	0.0	0.0	0.0
Capital income	0.1	0.2	0.2	0.1	0.1	0.1	0.1
Received government's transfers	0.7	1.2	1.5	1.8	2.0	2.2	3.2
Other revenues	0.4	0.2	0.1	0.1	0.1	0.1	0.0
Expenditures	24.7	22.5	21.5	19.6	18.4	17.8	18.0
Personnel	6.8	6.7	6.6	6.5	6.4	6.3	5.9
Other current expenditures	1.8	1.8	1.8	1.8	1.8	1.7	1.4
Social security benefits	4.1	4.4	4.5	4.	4.9	5.1	6.1
Investment	1.3	1.1	1.1	1.1	1.1	1.1	1.1
Interest	7.5	5.3	4.5	2.4	1.3	0.8	1.0
Transfers to state-owned enterprises	0.6	0.6	0.6	0.5	0.5	0.5	0.3
Transfers to social security institutions	0.7	1.2	1.5	1.8	2.0	2.2	3.2
Other transfers	2.7	2.7	2.6	2.5	2.4	2.3	2.2
Balance	−3.2	−3.5	−3.2	−1.6	−0.8	−0.4	−1.1
Deferred payments	0.3	0.1	0.1	0.1	0.1	0.1	0.0
Advances	0.3	0.1	0.1	0.1	0.1	0.1	0.0
Cash balance	−3.2	−3.5	−3.2	−1.6	−0.8	−0.4	−1.1

Source: ILO projections.

implicit – negotiation process between the public and the government. The ultimate choice of public finance instruments will reflect the popular trust or distrust of governments; the public perception of the role of the state; the trust or mistrust of private sector institutions, including the functioning of the capital markets; the perceived need of publicly guaranteed social and income security; and social values, such as the degree of societal solidarity and the acceptance or non-acceptance of income inequality.

Pension schemes make long-term promises. There are different ways to finance these promises. The accounting instruments necessary to monitor the full public cost of a national pension scheme and its financing, in the short and long run, are not yet developed. What is by no means clear, owing to the numerous direct and indirect links between the general government accounts and pension

Table 14.4 Social security account, Turkey, 1995–2005

Central government account	Percentage of GDP						
Base case	1995	1996	1997	1998	1999	2000	2005
Revenues	17.9	15.3	14.7	14.4	14.1	13.9	13.3
Direct taxes	6.4	6.5	6.6	6.7	6.7	6.8	7.2
Indirect taxes	7.6	6.3	5.8	5.6	5.4	5.2	4.9
Social security contributions	0.0	0.0	0.0	0.0	0.0	0.0	0.0
Other non-tax revenues	2.5	2.4	2.2	2.0	1.9	1.7	1.2
Grants	0.1	0.1	0.1	0.1	0.1	0.1	0.0
Annexed budget	0.1	0.1	0.1	0.1	0.1	0.1	0.0
Privatization revenues	1.2	0.0	0.0	0.0	0.0	0.0	0.0
Capital income	0.0	0.0	0.0	0.0	0.0	0.0	0.0
Received government's transfers	0.0	0.0	0.0	0.0	0.0	0.0	0.0
Other revenues	0.0	0.0	0.0	0.0	0.0	0.0	0.0
Expenditures	21.2	19.2	18.3	16.3	15.2	14.6	14.7
Personnel	6.7	6.6	6.5	6.4	6.3	6.2	5.7
Other current expenditures	1.3	1.3	1.3	1.3	1.3	1.2	0.9
Social assistance paid by ministries	0.1	0.1	0.1	0.1	0.1	0.0	0.0
Social security benefits	0.4	0.5	0.4	0.4	0.5	0.5	0.5
Investment	1.1	0.9	0.9	0.9	0.9	0.8	0.8
Interest	7.5	5.3	4.5	2.4	1.3	0.8	1.0
Transfers to SEEs	0.6	0.6	0.6	0.5	0.5	0.5	0.3
Transfers to social security institutions	0.7	1.2	1.5	1.8	2.0	2.2	3.2
Other transfers	2.7	2.7	2.6	2.5	2.4	2.3	2.2
Balance	−3.2	−3.9	−3.6	−1.9	−1.1	−0.7	−1.4
Deferred payments	0.3	0.1	0.1	0.1	0.1	0.1	0.0
Advances	0.3	0.1	0.1	0.1	0.1	0.1	0.0
Cash balance	−3.2	−3.9	−3.6	−1.9	−1.1	−0.7	−1.4

Social security account	Percentage of GDP						
Base case	1995	1996	1997	1998	1999	2000	2005
Revenues	4.3	4.9	5.1	5.3	5.5	5.7	6.7
Direct taxes	0.0	0.0	0.0	0.0	0.0	0.0	0.0
Indirect taxes	0.0	0.0	0.0	0.0	0.0	0.0	0.0
Social security contributions	3.1	3.3	3.3	3.3	3.3	3.3	3.4
Other non-tax revenues	0.0	0.0	0.0	0.0	0.0	0.0	0.0
Grants	0.0	0.0	0.0	0.0	0.0	0.0	0.0
Privatization revenues	0.0	0.0	0.0	0.0	0.0	0.0	0.0
Capital income	0.1	0.2	0.2	0.1	0.1	0.1	0.1
Received government's transfers	0.7	1.2	1.5	1.8	2.0	2.2	3.2
Other revenues	0.4	0.2	0.1	0.1	0.1	0.1	0.0

Table 14.4 Continued

Social security account	Percentage of GDP						
Base case	1995	1996	1997	1998	1999	2000	2005
Expenditures	4.3	4.6	4.8	5.1	5.3	5.5	6.5
Personnel	0.1	0.1	0.1	0.1	0.1	0.1	0.1
Other current expenditures	0.4	0.4	0.4	0.4	0.4	0.5	0.5
Social security benefits	3.7	3.8	4.0	4.3	4.5	4.7	5.6
Investment	0.2	0.2	0.2	0.2	0.2	0.2	0.3
Interest	0.0	0.0	0.0	0.0	0.0	0.0	0.0
Transfers to SEEs	0.0	0.0	0.0	0.0	0.0	0.0	0.0
Transfers to social security institutions	0.0	0.0	0.0	0.0	0.0	0.0	0.0
Other transfers	0.0	0.0	0.0	0.0	0.0	0.0	0.0
Balance	0.0	0.3	0.4	0.3	0.2	0.2	0.3
Deferred payments	0.0	0.0	0.0	0.0	0.0	0.0	0.0
Advances	0.0	0.0	0.0	0.0	0.0	0.0	0.0
Cash balance	0.0	0.3	0.4	0.3	0.2	0.2	0.3

Source: ILO projections.

financing and the pivotal role of governments, as at least a partial guarantor of income security, is that no one specific financing option is ultimately cheaper for governments and their financiers, the tax-paying and contributing citizens than the others.

ANNEX: PENSIONS IN THE HIERARCHY OF GOVERNMENT ACCOUNTS IN TURKEY[17]

In order to simplify the complex accounts at all non-social security levels of government, in this example accounts have been consolidated into one central government account (table 14.3). The social security account itself consolidates four different institutional accounts (table 14.4). The constituent institutional accounts have also been omitted here. The figures given are expenditure and income items expressed in percentage of GDP. Pensions constitute the dominant expenditure share in the row "social security benefits". The following tables also show an example of a hypothetical budget forecast which was established under a specific set of economic assumptions with the help of the ILO social budget model (tables 14.3, 14.4 and 14.5). The tables show that the social security scheme requires increasing government transfers as benefit expenditures increase and the "own income of the social security scheme" – social security contributions – virtually stagnate at least when measured as a percentage of GDP.

Figure 14.4 traces the share of the social security deficit within the total government deficit and the pension insurance deficit within the social security

Table 14.5   Summary of the social budget, Turkey, 1995–2005

Total nominal current expenditure in trillion TL	1995	1996	1997	1998	1999	2000	2005
	787	1 470	2 388	3 167	3 815	4 390	8 248
Total expenditure and income in % of GDP							
Pensions (three social security institutions aggregate)							
Pension insurance benefits	3.4	3.5	3.7	3.9	4.1	4.3	5.1
Old-age pensions	2.5	2.7	2.8	3.0	3.1	3.3	4.1
Invalidity pensions	0.1	0.1	0.1	0.1	0.1	0.1	0.1
Survivors' pensions	0.6	0.6	0.6	0.6	0.6	0.6	0.7
Orphans' pensions	0.2	0.2	0.2	0.2	0.2	0.2	0.3
Grants	0.0	0.0	0.0	0.0	0.0	0.0	0.0
Administrative expenditure	0.1	0.1	0.1	0.1	0.1	0.1	0.1
Subtotal	3.4	3.6	3.8	4.0	4.2	4.4	5.3
Unemployment insurance							
Subtotal	0.0	0.0	0.1	0.1	0.1	0.1	0.1
Short-term benefits							
Subtotal	0.1	0.1	0.1	0.1	0.1	0.1	0.1
Welfare by NGOs and others							
Subtotal	0.3	0.2	0.2	0.2	0.2	0.2	0.2
Health							
Subtotal	4.2	4.3	4.4	4.4	4.5	4.6	4.9
Military personnel scheme							
Subtotal	0.8	0.7	0.7	0.7	0.7	0.7	0.6
Private banks' schemes							
Subtotal	0.4	0.4	0.4	0.4	0.4	0.4	0.4
Employers' social benefits							
Subtotal	0.9	1.0	0.9	0.9	0.9	0.9	0.9
Total current expenditure	10.0	10.3	10.5	10.8	11.0	11.3	12.5
Change of reserves, unemployment fund	0.0	0.3	0.4	0.3	0.2	0.2	0.3
Total social expenditure	10.0	10.6	10.8	11.0	11.3	11.5	12.8
Social protection income	10.0	10.6	10.8	11.0	11.3	11.5	12.8
Social insurance contributions	3.1	3.3	3.3	3.3	3.3	3.3	3.4
Pension scheme	2.2	2.2	2.2	2.2	2.1	2.1	2.2
Health insurance scheme	0.9	0.9	0.9	0.9	0.9	0.9	0.9
Unemployment fund	0.0	0.2	0.3	0.3	0.3	0.3	0.3
Other income (including imputed contributions)	2.7	2.7	2.7	2.7	2.7	2.7	2.8
Investment income	0.1	0.2	0.2	0.2	0.1	0.1	0.1
Pension scheme	0.1	0.1	0.1	0.0	0.0	0.0	0.0
Health scheme	0.0	0.0	0.0	0.0	0.0	0.0	0.0
Short-term benefit scheme	0.0	0.0	0.0	0.0	0.0	0.0	0.0
Unemployment fund	0.0	0.1	0.2	0.1	0.1	0.1	0.1
Income from general revenues	4.0	4.4	4.6	4.8	5.1	5.3	6.5

Source: ILO projections.

Figure 14.4 Government, social security and pension insurance deficit, Turkey 1995–2005

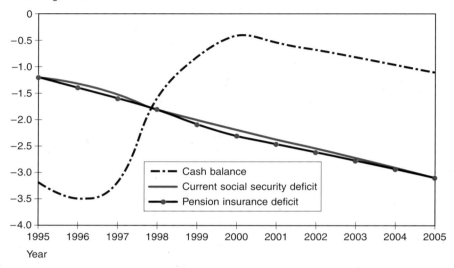

Source: ILO projections.

deficit. It shows that the social security account would be in surplus if the pension insurance (which is the combination of all pension branches of all social security institutions) was not in a deficit. Furthermore it also shows that the government deficit could be avoided for most of the projection period if the social security account could be kept positive. In this case, the current government deficit can be traced back clearly to the social security scheme, and to the pension scheme in particular. The total extent of government social expenditure is identified in the national social budget which combines the government subsidies to the social insurance schemes, government contributions as an employer and the direct government outlays for social transfers into one item, "Income from general revenues".

Notes

[1] See United Nations (1969, p. 25).

[2] See International Monetary Fund (1997a, 1997b).

[3] For example, if a country introduces a new pension scheme with a relatively generous pension formula (as was the case in many countries in Africa, the Caribbean and Latin America) which is financed through partial funding, that is through a contribution rate which, in the initial years, is much higher than the contributions which would be needed in order to cover the initially low cost, then the government could borrow from the schemes and could, for example, invest in their national infrastructure. It could, for example, finance an extensive health care infrastructure.

Proper social budgeting will show that the flow of money between the schemes and the government accounts will subside at some point, and even have to be reversed, or contribution rates in the pension schemes will need to be increased. The government's financial planning has to prepare for these events: it either has to prepare the public well in advance for higher contribution rates or it has to be prepared to redeem some of its loans and may have to suppress other expenditure (for example, on health care and other social transfers) in order to be in a position to retrieve funds for the scheme. The same would be the case if the government were to borrow from private pension insurance schemes.

[4] More details on the principles of social budgeting are explained in Scholz et al., (2000).

[5] See, for example, ILO (1994a, pp. 65–66).

[6] National accounting adds, in this context, an interesting connotation to the debate on funded versus unfunded pay-as-you-go financing of pension schemes. If an allegedly funded social security scheme invests all its reserves in government investment facilities, and if the government pays the correct (inflation-indexed) interest rates and correctly redeems capital borrowed, then the pension scheme is no more than a mixed contribution and tax financed pay-as-you-go scheme, as liabilities for interest payments and redemption must be financed by general taxation. On the level of the consolidated government account the scheme turns into a pay-as-you-go scheme.

[7] On the other hand, the fact that governments directly provide benefits does not automatically mean that the schemes are fully financed by general taxation. Governments might well execute a social insurance type of arrangement which collects contributions in the same way as an autonomous social insurance scheme (as for example, in the United States). Even schemes with universal benefits for every resident might collect contributions (or earmarked taxes) which help to finance the benefits (such as in the United Kingdom).

[8] Including pensions, short-term benefits, health, unemployment benefits and social assistance.

[9] See Heller (1998).

[10] See World Bank (1994, pp. 139–40).

[11] See Heller (1998, p. 17).

[12] This also means, by implication, that, in any scheme where such a level of reserves is required at any given point in time, total annual contributions paid in any future years must be equal to the present value of all future pension rights which are derived from this annual contribution.

[13] The model was used to project long-term social expenditure in OECD and Central and Eastern Europe. Details of the methodology and the assumptions are described in Latulippe (1997). The central assumption of the model is a 2 per cent per annum average real growth over the projection period. Total employment is assumed to grow by an average of 1 per cent per annum. The long-term average real interest rate is assumed to be 3 per cent.

[14] In this context the appropriate financial planning instrument for national social policy, and hence pension policy, is comprehensive national social expenditure accounting and planning in the form of national social budgets.

[15] See, for example, the reasoning of Besharov (1998) on the "tax ceiling" in OECD countries.

[16] See, for example, Tanzi (1996, p. 31) and Orsmond (1996, pp. 8 and 9).

[17] The data for the example are taken from: ILO (1996b). The projections are based on an annual real GDP growth rate of 5.9 per cent, an annual growth of employment of 2.3 per cent and constant social security legislation and administrative practice.

CONCLUSION TO PART I

Part I discusses issues in the structure of social security pension systems as they have emerged throughout the world. Two overarching conclusions stand out. In the first place, social security pension systems are extremely variegated in the details of their design and operation, and these details are of vital importance in providing income protection in old age for the greater part of the population. Although it is possible to establish some general categories of different types of schemes – funded or unfunded, tax- or contribution-financed, mature or immature – it is the details of how the parameters of these schemes are set, the way in which different social groups are treated, the existence of floors and ceilings to both contributions and benefits, and the extent to which regulations or administrative discretion determine the benefits to be received that make the difference between a scheme which is effective and efficient and one which is not. In many cases these particular differences emerge from the cultural, historical and political background of the country concerned and the adaption of societal values to them. But they also mean that it is not possible to provide a simple taxonomy of social security pension schemes, or to label one kind of scheme better than another, although there are a number of underlying value judgements which are common to all. The devil is in the details.

Second, it will be apparent from the discussion that many social security pension schemes do not work very well. A primary conclusion of this part of the book is that, for most workers of the world, the most important social security pension issue is not how benefits are financed, or their value determined, but the fact that they are not covered by a social security pension system. This problem occurs primarily in developing countries. The developed countries generally have high coverage rates, and the problem of lack of coverage is generally limited to self-employed workers and workers in the underground or informal economy. These types of workers also tend to have low coverage rates in developing countries, but because of the different structure of those economies their importance in the workforce is much greater there.

Equally important in many countries is the question of governance. A country can have a well-designed social security pension system but the system can fail to meet its goals if it is poorly governed. Many of the problems of social security systems in developing countries result from poor governance and can be resolved by improvements in governance rather than major reforms to the overall design of the system.

The first three chapters of Part I discuss the main types of social security pension benefits. A conclusion running across the three chapters is that the entitlement conditions – the requirements for qualifying to receive benefits – are an important aspect of the structure of benefits. Particularly for disability and social assistance benefits, the entitlement conditions may ease or tighten according to bureaucratic interpretation or application of the rules. Because of budgetary pressures, many countries are seeking to reduce the generosity of benefits. This can be done as an equal percentage reduction for all beneficiaries or as a selective reduction. A selective reduction that reduces benefits relatively more for upper-income workers may be fairer because upper-income workers generally have other sources of income and consequently depend less on social security benefits than do lower-income workers.

In Chapter 6, on the financing of pension programmes, it is noted that financing is generally shared between workers and employers. In an attempt to encourage coverage through voluntary compliance by more self-employed workers, and even in some cases to encourage self-employment, those workers have been charged a lower rate than the total rate charged to workers and employers. Other countries have charged self-employed workers a rate equal to the sum of the employee and employer rate on the theory that, ultimately, the employee bears through reduced pay the rate paid by the employer.

In Chapter 7, on the management of investment of funded social security pension schemes, some of the problems associated with individual management of funded schemes are discussed. If pension policy gives individuals responsibility for managing the investments of their defined contribution retirement schemes, that policy should also ensure that workers have sufficient financial knowledge to make wise decisions. Experience has shown that workers tend to be conservative in their investment decisions, which causes them to receive a low expected rate of return and low benefits in comparison to what they would have received had they invested in higher risk assets.

Chapter 8, on coverage, indicates that lack of coverage tends to be a problem among workers with particular characteristics: informal sector, agriculture, low-wage, household workers and the self-employed. In some countries a special scheme with lower contributions and benefits than the general scheme may be better suited to the needs of these workers.

Chapter 9, on governance, suggests that in many countries the problems with the social security system can be considered as problems of poor governance. Sometimes these problems arise because of politicization of the social security institution and can be resolved by creating an independent administrative structure.

Chapter 10, on contribution evasion, indicates that the problem is widespread in developing countries and, in some countries, so severe that governments have suspended paying old-age benefits. A fundamental reason why contribution evasion occurs is the same reason why social security contributions are mandatory: some workers will not voluntarily save adequately for their retirement. In some countries contribution evasion is primarily a result of high inflation. In other countries corruption and lack of trust in the government are important reasons.

Chapter 11, on pension transfers and the redistribution of income, indicates ways that pension systems can be designed so as to be progressive, providing low-income workers with a higher rate of return on their contributions than upper-income workers. While progressive features are commonly built into the structure of defined benefit plans, that is rarely the case with defined contribution plans.

Chapter 12, on risks to individuals, indicates that relying on defined contribution plans may lead to considerable oversaving or undersaving, in comparison with that needed to reach a target replacement rate, depending on the performance of capital markets and wage growth rates near the point of retirement.

Chapter 13, on economic effects of social security pension systems, finds little support for large effects of old-age benefits schemes in labour or capital markets. In many countries disability benefits schemes and, to a lesser extent, special early retirement schemes and unemployment benefits are the primary paths to early retirement. Evidence concerning effects of unfunded social security schemes on savings, or effects of switching to funded schemes, is mixed, but does not consistently indicate a negative effect of unfunded schemes or a positive effect of switching to funding. Other government policies aimed specifically at encouraging savings, such as tax policies, are more appropriate tools for influencing national savings.

Chapter 14, on the consequences for public finances, points out weaknesses in some of the standard concepts used to measure the effects of social security pension finances on public finances. It argues that a commonly used measure of implicit pension debt is misleading, and that social security financing is adequate if projections indicate that in each period revenue plus reserves are sufficient to meet benefit payments.

For many countries expenditure on social security pensions, and the revenue which is collected to pay for them, are now large and significant proportions of national income and of government revenue. This sets a limit to what a country can afford. Conversely the low level of benefits and the small proportion of the population which is covered represent an obstacle to the achievement of better and more equitable income protection in old age. Reconciling these two constraints involves not only a question of normative values but, as the wave of pension reforms around the world suggests, one which involves better coverage, governance and the design of pension schemes.

REFORM: THE SEARCH FOR A NEW BALANCE

Part II provides policy analysis and major policy prescriptions. While countries differ widely in their economic and social circumstances, and no one pension system is right for all countries, nevertheless general guidance can be useful.

Chapter 15 discusses the normative basis for policy. The normative basis reflects people's views on desirable goals for a social security pension system. It refers to ILO Conventions which provide explicit but general guidance on the structure of retirement income systems, for example concerning minimum target replacement rates. Two key aspects refer to the need to provide a guaranteed and predictable replacement rate on retirement and the need to involve workers, employers and governments in a tripartite management of the schemes.

The following two chapters present policy towards extending coverage and improving governance, the two most important policy issues in many developing countries. Chapter 16 discusses extending coverage to the informal sector. In some cases special programmes need to be designed specifically to meet the needs of informal sector workers; in other cases legislative restrictions on coverage in the old-age benefits programme need to be eased. Chapter 17 discusses improving governance, management and compliance. Management needs to be structured so that employers and workers have input into the structure of social security programmes. In some cases it may be useful to have the formal input of these groups through their participation in management committees.

Chapter 18 analyses issues in setting the minimum age at which old-age pension benefits can be received. With life expectancy increasing and the age at retirement decreasing in many countries, the percentage of adult life spent in retirement has increased considerably. The minimum age at which old-age benefits can be received has an important effect on the cost of benefits providing a given target replacement rate, such as the rate of 40 per cent set out in ILO Convention 102.

Chapter 19 develops pluralistic designs and flexible structures for old-age benefits systems. To meet the goals of alleviating poverty in old age and reducing risk in retirement income, it is desirable that retirement income be provided through several sources. Providing retirement income through multiple sources increases the flexibility of the system in meeting the needs of workers in different situations.

Chapter 20 discusses the reform process and its political management. Many countries have found that it takes years to enact reforms once the need for reform has been agreed upon. This chapter provides strategies for successfully managing the reform process to reduce resistance to reform and reach consensus.

THE NORMATIVE BASIS FOR POLICY

15

This chapter discusses the normative principles underlying the design of pension schemes, and their background. Of particular importance is the need for pension schemes to provide some guarantee as to eventual replacement rates and the chapter goes on to propose a three-tier structure comprising a mixture of pay-as-you-go and defined contribution schemes. Most of this book is related to the considerations of this chapter, but especially relevant are the general overview and main issues (Chapter 1) and the discussion of pluralistic designs and flexible structures (Chapter 19).

A large number of the considerations which affect the reform and development of pension schemes, or even their existence, are normative ones, based on the values which society places on the provision of income security in old age, and on the amount of money which it is prepared to put aside for this purpose. They include such questions as who should receive a pension, and how much; who should contribute, and what amount; how the schemes should be managed, whether public or private; at what age pensions should begin; whether contingencies, other than old age, should be taken into account; whether the schemes should be universal and compulsory, or voluntary and selective; and how they should respond to changing circumstances. Of course all such issues also have their economic aspects, which interact strongly with the normative ones, but unless we are clear about the moral and social objectives, as well as the economic ones, we will not have a precise idea of the purpose of pension schemes and how they should be structured, nor will we possess any criteria for assessing how successful they are. For the most part the normative criteria are treated as axiomatic: that is, as criteria whose validity is self-evident. Clearly this is uncertain ground. Everyone will have his or her own individual criteria, which are likely to differ from everyone else's. On the other hand, the forming of a collective policy, especially one which is universal and compulsory, requires the adoption of a consensus, embodied in legislation, which determines not only the promises made from one generation to the next but also the safeguards which protect those who are saving for their own retirement.

At an international level, these criteria have been extensively discussed, many times, by the International Labour Organization and have been consecrated in a number of International Labour Standards – Conventions and Recommendations – which codify the understanding of the international community as to what does, and what does not, constitute an appropriate structure and framework for pension schemes. Technical Brief 2 provides a list of such International Labour Standards. They are not immutable, having been changed a number of times in the history of the ILO, nor have they all been ratified by all countries, but they nevertheless provide a comprehensive view of what the world community regards as an acceptable basis.

It is also important to appreciate something about the way in which pension schemes have developed, and the consequences of this development for the normative basis of policy. At the beginning of the twentieth century, even in the developed economies, few workers possessed the security of a retirement pension. Most worked until they were in their late sixties, then spent a brief retirement living with their children until they died in their early seventies. To be old generally meant to be poor. Being disabled signified that poverty began earlier. To survive, for the wage earner, implied that poverty lasted longer. No support from the children meant being thrown back on the Poor Laws.

Gradually, through the first part of this century, pension schemes became more widely adopted. Mostly they took the form of occupational schemes whose coverage was restricted and benefits small in relation to previous income. Their principal objective was the prevention of poverty in old age, and they generally had the support of employers who were concerned about the consequences of laying off older workers. Up to this point the principal moral and normative values underlying the schemes concerned the prevention of poverty in old age.

From the middle of the century, however, in the aftermath of the Second World War and in the light of the Beveridge Report,[1] more universal pension programmes came into being: compulsory, comprehensive and contributory, although still with benefit rates which could scarcely lift the recipient out of poverty. In addition to the Beveridge Report in the United Kingdom, other countries adopted similar criteria for social security schemes, and by 1952 there was sufficient consensus in the ILO for the adoption of the Social Security (Minimum Standards) Convention, 1952 (No. 102), which, for the first time at an international level, established normative criteria not only for the provision of retirement pensions but also for all other forms of social security. Subsequently coverage, benefits and expenditure increased rapidly and, as progressive numbers of colonies acquired independence, pension schemes also began to emerge in developing countries where previously none had existed. From 1960 onwards, expenditure on retirement benefits (in the developed countries) increased at more than twice the growth of GDP (see figure 15.1). Coverage became almost universal and pensions began to be couched in terms of

Figure 15.1   OECD countries: Public social expenditure on old age as a percentage of GDP

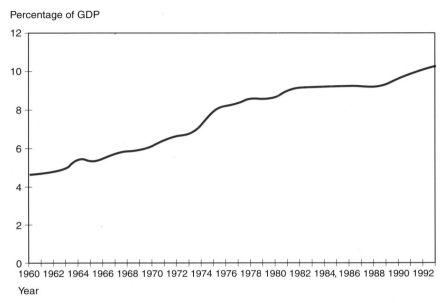

Source: OECD estimates of social expenditure: Linked series 1960-80 and 1980-93.

replacement rates which set the benefit level at between half and two-thirds of income when in work. As economies grew and pension programmes multiplied in developing countries, the provisions of this Convention were modified, improved and expanded.

The expansion of retirement pension schemes and their largely public nature meant that the discussion of the normative basis for social security pension schemes acquired a much more complex character. There were a number of reasons. In the first place pension programmes, as they were designed in the developed countries in the late 1930s, 1940s and the early 1950s, did not anticipate a number of trends which were later to have a large impact on their growth. They did not foresee the expansion of female employment and the subsequent increase in the proportion of women with their own entitlement to a pension. This turned out to be inconsistent with the earlier picture of women's pensions being derived from those of the male wage earner. Nor, looking further ahead, did they anticipate the effect which the growth of unemployment (at least in Europe) would have on older workers from the 1970s onwards, and the demand which it would generate for early retirement provisions. The 1970s, and the first half of the 1980s, were also a period of high inflation, and the consequences of this for the revaluation of pensions in payment had also not been fully anticipated. Nor did the programmes foresee the demographic changes which are currently imposing concerns about the future viability of the schemes: the "baby boom" of the postwar period followed by the sharp decline in birth rates across most OECD countries, and the substantial and prolonged increase in longevity and thus in the span of retirement. These demographic changes implied a large increase in the proportion of older people in the population and are currently generating concerns about the financing of pensions well into the twenty-first century. Finally the scale of pension programmes was not envisaged: pension programmes now average 10.5 per cent of gross national income across OECD countries, to the point where they are a large, and relatively inflexible, element of fiscal policies. Their management demands a complex structure of contributions, benefits and compliance. Formulating a normative basis to handle these issues became complex and has been made more so by the large number of developing and middle-income countries with serious pension issues to resolve (especially those concerned with extending the coverage of pension schemes) and, more recently, by a recasting of the pension policies of those countries in the midst of transition from planned to market economies.

Second, and as important as the previous issues, were the consequences of the schemes' success. For the developed countries at least, the incidence of poverty in old age has greatly diminished since the 1940s and 1950s, in relative as well as absolute terms. In large part this has been due to extensions in the coverage of social security schemes and to the increase in benefits. But it can also be attributed to the general growth of real incomes and savings, especially in the form of housing. The focus of the normative basis of pension schemes shifted towards the provision of retirement income for all members of the population, especially those workers whose earned incomes were clustered around the middle of the income distribution. For developing and middle-income countries, the impact of pension schemes on poverty among the elderly has been much less: their levels of coverage and benefits have been much smaller and many of them have been adversely affected by processes of structural economic adjustment and transition from a planned to a market economy. This raises questions of the appropriateness of earlier normative standards, and whether or not there now exist two types of problems and two sets of normative criteria: one for countries which may be considering whether they have developed too generous a pension system; one for countries where pension schemes need to be expanded rather than contracted.

Finally the acceptance of state intervention in all parts of the economy, which prevailed during the 1950s and 1960s, began to be reversed in the mid-1970s, and has continued. With a greatly reduced risk of poverty there are thoughts of moving away from public pay-as-you-go social security pension plans towards defined contribution schemes and greater individual responsibility, which place priority on a tight connection between individual contributions and benefits and reduce the emphasis given to solidarity between income classes.

All these considerations create a need to re-examine the normative basis established when the schemes were first begun, especially as far as those in the developed countries are concerned, although for the developing, transitional and middle-income countries many of the original concerns remain: chief among them, as the first part of this book has set out, are the questions of coverage, governance and the prevention of poverty in old age. But whichever category a country falls into, revised normative criteria will be needed to examine closer relationships between pension schemes and needs, to provide more scope for individual choice and to identify closer relationships between social costs and economic efficiency.

THE GUIDING PRINCIPLES OF PENSION REFORM AND DEVELOPMENT

General

The general objectives for the benefit structure of pension schemes can be thought of in terms of five components:[2]

1. the extension of coverage to all members of the population;

2. protection against poverty in old age, during disability or on death of the wage earner for all members of the population;

3. provision of an income, in replacement of earnings lost as a result of voluntary or involuntary retirement for all those who have contributed;

4. adjustment of this income to take account of inflation and, at least to some extent, of the general rise in living standards;

5. creation of an environment for the development of additional voluntary provisions for retirement income.

Other criteria and principles are discussed below, but it is clear from this general statement that some form of universal coverage is a priority; that pension schemes should at least encompass the original aim of preventing poverty in old age, ensure the provision of an earnings-related pension for workers whose income is above the poverty line, provide the opportunity for workers to add to the benefits provided by the (mandatory) schemes, and protect income against inflation and also adjust, at least partially, to the rise in real wages. To this extent the five principles above reflect not only the original anti-poverty motivations for pension schemes but also the complexities involved in providing earnings-related pensions for the average worker and the other issues which have evolved over the second half of this century.

Nevertheless the five points indicated above leave a great deal unsaid and unspecified. There are a number of other criteria which must also be taken into account.

Coverage

Ideally pension schemes should cover the whole population. We are all going to grow old and we will all need an income when we do. This, together with the principle of compulsory affiliation, is the quid pro quo for the state's responsibility to provide a minimum income in old age to all citizens, regardless of their previous employment or contribution history. But 100 per cent coverage is not always possible. As previous chapters have discussed, in many developing economies a large proportion of the economically active population does not possess a regular job whose earnings can be monitored, and on which contributions can be levied. Even in developed economies a significant proportion of the labour force is self-employed. And in all economies there will always be some people who are simply unemployed. This clearly limits the number of people who can be brought under the umbrella of a formal social security pension scheme. Other factors are important, especially the capacity of the pensions agency to force employers and their workers to comply with mandatory registration. As a consequence, some countries do not possess the fiscal means to provide minimum anti-poverty pensions for all citizens regardless of their contribution history. The International Labour Standards recognize the problem and attempt to set minimum standards: the Social Security (Minimum Standards) Convention, 1952 (No. 102), sets a minimum coverage of 50 per cent of all employees, or 20 per cent of all residents, and these levels were increased in the Invalidity, Old-Age and Survivors' Benefit Convention, 1967 (No. 128), to all employees, or 75 per cent of the economically active population, or all residents below a certain means-tested income limit. These criteria are rarely completely fulfilled, but full coverage remains the ideal.

Compulsory affiliation

Whatever the financing regime, compulsory affiliation by all workers and employers is important for two main reasons. First, where the financing of minimum anti-poverty pensions relies on the revenue collected by the general pension scheme, there must be no possibility for individuals to opt out simply to avoid their share of supporting those on low incomes: the burden must be equitably spread over a large population of the non-poor. Second, and perhaps more important, is the fear that a large part of the population is myopic. There is substantial evidence that, left to themselves, many individuals will be too shortsighted to save enough for their retirement and will become a burden on the state when, given a push, they could have contributed sufficiently for their retirement.

Solidarity

The principle of solidarity, reflected in the second of the five general criteria set out above, is what justifies the existence of social security pension schemes in addition to individual protection measures, including those based on insurance mechanisms or individual savings. This principle applies first and foremost to financing techniques. Irrespective of the approach chosen for the financing of pension schemes (full or partial funding, pay-as-you-go, general taxation or a combination of these), collective financing is indispensable to ensure that money is available to support the incomes of the most vulnerable. This does not necessarily apply a priori only to low-income categories but to all those who, through the occurrence of social risks, lose a substantial portion of their earning capacities.

One form which this protection can take is that of means-tested social assistance, under which the basic support for a minimum income is provided from general taxation. This is the option chosen in a number of countries, such as the United Kingdom. In other countries the financial support is provided out of the contributions for the general pension scheme, and reflects the solidarity inherent in them. Whichever is the case, two points need to be noted. First, the responsibility for ensuring a minimum income in old age lies with the state, which must draw on general taxation where individuals cannot afford to buy adequate protection from the market or cannot afford adequate contributions to public schemes in the case of old age, invalidity or death of the wage earner. Second, and this applies to a number of developing countries, the capacity of the state to make such provision depends not only on the taxable capacity of the country but also on the distribution of income within it. If large numbers of the elderly require basic support – because there are a minority of rich people – the task of providing it becomes that much more difficult.

Equality of treatment

Equality of treatment corresponds to the fact that the Universal Declaration of Human Rights,[3] according to which every human being has the right to social security, prohibits discrimination of any kind as to race, colour, sex, language, religion, political or other opinion, national or social origin, property, birth or other status (article 2.1). In the social security field this type of preoccupation is of particular importance concerning discrimination based on sex,[4] on nationality and on residence. But achieving equality, even with the best will in the world, is by no means an easy task, the two most awkward areas concerning women and migrants.

As far as differences of treatment between men and women are concerned, there are of course obvious cases of discrimination which need to be eliminated, where different rules and conditions are applied to men and women workers. But there is also a range of other areas where application of the same rules to men and women results in different outcomes. This is the case, for example, where women are obliged to take a number of years away from work to bring up young children, and in so doing lose years of contributions towards pension entitlements. There are other cases where a woman's right to a pension is derived from that of her husband and where she may lose it if she becomes divorced or separated. And there are yet other situations where discrimination, in terms of wages and earnings, means that a woman's entitlement to a pension is also lower than it should be. Conversely, the higher life expectancy of women can provide them with a longer (if lower) pension than their male counterparts. The experiences of different cohorts also matter. Later cohorts of women have higher participation rates (and also higher levels of skills, training and education) which means they are less reliant on pension rights derived from those of their husbands. These differences are slowly being addressed in most developed countries, in ways which take account of the differences in life experiences as well as removing the most obvious forms of discrimination, although they are much less adequately tackled in less developed countries.[5]

The treatment of migrant workers can also present problems. Migrant workers who pay social security contributions in their host country can also receive benefits for health care, unemployment and other short-term cash benefits such as family allowances. But in the case of pensions and long-term cash benefits the problem becomes complicated because the right to a benefit is accumulated and paid over a long period, and because it is necessary to combine benefits and entitlements from two or more countries. This is usually done by calculating the discounted present value of the amounts due in each country, and combining them through some form of clearing house. But this can create some unfairness where benefits are related to contributions in a non-linear way, or where the benefit formulas include a degree of redistribution towards those of lower incomes. Many countries have concluded bilateral and multilateral agreements to resolve the problem.

Guaranteed and predictable benefits

Although the prevention of poverty is one of the cornerstones of the normative basis, the other is the provision of a retirement income – for those workers whose lifetime incomes are generally above the poverty line – which does not differ too greatly from the income received while in work. In essence, this means an earnings-related pension. Considerations of individual equity mean that such a pension should be financed during the working career by contributions which are also earnings related. There are numerous formulas which can reflect this principle, some more so than others,[6] but there is general recognition that once the formula is determined, the pension amount should be predictable and guaranteed. This raises difficult questions about how to cope with risk. As Chapter 12 has argued, some forms of pension financing, especially those in which benefits are related to the investment performance of accumulated savings, place the risks on the pension recipient. Other forms of financing, especially pay-as-you-go schemes, pass the risk back to the community as a whole. The risks may be large. They depend upon the rate of increase of real earnings, the rate of return on investment, whether or not the burden of demographic change is to be met by present contributors or by present beneficiaries, and who will bear the cost of increasing longevity.

Indexation

Indexation of benefits reflects the view that pensions should be adjusted to take account of price movements and possibly also to take account of movements in real wages. As far as indexation to prices is concerned, the point is a fairly obvious one and does not need elaborating: contributors are entitled to benefits which reflect the real value of their contributions and should not be placed in a position where, after relatively few years as retirees, inflation can erode a substantial part of their benefits. Many countries have now established automatic mechanisms for the adjustment of pensions. As far as indexation of benefits to real wages is concerned, the point is more debatable. The case for indexation to real wages is based on the view that retirees are entitled to a share of the general growth of productivity as well as protection against inflation. There would seem to be some natural justice in this view, but relatively few countries have gone so far as to establish automatic legislation which provides it. Most rely on ad hoc adjustments to pension levels at irregular intervals. Clearly some sort of adjustment is required if pensioners' incomes are not to be left gradually behind the incomes of those in the remainder of the population.

Democratic management

The participation of workers' and employers' representatives in the management of social security schemes is the direct consequence of financing through contributions. The aspect is a crucial one since it makes reference to the free use of salary whose suspension through the introduction of social security contributions (deferred salaries) becomes acceptable only when workers have, through their representatives, the right to influence the use of what, at the end of the day, remains their money. Application of this principle clearly becomes much more difficult when the pension scheme is of a defined contribution type, operated through private pension funds but nevertheless mandatory. In this case the equivalent protection, as far as the management of the funds is concerned, must be the right of workers to change from one fund to another, depending on performance. A sufficient number of pension agencies must exist for the workers' selection to be a real one, and sufficient transparency concerning their performance should be available for workers to be able to choose.

State responsibility

It follows from the normative principles outlined above that the state has a responsibility to ensure that the conditions of pension schemes and the delivery of benefits are fulfilled. This includes not only the setting of the framework of the schemes but also responsibility for their general management and efficiency, which stems from the compulsory nature of the schemes. But it does not necessarily imply that the state should become directly involved in the operation of the schemes itself. This may be left to other agencies (quasi state bodies, or even private sector institutions) but, where the state does not operate the schemes itself, it must establish a wide range of prudential regulations, coupled with rigorous auditing processes, which safeguard individual contributions over a long time, and ensure that the benefits are efficiently delivered.

Ceilings

The provision of earnings-related pensions, based on earnings-related contributions, is not without limit. It is intended to provide income security to the broad spectrum of workers in the middle range of incomes and is not intended as a vehicle to reinforce the retirement incomes of those with high incomes. Almost all social security pension programmes therefore impose an upper limit on the value of retirement benefits and consequently an upper limit, also, on the level and rate of contributions. For those workers (including the self-employed) with relatively high incomes who seek to ensure a pension corresponding to their lifetime incomes, or even for those workers on lower incomes who wish to ensure a replacement rate higher than that provided by the mandatory public scheme, the state should ensure that adequate means are available to do so. Generally this implies the use of private or occupational pension schemes in which the individual can save on a voluntary basis. But it also implies that the state has an obligation to regulate such funds and to ensure that the pension contract – which can extend for a long time – is properly fulfilled.

IMPLICATIONS OF THE PRINCIPLES

The implications of these principles in terms of the design, management and operation of pension schemes can present difficulties in reality. The main issues centre around questions of universal coverage and the question of using defined contribution, individual savings accounts as a replacement for public defined benefit schemes.

Universal coverage

Although universal coverage remains the ideal, few countries are able to achieve it within the confines of a contributory system. The large size of the informal sector in developing countries in Asia, Africa and Latin America prevents countries from recording the incomes, many of which are in kind rather than cash, of those who are self-employed, or collecting contributions from them. The boundary between the informal and formal sectors of the economy is a grey one and many countries, for practical reasons, are obliged to limit the scope of their pension schemes to firms with five, or even ten or more, employees.

The same is true in advanced economies and in economies in transition, where the number of self-employed persons has grown substantially in recent years, although it remains much smaller than in developing countries. Where countries (such as Turkey) have tried to compel registration by informal workers, the attempt has not generally been successful. This leaves such countries in a quandary if they still wish to provide anti-poverty minimum pensions in old age. One approach is to make participation by the self-employed voluntary and to provide a flat-rate minimum pension which is separate from, and higher than, the basic anti-poverty pension. This would permit a degree of solidarity within the pension schemes, financed mainly by the contributions from formal sector workers, and it would leave the anti-poverty pension to be financed directly from general taxation. But the countries which have large informal sectors have problems collecting sufficient taxes and hence in financing anti-poverty pensions on any significant scale. And it raises the question of incentives: if those who are poor throughout their working lives know that, when they grow old, they will receive a state-financed anti-poverty pension, they may be unwilling to contribute to the additional amount provided by the basic flat-rate pensions. As a result, anti-poverty pensions in such countries are not high enough to bring many individuals out of poverty. And many of the self-employed cannot afford, do not wish, or are too myopic, to make the necessary contributions voluntarily. They may also be sceptical about the reliability of the state's promises actually being fulfilled.

The dilemma is a vital one for the expansion of pension schemes in developing countries, and it is one to which formal social security schemes do not have a ready answer. In the end it means that a majority of workers in developing countries must rely on the support of children or family members, a social contract which has become less viable given increased rates of urbanization and exposure to economic recession.

Funded or unfunded, private or public, defined contribution or defined benefit schemes

Much debate has recently developed around the choice of regime for pension programmes. Technically it is possible to design a pension scheme which is fully funded or pay-as-you-go, operated by public or by private agencies, or of the defined contribution or defined benefit type. Any permutation – or any gradation – of these aspects is technically feasible and the choice of an optimal design has been much discussed among academics and practitioners, and in the media. Much of the debate has focused on the need to meet the pension requirements of an ageing population and on the impact of pension design on incentives in the labour market, especially in a period of high unemployment. It has also reflected, although rarely explicitly, views about individual equity, the extent to which contributors to a pension scheme should be obliged to contribute to the redistribution of income to the poor, and the degree to which individuals should be responsible for their own social protection in old age. As previous chapters have shown, much of the controversy which this has provoked has been misguided: funded schemes do not provide additional protection against ageing populations; private schemes are not necessarily cheaper to administer than public ones, nor are they necessarily more efficient at investing contributors' money. But as far as the general principles affecting pension schemes are concerned, the argument can be reduced to two main issues: whether fully funded individual accounts can provide the necessary guarantees required to support individual pensions, and the question of democratic management.

Under public pay-as-you-go social security pension schemes, risks are borne by contributors. The pension which an individual will receive is not affected by interest rates, present or future rates of unemployment or demographic developments which affect the ageing of populations or the longevity of the population. Nor is the individual affected by rates of inflation, now or in the future. Provided governments stick to their promises, the future pension is predictable and guaranteed, depending only on the earnings and contribution profile of the individual and the benefit formulas in force. There is always the risk, of course, that the governments will not stick to their promises, or that the public pension scheme will be mismanaged, and for many people – especially in developing countries – this risk is a major one.

With a defined contribution scheme, however, risks are largely borne by pensioners and their pension is not predictable. Contribution rates are fixed and the amount of capital which will be accumulated by the time of retirement is determined by interest rates, which are variable and uncertain. The amount of the pension will also be affected by the expectancy of life at retirement, and the rate of interest which will apply to the annuity to be obtained from the capital accumulated. These risks are large, as much as 30 per cent of the ultimate pension, and they are volatile, as recent developments in capital markets have shown. They will also be affected by the reaction of capital markets to demographic changes. And under a defined contribution scheme the ultimate level of pensions will also be affected by the expected length of retirement both for the pensioner and for his survivors. Finally, under a defined contribution scheme which reckons an individual's pension entitlement entirely in terms of his own contribution, there is no scope for solidarity with those on low incomes: any basic or anti-poverty pension will need to come from general revenues.

Clearly pension schemes of the defined contribution type cannot meet some of the principles set out above. They cannot provide a guaranteed retirement income, nor the degree of solidarity necessary to provide anti-poverty minimum pensions. Where they are mandatory, but their management is placed in private hands, they do not meet the principle of democratic management. It is much more difficult for them to provide benefits which are fully indexed against inflation.[7] And, where they are in the hands of private agencies, they require a high level of state regulation and supervision. Of these the failure or absence of a guarantee is the most serious.

That said, there are some economic advantages. Mandatory defined contribution schemes may stimulate the growth of capital markets, create fewer distortions in the labour market and are much less susceptible to the risk of overpromising on the part of government, or bad governance and management (although contributors may be susceptible to over-generous advertising as to rates of return by private pension agencies).

One compromise (and there are many possible ones) might be to think in terms of a two- or three-tier structure of pensions composed in the following way:

- a lower tier which would provide a basic anti-poverty pension, available to all citizens and financed from general revenues;
- a broad public social security pension, financed by compulsory contributions, which would provide a moderate replacement rate for all who contributed to it;
- an optional defined contribution tier, possibly privately managed and operated, which would provide a pension supplementary to the public one.

Much would depend upon the extent of the different tiers. A moderate replacement rate for the second tier might mean something between 40 or 50 per cent of previous earnings.[8] This would leave any further increase in the replacement rate to be financed by a scheme of the defined contribution type: voluntary, possibly occupational, perhaps privately managed, but well regulated by the state. The risks associated with this last tier would have much less impact on individual pensions since they would apply only to the supplement above the social security pension and not to the whole pension. Such a scheme might still have difficulties in financing the first anti-poverty tier from general revenues, particularly if the country were in a weak fiscal situation, but it would also provide scope for the provision of pensions higher than the ceiling imposed by the middle social security tier. It would also impose on the state the double duty, not only of setting the parameters of the mandatory social security tier and ensuring that they are implemented, but also of establishing the prudential regulations and the monitoring of the voluntary defined contribution tier. But it would provide an acceptable compromise between the two kinds of risk: the political risks associated with the implementation of the public social security tier and the market risks associated with the defined contribution one. Risks, including the risks associated with ageing populations, would be shared between contributors and pensioners.

The use of a defined contribution scheme as the financing mechanism for the third, voluntary tier also raises the question of its management and, in particular, may conflict with the principle of democratic management of pension schemes indicated above. In principle, voluntary coverage may be taken into account in the assessment of pension schemes only when it (a) is controlled by the state or managed by the social partners, (b) it is also applicable to low-income workers, and (c) it meets the general requirements of compulsory social security schemes, including collective financing, periodicity and predictability of benefits, legal protection and financial guarantees. These conditions are difficult to fulfil if the voluntary third tier is also to be privately managed. One way to solve the problem is to ensure that contributors and pensioners have an adequate choice of the private agency which will manage their supplementary pension. As already indicated, there must exist a significant range of competitive private sector agencies from which to choose, contributors must be able to move from one agency to another at any time, pensioners must be able to choose the agency which will provide their annuity,[9] the private agencies must be regulated and monitored by the state, and their performance must be transparent so that workers have a reasonable basis for choice. And, of course, benefits must be indexed.

Notes

[1] Beveridge (1942).

[2] See Iyer (1993).

[3] And the associated International Covenant on Economic, Social and Cultural Rights, 1966.

[4] Article 11.1 of the UN Convention on the Elimination of All Forms of Discrimination Against Women, 1979, makes an explicit reference to social security (retirement and disability pensions).

[5] See Brocas et al. (1990).

[6] The most equitable being those formulas which link pension amounts to average *lifetime* earnings, rather than simply earnings over the last few years before retirement.

[7] Very difficult, but not impossible. Generally this would require the use of indexed bonds, issued by the Central Bank, in formulating the annuity to be based on the accumulated capital.

[8] The Social Security (Minimum Standards) Convention, 1952 (No. 102), stipulates that after 30 years of coverage a retirement pension should not represent less than 40 per cent of previous earnings. This might mean the earnings over the last several years or over average lifetime earnings. It should be noted that 40 per cent of the national average wage is within the normal range of relative national poverty lines used by UNICEF for different developing countries.

[9] Which may be different from the agency to which they have paid contributions.

EXTENDING COVERAGE

16

This chapter reviews policies for extending the coverage of pension schemes, both within the formal sector of the labour market and to the informal and self-employed sector. Related issues which are dealt with elsewhere in the book include a broad discussion of problems relating to coverage (Chapter 8) and some of the normative issues (Chapter 15).

Most workers in developing countries will not be entitled to a social security pension when they can no longer work because of old age or invalidity. Furthermore the majority of families are not protected against financial insecurity on the death of the principal income earner. The categories of persons most likely to be excluded were identified in Chapter 8 and reference was made to initiatives which some countries have taken to respond to the problem. We now discuss some of the policy options which could be appropriate.

A number of common considerations lie behind these policy options.

1. There is unlikely to be in any country only one solution to the goal of universal coverage.

2. In developing countries it may be unrealistic to rely on an extension of a social insurance scheme designed for the formal sector as a means of covering the self-employed and those in the informal sector.

3. High levels of coverage depend on a high degree of consensus and the latter depends on the scheme being related to the needs and circumstances of those that it seeks to cover.

4. Achieving an extension of coverage is interdependent with good governance and scheme design.

Policy options include the following:

- extending, without a significant modification of the contribution and benefit structure, existing schemes to cover excluded groups;
- restructuring or adapting existing schemes to facilitate coverage of excluded groups;

- designing special schemes for excluded groups;
- introducing tax-based universal or selective schemes;
- encouraging the development of special schemes based on self-help or mutual insurance principles.

The first three approaches seek, each to a different extent, to bring the excluded within the scope of the existing system and imply the general application of at least some social security principles, particularly contributory-based entitlement and compulsory insurability and related obligations that ensure compliance. The fourth breaks the contributory link and presumes, with financing from general taxation, the payment of benefit based on evidence of a contingency such as old age or low income. The fifth presumes that, at least for some of those excluded, coverage under a public social security scheme is unrealistic and implies that private and group arrangements based on mutual support might be the only solution. The following paragraphs discuss these policy options.

EXTENDING EXISTING SOCIAL INSURANCE SCHEMES

This approach presumes that the national economy will grow, causing the formal sector to increase and the informal one to decrease so that the number of small and intermittent enterprises will decline in relative terms. This assumption of classical development theory has not been substantiated in practice in most developing countries, and this approach is likely to produce only a limited extension of coverage within the time span of one generation. It was recently estimated for India that about 10 per cent of the workforce is covered by formal social insurance schemes, down from 13 per cent during the mid-1980s.

Nevertheless governments can take a number of practical steps to improve opportunities for extension. Where coverage is restricted under the law by the exclusion of those who work for small employers or in certain occupations such as agriculture, these restrictions may be removed or reduced by statute (see box 16.1). In principle, and in a fully developed scheme, no one who is working as an employee should be excluded from protection. Since such persons were excluded for administrative considerations, they can be brought effectively under the scheme only if the administrative implications are addressed. These apply to employers, workers and to the social security scheme itself. Time must be allowed for the necessary preparations to be made. If a timetable is prescribed in the legislation, this may provide the discipline to ensure that administrative steps are taken to prepare for the extension of coverage and it also has the advantage of avoiding further rounds of negotiation and political reflection.

The best approach would be for social security legislation to cover all employees, but to permit certain exceptions. These might be divided into two categories: those who are to be permanently excluded from coverage (perhaps,

> **Box 16.1 Extending social security coverage to government and military workers**
>
> In many countries government employees and the military are covered by generous pensions financed out of government general revenue and are excluded from coverage under the national social security system. These generous pensions are part of the compensation received by people working in these occupations, and may be used by the government to attract qualified people to those jobs. Nonetheless it is desirable for several reasons to include government employees and the military in the national social security system. First, it helps to foster a sense of national solidarity that all citizens of the country are treated equally under the national social security system, rather than some groups receiving privileged treatment. Second, in small countries, it enables the social security system to benefit, with increased efficiency from economies of scale.
>
> There is a growing tendency towards including government employees and the military in the national social security system. All new government employees have been included in the United States social security system since 1983, in the Irish and Jordanian social security systems since 1995, and it is envisaged in the new legislation enacted in Zambia in 1998 to establish a national pensions scheme. It may be considered expedient, as it was by these countries, to restrict coverage to new employees, since current employees had been hired with the expectation that they would be covered under their existing system. Those employees could be given the option of switching.
>
> In making this change it may be advisable to start a new occupational pension scheme for government and military employees, to supplement their benefits received from the social security scheme.

in some circumstances, members of the armed forces who have their own scheme, and employees of foreign governments or international organizations) and those who it is foreseen would eventually be brought within the scope of the scheme. The exclusion of the first group could be provided in the legislation while the second group (including those who work for small employers, agricultural workers, domestic workers and casual workers) could be recognized in a schedule in legislation.

Any enlargement of coverage under the social security scheme can only be achieved with the concurrent improvement of its administrative capacity and governance (see Chapters 9 and 17). However, with respect to the specific issues related to the extension of coverage, the administrators of social security schemes often find it difficult to deal with the special circumstances of the self-employed and casual wage workers. When such schemes are extended to smaller enterprises, each new employer has to be identified, registered, educated and persuaded to comply with all the rules of the scheme in so far as they relate to the registration of employees and to the mode and timing of the payment of contributions. In the case of casual workers, contributions are difficult to secure, and maintaining up-to-date and correct records is administratively complicated when such persons work intermittently and irregularly for different employers. There is also a conflict with the underlying concept of the receipt of benefits for replacement income, if the income to be replaced cannot be determined easily.

Other administrative reforms may improve compliance and enforcement. An example is the development of cooperation with other public agencies, such as tax authorities, to identify individuals and businesses who should be covered by the social security scheme. Improved governance, supported by effective public relations and educational activities to increase awareness as to rights and obligations, needs to be underpinned by compliance and enforcement procedures and powers that reinforce the mandatory character of the scheme.

The extension of coverage in a mandatory scheme should depend on the capacity to enforce it. Where a country has decided to broaden the scope on a mandatory basis without a supporting administrative infrastructure, the solidarity and redistributive basis of the scheme may be threatened and insured persons may strategically plan the payment of their contributions so that they maximize the benefit of their participation in the scheme. An example is provided by the Philippines, where the Social Security System scheme was developed to provide universal coverage but was restricted in its enforcement by a combination of public sector restraints on resources and a soft compliance policy.

ADAPTING EXISTING SOCIAL INSURANCE SCHEMES

Extending coverage by adapting existing schemes relies on the view that the existing schemes are inappropriate for many of those not covered and also for some who are covered but are evading contributions. This may be because the contribution rate is high – for instance, because the self-employed would be expected to contribute at the same rate as the combined employer/employee contribution – or because the benefit package does not match the perceived priorities of those excluded.

One approach for the self-employed would be to permit a degree of choice in the selection of insurable earnings used for the calculation of contribution liability. This could be achieved by prescribing minimum insurable earnings levels for different occupations (Egypt, for example, follows this approach). Consideration might also be given to revising the benefit and contribution structure to facilitate the entry of the self-employed and informal sector workers. The design could have a structure with two components. The first component would be mandatory in order to provide entitlement to a basic flat-rate pension (subject to satisfaction of a prescribed period of insurability and with considerable variation depending on national circumstances). This basic component could be applicable to all gainfully occupied persons and would require a relatively low contribution rate or even be replaced by a flat-rate contribution for workers in the informal sector. The second component would provide an earnings-related benefit on a defined benefit basis. This component would be applicable only to formal sector employees and possibly the higher income self-employed. (This system is also discussed in Chapter 19.) Since it seeks to address the problem of low coverage, it is designed to provide a more realistic entry threshold for the self-employed and for informal sector workers. Such workers would be within the scope of the national scheme but on a basis which neither strained the solidarity principle of the scheme nor represented a major contribution burden for them. Where the scheme covers a range of benefits other than pensions, some flexibility could be allowed as to the coverage of groups such as the self-employed, domestic and casual workers.

Another possible adaptation of existing schemes is to introduce defined contribution principles to provide a clear link between individual contributions paid and pension entitlement. However this is inappropriate in the case of protection for invalidity or surviving dependants since insurance must be provided against the risk that these contingencies occur early in the life of an insured person. In the context of extending coverage for a retirement pension, there is no clear evidence that a defined contribution system is more likely to encourage compliance among the self-employed and informal sector workers. On the contrary, the absence of any redistributive element (except perhaps in a basic anti-poverty tier) is likely to lead to such persons choosing to place any spare resources in other forms of savings.

The experience of the defined contribution schemes in Latin America (see box 16.2) and of the provident funds in Asia and Africa does not suggest that such schemes provide a substantive solution to the problem of covering the self-employed or those working in agriculture. Furthermore the low level of contribution liability of these workers, and difficulties in securing their compliance, tend to result in private pension fund providers making limited efforts to attract and maintain their membership. If their coverage were considered desirable, as part of a poverty alleviation programme, the government could consider special intervention in the scheme to stimulate participation by the self-employed, such as through a subsidy directed at either guaranteeing an interest rate above the market rate, guaranteeing a minimum pension, covering the risk associated with invalidity or death, or treating contributions as tax deductible.

SPECIAL SCHEMES FOR THE SELF-EMPLOYED AND THE INFORMAL SECTOR

The above reference (on the possible application of defined contribution principles to the development of an income maintenance scheme for the self-employed and the informal sector) leads to consideration of whether it is feasible to design special schemes for the self-employed, or other sections of the labour force, who do not fit within the parameters of a redistributive social security scheme. There

Box 16.2 A comparison of the apparent advantages and actual experience concerning coverage under defined contribution schemes in Latin America

Apparent advantages	Effects in practice
Easier threshold to entry due to incentives noted below	Increased barriers for entry when insured person's contribution is increased (Bolivia, Colombia, El Salvador, Peru), plus high administration and commission fees, no solidarity (subsidies for self-employed), and unattractive to private pension funds because of low contribution and burden of compliance for lower-income workers
No employer's contribution	Where this has been done, the insured person's contributions have been increased (except Chile), hence higher barrier to entry (in Latin America, employer's contribution has not been eliminated in Argentina, Colombia, El Salvador, Mexico and Uruguay)
Competition reduces administrative costs thus facilitating coverage	Administrative costs are high
Direct link between insured person's contributions and benefit is an incentive to register and pay	Compliance (active/affiliate ratio) is about 50 per cent in five countries for which data are available
Minimum pension is guaranteed hence another incentive to join	Many of the low-income insured (estimated as 50 per cent or more in Chile) cheat the system, minimize their contribution to maximize state subsidy

are essentially two ways of doing this: either designing a special public scheme which corresponds to the needs and circumstances of the excluded group but which is administratively and financially distinct from the scheme for formal sector workers, and is either financed wholly by those insured or partially, with a government subsidy; or encouraging (and assisting) the development of mutual support systems covering occupational groups or communities.

An example of the first approach would be to design benefit packages for the self-employed and the informal sector which would make a basic core of social protection obligatory for all gainfully occupied persons, but give a more comprehensive protection, on an optional basis, for those satisfying tests of membership. Survivors' and invalidity benefits could be the priority components of such a core package. Public social insurance schemes would have a comparative advantage in providing such benefits because insurance against these risks requires a large pool of contributors.

Various problems would need to be addressed, however. Since many persons at some period of their working lives would be insured under the principal scheme, consideration would have to be given as to how this could be linked with membership of a special scheme. Such an arrangement implies the need for transfer of information and funds. Furthermore, even though the special scheme would be designed specifically to appeal to excluded groups, it would probably fail if membership were voluntary since moral hazard considerations would cause members to seek to maximize their entitlement in relation to their contribution liability. But ensuring compliance in a compulsory scheme would also be difficult, depending on the categories of persons included. If a significant percentage of those covered saw no advantage in such a scheme or felt unable to afford to pay the contribution, the effect of this would be to undermine both its financial viability and its solidarity base. The government could either subsidize the scheme to ensure a higher level of participation, as is done in Ecuador, the Islamic Republic of Iran, the Republic of Korea and Turkey, or establish earmarked taxes specifically designed to support the social security pension scheme.

A special scheme could also be considered in countries with many domestic workers. Such employment is, in general, stable with limited turnover. Simplicity would be an essential feature of such a scheme and a flat-rate scheme may be advisable. Similarly, special schemes could be established for agricultural workers through a levy on produce and for construction workers by a levy on the overall construction site contract.

As regards the approach based on mutual support, over the past decade many new self-financed schemes have emerged that are managed by, or at least for, various groups of informal sector workers. These schemes often have their origins in community- or occupation-based support systems established to enable their members to cope with common problems. They are as likely to be concerned with promoting income-generating activities as with insurance, but many have savings and credit systems to pool resources to meet social protection needs, although these normally relate to sickness, disability and death rather than to retirement.

The success of such schemes and the extent to which they can be replicated elsewhere depends on the following:

- the commitment and charisma of one person or a small group of people;
- whether there is a consensus on the priority contingencies which should be covered;
- the scope for "sound control" among the members and the prospects for reciprocity of entitlement;

- access to external resources that will ensure long-term financial viability;
- the capacity of the scheme's administrators (who are often unpaid);
- opportunities for pooling between different but similar schemes;
- opportunities for linkage with private insurance or possibly social insurance schemes.

For lack of these conditions, many schemes founder after a short period. To promote stability they need encouragement in the form of tax concessions or financial and administrative support, possibly from the social security system. However careful consideration needs to be given to the relationship between such schemes and the social security scheme. Some of these self-help schemes have been established by individuals and small employers who are legally insurable under the national social security scheme. Perhaps such coverage under the national social security programme is premature, but it is inadvisable to legitimize evasion through support for an informal arrangement covering workers who were also legally covered by the national scheme. On the other hand, it may be that the social security programme should be modified to better suit the circumstances of certain sections of the labour force.

One fundamental question is whether mutual support schemes should be encouraged as a supplement or as an alternative to a basic national social security scheme. In most cases, taking on the additional role as a provider of a basic pension would require a level of resources and administrative capacity significantly beyond that which the scheme currently possesses. Furthermore providing for a pension on retirement may not be seen by the participants of such schemes as a priority, but to open the possibility, and to encourage participation in a special scheme organized by an informal sector association may compromise efforts to strengthen and extend the formal sector scheme which will be trying to maintain the principle of compulsory insurability and uniformity. Thus a dilemma confronts policy makers and a balance needs to be struck between strengthening and extending the formal sector public scheme and encouraging those clearly outside its scope to make separate arrangements.

There may be scope for using self-help associations as agencies on behalf of the national social security scheme for the administration of a basic pension scheme. They could facilitate the registration of their members and the collection of contributions, and be reimbursed for this. They could even be rewarded for increasing coverage. This is effectively the arrangement in those countries where members of cooperatives are insurable under the social security scheme. The social security system scheme in the Philippines is pursuing a progressive policy of contacts with informal sector associations to forge links to identify and remove obstacles to coverage. Training of managers of informal schemes could be contemplated.

Most mutual support schemes for informal sector workers are organized either by communities, or by persons with similar occupations or trading activities. While this may generate the trust that must underpin any social insurance scheme, it may be insufficient to ensure such schemes' extension and replication. Area-based schemes might be both easier to establish and more sustainable because they would have the backing of the government itself. Such schemes could be developed as pilot projects focusing on workers who are above the poverty line but outside the formal sector with its statutory protection. Membership might be open to all workers in a defined geographical area, irrespective of the nature and duration of employment or the place of work.

The range of benefits would depend on the level of funds available both from the contributions of members and from other sources. Basic benefits may include insurance against death or invalidity, health insurance and scheme benefits. Contributions would have to be mandatory, but could be flat rate. Members could be given the option to select from among different premium amounts with corresponding benefit packages worked out on an actuarial basis. Some other possible sources of finance which could be considered by the government include flat-rate levies on selected employers, and additional taxation or social security levies linked to specific items (such as electricity consumption, clearance of negotiable instruments, motor vehicles and licences).

Administrative responsibilities could be given to local government bodies, perhaps in collaboration with national bodies. The management of the finances and benefits could be entrusted to a professional insurance agency. It would be desirable to use the existing administrative mechanism as far as possible.

DEVELOPING TAX-FINANCED PENSION SCHEMES

Three variants of tax-financed schemes might be considered here.

1. Schemes could provide flat-rate benefits, based on subsistence levels, for all those over a prescribed age and who are permanently and totally disabled. Those entitled to a pension from another source would be excluded. Such pensions would be financed from taxes and this could include indirect taxes or special levies on produce. A problem with such a tax-based approach is the difficulty in many developing countries of collecting taxes and also the narrow tax base. Even if it were possible to collect more tax, a universal pension scheme might not attract priority over improvements in primary health care. There is also a risk that such a scheme would cause higher evasion under any contributory scheme which was operating simultaneously in the country.

2. A tax-financed scheme could be aimed at the poor through the application of a social assistance system based on a means test. This option might help to solve the problem of low coverage under social insurance pension schemes in that a social assistance scheme would ensure a subsistence level income. It could also be complementary to a defined contribution mandatory savings scheme. Many of those working in developing countries in the urban informal sector, and in agriculture, are subject to periods of unemployment and underemployment and also earn so little when they work that they are

417

unable to contribute to their future social protection. For such people, social protection is best supplied through schemes provided directly by the state. However, it is also equally difficult to distinguish those who have the resources from those who do not.

3. A general poverty alleviation programme could include provision to provide assistance to the most vulnerable groups. Most developing countries cannot afford a social assistance system covering the poor and are thus unable to establish a comprehensive safety net. Many such countries do, however, have more general poverty alleviation programmes and these should contain an appropriate mix of income-generating infrastructure development and income-support measures. It may be necessary, when establishing target groups, to take account of the very old (such as those over 65) and the disabled. Drèze and Sen (1989 and 1991), for example, see income support for widows without adult sons as representing a significant step towards relieving an important social problem in India involving some 30 million widows who suffer from much higher rates of poverty and deprivation than the general population.

Even where criteria for selection are less demanding, there is evidence that cash payments to the elderly can greatly improve old-age security. For example, in South Africa a cash transfer about twice the median income of African households, where eligibility is determined on the basis of age irrespective of previous contributions, has been an effective tool for redistribution, as it has mainly benefited poorer African households. This redistributive effect is largely driven by a low take-up rate by white households and the fact that efforts were made to reach poorer African households in rural areas. Interestingly, because the elderly poor in South Africa also tend to live in extended families containing poor children, and because the cash payment was shared within the household like any other source of income, the scheme was also effective in reducing child poverty and poverty overall.

Tax reform and social protection are strongly linked, and financing reforms should be seen as integral to rethinking how to provide social protection for the elderly poor effectively. Tax reform in this context should be in the direction of broadening the revenue base with a much stronger focus on domestic indirect taxes (such as sales taxes and VAT), as opposed to direct income or social security taxes. These taxes, though non-distributive, are much easier to collect and can be applied to a much wider tax base than is the case with income or social security taxes. Because they are less conspicuous, and are not directed at particular groups, they do not run into the same evasion and political economy problems faced in the collection of individual income and social security taxes. In essence informational, incentive and administrative constraints impose severe limits on the scope for redistribution via taxation in developing countries, therefore the focus of tax reform to promote social protection should be on creating a broad-based, buoyant and stable revenue base.

There is now a large body of evidence which suggests that switching expenditures within an overall governing budget towards, for example, the social sectors (such as health and education) can have a large pay-off in terms of improving the welfare of citizens, including that of the elderly. Understanding the budget process, and the political economy of how the overall pattern of expenditures is determined, is central to understanding how this type of expenditure reform might be accomplished. Given a typically strong demand for basic social services by the general population, the viability of this type of reform would appear to hinge on whether there are political institutions in place which effectively aggregate these preferences (for example, via voting) so that they are reflected in government allocation decisions.

The difficulties associated with the administration of a social assistance scheme should not be underestimated. These include the following:

- the determination of the poverty line or threshold,
- the design of the system,
- the basis for distinguishing those persons among the many who are poor who are most vulnerable,
- the determination as to what extent account should be taken of support provided (or expected) from other members of the household and family.

A recent field study on the application of the Indian old-age social assistance scheme in Gujarat, Orissa and Uttar Pradesh (Sankaran, 1998) showed various cases of patronage – for example at the selection stage, and of abuse, in particular in the case of cash payments. It also highlighted problems in determining a suitable means test.

Thus, in assessing the cost-effectiveness of social assistance programmes, some of the following issues need to be addressed.

1. What are the responsibilities of the central and local government in the financing, administering and fixing of the social assistance benefits?

2. What should be the criteria for the means test (income, land, assets) and at what level of government should eligibility be determined?

3. How can corruption-free mechanisms be designed?

4. How can administrative costs be controlled?

5. How should social assistance and social policy interventions, such as food for work and employment guarantee schemes, be coordinated?

Given the dominant role that informal mechanisms play in supporting the elderly poor in developing countries, it is essential to consider, in the design of social assistance programmes, how such schemes would affect the incentives to provide private support. There is a possibility, for example, that children may reduce transfers to parents if the latter begin to receive state transfers, thus diluting the welfare impact of a given programme. The available empirical evidence on this suggests that there is a moderate trade-off between public and private financial transfers; however this is not dollar for dollar so public support measures still improve the welfare of the elderly. Incentives to provide private support appear not to be completely undermined by public support.

More importantly there are a range of circumstances where complementarities may exist between private and public support. Rather than crowding out private support, public support measures may actually strengthen incentives to care for the elderly leading to a crowding in of private support. These complementarities may be particularly strong in extended or geographically proximate households. Within families living together, or close together, the elderly play a productive role in providing a range of services, such as child care and domestic work, in exchange for which they receive housing, food and health care. If the effect of a public support measure is to reduce their cost to the family (for example through subsidized health care) then the incentives to provide support for them will tend to be strengthened as their value to the household is enhanced. These effects will be even stronger when the elderly can directly contribute monetary resources to the household, as is the case when they receive a cash payment from the state. It can be argued, for instance, that a widowed, or elderly dependant, who receives, say, a cash payment from the state may be less – rather than more – vulnerable to neglect within the household, in so far as the availability of an independent source of income increases his or her bargaining power vis-à-vis other household members. Household formation and the configuration of caring arrangements are endogenous, therefore measures that reduce the costs of caring for the elderly and increase the benefits of having them present in the household may encourage the formation of extended households or, at a minimum, will improve the functioning of the exchange market between related individuals.

Given the variety of situations in different countries, with differing levels of economic development as well as institutional capacity, it is inappropriate to propose policy conclusions of general application. Furthermore in most countries there is no one solution to the problem of extending coverage and the policy options discussed are not mutually exclusive. The problem varies in form and significance, depending on the degree of development and a range of other factors.

Broadly there are three types of countries. The first consists of the developed countries, where the problems of coverage are of relatively limited significance. Here the emphasis needs to be on ensuring that social security and employment legislation are adapted to take account of new forms of contractual relationships, steps are taken to improve compliance and, where this has not already been done, mechanisms are established to cover the self-employed.

The second consists of the middle-income countries, some of which have well-developed social security institutions. Here the general approach should be to progressively cover the labour force through an extension of the social insurance programme. Where resources permit, consideration should be given to the establishment of a universal flat-rate pension scheme or more selective protection through social assistance.

Third, there is a large group of low-income countries where a rapid increase in social protection for income security on termination of employment is difficult to attain. Universal schemes, whether based on residence or on means, are the most effective ways of ensuring high coverage, particularly of the poor. But such schemes are seen by most developing countries as beyond their resources and often as being of relatively low priority. Moreover in many such countries it has not even proved possible to ensure that those who are gainfully occupied in the formal sector make some provision for their future.

New approaches to social assistance are required that can encompass people in financial need who cannot be reached by policies for employment and who cannot (and/or have not been able to) contribute to self-financed social insurance schemes. The advantage of social assistance benefits is that they can be directed to those most in need, such as children, the disabled and the retired. However they require a sophisticated administration to determine who is really deserving and to make sure that the benefits reach the target population effectively. Accordingly the costs of delivering the benefits are often high, and without a tight benefit administration there are likely to be leakages or corruption. Naturally the size of any social assistance schemes must depend on the resources, administrative capacity and priorities of the countries concerned.

Beyond the tax-financed universal and social assistance schemes, various policy options have been discussed and reference has been made to international experience. Those who work as employees for small businesses should be brought within the scope of the formal social security scheme, but this must be carefully planned and preceded by a strengthening of the administrative capacity and the education of the employers and workers. Insurability should be mandatory and be seen to be so. The process of extension of coverage to this sector has generally been slow and it has not been accompanied by sufficient efforts to establish the essential administrative functions. However this sector is the easiest to address and should be given priority since the needs and circumstances of its employees are virtually indistinguishable from those of employees already covered.

Attempts by governments to integrate self-employed workers into public social insurance pension schemes have met with mixed success. Some self-employed workers who are part of, or close to, the formal sector (such as the professional self-employed, shopkeepers and employers) may be induced to join such schemes, particularly if there is scope for them to select the level of their participation. If, on the other hand, the self-employed are obliged to pay both the employers' and workers' contributions, evasion is likely if they identify what seem to them to be better opportunities elsewhere for protecting their future. Some liaison with the tax authorities would seem essential and there may even be scope for integrating the collection of tax and social security contributions from the self-employed.

Special schemes for the self-employed may have more success if the government is willing to subsidize the coverage to make it attractive, but there are limits to the extent that other contributors or taxpayers will be prepared to subsidize those who are seen as having the opportunity of participating in the scheme on a basis which is determined by their best interests. Self-employed workers have much greater opportunities for non-compliance than employees working in formal sector enterprises. In some developing countries, governments have attempted to create special schemes for casual and home workers outside the formal sector. These have had some success, in particular where such schemes could be supported by earmarked taxes. In those countries where coverage is low because many workers are engaged in informal sector activities, or are working on their own account, consideration could be given to designing the scheme to take account of this fundamental problem. Instead of designing a scheme for the minority of the labour force that is in the formal sector, it would be better to design one that takes account of the needs and circumstances of the majority. Such a scheme could include optional additional provision or it could be a basic social protection package. Where possible, excluded groups should be brought at least partially within the scope of the principal scheme where there would be some scope for the application of solidarity principles.

The self-financed informal sector schemes are fragile and subject to collapse. Nevertheless they keep springing up because they fulfil basic needs. Most of the self-financed social insurance schemes for informal sector workers are organized on an occupational or sectoral basis. While such bases may be good for generating the necessary trust that must be the foundation of any social insurance scheme, they may not have the capacity to provide long-term income security for their members and are more likely to be able to meet short-term needs, such as health care and lump-sum assistance, to alleviate family distress. There may be more scope for area-based schemes which are more replicable, and which imply the backing of the government itself. Bringing social protection provision down to a lower level of government, explaining responsibility to communities or NGOs may improve matters because these providers may be more accountable and have a higher valuation of the preferences of the elderly poor.

Greater priority needs to be given to achieving a wider coverage under pension schemes. There is a need for more research on the social security priorities and contributory capacities of the non-covered population, as well as on the various mechanisms that could be used to extend coverage through the adaptation of existing formal social security programmes. There is scope for innovation and experimentation based on a general recognition that no one solution is appropriate for all situations.

Living standards are tied to economic growth and in the long term provide the basis for improved and broader-based social protection schemes, whether these are financed by contributions from those covered or through taxes, as in the case of social assistance or basic income schemes. In the meantime the approach for developing countries should take account of the following:

- revising schemes to facilitate partial membership by the self-employed, domestic workers, agricultural workers and those with a regular income from informal sector activities;
- setting time limits for such an extension;
- strengthening the administrative capacity of the social security scheme, particularly in compliance, record-keeping and financial management;
- undertaking education and public awareness programmes to improve the image of the social security system;
- encouraging the development of mutual support schemes for those outside the scope of extended coverage and as supplementary protection for those only covered for basic protection: concentrating on the organized informal sector;
- enlisting the support of cooperatives and self-help schemes in the administration of the national social security scheme;
- developing social assistance schemes aimed at the absolute poor within prescribed vulnerable groups;
- ensuring that social protection is integrated and consistent with other development programmes for the informal sector, such as improving access to credit and savings mechanisms, bolstering community and informal sector support and ensuring the provision of basic social services.

In the countries in transition, the scale of the problem is not as severe, and its consequences are cushioned to some extent by social assistance schemes. But it is essential for social security schemes to complete their own process of transition to enable them to take on the new responsibilities of administering social security schemes for the private sector. The basic mechanisms and provisions exist to improve the level of coverage, but registration, collection and compliance provisions need to be strengthened and the legislation revised to fit the new situation, all in the context of efforts to develop a relationship with representatives of private sector workers and employers.

Finally the implementation of defined contribution schemes, and the privatization of social security administration, will not contribute to increased coverage (unless this is subsidized in some way by government). First, the individualization of responsibility for social protection restricts the scope for redistribution to those with lower incomes and intermittent employment records – the bulk of those excluded from coverage. Schemes based solely on individual savings are unattractive to the poor. Second, private sector administration would not be attracted to the task of administering schemes for the self-employed and the informal sector and this approach would have the effect of aggravating the fundamental problem of the provision of adequate social protection.

IMPROVING GOVERNANCE, MANAGEMENT AND COMPLIANCE 17

PLANNING, POLICY AND COORDINATION ISSUES

Chapter 9 draws attention to the fundamental importance of good governance if social security objectives are to be met. It also identified the principal problems that are being experienced by social security schemes throughout the world. Recognizing that governance embraces each aspect of the implementation of the scheme, from its conception to its operation, the chapter categorized these problems according to whether they occurred at the strategic or macro-policy level, at the institutional or operational level. This chapter looks more closely at what might be done to address these problems. It then discusses some key issues which relate to the overall approach to the objective of achieving good governance of social security schemes. Among related topics discussed elsewhere in the book, issues relating to governance are covered in Chapter 9, contribution evasion is analysed in Chapter 10 and issues relating to design are discussed in Chapter 19.

Social protection issues are invariably both complex and wide-ranging. They involve difficult decisions as to priorities and the allocation of resources. Within the government, responsibility for social protection is likely to be divided between several different departments. Even in the relatively narrow context of pensions, there may be separate statutory schemes for the private sector, the self-employed, public servants and the armed forces and, as regards risks, for employment injury as well as for retirement, invalidity (disability) and survivors. In addition there will often be occupational schemes and private pension funds and there may also be a social assistance scheme providing a safety net. The roles and interrelationships of these different segments of the social protection system need to be clear and, furthermore, they should each represent a component in a long-term strategy which provides a policy framework for development. Problems will inevitably emerge which need to be tackled, but it is preferable if this can be done in a strategic context rather than on an ad hoc basis. It is thus advisable for governments to formulate an overall national social protection strategy within which objectives, roles and responsibilities can be defined and development monitored.

The absence of such a strategy often illustrates two other weaknesses. First, there is a need for some coordinating mechanism to ensure that the development of social protection as a whole is consistent with the overall objectives. There should be policy cohesion between the different initiatives of individual government departments. This implies the need for an interdepartmental committee or some other administrative mechanism, established at a high level and with the power to ask individual ministers to reconsider policies, if necessary, in the broader context. Such a committee or authority could be the responsibility of the central planning authority, or of a subcommittee of the cabinet, or it may be that less formal coordination arrangements between departments can be established. But without coordination at the policy level there is the risk of inconsistency.

Second, coordination and the development of social protection strategies depend on information and analysis to enable informed choices to be made on policy options. A quantitative analysis of the implications of different options, in both the wider macroeconomic context and the narrower social protection context, is essential to this. The application of social budget modelling techniques (described in Technical Brief 1) represents a useful tool in this process. Since this analysis must be interdepartmental, it presumes that the planning process – and the capacity to make it so – exists, as well as the skills.

Another essential ingredient of the planning process is consultation with those affected by the proposed scheme in order to make them aware of the reason for the reform, what it is trying to achieve and what it will mean to them in obligations and entitlements. The need for transparency starts with the conception of the scheme. This is discussed further in Chapter 20.

When policy decisions have been taken, and the reforms designed, the process of drafting and enacting legislation must begin. Drafting skills and specialist knowledge of social security issues are essential, but the legislative system may be cumbersome and may inhibit the introduction of straightforward reforms which are not subject to dispute. Fundamental reforms, which require the preparation of new principal legislation, will inevitably take time to process but there should be sufficient flexibility in the legislative system to permit matters of a subordinate or recurring nature to be enacted under ministerial powers.

The process of reform of the social protection system can be lengthy and timetables are often unrealistic. Since the issues can be highly political, it is common for there to be a long period of consultation, reflection and consensus building, which tends to result in a desire for speedy implementation once the policy has been settled. The failure to take account of the time necessary to prepare the systems and the public for the new requirements has resulted in some schemes being introduced prematurely and unsuccessfully. In the experience of the ILO through its technical cooperation programme, it takes a minimum of 12 months (and 24 months would generally be more realistic) from the date of enactment of the principal legislation to complete preparations for the implementation of social security pension schemes.

INSTITUTIONAL ISSUES

A key issue in securing the good governance of either a new social security scheme or an existing one is the choice of the institutional arrangements. There are basically three choices, but with considerable scope for modification of each:

- direct administration by a government department;
- administration by an autonomous public institution with a supervisory board of directors or trustees;
- private administration by insurance companies and pension funds.

In each case a government department retains responsibility for policy and for the overall performance of the scheme. Thus the responsible minister has to account to the public for the overall effectiveness of the scheme. (These different institutional arrangements are discussed in Chapter 4.) They all have the same objectives and their differences reflect varying viewpoints as to the best way of meeting these objectives, but each presumes a need for a degree of supervision and control over the resources that it provides. Thus the choice of a government system presumes that well-established systems for audit and budgeting will apply to the public social security system and this should be integrated with other national priorities; or the choice of an autonomous public institution based on the notion that social security finances are distinct from those of the government and that the different interests of the stakeholders (government, contributors and beneficiaries) should be reflected in the management of the scheme; or the choice of private organizations, operating under statutory regulation and in a competitive environment, will ensure that the scheme provides good service to its customers and that the resources are managed efficiently.

It has already been noted that the majority of social security pension schemes are administered by autonomous public institutions with a supervisory board which represents the principal stakeholders. But it has also been noted that in many countries the governance of these social security schemes has been unsatisfactory and that these public institutions have not performed in the way that was envisaged. It has proved difficult for many of these institutions in developing countries to apply the delicate balance of interests and power implicit in the concept and it has been a common experience for the scheme to be heavily controlled by the state, particularly during times of economic adversity or political uncertainty.

This has tended to result in different approaches to governance reform. One approach is to move along the spectrum towards privatization, while another is to maintain the present arrangements but to concentrate on reforming those aspects which do not work well. There are, however, alternative approaches which seek to improve efficiency through a specialization of functions, or which give priority to integration and rationalization and which thus favour the unification of schemes. These approaches are discussed in the following paragraphs.

REVIEWING PUBLIC/PRIVATE RESPONSIBILITY FOR PENSIONS

In some countries, particularly in Latin America, the problems and issues discussed in Chapter 4 have, to some extent, undermined the validity of social security schemes based on social insurance principles. A linkage exists between the concept and the performance, particularly in the minds of those who advocate a reduced role for the state in relation to social protection and who regard private sector management as inherently more efficient than the public sector. There is often a connection with the philosophy which lies behind a national structural adjustment programme for the economy, in which the role of the state would be scaled down and instead private sector development would be promoted to revitalize the economy. To what extent is privatization the answer for improved governance of social security?

First, the debate concerning the privatization of social protection is essentially on two levels: one relates to the responsibility for providing it, and thus to its structure, and the other to the management of it. At the structural level, those who argue against the principles of social insurance maintain that social security overprotects individuals and removes their freedom of choice, on the basis that they are somehow incapable of making rational decisions as to what is best for them. It is argued that the state should withdraw to a position in which it provides a minimum level of protection and then creates and encourages an environment under which private arrangements can be made. But it is invariably recognized by proponents of this approach that it is necessary to counteract individual myopia by imposing mandatory obligations to contribute to social protection.

At the administrative or institutional level it is argued that the social security institutions are not subject to market competition (they are effectively monopolies) and they are not required to make a profit. Administrators consequently pay insufficient regard to the financial implications of the decisions they are obliged to make. The increasing acceptance of neoliberal thinking which stresses the rights of individuals to choose has combined with a disillusionment as to the value of state intervention and has provided the momentum for the privatization of social security. There was a tendency to assume that the competitive forces of the market place would have a generally beneficial effect, but there is little information or research as to how this would be achieved in practice with a system that owed its existence to the need to counteract the harshness and inequalities of the marketplace. Experience in those countries where private schemes have taken on a more significant role has revealed that the problems experienced by public schemes are by no means exclusive to those schemes.

1. Employers may be unwilling to provide the necessary information on the different pension plans relating to their employees and may also fail to deduct contributions or simply fail to pay them.

2. There is an inherent contradiction between the objectives of a mandatory social security scheme which seeks to counteract myopia and to provide social protection on a broad basis, and the motives and approach of a private sector organization, which seeks to maximize income and minimize expenditure. All things being equal, such organizations will tend to ignore or pay less attention to the lower paid, those in irregular employment and those reluctant to participate.

3. Decisions taken as to the structure of the scheme will determine the role to be undertaken by the state, but the state cannot remove itself from the overall responsibility to ensure that social protection is provided for its citizens.

4. Provisions which relate to income replacement on termination of employment require an array of administrative procedures, both to monitor the establishment of entitlement and then to make pension payments. These tasks must be carried out either under a publicly managed defined benefit scheme or under a privately managed mandatory retirement savings scheme which is subject to the necessary compliance measures to ensure that employers and workers are registered and pay the contributions that are due. In the case of mandatory retirement savings schemes, such as have been introduced in Latin America, the tasks may be spread among many approved pension funds which are also obliged to invest pension funds and provide annuities at the point of retirement. Administration is complicated by the opportunity which must be afforded to individual members to switch from one fund to another. The scale and complexity of the responsibility, combined with the fact that pension funds are profit making, have obvious implications for the application of the scheme at the lower end of the market (among lower-paid workers or among employers with a high turnover of workers) and obliges the establishment of a public supervisory authority whose task it is to make sure that employers, workers and pension funds all meet their obligations.

5. Since the scheme must be mandatory, some measures must be taken to ensure compliance, and these should be conditional not on the profit motive but on the need to counteract myopia and avoid inequity (those who do not comply will nevertheless qualify on a means-tested basis for the basic pension). Experience in Chile illustrates that non-compliance remains a problem in spite of the establishment of the resources allocated for the implementation of an efficient regulatory authority.

6. In those countries where there is considerable reliance on occupational pension schemes or on personal pension plans, it is also essential for a regulatory

framework to be established to protect individuals, whether or not such arrangements are compulsory. It is also relevant to note that there have been, in recent years, a number of scandals relating to private pension funds in such mature economies as Germany and the United Kingdom. In the latter the Maxwell affair involved the misappropriation of large sums of money from pension funds and the misselling scandal involving improper sales practices to persuade people to switch from the public scheme, or from occupational pension schemes, to inappropriate personal pension plans.

Thus the level of government intervention required where there are mandatory retirement savings schemes or considerable reliance on occupational or personal pension plans is at least as great as that required where there are wholly public schemes, and this intervention is probably more complex because it has to be exercised through private organizations. Furthermore government intervention leaves the opportunity open for political manipulation. This leaves open the question as to whether mandatory privately administered retirement savings schemes are more efficient and whether they better meet the objectives of good governance. The evidence is not conclusive either way, and comparisons are difficult because of conceptual and functional differences between the systems. There is, for example, a striking contrast between the voluminous and complicated regulations governing private pensions in the United Kingdom and the simple regulations governing complementary pension schemes in France, where all decisions must be taken jointly by employers' and workers' representatives. Furthermore administrative costs for established defined benefit schemes in OECD countries average about 3 per cent of benefit expenditure and there are many examples of pension schemes being implemented in developing countries with low administrative costs.

In terms of the transparency of the respective systems, it is apparent that insured persons are often as confused about the provisions of a mandatory retirement savings scheme as those of a public scheme. Indeed it seems that many people find it difficult to make the choices envisaged under the private systems and are thus susceptible to advice and guidance for which they must invariably pay. The uncertainty extends, in particular, to the level of benefit to be provided. Thus the mandatory retirement savings schemes lack the predictability which many regard as an integral part of social protection. Neither does privatization protect individuals against political risks, since crucial aspects of the scheme especially the level of benefits, may still be seriously affected by public policy decisions. Public policy can place limits on the investment decisions of private pension funds and it determines how contributions, capital gains and the pensions themselves are taxed. It also affects interest rates, and thus the growth rate of pension investments and the value of annuities purchased.

It is often argued that members of a defined contribution scheme will be less inclined to evade payment since the level of benefits they receive is directly related to the level of contributions they have paid. This hypothesis is questionable, for two reasons.

1. A typical defined benefit scheme also provides benefits which are related both to earnings and contributions. Although there is provision for insurance cover in respect of death and invalidity, and for redistribution to the lower paid, there is generally a linkage between contributions and benefits and many schemes are being modified to strengthen that linkage.

2. Even under defined contribution schemes, employers choose not to pay (or at least to delay payment). Sometimes such a decision is reinforced by collusion with workers who are anxious either to keep their jobs or to maximize their take-home pay because they give a higher priority to current needs.

A shift in responsibility from public sector to private sector management can take many forms. First, there is a spontaneous trend, particularly where private arrangements have developed in a void created by the failure of public sector schemes to provide adequate social protection, in terms of either coverage or level. Second, some countries have a more programmed approach to increased private sector responsibility which is the reflection of specific policy initiatives and where, for example, in the pension context, the public scheme has been reduced to represent a basic tier of protection, with additional pension entitlement being dependent on individual membership of private pension funds.

Some countries have introduced private sector participation in the administration of the social security scheme. If the scheme lacks the expertise to operate a computerized record system, this task could be contracted to a private sector organization. This was done in Thailand and Uganda, but at least for some time in both countries there were problems since it was difficult both to obtain the required information in good time from employers and to ensure that the contracted company gave sufficient priority to the processing of the data. Similarly many schemes lack the specialist knowledge needed to take full advantage of investment opportunities: thus responsibility for the management of the investment of social security funds could be contracted to private investment managers as an alternative to establishing their own investment department. Many schemes do not have their own actuarial services. Consideration should therefore be given to identifying tasks which could be better performed by private specialist companies. Management contracts could then be devised to set out the requirements of the task and these contracts could be backed up by supervision and penalties in the event of failure to comply with the contractual obligations.

MAKING PUBLIC SOCIAL SECURITY INSTITUTIONS MORE EFFECTIVE

Whether the structure of the social security scheme is private or public, the state must play a major role in ensuring that it meets its objectives. Where the administration is entrusted to the private sector, significant supervision will be needed by a public sector body. Efficiencies through competition may be counteracted by the loss of economies of scale or because of advertising costs of private organizations. It is not easy to reconcile the motives of private, for-profit organizations, with the task of administering a truly universal social security scheme. This tends to suggest a need for the establishment of well-managed autonomous public institutions charged with the task of administering public social security schemes providing at least a core of social protection on a uniform basis, and empowered to do so in a way which takes advantage of techniques of efficient management applied by successful private sector organizations.

Social security schemes financed by employers' and workers' contributions are obliged to give priority to the interests of their contributors and beneficiaries who should, as a consequence, have the opportunity to participate in the supervision of their scheme. At the same time, the scheme has the opportunity to use some of the resources derived from these contributions to administer the scheme and the obligation to do so in the most efficient way. Can truly autonomous public institutions be established which can combine the advantages of public and private management? Experience, discussed in Chapter 4, suggests that many developing countries (and even higher-income countries and countries in transition) have found it difficult to establish a public institution responsible for the administration of a social security scheme which is truly autonomous, achieves the delicate balance of representation of the interests of the government, the contributors and the beneficiaries and is able to operate with an acceptable level of efficiency. Nevertheless in many such countries there are no clear indications that large-scale privatization would result in more effective systems and it may be more appropriate, in the reform process, to give priority to addressing the weaknesses in the public institution which limit their effectiveness.

IMPROVING THE COLLECTION OF CONTRIBUTIONS

All social security schemes depend on information provided by employers and insured persons and on their capacity to organize and record this information. Much of this information is given by employers and individuals to different government agencies for different purposes. This represents a considerable burden which is reflected in lower levels of accuracy and compliance.

This provides the basis for an approach to governance reform founded on the premise that the separation of the administrative functions of a social security scheme would provide an opportunity for greater specialization to focus on the problems of each function. An example of this relates to the collection and enforcement of contributions. It is argued not only that compliance levels are low, but also that the collection procedures duplicate those employed by the authorities to collect income tax since, in many countries, this is also deducted at source and then paid over by employers. It is also argued that the tax authority specializes in the collection of public funds, is not hampered by welfare considerations and generally has special powers to enforce payment. Accordingly it is suggested that the tax authority should collect social security contributions together with tax or, alternatively, that a separate revenue collection agency should be established to collect all public revenue. Such a system is already in operation in a number of industrialized countries where social insurance schemes exist (for example Sweden, the United Kingdom and the United States). In the United Kingdom social insurance contributions and income tax are collected by the Inland Revenue which transfers the amounts collected to the social security fund and also provides the Department of Social Security with copies of the documents submitted by employers showing the amounts paid by each insured worker. Enforcement action is also, in general, taken by the Inland Revenue but disputed liability is the responsibility of the Department of Social Security which also, through its Contributions Agency, carries out compliance checks on employers and enforces the liability of the self-employed through its own inspectorate. There is scope for arrangements of this kind to work satisfactorily in developed countries where interdepartmental agreements can be devised and implemented without great difficulty.

A unified system for collecting tax and social security contributions may be cheaper, but an evaluation would need to consider the cost of changing a well-established dual system. Other developed countries (for example France, Germany and Japan) prefer, however, to have separate systems for the collection of tax and social security and the application of a unified system would be rather more difficult in developing countries for a number of reasons:

- Contributions collected by the tax authority need to be transferred to the social security fund.

- Equal priority would need to be given in the collection and enforcement process to both tax and social security liabilities.

- Social security contributions might come to be regarded merely as another tax and thus compliance might suffer.

- Social insurance principles of solidarity and uniformity might be prejudiced.

- If social security contributions are collected by another public agency, particularly one closely connected with central revenue collection functions such as the Ministry of Finance, the financial independence and autonomy of the social security institution might be weakened.

The introduction of a unified system would also imply the need to harmonize taxable and insurable earnings and definitions as to the status of workers/taxpayers. A unified registration system would also be necessary. Furthermore data requirements for determining long-term entitlement to pension would be more demanding than those relating to annual tax liability.

In developing countries the tax systems often display greater weaknesses and lower compliance rates than the social security system. Some of the countries in Central and Eastern Europe have introduced a unified system and here the circumstances may be favourable in that the functions relating to the collection and enforcement of contributions are new, the social insurance concept is not well established and there is no tradition of a distinct social security contribution paid by workers. However, in those countries, tax authorities are often far less successful in collecting revenue than are social security institutions.

Collection practice varies among the mandatory savings schemes in Latin America. In Chile where there is no employers' contribution, the employer is obliged to deduct the contribution from the worker and pay this to the appropriate agency (AFP) with whom the worker is registered. The system is supervised by a superintendency of AFPs but there is no central collection agency. Similar arrangements apply in Peru. In Uruguay all contribution deductions are passed to the public institution (BPS), which administers the basic pension scheme; BPS then passes on contributions for the second-tier pension to the appropriate pension fund. In Argentina a unified revenue collection agency has been introduced which includes responsibility for collection on behalf of approved private pension funds.

THE UNIFICATION OF SOCIAL SECURITY SCHEMES

The unification approach is the reverse of the specialization approach and derives its appeal from two sources: first, where the social security system is fragmented between different sections of the population or different risks with duplicated functions and inconsistencies; second, from the viewpoint of employers and insured persons it may be argued that there should be one point of contact for social security obligations and entitlements. Many countries, such as France, Germany, Japan and the Republic of Korea, have developed systems with different specialist agencies administering different schemes, sometimes in respect of different occupational groups. Some developing countries have done the same (for example, Gabon, India, Pakistan, the Philippines and Senegal). Such an approach reduces the range of risk pooling since those insured are more homogeneous, but it could be argued to be inconsistent with social insurance principles and, in the governance context, to lead to a duplication of functions and to higher aggregate administrative uses. The increasing development of health insurance schemes provides an example of the arguments for and against specialization or unification. The nature of the benefit has little in common with pensions. Indeed its linkage with pensions could have compliance implications, since people might be more inclined to insure against health care costs than save for their pensions. On this basis one could make a case for specialization. On the other hand, the two benefits require similar administrative mechanisms and insure the same people.

433

There are conflicting considerations relating to the specialization/unification question and, furthermore, it is rare for the issue to be considered on a level playing field. Political considerations and an inclination to preserve the status quo may well be dominant factors. Consequently there is no one approach which can be promoted with confidence internationally. Moreover, what is already established and accepted in any country presents a powerful obstacle to a radical restructuring of institutional responsibilities.

CONCLUSIONS

Issues of governance lie at the heart of the debate on how to best provide more effective social protection. But the debate is distorted by misconceptions and by a firm adherence to certain basic principles as regards, for example, the role of the state. It is also worth noting that a mandatory system which collects contributions from people – including some with low incomes – and retains these for perhaps 30 years, will never be popular and is unlikely to work better than the level of economic and political development in the country permits. The overriding objective should be to create a realistic scheme which commands a broad consensus and then, having regard to all relevant aspects in the country, to establish a system of governance that has the best chance of delivering the essential services.

There are many systems of administration in the spectrum between reliance on private insurance and direct administration by central government and it is difficult, and probably inappropriate, to try to reach any general conclusion as to which system is best. Both extremes of the spectrum seem to present obvious disadvantages with the scheme being susceptible to the influence of either the government or the shareholders and managers of insurance and investment management companies. The nature of the scheme is a crucial consideration. It is difficult to envisage a public pay-as-you-go defined benefit scheme administered wholly under private sector management, although certain functions may be contracted to private sector specialists in the interests of efficiency. A truly autonomous public scheme should be able to display many of the characteristics of efficiency associated with private enterprise, but it should also respect the principles of social security.

To some extent the debate about the relative merits of private and public management is a false one: there is only good management and bad management. Although attractive concepts are at the mercy of human beings, some stand a better chance than others. If the establishment of a mandatory scheme based on the collection of contributions from employers and workers is being considered, the model of an autonomous public social security institution, with its own legal identity and powers, and subject to the control of a tripartite management board, seems to present prospects for a balanced approach. It provides an opportunity for participation by the stakeholders and for the implementation of efficient administrative techniques and effective human resource development. But it has to be conceded that, in practice and thus far in many countries, the model looks better in principle than in practice and much needs to be done to achieve the right balance and to provide the right basis for effective governance. (See Regional Brief 2 on Africa and, in particular, the statement of the Commission on Social Protection and Social Dialogue issued on behalf of all African countries in the CFA zone in Yaounde in 1997, which calls for the reform of social security institutions with a view to ensuring that they function with the autonomy envisaged in their legislation.)

Where public accountability systems exist with a sophisticated democratic framework of public scrutiny, the objectives of a social security system can be achieved through direct public management without the direct participation of employers' and workers' representatives. Still in such cases some form of consultative process is desirable. This argument also applies to schemes financed wholly from general tax revenues which are invariably administered directly by government.

It is difficult to restructure social security institutions once they have been established. The exception is where there is a climate of radical reform, such as has existed in recent years in Central and Eastern Europe. In any event many of the weaknesses in the governance of social security would not necessarily be solved by privatization, specialization or unification: they may only appear in another form or be replaced by different problems. For many countries, therefore, the most realistic and effective approach would be to seek improvement within the present structure. There are certain key problems here which have already been mentioned but which deserve to be highlighted.

1. The need to improve the basic administrative functions such as maintaining records and making payments accurately and on time. Where these functions depend on the cooperation of employers and insured persons special emphasis should be placed on making the procedures and tasks as simple as possible: this implies the need for simplification both in procedural and institutional terms, and consideration should be given to rationalizing social security obligations to avoid employers and insured persons having to deal with several institutions and to provide detailed information to each; independent appeals systems should be established to resolve disputed decisions on benefit claims and contribution liability.

2. Increase income by focusing on improving compliance and investment performance. Compliance is a particular problem and a compliance and enforcement policy needs to be established and supported by the allocation of resources, including trained inspectors and effective penalties and enforcement mechanisms; workers should be encouraged to report non-compliance by their employers and should be provided with an annual social security statement by the institution so that they can check the progress of their membership.

3. The need to control administrative expenditure by means of a thorough examination of procedures, the allocation of functions, staffing levels and non-essential expenditure.

4. The need to improve the service to the clients through increased transparency and accessibility, and by generally restoring confidence in a system which exists for the benefit of insured persons and not its administrators. Transparency could often be improved by better public relations activities aimed at making social security obligations and rights simple to understand and by emphasizing (where appropriate) the linkage between benefit entitlement and contributions.

Many social security schemes seem to have lost sight of the basic objectives of the scheme. This may be attributable, in some cases, to poor working conditions and low expectations for staff. These issues also need to be addressed so that an environment of responsibility and motivation is created.

Operational weaknesses are often a consequence of failures elsewhere in the governance structure, in the institutional arrangements (for example, the chief executive may be appointed on political criteria rather than on merit) or in the policy decisions over the choice of scheme (thus the scheme selected may be difficult to implement effectively). But the effectiveness of social security schemes is judged by their members at the operational level and in relation to the efficiency in maintaining records, answering enquiries and providing adequate levels of benefit in accordance with clear rules of entitlement and without delay. Many schemes have not yet been able to meet these expectations and are unable to maintain a working consensus with their contributors and insured persons. Problems are often compounded by the general absence of any mechanisms to monitor performance in key areas and thus to provide a basis for addressing the problem. Many schemes tend to rely on informal and irregular subjective judgements when faced with uncertainty, a lack of clarity or conflicting demands and lack a reference point against which to measure the problem. It would be relatively easy to separate the basic objectives of the administration of a social security scheme into broad sections such as the liability and payment of contributions, maintenance of records, payment of benefits, management of finance and general administration, and to identify the key functions the performance of which lies at the core of each section's objective, such as the number of active insured contributors or the number of claims for benefit received and still outstanding. Targets could then be set for the performance of these functions, measured, evaluated and revised as appropriate. A system of performance indicators is only successful if it is supported by the management and staff and if it relates back to the objectives of the scheme and to the perspectives and needs of its contributors and beneficiaries.

INFLUENCING THE AGE OF RETIREMENT

18

This chapter discusses policy issues involved in setting the minimum retirement age and concerns about the actual age at which workers retire. Among related issues presented elsewhere in the book, the minimum retirement age as a requirement for receipt of retirement benefits is considered in Chapter 3. The effect of increasing life expectancy on the cost of retirement benefits is dealt with in Chapter 11, on pension transfers and redistribution. The impact of the minimum retirement age on worker retirement is analysed in Chapter 13, on the economic effects of pension schemes, which indicates that both defined benefit and defined contribution plans may influence retirement age. Minimum retirement age in a number of countries is discussed in the regional briefs, particularly Regional Brief 4 on Arab states of the Middle East.

The minimum age at which social security retirement benefits can be received has an important effect on the cost of the social security scheme. The cost of benefits providing a target replacement rate of, say, 40 per cent will be lowered if the minimum age at which benefits can be received is raised.

Policy concerning the minimum age at which retirement benefits can be received is affected by a number of demographic and economic factors. In many countries the increase in life expectancy, combined with a decline in the age at retirement, has caused a considerable increase in the percentage of adult life spent in retirement. Economic and demographic factors affecting the choice of a minimum age for social security pension benefits require a balancing of the costs of social security against the desire of workers to retire and receive retirement benefits.

RETIREMENT AND RETIREMENT POLICY

In western Europe social security retirement benefits play only a small role in determining retirement age. The minimum age at which they can be received is just one element of retirement policy. In western Europe most workers retire before the minimum age at which social security retirement benefits can be received. In Belgium, France, Germany and Luxembourg only one in three or four older workers, and a considerably smaller number in the Netherlands, directly receives benefits from the social security retirement scheme on leaving the labour force.

Retirement policy can be flexible, allowing workers a range of ages over which they may retire without penalty, or it can be structured to induce retirement at particular ages. Retirement policy can promote the withdrawal of older workers from the workforce or it can encourage older workers to continue working or to re-enter the workforce if they have left it. Legal protection against age discrimination can facilitate work at older ages, while permitting employers to set a mandatory retirement age may discourage it.

Retirement has quite a different meaning in developed countries than in developing ones. The transition from work to retirement in developed countries can be an abrupt change from full-time work to full-time retirement, it can include a period of part-time work, involve full-time retirement followed by re-entry into the labour market and a subsequent second retirement, or leaving one's career job and taking a bridge job before fully retiring.

The elderly poor in developing countries are generally not covered by social security. Their exit from the labour force generally does not follow any of these patterns. They work with diminished vigour until they can no longer work. As they grow older they may change to tasks that are less physically demanding, with younger family members taking over the more difficult tasks.

The need to raise the minimum retirement age

The minimum retirement age is the earliest age at which a worker can receive social security retirement benefits. It is an important parameter in designing a social security scheme in some countries because of its potential effect on system costs and retirement age. During the 1990s a common criticism of the social security schemes of Central and Eastern Europe was that they allowed retirement at too young an age.

A common criticism in OECD countries is that, because of their increase in life expectancy, their minimum retirement age should be raised. In discussing raising the minimum retirement age in OECD countries, critics often note that the fraction of life spent in retirement has increased. The common analysis for both regions assumes that there is a formula for determining retirement age relative to international norms or life expectancy. This chapter provides a framework for analysing these criticisms.

In examining the minimum retirement ages set by social security schemes in different countries, as indicated in the regional briefs, several facts are evident. First, once the minimum retirement age is set, it tends to stay the same for many years. Second, at some point most OECD countries have reduced their social security minimum retirement age. Third, more recently OECD countries have reduced the benefits available to workers retiring at the minimum retirement age. Fourth, many countries have established lower minimum retirement ages for women than for men, but the trend is towards raising the minimum age for women to that for men. Fifth, in countries having a number of different social security programmes, privileged groups tend to establish low retirement ages for themselves. Sixth, during the 1990s some countries increased the minimum retirement age, but with the effective date of the increase generally early in the 21st century. These facts provide the background for analysing policy towards the minimum retirement age.

Economic considerations in determining the minimum retirement age

The minimum retirement age under social security should be set taking into account life expectancy and ability to pay. A simple way to think about the minimum age, incorporating life expectancy and ability to afford retirement at different ages, would be to determine an appropriate ratio of retirement to work years for the average pensioner. The lower the ratio, the lower the savings or contribution rate needed by the worker to fund retirement. In developed countries the ratio of retirement to work years is roughly one to two, there being roughly 20 years of retirement and 40 years of work. In these countries many people have the luxury of retiring while still in good health, so that they can enjoy an active retirement.

Because of their lower income, developing countries are less able to afford retirement. In these countries the minimum retirement age should be related to the age at which many people can no longer work. The ratio of retirement to work years is generally less than in developed countries because of the greater difficulty in paying for retirement. In most developed countries, the minimum retirement age is at least 60, and reaches 65 or as high as 67 in some countries (see table 18.1). In developing countries with shorter life expectancies it is frequently 55, but may be as young as 46 or less. It is age 60 for most African countries.

The life cycle model

The life cycle model of consumption, savings and labour supply provides a more formal way to think about retirement age. It posits that individuals save while working to pay for their retirement. In the absence of government programmes, workers choose a retirement age depending in part on how much they are able to save. If they save a high fraction of their earnings while working, they can retire at an earlier age and finance a longer retirement. Retirement age depends on the age at which people start working (which affects the length of the period during which they save), the amount of savings they accumulate while working and life expectancy.

People with higher lifetime wealth tend to consume greater lifetime leisure. With increasing wealth people tend to spend more years in retirement. Increasing

Table 18.1 Minimum pensionable age in social security, selected countries, 1997

Country	Age
Kuwait	45 for men, 40 for women
Yemen	45
Jordan	46
Zambia	50
Pakistan	55 for men, 50 for women
Burkina Faso	55
Luxembourg	57
Bulgaria	60 for men, 55 for women
Canada	60
United States	62
Netherlands	65
Norway	67

Sources: National social security legislation.

Note: These ages generally require a minimum number of years of covered employment.

wealth is also associated with greater life expectancy. Thus greater life expectancy does not automatically translate into an increase in the desired minimum retirement age. Assuming that years of healthy, active life increase with higher life expectancy, such higher life expectancy would lead to a postponement of retirement. If wealth has also risen, however, it is unclear in terms of the life-cycle planning of workers whether the minimum retirement age should be raised. In OECD countries the ratio of retirement years to work years has increased over time (see box 18.1).

Pay-as-you-go financing

With pay-as-you-go social security the system dependency ratio is an important aspect of financing. It can be measured as the ratio of social security beneficiaries to workers. The higher this ratio, the more difficult it is to provide social security benefits. Thus with pay-as-you-go financing the optimal minimum retirement age will depend on the system dependency ratio: the higher it is, the higher the optimal minimum age for retirement.

The savings considerations of workers in the life cycle model and the effect of their wealth on the demand for leisure determine the demand for a given retirement age. Pay-as-you-go financing and the system dependency ratio can be thought of as determining the costs of benefits provided through social security. The higher the system dependency ratio, the greater the cost of providing retirement benefits.

The physical demands of work also affect the age at which workers retire. Workers retire at younger ages in physically demanding occupations, such as

Box 18.1 Retirement experience and the cost of providing pensions in developed countries

The last four decades of the twentieth century witnessed a widespread tendency for workers in industrialized countries to retire earlier.[1] A retiree may be defined as a person who has withdrawn from the labour market and is no longer economically active. The effective retirement age may be estimated from the reduction of labour force activity rates with age. Retirement is then not linked directly to the entitlement to retirement pensions, although the cessation of economic activity is associated normally with the payment of retirement pensions or other long-term or bridging benefits.

In the OECD countries the average effective retirement age decreased by five years, from 66 in 1950 to 61 in 1990. As shown in table 18.2, the effective retirement age decreased throughout the period in all the regions except in Japan, where it increased slightly between 1950 and 1970 and decreased over the following 20 years. Average retirement age varies between regions and sexes. In 1990, the average retirement age was 59.3 in Central and Eastern Europe and 59.2 in the countries of western Europe. By comparison, it was 65.5 in Japan and 62.6 in North America. The average retirement age was three years higher for males than for females.

Current generations of retirees enjoy longer retirement than their predecessors because of both a lower retirement age and a longer life expectancy. The duration of retirement increased from 12.5 years on average in 1950 to 18.9 years in 1990. It is higher for females than for males: females retire earlier and have longer life expectancy. In 1990 the gender difference in the duration of retirement averaged 5.8 years: 22.6 years for females versus 16.8 years for males.

Table 18.2 Effective retirement age and expected duration of retirement

Region	Effective retirement age		Expected duration of retirement	
	1950	1990	1950	1990
Japan	66.2	65.5	12.0	17.8
North America	65.9	62.6	13.1	18.1
Oceania	65.3	60.0	13.2	20.5
Northern Europe	67.2	61.9	12.2	18.7
Southern Europe	69.0	60.1	10.5	19.9
Western Europe	65.7	59.3	12.8	20.7
Central and Eastern Europe	65.0	59.2	12.8	18.6
Average w/o Central and Eastern Europe	66.5	61.8	12.4	19.0
All countries	66.0	61.0	12.5	18.9

Source: Latulippe (1996)

Using those figures of average retirement age (61) and duration of retirement (18.9 years) makes it possible to compare the number of years spent in retirement with the number of working years. This is called the passivity ratio. Assuming that people who retired in 1990 joined the labour market at age 20 and worked continuously until retirement, the passivity ratio is 45 per cent. By comparison people who retired at the age of 66 in 1950 with an expected duration of retirement of 12.5 years had a passivity ratio of 25 per cent, assuming an earlier entry age of 17. This trend towards an increase in the passivity ratio will continue in the future if retirement age is not increased.

mining, the military, the police and the fire service. Often legislation has created special pension schemes for these occupations. The physical demands of work set a limit on the age up to which people are able to continue working. Because the physical demands of work have decreased over time for most workers, that would tend to raise the average retirement age.

Thus six factors have been identified that affect what the minimum age of retirement through social security should be (the sign of the predicted effect of an increase in the factor on the minimum retirement age that will best meet the needs of society is indicated in parentheses): age at which people start working (+), life expectancy (+), problem of disability (−), physical demands of work (−), the system dependency ratio (+) and lifetime wealth (−).

This model can be applied to analysing the minimum retirement age in Central and Eastern Europe compared to western Europe. Life expectancy, average age at which work starts, and lifetime incomes are lower in Central and Eastern Europe and the prevalence of disability is higher than in western Europe, while the comparison of the system dependency ratio depends on the countries compared and the physical demands of work are higher on average. On the basis of lower life expectancy, lower age at which work starts and greater physical demands of work, the retirement age should be lower in the countries of Central and Eastern Europe. Since lifetime income is lower, it would be expected that fewer years and a lower percentage of life would be spent in retirement in those countries, which would raise the retirement age (see table 18.3).

In developed countries, life expectancy, the age at which work starts, and lifetime income have increased. The first two changes would increase retirement age while the last would decrease it. The system dependency ratio has increased and the physical demands of work have decreased, both of which would increase retirement age. Thus, assuming that the effect of increased wealth is not predominant, the age at retirement should be increased. Empirical evidence over most of the twentieth century, with falling retirement ages, indicates that for that period the effect of increasing wealth has predominated.

Table 18.3   OECD countries with current or future legislated minimum pensionable age of 65 or older for social security benefits

Country	Gender to which minimum pensionable age applies	Age	Effective date if later than 1998
Australia	men and women	65	2013 (women)
Germany	men and women	65	2001 (men), 2004 (women)
Iceland	men and women	67	
Ireland	men and women	65	
Netherlands	men and women	65	
New Zealand	men and women	65	2001
Norway	men and women	67	
Switzerland	men	65	
United Kingdom	men and women	65	2013 (women)

Source: National social security legislation.

POLICY OPTIONS

An alternative that governments have considered to raising the minimum retirement age is to cut the benefits available at that age. This alternative preserves the option of retiring at a particular age, but the reduced benefits encourage workers to retire later. Raising the minimum retirement age may pose serious difficulties for individuals with moderate disabilities who are unable to qualify for disability benefits but have difficulty working. This problem could be addressed by easing the rules for qualifying for disability benefits.

Some countries have allowed retirement on the basis of a minimum number of years of work, with no minimum age. Turkish men initially covered under the social security scheme before January 1976 can retire after 25 years of work, with some retiring as early as age 43. Turkish women can retire after 20 years of work, so that some retire as early as age 38. In Kuwait women can retire after 15 years of work. In Italy, until the mid-1990s some workers were eligible for "baby pensions", meaning they could qualify for them at young ages on the basis solely of years of work. Countries that have allowed retirement with no minimum retirement age have found that some workers retire at young ages and have lengthy retirement periods. It is expensive to provide retirement benefits for these workers. Retirement eligibility requirements should always be set as a minimum age, in conjunction with minimum years of work, rather than solely as minimum years of work.

POLICY CONSIDERATIONS

Increasing life expectancy requires some adjustment in preparing for retirement. Unless workers are willing to increase their personal saving rates for retirement,

443

all countries need either to raise their minimum retirement age over time as life expectancy increases or to raise their social security contribution rate. This applies both to countries with defined benefit and to those with defined contribution schemes. If countries with defined contribution schemes fail to raise the minimum retirement age or contribution rate as life expectancy increases, they will have more and more beneficiaries with low annual benefits, as the account balances accumulated at retirement will need to fund an ever longer retirement period.

A country that has decided to raise the minimum retirement age must consider how best to do this. A gradual phase-in period is seen by the public as fairer than an abrupt change. If the retirement age is raised gradually, the effect of this is borne by a number of age groups and no one age group sees itself as being singled out. Raising the minimum retirement age should be done with a lag following the decision so that it does not affect workers near retirement who have insufficient time to adjust their savings and retirement plans.

Raising the minimum retirement age in defined benefit schemes is usually done in a way that reduces the lifetime benefits workers can expect to receive. An alternative way of viewing the change, however, is that increases in life expectancy raise lifetime benefits and raising the minimum retirement age is done to keep lifetime benefits constant. This is similar to the concept of price indexing benefits, where nominal benefits are raised to maintain real benefits constant with increases in prices.[2]

How far in advance should an increase in minimum retirement age be announced? Above what age should people not be adversely affected? The longer the time before the first increase in retirement age occurs, and the slower the speed with which the change occurs once it starts, the lower are the budgetary savings. Variations in these parameters do not affect different age groups in the same way. Thus the decision on the timing of raising the retirement age must be based on the trade-off in terms of the benefits of minimizing the disruption of people's lives with a slow phase-in versus the budgetary gains of a fast phase-in.

When the minimum retirement age for receipt of social security benefits is raised, the result could be an increase in labour supply as workers decide to retire at an older age. This might be offset to some extent by decreased labour supply at younger ages as workers shift leisure hours to earlier in life. Alternatively it could mean only a cut in benefits, with workers continuing to retire at the same age but with lower benefits.

Raising the minimum retirement age affects other social programmes. It may cause older workers to increase their benefit claims for unemployment insurance, disability insurance and social assistance. The increases in these benefits must be considered in determining the total benefit savings that occur by raising the retirement age.

Equity

Considerations of fairness play an important role in discussions of raising the minimum retirement age. Is it fair that women, who have longer life expectancy, are permitted to retire earlier than men? The arguments made in favour of allowing earlier retirement for women are that wives tend to be several years younger than husbands and allowing females to retire earlier than males allows husbands and wives to retire at about the same time. Furthermore, in countries where women rear many children, it is argued that women have the double burden of work and child rearing and thus have earned an earlier retirement. In Algeria and Tunisia child-rearing responsibilities are explicitly taken into account in setting the minimum retirement age for women. Beliefs concerning fairness have changed, however, and in many countries it is now felt that this difference in treatment of the two sexes is unfair. Thus many countries have decided to gradually raise the minimum retirement age for women until it reaches the level for men. In the European Union occupational pension plans are required to have equal retirement ages for both men and women.

Raising the minimum retirement age affects people in different ways. Its effect is felt most strongly by people with short life expectancy, because raising the retirement age is a greater percentage reduction in years of benefit receipt for them than for workers with longer life expectancy.

Raising the retirement age poses difficult policy issues. Workers have accrued entitlements to benefits and in some countries these accrued entitlements cannot legally be reduced. In all countries, even if there is not a legal issue, there is the question of workers' moral claim to the entitlements. Raising the retirement age can be done so that benefits received at the higher age are the benefits that would have been received if retirement had been postponed, which in the long run will have little effect on total benefit payments. Alternatively benefits can be provided at the new higher minimum retirement age than would have been provided at the previous minimum retirement age, which reduces lifetime benefits.

Pathways to early retirement

Early retirement can be financed in a number of different ways. It can be financed through social security retirement benefits, special government programmes that provide early retirement benefits, occupational pension benefits, disability benefits, unemployment benefits and savings. In countries that have a high minimum retirement age of 67, such as Denmark and Norway, many workers take earlier retirement by qualifying for disability benefits or special early retirement programmes (see box 18.2).

In western Europe, retirement policy has been greatly affected by high unemployment rates. Countries have encouraged older workers to leave the labour force in an attempt to make more jobs available for younger workers.

Box 18.2 Early retirement in Denmark: The Post-Employment Wage Plan
The Danish pension scheme has several characteristic features. First, while
the official retirement age via the social security pension (*Folkepension*) is
high at age 67, the actual average age of retirement is much lower: 62 for
males and 60 for females. Several early retirement options make this possible.
Second, social security is available to all older people in Denmark, regardless
of previous labour market attachment. Third, the decision to retire is generally
not reversed, with few transitions back to work after people retire. Fourth,
private pensions are a small fraction of the total pension structure. Fifth,
many of the early retirement plans are only available to workers who have
been affiliated to an unemployment union for many years, and therefore
mostly popular among workers in blue-collar jobs. Sixth, there has been a
dramatic growth in the numbers opting for early retirement, particularly after
the introduction of the Post-Employment Wage (PEW) in 1979. Finally, replacement rates are relatively high under the Danish pension scheme. Under the
PEW, for instance, retirees are entitled to 90 per cent of previous wage earnings
for the first two-and-a-half years and 82 per cent of previous earnings over the
next four-and-a-half years if they retire before 63. If early retirement is taken
after 63 but before 67, retirees are entitled to a 90 per cent replacement rate
for the entire period under the PEW.

The PEW plan allows early retirement starting at age 60 to workers who
had been members of an unemployment insurance fund originally for at least
ten of the previous 20 years (now increased to 20 of the previous 25 years).
It was introduced by the government in 1979 mainly in an attempt to curb
long-term unemployment and to create jobs for the young unemployed.
While the first objective was more or less served, job creation did not
result as it was difficult to fill jobs vacated by older, trained personnel
with young, inexperienced new entrants. After its introduction in 1979 there
was an immediate drop in labour force participation rates for older workers.
For males in the 60–64 age group (the eligible age group), participation rates
fell 18 percentage points from 70 per cent to 52 per cent immediately after
the introduction of the PEW. Among women, participation rates decreased
only slightly because of the opposing effects of two trends: first, a decrease
in participation rates among elderly women because of the availability of
early retirement plans; and second, increases in women's labour market
participation at all ages (Pedersen and Smith, 1996). The PEW has proved
to be popular and an increasing number of workers say they expect to
retire through the PEW. In the 18–66 age group, 63 per cent of women and
60 per cent of males expect to retire through the PEW (Pedersen and
Smith, 1995).

The PEW may be a mixed blessing for the elderly. While most older workers
prefer to retire earlier than the minimum age for social security benefits of 67,
recent surveys have shown that many feel the hours' constraint of the PEW is
too restrictive. Under the PEW, retirees can only work a maximum of 200
hours a year or else forfeit their benefits. A gradual phase-in of retirement
between the ages of 60 and 67 is seen as the most desirable option by most
elderly. Partial retirement options are available but participation has been
low because of financial disincentives.

The PEW plan has proved to be costly to the Danish welfare state. Analysts are considering the likely effects of a cut in its generosity or availability. Christensen and Datta Gupta (1998) looked at the effect on the retirement age and government budget of two alternative changes in the PEW plan: first, a 25 per cent decrease in PEW benefits accompanied by a relaxation of the hours' constraint from a maximum of 200 hours a year up to a maximum of 705 hours a year (15 hours per week for 47 weeks), thus making the reformed PEW programme more attractive to workers; and second, an increase in the age of first receipt of the PEW from 60 to 62. The effects of the two reforms are compared across married females and males.

They found that women defer retirement more than males following the reduction in benefits and relaxation of hours' constraint (a 0.65 years average deferral for women compared to 0.2 years average deferral for males). In terms of the effect of these reforms on the government budget, the researchers have calculated government savings, which are pre-reform expenditures minus post-reform expenditures (where expenditures include all government outlays on PEW and other early retirement plans) to those in the 60–66 age group plus unemployment insurance benefits to those out of work, less tax revenues from those working full-time or part-time or doing supplementary work on the PEW. The savings are per capita figures and cover a seven-year period (ages 60 to 66) to reflect society's burden associated with this cohort. Under this reform, savings are greater for males than for females.

Comparing the two policy changes, deferral of retirement age is greatest under the second reform, that is, raising the eligibility age. In terms of budget-ary implications reducing benefits, plus increasing maximum allowable hours of work, entails at least 50 per cent more savings than raising the eligibility age. This is true for all population groups, except for unskilled workers (both females and males), for whom increasing the eligibility age entails more savings.

The Danish government faces a distributional challenge if these alternative policies are to be considered. Reducing benefits while increasing hours of work is fiscally more attractive than raising the eligibility age yet entails lower savings for unskilled workers, a key subgroup of workers which is therefore at a relative advantage if the first reform is adopted. For both reforms, females are at a relative advantage to males, since savings are greater for males in almost all cases, again a distributional issue that needs to be faced. However, from pure cost considerations, reducing benefits while relaxing the hours' con-straint emerges as the winner.

Many European countries have provided extended unemployment benefits for older workers as a bridge to retirement. These schemes have often been com-bined with policies to encourage youth employment, with clauses requiring the replacement of departing older workers by younger workers. Examples are the early retirement solidarity contract in France, the early retirement pro-grammes in Germany and Luxembourg, and the job release schemes in the United Kingdom. Also countries have made it easier for workers to qualify for disability benefits when unemployment is high by relating eligibility to ability to find work. These policies have disguised the true level and cost of unemployment and although they have encouraged earlier retirement they appear to have had little effect on reducing the unemployment of the young.

In Canada, the United Kingdom and the United States some employers have introduced private pension schemes to encourage older workers to retire early. This path to early retirement is more important in these countries than elsewhere.

Many countries allow early retirement in some physically demanding occupations. While in most countries this only affects a small percentage of the workforce, in Central and Eastern Europe the practice of special early retirement for specified occupations is widespread. While early retirement in certain physically demanding occupations may efficiently use early retirement benefits, this practice should be applied selectively. Politically powerful groups can abuse it by winning generous early retirement benefits unjustified by the physical demands of their work. In the countries of the former Soviet Union, generous early retirement benefits rewarded work in certain occupations, rather than being based solely on physical demands.

Special preferences in the form of early minimum retirement ages in the social security retirement benefit scheme are not the best way to accommodate the special circumstances in industries with hazardous or arduous work. They essentially tax all workers to subsidize the price of the commodity or service being produced in the one industry. Such indirect subsidies are inefficient. Economic efficiency is sacrificed to the extent that the subsidized commodity competes with unsubsidized commodities because the prices consumers face are distorted, thus biasing their purchasing decisions.

Indirect subsidies in the form of retirement age preferences discourage employers from making capital investments that could make the work less dangerous or strenuous. In countries with multi-tier retirement income schemes, an occupational pension benefit can allow employees to stop working before they become eligible for social security retirement benefits. To avoid providing excessively high replacement rates, the occupation-specific benefit can be integrated with the government-financed benefit. Benefit integration results in the occupational pension benefit being reduced once the worker reaches the minimum age for social security benefits.

While workers doing physically demanding or dangerous work may need to retire sooner than those in occupations with fewer such demands, this is unlikely to be true of workers engaged in intellectually demanding work. Nonetheless in Poland journalists and teachers are among those eligible for early retirement based on the demands of their work.

In some occupations the productive working life is unusually short. Few ballet dancers perform past their 30s. Some social security schemes attempt to accommodate such occupations. In Poland ballerinas are eligible for early retirement benefits. The needs of such people are best accommodated through second careers, however, since a retirement benefit awarded at an age when some people are only beginning their active work life is prohibitively expensive.

Defined benefit social security schemes often increase benefits for workers postponing retirement past the minimum retirement age. This is done to compensate for the loss in benefits due to their being received later and for a shorter period. Some countries have tried to make this increase actuarially equivalent, meaning that for workers with the actuarial life expectancy, the increase in annual benefits with postponement of retirement is sufficiently large for the expected lifetime value of benefits not to be affected by workers postponing retirement. An advantage of making benefit adjustments actuarially equivalent is that it is thought to minimize the effect of the retirement scheme on the decision of workers on the age at which they retire. Workers with short life expectancies, however, would still be induced to retire since that adjustment would be insufficient to maintain their expected lifetime value of benefits if they postponed retirement.

Some countries, such as Sweden, allow older workers to work part-time and receive proportionally reduced benefits. This option allows workers to move gradually from full-time work to full-time retirement. It is thought that many workers would prefer a gradual transition to retirement rather than an abrupt one. Other countries, such as Japan, have an earnings test that permits labour earnings up to a certain level and full or partial benefit receipt (see box 18.3).

POSTPONED RETIREMENT

Countries have a number of policies to choose from when trying to raise the age at which workers retire. They can raise the age at which benefits are first paid in social security. Alternatively they can leave the minimum age unchanged but reduce the benefits available at that age. Sweden has enacted an innovative reform that automatically reduces benefits received at retirement to take into account increases in life expectancy. There are several related options. They can make it more difficult to qualify for benefits at the minimum age by raising the number of years of service required to qualify, as in France, or reward postponed retirement by raising the percentage increase in benefits with postponed retirement.

To encourage later retirement beyond a certain age, the condition for benefit receipt may be liberalized. Beyond a certain age, people may be allowed to continue working and to receive their social security benefits at the same time. While an earnings test may apply at earlier ages, in most countries it does not apply above a maximum age. The marginal increase in benefits with postponed retirement may be smaller than at earlier ages once a certain age has been reached, which discourages postponed retirement. Because a one-year postponement of retirement at older ages is a greater percentage reduction in expected years of benefit receipt, the increase in benefits with postponement should last longer.

Box 18.3 Partial retirement: Lessons to be drawn from OECD countries

The terms "partial retirement", "phased retirement" or "gradual retirement" refer to a transition period of part-time work between the career job and retirement which includes either partial or full payment of a pension. Partial retirement is different from the related concept of flexible retirement age, where workers are given a range of ages over which they can retire, but the transition from work to retirement is abrupt. Yet another transition pattern is intermittent full-time work at older ages, as an older worker may leave a career job, be out of the labour force for a while and then return for a period to a full-time job. Although that pattern of work does not involve part-time work, some government programmes consider it to be partial retirement.

Potential benefits

Partial retirement provides workers with an adjustment period between their career of full-time work and full-time retirement. A gradual transition gives workers a period to adjust to the greater amount of non-work time, to develop new interests and activities, and to face a gradual reduction of income. It could also reduce health problems among elderly workers by providing workers in need of it greater flexibility in dealing with health needs while giving them more opportunity for continued employment.

Partial retirement may also have positive effects on the labour market. The greater flexibility may improve worker morale and reduce absenteeism. It may allow the retaining of skilled older workers, or, more generally, partial retirement may lead to later full-time retirement and greater total labour supply. Finally partial retirement could reduce the financial burden on social security pensions if receipt of full benefits is delayed and the adjustment of benefits with postponed retirement is less than actuarially equivalent, thus resulting in a reduction of lifetime benefits.

Potential drawbacks

The partial retirement option could result in an earlier partial retirement than would have occurred under full retirement, with less total labour supply. Accordingly it could increase rather than reduce the burden on social security, especially if financial incentives are provided to encourage people to opt for partial retirement or if governments subsidize training of older workers who wish to delay retirement.

Also fixed costs of employment, both for employees and employers, may make partial retirement an undesirable option. Overhead costs may be increased and productivity reduced if more people with reduced working time are needed to do the job. The availability of partial retirement benefits could legitimize precarious job conditions for older workers: workers could be constrained to accept part-time work, along with job reclassification, as they get older. This could be especially important in a context of corporate restructuring or downsizing.

Several OECD countries have policies that allow or encourage workers to take partial retirement. In most countries few workers have taken advantage of the option, while in a few countries the option has been popular. The following lessons can be drawn from the experience of the OECD countries with respect to partial retirement.

1. Workers are sensitive to the financial incentives embedded in the programmes. Workers consider the income earned and hours worked – required by full-time work and partial retirement – and compare that to the retirement benefits received in full retirement. Workers will be less inclined to opt for partial retirement if they are provided with good pensions for full retirement. Employers also look at the costs and benefits of providing partial retirement. A generous early retirement programme at no direct cost to the employers will make it unlikely that many workers will opt for partial retirement.

2. The availability of part-time work, training for older workers and the flexibility of work patterns are also critical factors in the successful implementation of a partial retirement programme.

3. The effect of partial retirement on the pension scheme and the labour market is not clear. Countries where part-time work is more popular among older workers tend to have a higher average retirement age. This does not mean that the total number of hours worked in late career by individuals is greater, since they work a reduced number of hours. Moreover the introduction of partial retirement provisions could modify the work and retirement behaviour of individuals, depending on the retirement provisions, the personal circumstances and the social and economic situation.

4. Partial retirement policy can be carried out either through social security or special national programmes, or through policy encouraging employers to offer partial retirement benefits through employer-provided pension plans. Although the United States does not have a formal partial retirement programme, the percentage of older workers who combine work and pension in the United States is high compared to other countries.

5. The distributional effects of government-supported partial retirement programmes should be considered. These programmes may be used primarily by upper-income workers but supported by all workers out of general revenue. They could also be used either by people with limited pension entitlements or by career workers, depending on how the partial pension is calculated and its effect on the pension paid at the time of full retirement.

In past years, the priority of governments was towards early retirement as a way to buy out older workers from the labour market. Now some governments are trying to encourage later retirement. Partial retirement, designed to encourage people to stay in the labour market, could become more popular.

OTHER GOVERNMENT POLICIES AFFECTING RETIREMENT AGE

The minimum age at which workers can receive occupational pension benefits may also affect the age at retirement. In Denmark that minimum age is 67 for receipt of benefits from a tax-favoured occupational pension, but as indicated

451

in box 18.2, other programmes facilitate early retirement. In Canada the minimum age is 55.

Retirement age may be affected by regulations governing the generosity of accrual of benefits with delayed retirement in occupational pensions. Laws may require that occupational defined benefit plans increase benefits for delayed retirement up to a certain age. Laws limiting the ability of employers to require retirement may encourage continued work. Employers, however, can substitute financial inducements for mandatory retirement rules and possibly achieve the same retirement ages.

For several decades following the end of the Second World War, many OECD countries enacted programmes to facilitate early retirement. Now these countries, and countries in Central and Eastern Europe, are considering ways to encourage workers to postpone retirement.

Countries seeking to raise the retirement age of their workers have a number of policies they can pursue. In both defined benefit and defined contribution schemes, with increasing life expectancy it becomes increasingly expensive to finance old-age benefits. The speed with which an increase in the minimum retirement age is instituted depends on the trade-off between the budgetary savings from a rapid raising of the retirement age and the disruption of the lives of older workers that would come. An increase in the minimum retirement age may increase the labour supply of older workers or it may simply reduce their social security benefits. In the latter case it would probably increase the claims on other government-provided benefits, which should be recognized when measuring budgetary savings.

Notes

[1] Retirement has a different meaning for large segments of the population of less developed countries. The nature of work might change over the years but people often do not actually retire unless obliged to do so for reasons of sickness or disability.

[2] This interpretation was suggested by Robert Myers.

DEVELOPING PLURALISTIC DESIGNS AND FLEXIBLE STRUCTURES

19

This chapter discusses the structure of retirement income schemes, bringing together the issues of risk, costs, progressivity, governance and the need to extend coverage that are discussed in earlier chapters. It studies the role of pay-as-you-go schemes versus funded schemes, defined contribution versus defined benefit schemes, mandatory versus voluntary benefits, and public versus private benefits. It investigates what economic, demographic, political or institutional factors cause the answers to these questions to differ in different regions of the world. The chapter first analyses the determinants of retirement income schemes, focusing on the roles of political philosophies, governance capabilities and rates of return on alternative sources of financing, including the role of costs. It presents different structures of retirement income schemes for developed and developing countries.

While the issue is beyond the scope of this chapter, countries need to consider the structure of retirement income schemes within the larger framework of social expenditures. A balance must be struck between the well-being of the elderly and the non-elderly. In addition, developed countries need to balance health care expenditures on the elderly and cash benefits they receive.

The chapter draws on material introduced and discussed in greater detail earlier in the book, such as the issue of extending coverage in developing countries, where coverage is low (Chapter 8), governance as an important aspect of pension policy (Chapter 9), and the risks of different types of retirement income schemes (Chapter 12).

There is no one universal perfect retirement income scheme. The level of economic development, the population age structure and political factors affect the retirement income scheme appropriate for different countries. As the economic, demographic and political situation in a country alters, changes in retirement income schemes may also be required. Because of the interaction between social security retirement benefit schemes and economic development, retirement income schemes evolve over time and different systems may operate more successfully in different countries.

Table 19.1   The increase in the number of countries with mandatory old-age security programmes

Year	Number of countries
1940	33
1949	44
1958	58
1967	92
1977	114
1987	130
1989	135
1993	155
1995	166
1997	166

Source: US Social Security Administration (1995, 1997).

Retirement income schemes are often characterized as composed of a number of tiers. A tier refers to a source, or a group of similar sources, of retirement income. Such a characterization is generally a simplification of reality but it aids in understanding the general structure of a retirement income scheme. Originally, in all countries, retirement income was provided for elderly persons by other family members, primarily their children. Gradually a social safety net developed as government began taking responsibility for providing retirement income. The earliest government systems focused on means-tested assistance programmes. They were followed by government-sponsored social insurance, which first developed about a century ago. In many countries, such as the Netherlands, Norway and Sweden, social security retirement income schemes initially only provided flat benefits, often with an earnings-related benefit added later. Over time, the number of countries with social security schemes has increased, and recently Comoros and Thailand have indicated that they intend to institute social security schemes to provide retirement benefits. At the end of the twentieth century, most countries have such systems (table 19.1).

Employer-provided pensions are another source of retirement income. Among large employers they predated social security programmes in many developed countries and have grown in importance during the second half of the twentieth century in about a dozen developed countries. In most other countries, however, their role is minimal.

Over time, retirement income schemes in developed countries have become increasingly complex and retirement income is being provided by an increasing number of sources with different characteristics. Increasing complexity is desirable because it provides greater diversification against risks.

DETERMINANTS OF THE STRUCTURE OF RETIREMENT INCOME SCHEMES

Three factors are of key importance in determining the structure of retirement income schemes. Two involve a comparison of the government and the private sector, while the third is a comparison of pay-as-you-go and funding:

- political philosophies which incorporate values concerning the appropriate role of government versus the private sector responsibilities of individuals and families;

- governance capabilities of government – its capability to collect contributions, manage investments, and pay benefits – versus the capability of private financial market institutions;

- the risk and expected rate of return of pay-as-you-go retirement benefits versus those of funded benefits.

Political philosophies: Individuals versus social insurance

The role of government in retirement income schemes is affected by the prevailing political philosophy. Within each country the prevailing political philosophy affects the role of state versus individual responsibility, and correspondingly, compulsion versus free choice. Competing political philosophies are based on different concepts as to how society can best meet human needs. They differ in their views of the ability of individuals to meet their own needs.

According to the *laissez-faire philosophy*, the state has no responsibility for the retirement income of the individual. Thus the state should not require retirement saving by individuals. Individuals should be free to make their own decisions, including their own mistakes, without the interference of a government bureaucrat. Individuals know best their own interest. High-level bureaucrats, who are more educated than the general population, tend to view their values as superior and impose them on others. Besides, according to this view, bureaucrats are inefficient in managing programmes because they are not subject to competition and the profit motive. For this reason it is thought that government programmes are less well managed than private sector programmes.

All individuals belong to families. According to the laissez-faire philosophy, the family has primary responsibility for its members. Beyond that, private charity has a role to play in caring for the needy lacking adequate support from their families. Governmental programmes displace the rightful primary roles of individual responsibility, family and charity. Elements of this expression, with its focus on individual responsibility and minimizing the role of the government, frequently enter debates over the structure of retirement income schemes.

Social security policy makers universally accept that the state has a role. Recognizing the important roles of individuals, families, charities and employers in providing retirement income security, there are reasons why the state must also have a role. While most decisions are best left to individuals, decisions concerning retirement savings are particularly difficult for individuals to make because of the long time frame involved, extending 50 or more years for young workers.

Within this consensus, people differ over the proper role of state versus private responsibility. Some favouring a laissez-faire approach, sometimes referred to as neo-liberals, feel that the government should be restricted to mandating a minimum level of saving, regulating the voluntary part of the retirement income scheme and providing a social safety net. This individualistic approach favours retirement income provided through mandatory defined contribution plans managed in the private sector, with minimal income transfers through government programmes. It places considerable responsibility on the individual and mistrusts government, arguing that government mismanages programmes and resources. Activities should be left as much as possible to the private sector, which is believed to be more efficient.

Adherents of the *social insurance approach* argue that government should reduce the effects of risks facing individuals. It should make their lives more economically secure by providing social insurance. This approach sees the fundamental purposes of social security as being to relieve poverty, to reduce income inequality from that determined by market forces and to provide a guarantee of security against social and economic risks. It views the market as producing a distribution of income that is socially unjust, being too unequal. Social insurance has an important role in achieving social justice by distributing resources more fairly. It helps reduce social conflict and achieve social solidarity. The traditional social security programmes in Europe, Japan and North and South America are social insurance plans designed to provide income transfers between groups. The social insurance approach uses government to facilitate intergenerational transfers and transfers across income groups within a generation.

The social insurance approach is the dominant approach worldwide. Out of 160 countries in 1998 with social security retirement benefits programmes, more than 125 countries had traditional contributory defined benefit earnings-related programmes.

Political philosophies and goals

The basic goal of social security retirement benefits programmes is to provide security for vulnerable people in society. In old age, they do so by reducing or preventing poverty among the elderly. To meet this goal requires a system that transfers income to low-income elderly. Often, when social security schemes are first started, their primary focus is on this goal (Wheeler and Kearney, 1996). One of the challenges in designing social security schemes is to develop a system that alleviates poverty but does not discourage work and saving by low-income workers.

As social security systems have developed, they have adopted a more ambitious goal. The goal, an adequate retirement income for all elderly, extends the responsibility of social security beyond that to the poorest segment of society. This goal is sometimes expressed as the smoothing of lifetime consumption so that it does not fall precipitously at retirement. Retirement income adequacy can be measured by the replacement rate: the percentage of income while working that retirement income replaces. The target replacement rate should be higher for low-income workers than for high-income workers because the consumption of low-income workers is a higher percentage of their income. One possible goal is to provide a replacement rate from all sources of retirement income such that workers with average and below-average income have the same standard of living in retirement as they have while working.

The social insurance approach favours a government role to alleviate economic risk. Governments can do so through mandatory risk sharing. Social insurance can reduce the effects of risks workers and their families face by providing insurance unavailable in the market. There are at least two significant sources of risk to individuals that the market does not provide insurance against but for which social security social insurance can be structured so that it does.

First, social insurance can provide insurance against being poor. Poverty has numerous causes, but in every society the circumstances of the family one is born into have a large effect on one's economic well-being. The economic circumstances of one's birth are, in many countries, the largest risk factor affecting an individual's lifetime income. Social security can insure against the economic risks associated with being born to a poor family by providing income transfers to retirees who have had low lifetime earnings. These transfers reduce the economic effects of risk in society, making everyone better off (Rawls, 1971).

Upper-income workers could have had the misfortune of being born poor. They or their children may suffer economic misfortune. They receive an insurance benefit from a social security scheme that is of value to them even if they do not make a claim on the insurance. If these risks decrease as countries develop, that would reduce the need for social insurance. Statistical evidence indicates that in the United States a person's socioeconomic background has declined in importance over time as a determinant of the person's income as an adult (Urban Institute, 1997).

Second, social insurance can provide insurance against wage variability. The market does not provide insurance against wage variability. While large employers may provide some implicit insurance against it for some workers, most workers bear this risk entirely on their own. Social insurance programmes can reduce the effects of risks workers face owing to the variability in their wages through drop-out years, where workers can drop out low-earnings years when calculating their social security retirement benefits. Social insurance programmes can also exclude low earnings from liability for payroll tax payments,

457

or exclude low benefits from income taxation, and provide higher benefits relative to earnings for low-income beneficiaries.

By moderating the risks that workers face in free market economies, social insurance sustains support for market capitalism. Because of risk sharing across participants in a single national plan, social insurance fosters a sense of national solidarity and reduces social conflict. In well-developed social insurance schemes, essentially all members of society are connected in a risk-sharing pool.

Macroeconomic goals, such as encouraging economic growth, are secondary goals of social security, not because their importance is secondary but because other policies and programmes of government are better suited to meeting these goals. Governments have other policy instruments that are more directly designed to encourage growth, such as a tax policy concerning saving and investment, policies towards education and infrastructure development. Nonetheless an important goal of social security is not to discourage savings and growth. Related macroeconomic goals include full employment and labour market flexibility; microeconomic goals include lack of distortion of incentives in labour and capital markets.

Governance capability as a determinant of retirement income structure

Governments differ in their ability to manage social security schemes. Some countries have efficient, professional civil servants, while in other countries civil servants are inefficient or corrupt. The relative efficiency of the public sector versus the private sector is a factor in determining their relative importance in providing retirement income. Even when considerable responsibility for providing retirement income is entrusted to the private sector, however, the government still retains an important role as a regulator. Thus the government's capacity to regulate needs to be considered when analysing the relative roles of the public and private sectors.

Small countries may lack workers with the specialized skills needed to run some social security schemes, such as actuaries, economists or lawyers trained in the social security field, nor do they have the capability to regulate financial market investments. Although 40 per cent of the world's population live in China and India, most countries are small. In 1995 roughly half the countries in the world – more than 80 – had populations of fewer than two million people.

The governance requirements differ for different types of social security schemes. A traditional pay-as-you-go defined benefit scheme requires the ability to collect contributions, keep records concerning contributions and make benefit payments. A funded defined contribution scheme has all those requirements, as well as requiring the ability to regulate capital markets and multiple financial institutions managing funds. For developing countries with weak governance capabilities, a pay-as-you-go scheme may be easier to regulate.

Rates of return and risk on alternative sources of financing

Social security schemes provide mandatory retirement benefits. An approach to analysing pay-as-you-go versus funding concerning their mandatory savings role compares the rates of return of the two financing methods[1]. Under simplifying assumptions, the internal rate of return to pay-as-you-go social security equals the growth rate of the labour force plus the wage growth rate[2]. Because declining population growth due to declining fertility generally accompanies growth in per capita income, a decline in social security's rate of return appears inevitably to accompany economic development[3]. (Information on population growth in different countries is presented in the Statistical Annex.) Thus it appears likely that as the population growth rate declines, the role of pay-as-you-go social security will decline relative to funded benefits. An implication often drawn is that, when the implicit rate of return on social security falls below the market rate of return, social security participants would be better off had they invested in the market rather than participated in social security.

Comparing only the rates of return to funded and unfunded social security is incomplete because it ignores risk. It does not consider social security as an asset in a portfolio of assets. In particular, evaluation of social security as an investment should consider not only its rate of return but also its riskiness and the covariance of its return with other assets, both marketable and non-marketable, in the household portfolio[4]. Even with a low rate of return, social security may be a valuable part of a retirement income portfolio because of its low risk in many countries and the low or negative correlation of its rate of return with the rate of return on other assets. Any financial evaluation of social security also needs to incorporate the value of the insurance it provides.

The risk and rate of return on pay-as-you-go social security varies across time and across countries. When economic growth is robust, a pay-as-you-go scheme is more desirable. The Republic of Korea experienced rapid economic growth at an average annual rate of 7.7 per cent over the period 1980–94, while Brazil experienced economic decline, with an average annual growth rate of −0.54 per cent. While economic growth has been experienced over long periods in the developed countries, among developing countries long periods of decline are common. A quarter of the 60 countries with initial per capita GDP of less than $1,000 in 1960 had negative average annual growth rates through the mid-1990s, and a third had growth rates of less than 0.05 per cent (Pritchett, 1997).

The strength of labour markets should be compared with the strength of capital markets. Pay-as-you-go financing is based on labour markets while funding is based on capital markets. In small countries funding based on the labour market may be relatively riskier than in large countries because there is limited diversification of the risks affecting the labour market. At the same time small countries can take advantage of international diversification of capital markets. Well-managed funded systems have a small to moderate risk of a large loss occurring quickly, whereas well-managed pay-as-you-go schemes do not face such risks. The demographic changes that affect pension systems generally occur over a period of years, allowing workers and social security schemes time to adjust. Generally pay-as-you go systems are less risky than funded systems.

Capital markets in many countries are poorly regulated. Thus stockholders' rights may be poorly protected. Many countries' markets trade few stocks, and have relatively light trading in some stocks. Most countries, as of the late 1990s, did not have national stock markets, and in those where they did exist the markets were risky. Statistical evidence indicates that the emerging stock markets are more volatile than the well-developed stock markets (Richards, 1996). In 1995, when the International Finance Corporation stock market price index for the United States increased by 34 per cent, 35 of the world's 78 national stock markets lost money (International Finance Corporation, 1996). In 1998, stock markets in Asia suffered large losses. (See the Statistical Annex for information on national stock markets around the world.)

Even well-developed capital markets have considerable risks. Between 1950 and 1990 in the United States, with its large, well-developed and reasonably well-regulated stock market, declines of 10 per cent or more in the Standard & Poor's 500 index occurred on average every 18 months, and declines of 20 per cent or more occurred on average every 78 months. Far more dramatic is the experience in Japan – the world's second largest economy – where the Japanese Nikkei stock market index reached a peak of more than 40,000 in December 1989. During the early 1990s it lost more than half its value and by 1998 was trading at times below 13,000. Thus a decline of more than 60 per cent in the Japanese stock market persisted for more than eight years.

Risk can be reduced through diversification. The risks to retirement income can be reduced by providing retirement income from different sources. The risk-return mix in a retirement income scheme may be optimized in some countries when workers participate at the same time in both unfunded defined benefit plans and funded defined contribution plans. When participating in both types of plans, the worker effectively has a defined contribution plan with a guaranteed minimum benefit. Countries can trade off the level of the minimum benefit against the size of the expected defined contribution benefit. Combining the two offers the downside protection of defined benefit plans, yet allows workers to invest in high expected return assets.

In most countries the greater the reliance on a funded defined contribution plan, the greater is the uncertainty as to the benefit level most workers will receive. At least in countries with well-run defined benefit plans, those plans are less risky for most workers than defined contribution plans. This is because labour market financing is generally less risky than capital market financing. It is also because the adverse effects on a worker's benefit entitlements resulting from that worker's unemployment are typically much more severe in defined contribution schemes than in traditional defined benefit schemes. For this reason recognizing the risk aversion of most workers, for countries that can provide defined benefit plans with low risk, a sizeable portion of the retirement benefit should be provided through a defined benefit plan. The greater the risk in the defined benefit plan, however, the lower is the amount that should be provided through it relative to a funded defined contribution plan.

A mixed system offers the most diversification against risks (see Chapter 12). In such a system many workers have both unfunded defined benefit and funded defined contribution plans. Risks are reduced in a mixed system because unfunded plans and funded plans are subject to different risks that are not perfectly correlated. A pay-as-you-go social security scheme is subject to risks to the level of its contribution base of national wage earnings, but is not directly subject to financial market risk. By comparison the situation is reversed for funded plans, since they are subject to financial market risks considerably more than labour market risks. In both defined benefit and defined contribution plans, retirement income is subject to labour market risks, such as unemployment, which reduce the accrual of retirement income.

Administrative costs of individual accounts

Administrative costs of pension funds reduce realized investment returns, lowering the pension in the case of defined contribution funds and increasing the cost to the sponsor for defined benefit funds. They need to be considered in the light of investment performance which may compound or offset differences in costs.

Conceptual problems arise in the measurement of administrative costs. Because of economies of scale, large schemes tend to have lower administrative costs relative to their size than do small ones. Funded schemes tend to have higher administrative costs relative to their contributions received than do unfunded ones because of the costs of managing investments. Thus higher costs do not necessarily imply less efficient management but, in the case of funding, they may indicate that more activities are being carried out.

The issue of personal pension costs arises for Chile. There a major problem is that the ability of investors to switch managers, which is necessary in order to ensure competition among management companies, generates high promotional expenditures (30 per cent of total costs). This contributes to high overall management expenses equivalent to 15 per cent of contributions, 1.5 per cent of wages and 1.6 per cent of fund assets (James and Vittas, 1995).[5] These nonetheless represent an advance on the start of the programme when costs were proportionally much higher: 14.5 per cent of assets in 1982. These fees are composed of fund management fees, costs of administering contributions and pension payments, advertising costs and administrative fees for switching accounts. The Chilean system remains small (the size of a large occupational defined benefit fund in an OECD country), however, so reductions in costs due to further scale economies may be envisaged.[6]

461

There is a major contrast with efficient provident funds, as in Malaysia or Singapore. In Malaysia operating costs in 1991 were 1.7 per cent of annual contributions, around a tenth of those quoted for Chile. According to Bateman and Piggott (1997), this is linked to the existence of a single investment fund. In Singapore total operating costs in 1990 were 0.5 per cent of annual contributions and 0.1 per cent of accumulated assets. This also compares favourably with employer-based pension funds in OECD countries, although the ratio to contributions is affected by the high contribution rate of around 40 per cent.

Administrative costs of occupational pension funds are available for a selection of OECD countries. They suggest generally that the administrative costs for occupational funds, as for Australia and Switzerland, are intermediate between those of centralized public funds and personal accounts. The data imply economies of scale in asset management and pension administration, which has been confirmed by various studies. United States data (Turner and Beller, 1989) show that costs are greater for small occupational funds than large, and for defined benefit relative to defined contribution. The higher costs for occupational defined benefit plans than for defined contribution plans in the United States are at least partially due to the costs of complying with regulations. For funds with assets of $1 million in 1985, costs were 2 per cent of assets per year for defined benefit and 1.4 per cent for defined contribution. For plans with assets of $150 million, the costs were 0.7 per cent and 0.2 per cent, respectively. An alternative way of expressing costs is in terms of contributions. Andrews (1993) notes a figure of 8.3 per cent of contributions for United States defined benefit funds and 4 per cent for defined contribution. For the United Kingdom, Hannah (1986) quotes administrative expense to cash flow ratios of 6 per cent for medium-sized companies with insured schemes, 2 per cent for large defined benefit schemes and 1 per cent for social security. The data from the latest survey by the United Kingdom Government Actuary (outlined in Davis, 1997) show that schemes with fewer than 11 members had average costs of 9 per cent of income, which fell to 3–4 per cent for schemes with up to 10,000 members and 1.4 per cent for schemes with 10,000 and over. Costs as a proportion of assets were 1.1 per cent, 0.3–0.5 per cent and 0.1 per cent for the corresponding size classes.

Administrative costs of individual accounts affect the net rate of return that workers receive from social security and may affect the structure of retirement income schemes for low-income workers. The costs of individual accounts are largely fixed costs, not varying with the size of the account. For example, the cost of producing an account statement and mailing it to a participant is the same for a small balance of $100 or a large one of $100,000. Because their costs are fixed costs per account, profit-making institutions tend to charge fixed fees to manage individual accounts.

Administrative costs vary considerably across different types of retirement income plans, affecting their relative role in a retirement income system. The least cost plan is not necessarily the best since plans also differ in the services

Table 19.2 Administrative cost of Dutch old-age pensions
(percentage of total contributions, 1993)

Type of plan	Cost (%)
Mandatory social insurance	1.2
Firm-based pension funds	4.4
Private group pension insurance	7.2
Private individual pension insurance	21.1

Source: Aarts and De Jong, 1997.

they provide. In the Netherlands, individual account defined contribution plans are 20 times more expensive to administer than the national social defined benefit plans (table 19.2). Because these statistics are for a single country, they are not affected by differences across countries that make cross-country comparisons of plans of different types difficult. Also these statistics incorporate the cost of annuitization of individual accounts, often ignored in this type of consideration. They do not include, however, the cost of adverse selection, which further reduces the monthly benefits provided by individual account plans because their clientele tend to be relatively long-lived. These statistics are affected, however, by economies of scale, with the individual account defined contribution plans having higher costs in part because they do not cover all workers in the Netherlands and thus do not benefit from economies of scale to the same extent as the national social insurance. They also have higher costs because of the costs of managing investments.

The problem of fixed costs for small individual accounts can be managed several ways. First, subsidies for small accounts from large accounts can be mandated by requiring that fees be a fixed percentage of assets or contributions. A problem with this approach is that profit-maximizing firms will prefer large accounts to small accounts when the fees are charged this way since large accounts will be more profitable. The firms may seek other ways to attract large account balances and discourage low-income workers from participating in their fund. Second, workers below a threshold of earnings or hours can be excluded from mandatory contributions, as in Australia and Denmark. Workers working fewer than ten hours a week are excluded in Denmark while workers earning below a threshold are excluded in Australia. Third, all workers can be given a flat government subsidy for their accounts, as in Mexico. Fourth, the government could give a selective flat subsidy for the accounts of low-income workers. Fifth, the government could run a clearinghouse for the collection of contributions, the allocation of contributions to fund managers and the disbursement of benefits, as is done in the Thrift Savings Plan for Federal Government workers in the United States. In this plan the government mandates

463

subsidization of small accounts by charging a fixed percentage administrative fee relative to account balances.

It may be desirable for lower-income workers to be covered by fewer sources of benefits than upper-income workers because of the fixed costs for managing financial accounts. In particular it may be desirable not to extend mandatory funding to lower income workers.

Administrative costs may be a problem in small developing countries (James and Palacios, 1995) and can be particularly burdensome, as the wages of workers involved in the provision of benefits tend to be higher than average wages, while the reverse is more likely to be the case in developed countries. Also small countries have high expenses because they are unable to fully attain economies of scale.

THE STRUCTURE OF RETIREMENT INCOME SCHEMES

Analysts typically characterize retirement income schemes in developed countries as having three tiers. However, because analysts have stressed different functions or attributes of retirement income schemes, they have differed as to what the three tiers are. Sometimes they have divided the tiers according to the provider of retirement income: government, employers, families or individuals. Sometimes they have divided the tiers according to their purpose: anti-poverty, income replacement and supplementary (World Bank, 1994). In this case, the government provides minimal anti-poverty benefits, the government or private sector provides mandatory funded benefits, and individuals and families provide supplementary benefits. Two Canadian policy analysts have characterized the Canadian retirement income scheme as having three tiers based on the type of funding: a general revenue-funded anti-poverty tier, a largely unfunded social insurance defined benefit plan tier and a voluntary funded occupational pension plan tier (Banting and Boadway, 1996). The multiple-tier approach is often best understood not as an empirical statement about the way retirement income schemes actually are, but as a statement about how they should be structured. For some countries the tier approach is a simplified way to conceptualize a complex retirement income scheme.

This book stresses the roles of the retirement income scheme in reducing poverty and providing low-risk retirement income. To do that, retirement income must have an element that is redistributive and it must be provided from diversified sources. The relative importance of the different sources will depend on their rate of return and risk. Whether the sources are managed in the public or private sector will depend on political philosophies towards individual and private sector responsibilities versus the role of the government and views as to the relative governance capabilities of the private and public sectors.

These statements concerning the structure of retirement income schemes can be remade in the customary framework of tiers. To reduce risk through risk diversification, the best approach for developed countries can be characterized as a three-tier system plus a social safety net, with the tiers being determined by their risk and redistributive characteristics. The essential aspect of this approach is not a particular number of tiers but that retirement income be provided from different sources having different risk characteristics in order to diversify risk. This approach stresses the desirability of increasing complexity in retirement income schemes as they develop to allow for greater diversification of retirement income risks.

The social safety net is a government-provided anti-poverty benefit. It includes means-tested and income-tested benefits for low-income elderly and universal flat-rate benefits that are primarily designed as anti-poverty benefits. Flat-rate benefits are equal for all recipients. It should be stressed that the important point in analysing a retirement income scheme is not whether a particular programme is a safety net programme, or first-tier programme, but that the system has a safety net benefit, an unfunded benefit and a funded benefit. (Social assistance benefits are discussed in Chapter 5.)

The primary characteristics of the first-tier programmes are that they are mandatory and unfunded. Thus they include mandatory unfunded defined benefit schemes or notional (unfunded) defined contribution schemes provided through the government social security scheme. This tier is the traditional pay-as-you-go social security scheme found in most countries. It generally provides social insurance for workers against some economic risks by spreading the effects of risk across the population. In countries where this type of benefit can be provided with low risk, it should form the basis of the retirement income scheme. Since a desirable characteristic of retirement income benefits is that they are transparent, in the sense that their value is clearly known in advance, these benefits should generally be the most important source of retirement income.

The second tier is funded and could be mandatory or voluntary. These programmes could be provided by the government, or by private sector institutions, depending on views on the role and capability of government in society. This tier could be combined with the first tier as a single partially funded plan. It includes funded occupational pension plans and funded individual pension accounts. When it is provided through the private sector it reduces the role of the government. While retirement income schemes generally need a funded source of retirement income, it is not essential in all countries that the sources be mandatory. Box 19.1 and Chapter 7 discuss issues relating to national readiness for funded pensions.

The third tier comprises voluntary and supplementary non-pension sources of retirement income. It includes private savings, labour earnings, support from family members and charity. In some countries saving in the form of housing is an important aspect of retirement savings in the third tier. Housing can be used both as an investment that is liquidated in retirement and as a source of services that are paid for before retirement.

As well as having different risk characteristics, the three tiers are distinguished by three factors: (1) whether they are solely anti-poverty benefits

Box 19.1 National readiness for individual account plans

With the growing popularity of funded defined contribution plans around the world, it is becoming clear that many countries, both developed and those less so, are not fully prepared for what these plans require.

The government that formulates and adopts the plan may not be ready for it. Hungary adopted legislation providing for a funded defined contribution tier in its social security programme late in 1997 but did not have the computer systems necessary to collect contributions and transmit them to the proper funds. Many developing and transition economies are debating individual defined contribution plans without having reliable and auditable systems for tracking wages throughout the employee's career and making sure that payroll tax contributions are made. In many such countries the principal method for maintaining and documenting one's earnings history continues to be the labour book. This notebook is maintained by the employee, who is responsible for obtaining certification of employment history from successive employers. But active resale markets in labour books are common, weakening their probative value, and without accurate wage and contribution records it is not possible to verify benefit entitlements. Experience with defined contribution plans around the world points to a set of criteria for determining whether a country is ready for such a plan and could successfully implement one. These criteria are not intended to be exhaustive, but rather represent lessons drawn from pitfalls countries have already encountered.

Integrity of the payroll and benefit systems

The foundation for a well-functioning defined contribution-based retirement scheme is an accurate, efficient and, above all, auditable payroll system. Employers should know how many employees they have and how much they pay them, as well as some key facts about them, such as their age and length of service. The civil service of Pakistan, for example, does not meet these criteria. People should not be on the payroll unless they are actually employed. Dead people, imaginary people (called "ghost workers" in some countries) and people who have gone on to other employment should not be getting paid by their former employer. If employers do not have this information, they cannot provide it to the social security institution. Employers should not only know these things about their staff; they should also be willing and able to transmit accurate information to appropriate government regulatory and revenue-collecting agencies. South Africa is an example of a country with a limited capacity to audit payrolls.

Accurate payroll records are important in pay-as-you-go defined benefit retirement schemes as well, but the record-keeping demands of defined contribution plans are greater. In transition and developing economies, pay-as-you-go defined benefit plans typically base benefits on final pay. Most people can document what they earned last year, though the pension agency may have to take verification of the pensioner's length of service on faith. But benefits in defined contribution plans are effectively based on the participant's entire work career, so earnings records have to cover that career as well. Poor records will reduce confidence in the system, discourage compliance and, in plans with government-sponsored minimum benefit guarantees, cost the government money.

Convincing the public
It is said, perhaps apocryphally, that even Albert Einstein did not understand the power of compound interest. And Einstein did not face the problem of inconsistent and uninformative accounting standards prevalent in many developing and transition economies (see Chapter 7). Most people also have trouble seeing far into the future, though people may be better able to envision the intermediate than the long term (Korczyk, 1998). Finally people say they do not feel as confident choosing investments, even for non-retirement saving, as they do buying a car or household appliance (Cutler, 1996). Educating people about saving for retirement thus faces formidable hurdles. For example, in Kazakhstan, a group of key government officials travelled around the country giving speeches and appearing on television and call-in radio shows to present their case for pension reform (see Regional Brief 5).

How to invest
The next task needed to ensure that employees are ready for defined contribution plans is education about risk-return trade-offs. Employees need to understand more than the fact that greater expected return requires taking greater risks. They need to understand that different managers can trade risk against return differently, but that risk-return combinations that sound too good to be true probably are. They also need to understand the risk-return combinations appropriate at various ages or life cycle stages.

Account-switching experience in some Latin American defined contribution plans also suggests the need for participant education about buying and selling financial assets. Participants should understand at least the basics of such concepts as asset diversification, market timing, value investing and cost averaging to avoid overreacting to short-term business cycle fluctuations – or overblown solicitations from investment managers – and to build assets for the long term.

Not all countries wishing to adopt defined contribution plans have the preconditions present for doing so successfully. These preconditions include prepared employers, educated employees, and reformed and prepared social security schemes. Countries proceeding without at least these preconditions may face problems in achieving their policy goals.

(safety net) or general benefits (first, second and third tiers); (2) whether they are unfunded (safety net, first tier) or funded (second tier);[7] and (3) whether they are mandatory (first and possibly second tier) or voluntary (third tier). The government manages the first tier and may manage the second. The household sector manages the third tier. Private sector firms may manage the second tier. It is expected that every country will have a safety net and the first and third tiers. For many countries a funded tier may not be feasible. For others, it may be feasible but should be voluntary. For some countries, with well-developed capital markets and a poor governmental ability to manage an unfunded system, a mandatory funded tier may be desirable, but the government's ability to manage or regulate a mandatory funded tier must also be considered.

A social insurance approach containing a pay-as-you-go plan combined with some funding provides better risk diversification than an approach based solely on capital markets. The social security benefits provided by pay-as-you-go systems are not subject to capital market risks. The benefits individuals accumulate in pay-as-you-go social security schemes have risks that have low correlation with capital market risks. Thus the inclusion of these benefits in the retirement income of individuals helps diversify their retirement income portfolios.

FIRST TIER

Countries with low coverage

Different types of retirement income schemes are appropriate for developing and developed countries. Countries where a sizeable percentage of the labour force does not participate in social security should consider instituting a multi-tier scheme to deal with the problem of extending coverage. Extremely poor workers would be covered by a means-tested social assistance pension to the extent permitted by budgetary considerations. The first tier would be composed of two parts. The part would provide a basic flat-rate benefit, which could be structured so as to increase with years of contributions. This part would be designed to meet the social goal of providing a minimum benefit that prevented poverty in old age. The second part would be an earnings-related benefit to which only workers earning above a minimum amount would contribute. It would provide earnings-related benefits for upper-income workers. This part would be designed to meet the social goal of providing income replacement for middle- and upper-income workers. The structure of the system could vary across countries depending on the minimum earnings level for participation in the earnings-related benefit. Figure 19.1 illustrates the system, with a flat-rate benefit covering most workers and pay-as-you-go and funded benefits only covering higher-income workers.

For developing countries, to keep the flat-rate benefit affordable at a low level of financing, eligibility for benefits could be limited to only disability and survivors' benefits, or could provide retirement benefits starting at a relatively old age compared to the life expectancy in the country, say 65 or 70 in most developing countries. The flat-rate benefit could be financed in different ways. It could be financed as a separate fund on a pay-as-you-go basis and have a low mandatory contribution rate, say 2, 3 or 4 per cent. Thus, it would be redistributive from higher-income to lower-income workers, but would maintain an incentive to contribute because contributions in more years lead to greater benefits. The extent of the redistribution would be greater the higher the earnings ceiling on taxable earnings. An alternative way to finance the flat-rate benefit would be to finance it out of the same fund as the earnings-related benefit. As a further alternative, general government revenue could be used to subsidize the flat-rate benefit.

Figure 19.1   A possible retirement income scheme for a developing country

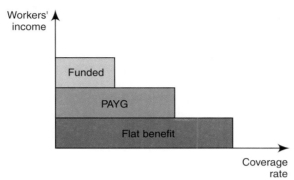

Source: ILO compilation.

To reduce the administrative costs of the flat-rate benefit, contributions of people only participating in that part could be collected quarterly. Contributions for workers participating in both tiers could be collected monthly. To simplify administration for employers, all workers in enterprises with at least a minimum number of workers could automatically be included in both parts.

While the goal of the flat-rate benefit is to extend coverage to all workers, in some developing countries a sizeable percentage of the workforce may still be excluded. Excluded groups might be the poor, the young, or employees working few hours in the formal sector. As countries developed, coverage of the flat rate benefit, and eventually of the earnings-related benefit, could be gradually extended so that it included all workers.

The third tier would include voluntary savings. This tier would be designed to meet the social goal of allowing upper-income workers to supplement their mandatory benefits through voluntary saving. Uruguay has a retirement income scheme similar to this. It has two mandatory tiers – a social insurance benefit and an individual account defined contribution plan – but low-income workers only participate in the first tier. Workers earning above an earnings ceiling are not required to make contributions above the ceiling but may save voluntarily from that segment of their income. In Switzerland low-income workers are not required to participate in the mandatory supplementary employer-provided pensions. The Irish pension scheme, discussed in box 19.2, provides an alternative model that may be appealing for developing countries.

Developed countries

One of the most important issues in designing retirement income schemes is how large the role of the pay-as-you-go social security scheme should be in the retirement income scheme. Should it provide generous benefits at all income levels,

Box 19.2 Social security in ireland: A model for pension reform
Of the 26 OECD countries which have social insurance schemes, Ireland has
the fifth lowest social security contribution rate and the third lowest contribution
rate for programmes covering old age, disability and death. In addition it is
expected to have the closest balance between pensions expenditure and contributions of all of the OECD countries over the next 75 years. This is shown in
the 1996 OECD study, *Ageing in OECD countries: A critical policy challenge,*
which estimates the net present value of the expected deficit as a percentage
of GDP over the period 1994–2070.

Ireland has both contributory and non-contributory retirement pension
schemes which cover employees and the self-employed. Total expenditure
on these schemes amounted to 4.8 per cent of GNP in 1996. It is projected to
fall to 2.6 per cent in 2056 if pension benefits are increased in line with
prices or to increase to 8 per cent if pensions are indexed in line with average
earnings. The administrative cost of the contributory schemes is low, 2 per cent
of contributions, compared with occupational schemes, 5 per cent of contributions. The way in which social security is provided in Ireland may, therefore,
serve as a model for countries which are interested in reforming their pension
schemes using social insurance principles. Such an approach would facilitate
the provision of basic pensions at costs which are affordable now and which
will continue to be affordable in the future.

Overview of retirement programmes in Ireland
The main difference in the way in which social insurance pensions are provided
in Ireland and other OECD countries is that the contributions are pay-related
while the benefits are flat-rate. Means-tested non-contributory pensions are
financed out of general tax revenue. Insured members of the working population who satisfy the contribution conditions qualify for flat-rate pensions as of
right. Those who do not satisfy the contribution conditions may qualify for a
flat-rate non-contributory retirement pension if they pass a means test.

There are two social insurance schemes, the Retirement Pension Scheme
and the Old-Age (Contributory) Pension Scheme, and one social assistance
scheme, the Old-Age (Non-Contributory) Pension Scheme. The contributory
schemes pay pensions to people reaching age 65 and 66, respectively. Eligibility for a retirement pension requires retirement from insurable employment but
this condition does not apply on reaching age 66. The pensions which are payable are sufficient to keep most elderly people out of poverty when account is
taken of other sources of income and benefits-in-kind, such as free travel on
public transport, free electricity, free telephone rental and a carer's allowance
payable to someone to look after an old person when full-time care and attention are needed.

About half of the labour force is covered by an occupational or personal
pension scheme which will provide a retirement income related to final salary.
Most organizations with more than 50 employees have an occupational
scheme.

Qualification conditions
To qualify for a pension an applicant must have started paying Pay-Related
Social Insurance (PRIS) at least ten years before retirement. For the maximum

retirement pension the applicant must have paid a total of at least 156 weeks' PRIS and maintained a yearly average of at least 48 weeks' paid or credited contributions since 1979 or at least 24 weeks' paid or credited contributions since 1953 (or commencement of employment, if later). For the minimum retirement pension, a yearly average of 24 weeks' contributions is required. For the Old Age (Contributory) Pension, the contribution conditions are similar except that, for the minimum pension, a yearly average of at least ten weeks' paid or credited contributions is required.

Contribution rates

Employer, employee and self-employed contributions are proportional to earnings up to an income ceiling of about one-and-a-half times average industrial earnings for the employee and 1.8 times for the employer. There is a lower earnings limit equal to around 10 per cent of average industrial earnings below which PRIS contributions are not payable. Above this limit there are earnings thresholds on which the PRIS contribution varies by slice of income. There is no specific contribution rate for the two contributory old-age pension schemes because there is a unified social insurance scheme which provides cover for the contingencies of unemployment, illness, death of a spouse and old age. However, an *Actuarial review of social welfare pensions* recently carried out for the Irish government estimates that the payment for the contributory old-age pension scheme by the employer is 5.3 per cent and 2.8 per cent for the employee up to the employer and employee income ceilings. In addition there is a contribution equal to about 1.5 per cent of total earnings by the state out of general tax revenue to cover the gap between pension expenditures and contributions.

Contribution rates have increased slowly from the relatively low levels which existed when the contributory old-age pension scheme was introduced in 1960. The actuarial review mentioned above shows that the employer and employee contributions will grow moderately in the period up to 2046 to 6.3 and 3.3 per cent, respectively, if pensions are indexed in line with prices and, more significantly, to 17.3 and 9.2 per cent if they are indexed in line with average earnings.

Indexation

Although there is no legal obligation to index pensions in line with prices or earnings, the practice has been to increase them in line with average male industrial earnings. Consequently pensioners in Ireland have shared in increasing prosperity along with the working population. This contrasts sharply with experience in the United Kingdom where pensioners have not shared in the increase in living standards because of a decision taken by the Conservative government in the 1980s to increase pensions only in line with prices.

Social security coverage and number of beneficiaries

When the contributory old-age pension scheme was introduced in 1960 almost two-thirds of the labour force were covered by the scheme. The coverage rate has increased steadily over the years following the phasing out of regulations which restricted coverage to blue-collar workers and to persons earning less than a specified level. Today virtually 100 per cent of the labour force is covered by the scheme. Because the scheme is financed on a pay-as-you-go basis, it was possible to provide pension benefits immediately for qualified persons. Thus, in 1961, the year after the scheme was introduced, 9 per cent of those aged 65 and over received a contributory old-age pension. As the scheme has matured and more and more people have met the qualifying conditions, the percentage of the elderly population in receipt of a contributory pension has increased steadily. Thus, in 1996, 44 per cent of the elderly population were in receipt of a contributory old-age pension. It is projected that by 2026 almost 95 per cent of those aged 65 and over will receive a contributory old-age pension.

The growth in the percentage of the population receiving a contributory old-age pension will be matched in the long term by a decline in the percentage in receipt of a non-contributory pension. At the time that the contributory scheme was introduced almost two-fifths of those aged 65 and over were receiving a non-contributory pension. The proportion fell to one-third in 1996 and it is projected to fall to less than one-twentieth by 2026.

Ireland has succeeded in having relatively low pension costs mainly because its social security pension schemes are strongly redistributive, with flat-rate social insurance pensions being financed out of earnings-related contributions, and flat-rate social assistance pensions being financed out of general taxation. It also has a higher statutory retirement age for men and women, 66, than the OECD averages (64 for men and 62 for women) and lower life expectancy, 75.2 years at birth, than the OECD average (76 years at birth). Its social insurance pension scheme is straightforward to administer and its high coverage rate provides economies of scale which keep administrative costs low.

provide flat, or relatively flat, benefits that are adequate for middle- and lower-income workers but require supplementation for upper-income workers, or only provide anti-poverty benefits?

The income replacement rate workers need depends on the comparison of the costs of maintaining a similar standard of living while retired with those while working. Thus, for example, it depends on the extent to which the individual is responsible for paying for his own medical care and on the difference in tax treatment between workers and retirees.

It is not possible to know whether a given replacement rate provided by social security is too high or too low without knowing whether workers are eligible for retirement benefits from other sources. A given replacement rate may be adequate if universal health care coverage is available for retirees, but not if retirees must pay for health care or health care insurance from their own budget.

The share of retirement benefit expenditures relative to GDP measures the overall size of the retirement income scheme. Retirement income benefits compete with all other expenditures in terms of the share they take of GDP. An overly generous retirement income scheme will crowd out other worthwhile expenditures.

SECOND TIER

Government management of a funded tier

Government bureaucracies have been thought to be inefficient at managing programmes in comparison to the private sector. This inefficiency arises because they are not subject to competition and the profit motive. Government management of provident funds has frequently been unsuccessful and many countries with provident funds have converted to pay-as-you-go schemes. Experience has shown, however, that government bureaucracies can be more efficient at managing social security programmes than private sector organizations. This occurs for several reasons. First, the private sector has advertising and marketing costs; second, the private sector does not fully benefit from economies of scale, especially in small countries, as there are multiple small institutions managing social security funds; and third, the private sector may be too small to accommodate a sufficient number of fund management firms for a competitive market.

With government management of a funded tier, having the government manage investments in the stock market raises several difficult issues. The volatility, or risk, of stocks is considerably greater than that of Treasury bills. Social security might be underfunded in any given year if the stock market did not perform well. Another issue of concern with government management of social security stock investments is how to keep the management of the investments from becoming politicized. The government could use the financial power associated with its investments to reward or punish firms or industries. To prevent this occurring, the financial management may need to be done by private sector firms. Even with private firm management, to prevent politicization of investment, the investment policy may need to be a passive policy of investing in a broad market index rather than picking individual stocks.

The role of voluntary funded occupational pension plans

Private or occupational pensions that are funded play an important role in the retirement income schemes of about a dozen developed countries. These include Canada, Japan, the Netherlands, the United Kingdom and the United States. Even there, however, their role is important only for people in the upper half of the income distribution. Overall, the role of private pensions is much smaller than that of social security. Because of problems facing pay-as-you-go social security schemes, many countries are increasingly turning towards private pensions as a potential source of retirement income. That raises the question of whether private pensions can take on an expanded role in providing retirement income.

The role of occupational pensions in providing retirement income varies across countries as a consequence of differences in government policy and economic development. An important determinant of the role of occupational pensions is the generosity of social security benefits. In planning their level of consumption over their lifetime, workers take into account their lifetime income. This determines a desired level of consumption in retirement. Because occupational pensions typically are more likely to be provided for higher-income workers than for lower-income workers, the generosity of the social security scheme for the former is particularly important in determining the role of occupational pensions. Italy, for example, has generous social security benefits for high-income workers and it has a relatively small occupational pension scheme.

A second important way that government policy affects the size of the occupational pension scheme is through the income tax system. As a practical matter, it appears that a tax subsidy is necessary to encourage the development of an occupational pension scheme. All countries with sizeable occupational pension schemes provide preferential income tax treatment for occupational pensions compared to other financial assets that can be used for saving for retirement (see box 19.3). Typically the tax preference takes the form of exempting pension contributions and pension asset income from taxation. Pensions are taxed only when the worker receives pension benefits. Some countries, such as the Bahamas, do not have a personal income tax system, and thus cannot use this policy tool to encourage occupational pension plans.

Preferential tax treatment for pensions reduces the tax base, raising the tax rate on all other taxable sources of income. A narrow tax base with a relatively high tax rate will cause greater economic distortions than a broad tax base with low levels. Middle- and upper-income groups tend to be the main beneficiaries of the tax preference.

A third aspect of government policy that affects the role of occupational pensions is government regulation. Government regulations may either encourage or discourage workers to demand, and employers to provide, occupational pensions. Government regulations determine the allowable features of occupational pension plans. For example, they determine whether employees may receive a tax deduction for contributions or whether only employers may receive a tax deduction. Government regulations determine whether all workers that work for an employer must be provided with a pension, or whether the employer may establish a pension plan but cover only some workers.

Effective occupational pension policy requires a skilled government bureaucracy. To establish and carry out policies governing pensions requires development of a knowledgeable, capable and honest governmental bureaucracy. When government bureaucrats can be bribed to ignore pension laws, a pension scheme is less likely to develop.

Box 19.3 Tax expenditures

Many developed countries provide tax concessions for occupational pensions that are called tax expenditures. Tax expenditures reduce the net position of the government budget from what it would have been had pensions been taxed equivalently to other forms of savings. All countries with well-developed voluntary occupational pension schemes provide such tax concessions, and those concessions appear to be necessary for the voluntary development of systems that provide widespread coverage. An advantage of tax expenditures is that they require less government administration than direct provision, making them attractive to governments intent on reducing the role of the state. Usually, however, the state then becomes involved in extensive regulation of occupational pensions to protect the rights of workers. In countries that rely heavily on funded occupational pensions, tax expenditures for pensions are a major non-transparent form of social welfare that favours middle- and upper-income workers (Sinfield, 1998).

Tax expenditures tend to favour middle- and upper-income workers because they are more likely than low-income workers to participate in an occupational pension scheme, their marginal tax rates are often higher and their pension assets, which are sheltered from taxation, are greater. In 1993, in the United Kingdom tax expenditures for pensions cost taxpayers considerably more than all means-tested assistance for the poorest old people (Sinfield, 1993). Because of the large amount of assets in occupational pensions in some countries, in particular the Netherlands, the United Kingdom and the United States, the tax expenditures on pensions are often the largest tax expenditures in those countries. In the United Kingdom the revenue cost of the tax expenditures on pensions is about 15 per cent, as large as personal income tax revenues. In Ireland in 1989 tax expenditures on occupational pensions are estimated to have cost the equivalent of 36 per cent of annual expenditure on state contributory retirement pensions.

A greater role for occupational pensions in the retirement income scheme may increase income inequality and poverty among the aged. Traditional social security programmes tend to redistribute income towards lower-income workers. Occupational pension plans do not. Thus, if occupational pension plans partially replace social security, the inequality of the income distribution may increase. If an increase in the role of occupational pension plans was associated with a general reduction in social security, low-income workers would be worse off. Their social security benefits would be reduced while it would be unlikely that they would receive occupational pension benefits. This change, conversely, would benefit high-income workers who would have lower social security benefits, but disproportionately lower social security taxes.

DEFINED BENEFIT VERSUS DEFINED CONTRIBUTION PLANS

First-tier plans are defined benefit plans in most countries, the exceptions being countries with provident funds or mandatory privately managed defined

Table 19.3 Defined contribution plans in selected countries

Type of plan	Country	Name of plan	Contribution formula
Mandatory, funded	Australia	Superannuation guarantee charge	15% by 2003
	Sweden	Premium reserve account	2%
	Mexico	Administradoras de Fondos De Retiro	6.5%
	Chile	Administradoras de Fondos de Pensiones	10% required, 20% max.
Contracted out, funded	United Kingdom	Approved personal pension	4.6%
Mandatory, unfunded	Sweden		16.5%
	France	ARRCO (employees)	6% min.
		AGIRC (managerial staff)	16%*
Voluntary, group	USA	401(k), profit sharing, money purchase	18% max.
	Canada	Registered pension plan	18% max. C$13 500
	United Kingdom	Personal pensions	17.5%
Voluntary, individual	USA	Individual retirement account	$2 000 max.
	Canada	Registered retirement savings plan	18% max. C$13 500 max.

* Of portion of earnings over social security ceiling.

Note: There are generally minimum and maximum limitations on the earnings to which the contribution rates apply. Maximum contribution rates in voluntary plans may be lower if the worker contributes to another plan. The maximum contribution rate in the United Kingdom for personal pensions is higher for workers aged 40 and older.

Sources: Country legislation.

contribution plans. Many countries with provident funds have converted to defined benefit plans based on social insurance principles. Second-tier plans could be defined benefit or defined contribution, or both. Both defined benefit and defined contribution plans may have a role in a retirement income scheme.

Defined contribution plans around the world differ considerably in their features. However, when defined contribution plans are a major part of the retirement income scheme, their required contribution rate generally ranges from 10 to 15 per cent. When they are voluntary, their maximum allowed contribution rate tends to be in the range of 17 to 20 per cent (table 19.3). As discussed in Chapter 12, defined benefit and defined contribution plans differ greatly in the amount and type of risks borne by participants. In defined contribution plans the worker bears the investment risk, although most government-mandated defined contribution plans receive some form of government guarantee. Because the worker's benefit is tied to the rate of return on the assets in his or her account, a downturn in asset markets at the point of retirement may greatly reduce a worker's retirement income.

Social safety net: Anti-poverty means-tested benefits

Means-tested programmes have an important role in retirement income schemes. They also have several weaknesses. They might motivate people with low income and low assets to reduce their economic resources in order to qualify for the programmes, or discourage savings and work and encourage the elderly to transfer their resources to their children in order to qualify. Means-tested programmes usually have incentives that motivate some people to cheat to obtain benefits. They may allow the administration scope of discretion when determining if the claimant really is needy, which can be humiliating. Means-tested benefits can be constructed to give the claimant a legally enforceable right to a certain benefit, provided he or she can document that his or her registered means (income and assets) are below legally specified limits. Such benefits are not necessarily stigmatizing to claim. In countries such as the United Kingdom, however, many people who qualify for these programmes do not apply for benefits because of the stigma, reducing the effectiveness of the programmes in reaching the target population. Means testing greatly increases the administrative cost of a programme.

Means-tested programmes sometimes are based on the mistaken view that accurate provision of benefits is possible only by awarding benefits on the basis of an income test. The poor can be identified in an alternative manner. They can be identified by poverty indicators: family or individual characteristics correlated with poverty. In some countries good indicators are poor health or old age. In Egypt unmarried women aged 50 and older can receive a social assistance pension, in recognition that women in that age group may have limited work opportunities.

A flat benefit is a type of anti-poverty benefit. It is, by definition, not related to individual earnings. Thus there is no relationship between the tax payments that fund it and the benefit received. The financing of this type of benefit leads to distortions caused by taxes, such as discouraging labour supply. A guaranteed minimum benefit encourages tax evasion by low-income workers because it reduces the marginal benefit they receive based on their tax payments. By evading contributions low-income workers can qualify for a minimum benefit, which may about equal their benefit had they fully contributed.

These incentive problems can be limited by focusing social assistance programmes on groups who are not expected to work, such as people above a threshold age, say age 70. When resources are severely limited, such a strict qualifying condition assures efficient allocation of benefits. In spite of their weaknesses, social assistance benefits are a necessary part of retirement income schemes. The alleviation of poverty should take the highest priority among social policy objectives.

There is no perfect social security system. All pension schemes are the result of political and economic trade-offs, and require good management to function well. They must cope with macroeconomic uncertainties: inflation, unemployment, wage growth rate, changes in demographics and interest rates.

A wide range of social security schemes is capable of meeting the goals of society, but the following general recommendations apply for most developed countries. There should be a poverty reduction programme, an unfunded social insurance programme subject to labour market risks, a funded programme subject to capital market risks, and private savings. The relative importance of these sources of retirement income varies across countries depending on their dominant political philosophy, the capacity for governance in the public sector versus the private sector, and the relative rates of return and risks of different sources of retirement income. There should be compulsory participation in a unified national pay-as-you-go system without special treatment for favoured groups. While a mandatory funded programme is not desirable for many countries, if the funded programme is mandatory, consideration needs to be given to the problem of fixed costs that are a relatively heavy burden for small accounts.

In developing countries with poorly developed capital markets and regulatory capacity a simple system may be preferable, with an anti-poverty benefit, private savings and a pay-as-you-go tier. The essential aspects of these recommendations are that developing countries should take steps to expand coverage and that, as countries develop, they should provide retirement income from multiple sources to diversify risks. This recommendation is merely a restatement of the adage, "Don't put all your eggs in one basket", or the associated financial market advice that risk-averse investors should diversify their sources of income. Exactly how many different sources, and the relative weight given to each, should only be decided after an analysis of the particular situation of a country. Within a broader framework, spending in society on retirement income needs to be balanced against spending on health care, education and other priorities.

ANNEX: ADMINISTRATIVE COSTS IN PUBLIC AND PRIVATE PENSION PLANS: WHAT MAKES THE DIFFERENCE?

It is reasonable to expect that the cost of collecting contributions, managing participant records, investing accumulated balances, determining benefit eligibility and distributing benefits would differ between publicly managed and privatized plans. These costs are charged to participants both in government plans and in those sponsored by private employers, though not all such costs are always charged to participants in either type of plan. Administrative costs should thus be considered in the adoption or modification of national retirement schemes.

This analysis discusses some of the major issues of definition, measurement and interpretation in evaluating pension programme administrative costs, some of the principal factors that determine costs and concludes with an assessment of options facing policy makers. The analysis is limited to plan-level costs. It thus does not consider the distributional effects of alternative allocations of plan costs to participants (for example, flat fees on all accounts versus flat percentage charges on all contributions or assets versus graduated flat or percentage charges). Once a given plan design, with a given level of aggregate costs, is selected, it is possible to achieve any distributional result by means of appropriate fee structures. The distributional effects of plan costs on participants should therefore not generally be a consideration in the selection of plan design.

What to include in costs

Whether the goal is to compare administrative costs across countries or to evaluate the cost impact of change in one country's programme, the first step should be to decide on a comprehensive definition of plan administrative costs. Administrative costs should include the full resource costs of turning revenues into benefits.

Measuring these costs for government programmes turns out to be difficult. Government agencies often do not purchase their inputs in competitive markets; an example is the use of public buildings and land for government agencies. Government programmes may benefit from economies of scale such as the collection of payroll and other taxes by the central tax authority. When, as in the United States, employers pay payroll and income taxes on one form, with one remittance, and send them to one address, the costs of tax enforcement may be difficult to allocate among the revenue streams collected. Differences between government and private accounting procedures can also cause measurement problems. For example, private entities report charges for depreciation of fixed assets, while government agencies do not.

It is also important to note, however, that costs may also not be fully allocated to participants in purely private pension schemes, such as employer-sponsored plans in the United States. Employers' costs that are not passed on to participants may include the costs of office space, personnel to manage pension plan record keeping and other functions, and participant information efforts.

Measuring administrative costs is further complicated by the fact that administrative and benefit costs are inherently fungible. One national plan may perform meticulous actuarial projections that provide advance warning of demographic hazards and allow the country to consider benefit changes, tax changes or other changes in public spending priorities in advance of spending increases that would otherwise occur. Another country may invest minimal resources in projecting future trends, but be faced with unexpected benefit liabilities as a result. The higher administrative costs resulting from actuarial projections in the first plan can be translated into benefit savings, while the lower administrative costs in the second can increase benefit costs.

Monitoring the integrity of the payments process provides another example of the trade-offs between administrative and benefit costs. Many countries face problems in tracking their pensioners. People may collect multiple pensions when only one is legitimately payable, or payments may continue to be made to people who are dead. While dead pensioners are a problem to some degree in almost every pension scheme, some countries with weak governmental infrastructure have faced particular problems, especially in rural areas. A pensioner may die and be buried on the family's land. No death certificate is issued, and the family continues to collect the pension. Investing in administrative infrastructure can limit such wrongful benefit payments.

If the administrative costs of retirement income plans are defined to include all costs incurred by government agencies, employers and individuals, the true costs of administering pension programmes are probably never measured. In countries where public bureaucracies do not work well, pensioners may face a difficult application process, receive incorrect benefit amounts and may even have to bribe government employees to draw attention to their case. Competitive systems may reduce these bureaucratic costs,[8] but, in turn, require regulation, which is not cost-free itself (James and Palacios, 1995).

Measures of plan costs

Cost figures must be applied to a unit of output. A number of ratios are commonly used to evaluate and compare administrative costs. All of these ratios are informative but partial in nature. None of these measures takes account of service quality or plan characteristics (redistributive or not, adequate replacement rate or not), both of which can be considered elements of plan output.

Costs relative to contributions or benefits

Costs as a percentage of contributions or benefits can be used to assess administrative efficiency. But these costs reflect not only efficiency, but also a country's demographic structure, system maturity and income level (James and Palacios, 1994). These costs will be highest in countries with young populations and immature pension schemes (that is, a low ratio of pensioners to contributors). These countries will have low total benefit payments but must still pay for collecting taxes and keeping records.

Costs relative to assets

This measure would be used in private or privately managed plans, but not in publicly managed programmes that accumulate few assets. Mutual funds and other investment managers, who might be expected to take an active role in a privatized retirement income scheme, often express their fees as a percentage of assets under management. Larger mutual funds tend to benefit from scale economies (Baumol et al. 1990)[9]. In the United States market, it has also been the case that mutual funds aimed at the institutional (employer-sponsored pension) market have lower administrative costs and are less likely to charge loads (commissions levied at the time the investor purchases or sells shares) (Mitchell, 1996). A privatized United States social security scheme might be able to benefit from such market segmentation – or it might not. Pharmaceutical manufacturers in the United States, for example, were very reluctant to give Medicaid, the joint federal-state health care coverage programme for poor people, the same bulk-purchase rates they give to their best private sector customers.

Costs per plan member

This measure avoids the bias against young countries with immature systems that is inherent in cost measures based on plan flows, but it does not control the quality of services provided, the price of labour and capital, or economies of scale. On this measure, small, high-wage countries have the highest administrative costs. It is generally agreed that this measure is the best simple index of administrative efficiency, though some observers caution that it should be used only to compare countries with roughly equal system sizes and per capita incomes (James and Palacios, 1995).

Costs relative to per capita income

Unlike costs per member, this measure is independent of national currency. It offers some adjustments for inter-country differences that others do not. It shifts costs per member down more for high-income than for low-income countries, which can serve as an adjustment for higher input prices and higher quality services in the former countries. On this measure, small, poor countries have the highest administrative costs, while industrial countries have the lowest (ibid.). But high-income countries are also more productive, so comparing administrative costs with income gives them "credit" for more system efficiency than they may really display.

Interpreting cost differences

Administrative costs do not measure plan quality or cost-effectiveness, but only the cost of inputs into the benefit delivery process. Cost-effectiveness depends on many other aspects of a plan. Consider two hypothetical countries with identical administrative costs but differing levels of service. In one country benefits are delivered to pensioners on time and in the correct amounts, while in the other country benefit qualification is arduous and delays in payments are common as are incorrect payments. Most people would agree that the first programme was more cost-effective than the second.

Suppose that the benefit structure in one country is compressed (inflation has compressed benefit structures in many transition economies) and in the other more dispersed. Even if the cost of calculating and updating earnings-based benefits were identical in the two countries, the first plan would be arguably less cost-effective than the second, since an equal effort must be devoted in calculating the small and large benefit increments.

Finally administrative cost comparisons, especially between publicly and privately managed plans, do not account for differences in the political goals of systems (Mitchell, 1996). The United States social security system, for example, is in part an earnings insurance programme and in part a redistributive transfer programme. A private programme might not have as strong a redistributive bent, if any. If it did not, then cost comparisons between social security and private alternatives would be based on different output measures.

Factors influencing pension scheme costs

Defined benefit or defined contribution?

A major factor determining pension scheme cost differences is the type of plan. Defined benefit plans offer a specified benefit, which the sponsor (the government in a national plan or the employer in a private plan) is left to fund. Advance-funded defined benefit plans, which are typically found only among private employer-sponsored plans, are expensive to operate in part because they require actuarial services to ensure that asset accumulation is on target[10]. In the United States, defined benefit plans must also pay insurance premiums to the Pension Benefit Guaranty Corporation (PBGC), a government agency that insures benefits against plan insolvency. In 1993, the most recent year for which data are available, average administrative expenses were $115 per participant for defined benefit plans and $53 per participant for defined contribution plans (calculations based on US Department of Labor, 1997).

The typical United States defined contribution plan, however, is a bare-bones plan by international standards. United States plans function much like savings accounts, with the participants' claims limited to contributions plus investment earnings. In contrast, in many social security individual account plans in other countries, participants may receive benefits from minimum benefit guarantees and investment return guarantees, and the benefit is paid out in annuity form. Such plans would incur many of the costs typically attached to defined benefit plans.

Funded or pay-as-you-go?

Funded plans incur certain costs that pay-as-you-go plans do not. Plans that accumulate assets, whether these plans are private or public, must provide for their investment. Balances held in the United States social security scheme are, by law, invested in special Treasury securities, so expenses for investment management are minimal. But in other countries investment restrictions may not translate into administrative cost savings. In Hungary's third-pillar voluntary pension accounts, for example, some plans are restricted to investing in government securities until their assets increase to a certain level, but some investment managers charge as much as 9 per cent of contributions while investing solely in government securities, whereas others charge 5 per cent to manage a fully diversified portfolio.

In countries with broad asset markets and rapid growth, funding may be preferable to pay-as-you-go finance, since higher investment returns can fund a higher level of benefits. In countries with high inflation and narrower asset markets, the benefits of advance funding may be smaller relative to the administrative costs of maintaining pension balances. The benefits of advance funding may also depend on whether pension funds are subject to investment restrictions, including limits on the share of assets that can be invested in private securities. Such restrictions will tend to channel plan assets to lower-paying uses, such as the purchase of government debt.

Investment management strategies

While funded plans incur investment management costs, these costs may vary dramatically according to the investment technique used. Some pension funds are actively managed, with extensive effort devoted to selecting and trading securities. But mutual funds using passive investment techniques, called index funds, are increasingly popular in the United States. Rather than devote an extensive effort to researching and selecting investments, these funds hold broadly diversified portfolios designed to match a market index, such as the Dow Jones Industrials or the Standard & Poor's 500. Index funds have lower turnover than actively managed funds, since securities are traded primarily when the index changes. Index funds thus have lower expense ratios, ranging from one-third to one-half of those of actively managed funds (Mitchell, 1996).

Centralized or competitive?

A government-run retirement income scheme will typically be centralized and operated through the central government. A privatized system, however, will revolve around competing private investment managers. Competition in a privatized national retirement system raises marketing expenses and reduces economies of scale. It has been argued that these costs are offset by more and better service (James and Palacios, 1995), but some systems may lack reasonable brakes on the availability of service. An estimated one in two active accounts in Chile is switched annually among investment managers (Vittas, 1997a). What appears to be highly responsive service may instead be churning, which results in higher and unproductive administrative costs.

The degree of centralization may also affect the quality and cost of contribution enforcement. Evasion is probably easier in a decentralized individual account system, though many other factors may encourage evasion as well.

Availability of infrastructure

Information exchanges among developed, transition and developing economies allow less advanced countries to learn what works, how to fix what does not, and which mistakes to avoid. But a plan that works in a country with a developed infrastructure (a well-functioning postal service and other communications services, sound banks, reliable payroll records) may not work, or work as efficiently, in a country where the financial and governmental infrastructure is shakier.

A country's ability to enforce contributions and monitor the integrity of the payments process will also influence its administrative costs, especially but not exclusively in a funded, individual account plan. Countries where source withholding from public enterprises has been the primary method of tax collection often do not have in place the enforcement techniques necessary to deal with emerging private sector enterprises, which are typically not plugged into source withholding mechanisms. Ineffective enforcement will increase the resource costs of collecting a given amount of contributions (or reduce the collection efficiency of a given amount of enforcement spending).

Monitoring the integrity of the payments process can present special problems in countries with weak communication infrastructures and enforcement techniques. Participants should get all the benefits – and only those benefits – to which they are entitled. In some transition economies, complex inflation indexing formulas and inadequate technology delay promised updates in pension benefits. And verifying the eligibility status of pensioners may be costly if valid and up-to-date address and other records are not available.

The structure of benefits

In general a flat benefit is less costly to administer than an earnings-based benefit. Administering a flat benefit requires basic eligibility information about the prospective recipient (age, covered work history, perhaps residence or citizenship status), while an earnings-based benefit requires the basic information plus earnings history for the covered period less years not being counted, if any.

Adding a flat benefit to an earnings-based plan as a benefit floor – as done in Hungary (the second pillar) and other countries – is not cost-free from an administrative standpoint. If beneficiaries are to receive the greater of their earned benefit or the statutory minimum, as in the Hungarian second pillar, the earnings-based benefit must be calculated and verified to avoid unwarranted government subsidies.

Public consensus

One important factor in determining administrative costs can be the degree of public consensus or support a plan enjoys. In the United States, for example, survey after survey suggests that many working-age Americans fear that they will not be able to rely on social security benefits in the same way that their parents' and grandparents' generations have done. At the same time, however, research also shows that many people are willing to support the programme and willingly pay payroll taxes to do so because they agree with its goals (Korczyk, 1990). Given this level of support, employees want their employers to make required contributions on their behalf, and will take action to ensure that this is done. But in a country where tax evasion is less a crime than a national sport, the retirement system will face added administrative costs when it does not enjoy public support.

Administrative costs are, and should be, a consideration in evaluating retirement income policy options. But cost comparisons, whether among different countries with the same pension scheme or among alternative pension schemes for a given country, are subject to numerous qualifications and uncertainties. These considerations include demographic structure, income and the availability and quality of governmental and financial infrastructure. Therefore it is likely that the best way to compare administrative costs across countries is to compare actual costs with those that would be expected on the basis of the countries' characteristics (James and Palacios, 1995).

While inter-country comparisons are difficult, requiring multivariate statistical analysis, comparing the costs of alternative schemes in the same country can be even harder. A country considering replacing or augmenting its retirement income system with one of a different design is likely to be motivated not just by cost issues, but also by differences in the "output" expected from the system. Public and private schemes are likely to differ in characteristics such as redistribution, investment return, benefit levels, impact on national saving, participant choice and service quality, all of which are dimensions of a system's output.

Notes

[1] See Samuelson (1958) and Aaron (1966).

[2] Among other things, this assumes that labour force participation rates, the social security coverage rate, payroll contribution rate and hours of work per worker are constant.

[3] After an initial period, declining fertility is accompanied by increased female labour force participation, which increases the rate of growth of the labour force.

[4] Bailey and Turner (1997).

[5] Diamond (1993) quotes a higher figure of 2.9 per cent of wages and 30 per cent of contributions.

[6] On the other hand, evidence from the United Kingdom tends to confirm the result for Chile that the costs of personal pensions are high, given the lack of economies of scale of management, advertising and the high costs and compliance with the regulatory regime – as well as possible monopoly rents. Note in addition that United Kingdom personal pensions are usually not transferable

without major cost. Blake (1995) suggests that an initial transfer into a personal scheme may cost 25 per cent of the transfer value, with annual commissions of 2.5 per cent of the annual premium. The Institute of Actuaries considers that 10–20 per cent of contributions may be absorbed in fees over the entire span of a personal pension contract. In a detailed survey of 90 providers, Walford (1993) estimated that the various charges would reduce returns on a five-year pension plan by 13 per cent on average, but with quite a wide distribution from 8.5 per cent for the 10 per cent of employers with the lowest charges to 18 per cent for the worst 10 per cent. Annuity fees, which do not apply to occupational defined benefit plans, impose a further burden. Meanwhile expense ratios for United States 401(k) plans holding mutual funds are 80–188 basis points, with an extra 6–32 basis points for an annuity option (Mitchell, 1996).

[7] Tier 3 contains both funded and unfunded sources of retirement income.

[8] On the other hand, anyone who has ever had to straighten out an insurance claim in the highly competitive US private health care market might disagree.

[9] But bigger is not always better. Some funds (Fidelity Magellan is a prominent US example) can become "too" big. A fund can become so large that its trades move the market and maintaining a diversified portfolio becomes complicated.

[10] Actuarial projections should also be used to ensure that national social security plans funded on a pay-as-you-go basis are financially sustainable. In practice, however, retirement schemes in many countries simply project their benefit obligations from year to year based on past experience without any long-term assessments. While this approach is riskier to the national budget, it may result in lower administrative costs, at least in the short term.

THE REFORM PROCESS AND ITS POLITICAL MANAGEMENT

20

Countries have encountered problems in the political process of deciding on and implementing social security pension reform. Many of them have found that, once the need for reform has become apparent, the process of reaching a consensus on the reform to be implemented has taken years.

The reform process may be slow because it has considerable risks for politicians and government bureaucrats responsible for it, as well as for the workers and employers ultimately affected by it. Social security pension reform needs to be researched and considered carefully. Thought should also be given to the way to manage reform. Managing the process of reform is an important aspect of the governance of social security schemes.

This chapter suggests strategies that may facilitate the reform process. In discussing the reform process, it considers broadly any changes that require a modification in social security legislation. It is sometimes useful to distinguish between reform that changes the parameters of an existing system (parametric reform), such as raising the retirement age, and reform that changes the entire structure (structural reform), such as substituting a pay-as-you-go defined benefit scheme for a provident fund. A third type of reform is improving governance, where the basic parameters and structure are not changed but steps are taken to improve the functioning of the existing system. While the amount of political effort differs between reforms, the process proposed here may be useful for all three types.

DIFFERENT REFORM PROCESSES

Many of the problems of social security can be resolved through improvements in governance. Some changes in governance, such as establishing a computerized record-keeping system, are reforms internal to the structure of the social security institution. Technical reforms of the management and operations of the social security institution generally need not involve the political process, but they have their own political process within the government bureaucracy.

Major reforms, such as increasing the minimum age at which pensions may be payable, or changing the type of social security scheme, require a complex interaction of the government with workers and employers. Major reforms in a democracy require use of the political process to secure changes in social security legislation.

Different political structures also require different reform processes. In some countries pressure groups play an important role in democratic-pluralist political systems. Pressure groups may include trade unions, employers' organizations and financial sector service providers, such as investment management companies and life insurance companies. The age distribution of the population may play a role, with older workers and retirees forming political interest groups. In other countries the government may be able to introduce changes relatively easily on its own initiative. The exact form of the reform process may also be affected by whether there is a single dominant political party, two competing parties or a number of parties. Nevertheless, in each of these situations, within the group or groups ultimately making the decision, a process is needed to build a consensus.

REACHING CONSENSUS ON SOCIAL SECURITY REFORM

Identifying the problem

The first step in a social security reform is recognizing that a problem exists. The problem may be evident to all, such as benefits not being paid owing to a shortfall of revenues. The level of benefits may be deemed inadequate or too high. That many people are not covered by the social security retirement benefits scheme may be recognized as a serious problem. Or the problem may be that politically powerful groups receive privileged benefits unavailable to the general populace.

Social security policy making should not be done solely in response to immediate crises. It is desirable that planning should occur over a long time horizon. Thus the step of realizing that a problem exists may require an actuarial projection, as discussed in Technical Brief 1.

Depending on the type of problem and the political situation in the country, the group relevant for consensus building may be internal to the government, may be within a single political party or may involve two or more political parties. The remainder of the chapter discusses the case where the relevant public is society at large.

Involving the relevant public in discussion of the problem

A key element in building a consensus is involving various groups in the process. Relevant groups include workers and their organizations and employers and their organizations (see box 20.1). There needs to be public discussion of the

Box 20.1 Labour unions' role in pension reform

Organized labour has been a key constituent initiating, expanding, presiding over and negotiating the alteration of social insurance schemes in many countries. In some countries labour unions helped build a private-public mix of employer-, worker- and state-financed retirement; the systems in Australia, France, the Netherlands, the United Kingdom and the United States are notable examples. In other countries organized labour functions as a general advocate for social spending for workers and families and political coalitions for more pensions (Argentina, Italy, Mexico and some Scandinavian countries are examples).

Labour unions, especially in Europe and Latin America, are developing proposals for reforms that attempt to shape pension reform and resist retrenchment. Latin American unions have a number of demands: to have labour union representation on the management board of the companies that manage the individual accounts, to allow workers to join pension funds as a group, and to direct the investments into projects that meet regional development goals. The Inter-American Development Bank shares the latter objective, and it and Argentine and Chilean unions have a joint partnership to leverage pension fund investments into economically directed investments. Argentine unions have control over some major pension fund management companies, though this is not the case in Chile, El Salvador, Mexico, Peru or Venezuela.

French, Israeli and Italian workers in 1994, 1996 and 1997 staged prominent and successful national protests which stalled state pension retrenchment. By 1995 the French government had minimized pension cuts by diminishing military spending instead. In August 1995 the three Italian labour federations supported a supplemental private pension scheme, advance funded by workers and employers. The Italian case represents a stark example of the new politics of retrenchment.

Expanding a welfare state has different politics from reducing one. Labour unions can provoke politicians who are ready to take credit for expansions, but the strategy changes when politicians wish to avoid blame for a reduction. Retrenchments cause immediate losses for a few and often steady erosion for many. Unions can highlight these losses. Public budget deficits may justify retrenchment, but the combination of large deficits and conservative governments interfere with joint negotiations and bargained retrenchment.

Not only does retrenchment politics create identifiable and concentrated immediate losers, it also faces another labour constituency: the workers who make up the professional and service staffs of the agencies. These blocs can create their own protective force even if organized labour is weak or weakened. This all leads politicians to lower the visibility of the retrenchment by making reforms that are technical and complicated. This hinders trade union involvement.

In the United Kingdom the Thatcher Government tried to diminish the relatively new state earnings-related pension scheme but faced opposition from the Labour Party and major insurance companies. In 1986 the Tories succeeded in a more gradual replacement of state pensions by private pension alternatives by appealing directly to employees, claiming the private system was better than the state system, using complicated assumptions and financial return projections.

In 1997 United States organized labour faced a more direct test of its ability to stave off retrenchment. For the first time, the quadrennial Social Security Advisory Council was seriously split between proposals to create individual advance-funded pension accounts and one calling for maintenance of the system's basic structure. Organized labour argued that the privatizing agenda is a thinly disguised campaign to promote the self-interest of the financial services industry. This is a twist to classic retrenchment politics that focuses on the losers; instead organized labour focused on the narrow and well-off business interests.

In Central and Eastern Europe, labour plays a complex role of crafting industrial relations rights while attempting to influence pension reform. This region is exposed to sophisticated and vigorous attempts by western insurance and money management companies to institute individual defined contribution accounts to displace contributions to defined benefit state schemes. The Central and Eastern European trade unions, notably in the Czech Republic, Hungary, Poland and Ukraine, have accepted the need for a private-public mix and emphasize the need for a defined benefit scheme, supplemented by a system of bargained and jointly managed private pensions.

Organized labour will resist retrenchment that lacks generous support for the poor elderly, resist defined contribution accounts, advocate a worker- and employer-financed retirement and promote joint administration in the management and investment of retirement funds.

problem. The government needs to educate the public and the various groups about the seriousness of the problem and the need for change. The government may need to commission studies that document the nature of the problem and its consequences. It may need to have a public information campaign to alert the public to the seriousness of the problem, especially if the problem is one that is not immediate but that is foreseen in the future, for example arising from the changing age structure of the population.

Determining the causes of the problem

After reaching a consensus that a problem exists, the next step is to determine the causes of the problem. Technical experts such as accountants, actuaries, economists and lawyers may need to be involved. In countries lacking specialized technical expertise, outside experts from international organizations such as the ILO may be needed to provide assistance in determining the causes of the problem.

Developing reform process infrastructure

Early in the reform process investments should be made in the development of a reform process infrastructure. Such investments include training technical personnel in the social security institution, educating politicians about the issues and educating workers' and employers' groups and journalists about the issues so that the debate, and subsequent decision making, are better informed. In addition investments may need to be made to strengthen the parliamentary process. This might include the establishment of special committees in parliament with responsibility for the oversight of social security, and the development of expertise in parliament and among parliamentary staff.

Agreeing on causes

The next level of consensus building is to reach agreement on the causes. This stage may require meetings or conferences where the problem is discussed and various theories as to its causes are debated. If a consensus among experts exists as to the causes, this should be communicated to the responsible officials in the social security institution and to members of parliament.

Establishing a clear statement of guiding principles

The development of a statement of guiding principles or goals for reform, as suggested in Chapter 15 on the normative basis for policy, provides a clarity of purpose. Disagreements may occur over the goals of reform, with such disagreements often based on philosophical differences over the role of government versus individual responsibility. If a consensus can be reached on the guiding principles for reform, doctrinal and ideological disputes will be reduced.

Pension reform usually has five goals (Tambouri, 1998): (a) social acceptability, (b) financial sustainability, (c) political feasibility, (d) non-distortion of labour and capital, (e) client-friendly management and administration. The goal of the adequacy of pensions can be considered as an aspect of social acceptability. Other goals, such as increasing savings, developing a domestic capital market or reducing the role of the state may also be important in some countries. The goal of political feasibility is likely to limit the ability of a country to achieve the other goals.

Developing alternative solutions

Once the causes of the problem have been identified, a process needs to be set in place to develop alternative solutions that are technically feasible. Different options need to be proposed and studied, perhaps with the assistance of international organizations. In some cases it may be desirable to encourage workers' and employers' groups to propose solutions. It is often useful to examine what other countries have done.

Once several leading contenders have been established as alternatives, it is necessary to determine the cost of alternative solutions. This frequently requires the use of actuarial models, such as are described in Technical Brief 1. Also, the effects of alternative solutions should be studied, with thought being given to possible unintended effects. How different groups are affected by alternative solutions should also be considered. Often reforms involve trade-offs between various goals and between groups. It is desirable to clarify the trade-offs and the winners and losers.

Debating alternative strategies and policies

In considering alternatives a strategic decision needs to be made regarding parametric or governance reform versus structural reform. Often, governance reform and parametric reform rather than structural reform are needed, though at times structural reform may also be required.

The timing of reform is an important strategic issue. There are two dimensions of timing. First, should reform occur gradually over a period of time, or should it take the "big bang" approach, with the implementation occurring all in one go? Second, should reform occur after a short implementation period or should it be postponed? Some analysts argue for the "big bang" approach to major reform, arguing that the economic costs of the transition are ultimately less because of the short time involved, though the transition may involve a relatively short period of economic difficulty. A "big bang" approach may be desirable if a major change of structure is being undertaken. For some reforms it is desirable to announce them years in advance so that workers can adjust their plans to take the reform into account. However the longer they are postponed the further off are the benefits of the reform. In implementing reform it is important to take account of acquired rights and not to change benefit amounts retrospectively, or at least to limit such changes to workers many years from retirement.

Educating the public

At all stages of the process an effort should be made to inform and educate the public. This would involve campaigns of public information and public relations. Written material about the reform should be prepared for employees and employers. Information should be disseminated through newspapers, radio, television, brochures and training material and, in some countries, over the Internet. Government officials should give speeches and meet leaders of workers' and employers' groups. Journalists should be briefed.

As part of the effort to provide public information and consultation with different groups, the government may draft a preliminary proposal, called a Green Paper in some countries, such as the United Kingdom, in which the leading alternative or alternatives for reform are discussed. This paper provides interested groups with the opportunity to submit their comments or suggestions for change.

Dealing with disagreements over reform

An important element in building a consensus is determining the sources of disagreements over reform. Some disagreements occur between the winners and losers. Disagreements may occur over the likely effects of reform, which to some extent may be unknown and to some extent predictable, but with people disagreeing in their predictions.

An effort should be made to understand the reasons why there are disagreements and to reduce the areas of disagreement. Discussions should be held about whether goals can be pursued by alternative policy tools, such as tax policy. All parties should attempt to understand the viewpoint of those not agreeing with them, which requires a minimum level of goodwill in the political system.

Sometimes disagreements can be reduced or resolved by proposing a different perspective from which to view a reform. For example, an increase in the minimum age at which benefits can be received may be viewed as a benefit cut, or as a way of indexing lifetime benefits so that they are not increased by increasing life expectancy. It may be useful to undertake economic and actuarial studies to determine the extent to which differences of opinion, based on views as to facts or on beliefs about effects, can be resolved by providing more or better information. Some differences about social security reform are due to different views concerning the effect of social security schemes on economic growth, but these differences may not be easily reconciled because of the difficulty of solving the underlying economic issues concerning the functioning of the economy.

The process may require parties to accept differences of opinion and seek compromise. Compromise may be an important aspect of the reform process. Finally there may need to be the acceptance that some people may be made worse off by a reform. This happens, for example, with reforms that reduce the overly generous benefits previously enjoyed by some groups. Governments need to try to avoid giving in to pressure which will undermine the effect of reform, for example by excluding certain privileged groups. Dealing with groups whose privileges are being curtailed can be a difficult aspect of the reform process. Sometimes, however, incentives need to be offered to certain groups to ensure the passage of reform.

Increasing social acceptability of reform

One strategy for increasing social acceptability of reform is to introduce it gradually. If governments wait to make reforms until the need is imminent, they will not have the option of implementing the reform gradually or with a delay. It is desirable to try to anticipate the need for reform far into the future. Implementing a reform rapidly that adversely affects retirees and workers near retirement age undermines trust in the social security scheme because workers and retirees will believe that the system cannot be depended on to provide a stable source of benefits.

If reform is introduced gradually, the group that is most adversely affected by it will be young workers and their retirement will be many years in the future.

Social acceptability and political feasibility of reforms are also increased by giving workers options. For example, major reforms often give the current working generation the option of remaining in the present system or switching to the reformed system. Introducing reforms gradually and providing flexibility and choice reduce individual opposition to reform. When a reform involves reducing benefits it may be necessary to direct benefits more towards the poor to ensure that they are not adversely affected.

Reaching consensus on solution

After alternative reforms have been proposed, studied and debated, and their costs and effects analysed, it is time to strive for a consensus on a solution. Sometimes a consensus can be reached on reforms by achieving a consensus on the nature of the problem, its causes and on the goals of the social security scheme. Stated alternatively, it is unlikely that a consensus will be reached on social security reform while there are differences over the causes of the problem and the goals of social security.

In reaching a consensus different pressure groups may try to build coalitions to support their position. Formal and informal methods of consultation may be needed between the government and different groups, as well as within groups. Formal consultations may involve public conferences or hearings where groups may make presentations. Informal consultation may involve telephone calls and meetings with an ostensibly social purpose, such as meeting for lunch. Also, some consultation of both types may be most effective at public events while at other times it may be most effective if done privately.

Drafting of proposed reforms

The government then needs to draft a proposed reform. In some countries, such as the United Kingdom, this is called a White Paper. The reform would be debated and perhaps modified in response to objections raised. At this point government leaders need to be actively involved in gaining support for the reform both in parliament and among the general populace. The proposed reform needs to be translated into a draft law and regulations. Countries differ as to the amount of detail they wish to embody in law versus the amount they wish to cast in regulations. Again public input should be sought on the draft law and regulations, and they should be modified accordingly. Finally parliament enacts the law and the government publishes the associated regulations.

IMPLEMENTING REFORM

Once the political process has culminated in the enactment of the reform law, it is time to implement the reform. There is a tendency for the period of implementation to be rushed to seek to give effect to the political decision and the law.

This is a mistake. It is essential to allow enough time for the reform to be introduced smoothly, otherwise it will provoke an adverse reaction. A reform may involve major structural changes, but a sufficient period needs to be allowed to prepare the institutional structure to implement those changes. Social investments need to be made to develop the implementation infrastructure. This includes training government personnel regarding the requirements of the law and in the necessary skills to implement the law, and the development of programmes to implement and enforce the law. An alternative that may be useful, especially for small countries, is to import people with needed specialized skills.

It is necessary to educate employees and employers about their new responsibilities under reform. It may also be necessary to have a public information campaign to increase acceptance of the reform.

Evaluating reform

To ensure the success of the reform, after it is instituted it is necessary to evaluate how it is actually working and to be prepared to make adjustments. Evaluation of the reform by workers' and employers' groups should be encouraged. The government should seek public input on the evaluation of the reform.

Adjusting reform

Most reforms need to be modified after experience has developed of the way how they function. Also adjustments sometimes should be made as employers, workers and government gain experience with reform and are capable of handling a more sophisticated system. The government should propose adjustments to the reform and receive public input on the proposed adjustments. The adjustments should then be modified and implemented. After the initial adjustments the functioning of the social security scheme should be periodically evaluated. Japan evaluates its social security scheme on a five-year cycle. A regular pattern of evaluation provides assurance that problems will be dealt with, while providing a level of certainty that the system will also have periods of stability.

CONCLUSION TO PART II

The main conclusion of Part II is that different types of retirement pension systems are appropriate for different countries. Typically, pluralistic systems that diversify retirement income sources to reduce risk and have a redistributive function aimed at alleviating poverty are desirable. Chapter 15, on the normative basis for policy, argues that the primary goals for social security old-age benefits should be the alleviation of poverty and the provision of low-risk benefits. While encouraging saving is an important goal for many countries, that goal can be better accomplished, and without the sacrifice of other social security goals, by other policies, such as a tax policy towards savings and investment. The ILO social security Conventions provide guidance as to the minimum level of generosity of benefits, specifying a 40 per cent replacement for a manual worker after 30 years of work. This can be considered also to require obtaining a reasonable retirement age relative to life expectancy in the country. But it is also a minimum level of income in old age which requires the guarantee of a social security retirement pension.

For most developed countries, meeting the goal of providing low-risk retirement income requires a scheme that has a pay-as-you-go element which is subject primarily to labour market risks and has a funded element that is subject primarily to capital market risks. These two elements could be in one or several programmes.

For developing countries with low coverage and high proportions of their workers in the informal sector, priority needs to be given to expanding coverage. This is a difficult task, mainly because of the problems of bringing informal workers within the ambit of formal social security schemes. The issue is discussed in Chapter 16. Imaginative and new approaches will be required which will need to build on the institutions and solidarity of the informal sector itself at the same time that the scope of the formal social security schemes is extended and their governance improved. This would be assisted by having special schemes designed for workers in the informal sector. They might be broader in scope than conventional social security schemes and cover a wider range of contingencies, but would need to be simpler to manage and administer. It would require special schemes be constructed, or special treatment be provided for those workers to make the scheme better fit their needs and their limited capacity for contributing; but the level of benefits might need to be restricted.

Chapter 17, on improving governance, management and compliance, argues that governance can be improved by involving workers and employers in the process. The way they would be involved depends on the circumstance of the country but, in some cases, it would involve tripartite (worker, employer, government) participation in a management board. In other cases, participation could occur through lobbying, voting and otherwise being involved in the political process.

Chapter 18, on influencing the age of retirement, discusses issues in determining the minimum age at which retirement benefits can be received from social security pension schemes. Wealthier countries can afford longer retirement periods. With increases in life expectancy the retirement period increases. Population ageing, raising the number of retirees relative to workers, raises the cost of providing benefits. These are some of the issues that need to be considered in setting the minimum age at which benefits can be received.

Chapter 19, on developing pluralistic designs and flexible structures, argues that, to meet the goals of alleviating poverty in old age and providing low-risk retirement benefits, different approaches are needed for developing and developed countries but, generally, multiple sources of benefits are needed.

Chapter 20, on the reform process and its political management, presents strategies for reaching consensus on reforms. Making reforms gradually, and allowing for options, are two strategies to reduce opposition to reform. Consultation with workers and employers is needed at all stages of reform. The government may need to educate the public about the problems and issues, and investments may be needed in strengthening the skills and knowledge of staff and parliamentarians involved in the process.

The development of social security pension schemes is an integral part of general social and economic development but, as both parts of this book have set out, for most countries in the world, their current state of development of pension schemes falls far short of what should be achieved and what can be achieved. To improve things will take time. But the activity concerning pension development and reform which has been launched in almost all countries in the world over the last two decades suggests that the process is under way.

ASIA AND THE PACIFIC

SOCIOECONOMIC OVERVIEW

The extended family is a fundamental socioeconomic feature of most Asian societies.[1] Most elderly in Asia live with one or more of their children, but the trend is to supplement traditional family support with social security retirement pension benefits.[2] The main limitation of the family is that it is a small group and, with urbanization and industrialization, the tendency is for families to become both smaller and more widely dispersed.

Rapid economic development, especially in East Asia, has drawn many more members of the labour force into wage employment. Between 1980 and 1995 (in Thailand, 1996) the number of employees as a percentage of the economically active population grew in Malaysia from 54 to 73 per cent, in Pakistan from 22 to 33 per cent and in Thailand from 22 to 37 per cent.[3] This trend has led to a growing need for social security pensions. For, while the self-employed may usually continue to work as long as they feel fit to do so, employees are typically required to retire at a certain age and it may then be difficult for them to find other work, whether for another employer or on their own account. Entry into wage employment increases the need for social protection, but it does not guarantee that this need will be met: much of the new employment being created is in small enterprises not covered by social security, or in the informal sector in enterprises which disregard or are not affected by social security legislation.

Demographic ageing will affect Asia dramatically more than other regions in the next few decades. Whereas Asia in 1985 accounted for 28 per cent of the world's elderly, defined as those over age 60, that figure is expected to increase to 58 per cent by the year 2025.[4] At the same time, rapid economic development in many countries of the region, up to the Asian financial crisis starting in 1997, was drawing more of the labour force out of self-employment – particularly in agriculture – and into wage employment, thereby subjecting an increasing proportion of Asia's labour force to mandatory retirement practices.

499

The financial crisis, which started in Thailand in mid-1997 and subsequently spread to most of the economies of East and South-East Asia, revealed serious weaknesses in the systems of financial regulation in these countries. Volatility in currency and capital markets was far greater than appeared to be justified by economic fundamentals. In order to restore economic stability, restrictive fiscal measures were implemented which sharply reduced output growth and employment in the short term. In the future these economies are not likely to return to the rapid growth rates they achieved in the mid-1990s.

Open unemployment in most Asian economies has tended, until recently, to be low, in part owing to favourable economic trends, and partly because the lack of unemployment benefits has discouraged the unemployed from registering as such and encouraged them to make do with temporary or part-time work, or to resort to informal sector activities. The increase in open unemployment, resulting from the financial crisis in East Asia, has significant implications for workers' long-term economic security. For many, especially in countries like the Republic of Korea, the crisis spells the end of what they thought was lifetime employment. Those affected are unable to continue saving for their old age or to build up long-term benefit entitlements. Indeed many are being obliged to consume all or part of their savings and, in certain countries, to make withdrawals from statutory or non-statutory provident funds in order to help them weather the crisis.

Even where savings are not being spent, their value has in many cases been drastically reduced by steep falls in the prices of financial assets, particularly equities, and by currency devaluation and inflation. These developments have hit not only personal savings, but also the investments of company provident funds in countries such as Thailand, where tax breaks have encouraged the growth of such funds. National provident funds have not entirely escaped, but the restrictions placed on their investment policies mean that most of them have only had limited exposure to the decline in equities' markets.

OVERVIEW OF SOCIAL SECURITY SYSTEMS

Social security in the Asia and Pacific region varies considerably in scope and coverage, but generally it tends to be less developed than in other parts of the world with comparable levels of economic development. For old age, invalidity and survivors in many countries only have provident funds paying lump-sum benefits. Social health insurance schemes often leave much of the cost of treatment to be covered by the patient and sometimes exclude family dependants of the insured worker. In numerous countries employment injury is still employers' liability, which means that accident victims often find it difficult, or even impossible, to obtain their full entitlements, given the adversarial nature of this system and their typically weak bargaining position. Sickness and maternity benefits tend to be minimal and are frequently employers' liability rather than being covered by a social insurance scheme, which tends to make life more difficult for workers with health problems and women of child-bearing age. Unemployment benefits exist in few countries of the region, though severance pay entitlements (again employers' liability) may be substantial for those with long employment in a particular enterprise. Family allowances rarely form part of national social security provisions, though employees of the state and larger companies sometimes receive them.

The region is characterized by diversity in the systems used to provide people with pensions or other benefits when they reach old age, or when their income is interrupted owing to invalidity or death of the primary wage earner. This diversity in part reflects the fact that Asian countries are at greatly different stages of economic development. Social, cultural and political factors have also played an important role.

One striking feature of the region is the large number of countries with no mandatory retirement pension scheme. Most of these countries are former British colonies and the main reason they do not have a retirement pension scheme is that they have provident funds, usually with mandatory coverage of employees in the private sector. A provident fund does not fulfil the same function, as it does not provide a replacement income for the length of retirement. Once a provident fund is in place, experience has shown that it is difficult to replace it with a pension scheme.

In many Asian countries with provident funds catering to private sector employees, the majority of pensioners are former public servants or their dependants. The public service is commonly viewed as privileged in this respect. It must be borne in mind, however, that pensions are just one component of an overall remuneration package; certain other elements, in particular the salary, are often less generous than in the private sector. Public service pensions are calculated on the basis of these salaries and thus may be correspondingly low. Public sector pensions also have their own special characteristics; for example, in some, employees who do not remain in the public service until retirement may lose all entitlement to a pension.

Countries in the region less exposed to British influence have for the most part set up social security pension schemes to cover employees and sometimes also the self-employed. These include countries as diverse as the Republic of Korea, the Philippines and Viet Nam. Pakistan, despite its strong British connections, opted for a social security defined benefit pension scheme in the 1970s. India has also recently established a social insurance defined benefit pension scheme, though this did not happen until half a century after the end of British rule and the design of the new scheme is heavily marked by its provident fund origins.

Not only do retirement pension schemes differ widely between countries in the region, but within the largest country, China, in the last decade wide differences in pension schemes have developed between the various provinces and cities, although the national authorities have recently recognized the need for a return to a unified national system (see box RB1.1). The existing differences

Box RB1.1 China

For more than 30 years, China has had a social security retirement pension scheme for its urban working population with a scope similar to that provided by OECD countries. Following the general economic reform in the 1980s, however, it was no longer able to provide the target population with adequate and effective protection as it successfully did in the central planning era.

The reform initially started from a few selected localities in 1984 and was then quickly expanded to the rest of the country. To provide guidelines for the pension reform, the State Council approved basic principles, which included ultimately universal coverage by the basic public pension provision, cost sharing between the state, employers and workers and a three-tier pension scheme – the compulsory basic pension tier combining a social insurance element and a funded individual account.

Recent policy development

Extending personal coverage. State sector workers, who were the target group of the retirement pension scheme, constituted more than 90 per cent of the urban workforce in the central planning era. The number of non-state sector employees has increased significantly as economic reform and rural immigration have greatly changed the composition of the urban population and economy, and the need for protecting those workers and their families not yet covered is essential.

The new Labour Law of 1994 stipulated that coverage should eventually be extended to all salaried workers regardless of the nature of their employment or ownership of the enterprise. Accordingly, the Ministry of Labour, in May 1995, launched a four-year national campaign for the extension of coverage to uninsured urban workers and envisaged achieving its goal by 1999. Decree 26 (1997) on setting up a unified basic old-age insurance for urban workers, issued by the State Council on 16 July 1997, requires that coverage should be gradually expanded to all enterprises and their workers, as well as the self-employed.

Broadly, problems are associated with covering three main categories of employees: those of the state sector, the non-state sector and the rest of the population. Within the state sector, hundreds of thousands of previously covered workers and retirees have been deprived of the entitlement to protection owing to the unwillingness, or the lack of financial capacity, of their enterprises to continue making financial contributions to the schemes. This problem is particularly grave in some old industrial enterprises that are important in some local economies, and it is believed that redundant workers, amounting to an estimated 15–20 million in 1997, and retirees are the most vulnerable people in this situation.

As far as state sector workers are concerned, a number of policy questions have to be answered:

- How should the following conflicting realities be reconciled? For political reasons, pension funds must continue to pay benefits to current retirees of enterprises who have stopped contributing to the funds as a result of financial difficulties or other problems. Yet because of financial reasons, and in the long term, the funds cannot afford to do this.

- Should state sector workers be covered uniformly by the same scheme or separately because of their different employment, economic and demographic natures?
- Should there be a national programme or local ones?
- Do the current pension agencies have the required operational capacity in terms of both human resources and infrastructure?

The situation for the rest of the population varies. Workers in township and village enterprises merit being considered first, not only because of the size of this workforce – accounting for 128 million employees in 1995 – but also because their circumstances are similar to those of the private sector. Therefore the same policies should also apply to this group of workers. Much closer coordination between related government departments, however, is vital. The second large group is that of the 80–100 million rural immigrant workers looking for jobs in cities. Because of their high mobility and frequent changes in employment, the difficulty in covering them with a social security scheme is considerable. Finally the extension of coverage to the vast rural population would be the most difficult task and is not likely to be a short-term objective for the government.

Governance
At the strategic or macro-policy level. After years of discussion and consultation among all parties involved, a broad national pension strategy was finally formulated. Since its legal framework is based on a law of the 1950s, an effort has been made to reformulate a Social Insurance Law and Old-Age Pension Bill; but there is a lack of an efficient and effective mechanism for policy coordination and coherence at the macro level. As far as the role of employees and employers is concerned, trade unions are usually active in the policy-making process while employers' organizations are traditionally absent.

At the institution level. Operational agencies were set up and separated from the government's policy-making function in the mid-1990s. Their autonomy, however, is limited as their pension boards are usually dominated by representatives of government, and chief executives are therefore normally appointed directly by the government.

At the operation level. The registration of enterprises and their established employees in the state sector is generally accurate and on time, but some difficulties are encountered with small enterprises in the private sector and workers with temporary status. Computerization has greatly improved the quality of record-keeping, information exchange, analysis and dissemination at the national level. With the computerization and cooperation of the banking system, the processing of benefit claims and benefit delivery has been improved. Most enterprises respect the law and fulfil their duties with respect to paying contributions. Despite the existence of an appeals mechanism, individuals rarely use it.

Design of the pension model
The basic social security retirement pension formula introduced in June 1997 has two components: a universal flat-rate part and an individual account. The

former is fixed at 20 per cent of current regional average income and is payable to each insured person at the time of retirement, provided prescribed conditions are met. The amount of monthly benefit financed by the second tier is equal to the overall balance cumulated by the time of retirement in the individual account divided by 120. A global pension equal to around 58 per cent of the previous income is expected to be obtained by an insured person satisfying the prescribed contributory period. Once the benefit level is determined, it is paid periodically until death, irrespective of the financial status of the individual account. Nevertheless the family can inherit a part of the balance, if any, left on the insured person's personal account at the time of his or her death.

Regarding contributions, 11 per cent of payroll is earmarked for the individual's account. From this, 3 per cent is paid by workers at the beginning and is then progressively increased to 8 per cent. The difference is covered by part of the employer's contributions, which mostly go to the solidarity pooling funds to take care of the flat-rate benefit component, the continuing payment of the second component once the individual account is exhausted and towards benefits for the current generation of retirees.

are not mere details; in fact they amount to radically different approaches, with some places having established mandatory defined contribution savings schemes, while others have schemes which are defined benefit based on social insurance.

EXISTING PENSION ARRANGEMENTS

Restricted coverage

The most obvious feature of social security retirement pensions in Asia and the Pacific is the incomplete coverage of the schemes in most countries, the principal exceptions being Australia, Japan and New Zealand, which are discussed in the brief on OECD countries. Contributory schemes in the region usually exclude the self-employed and often also exclude many employees, for example those in enterprises with fewer than ten workers, or those with earnings above a specified maximum. Numerous countries are reviewing the coverage of their schemes. Expanding coverage is widely regarded as a high priority, since the employees in small enterprises who are most often excluded tend, also, to have low earnings and little with which to support themselves in old age. There are difficult administrative problems involved in extending coverage to small enterprises, but the exclusion of such enterprises is in itself a source of considerable problems, as it is notoriously difficult for social security institutions to ascertain the precise number of employees in an enterprise. Useful experience has been gained by certain countries in the region which have extended their schemes to cover employees regardless of the size of the enterprise, for example Malaysia.

Extension of social security pension coverage to self-employed workers is probably the greatest challenge facing social security schemes in the region. The Republic of Korea took this step in 1995 by obliging farmers, fishermen and rural self-employed to contribute 3 per cent of earnings, a rate which is to be increased by 3 per cent every five years until it reaches 9 per cent. The government is subsidizing the administration of the scheme for the self-employed and the cost of providing protection for lower-income farmers and fishermen. Most self-employed persons are subject to compulsory coverage in the Philippines. Many other countries offer voluntary coverage to the self-employed, but in most cases the numbers who choose to contribute are minimal. Even where coverage is in principle compulsory, many self-employed persons evade the payment of contributions.

In Viet Nam certain groups have, with the guidance of the government, established pension schemes to provide income support to their members on retirement. These include both urban informal sector workers who are members of cooperative associations, and rural workers, in particular farmers who are members of the Viet Nam Farmers' Union. In the case of the latter, there are several well-established pension schemes in which annual contributions to the value of 80 kg. of rice are paid over 20 years, which gives a person a pension entitlement of approximately 6 kg. of rice per month.

Absence of periodical benefits

Lump-sum benefits do not provide social protection against the risk of outliving one's income. The need for periodical benefits is increasingly acknowledged among the countries which have national provident funds, such as Fiji, India, Malaysia and Singapore. The Fiji National Provident Fund offers its members a choice between the traditional lump-sum benefit and a pension for life. Members are encouraged to take the pension, as the annuity factors used to convert individual balances into pensions are extremely generous: 25 per cent for single-life pensions and 16.7 per cent for joint-life pensions. These are to be compared with the actuarial annuity factors which have been calculated as 10 per cent and 8 per cent, respectively. In spite of this enormous incentive to opt for a pension, most members continue to take the lump sum. Only about 10 per cent of balances are converted into pensions.

The experience of Fiji suggests that, when individuals are allowed to choose between a lump sum and a periodical benefit, there is a strong tendency to opt for the former, even if it is highly disadvantageous to do so. This is no doubt the result in many cases of shortsightedness and irrationality. Only in specific circumstances could such behaviour be regarded as rational (for example, if the Fund was likely to go bankrupt or to pay a rate of interest well below the rate of inflation, if the individual was in urgent need of capital not otherwise available, or if social assistance benefits were provided for people not receiving a pension). The result of granting beneficiaries freedom of choice is doubly undesirable from a social point of view. On the one hand, most people (including the poorly educated) deprive themselves of any regular income in retirement; on the other hand, the minority of members (probably more highly educated and better off) who do opt for a pension are heavily subsidized by the others (because of the generous annuity factors used).

Other countries have recognized that an element of compulsion is necessary. In Singapore, it was decided that members of the Central Provident Fund must set aside a minimum sum in their retirement account at age 55 to finance a regular monthly benefit. Until 1995 members could satisfy the minimum sum requirement by pledging their property. However by July 2002 at least half of the minimum sum requirement will have to consist of cash in the member's retirement account.

A more satisfactory solution requires fundamental reform. In recent years the main example of such a reform is to be found in India. Details of the new Indian pension scheme for employees are given in box RB1.2.

MAJOR DEVELOPMENTS AND REFORM INITIATIVES

Pension reform measures in Asia and the Pacific fall into three categories. There are reforms of existing national provident funds, entailing the introduction of pension benefits, as in India. There are reforms of existing pension schemes, notably in the economies in transition and in the more highly developed countries, such as Japan.[5] Finally some countries, such as Thailand, which have hitherto had no social security retirement pension scheme, are establishing a national pension scheme for employees.

From provident fund to pension scheme

In 1995 India partially converted its Employee Provident Fund into a defined benefit social security retirement pension scheme. Only the employers' contribution is used to finance the pension, which is a percentage of covered earnings in the final year of employment (50 per cent for those with 33 years of insured employment, rising to a maximum of 60 per cent for those with more years of service). This scheme has the potential to provide significant income protection for retired employees and, thanks to transitional provisions, is already paying pensions to a certain number. The workers' own contributions continue to be paid into individual savings accounts.

However the new Indian pension scheme betrays its provident fund origins in a number of ways which undermine the social protection it offers in retirement. For instance:

- retirees are given the option to commute one-third of their pension entitlement to a lump sum (in spite of the fact that they already have access to the balance in their provident fund account, to which their own contributions continue to be paid);

Box RB1.2 India

The Indian Constitution stipulates that "The State shall within the limits of its economic capacity and development, make effective provision for securing the right to public assistance in case of unemployment, old age, sickness, disablement and other cases of undeserved wants." (Article 41). The first schemes established to provide social security benefits in India were provident funds. The Employees' Provident Fund, which is by far the largest in India, was introduced in 1952 to cover the workers in the organized sector. It provides lumpsum benefits for people who are retired or have been out of covered employment for a certain period. Advances for life insurance policies, house building, medical treatment, marriage and higher education are also provided.

Over the years steps were taken to provide better income-maintenance protection in case of retirement, death and invalidity. Starting in 1971, part of the provident fund contributions was used to provide monthly pensions to surviving dependants. The Employees' Pension Scheme was introduced in 1995. It provides earnings-related pensions on a defined benefit basis in respect of retirement, invalidity and, in the case of death, to surviving dependants. Approximately 50 per cent of total contributions paid to the Employees' Provident Fund are now used to finance the new Employees' Pension Scheme.

The basic objectives of the provident fund were undermined by the various types of intermediate withdrawals available to members. The establishment of the pension scheme is a significant development in this regard, since protection in old age is now ensured by a pension and no longer depends on the balance remaining in the member's provident fund account.

The organization responsible for administering the Employees' Provident Fund and the Employees' Pension Scheme functions under the overall superintendence of the policies framed by the central board of trustees, made up of representatives of central and state governments, employers and workers under the chairmanship of the Minister of Labour. The organization is also responsible for the supervision of the provident funds of exempted enterprises. Exemption from coverage under the provident fund may be granted to employers who have established trust funds that provide at least equivalent benefits. A minority of covered workers participate in private contracted-out schemes rather than the Employees' Provident Fund (24 per cent of workers and 1 per cent of enterprises in 1996).

The ILO estimates that out of a labour force of 375 million workers in the early 1990s, 10 per cent were covered by formal sector social security schemes (ILO, 1997b). Out of the remaining 335 million, perhaps 50 million were in regular wage employment, but the vast majority were either self-employed or casual labourers. Only a tiny minority of those workers benefit from alternative forms of social security protection, such as welfare funds or social assistance.

Action could be taken to extend the application of the Employees' Provident Fund and the Employees' Pension Scheme to a larger number of regular workers, some self-employed and some categories of casual and contract labour. It would require concrete measures, such as amending the provisions that exclude from coverage workers employed by small enterprises, workers earning a salary above the ceiling, or workers employed by enterprises not falling within the list of covered industries.

Providing social security for a significantly larger proportion of the Indian population would also require more comprehensive measures that should become part of a national social security policy. An ILO report concluded that key issues in this national policy should address the following:

- the structure, financing and administration of social security schemes for the formal sector;
- the extent to which existing formal sector schemes can be applied to other sectors of the labour force;
- the scope for the development of area or occupation-based schemes for workers in the informal sector through non-governmental organizations;
- the establishment of a national uniform package of assistance for the absolute poor.

- retirees are also offered the option to receive a pension for a fixed period of 20 years, with a so-called return of capital bonus (100 times the original pension) being paid at the end of this period. This is a tempting option for those who think they may die within 20 years and who wish to leave the balance of the pension plus the bonus to their heirs; but it will leave an increasing number of old pensioners destitute, as with the rise in life expectancy more survive beyond their allotted 20 years;

- at any time during their first ten years of coverage, insured employees may leave their job, then apply for a withdrawal benefit; if and when they resume employment, their accumulation of pension entitlements will have to start again from zero. Nothing in the law prevents the improvident from doing this repeatedly and thereby reaching old age with few or no pension entitlements, though such behaviour may be discouraged by the fear of not finding another job;

- the potential of the scheme to ensure an adequate income in old age is also undermined by an early retirement provision which allows anyone with 20 years' service to draw a pension at age 50: the income replacement rate would then be as low as 24 per cent, compared with approximately 43 per cent for those continuing in employment until the standard pensionable age of 58. The risk that early retirement will lead to poverty is compounded by the scheme providing no guaranteed indexation of pensions in payment.

While there is room for improvement, the 1995 reform constitutes a considerable step forward in terms of retirement income security. The fact that a number of compromises had to be made is testimony to the political difficulties involved in moving from a provident fund to a pension scheme. Many workers are not only eager to get the money as soon as possible, they are also suspicious of the intentions of governments proposing such reforms, and believe that they are better able to manage their savings than a pension fund. Overcoming these attitudes is not easy. The Indian reform was successfully carried to completion thanks to the support it received from knowledgeable workers' representatives in whom the majority of workers placed their trust.

Other countries, such as Malaysia, have been studying the adequacy of existing provisions and the feasibility of providing a lifetime pension. A survey conducted for the Employees' Provident Fund in 1995 showed that its lump-sum retirement benefits were found by the majority of retirees to be inadequate to sustain life after retirement. In most cases the benefits were exhausted within three years of receipt at age 55. The Fund already offers its members the option of taking a phased withdrawal of the balance from age 55 for a term of five, ten, 15 or 20 years, subject to a minimum balance and a minimum payment per month. It was reported in 1996 that in the previous year, fewer than 120 people had opted for a phased withdrawal. In the light of experience elsewhere (for example, Fiji and Indonesia, which introduced a withdrawal option in 1993), the failure of this option to attract much interest in comparison to lump-sum benefits is not surprising. Other possibilities, such as a social insurance defined benefit pension, are now being considered.

Reforms of existing pension schemes

A number of countries in the Asia and Pacific region are undergoing a process of profound structural change, in particular those engaged in the transition to a market economy. Pension reform in these countries is closely tied to the broader issue of economic reform.

The civil service and state-owned enterprises have accounted for a high proportion of total formal employment in countries such as China,[6] the Lao People's Democratic Republic and Viet Nam, but in all these countries economic policy is aiming to trim the civil service, to reduce the role of state-owned enterprises, and in particular to come to grips with the problem of the large number of such enterprises which are making a loss.

Extending pension coverage to private sector employment

In the past generally only workers in the public sector have enjoyed pension scheme coverage. If coverage is not extended to the private sector, workers may be less willing to move out of the public sector, particularly as this could mean losing past service entitlements. It is therefore important to establish pension insurance for private sector employees, and also to have provisions to protect past-service entitlements of employees leaving the public sector.

The government of the Lao People's Democratic Republic has identified the extension of social security to private sector employees as a top priority. In China the Ministry of Labour has recognized that about 30 million workers, or 25 per cent of all urban employees, are not yet protected by the pensions' pooling schemes[7], now redefined as two-tier schemes: social pooling and individual account. Those excluded are mainly workers in private companies, foreign companies and joint ventures. In 1995 the Ministry launched a national campaign aiming to expand coverage to employees in all types of urban enterprises, as well as to the self-employed. However, for township and village enterprises, which had 128 million employees in 1995, status remains ambiguous, and a large number of migrant rural labourers coming to work in urban areas continue to be excluded from coverage.

Viet Nam extended compulsory social security retirement pension coverage to the private sector in 1993, but compliance appears to be extremely low. It was estimated that the total number of employees covered in 1995 should have been about 5 million, but actual coverage was only about 3 million, which was barely the number employed in the state-owned enterprises alone.

The problem of the pension liabilities of state-owned enterprises

In certain socialist countries state-owned enterprises were individually liable to provide benefits for their present and former employees. This type of arrangement is inconsistent with the needs of a market economy, since in practice it makes it virtually impossible, in social and political terms, to allow loss-making state-owned enterprises to go bankrupt. It is therefore vital to relieve enterprises of these financial liabilities through a social insurance, or risk-pooling, mechanism.

China is particularly interesting in this respect. From the early 1950s until the Cultural Revolution in 1966, a national social insurance defined benefit retirement pension scheme was operated by the All-China Federation of Trade Unions (ACFTU) covering workers in urban enterprises. All enterprises paid a uniform rate of contribution (3 per cent of the total wage bill). Part of this contribution (70 per cent) was retained within the enterprise to pay benefits (in accordance with national legislation) while the remaining 30 per cent was paid to the ACFTU. Any enterprise which had to pay more in benefits than the amount of its contributions received a compensatory payment from the local trade union, while those with a surplus of contributions over benefits paid this to the union. The ACFTU in turn covered the deficits and collected the surpluses of local unions. Thus, as in most other countries, the financial liability for providing benefits is not with the enterprise itself, but with the social security scheme.

In 1966 the Cultural Revolution commenced, leading to almost total economic collapse. In 1969 the Ministry of Finance issued a paper entitled Views on the reform of some financial schemes in state-owned enterprises. This stipulated that all state-owned enterprises should stop drawing on trade union social insurance funds. As a result the financial burden of providing benefits was transferred from a national system to the individual enterprises. Older enterprises, with a high proportion of pensioners, were placed at a great disadvantage while newly established enterprises could afford generous welfare benefits.[8]

From 1984 pension pooling arrangements started to be introduced at the county level in order to ease the burden on individual enterprises. By 1996 virtually all of them – as well as large or medium-size collective enterprises – were covered by a pooling scheme (in 1995 there were 2,849 such schemes at the county, city or district level).[9] The government has recognized that a higher level of pension pooling is necessary in order to facilitate labour mobility, and to compensate for widely diverging contribution rates in different localities.

Pensions for workers in state-owned enterprises are also a major issue in the Lao People's Democratic Republic, although the problem there has been different from that in China. In the past employees of these enterprises were covered by the civil service pension scheme. A reform adopted in 1993, however, excluded them from that scheme. Many state-owned enterprises have been privatized in the Lao People's Democratic Republic: the number of state-owned enterprises was reduced from about 600 in the late 1980s to 90 in 1996. There are now no clear guidelines concerning the pension rights of the employees in the remaining enterprises and the actions being taken by individual enterprises vary considerably. It has been reported that some retired employees are being paid pensions by the ministries formerly responsible: for example, Lao Beer pensioners are getting pensions from the Ministry of Industry. Some state-owned enterprises are paying their pensioners out of their salary budget and are concerned about the future cost of doing so. Some are still collecting from their employees the 6 per cent contribution payable by civil servants, while others are not.[10]

Thus, in the case of the Lao People's Democratic Republic, at least some of the state-owned enterprises which remain in existence have had to assume the liability for paying pensions from their own funds. In other cases employees have lost their pension entitlements as a result of being excluded from the civil service pension scheme (which has been in operation since 1986). The real difficulty is that the Lao People's Democratic Republic does not yet possess any social security pension scheme for employees in the private sector. The ideal solution would be for such a scheme to also cover the employees of state-owned enterprises, as this would allow labour mobility to take place without loss of pension rights and place the state-owned enterprises on an equal footing with private employers. How to finance past service entitlements will require special consideration, but this is less of a problem than in other countries, as in the Lao People's Democratic Republic the scheme has been in existence for just over ten years.

The cost of honouring past-service pension entitlements is difficult for the economies in transition. Until recently the only workers with pension entitlements were those employed in the public sector. Now, for example in China and Viet Nam, pension coverage has been, or is being, extended to cover employees in the expanding private sector. At present most pensioners are former public sector employees, while in the years to come an increasingly large percentage of contributors – ultimately perhaps the majority – will be working in the private sector. How should the pensions of the former be financed, given that all these countries have been operating on a pay-as-you-go basis?

If there were to be a single social insurance scheme covering employees in state-owned enterprises and in private enterprises, the changing structure of employment need not cause any problem. The current contributions of all active workers could be used to pay current pensions. From an equity viewpoint, this approach has much to recommend it, for financing past pension commitments from current pension contributions places the burden on those who will in due course receive pensions themselves.

When state-owned enterprises and the expanding private sector are covered by separate schemes it is inevitable that the former will have an increasingly large deficit. As this deficit ultimately could not be financed by the enterprises themselves, there would be little choice but to subsidize the scheme from general government revenue. This option spreads the cost of honouring past entitlements among all taxpayers, many of whom may themselves not be covered by any pension scheme. In Viet Nam, although both sectors come under the same scheme, the state has assumed financial responsibility for pre-1995 pension entitlements and is currently subsidizing about 90 per cent of total pension expenditure.

It is unclear how China will resolve this issue. The government anticipates overcoming it ultimately by extending coverage to non-public sectors, such as joint-venture and private enterprises. The Ministry of Labour and the State Council for Restructuring the Economic System, however, have agreed that the national pension scheme should include a substantial individual savings component (to which 11 per cent of earnings, or more than half of the total pension contribution, would be directed). This would point more towards the solution based on government subsidies, as the residual contribution going to the pooling mechanism is unlikely to generate sufficient revenue to cover existing liabilities. It seems probable that the burden of past entitlements will be shared between current contributors and taxpayers. There is also a risk that the entitlements themselves may be eroded, for example through continued lack of full indexation of pensions in payment.

Implications of structural change for the administration of pensions

In the past state-owned enterprises were responsible for performing most of the administrative tasks connected with retirement pension schemes, even where they have not had to assume direct financial liability. As these were usually large enterprises, they had personnel departments with specialized staff who could do the work satisfactorily; and as they had soft budget constraints, the administrative costs were not perceived as a problem. Consequently the administrative role of the social security agency (Ministry or trade union) was relatively minor. With the transition to a market economy, this inevitably must change.

Private employers are neither willing nor even perhaps able to do all the administrative work which state-owned enterprises have done, particularly as most private enterprises are small and may not have a personnel department as such. The state-owned enterprises themselves must now operate with tighter budgets, so they are having to examine more carefully their administrative costs and concentrate far more than in the past on their core activities.

For financial reasons it is also important that retirement pension scheme administration be performed, or at least closely supervised, by the social security agency itself. Employers cannot be relied upon to administer social security mandatory contributions and benefits with the same financial rigour as a social security agency does. Indeed they have a strong incentive to underpay contributions and may connive with their employees to overclaim benefits. This could have happened to some extent in the past, but the ethos then was different and the absence of hard budget constraints meant that there was far less incentive to cheat the system. The social security system itself is now increasingly unable to rely on open-ended subsidies from the state, so it is under more pressure to collect the contributions which are due and to exercise strict control over the disbursement of benefits. All this points to the need for centralized record-keeping, which generally means a national social security database maintained by the social security institution. It will ultimately spell the end of record-keeping through "work books" or individual paper records kept by employers and they will be replaced by a computerized database operated by the social security agency. This means substantial investment in computer systems, but these will reduce running costs and improve financial control.

Establishment of new pension schemes

A small number of countries, which until now have had pension schemes only for government employees and no compulsory retirement benefit schemes for employees in the private sector, are now either establishing or envisaging the establishment of a new national pension scheme.

One of these countries is Thailand, which decided in 1990, with the adoption of its Social Security Act, to introduce a social insurance defined benefit pension scheme financed by contributions set at 3 per cent of covered earnings, payable by workers, employers and the government. The launch of the pension scheme was originally scheduled for 1996, but the legislation was amended in 1994 to postpone implementation until 1998.

Details of the pension scheme are not spelled out in legislation, but will be the subject of a royal decree. The coverage of the scheme will be the same as that of the existing social security scheme, which currently applies to enterprises with ten or more workers (and is to be extended to enterprises with five or more workers). The existing scheme, which is primarily a social health insurance scheme, also provides invalidity benefits, set at 50 per cent of previous earnings and payable for life. So the addition of a pension scheme to cover the other long-term contingencies is a logical next step in Thailand's development of a social security system.

As a result of demographic, social and economic changes, the need for income support in old age will increase enormously in Asia and the Pacific in the coming decades. Neither help from sons and daughters nor public assistance or private charity is equal to the task of providing income support on such a vast scale. Furthermore today's working generation in Asian countries aspires to a degree of financial independence in old age, an aspiration which can be satisfied only by acquiring pension entitlements during the active years. It is therefore urgent to establish adequate retirement pension schemes covering the majority of working people in the countries of the region.

Existing schemes often exclude those people most needing protection. Governments should therefore make it a priority to extend them to all employees, regardless of the size of the enterprise and, wherever feasible, to the self-employed. Meaningful social protection requires periodic benefits paid throughout retirement. It also requires minimum guarantees regarding the level of those benefits.

Where appropriate, pension schemes must adapt to structural change. In particular, state-owned enterprises should be relieved of pension liabilities, social security pension coverage should be extended to the emerging private sector and administrative responsibility for social security should be transferred from enterprises to suitably equipped social security institutions.

Notes

[1] Australia, Japan and New Zealand and are discussed in Regional Brief 6, on the OECD region.

[2] Schulz (1997, p. 26).

[3] Source: ILO Bureau of Labour Statistics. The figure for Thailand is for 1996.

[4] Schulz (1997, p. 7).

[5] For more details, see Regional Brief 6, on OECD countries.

[6] About one third of the workers covered by formal sector social security schemes work for the central, state and local governments.

[7] Twenty-one years after the beginning of economic reform, this portion is declining to less than 60 per cent of urban employment.

[8] Hu (1997).

[9] Wenruo (1997).

[10] Hu (1997).

AFRICA

In pre-colonial Africa, social protection for the poor or those unable to support themselves was a matter principally for the extended family although, within the community, charitable or religious organizations also played an important role. During the colonial period, new systems of organized social protection emerged to support economic development. Initially the colonial powers extended their own social security systems to their expatriates. The extension of such provisions to African workers varied but where it was effected it was concentrated on urban and industrial workers mainly to stabilize the workforce or to appease the trade unions that had been mobilized to combat injustices. However the majority of the population remained without coverage under a social security scheme.

Against this background, several distinct patterns of social protection developed in Africa which, to a great extent, reflect different colonial traditions. In North Africa, where the proximity to Europe was a major factor, are to be found the oldest and most comprehensive schemes, with pension schemes based on social insurance principles operating in Algeria, Egypt, Libyan Arab Jamahiriya, Morocco and Tunisia since the 1950s. The social security scheme in Egypt has developed to cover virtually all of the labour force and provides a wide range of benefits mostly on a social insurance basis through earnings-related contributions by employers and workers but with special provisions for casual workers. In the French colonies of sub-Saharan Africa, priority was given to the establishment of employment injury schemes. The pattern of development throughout the former French colonies in French West Africa and French Equatorial Africa tended to be standardized and family benefit and maternity benefit schemes were introduced in the early 1950s. A voluntary scheme – the West African Retirement Pensions Fund (IPRAO) – was established in a number of Francophone West African countries but compulsory pension schemes were not introduced until after independence, between 1960 and 1965. Given their common heritage and their close collaboration before and after independence many of the countries in Francophone Africa have similar schemes with pension provisions based on social insurance principles which provide a defined benefit determined by reference to length of service and average earnings.

In the former British colonies priority was also accorded to employment injury schemes but here the development of social insurance has been slower. The workers' compensation schemes were generally based on employer liability principles (Ghana, Nigeria, Kenya, United Republic of Tanzania, Swaziland) and only later were schemes developed which established a public institution and required the payment of contributions by employers to an employment injury fund (Zambia, Zimbabwe). The social security schemes were also generally more modest than those in Francophone Africa, and except in the case of provisions for public servants, did not tend to correspond to systems established in the United Kingdom. It was generally considered appropriate to restrict the introduction of pension schemes to permanent public servants, and a growing recognition of the need to provide some form of social protection to other workers in the organized sector led to the establishment of national provident funds in many former British colonies before and after independence. These covered non-pensionable public servants and the private sector. They were seen as simple to operate and provided a lump sum on retirement which would assist the worker on his anticipated return to his village. Some countries, such as Sierra Leone, did not establish either a pension scheme or a provident fund for private sector workers and, particularly in southern Africa (Botswana, Lesotho, Malawi and Zimbabwe), this development was considerably delayed; there was instead a greater reliance on occupational pension schemes and private pension funds. Unlike in the former French colonies, family benefits have not been introduced in English-speaking Africa.

The five former Portuguese colonies entered independence with only basic social security provisions and in the case of Angola and Mozambique the commitment to schemes based on social insurance principles has been inhibited by the consequences of civil wars. Internal and external conflict has had a serious effect on the development and operation of schemes in many countries, such as Ethiopia, Eritrea and Somalia (where there is no social protection for private sector workers in respect of income maintenance on retirement), and Liberia, the Republic of Congo and the Democratic Republic of the Congo, where schemes have been totally or substantially destroyed.

Finally three countries have chosen to introduce a pension scheme which places a greater emphasis on universality. Entitlement to a basic pension in South Africa is subject to a means test and the pensions are financed from taxation. For many workers this is replaced by an occupational pension, provided by their employers. Apart from the Workmen's Compensation scheme, which is financed by contributions from employers, pension benefits in South Africa are not financed in accordance with social insurance principles. The scheme in Mauritius combines elements of universality and social insurance with a basic pension paid to all residents without any means test and supplemented by earnings-related contributions paid by employers and workers. A similar scheme operates in Seychelles.

In general, and with certain exceptions, the coverage and effectiveness of existing social protection schemes relating to the contingencies of retirement, invalidity and death in Africa are weak. This is attributable to a number of factors, some political and economic and some which reflect failures in govern-ance at all levels, from the design of schemes to their operation. The schemes introduced by the colonial countries often took insufficient account of the socio-cultural context and thus proved limited and inappropriate. Since independence this has been compounded by adverse economic and political circumstances as well as by mismanagement, and many African schemes have failed to provide effective social protection even for the small minority of the population that they cover. There are, however, some encouraging signs that these issues are being addressed and some important developments have taken place in Africa in recent years.

SOCIAL PROTECTION AND ECONOMIC DEVELOPMENT IN AFRICA

As of 1997, 25 of the 35 countries in the world regarded as having a low level of human development are in Africa (UNDP, 1997). Within the continent, of the ten countries with the highest level of human development, five are in north Africa (Libyan A.J., Tunisia, Algeria, Egypt and Morocco) and five are in south-ern Africa (Botswana, Mauritius, Seychelles, South Africa and Swaziland).

Since 1986, in sub-Saharan Africa, per capita incomes have fallen by an average of 7 per cent annually. The decline in exports which led to the fall in tax revenues accentuated budget deficits. To balance the budget, countries resorted to borrowing which in turn increased the debt burden and the cost of servicing it. For countries in the CFA franc zone, there was a major currency devaluation in 1994. It had been expected that this would encourage growth: it led to growth, but it did not create jobs. There was even a fall in employment as a result of budgetary constraints. Public investment declined and there was a negative effect on jobs in both the public and private sectors. Domestic com-panies, generally importers of goods, were heavily affected. The first effect of privatization programmes, beneficial in the long run, was to reduce the labour force. In some cases, especially in the public sector, salaries were frozen or did not rise with prices. The reduction in domestic consumption led to the threat of business closures. Workers left the social protection system and thus lost the right to social security benefits. The phenomenon of exclusion was accentuated. For a large part of the population, these difficulties were exacerbated by a loss or reduction in income.

In less than a generation, the social and economic barriers in employment have changed. At the end of the 1970s it was generally believed that the formal sector would continue to employ a major and probably growing share of the active population. Thus only limited attention was paid to the relatively small number of people who had taken refuge in the informal sector. But three factors proved crucial. First, there was an explosion in demographic growth that every year produced large numbers of school-leavers seeking work. Second, a serious economic crisis reduced the absorptive capacity of the formal sector. Third, the pressure of the rural exodus forced many people to migrate to the towns to seek casual work. Thus the active population rose to more than 40 per cent in all countries, growing at a rate of 4.5 per cent per year, that is, slightly higher than the rate of population growth. The proportion of young people, especially first-time job-seekers, continues to rise. For the latter, the supply and demand ratio for employment is less than 7 per cent. The vast majority head for the informal sector. Data for the active population and the salaried population show that, at the current rate of growth, the ratio of employment of salaried workers could be no more than 2 or 3 per cent in the next 25 years. As this section of the population is the only one covered by the organized social security system, the viability of the system can be expected to deteriorate. This trend, which is applicable to most developing countries, is particularly marked in Africa, where societies are essentially rural, urbanization is fairly recent and the percentage of poor is high.

In sub-Saharan Africa nearly 75 per cent of the labour force (314 million people) still work outside the formal economy, often in subsistence agriculture or in low-income informal activities such as small-scale manufacturing and petty trading (ILO, 1997k). Open unemployment rates in urban areas doubled over the last 15 years to over 20 per cent and are expected to approach 30 per cent by the end of the century: on average 8.7 million new entrants to the labour market each year seek employment. These factors have obvious implications for poverty levels: 50 per cent of Africans are poor and more than 30 per cent of these live below the absolute poverty line. Despite the rise in GDP in some countries, per capita income has stayed the same or even fallen by as much as 30 or 40 per cent. Table RB2.1 illustrates the distribution of different categories of economically active persons in some French-speaking African countries.

Life expectancy at birth has improved by an average of four years every decade. Life expectancy at a retirement age of 55 was about 17 years in 1960; it rose to 19 years by 1990 and it is predicted that it will be 24 years by 2040 (see figure RB2.1).

These projections indicate that during the period up to 2030, the number of Africans between the ages of 60 and 75 will increase from 4 to 6 per cent of the population and those over 75 will increase from 1 to 3 per cent. While these are significant increases, the numbers are small; Africa will thus remain young until well into the twenty-first century and the implications of ageing for social security financing do not represent an immediate problem.

Figure RB2.1   Life expectancy at age 55 in Africa

Life expectancy (years)

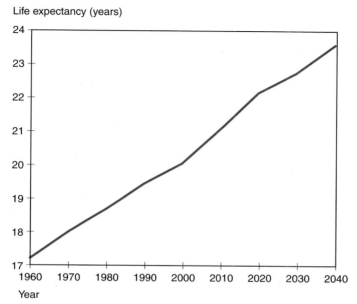

Year

ISSUES RELATING TO PENSION ARRANGEMENTS

Restrictions in coverage

In a few countries tax-financed social protection systems provide a measure of universal coverage for all residents, either on a means-tested (South Africa) or a universal basis to all residents who are within the scope of the contingency (Botswana, Mauritius, Namibia). Where the scheme is based on contributory principles, however, the level of coverage falls considerably and in most countries is effectively limited to the formal sector. Certain schemes cover, on a compulsory basis, all, or at least some, of the self-employed (for example, Algeria, Egypt, Tunisia) but many people evade their liability and thus the effective level of coverage is low. Although membership of schemes, in particular the provident funds, is open to the self-employed on a voluntary basis, in practice few take up this opportunity. Compliance is also a major problem in respect of those who are within the legislative scope of the scheme but who work for small employers or on a casual or informal basis.

Gabon is an example of a country which has made a special effort to extend coverage. In 1983 Gabon developed a complete social security system for non-salaried workers and the unemployed. This scheme is separate from the formal sector scheme and is administered by a public institution with financial and

519

administrative autonomy. The scope of risks covered is the same as for salaried workers: old age, invalidity, dependants, employment injury, health, family and maternity. As in the case of the countries which have established a universal scheme, the Gabon experience reflects the particular situation in the country and is not readily replicable elsewhere. During the period of formulation of the scheme (1980–82), favourable circumstances applied in Gabon, in that (a) the economic and financial situation was sound because of an abundance of well-exploited natural resources, (b) the salaried workers scheme was successful and provided a powerful encouragement to the authorities to extend social cover, and (c) unlike in other African countries, the categories without cover were a minority of the population.

In Benin, of the actively employed population (46 per cent) only salaried workers (5 per cent) are covered. Workers in the informal sector, self-employed and employers (59 per cent), domestic servants (24 per cent) and apprentices and others (12 per cent) have no protection. In Côte d'Ivoire, with a population of 14 million, 6.5 million people work in agriculture. None of them has social protection.

Thus, in most of Africa, the social insurance pension schemes and provident funds cover only a small part of the population, generally less than 10 per cent in total of the labour force plus their dependants, and represent in income distributed barely 1 per cent of GDP. Not only is this wholly unsatisfactory in social protection terms, in that the majority of the population are excluded, but the credibility and viability of the national social security scheme are adversely affected by its limited impact and by the falling number of contributors.

There has been a tendency in the past to view social protection reform in the context of its existing scope of coverage. Thus any extension in the range of existing benefits is considered with regard to the needs and capacity of those currently insured who are responsible for the financing of the scheme. In this context insufficient attention has been given to the problem of providing social protection for those not covered. Where efforts have been made in Africa to extend coverage they have basically taken one of two paths: integration within an existing scheme or the establishment of a separate scheme.

Governance

In those countries where contributory social security schemes have been established, almost all are administered by a public institution which enjoys, at least in law, if not always in practice, autonomous administrative and financial responsibility for the administration of the scheme. Policy responsibility lies with the minister but it was also common practice for the minister to appoint all the members of the board which supervises the scheme and the chief executive of the institution was also likely to be appointed by the president. It has generally proved difficult to achieve the level of democracy and tripartism in management consistent with the conceptual basis of the legislation. Direct

Table RB2.1 Distribution of the economically active population in certain French-speaking countries in Africa

Country	Total population (thousands)	Active population (thousands)	Salaried (a) sector/ state/parastatal	Salaried (b) private sector	Total salaried population	Employment ratio (%)	Salaried population/ active population (%)
Benin 1996	5 239	2 209	32 000	70 600	102 600	42.18	5.07
Côte d'Ivoire 1995	14 208	6 573	241 200	222 700	463 900	46.26	7.06
Niger 1994	8 867	4 497	40 774	18 600	59 374	50.72	1.32
Togo 1996	4 274	2 372	31 271	53 909	85 180	55.52	3.59
Cameroon 1996	13 400	5 226	161 700	368 717	530 417	39.00	10.15
Congo 1994	2 520	1 521	96 851	–	–	60.39	–
Gabon 1993	1 014	477	66 000	27 375	93 375	47.01	19.57
Equatorial Guinea 1994	390	152	11 245	10 294	22 169	39.20	14.50
Comoros 1991	446	126	–	–	31 625	28.31	25.00

Source: ILO technical cooperation reports.

involvement by the government for political or economic reasons resulted in many schemes not being administered in the best interests of the contributors and beneficiaries. There is, however, an increasing awareness of the need to introduce democratic principles into the supervision and management of national social security schemes, and some countries (Ghana and Uganda) have taken steps to ensure a higher level of autonomy for the social security institution.

Most of the contributory pension schemes in Africa are at least partially funded and thus the necessary prerequisites for a sound functioning of the social security scheme include in particular:

- conditions favourable to the development of employment,
- an adequately functioning financial market,
- the existence of investment opportunities,
- good governance and proper functioning of management institutions,
- promotion of social dialogue to consolidate the participation of the employers and workers in the management of the schemes.

In general these conditions have not been met. Weaknesses are found in the design of schemes and in their legislation which did not always take account of the national sociocultural context. Provisions which determine entitlement or exclusion have implications for patterns of dependency within the community. Legislative amendments have been made without prior assessment of the financial implications and, at the other extreme, there are examples of legislation which has not been implemented.

Administrative deficiencies are to be found in record maintenance, particularly in relation to the identification and registration of insured persons and in the processing of benefit claims, although to some extent this is attributable to weaknesses in public records. Sometimes, in the absence of records, the claimant is required to provide evidence of insurable employment and paid contributions. It is common for social security institutions to be overstaffed, with consequential burdens in administrative costs but with many of the staff insufficiently educated or inadequately trained. Personnel policies do not often permit recruitment or advancement based on merit. The inefficiencies in the system have implications for compliance and thus for the financing of the scheme. Weaknesses in the management information systems for social protection programmes have inhibited both the evaluation of performance and long-term development planning.

Financial management

An analysis of the balance sheets of schemes in Africa reveals common failings applicable to both assets and liabilities. On the liabilities side, the level of reserves is generally inadequate (or may not exist). On the assets side, investment policy and practice has often been unsatisfactory. A major part of the total investment by social security funds consists of loans to the state or public bodies and shareholdings. Instead of seeking to work with specialized financial institutions, the social security institutions have sometimes turned themselves into credit agencies. Mortgages have been granted directly, without any security. In many countries institutions have been obliged to deposit funds with the Treasury/Ministry of Finance and often such funds have been unproductive, inaccessible to the social security administration or with a zero real yield and uncertain liquidity. The funds invested elsewhere were often not subject to a defined policy or a formal plan. The sectors and enterprises that benefited were not always viable, many of the companies were wound up or were unable to meet payment schedules. The nature of the investments was similar to venture capital and the need to preserve the security of funds does not seem to have prevailed. Tangible assets, in particular in real estate, were not sufficiently substantial, and did not provide the required level of security.

The financial organization set up in some countries which led to capital accumulation was out of step with the financial markets or was not able to benefit from the existence of such markets. The management and investment of accumulated reserves suffered from adverse conditions. Within institutions it was not possible to create a regulatory system to provide an appropriate legal framework and a system of controls. The investments that were made did not comply with the rules and were not able to meet benefit commitments to insured persons. Savings were poorly rewarded, the cost of credit was high and difficulties encountered by clients with the financial institutions did not encourage access to medium- or long-term credit. In implementing development programmes, domestic saving, including social security funds, was little used. Instead there has been a reliance on external financing in spite of the implications for increasing the burden of foreign debt. The needs of the state for financing public enterprises (such as water and electricity supply companies) were covered as a priority by capital invested by international lenders. The interest rates offered were reduced and significant grace periods granted. This was prejudicial to the creation of national opportunities for investment of social security funds.

The difficulties encountered in making profitable investments led to an excessive accumulation of disposable and realizable securities. In some countries, for lack of opportunity, short-term deposits were made to the detriment of long-term investments. Some of the realizable securities seemed doubtful and institutions had to make provisions against them. In all countries credits were granted to third parties in the form of contributions recoverable from defaulting employers. The fall in the cash assets of social security institutions forced them into cash flow problems, sometimes leading to deferring payment of benefits. Restrictions affected liquidity and yields were uncertain and low. The yields from investments of social security funds in some places were subject to forced reductions by unilateral decision of the government. The security of funds invested was seriously affected. Guarantees, which were rarely demanded, were inadequate to protect against the insecurity of the investments. (The fact that it was the government which managed the reserves was an implicit guarantee.) This situation harmed real security aimed at maintaining purchasing power and the yield from investments. Sometimes the pursuit of yield has been at the expense of security.

Systems suffered from the effects of inflation, monetary devaluations and low interest rates. In Tanzania the 3,863.8 million shillings accumulated by the National Provident Fund were equivalent in 1986 to 241.4 million US dollars. In 1993 this amount had fallen to only 8.6 million dollars, or 28 times less, simply because of devaluations. At the same time the real rate of interest credited to accounts was negative. The nominal interest rate was 11 per cent, at a time when inflation was over 20 per cent. Those covered by the benefit scheme directly and personally assume the risks associated with the management of investments.

The level of social protection

Many African social security schemes have experienced difficulty in providing an effective level of income maintenance. This is true both of the pension schemes and of the provident funds, although the latter, with their reliance on lump-sum benefits based on accumulated savings in the form of contributions plus interest, have provided more dramatic examples. Thus, in the case of the Nigerian provident fund, in 1992 workers received on retirement a single lump-sum payment of barely 30 US dollars for careers of as much as 30 years. In Ghana, at the time when there was still a provident fund, while the contribution rate was 17.5 per cent of salary, the lump-sum payment to some workers at the end of a full career was sometimes the equivalent of four months' salary. Such examples of a loss in real terms of benefit rights were often the result of a combination of high inflation and inappropriate investment policies, but the level of protection was also commonly held down to low levels by the failure to increase the wages ceiling imposed to limit contribution liability (examples are provided by Kenya and Nigeria). In these circumstances, confidence in the system eroded totally.

In some French-speaking countries (such as Senegal), the defined benefit pension scheme determines the benefit through a points system (similar to the system used in France). Under this, a point (that is, the reference salary) is calculated as a function of the change in the average salary of the insured person. The benefit is then equal to the product of the total points acquired during the contribution years multiplied by the point value at the time when the benefit is calculated. The system is not easily understood by insured persons and in addition the level of benefits has not been maintained in real terms. Although intended to provide an automatic adjustment to take account of increases in earnings levels, the need to achieve a quasi-annual balance between income and expenditure, with the minimum impact on contribution rates, depended heavily on the economic and employment environment. Thus the value of the point has been held down, with a consequential fall in benefits in real terms.

Among the non-contributory pension schemes operating in some countries for public servants (as in Kenya, Sierra Leone and the United Republic of Tanzania) there has been a common failure to adjust payments to take account of increases in earnings or prices. Since the schemes are not based on contributions and generally do not contain any established adjustment mechanism, the real value of pensions has fallen in many countries. Similar problems have diminished the impact of workers' compensation schemes based on employer liability schemes, in that the prescribed levels of compensation payable have typically not been revised to take account of inflation.

DEVELOPMENTS AND OBJECTIVES

Most African countries have experienced significant changes over the past decade. This includes countries which have been newly established, such as Namibia and Eritrea, countries where there has been major political change reflecting democratic reforms (South Africa and Uganda) or conflict (Angola, Democratic Republic of the Congo, Liberia and Mozambique) and economic reforms with liberalization and deregulation policies, a reduced role for the state and increased responsibility and opportunities for private sector and individual initiative (Ethiopia, Ghana and the United Republic of Tanzania). In other countries this process is continuing (Nigeria and Somalia). These factors have major implications for the development of social security schemes, and democratic and economic reforms have been echoed in the structure and governance of social security schemes. The following paragraphs describe some of the initiatives which are being taken to improve social protection in respect of the long-term contingencies normally addressed by pension schemes.

Developments in French-speaking Africa

Because of their similarity in structure and administration, many of the French-speaking countries have experienced the same problems. The current conditions for the restructuring of the banking sector by which interest rates become a favoured instrument of monetary and financial policy should encourage the mobilization of domestic saving. This is the intention behind measures taken by the Central Bank of the West African States (BCEAO) in conjunction with the states for a regional approach to the restructuring and organization of the financial system of the countries in the West African Economic and Monetary Union (WAEMU) to stimulate the role of institutional investors, develop the financial market, liberalize interest rates, and introduce a competitive system and an adjudication system. Similar measures have been taken by the states of Central Africa. States also recognized the links between social protection, promotion of employment and social dialogue. In meetings in Dakar (1994), Abidjan (1996) and Yaounde (1997) these states emphasized that the process of extending the system of social protection could be promoted by rehabilitation and restoring the credibility of the existing systems.

The Commission on Social Protection and Social Dialogue (meeting in Yaounde in 1997 for countries in the CFA franc zone) issued a statement which included the following in its recommendations:

- Social protection systems should be specifically adapted to the new economic and social conditions but the pace of such adjustment should be set on a country-by-country basis.
- The extension of social cover to the whole population should be a priority.
- Social security institutions should be accorded greater autonomy (reforms are already being contemplated in some states, with priority being given to measures such as the rotation of chairmen for administrative boards, and the nomination of directors-general by the board).
- Personnel policies for social security staff should be improved with rewards linked to performance.
- Certain activities should be contracted to the private sector.
- Social protection should, in general, be structured with three levels but the system as a whole should be supervised by a permanent regulatory body.
- Social security institutions should be responsible for the management of reserves.

The extension of coverage

The experience in Africa reveals that the extension of social protection faces many problems and that there is no one model which can be readily applied. As a consequence of poverty, cultural considerations and traditional reliance on informal support systems, as well as mistrust of public administration, many Africans have a low propensity to participate in a long-term benefits scheme. But neither is there the capacity in most countries to finance a social protection safety net from taxation.

Table RB2.2 shows the cost of a safety net in Benin, on the assumption that 25 per cent of the total population is poor and that the absolute poverty line is equal to US$140 per person per year (Human Development Index Indicator). Merely as a result of population growth, the budget needed to cover the social security safety net would have to rise by 2.4 per cent per year over the period 1996–2050.

Increasing attention is therefore being paid to the possibility of people organizing themselves to help each other: at the community level, in cooperatives or in work associations. One of the main features of farming and the urban informal sector is their traditional organization which is solid and dynamic and does

Table RB2.2   Cost of a safety net in Benin

Year	Total population	Total in absolute poverty	Annual amount required to provide the absolute social security net (in US$)	Index
1996	5 239 100	1 309 775	183 368 500*	100
2000	6 266 000	1 566 500	219 310 000	120
2010	8 300 000	2 075 000	290 500 000	158
2020	10 843 000	2 710 750	379 505 000	207
2030	13 694 000	3 423 500	479 290 000	261
2040	16 404 000	4 101 000	574 140 000	313
2050	18 649 000	4 662 250	652 715 000	356

Source: ILO calculations.

* In 1995, Benin's total budget was US$340,000,000 (*Statesman's Yearbook*). Merely to provide this social security net to the poor would consume 53.9 per cent of the national budget.

not follow the formal sector. In farming some activities are organized simply to meet needs of supply and distribution. The structures necessary to establish a system of social protection should be identified so as to allow the identification of individuals and intermediaries who could play the role of the contributing employer. In such cases of traditional solidarity systems it would appear that associations or economic interest groups could play a major role provided that they were suitably prepared. The African experience suggests that, rather than create new organizations, it is preferable to respect local communities and to rely on existing organizations rooted in the local environment and cultural identities. The rural and informal sectors have their own organizations and self-support systems and greater emphasis in Africa should be placed on strengthening and developing organizations to which individuals have freely decided to belong.

Forms of community support are being revived. One of the great challenges for the extension of social protection will be the capacity to rejuvenate various forms of community support. There must be originality and inventiveness to meet to the maximum the social expectations of the majority of the people. The principal forms of community organization already exist. In Francophone Africa south of the Sahara, the tontine often occurs as a financial institution and a means of mutual assistance. Above all, it seems to be a system to encourage saving, and its members find in it a reliable way of forcing themselves to save. It is special in that it unites both formal and informal sector workers. In the case of cooperatives, these are generally defined as mutual assistance groups operating on a reciprocal basis, often groups of farmers, or artisans, living in the same village or district with the objective of improving their productive output and savings for their members and their families. Cooperatives operate in a wider area and include the majority of rural and urban craft workers and to a lesser extent those in the competitive informal sector.

These organizations vary widely, depending on the number of members. They are real solidarity systems organized according to their function and objectives. Mutual loan societies collect money for their members and return it in the form of investment and working capital loans to their businesses, in the form of social credits. Mutual loan societies are, in effect, enhanced tontines. Few of their members are workers at the informal subsistence level.

The needs of individuals are the same everywhere; the means of satisfying these needs are not. For workers in the modern sector institutional social security is there to satisfy specific needs such as loss of income or increased expenses. Satisfaction of such needs is most often expressed in monetary terms. The situation is different for farming communities and the urban informal sector. All suffer from scarcity of resources and goods, so their needs are basic and relate to those essential to the survival of the group. Nutrition levels are still poor in much of Africa and a national priority in many countries. Access to drinking water is also a prime concern, with major public health implications. Hygiene and sanitation, mainly in the large towns, are priority needs.

Development of pension schemes

Several countries are contemplating the introduction of pension schemes, either to replace national provident funds or to provide social protection, for the first time, for those who retire from employment.

Provident funds were established in most of the former British colonies (specifically in Gambia, Ghana, Kenya, Nigeria, Seychelles, Swaziland, the United Republic of Tanzania, Uganda and Zambia). The small Seychellois scheme was the first to be converted to a broader social security scheme in the late 1970s. The weaknesses of the provident fund system were, however, more generally exposed during the economic crisis of the 1980s, when it was found that the level of social protection in many countries was dramatically reduced by inflation. The Ghanaian provident fund, administered by the Social Security and National Insurance Trust, was converted in 1991 to a pension scheme based on social insurance principles, although lump-sum payments were retained for surviving dependants. The new scheme was also extended to cover most public servants.

Since then most of the remaining provident funds in Africa have taken steps towards conversion to social insurance based defined benefit systems. The National Provident Fund in Nigeria converted in 1994 and in both the United Republic of Tanzania and Zambia legislation was enacted in 1997 to introduce a national pension scheme based on social insurance principles. The process in each country has not been straightforward and it has proved necessary to modify initial proposals to take account of national circumstances. In the United Republic of Tanzania, where the contribution rate to the National Provident Fund was 20 per cent, it was found that a reasonable rate for a partially funded pension scheme was between 8 and 10 per cent. Rather than reduce the contribution rate it was decided to retain the provident fund at a lower level of contribution and then to phase this out as other social security benefits were introduced or as the pension contribution increased. The new system came into effect in 1998 and steps are being taken to replace the employers' liability workers' compensation scheme with an employment injury scheme also based on social insurance principles which will pay pensions for the first time in respect of serious permanent disablement and death cases arising from employment injury. In Zambia it was necessary to design a pension scheme which left scope for the continued reliance on occupational pension schemes.

Proposals for conversion have also been developed in Kenya and Uganda. In the case of Kenya, priority was given, however, to the establishment of a new public supervisory institution, the Retirement Benefits Authority, which would regulate and monitor the activities and investment practices of all retirement benefit schemes. In both these countries, and to a varying extent in much of English-speaking Africa, there has been a debate about the desired scope of the national pension scheme and the extent to which pension provision should be privatized. The debate has been influenced by the difficulties in governance experienced by many national provident funds and public pension schemes but the risks in relying heavily on private schemes where capital market development is fragile have also been recognized, as has the lack of experience in market regulation which is essential to ensure the success of a system where private pension funds play a significant role.

In those countries without the legacy of a national provident fund, progress in the development of social security schemes for private sector workers has been slow. In the case of Ethiopia and Eritrea this reflects the many years during which a centrally planned economy meant that most organized economic activity was owned by the State and the need to give priority to reconstruction in the period after the long conflict which led to the independence of Eritrea and to a change of government in Ethiopia. In Sierra Leone efforts to plan the introduction of a national social security scheme have also been inhibited by serious internal conflict. The national pension scheme established in Liberia in 1987 was also seriously disrupted by war.

In English-speaking southern Africa, social insurance principles are not yet strongly established, but important developments have taken place in recent years. After many years of preparation and debate in the face of differing views from the strongly established private pensions sector, the national social security scheme was established in Zimbabwe in 1990 with the creation of the National Social Security Authority. Initially this was focused on the existing workers' compensation scheme which was financed by contributions from employers paid into a central fund, but legislation was subsequently passed to establish a national pension scheme based on social insurance principles which covers all private sector workers and which will eventually extend to public servants and the self employed. A similar process has taken place in

Namibia, where legislation is currently being prepared to introduce a national pension scheme. In both countries the scheme reflects the national desire for a mixed social protection system in which occupational pension schemes and private pension funds will continue to play an important role. These considerations also apply in Swaziland and Botswana, but a national consensus has not yet been reached in either country on the respective roles of public and private schemes.

Important developments have taken place in improving both the scope and the level of social protection in Africa, but in general this has applied in a narrow perspective. Schemes have been introduced and others improved and new benefits have been introduced but almost nowhere has there been any significant impact on the major social protection problem in Africa – coverage. This issue has been discussed at length and in a global context in Chapters 8 and 16, but some specific reference to the African context is appropriate. First, the economic and fiscal situation is such that in most of sub-Saharan Africa the prospects for the introduction of a tax-based social safety net either on a universal or a means-tested basis are poor. This is a consequence of the large number of poor and the limited scope for increasing tax revenue. Second, most of the existing social security schemes cannot easily be extended to the self-employed and the informal sector because the threshold of entry in terms of their contribution and benefit structure is too high for most of those excluded and because the benefits provided are not consistent with the priorities of people living in poor circumstances whose social protection needs are essentially short term. Third, the administrative capacity of the existing public social security schemes is inadequate to take on the task of extending coverage.

What, then, can be done? There is no one solution to this fundamental problem. The overriding objective is to increase incomes and the standard of living by economic growth since social protection essentially depends on decisions being taken to allocate resources to prevent or alleviate hardship. But it is insufficient to rely on economic growth. Among those excluded in Africa there are many who have the capacity to contribute towards their social protection, and more careful consideration needs to be given to designing social security schemes which coincide more closely with their needs and circumstances. The reform and strengthening of the social security institutions both to improve their general efficiency and to make them more sensitive to their members would also be an important element. But beyond this there is a need particularly to put much greater emphasis on involving local communities in organizing and providing social protection for their people. In the rural areas where many workers are involved in producing and marketing a particular crop (such as cocoa in Ghana or tobacco in Malawi) there may be scope for financing basic social protection by a levy on the crop organized by the marketing association or by the community.

The second major issue affecting the development of social protection systems in Africa is governance. In many countries there is still a pressing need to improve the administrative performance of public social security schemes. The state must retain overall responsibility for the effectiveness of the system and will need to establish an efficient and comprehensive regulatory system to prevent abuses as serious as those which have occurred in the past. But there is scope for partial privatization to take advantage of private sector specialist skills. There is also in many countries a need to develop a new division of responsibility between public and private provision. Priority, however, should be given to strengthening the public systems through reforms which will ensure greater transparency in their operations, that give workers and employers an effective voice in management and supervision and that lead to recruitment and personnel policies which reward ability and performance.

LATIN AMERICA AND THE CARIBBEAN

In some countries in South America social security retirement pension schemes have a long history. Almost 50 years, however, separate the creation of the first scheme in South America and the last scheme in the Caribbean. Over this period nearly all schemes were originally designed according to European models and most in the region continue to be traditional social insurance schemes.

The countries of Latin America and the Caribbean are influenced by their colonial past. Latin America includes 19 countries that gained independence from Spain and Portugal in the nineteenth century, plus Haiti. The non-Latin Caribbean includes 14 countries which in the second half of the twentieth century became independent from France, Great Britain and the Netherlands. Most of these are middle-income countries and they have relatively high health standards; considerably better than for most countries in Africa and Asia.

As in other regions, social security schemes have been affected by the social, economic and demographic situations of the countries, which explain most of the evolution of the schemes as well as their shortcomings. In some countries high inflation, a low level of education of the population, rapid population growth, overprotected economies and corruption have contributed to problems in the social security scheme.

Retirement scheme reform is high on the political agenda of many countries in the region. During the 1980s and 1990s some questioned the basic functioning and structure of their retirement income schemes and embarked on radical reform. The results of many of the original systems were disappointing and coverage was low. As of the late 1990s, four of the 34 countries in the region had adopted mandatory defined contribution schemes and four had adopted voluntary defined contribution schemes. Other countries were actively considering adopting defined contribution schemes. Chile was the forerunner in the reform movement in 1981.

HISTORICAL PERSPECTIVE

The historical development of social security retirement pension schemes in the region can be examined by decades. Chile, in 1924, became the first country in the Americas to adopt a social security retirement benefit scheme, with Uruguay following in 1928. Several countries adopted schemes in the 1930s: Brazil (1934), Ecuador (1935) and Peru (1936).

The countries adopting schemes in the 1940s were influenced by the Beveridge report published in Great Britain and by the advice of the International Labour Organization based on international labour standards (Mesa-Lago, 1991a). These countries included Venezuela (1940), Panama (1941), Costa Rica (1941), Mexico (1943), Paraguay (1943), Colombia (1946), the Dominican Republic (1947), El Salvador (1949) and Bolivia (1949). In these countries a national social security institution was established but initially coverage was limited to the capital and the main cities. Prior to the establishment of the national system special schemes had been established for certain occupational groups, such as the armed forces and civil servants, and in most countries some or all of the occupations covered by such schemes were excluded from the general social security scheme.

All of the countries of South America have had social security retirement benefit schemes for at least 50 years. The early countries in the region were truly pioneers in the development of social security, with the countries of North America adopting their schemes later: the United States in 1934, Canada in 1951. By comparison, by 1950, only three African and two Asian countries had enacted social security retirement benefits schemes (Mesa-Lago, 1991a).

The initial tendency to develop special schemes for particular occupational groups resulted in the establishment of a number of social security institutions in some countries and thus in a stratified social insurance system, with relatively small privileged groups having generous benefits while the majority of the population had less generous protection.

In the 1950s, 1960s and 1970s a number of Caribbean and Central American countries adopted retirement benefit schemes. During the 1950s schemes were adopted by Haiti (1951), Honduras (1952), Nicaragua (1955), Bahamas (1956) and Jamaica (1958). Barbados adopted its scheme in 1966 and Bermuda in 1967. During the 1970s schemes were adopted by Saint Lucia (1970), Saint Kitts and Nevis (1970), Saint Vincent and the Grenadines (1970), Trinidad and Tobago (1971) and Antigua and Barbuda (1972). The schemes adopted by Saint Lucia, Saint Kitts and Nevis and Saint Vincent and the Grenadines were provident funds that were all converted to social insurance defined benefit schemes later in the 1970s. At about the same time, a number of countries that had previously established retirement benefit schemes in urban areas also extended coverage to rural areas. These countries included Argentina, Brazil, Colombia and Ecuador.

533

During the 1980s and 1990s a number of countries adopted either voluntary or mandatory defined contribution schemes to replace partially or completely their traditional social insurance defined benefit schemes. These countries were Chile (1981), Peru (1992), Colombia (1993), Argentina (1993), Uruguay (1995), Mexico (1995–1996), Bolivia (1996) and El Salvador (1996). In the late 1990s Costa Rica and other countries were actively considering such a change.

COVERAGE

Because of the large informal sector in this region, many workers are not covered by social security retirement benefit schemes, either because their type of employment is not covered or because they are covered under the law but they or their employers evade making contributions. All salaried employees are insurable in two-thirds of the countries of the region. Self-employed workers are only compulsorily covered in 11 countries (Mesa-Lago, 1994). Argentina and Uruguay are the only countries with defined contribution schemes that have mandated coverage of the self-employed. The system in Jamaica has compulsory coverage for the self-employed and rural workers but contribution evasion among the self-employed is widespread. Statistics from 1987 indicated that there were 329,000 self-employed workers (one-third of the workforce) but only 19,000 were members of the scheme, with a mere 8,400 contributing regularly (ILO, 1992). In Chile coverage for the self-employed is voluntary because of the difficulty in enforcing coverage for this group and few among them choose to participate. Coverage for the self-employed is also voluntary in 11 countries, including Bolivia, Colombia, El Salvador and Mexico. Often, when the self-employed have the option of joining, the contribution rate payable is much higher than that for employees, since employers generally also contribute for the latter. Costa Rica has succeeded in expanding coverage among the self-employed, partly by prescribing contribution rates that are lower than the combined rate for employers and employees. A reform proposal in Costa Rica in 1998 stipulates mandatory coverage of the self-employed.

Because the reforms of social security in Latin America have not attempted to include traditionally excluded groups, or to completely eliminate the schemes of privileged groups, this has produced a patchwork of social security retirement pension schemes that includes the following:

- groups not covered,
- schemes for privileged groups,
- schemes that are not reformed (municipal and governmental),
- reformed old schemes,
- new schemes.

Thus an effect of the reforms has been an increase in the number of institutions providing retirement benefits, which has increased the complexity of the task of ensuring that the required contributions are, in fact, actually paid. The reforms, however, have standardized entitlement conditions for the large majority of the insured.

Public employees are included in the social security scheme in Jamaica but they are permitted to retire earlier than other employees covered by the scheme. As a result, in 1989, 27 per cent of social security expenditure went to public employees, while they represented 7 per cent of the workforce.

The military and government employees are typically covered by special schemes in the region. The military are covered by special schemes in all countries, except in Costa Rica (which does not have armed forces) and Bolivia which included them in the reform of 1996. Government employees are covered by special schemes in Brazil, the Dominican Republic, Mexico, Paraguay and Venezuela. Government employees in Peru can join the new social security retirement scheme, and provincial government employees in Argentina can sign agreements with the central government to join the new social security retirement scheme.

In some countries workers are excluded from coverage according to their level of earnings. In Antigua and Barbuda family and casual workers who receive low wages are not covered. In the Dominican Republic, on the other hand, white-collar workers are not covered if they earn more than a low level of earnings.

Special groups of workers are excluded from the social security retirement pension scheme in some countries. Among the countries with defined contribution social security retirement pension schemes the following categories of workers are excluded: Argentina, employees of municipalities; Colombia and Mexico, petroleum workers, electricity workers, telephone workers, banking system workers, congress members; Peru, government employees; and, in Uruguay, employees of banks. The military are excluded from all the defined contribution schemes and are covered by more generous tax-financed schemes, except in Bolivia. In Colombia, workers not excluded have the choice of a defined contribution account managed in the private sector or the scheme administered by the social security institution (ISS). About 75 per cent of workers have chosen the social security institution.

The percentage of the workforce actually covered by social security retirement benefits schemes in these countries varies with the level of economic development, which is also correlated with the age of the social security scheme. Countries that are more developed started their social security schemes earlier and thus have older schemes and, because of their greater development and the age of their social security systems, tend to cover a higher percentage of the workforce. A structural barrier to the extension of coverage has been the model of social insurance financed with wage contributions. In the least developed countries in the region the majority of the labour force are not salaried but are self-employed, domestic servants, unpaid family workers, owners of small enterprises, small-scale farmers and peasants (Mesa-Lago, 1994). The state decision and will to extend coverage, however, are important aspects of the extent of coverage.

BENEFITS

With defined benefit social security pensions, benefits are based on earnings at the end of the worker's career and in some cases the benefit formula provides generous benefits. In Brazil retirement benefits are 70 per cent of average earnings in the last 36 months plus 1 per cent of average earnings for each year of contribution. After 30 years of contribution, a worker would receive the maximum benefit of 100 per cent of average earnings. In addition 13 monthly payments are made each year.

In Paraguay retirees may also receive up to 100 per cent of average earnings over the final three years of work and retire at age 55 with 30 years of work. The combination of the relatively young pensionable age and high benefits makes the retirement benefit formula one of the most generous in the world. By contrast, in the Bahamas the maximum benefit is 60 per cent of the worker's final average wages and the minimum age at which it can be received is 65.

In the countries with defined contribution schemes, the level of benefits is determined by the amount in the worker's account. Predicted replacement rates vary greatly depending on the assumptions as to the annual increase in real wages, real rates of return and the frequency with which contributions are made.

Six countries (Argentina, Chile, Colombia, El Salvador, Mexico and Uruguay) with defined contribution pension schemes guarantee a minimum pension but with diverse features. In Argentina the guarantee requires 30 years of contributions. Chile has a minimum benefit guarantee for workers who have contributed for 20 or more years. El Salvador has a similar guarantee for workers who have contributed for 25 or more years, but it is also limited by the availability of fiscal resources. Bolivia does not provide such a guarantee and Peru established it in a law but has not implemented regulations. Chile also partially guarantees against insurance company bankruptcy pensions that have been converted into annuities with an insurance company.

Often there is no regular adjustment of pensions for inflation. Chile provides cost-of-living indexing, which is done monthly for workers who have chosen the option of annuity but not for workers receiving the minimum pension. Argentina adjusts the social insurance defined benefit pension annually. In Bolivia adjustment of benefit levels is based on an index related to the US dollar and in Venezuela adjustment is occasional. In El Salvador it is done according to the average of contributory wages, and in Uruguay it is based on constant pesos of 1995.

PENSIONABLE AGE

In most countries retirement benefits can be received between the ages of 55 and 60, with women being able to receive them at a younger age than men. In many countries retirement is not a requirement for receiving benefits. Men in Venezuela can receive benefits at age 60 and women at age 55 with retirement not being necessary. Urban employees in Brazil may receive benefits without retiring at age 65 for males and 60 for women, while rural employees may receive benefits five years earlier. A worker can retire in Paraguay at the age of 60 with 25 years of contributions or age 55 with 30 years. The minimum age at which benefits can be received in the Bahamas and Mexico is 65. Workers in the Dominican Republic can receive retirement benefits at age 60, but for workers who were first covered after age 45 it is 65.

In Bolivia workers can retire regardless of age when the accumulated fund in the individual's account is sufficient to finance at least 70 per cent of the individual's average wage in the previous five years. If this condition is not met, workers can retire at age 65. Argentina is increasing its minimum retirement age from 63 for men and 58 for women in 1997 to 65 and 60, respectively, in 2001. Peru has also chosen age 65, with retirement at younger ages if the pension fund is sufficiently large. A minimum retirement age is not set for the defined contribution scheme in Colombia: the only requirement concerning retirement is that the fund accumulated in the individual account be sufficient to finance a pension at least equal to 110 per cent of the minimum salary. In Uruguay men can retire at age 60 and women at age 56, but with the age for women being raised to age 60 by 2003. These ages are relatively young for Uruguay, given the long life expectancy of its population, while they are relatively high in Bolivia (65) and Peru (65).

MINIMUM PERIOD OF CONTRIBUTIONS

In Argentina a worker must contribute for 30 years to receive a pension from the social security defined benefit scheme. However an advanced-age pension can be received at age 70 with ten years of contributions. (For further discussion of the retirement benefits in Argentina, see box RB3.1.) In the Bahamas and Venezuela the minimum contribution period is 250 weeks, whereas in the Dominican Republic the minimum contribution period for a full pension is 800 weeks but a reduced pension is available with 400 weeks of contributions. In the defined contribution scheme in Chile there is no minimum contribution period for receiving a pension (Mesa-Lago, 1997a).

FINANCING

Most of the defined benefit social security schemes are financed by contributions from both employers and employees as a percentage of wages. Because of the large informal sector, however, a high percentage of workers in some countries are self-employed and thus no employer is involved in the financing. Most of these workers do not participate in the retirement benefits scheme of their country.

Box RB3.1 Argentina

In 1993 Argentina established a new social security retirement benefit scheme, taking effect in 1994: the Integrated System of Retirement and Pensions (*Sistema Integrado de Jubilaciones y Pensiones, SIJP*). The new system includes both a public defined benefit scheme, financed on a pay-as-you-go basis, and a private scheme based on funded defined contribution accounts. Until July 1996 workers could choose either scheme or change from the one originally selected. From that date everyone who enters the labour force becomes a member of the funded scheme.

The management of the system is the responsibility of several organizations: The National Administration of Social Security (*Administración Nacional de Seguridad Social, ANSeS*) – a public institution under the Ministry of Labour and Social Security – and the *Administradoras de Fondos de Jubilaciones y Pensiones* (AFJP), institutions which are controlled and supervised by the Superintendency of AFJP which is also under the supervision of the Ministry of Labour and Social Security.

Membership is mandatory for all workers aged 18 years or over who are employed or self-employed in the private sector, in the national public sector (except the army) and in local government institutions that decide to transfer their social insurance schemes to the new system. All other workers can join the new system voluntarily.

The system is financed by the contributions of workers and employers. The contribution rate for employed workers is 11 per cent of salary and the contribution of the employer is 16 per cent. Self-employed workers contribute 27 per cent. These contribution rates apply between maximum and minimum income levels. These revenues are supplemented by certain earmarked taxes.

The new system provides retirement, disability and death benefits. The retirement benefits have three components: Basic Universal Benefit (PBU) and Compensation Benefit (PC) paid by the public scheme and a third benefit that differs for each scheme. The public pension (PAP) is based on pay-as-you-go financing and the private pension is based on individual funded accounts.

An invalidity benefit is provided for the insured who have not fulfilled all the requirements for obtaining a retirement pension but who are totally disabled (a reduction of earning capacity by 66 per cent). The benefit paid by either scheme is the same. Those who are in the public scheme receive a benefit paid by that scheme. For the members in the private sector, the benefit is paid by the AFJP and is financed through the purchase of group insurance from a life insurance company. The survivors' pension replaces the income which the deceased person used to receive as a worker or pensioner and is paid to his dependants.

Several public and private institutions are responsible for managing the system. The AFJPs are public or private commercial companies whose function is to invest in various types of financial assets the funds deposited by members. They also pay benefits under the option of phased withdrawal of benefits. The National Bank of Argentina also serves as an AFJP to ensure the existence of at least one public AFJP.

Life insurance companies are public and private enterprises that protect the members of the AFJPs against the contingencies of invalidity and death. They also pay benefits in the form of life annuities.

The ANSeS is a public institution which is decentralized and autonomous and is under the Ministry of Labour and Social Security. Under the old system this institution was the only one in charge of the management of the social security scheme and up to 1992 it collected social security contributions. In the new system its functions are restricted, given the mixed nature of the system, but it continues performing major tasks such as the payment of benefits which are provided by the State (PBU and PC). The ANSeS also has authority to adopt provisions on specific matters related to the operation of the new system.

The Superintendency of AFJP is a decentralized body under the Ministry of Labour and Social Security which is responsible for the control, supervision and regulation of the private enterprises that manage the individual accounts. It has an important role with broad powers. It approves the operations of the AFJPs and controls their activities; it imposes legal sanctions on them when necessary and adopts regulations concerning institutional control, supervision of pensions, financing and health care.

The General Direction for Taxation *(Dirección General Impositiva)* is a public institution under the Ministry of Finance and Public Works that collects taxes and social security contributions which are later distributed among the AFJPs and ANSeS.

The coordination of the different public institutions dealing with social security is not explicitly provided for. This function, however, is entrusted to the General Secretary of the Ministry of Labour and Social Security under which are located the ANSeS and the SAFJP. Other public institutions that regulate aspects of the operation of the new system are the National Super-intendency for Insurance *(Superintedencia de Seguros de la Nación)*, the Central Bank of Argentina and the National Commission of Securities *(Comisión Nacional de Valores)*.

Some schemes receive financing from the government. Panama uses proceeds of a tax on alcohol to supplement mandatory payroll contributions to support social security, Ecuador provides a 40 per cent government subsidy on pensions for old age, and Uruguay uses proceeds from various taxes to help finance social security deficits. The social security defined benefit pension scheme in Chile – and other countries that have defined contribution schemes that will eventually replace the defined benefit scheme – requires substantial financial support from the government since it has most of the beneficiaries but few of the contributors.

In Cuba financing comes entirely from employers, with employees making no contribution. A pilot programme charging a wage contribution to workers began in 1998. Employees in Bermuda pay a flat amount rather than contributions being a percentage of earnings. Employers in the Bahamas pay a higher percentage of the combined employer-employee mandatory contribution for lower-wage workers than for higher-wage workers. In the defined contribution schemes in Chile, Mexico and Peru – but not Argentina – the financing comes entirely from the employee. In Bolivia part of the financing comes from the proceeds of the privatization of several state-owned industrial enterprises. Colombian workers who earn more than four times the minimum salary must pay a supplemental 1 per cent mandatory contribution which goes into a solidarity fund to expand coverage of low-income workers.

Contribution rates are fairly low in the Caribbean because they have relatively new systems with young populations and pay-as-you-go financing. In Haiti contribution rates are progressive, with the lowest-income employees and employers both paying 2 per cent, rising to 6 per cent each for the highest-income workers. The contribution rate is 2.5 per cent paid by both employees and employers in Jamaica. The total rate in the Bahamas is 8.8 per cent split between employees and employers. In the British Virgin Islands employees and employers each pay 3.25 per cent.

Contribution rates in Central America tend to be relatively low and are paid by employers, employees and the government. In Guatemala employees pay 1.5 per cent of earnings, the employer 3 per cent and the government 25 per cent of benefit cost, in Honduras employees, employers and government each pay 1 per cent, and in Nicaragua employees pay 1.75 per cent, employers 3.5 per cent and the government 0.25 per cent.

Contribution rates are higher in South America. For participants in defined contribution schemes, the mandatory contribution rate paid by them and their employer is at least 11 per cent. The total percentage contribution (employer plus employee if both contribute) is 11.8 per cent in Peru, 12.45 per cent in Mexico, 12.5 per cent in Bolivia, 13.1 per cent in Chile, 13.5 per cent in El Salvador, 13.5 per cent in Colombia, 27 per cent in Argentina and 27.5 per cent in Uruguay.

In Mexico and Uruguay contributions are paid to the national social security institution which then distributes them among the pension fund administrators. Argentina has a public central tax collection agency which receives the contributions and transfers them to the appropriate pension fund administrators. This system of a single collection agency appears to have economies of scale that reduce costs. In Chile, and other countries with defined contribution schemes, each employer must send the contributions to the appropriate pension fund administrator for each employee.

THE PENSION REFORM MOVEMENT

The pension reform movement has resulted in part from problems encountered by social security retirement pension schemes. In Latin America, these schemes have encountered the following problems:

- coexistence of multiple schemes, with powerful groups having generous schemes and little or no coverage for the poor,
- decline in contributors relative to beneficiaries,

- contribution evasion or late payments,
- low returns on investments,
- weak relation between contributions and benefits,
- excessive administrative costs and low efficiency.

With the exceptions of Argentina, Cuba and Uruguay, population ageing has not been the main cause of the financial problems of social security schemes. Instead those problems have been attributable to both economic factors (high inflation) and weaknesses in governance (including political involvement leading to inappropriate demands on investments, resource management and staffing, falling levels of coverage, and evasion). The growth of the informal sector, attributable in part to the restructuring of the labour market under economic reform programmes, has been a significant factor in Central and South America. The growth rate of the number of pensioners owing to longer life expectancy has not been offset by the expansion of formal employment.

Analysis of the pension reform processes in Latin America illustrates that they have been closely linked with political processes. The diversity of designs has been influenced more by political considerations than by a scientific approach to pension reform. In the pension reforms earlier in the century, all Latin American countries followed European models, while the major structural reforms at the end of the twentieth century have been influenced by the Chilean model, which has been considered an innovative paradigm. For further discussion of the system in Chile, see box RB3.2.

Groups traditionally excluded from pension schemes, such as agricultural workers, informal-sector workers and the self-employed, have not been considered in the reform processes. The underlying reason is their lack of political representation, but another important reason is that their low income creates a financial obstacle to their participation in social security retirement pension schemes. Nevertheless an innovation of recent reforms is that excluded groups now have the possibility of voluntarily affiliating to the new systems. Groups with strong political representation, such as the armed forces, civil servants, petrol companies and teachers, are frequently covered by generous retirement schemes, financed out of general revenues and they have frequently been excluded from the reform processes (Bonilla and Conte Grand, 1997).

In Argentina, Colombia, Uruguay and Mexico reforms of retirement and pension schemes have taken place in an environment characterized by consultations and bargaining among social actors. By contrast, the decisions regarding the reform processes in Chile and Peru were made at the highest level of government. Costa Rica has adopted an important reform of its schemes for special groups and has implemented the approach, for the first time in Latin America, of gradually complementing the partially funded social security scheme with a voluntary one of defined contribution accounts. A legal draft under consideration in 1998 makes this programme mandatory, converting the system into a mixed one.

Box RB3.2 Chile

Chile started a new defined contribution pension scheme in 1981. Unlike the old system, which entrusted fund management to public institutions, funds in the new system are administered by private corporations known as *Administradoras de Fondos de Pensiones* or Pension Fund Administrators (AFPs). AFPs must meet minimum capital and profitability requirements and are financed through commissions collected from employees. All new employees must enter the private pension scheme. Self-employed workers, however, have the option of remaining outside the system.

The AFPs invest payroll contributions after making deductions for administrative expenses. The charges and rates of return of the AFPs are widely publicized. Workers are allowed to move their funds among AFPs, thus creating a market for pensions.

Individuals are required to contribute 10 per cent of their pre-tax salary to a private pension fund of their choosing with an option to add to that amount. Voluntary contributions into the mandatory account held with an AFP are also deductible from income tax, as is the interest earned. An additional amount, ranging from 2.5 to 3.74 per cent of payroll, is levied to finance disability benefits and pre-retirement survivor benefits, and for administrative expenses. The average for 1997 was about 3 per cent. Employers do not contribute on behalf of their workers in the AFP system. Workers receive recognition bonds for their contributions in the former system. These bonds earn a real rate of return of 4 per cent.

Pensions are available for men at age 65 and for women at age 60. Benefits may be taken as either a price-indexed annuity, a phased withdrawal or some combination of the two. At retirement the individual must contract with an insurance company to convert his or her account balance to an annuity or contract with the AFP to organize an individual payout schedule.

Regulatory oversight is strictly maintained by requiring the AFPs to meet certain financial requirements and operating standards. Pension funds are legally defined as separate entities apart from the fund management. Because poorly developed capital markets in Chile offered few other investment opportunities, initial AFP fund investments were limited mostly to government bonds and bank deposits – both indexed against inflation. While portfolio diversification has increased over the years, investments continue to be restricted by law. Investment rules, aiming to ensure that AFP funds are conservatively invested with diversification of the portfolio, specify maximum limits on the percentage of the portfolio held in different types of assets.

The government provides a minimum pension to retirees whose individual pension accounts prove insufficient. That guarantee, however, applies only to those of pensionable age having contributed into the system at least 20 years. The government also provides a means-tested public assistance programme for the indigent elderly. It also guarantees the minimum profitability of AFPs by forcing them to set aside prescribed amounts in a profitability reserve whenever the investment return exceeds a prescribed percentage above the AFP industry average. Should the investment return fall too far below the average of all AFPs, the AFP is required to make up the difference through that profitability reserve. If that were inadequate, individual accounts would then be compensated from investment reserves. An AFP unable to finance the shortfall in the rate of return from its investment reserves is forced to liquidate, workers' individual accounts are transferred to other AFPs and the state makes up the shortfall. A further guarantee provided by the government involves the annuity payments for retirement, disability and survivors' pensions handled by failed insurance companies. This amounts to 100 per cent coverage of the minimum pension and 75 per cent of the difference between the minimum pension and the value of the original benefit up to an indexed ceiling.

Brazil has endorsed a reform of its retirement pension scheme, concentrating on improving its existing system and at the same time strengthening employer-provided pensions. In Colombia the approval of the new social security law emerged as a solution to the impossibility of obtaining consensus on either of the proposed alternatives, which were a modernization of the social insurance scheme or a defined contribution scheme. Finally it was agreed to let participants choose. All Latin American countries that have reformed their retirement benefit schemes have maintained invalidity and survivors' pensions by collective distribution of risks among participants.

Since the Chilean reform in 1981, with the exception of Uruguay which permits benefits only as life annuities, all other reforms have allowed the choice of phased withdrawal of benefits as an option. A major difference between the reformed and traditional schemes is that in the reformed system many workers choose the phased withdrawal option which does not offer the guarantee that benefits will be paid from the scheme for life.

In the defined contribution schemes workers are charged commission by the pension fund management companies to cover the expenses and profit of those companies. A factor subsidizing the costs of the reformed systems is that the commission is deducted from the worker's gross wage and is not considered as income to the worker and consequently is exempt from income tax. Thus a percentage of the commission is financed by the government, through a reduction in personal income taxes, and therefore the worker is less sensitive to the absolute difference in commissions between different providers.

The countries with major structural reforms resulting in the establishment of defined contribution plans can be divided into three groups (Mesa-Lago, 1997a). First, some countries (Bolivia, Chile, El Salvador and Mexico) have substituted a defined contribution scheme for the former defined benefits scheme. In these countries, the old system is closed to new entrants. Second, two countries – Argentina and Uruguay – have introduced a mixed system, with all workers participating in both the defined contribution scheme and the defined benefit social security scheme. In these countries the old system has been reformed and continues to operate alongside the new system, which is a mixed system providing a basic benefit through a social scheme and a supplementary benefit provided through a defined contribution scheme. In Argentina old workers can choose the reformed old system or the new mixed system, but all new workers must join the mixed system. In Uruguay low-income workers only participate in the social insurance scheme. Third, Colombia and Peru have maintained parallel schemes with workers choosing to participate in one. In these countries the defined contribution schemes compete with the defined benefit social security scheme (ibid.).

There are significant differences in the level of coverage of the economically active population among the eight countries (ibid.). In the southern cone countries of Argentina, Chile and Uruguay coverage of the economically active population is about 80 per cent; a similar coverage rate existed prior to the reforms. In Mexico, Colombia and Peru the coverage rate is 38, 35 and 32 per cent, respectively. In the least developed countries of El Salvador and Bolivia coverage is only 23 and 12 per cent, respectively. The size of the covered population also differs considerably, ranging from 11 million in Mexico, 8 million in Argentina and 6 million in Chile, to half a million in El Salvador and 356,000 in Bolivia. In Bolivia it is estimated that there are an additional 500,000 workers who evade contributions. The size of the covered population is important to allow competition among pension providers, which is fundamental for the systems to function properly. In Argentina and Uruguay coverage is legally mandatory for the self-employed but it is voluntary in the other six reform countries. In most of those six countries the informal sector, which mainly consists of the self-employed, is large, being the majority of the economically active population.

In all the countries with defined contribution schemes there is a large difference between the number of workers registered with the system (called affiliates) and those registered who actively contribute. In 1996 the ratios of active contributors to affiliates were 45 per cent in Peru, 53 per cent in Colombia, 52 per cent in Argentina, 54 per cent in Chile and 72 per cent in Uruguay. Possible explanations include that not all affiliates are actively employed and, because of the frequent switching among pension providers, there may be double counting of the number of affiliates, who have switched but are still retained on the records of the original provider.

Compulsory pension schemes around the world are generally administered by public institutions and, until the reform of the system in Chile, there was no case of private administration. The substitution of private administration for public was done in Chile because of disappointment with public administration. All pension fund administrators in Chile are private sector for-profit companies. In four countries individual accounts are administered solely by private for-profit corporations devoted exclusively to that purpose: Bolivia, Chile, El Salvador and Peru. In Argentina and Mexico, the public sector provides a pension fund administrator to give workers a choice. In Argentina, Colombia, Mexico and Uruguay there are a number of different types of pension fund administrators. These include private for-profit corporations, not-for-profit organizations, national social security institutions (Mexico and Uruguay), banks (including state banks in Argentina), insurance companies, unions, mutual aid societies and cooperatives. In all the countries there remains a public social security scheme that is administered by the government.

In Chile each pension fund administrator can only manage one fund but there have been proposals to change that. In Mexico administrators are allowed to manage multiple funds with different risk and return characteristics. The number of pension fund administrators is positively related to the number of workers in a country. In mid-1998 Argentina had 18 administrators, Mexico 17, Chile 12, Uruguay 6, Peru 5, El Salvador 5 (which had requested authorization) and Bolivia 2. Periodic reports are provided by the pension fund administrators to the affiliates and are important means by which affiliates can monitor the handling of their contributions. These are provided quarterly in Chile, Colombia and Peru, triennially in Argentina, biannually in El Salvador and Uruguay, and annually in Bolivia and Mexico (ibid.).

The government retains a role in the defined contribution schemes as system regulator. In Chile and Mexico the regulatory agency is a separate government organization financed by the government. The state regulatory agency is financed by the pension fund administrators in Argentina, Bolivia and El Salvador whereas in Peru the regulatory agency is financed by the pension fund administrators but is not supervised by the state. In Colombia the Superintendency of Banks regulates the pension fund administrators.

CONCLUSION

Latin America has become a leader in the pension reform movement around the world. Pension reform is continuing in the region itself, with countries having recently carried out reforms working to fully implement them and with other countries considering major changes incorporating defined contribution pension schemes. Nonetheless, as of the end of the 1990s, all of the countries in the Caribbean and the majority of the countries in Latin America retain traditional defined benefit social insurance schemes.

THE ARAB STATES OF THE MIDDLE EAST

The countries considered in this regional brief are the Arab states of the Middle East: Bahrain, Iraq, Jordan, Kuwait, Lebanon, Oman, Qatar, Saudi Arabia, Syria, United Arab Emirates and Yemen. In addition the territories under the Palestinian Authority have two pension schemes for civil servants (one operating in the West Bank and the other in Gaza) with different benefit structures.

The countries in this region have a long tradition of social and family solidarity that is reflected in their systems of government and social security arrangements. All the countries are members of the United Nations and the Arab League, and have attempted to follow the Conventions and Recommendations of the International Labour Office and the Arab Labour Organization in the development of their social security and social insurance schemes. This especially applies to the ILO Social Security (Minimum Standards) Convention, 1952 (No. 102), and Arab Conventions No. 1 of 1966, No. 6 of 1976 (labour standards and the need to promulgate specific laws on social insurance), No. 3 of 1971 (minimum standards of social insurance) and No. 24 of 1981 on the rights of Arab workers to social benefits when employed in other Arab countries. Given the countries' cultural similarities and mutual collaboration, these schemes display many similarities.

Priority has generally been given to providing protection against the contingencies of invalidity, disability and employment injury. The role and intervention of the state through appropriate legislation is a key factor in an analysis of social security and social insurance schemes. Complementary private or employer-based arrangements are not as well developed as in other regions.

While governments are responsible for the social security programmes, cooperation between employers and employees has been encouraged and, in most cases, the schemes are financed by contributions from both employers and employees, with the state covering any deficit. In most countries the schemes are relatively young, having to a great extent replaced traditional social protection schemes over little more than a generation ago.

SOCIOECONOMIC OVERVIEW

The countries of this region have been through considerable turmoil since the end of the Second World War. Their strategic position, first as a travel and trade route, followed by the discovery of oil, has at times contributed to conflicts, as have religious differences. Conflicts have significantly affected the development of social security schemes in Yemen, Lebanon and the Palestinian Authority.

With the exception of Yemen, which is poor, all the countries of the region have a fairly high life expectancy, with life expectancy at birth for females in most countries being 70 or higher, but only 50 in Yemen. The fertility rate in the region is also high, with 6.4 children per family in Saudi Arabia, 5.7 in Iraq and 7.6 in Yemen, but 3.1 in both Kuwait and Lebanon. Because of the high fertility rates, the countries of the region are not facing an immediate problem of population ageing. In Jordan, the population aged 60 and older in 1996 was 3.4 per cent of the total population. In Saudi Arabia and most of the other countries of the region more than 40 per cent of the population was younger than 15. In Bahrain in 1996 the ratio of pensioners to covered workers was 3.1 per cent (Bahrain, 1997). With the exception of Kuwait, which has a declining population, the combination of high life expectancy and high fertility is causing the population of the countries of the region to grow rapidly.

The general economic situation in the region over the 1980s and 1990s was a function of several adverse factors that slowed or halted growth in GDP. The region had a number of serious conflicts: the Iran–Iraq war, the Gulf War, the war in Lebanon and the Arab-Israeli conflict. Towards the end of the 1990s, however, countries again experienced economic growth. GDP per capita in the region differs greatly depending on which countries have oil. The two wealthiest countries in the region, United Arab Emirates and Kuwait, have per capita income exceeding that of many western European countries. Jordan and Syria have per capita income roughly comparable to that of Poland and Romania. Yemen has per capita income roughly comparable to that of India.

SOCIAL SECURITY RETIREMENT BENEFIT PROGRAMMES

The social security programmes in the Arab states have all been established since the 1950s. All the programmes are traditional defined benefit social insurance programmes. They generally provide both retirement benefits and employment injury benefits. Voluntary occupational pension schemes are not an important source of retirement income.

Iraq was one of the leaders in the region, establishing its retirement benefits programme in 1956. That programme was a provident fund, which was converted to a social insurance scheme in 1964. Syria followed in 1959. By contrast

Oman only started its programme in 1991. The programme in Yemen was also implemented that year, at the time of the reunification of the country. South Yemen had instituted a social security law in 1974 but social security varied among the different sultanates. Falling between these extremes, Saudi Arabia established its programme in 1969 and Kuwait did so in 1976. Prior to 1976 in Kuwait, and similarly for the other countries, schemes existed that provided retirement benefits for civil servants and the military.

The countries in the region are not facing an urgent need to reform caused by financial insolvency. The social security programmes are relatively new and have adequate funding to pay current benefits. Their populations are relatively young, and there is no talk in these countries of the need to raise the retirement age.

Coverage

While the coverage rates tend to be higher than in Africa and Asia, countries in the region generally do not cover all workers with their social security retirement benefit programmes. It is important to distinguish between the coverage of nationals and non-nationals since the labour market in this region is characterized by a large number of migrant workers, both between countries in the region and from those outside. Saudi Arabia, the United Arab Emirates, Kuwait and Jordan are major importers of foreign labour, while other countries, such as Syria, are exporters. This is reflected in the social security pensions. In spite of the international conventions which call for equality of treatment between nationals and non-nationals, some countries, such as Saudi Arabia, Oman, Bahrain and the United Arab Emirates, specifically exclude foreign workers from coverage under the pension schemes (although not under the employment injury scheme).

Other countries draw no distinction in law between national and non-national workers and bilateral agreements exist, such as between Jordan and Egypt, to ensure that pension rights are preserved or converted, when migrant workers return to their home countries. But many of the migrant workers (Syrians, Egyptians, Yemenis, as well as others from South-East Asia) work in host countries such as Jordan, Lebanon and Saudi Arabia in the informal sector, particularly in the construction or services sectors, and are thus effectively outside the scope of social security protection. The coverage of migrant workers in the region is a long-standing problem which shows little sign of being satisfactorily resolved.

As regards the coverage of national workers, typically such groups as the self-employed, casual and temporary workers, domestic servants and members of the family are excluded (although Kuwait and Bahrain cover some of the self-employed and Oman plans to do so). Some countries have chosen to limit coverage to those who work for larger employers: in Bahrain and Saudi Arabia, ten or more workers; in Jordan, five or more.

Retirement age

Some of the Arab states allow receipt of retirement benefits at ages that are young by international standards. These benefits will undoubtedly need to be reviewed in due course, since in most cases either early retirement is not penalized or the penalty is small (for example, a reduction of only 10 per cent is imposed under the Jordanian scheme for early retirement from age 46). In Yemen workers can retire at age 45 with 20 years of contributions; in Kuwait women can retire at age 40 with 20 years of contributions; in Lebanon both men and women can receive benefits at any age with 20 years of employment.

In Bahrain workers can receive retirement benefits at any age while continuing to work so long as they have 20 years of contributions. They receive reduced benefits for retirement before age 60 for men and 55 for women. Some female workers retire as young as 35. In Jordan both men and women can retire at age 46. Saudi Arabia, Bahrain and Iraq, however, all have set a minimum retirement age of 60 for men. In Saudi Arabia a worker can qualify for retirement benefits by working the 60 consecutive months immediately preceding retirement. Workers failing to meet qualifying conditions can receive a refund of their contributions.

In a number of the countries of the region the minimum retirement age is lower for women than for men. Those countries include Bahrain, Iraq, Kuwait and Oman, while in Jordan, Saudi Arabia and Syria the minimum retirement age is the same for both sexes. In Syria, both men and women can receive benefits at age 55 with 20 years of work. In most countries of the region, to receive retirement benefits the individual must have ceased working, or at least ceased working in the sectors of work covered by social security.

Benefits

Lebanon and Yemen differ from the other countries of the region in that, while they also have schemes based on social insurance principles, they pay lump-sum benefits rather than annuities.

In all countries of the region benefits are based on a short averaging period of earnings. In most of the countries benefits are based on the average of the final two years' earnings, but in Kuwait they are based on the final month and in Lebanon they are based on the final month or on the average of the final 12 months, whichever is higher. Apart from the problem that, on this basis, the pensions award does not reflect the lifetime pattern of earnings from labour, in some schemes earnings are manipulated so that the reference period will produce a higher rate of pension.

In Lebanon, although public servants and members of the armed forces receive pensions under special provisions, private sector employees are only entitled to a lump-sum payment on termination of service, which is financed by the employer and which is based on length of service and average earnings. Lebanon is considering starting a social insurance pension scheme, but proposals have not yet been formalized.

In Yemen the process of first unifying schemes following unification of the country (the south had a provident fund for the private sector and a pension scheme for civil servants, and the north a pension scheme for public servants) has been compounded by the desire to unify private and public sector schemes. All other countries with schemes pay pensions, although they generally have separate schemes for public servants. The pension formulas tend to be relatively generous, thus facilitating early retirement and affording limited scope for supplementary arrangements. In most countries of the region, the benefit is calculated at 2 per cent times years of service times the average wage during the reference period, with some countries providing minimum and maximum benefits. Kuwait provides 65 per cent of the last month's earnings plus 2 per cent of the last month's earnings times years of service above 15 years of service. Thus someone working 30 years would receive the maximum replacement rate of 95 per cent of the last month's earnings. This benefit could be received at age 50 for someone working continuously from age 20. Iraq has a relatively small difference between minimum and maximum benefits, the maximum being less than three times the minimum.

In Kuwait up to 25 per cent of the retirement benefit can be received as a lump-sum payment, which has caused some workers to retire in order to receive it. A Kuwaiti woman who has children can retire at any age after 15 years of work and be entitled to a pension for the remainder of her life and her children are entitled to receive a survivors' pension after her death. Kuwaitis working in arduous or dangerous occupations can retire at any age after 20 years of work. Because the self-employed do not receive a fixed income, they are free to declare the amount of income upon which they wish to make contributions. The contribution rate rises over higher income brackets in ten steps of one percentage point each, from 5 to 15 per cent, where 15 per cent equals the amount paid by employers and employees combined.

In Kuwait, with its provisions for early retirement, many doctors, teachers, engineers and other trained professionals, whose education was largely paid for by the Kuwaiti government, have retired before reaching age 40. This has created a loss of highly trained workers and a need to rely more heavily on foreign workers. The high cost of providing generous early retirement has led to a heavy financial burden on the scheme and pressure to reduce the availability of early retirement benefits. Because of this, Kuwaiti law has been amended to gradually phase in a fixed minimum retirement age of 45 for men and 40 for women. Starting in the year 2000, the fixed minimum retirement age will increase until it reaches 55 for men and 50 for women in the year 2020.

In most of the countries of the region benefits in payment are increased irregularly. In 1996 in Jordan benefits were increased by a flat amount or by 10 per cent, whichever was higher. For pensioners receiving the minimum

Table RB4.1 Summary of contributions for pension and lump sum on retirement

Country	Employer's contribution (%)	Employee's contribution (%)	State contribution
Saudi Arabia	8	5	Annual subsidy to cover the deficit
Bahrain	7	5	None
Iraq	12 (20 in oil sector)	5	None
Jordan	8	5	Cover of deficit
Kuwait	10	5	Annual subsidy of 10 of salaries
Lebanon (lump sum)	8.5	–	–
Oman	8	5	5 of remuneration
Syria	14	7	–
Yemen	9	6	6% as employer

benefit, which accounted for 80 per cent of pensioners, the increase was 30 per cent.

Financing

Across the Arab states – except Lebanon – both the employee and employer contribute towards the financing of retirement benefits, with the employer contributing at a higher rate than employees. In Lebanon only the employer contributes. Jordan and Oman have advance funding of benefits. Other countries, such as Syria, use pay-as-you-go financing.

Employee contributions across the region range from 5 to 7 per cent and employer contributions range from 7 to 14 per cent (see table RB4.1). In Bahrain employees who are voluntarily insured must pay both the employee (5 per cent) and employer (7 per cent) mandatory contribution. In Lebanon employees contribute nothing and employers contribute 8.5 per cent of payroll. In Iraq the employers' contribution for social security retirement benefits is considerably higher for oil companies (20 per cent) than for other companies (12 per cent). The employee contribution is 5 per cent. These contributions finance sickness, maternity and employment injury benefits as well as retirement benefits.

In some countries the government also contributes. In Saudi Arabia the actuarial balance of the social security scheme is reviewed at least annually. If the review reveals an actuarial deficit, the state will contribute to cover it. In Oman the government provides a subsidy equal to 5 per cent of total wages. Kuwait provides a large government subsidy of 10 per cent of total payroll. In Jordan the government provides financing for any deficit not financed by employer and employee contributions. In Yemen, by contrast, the government contributes 6 per cent for its employees while all other employers contribute 9 per cent.

Because the scheme in Jordan is fairly young, with few beneficiaries relative to workers contributing, it is building up assets. In 1996 it had assets equal to 17 per cent of GDP, while its expenditures equalled 0.8 per cent of GDP. Its rate of return on its funds that year was 8.1 per cent. It first started paying benefits in 1995. A covered worker in Jordan may make additional voluntary payments to get credit for past service that occurred before the social security law was enacted.

Administration of social security schemes

The administration of most of the social security retirement benefits schemes in the region involves the participation of representatives of both employers and employees. Generally the legislation establishes a public authority or corporation as an independent autonomous legal entity, but with a designated minister providing oversight (usually the Minister of Labour, but the Minister of Finance in the case of Kuwait). The managing institutions in most of the region are politically autonomous from the government, at least in principle. In reality the degree of political autonomy varies, with the politicians having a large influence over the management of the social security institutions in some countries.

The Saudi scheme is administered by an executive board which is composed of four members representing the state, three representing employers and three representing employees. Seventeen regional offices in the main cities are responsible for collecting contributions and paying benefits. In Bahrain the system has an executive board jointly composed of representatives of employers, employees and the state. Because of the small area of the country, all contributions are collected and benefits paid in the capital city. In Iraq, Jordan, Kuwait, Lebanon and Syria the system is also supervised by a tripartite executive board, with an equal number of representatives of employers and employees and a larger number of representatives of the state. Although the boards are intended to be supervisory and the institution autonomous, the scope of the autonomy varies and in some countries is effectively limited by a combination of factors such as the presence of the minister as chairman of the board, the appointment of board members by the minister and the limited experience of board members.

During the wars in North and South Yemen and Lebanon, social security records were destroyed as well as government facilities. Social security administrations are facing the difficult task of rebuilding the government infrastructure.

In Jordan the administrative expenditures of the social security institution were 4 per cent of total revenues in 1995 and 3.3 per cent in 1996. The percentage may have declined as a consequence of the increase in revenues as more workers were brought into the system (Jordan, 1997).

CENTRAL AND EASTERN EUROPE

SOCIOECONOMIC OVERVIEW

The transition countries of Central and Eastern Europe are often considered to be similar, and thus to face the same type of problems. While that was only partly true before the collapse of the centrally planned economies of the region, it has since become even less so. Differences are increasing across countries in their economic and social situation and also in their institutional solutions in the area of social protection.

Countries in the region differ considerably in their levels of economic development and living standards. Some countries, such as the Czech Republic, Hungary and Slovenia, have upper middle-level incomes. Other countries, such as Albania, Macedonia or Moldova, have a relatively low level of income. Average life expectancy at birth also varies significantly across the region, partly reflecting differences in living standards. Differences in per capita income levels and living standards are widening as a result of divergent economic performance among the countries.

During the economic transition from 1989 to 1996, GDP declined in nearly all countries of the region. The countries differ significantly, however, with regard both to the depth of output contraction and to prospects for a return to stable growth. Countries in the Central European Free Trade Agreement group (CEFTA) – the Czech Republic, Hungary, Poland, Slovakia and Slovenia – experienced the smallest decline in output: less than 20 per cent on average.[1] These countries also resumed economic growth in 1993 and were, on average, expected to achieve their pre-transition level of GDP in 1997. The economies of the countries of south-eastern Europe (Albania, Bulgaria, Croatia, the Former Yugoslav Republic of Macedonia, and Romania) contracted by as much as 30 per cent of GDP. Most of these countries were experiencing economic growth in the late 1990s, but it was slow and fragile. In the Baltic states of Estonia, Latvia and Lithuania, the contraction of output during the first half of the 1990s was the most severe and reached as much as 50 per cent of

GDP. All three resumed growth in the second half of the decade. In other former Soviet Union countries (Belarus, Moldova, Russian Federation and Ukraine) output was still contracting in the mid-1990s and growth prospects remain uncertain.

The transition from a centrally planned economy to a market economy has caused significant declines in output, employment, wages and indicators of health. These declines increase demand for social protection benefits. Not only do many more people require such benefits, but also in most countries more older workers are either forced, or encouraged, to retire early by the worsening labour market situation. This creates a greater number of beneficiaries and increases the demand for retirement income financing, which conflicts with shrinking public revenues.

Public revenues are shrinking for two reasons. One is purely economic: lower output, employment and wages reduce revenue from taxes and social security contributions. The privatization of the economy also makes collection of taxes and contributions increasingly difficult, as non-compliance and evasion grow. The second reason is more political in nature: one of the objectives of the transition, explicitly stated in many government programmes, is to make the state apparatus smaller and to restrict the redistribution of resources through the state budget. Political freedom is also making public revenues depend on society's willingness to pay taxes and mandatory contributions. The CEFTA countries have the highest levels of public revenue, even though such revenue is lower than in the past and decreasing. Public expenditure is nearly as high in some countries of the former Soviet Union as it is in the CEFTA group (higher in Ukraine, slightly lower in Russian Federation), but these countries have much larger deficits, which means that the actual level of revenue relative to GDP is significantly lower. In most of the other countries public expenditure has decreased dramatically, to well below 40 per cent of GDP, and the fact that many governments have large deficits demonstrates the difficulties in collecting taxes even at that level. Differences in expenditure and revenues among countries in the region are only partly due to prevailing policies. To a large extent they reflect differences in the governance of public finance, and in the ability to collect revenues at the desired level, which has important implications for social protection systems in these countries, particularly for pension schemes, which consume a large part of public spending.

OVERVIEW OF SOCIAL PROTECTION SYSTEMS

The social protection systems in most Central and Eastern European countries have features inherited from the systems of the former planned economies, which consisted of a visible (explicit) and an invisible (implicit) component. The visible institutionalized system of social security provided pensions, short-term cash benefits and health care. The implicit component added security through specific socialist income redistribution mechanisms, such as guaranteed employment, the provision of low-cost housing and heavily subsidized basic goods and services (for example food and services for large families, educational supplies, books and cultural goods and services). There was also a system of cash and in-kind benefits provided by state enterprises for employees, their families and retirees, such as cash allowances, subsidized recreational facilities and vacations, and subsidized short- and long-term loans.

The collapse of the command economies in Central and Eastern Europe ended the era of guaranteed full employment. As old state and emerging private enterprises struggle for survival in a market economy, they cannot afford to provide social employment. For the same reason they are moving away from providing social benefits and services. State enterprises are often still obliged to provide some social funds. In many countries of the region, however, the share of those employed by the state sector has radically decreased and private enterprises are, in most cases, neither obliged nor willing to provide social benefits.[2] These social functions of the labour market, along with many consumer subsidies, were transferred to the explicit social protection systems, which suddenly faced enormous new challenges.

In a majority of the centrally planned economies the provision and financing of explicit social security benefits (pensions, short-term benefits and health care) through social insurance contributions was replaced by government provision and financing. Social assistance, as well as welfare and unemployment benefits, played a small role. The unavoidable side effects of the difficult structural economic transition to a market economy during the first half of the 1990s have forced an adjustment to the emergence of unemployment and the rapid increase of poverty. Since 1990 unemployment benefit schemes have been introduced or adapted, and social assistance schemes developed for an increasing number of people who have fallen into poverty.

The emerging explicit social protection systems resemble the classic three-tier structure prevalent in western Europe:

- social assistance schemes, providing means-tested benefits for those in need;
- universal benefits, available to all citizens;
- social security schemes, providing benefits for employed or contributing members.

RETIREMENT, INVALIDITY AND SURVIVORS' BENEFITS

Social security pensions for the elderly and the disabled were part of the social protection systems in the former centrally planned economies of Central and Eastern Europe. Those pension schemes were designed to work in a different economic and social environment than the one that emerged in the late 1980s and the 1990s.

First, in the past, few countries in the region had high inflation rates. Price adjustments of controlled prices were made periodically and were usually followed by adjustments to pension levels. Most pension schemes thus had no automatic provisions for the indexation of pension benefits. After 1990 nearly all of the countries in the region had high and persistent inflation. To prevent benefits from deteriorating, adjustments were made, many of which were flat-rate adjustments distorting benefit structures. Some schemes, such as those of Bulgaria and Ukraine, have managed to maintain the differentiation between minimum and maximum pension levels, although flat-rate compensations have reduced the difference between minimum and maximum pensions (from a factor of three to two in Bulgaria). In other countries, such as Latvia and Lithuania, earnings-related pensions have degenerated into flat-rate pension schemes. Introduction of adjustment mechanisms became one of the first important changes in the pension schemes, although this was practical only when inflation rates decreased and stabilized.

Second, the region's pension schemes were designed for a situation of moderate differences in earnings. Earnings differences have increased dramatically in all transition economies.[3] At the same time, social security pensions were the only source of retirement security, with no supplementary pensions. Widening differences in earnings, coupled with the reduced differential between minimum and maximum pensions, are the source of complaints by higher earners and of pressure to make the present schemes more earnings-related and less redistributive. This in turn opens the possibility for supplementary pensions.

The former pension schemes granted relatively early retirement pensions, generally to men at age 60 and women at age 55 (except in Poland, where the ages were 65 and 60, respectively). Typical qualifying conditions were 25 years of contributions for men and 20 years for women. People such as miners, who worked under unhealthy or hazardous conditions, were allowed to draw retirement pensions earlier. Similarly, earlier retirement ages often applied to mothers with more than four or five children or with disabled children, and also to certain categories of people disabled from birth.

In many countries in the region, high unemployment induced governments to provide new regulations allowing earlier retirement for other categories of workers. As a result, actual retirement ages are much lower than the already low early retirement age. In addition pensioners may continue working in many countries, often without substantial reduction in benefits, but rising hidden or open unemployment has led to a sharp decline in pensioner employment in many countries. In Slovakia, for example, the proportion of working retirement pensioners fell from 33 per cent to 13 per cent over the period 1989–92.[4]

Retirement pension benefit formulas normally use a fixed percentage of reference income for the required minimum number of years, plus an increment for additional years of service. Reference income is usually an average over several years (the last years before retirement or the best years during a career), but the calculation might not take into account the full amount of individual income. Some countries define a number of income bands and calculate annual reference income as the sum of a descending series of factors times the width of the band.[5] Owing to this calculation method, the actual replacement rates of pensions are a decreasing function of income. Actual replacement rates are generous, and could reach 75 per cent of the reference income for 40 to 45 years of service and 50 per cent or 55 per cent for as little as 20 or 25 years of service (for example, in Slovakia and Ukraine).

Invalidity pensions are paid at two or three different rates, according to the degree of disability, but without crediting notional insurance periods from the start of invalidity up to the earliest retirement age, as is often done in western Europe. Survivors' pensions are paid as a percentage of the pension entitlement of the deceased. Retirement, invalidity and survivors' pensions are generally subject to a minimum and maximum pension provision. For example, in Ukraine the maximum is three times the minimum pension.

Social pensions for elderly people who do not otherwise qualify for a pension are paid five years after the normal retirement age. The social pension is less than or equal to the minimum pension for retirement, survivor and invalidity. Social and minimum pensions were originally linked to the minimum wage. This link, however, has been severed in many countries (for example, in Bulgaria, Russian Federation and Ukraine). In some of these countries minimum wages have been deliberately held at a low level, leading to the inequitable situation that minimum pensions are higher than minimum wages (for example, in the Russian Federation).

Many countries provide generous eligibility conditions for invalidity pensions, which are often used for early retirement. This is particularly true in Poland, where invalidity pensioners account for nearly 40 per cent of all pensioners. In many other countries – for example in Croatia, Hungary, Macedonia, F.Y.R. and Slovakia – invalidity pensioners exceed 20 per cent of the total (see table RB5.1).

The experience of pension schemes can be described by their average replacement rate (the average pension divided by average earnings subject to contributions) and the system dependency ratio (number of pensioners/number of contributors). The product of these two figures is the net pay-as-you-go contribution rate of the scheme (disregarding non-collection of contributions) expressed as a percentage of total insurable earnings of the insured population. Table RB5.2 summarizes these crucial indicators for selected countries.

The estimated net pay-as-you-go contribution rates in Central and Eastern Europe are at a normal level (if one takes into account that they are calculated the basis of on net incomes) for mature European pension schemes. The system dependency ratios, however, are high. They are much higher than demographic dependency ratios, which are the proportion of those older than working age to those in the working age (compare also table RB5.3). The main reasons for this are the high number of pensioners of working age and the high number of unemployed and thus non-contributing persons. The average financial ratios given above refer to an average of all pensions (retirement, invalidity and

Table RB5.1 Percentage distribution of pensioners by pension type, 1990–93

Country	1990	1991	1992	1993
Albania				
Retirement	75.3	77.1	79.1	79.9
Invalidity	8.4	7.1	6.5	5.9
Survivors'	16.3	15.8	14.4	14.2
Bulgaria				
Retirement	83.0	84.7	85.6	85.8
Invalidity	8.3	8.0	7.7	7.6
Survivors'	6.3	5.1	4.5	4.3
Croatia				
Retirement	46.1	n.a.	52.0	52.4
Invalidity	26.6	n.a.	22.7	22.5
Survivors'	27.3	n.a.	25.3	25.1
Czech Republic				
Retirement	54.5	54.9	55.1	54.9
Invalidity	18.4	18.5	18.7	19.1
Survivors'	27.1	26.6	26.2	26.0
Hungary				
Retirement	56.5	56.7	55.2	54.6
Invalidity	21.0	21.5	22.6	23.0
Survivors'	14.4	13.5	12.6	11.8
Lithuania				
Retirement	n.a.	79.7	79.1	78.7
Invalidity	n.a.	13.6	14.9	15.4
Survivors'	n.a.	6.7	6.0	5.9
Poland				
Retirement	41.9	44.9	45.8	46.0
Invalidity	39.0	37.5	37.4	37.3
Survivors'	10.1	16.6	16.4	16.3
Romania				
Retirement	74.8	75.2	73.9	72.7
Invalidity	7.3	7.6	8.8	10.3
Survivors'	17.9	17.2	17.3	17.0
Slovakia				
Retirement	50.4	51.1	51.1	50.7
Invalidity	22.2	22.1	22.7	23.1
Survivors'	51.5	52.4	26.3	26.2
The Former Yugoslav Republic of Macedonia				
Retirement	51.5	52.4	52.8	54.1
Invalidity	20.8	21.1	21.1	20.8
Survivors'	27.7	26.5	26.0	25.1

Source: World Bank (1996d).

Table RB5.2 Financial and demographic structure of selected pension schemes in Central and Eastern Europe, early 1990s

Country, year	Dependency ratio (%)	Financial ratio (%)	Net pay-as-you-go contribution rate (%)
Bulgaria, 1992	80	34	27
Czech Republic, 1992	61	37	23
Latvia, 1994	56	42	24
Lithuania, 1992	46	30	14
Slovakia, 1993	60	44	26
Ukraine, 1993	58	43	25
Russian Federation, 1993	49	42	21

Source: Data collected by ILO, Central and Eastern European Team, Budapest.

Table RB5.3 Pensioners as a percentage of contributors, Central and Eastern Europe (system dependency ratios in selected countries)

Country	1990	1991	1992	1993
Albania	0.22	0.27	0.35	0.97*
Bulgaria	0.55	0.65	0.78	0.80
Croatia	0.31	n. a.	0.40	0.43
Czech Republic	0.42	0.46	0.50	0.51
Hungary	0.47	0.50	0.58	0.66
Poland	0.40	0.45	0.49	0.53
Romania	0.34	0.38	0.43	0.49
Slovakia	0.39	0.45	0.50	0.53
The Former Yugoslav Republic of Macedonia	0.22	0.24	0.26	0.28

Note: *In 1993 state farms were privatized. Before privatization of agriculture, state farms paid social security contributions for their workers. Starting in 1993, workers were required to pay for themselves, but few did.

Source: Andrews and Rashid (1996).

survivor). The average statistical replacement rates of retirement pensions are generally only slightly higher than the overall averages. These figures demonstrate that in many Central and Eastern European countries, high system dependency ratios are offset by pensions that are low in relation to average wages, in spite of formerly generous pension schemes. The main reasons for this dichotomy are the absence of automatic pension adjustments for inflation and the limitations on maximum pension amounts.

The average replacement rate for the region as a whole was stable over the period 1989–94 at about 50 per cent (see table RB5.4). In CEFTA countries the average was higher – about 60 per cent, but with large differences between countries: from 45–46 per cent in the Czech Republic and Slovakia to well

Table RB5.4 Average replacement rates of retirement pensions, 1989–95 (as percentage of net wages), Central and Eastern Europe

Countries	1989	1990	1991	1992	1994	1995
Albania	76.9	74.2	74.6	45.5	44.0	54.2
Belarus	n.a.	25.7	38.8	21.8	37.2	34.7
Bulgaria	57.3	48.2	53.5	43.5	44.1	46.8
Croatia	na	73.0	62.8	56.6	62.0	na
Czech Republic	47.9	49.8	51.8	46.3	45.8	46.8
Estonia	38.5	33.2	n.a.	46.3	35.0	38.9
Hungary	63.1	62.6	64.3	60.9	59.6	56.9
Latvia	37.6	29.8	26.0	34.6	30.7	33.5
Lithuania	40.7	43.9	44.3	52.5	49.4	45.9
Moldova	41.5	43.5	35.9	63.6	64.1	53.5
Poland	44.6	65.0	76.2	72.5	72.8	74.8
Romania	54.9	46.5	44.6	43.1	49.2	49.2
Russian Federation	35.5	33.7	33.8	25.8	33.6	35.0
Slovakia	49.2	51.0	53.6	49.1	48.1	45.0
Slovenia	75.2	89.2	73.6	77.8	73.9	75.4
The Former Yugoslav Republic of Macedonia	na	8.5	67.3	75.8	82.3	na
CEFTA	*56.0*	*63.5*	*63.9*	*61.3*	*60.0*	*59.8*
South-eastern Europe	*63.0*	*64.1*	*60.6*	*52.9*	*56.3*	*50.1*
Baltic Republics	*39.2*	*35.6*	*35.2*	*44.5*	*38.4*	*39.4*
Former Soviet Union	*38.5*	*33.6*	*32.9*	*32.7*	*43.5*	*41.1*
Average	**51.0**	**51.7**	**51.5**	**49.1**	**51.2**	**50.5**

over 70 per cent in Poland and Slovenia. In south-eastern European countries average replacement rates fell from above 60 per cent to 50 per cent of the average wage. In the countries of the former Soviet Union, replacement rates are 40 per cent or less.

Total expenditure on pensions as a percentage of GDP is high on average for CEFTA countries, but this is mainly due to the high level reported for Poland (see table RB5.5). The figure for Poland is above 15 per cent, but this is not fully comparable with those of other countries because pension expenditure there includes personal income tax deducted from pension payments, while in other countries pension benefits are not taxed. Nevertheless net estimates show that Polish pension expenditure in comparable terms is approximately 13 per cent, which is still the highest in the region. In other CEFTA countries, pension expenditures are between 9 and 11 per cent of GDP.

Differences in expenditure levels are not due to different population age structures, which in fact are generally similar over the region. To a degree, they reflect differences in the generosity of the schemes, such as early retirement and entitlement to invalidity pensions. The various levels of expenditure, however, can be explained to a large extent by different policies towards retirement pensions. Some countries can only afford early retirement and other generous

Table RB5.5 Pension expenditure as percentage of GDP, Central and Eastern
Europe

Country	Source	1989	1990	1991	1992	1993	1994	1995
Albania	UNICEF, 1995	5.7	6.8	10.1	6.2	6.2	–	5.7
Belarus	UNICEF, 1995	–	6.2	6.4	5.7	6.0	–	–
Bulgaria	UNICEF, 1995	8.7	8.7	9.4	10.2	10.9	9.7	8.0
Croatia	Andrews and Rashid, 1996	–	13.6	10.6	6.0	6.2	–	–
Czech Republic	Ministry of Labour, 1996	8.3	8.0	7.8	8.4	8.4	8.4	9.0
Estonia	World Bank, 1996b	–	–	–	5.3	6.6	6.4	7.0
Hungary	ILO, 1997c	9.0	9.7	10.2	10.4	10.3	10.8	9.9
Latvia	UNICEF, 1995	6.3	5.8	7.8	6.2	9.9	11.8	–
Lithuania	UNICEF, 1995	4.9	5.5	6.1	5.8	5.1	6.3	6.7
Poland	ILO calculations	6.7	8.1	12.4	14.6	14.9	15.8	15.6
Romania	Andrews and Rashid, 1996	5.7	6.9	7.0	6.8	6.2	–	–
Russian Federation	UNICEF, 1995	5.9	6.0	6.6	7.3	6.4	5.9	–
Slovakia	ILO, 1995a	7.8	7.9	8.6	9.9	9.1	8.7	8.6
The Former Yugoslav Republic of Macedonia	Andrews and Rashid, 1996	–	10.4	11.4	11.4	15.6	–	–
CEFTA		*7.6*	*8.4*	*10.7*	*12.1*	*12.2*	*12.7*	*12.5*
South-eastern Europe		–	*9.0*	*8.5*	*7.3*	*7.1*	–	–
Baltic Republics		*5.6*	*5.7*	*7.0*	*5.8*	*7.3*	*9.5*	–
Former Soviet Union		–	*5.8*	*6.6*	*7.2*	*6.6*	–	–
Average		–	6.7	7.1	8.4	8.0	–	–

Note: Data for Poland for 1989–91 and 1992–95 are not comparable, since 1992 gross pension expenditure
includes personal income tax deducted from paid pensions. In most other countries, pension benefits are not
subject to taxation. Estimates show that net pension expenditure was 12.6 per cent of GDP in 1992 and 1993.

entitlement conditions because they pay low pensions. In other countries, such
as Poland, policies aimed at maintaining replacement rates at reasonable levels
must lead – if there are no significant changes in the system – to high expenditures, which will be difficult to afford in the long run.

Major developments and reform initiatives

The benefits provided by existing and newly created social protection systems
are not sufficient to handle current social problems. All Central and Eastern
European countries are trying to adapt their social protection systems to the
new economic, social and political environment. The state of the reform process
varies greatly from country to country. For the most part, however, reforms are
proceeding on parallel tracks: a short-term, ad hoc, track and a long-term,
structural track.

The earliest reforms were emergency responses to emerging problems. This
category included decrees providing new unemployment benefits and social
assistance benefits, or decrees repeatedly adjusting pension benefits to high
inflation. These elements were often part of more comprehensive reforms

which did not clear political hurdles fast enough to satisfy urgent needs. By the late 1990s the phase of emergency reactions to the new problems of poverty and open or hidden unemployment reached a consolidation stage. The benefit systems were in place, but were not yet functioning properly.

The second reform track represented an attempt to tackle long-term conceptual, design and financial issues relevant to the social protection system. This process began in many countries with a separation of social insurance funds and institutions from government administration (as in Albania, the Czech Republic, Hungary and Slovakia). Sometimes basic pension schemes were supplemented by voluntary tiers (for example, in the Czech Republic and Hungary). Comprehensive reform of basic pension schemes has been implemented thus far in the Czech Republic, Latvia and, most recently, also in Hungary (1998), Croatia and Poland (1999). All other countries in the region have debated reforms for several years, but only in a few of them had those debates reached the parliamentary stage by the end of 1998 (for example, Slovenia). Partial measures have been adopted in some countries, gradually phasing out privileges for special employment categories, initiating gradual increases in the retirement ages and modifying formulas for pension and entitlement conditions. Nearly everywhere reform concepts have been developed and are the subject of government discussion and public debate. In Bulgaria a White Paper on social security reform was drafted in 1994, but the shape of the future pension scheme was still under discussion four years later. (See box RB5.1 for further information about pension reform in Bulgaria.)

The social protection systems reform proposals in Central and Eastern Europe, discussed or emerging from the debates on reform in the late 1990s, typically include the following:

- modified social insurance retirement pensions with a higher retirement age and longer contributory period required, providing benefits through purely, or almost purely, earnings/contributions-related benefit formulas. These reforms are normally combined with supplementary (voluntary or mandatory, private or occupational) second- and third-tier pension schemes to complement statutory social security benefits;
- lower replacement rates for maternity and sickness benefits;
- consolidation of unemployment benefit schemes;[6]
- improved social assistance benefits, resulting from better definitions of eligibility and the construction of new or reshaped delivery networks;
- a mixed health care delivery and financing system, in which personal health care benefits would be provided and financed by new health insurance schemes, with public health services remaining in the realm of the government and shared service delivery between the public and private sectors;
- streamlining of usually elaborate family benefit schemes, with many benefits becoming income related;

Box RB5.1 Bulgaria

Bulgaria's social security scheme was started in 1957. Until 1995 the Ministry of Labour and Social Welfare was responsible for its operation. Since then the National Social Security Institute has managed Bulgaria's social protection system as an autonomous tripartite body. It relies on the state, however, as its guarantor to finance its annual deficits.

Bulgaria's social insurance scheme is based on the defined benefit approach with universal coverage, including employees from the private and public sectors, self-employed workers, members of cooperatives and professional associations. Coverage has remained stable since 1990. The National Social Security Institution provides wide protection for the contingencies of retirement, invalidity, death and employment injury. Through its regular pension payments, the National Social Security Institution has also provided different types of social assistance benefits – for example, family and electricity allowances – which accounted for nearly 10 per cent of the National Social Security Insurance benefit expenditure in 1996 and contributed to the deterioration of the financial situation of the institution.

Social security benefits have traditionally been financed solely from employers' contributions. Only in recent years have employee contributions, set at 2 per cent of insurable earnings, been levied. Contribution rates vary according to employment categories as determined by the Labour Code of Bulgaria: a contribution rate of 52 per cent of insurable earnings is payable by those in the most arduous employment (Category I), 47 and 37 per cent by those in Employment Categories II and III, respectively. The overall average contribution rate was 39 per cent in 1996. In 1996 about 80 per cent of workers were in Employment Category III, under which the normal retirement age is 55 for women and 60 for men, and the required service for a full pension is 20 years and 25 years, respectively.

In exchange for paying higher contribution rates, workers under Employment Categories I and II have been entitled to favourable eligibility conditions for receiving retirement pension. For example, they can retire as early as age 47 for women and age 52 for men if they satisfy a minimum required period of 15 years' service. Although the government intended that the higher contribution rates would compensate for the additional cost of providing more generous provisions for these Employment Categories, there has been cross-subsidization coming from Employment Category III. This factor contributed to the deteriorating financial situation of the social protection system of Bulgaria and was further compounded by strong pressures coming from trade unions to entitle their members to be classified under the more favoured Employment Categories I and II.

The financial situation of the National Social Security Institution has been markedly affected by the ageing problem of Bulgaria, which is well ahead of most other countries in the world, as low fertility rates have prevailed for many years. After a steep decline at the beginning of the 1990s the number of contributors remained fairly stable over recent years at nearly 3.1 million in 1996, who represented 37 per cent of the 8.4 million general population and 80 per cent of the labour force. The number of pensioners, however, has increased since 1990, especially in the initial years of transition, while the number remained relatively stable after 1993 with approximately 2.3 million pensioners in 1996, of whom 87 per cent received lifetime retirement pensions. This implies an old-age National Social Security Insurance dependency ratio of 59 retirement pensioners per 100 contributions, which is high compared to the corresponding ratio for the general population of 36 people aged 60 and older per 100 people aged 15 to 59.

Since 1990 the government has taken various initiatives to adapt to a new economic and social environment but these moves have generally been regarded as too slow. An apparent consequence was the economic turmoil of 1996–97, with inflation soaring in 1997. Thus in addition to having a demographic problem, the National Social Security Institute had to deal with hyper-inflation which was not a major issue before the reform process stalled. Reforms adopted by the government to make pensions more equitable for all pensioners, through the use of individual coefficients that harmonize the past earnings level of all individuals in reference to the national average wage, turned out to be futile because of high inflation.

Since April 1996 the National Social Security Insurance has reinforced the earnings-related basis of its pension formula, defined as the individual co-efficient in reference to the national average wage times the individual replacement rate (calculated as 55 per cent plus 2 per cent times years of service in excess of the minimum requirement) times the past 3-year national average wage. Under hyper-inflation almost any mechanism for updating the national average wage must fail because prices are increasing so fast, and the government could not provide adequate benefit protection. Instead temporary income measures were adopted through the granting of uniform flat compensation supplements to all pensioners which led to an equalization of pensioners' incomes – in contrast to the earlier measures aimed at reinforcement of the earnings-related aspect of the pension formula. The inadequacy of the income measures taken is reflected by the fact that in 1997 only about 6.5 per cent of GDP was redistributed to eligible persons, whereas in 1995 this rate was 9.5 per cent.

The ILO strongly recommended to the government the use of an alternative method to index National Social Security Institute benefits on the basis of projected inflation rates, so that the purchasing power of pensions could be stabilized (at low levels) without creating undue pressure on the scheme's finances. The National Social Security Institute took advantage of the flexibility of its defined benefit scheme for adjusting its benefits in payment. Also the ILO stressed to the National Social Security Institute the need to gradually harmonize benefit provisions for all insured persons by eliminating special privileges on the basis of employment groups, to provide social assistance benefits outside the scope of the National Social Security Institute regular benefits and to strengthen the institute's administrative system in order to enhance compliance in reporting and paying contributions to the scheme. Reporting procedures were improved through the establishment and maintenance of individual records on the insured population as opposed to individual data that were decentralized at the employer level in the past.

The fundamental problem facing Bulgaria – the low contributor to pensioner ratio – should be dealt with through two significant changes: (1) raising the retirement age; and (2) increasing employment (in order to compensate for the losses that accrued at the beginning of the 1990s). These changes are outside the policy responsibility and capacity of the National Social Security Institute and must be achieved through other means.

- replacement of general housing subsidies with housing allowances earmarked for low-income households.

Implicit social protection benefits (such as consumer subsidies and social employment) will, in the future, only play a marginal role. In view of budgetary shortages and increasing demands on social protection systems, governments are increasingly seeking off-budget financing for social security. The most prominent means of off-loading a portion of the social protection burden from the government budget is to reintroduce social insurance financing[7]. Governments try to use the social insurance mechanism to move away from the financing of personal social security, such as earnings-related individual pensions and personal health services, while concentrating on the financing of anti-poverty benefits (for example, social assistance schemes, and social insurance contributions for the needy) and ensuring transfers to families with children. Disconnecting personal social security benefits from the government budget also yields an advantage for those insured: their future benefit levels may be less vulnerable to the adverse effects of shrinking government budgets.

The assignment of parts of the benefit delivery system to quasi-autonomous social insurance schemes will also have implications for the governance of social protection. In some countries, employers and trade unions will exercise stronger oversight of the social protection system[8].

A typical pattern for the new financial structure of the overall reforms is summarized in table RB5.6. This general pattern can be observed in Bulgaria, Latvia,[9] Lithuania, Russia and Ukraine.

The net balance of shifts in financing can be calculated for specific countries. In Bulgaria, for example, reform could yield a slight net reduction of government social expenditure (based on the assumption that the government will pay social insurance contributions for those who cannot pay). The strategic advantage for the ministries of finance in restructured social security financing lies in cutting budgetary links with the two major expenditure categories of pensions and personal health services, which generally account for about two-thirds of overall national social protection expenditure. These two items will have the biggest cost increases in the near, and longer-term, future.

The reform process is complex and inevitably fraught with problems, of which the most obvious are the lack of coordination and other deficiencies in the management of change and insufficient analytical back-up. The immense complexity of social protection systems, and uncertainty about the economic

Table RB5.6   Post-reform financing structures of Central and Eastern European social protection systems

Social protection component	Financed through:	Replacing financing through:	Expected net shift
Social insurance Pensions and short-term benefits	Social insurance contributions of employers and increasing employee contributions, with state contributions to the needy	Employer payroll levies with direct links to general budget	To employers and gradually to employees
Unemployment benefits	Social insurance contributions of employers and employees (financing unemployment benefits, employment policy and employment services)	Previously budgeted financing only for marginal expenditure (in place since the early 1990s)	To employees and employers
Universal benefits Health care	*Personal health services* through social insurance contributions of employees, employers and the government (for the needy)	General taxation	To employers and employees
	Public health services through general and local taxes		To local governments
Family benefits	General taxation (financing streamlined benefits)	General taxation and, to some extent, social insurance	General taxation
Social assistance	General and local taxes	On a smaller scale, mainly financed from central government tax revenue	Increasing role of local taxes

and financial sustainability of long-term social commitments, are playing an increasing role. Stalemate in the political decision-making process in many countries slows the reform process. But delays are also caused by factors rooted in these countries' governance and administrative systems, which are not yet geared to engineer far-reaching reforms in pluralistic societies.

Pension reforms undertaken or discussed in some Central and Eastern European countries[10]

Many countries in the region during the late 1990s were making modest changes in their pension schemes and were discussing fundamental reform measures. A full legal framework for private pension funds has only been introduced in the Czech Republic, Hungary, Poland and Slovakia. Russia also has private pension funds, but foundations of the regulatory framework were adopted only in 1998. Only in the Czech Republic and Hungary have these voluntary pension funds started to play a more important role (with coverage reaching 33 per cent and 15 per cent, respectively, of the labour force in 1997). Several countries have started the process of increasing the retirement age. The Czech Republic, Latvia, Hungary and, most recently, Poland and Croatia are the only ones to have begun implementing completely new laws relating to social security pensions. In many countries discussion concentrates on issues concerning the role of a new mandatory funded pillar in the pension scheme. This is despite the fact that, as in the case of Hungary[11] and Poland,[12] the present pay-as-you-go systems can be made financially sustainable after necessary modifications (such as an increased retirement age and tightened eligibility conditions). Below we present examples of reforms already introduced or discussed.

Albania

The legal basis for a three-tier pension scheme has been established (basic compulsory pension insurance, occupational pension plans and additional voluntary pension insurance), but laws on occupational pensions have not yet been implemented (apart from additional pension provisions for civil servants). The process of a gradual increase in retirement ages and required contributory periods for special employment categories has begun. Employee contributions have been introduced (up to 10 per cent of monthly wages). Qualifying conditions for invalidity pensions have been tightened.

Belarus

The upper level of employers' contributions (which are differentiated) was decreased from 40.8 per cent to 35 per cent, and benefit indexation introduced.

Bulgaria

A gradual increase in the retirement age to 63 years for both men and women has been initiated and a 2 per cent employee contribution introduced. The National Social Insurance Institute, which manages pensions and short-term benefits, has been separated from government administration.

Croatia

After four years of discussion, a new draft law on social security pensions was presented to the public in 1997. The new law was adopted by the parliament in the summer of 1998. The pay-as-you-go social security pension scheme will be made purely contribution-related (based on a points system). The retirement age will be gradually increased. The law includes provisions for the introduction of a mandatory, fully funded tier.

Czech Republic

A two-tier pension scheme was established, with a defined benefit pay-as-you-go pension having a flat rate and earnings-related component as the first tier. The retirement age is gradually being increased to 62 for men and 57–61 for women, depending on the number of children they have raised. The period of earnings used in the benefit formula was increased to 30 years. A second voluntary tier is supported by state contributions. However in 1997 public debate was reopened on the proposal to also introduce a mandatory fully funded tier into the retirement pension scheme.

Estonia

A gradual increase in the minimum retirement age to 65/60 for men/women has been introduced, to be completed by 2003.

Hungary

In Hungary an autonomous National Pension Fund, supervised by employers and trade unions was established in 1991, but it was put back under direct state supervision in the summer of 1998. A voluntary pension tier was introduced in 1995 (based on mutual funds). After two years of preparatory work and intense public debate, parliament passed a new pension law in the summer of 1997. From the beginning of 1998, a new system has started to be gradually implemented consisting of two mandatory tiers. One tier will be pay-as-you-go defined benefit, and purely earnings-related (financed by three-quarters of the total present pension contributions), providing a replacement rate of 40% after 35 years of contributions. The second tier will be a fully funded individual retirement savings scheme. The new system will be compulsory for all new entrants to the labour market. Persons under 47 years of age at the beginning of 1998 may opt for the new system or stay in the current system.

Latvia

The retirement age for women is being gradually increased to 60. A new, three-tier system was introduced in the late 1990s. The first tier is pay-as-you-go and defined contribution (based on "notional funding"). The second tier will be a relatively small mandatory defined contribution tier, fully funded and privately managed. The third tier is voluntary and supplementary, through occupational and individual pension plans.

Poland

After several years of debating various reform proposals, an outline of the reform was approved by parliament in 1997. After most of the new laws had been finally adopted at the end of 1998, implementation of the reform started at the beginning of 1999.The former social security system is gradually being replaced by a system consisting of two mandatory pillars: the first financed on a pay-as-you-go but defined contribution basis (similar in design to the system introduced in Latvia) and the second a fully funded and privately managed defined contribution scheme. Everybody covered by the social insurance scheme, and younger than 50, enters the notional defined contribution tier (with the initial "notional capital" being assigned for all those with the acquired rights under the old scheme). One-third of the contributions to the retirement pension scheme will go to the second fully funded tier, which is obligatory for anyone younger than 30. Those between 30 and 50 years old at the time the reform took effect can choose between having all their contributions going to the notional defined contribution scheme or opting to have one-third going to the licensed private pension funds. The pension fund managers must place their funds with custodial banks. As of 1998, 22 companies had applied for licences to be pension fund managers. Among other regulations, limits have been set for investments: funds can invest up to 40 per cent in the primary stock market shares, 5 per cent in foreign shares, 10 per cent in the secondary stock market, 10 per cent in National Investment Funds, 10 per cent in National Bank bonds and 15 per cent in municipality bonds. The pension fund managers must place their funds with custodial banks. (Box RB5.2 compares the pension reforms of Hungary and Poland.)

CONCEPTUAL DEFICIENCIES AND PRIORITY PROBLEMS

The initial changes made in pension schemes understandably reacted to immediate social needs with insufficient time to develop a coherent concept for reform. Benefit reforms tend to proceed in departmental isolation and sometimes lack clear priorities. Although to some extent contrary to the most urgent needs and logical priorities, debates on national reform often focus on cash social security benefits. The upgrading of social assistance schemes plays a minor role in the present debate, in spite of the grave problem of poverty. Blueprints for new pension schemes are often discussed without reference to social assistance schemes. Health schemes are developed without regard to possible cooperation with other social protection subsystems, while housing and other subsidies are cut without the impact on social assistance schemes being assessed.

Lack of national consensus

Social protection reforms affect several generations. They require a broader social consensus than short-lived parliamentary majorities. No social protection system can be sustained without widespread public acceptance. Achieving consensus depends on a dialogue between the government, major societal groups and, notably, the chief contributors of the social security system (employers and employees) as well as the general public. Such a dialogue, however, is

Box RB5.2 Retirement pension reforms in Hungary and Poland
At the end of 1998 Hungary and Poland were the only two transition countries in Central and Eastern Europe to introduce a mandatory funded component of a significant size into their reformed pension schemes, and to actually start implementing such a reform.

Pre-reform systems
Both countries had defined benefit, pay-as-you-go financed pension schemes, covering practically all employed persons (in the Polish case, there is a separate scheme for farmers which stays intact under the current reform) and providing retirement, invalidity and survivors' pensions. In both countries, the systems provided replacement rates of over 70 per cent after 40 years of contributions for those with previous earnings close to average, but these rates were much lower for all those with higher earnings. Polish schemes were generally more generous, and this can be seen when one looks at the overall costs: Poland was spending, in the mid-1990s, about 14 per cent of GDP on all pensions (including invalidity, survivors' and farmers' pensions), while in Hungary it was about 10 per cent of GDP – still relatively high compared with many other Central and Eastern European countries.

New system: First tier
In Hungary the defined benefit first-tier pension will be a percentage of average adjusted past earnings subject to contributions (1.22 per cent for each year of the contributory period). Thus, after 40 years of contributions it will give a replacement rate of 48.8 per cent. Retirement age will be increased to 62.

In Poland the first tier will be a notional defined contribution one. All the contributions paid will be recorded into the individual notional account. The accumulated amount will be increased every year by an index calculated as a weighted average of the consumer price index (with weight 25 per cent) and of the growth index of the sum of earnings subject to contributions (75 per cent). The pension will equal accumulated notional capital, divided by the average statistical life expectancy at the age equal to the age of the person retiring (minimum retirement age will be 60 for women and 65 for men). Final replacement rates will depend on the long-term future trend of real wages and employment (number of contributors). If the number of contributors is more or less stable, the replacement rate will not exceed 30 per cent after 40 years of service.

Poland also introduced a Demographic Reserve Fund which will be financed by a contribution of 1 per cent of the gross earnings. Resources of this fund cannot be used before the year 2009.

Funded tier
Eventually, in both countries, contributions to the funded tier will be at the level of 7–8 per cent of gross earnings. Replacement rates will, of course, depend on long-term rates of return of the pension funds compared with real wage growth. If the rate of return does not exceed real wage growth, one can expect a replacement rate of about 20 per cent after 40 years of contributions.

Hungarian regulations allow even relatively small pension funds to enter the second tier. They also allow various ownership forms, including mutual funds. Polish law is much more restrictive in this area, and only allows relatively big shareholders' companies to have licences to manage the funds (with at least 4 million ECU of the initial capital).

Although there were many pension funds licensed at the beginning of the Hungarian reform, after one year the five biggest funds had 80 per cent of all the participants in the second tier. In Poland more than 20 companies were licensed, most of them, as in Hungary, being a joint venture of big banks and insurance companies. Contributors are free to choose funds and can switch between them. In Hungary switching between funds can be frequent, and is less costly to the participants than in the case of the Polish regulations.

Benefits can be paid in the form of various types of life annuities. In Hungary pension funds accumulating contributions will also be responsible for distributing benefits. Polish law on the distribution of benefits had not been passed at the end of 1998, but the draft provides for the existence of special licensed insurance companies which would take care of the distribution.

Minimum pension provisions and guarantees

In Hungary there is no overall minimum pension guarantee within the new system. Instead there will be means-tested social assistance type benefits for the elderly. There is also a minimum guaranteed pension within the funded tier: 25 per cent of a member's first-tier pension (after at least 15 years of contributions). In Poland the law introduced an overall minimum pension guarantee: if a person's pension (from both tiers, after not less than 20/25 years of contributions) is lower than a minimum pension, then such a pension will be increased to the minimum level (this will be financed by the state budget).

In the two countries there are similar regulations aimed at increasing the security of the funded pensions (such as minimum rates of return requirements, guarantee funds, investment rules, and custodianship).

Indexation

In Hungary first-tier benefits will be adjusted in line with a weighted average of price and wages growth (50–50). There are no provisions for indexing second-tier pensions. In Poland the indexation coefficient (to be decided by the parliament every year) should not be lower than the price increase plus (if real wages grow) 20 per cent of the average wage increase. Indexation of the second-tier benefits is also envisaged, but the form has not been specified.

Opting out and transition

In both countries the new, two-tier system is mandatory for new entrants to the labour market (in Poland to all those younger than 30 at the start of the reform). In Hungary all the others had a choice, either to stay in the old system (with slightly modified rules) or to join the new two-tier one. In Poland all those older than 50 must stay in the old system, with the others automatically joining the new first tier. To account for acquired rights, initial capital will be calculated and assigned to the individual notional accounts. People between 30 and 50 years old can direct their contributions only to the first tier or may decide to allocate part of it to the chosen private pension fund.

Contributors in Hungary were given two years to make their choice. During the first year many more than expected opted for the two-tier system (1.2 million compared with 0.7 million). In Poland the time given for a similar decision is much shorter (less than one year). Polish contributors will have a harder choice as there is no possibility of reversing the decision, as in Hungary.

Problems of implementation

In both countries reform is being implemented gradually, thus the transition period will be long. However even such a gradual transition is costly: as a result of channelling part of the contributions to the funded tier for many years there will be a deficit (additional to the pre-reform one, significant in size in both countries) in the pay-as-you-go one. Official forecasts estimate this deficit to be as much as 2 per cent of GDP. In the first year of the Hungarian reform the deficit was higher than expected as many more than anticipated opted for the funded tier. This resulted in the government deciding to reincorporate the National Pension Fund into the state budget and to suspend the increase – scheduled for 1999 – in the portion of contributions to be channelled to the second tier.

In Hungary and Poland there are many provisions for early retirement, and for other special retirement conditions for those employed in hazardous and special occupations. Difficult negotiations with interested occupational groups are expected to take place in both countries before new solutions, suitable to the reformed systems, can be found.

All those who can make a choice between systems are under strong pressure from the competing pension funds to select a two-tier system. Taking into account all the other information problems with making a choice in such a situation, there are doubts concerning the extent to which interested persons are really able to choose rationally. From this point of view the possibility – existing only in Hungary – to reverse the original decision might be an advantage (however disadvantageous it is for the private pension fund itself).

The actual outcome of all these decisions – personal ones, as well as with regard to the design of the system – will only become known after several years, and only then will it be possible to evaluate fully the reforms undertaken.

still lacking or is not yet of sufficient quality. Central government reform plans are too infrequently discussed with employers and workers, local governments and the public, or are not discussed in sufficient detail. Maintaining public consensus also requires the involvement of government, employers and beneficiaries in the social protection system, in a well-balanced national system of social protection governance. Such involvement, in turn, requires a willingness to accept responsibilities, change old power structures and collaborate actively. The emerging employers' organizations are often not fully aware of their societal responsibilities and trade unions often find it hard to exchange their old power bases for new ones.[13]

Deficient management of change

The lack of coordination, or even communication, between government agencies in the reform process is often striking. Ministries and institutions planning reforms often hardly communicate with each other. The lack of national management and coordination has slowed the reform process in many Central and Eastern European countries. Another impediment is the lack of a transition process between the legal design of the social protection system and the implementation of reforms. Organizational reforms may involve many institutions at the national and regional level and numerous procedural changes within existing organizations, which must be complemented by new procedures. They require detailed master plans for the transition and considerable project management. In many countries the overall leadership of the reform process is unclear. Working groups within Ministries of Social Protection, for example, often compete with the social affairs divisions in Ministries of Finance, with the staffs of vice-premiers or of the Council of Ministers, or with research teams assigned by parliamentary social commissions.

Lack of financial and economic planning

Even minor reforms of social protection systems in industrialized countries trigger extensive research. The reform processes in Central and Eastern European countries often lack sufficient quantitative analysis. Reform laws are often drafted without actuarial or other quantitative studies. Cost-benefit analyses or analyses of the distributive effects of reform measures are also often missing.

Skill and methodology gaps

Reforms which aim at new national management of transfer systems that reallocate 20 to 30 per cent of GDP should be executed by well-prepared managerial and technical staff. While well-educated analysts, managers and administrators are in sufficient supply, the skills and methodology needed for the successful operation of major independent social service agencies are lacking. For example, local welfare officers who formerly administered institutions for the disabled or orphanages now administer major social assistance cash benefit programmes. Pension managers who used to administer benefit payments relying on data and services from state enterprises now administer independent pension schemes.

Countries in Central and Eastern Europe differ in their living standards and the differences have increased during the economic transition to market economies. The social protection systems of most countries in the region have features inherited from the systems of the former planned economies. The earliest reforms in the region were emergency responses to emerging problems. Later reforms represented an effort to deal with long-term conceptual, design and financial issues.

All the pension reforms implemented or debated in the region will eventually lead to higher retirement ages, lower replacement rates provided by the mandatory schemes (particularly for all those with relatively short contributory periods) and much higher differentiation of pensions. New design of the pension formulas, together with defined contribution components, may in the future effectively stimulate later retirement and reduce pension entitlements. At the same time, new pension schemes may, in the future, leave many of those with incomplete working careers and/or low earnings with insufficient protection in old age. Pension schemes reformed along these lines thus have to be complemented by effective social assistance systems. Developments of the latter have until now been, both conceptually and in practice, lagging behind other social reforms.

Notes

[1] Romania became a member of CEFTA on 1 July 1997. However the data used in this brief relate to the period prior to Romania's accession to the organization.

[2] See, for example, Freinkman and Starodubrovskaya, *Restructuring of Enterprise Social Assets in Russia*, Policy Research Working Paper 1635, Washington, World Bank, 1996. See also Commander and Schankerman (1995).

[3] See M. Rutkowski, *Changes in the Wage Structure during Economic Transition in Central and Eastern Europe*, Washington, World Bank, 1996.

[4] Ministry of Labour, Social Affairs and Family (1993).

[5] In Ukraine, for example, the reference wage is calculated as 100 per cent of the first four bands, 85 per cent of the fifth band, 70 per cent of the sixth and so on until 15 per cent of the tenth. Income in excess of the tenth band is not taken into account (each band represents one minimum wage).

[6] In many countries these schemes were quite generous when implemented. Replacement rates have since been cut, eligibility has been restricted and duration shortened.

[7] See I. Topinska, "Changing Financial Pattern: From the Collective to Individualistic Financing of Social Risk", in W. van Ginneken (1996a).

[8] However, the most recent events in Hungary show that in some cases autonomy of the social insurance funds and tripartite governance may be weakened rather than strengthened as a result of the reform: during the first year of the implementation of the pension reform, in the situation of the growing deficits of the social insurance fund, the government decided to abolish bipartite self-governing bodies of the social insurance funds and to incorporate the funds into the state budget.

[9] The case of Latvia shows a slight deviation from the general pattern, as it does not embrace the introduction of a fully fledged social health insurance scheme, but aims for a health care financing system which combines elements of health insurance with that of a national health service.

[10] See also, for example, ISSA (1996b, pp. 14–24).

[11] Hungarian experts analysed reform proposals for enhancing the present pay-as-you-go system by introducing measures to increase the retirement age, improve the collection of contributions and tighten eligibility conditions. Analysis showed that these measures could ensure long-term financial sustainability of the pension scheme. See Simonovits (1997). See also the projections presented in Augusztinovics (1995).

[12] Even authors of the recent and most radical proposal for pension reform in Poland agree that it is possible to stabilize the costs of pensions in the long run through rationalization (an increase in the retirement age, extension of the calculation base period, and a switch to price indexation) of the present pension system in Poland. However, after admitting this they say: "rationalization alone is

neither sufficient nor desirable. It would not be sufficient because social insurance reform should, if possible, create new opportunities and perspectives for the generation which still has many working years before it. ... [It] would also not be desirable because the present crisis is a crisis of all single pillar pay-as-you-go pension systems in general" (Office of the Government Plenipotentiary for Social Security Reform 1997, pp. 2–3).

[13] In many CIS countries, for example, unions still control the social insurance fund providing short-term benefits, execute the activities of the labour inspectorate and administer a variety of other social benefits at the enterprise level. Union-based provisions of statutory social security might soon become incompatible with the new economic environment, but union representation on the boards of social security system could strengthen the public acceptance of the social security system.

THE OECD COUNTRIES

The Organization for Economic Cooperation and Development (OECD) seeks to encourage economic cooperation among the leading economies. Of the 20 original member countries when it was founded in 1961, only two were outside western Europe: Canada and the United States. Since then economic progress has caused the OECD to broaden its geographic scope. Four Asian-Pacific nations have joined: Australia, Japan, Korea and New Zealand. Recently, with the fall of communism, three nations from eastern Europe – the Czech Republic, Hungary and Poland have also joined. There is also a member country in Latin America: Mexico.

OECD countries spend on average 10 per cent of their gross domestic product (GDP) on old-age retirement benefits, exceeding their health care spending. OECD countries rely primarily on pay-as-you-go defined benefit systems for providing social security retirement benefits. Pension benefits are based on the worker's earnings, years of service and age at retirement. The pay-as-you-go social security systems are frequently supplemented by voluntary funded schemes, mostly operated by the private sector.

Most OECD countries are considering changes in their retirement income schemes. Reforms during the 1990s mainly responded to economic pressures from slow economic growth, high rates of unemployment and, in many countries, rising government deficits (Myles and Quadagno, 1997). A number of western European countries have cut the budgetary costs of their social security retirement pension scheme to meet the Maastricht Treaty requirements for qualifying to join in a common European currency. Countries are also considering longer-term reforms to ensure the financial viability of their schemes in the face of population ageing.

This regional brief surveys social security policy and reform issues in the OECD region for the 24 countries that were members in 1993 but excluding the five most recent members (the Czech Republic, Hungary, Korea, Mexico and Poland) which are covered in the briefs on their respective regions.

576

OVERVIEW OF THE ECONOMIC ENVIRONMENT

Early retirement

The cost of social security retirement pension benefits depends not only on the population age structure but also on the extent to which older people work. Along with population ageing, perhaps the most important change in OECD labour markets over the last two decades was a massive movement among older workers to early retirement. Across OECD countries labour force participation rates of men aged 55 and older have declined for the last 20 years. The levels and downward trends differ between countries, but in all cases the majority of men have stopped full-time work several years before the age of legal entitlement to full social security retirement pensions.

Scheme dependency ratio

The retirement benefit scheme dependency ratio is the ratio of pensioners to active workers. In contrast to the retirement dependency ratio, which is determined solely by the age structure of the population, the scheme dependency ratio is affected by the unemployment rate, the labour force participation rate of women and men, and early retirement. Germany's scheme dependency ratio is considerably higher than its old-age dependency ratio. The large difference between the ratios is due to the high number of early retirement and disability pensions, the long education period in Germany resulting in late entry into the labour market, and the fairly low labour force participation rate of women (Queisser, 1996b).

In Germany, as in many OECD countries, social security financing problems have been caused not so much by population ageing as by other factors affecting the scheme dependency ratio and benefit generosity. Considering all the OECD countries, 70 per cent of the increase in the scheme dependency ratio was in recent years due to changes in the entry and retirement ages, while only 30 per cent was due to changes in the age structure of the population (Latulippe, 1997).

OVERVIEW OF OECD SOCIAL SECURITY SYSTEMS

Early development and basic structure

The first social security retirement pension benefit schemes in OECD countries originated at the end of the nineteenth century. By the beginning of the twentieth century, Australia, Belgium, France and New Zealand had non-contributory social security pension schemes (Mouton, 1984). The retirement benefit scheme of most OECD countries, while predating the Second World War, were developed in their current form just after the war, and thus have existed in their current forms for more than 50 years (ILO, 1989a).

Most OECD countries have retirement income schemes characterized as consisting of three tiers, though analysts differ as to how they apply the tier analogy. According to many analysts, the first tier is the retirement pension benefits the state provides through social security schemes. The second tier is the occupational plans that employers provide. Australia, France and Switzerland have a mandatory second tier. For most countries, the second tier is voluntary but it receives support from the government through favourable tax treatment. The third tier is individual pension schemes and private savings provided by individuals. Most countries also have anti-poverty programmes as part of their social security pension systems, and in addition many older households, primarily in Japan, Sweden and the United States, receive income from work.

The characterization of OECD retirement income schemes as having three tiers does not mean that all workers receive income from every tier. For most OECD countries, the bottom 40 per cent of the income distribution of retirees has a one-tier system: social security retirement benefits. They receive little income from occupational pensions or private savings (Rein and Turner, 1999). While all of the first-tier social security schemes in OECD countries are based on the concept of social insurance, with some redistribution within the system, the structures of the schemes differ considerably across countries.

Universal benefits

The OECD retirement income schemes have developed along two paths. A number of OECD countries before the Second World War provided means-tested benefits for the elderly poor. Influenced by the Beveridge report in England (Beveridge, 1942), after the Second World War means tests were relaxed and a universal flat benefit was provided for all citizens. Entitlement was based on age and residency, rather than earnings. This path was followed by the Nordic countries (Denmark, Finland, Norway, Sweden), the Netherlands, Switzerland and most Anglo-Saxon countries (Australia, Canada, New Zealand), excluding the United States (ILO, 1989a; Myles and Quadagno, 1997).

Ireland's social security scheme provides a flat-rate retirement benefit rather than an income-related one, but this is for workers only (see box 19.2). The Netherlands also has a flat rate pension. In the Netherlands most employees are required to be covered by a supplementary scheme but this is not the case in Ireland. The basic pension is also independent of salary in Iceland and Norway. The United Kingdom started a flat-rate pension scheme in 1948, but entitlement was based on the payment of contributions for a prescribed period.

Most countries that began with a flat-rate pension scheme later added an earnings-related pension scheme. Starting in the 1950s, the Nordic countries, plus Canada, added an earnings-related pension scheme to their flat-rate pension. Sweden started its earnings-related scheme in 1960. The United Kingdom joined the group in 1975 when it began the state earnings-related pension scheme (SERPS). Pure universal retirement income schemes remain only in Denmark, Ireland, the Netherlands and New Zealand.

Finland, Ireland, the Netherlands, Norway, Sweden and the United Kingdom finance the basic benefit mainly from payroll contributions, and it is related to earnings, whereas in Australia, Canada, Denmark and New Zealand it is financed from general revenue and is not related to the worker's earnings.

New Zealand's universal pension is its only social security retirement pension. New Zealand is an extreme case, where private pension coverage is also low and there are no tax subsidies for pension contributions or savings (Myles and Quadagno, 1997). Housing is used relatively more for retirement savings in New Zealand than elsewhere. Canada, Denmark, Japan, the Netherlands and Sweden provide a universal retirement benefit unrelated to work, as well as providing an earnings-related benefit. Denmark bases entitlement to a pension on citizenship or residence (Ostrup, 1996). Switzerland and the United States provide benefits for non-working spouses based on the working spouse's earnings.

Iceland in 1992 shifted from a universal flat-rate retirement benefit to a means-tested benefit. Thousands of pensioners had their benefits reduced or eliminated, without any transition measures for existing pensioners or those close to retirement (Beattie and McGillivray, 1995).

Earnings-related benefits

Differing from the universal and flat benefit schemes, the second line of development of retirement income schemes in OECD countries follows the earnings-related social insurance model adopted by Bismarck in Germany in 1889. The "Bismarck" countries include Austria, Belgium, France, Germany, Italy, Spain and the United States. Financing is based on a mix of employer and employee contributions, sometimes supplemented by financing from government general revenue (Myles and Quadagno, 1997).

Social security retirement benefit schemes across a number of countries have tended to converge (ILO, 1984b). Countries with earnings-related benefits have added minimum benefits. The United States has added a minimum benefit for low-income workers with many years of coverage. As noted earlier, many countries with flat benefits have added earnings-related benefits.

Means-tested benefits

Australia, Finland and New Zealand only provide means-tested social security benefits. Most benefits in these countries are provided through mandatory employer-provided plans. Canada, Finland, the Netherlands and New Zealand provide a means-tested benefit by testing against income but not assets. The result is a guaranteed minimum income. Norway has means-tested benefits that test only against social security pension, and the result is a guaranteed minimum pension. In the United States benefits are provided through the Supplemental Security Income (SSI) programme with means testing of both income and assets (Myles and Quadagno, 1997).

Canada's flat-rate benefit is means tested but the earnings-related benefits are not. The earnings test reduces benefits for workers earning above a certain amount. In countries with an earnings test, this usually does not apply to workers above a certain age. In Japan and the United States the earnings test applies up to age 70. Finland's retirement social security benefit is means tested. No social security retirement benefit is paid if the mandatory TEL pension is above a certain amount. Approximately half of new pensioners do not receive a social security retirement benefit.

Replacement rates

The English-speaking countries (Australia, Canada, Ireland, New Zealand, the United Kingdom and the United States) all have social security systems that provide low or moderate replacement rates. These and other countries with low or moderate expenditures spend a relatively low percentage of their GDP on social security retirement pensions: Canada 6.5 per cent, Finland 7.2 per cent, Ireland 4.4 per cent, Japan 6.3 per cent, United Kingdom 7.0 per cent and the United States 7.4 per cent (OECD, 1995a). The percentage of GDP spent on social security retirement pensions is affected both by benefit levels and by the percentage of the population receiving benefits.

In Canada and the United States, the average income replacement rate is about 40 per cent. The replacement rate is lower for highly paid workers and higher for lower-paid workers. In these countries occupational voluntary pensions play an important role.

Portugal and Spain have more generous social security retirement pension schemes with replacement rates exceeding 75 per cent, while Austria, Iceland and Italy have rates close to, or exceeding, 90 per cent. Finland, France, Germany, Luxembourg and Norway have replacement rates of between 50 per cent and 75 per cent. In Finland, France, Luxembourg and Norway the replacement rate decreases as the salary increases.

In Finland, Iceland, Norway, the United States and, to a lesser extent, France the replacement rate for a retired person with a dependent spouse is greater than that for a single person. This is the case in countries where the retirement pension for the former employee is supplemented by a pension paid to the spouse.

Unified national systems

Most OECD countries provide social security retirement benefits schemes that are near universal in their coverage of workers, although often excluding the government bureaucracy and the military. Sometimes the self-employed are also excluded, as in Germany where they can contribute voluntarily and in the United Kingdom for the earnings-related benefits.

Germany's social security system is institutionally fragmented although the rules governing contributions and benefits are similar in different schemes. Three different schemes serve private sector employees, but within each scheme a number of different institutions manage plans for different occupational groups. Farmers, artists and other groups of self-employed workers have their own schemes (Queisser, 1996b).

Most countries, however, have moved towards unifying schemes, bringing workers formerly covered under separate schemes under a single national scheme. For example, in 1984 Belgium considerably reduced differences in eligibility conditions and methods of calculating pensions between the schemes for civil servants, employees and the self-employed. In 1985 Spain integrated a number of special pension schemes into the general scheme to cover different groups. The United States in 1983 brought newly hired civil servants in the federal (national) government under the social security scheme. Greece has numerous schemes covering different segments of the workforce, but a reform in 1992 required all schemes to adopt similar provisions for new entrants with a phased-in alignment of provisions for all other employees (Petridou, 1996). Italy in 1995 created a single scheme covering employees in the public and private sectors and the self-employed. This scheme replaced roughly 50 compulsory schemes that had treated categories of workers differently, causing inequities in retirement income.

Financing

Most OECD countries finance retirement benefits on a pay-as-you-go basis. Canada, Denmark, Japan, Sweden and the United States, however, have partial funding of defined benefit social security retirement benefits. The partial funding in the United States is temporary, as the fund is projected to be depleted when the "baby boom" generation retires. In Japan the social security funds can be invested in the private sector. Between fiscal years 1993 and 1996, because of weakness in Japanese capital markets, investment losses in the social security fund totalled 1.4 trillion yen from the 23 trillion yen fund.

Germany subsidizes social security retirement benefits in the former East Germany, which would otherwise have difficulty supporting the level of benefits because of high unemployment. The German government also subsidizes the general social security retirement benefit scheme, financed out of general tax revenues. This subsidy covers the cost of benefits not directly related to the concept of retirement insurance, such as credits for non-contributory periods due to education, military service or child rearing. In Japan one-third of the funding for social security retirement benefits is provided by the government out of general revenues, so there is tripartite financing: by government, employers and employees.

Defined benefit versus defined contribution

Most of the social security schemes in OECD countries are defined benefit schemes. Some countries, however, are moving towards defined contribution schemes. The mandatory employer-provided plans in Australia are defined contribution plans. In the United Kingdom workers are permitted to contract out of the earnings-related part of social security and replace that defined benefit scheme with an individual account defined contribution scheme. This may reflect a trend towards increasing popularity of conservative ideology. For example, the 1988 reform in the United Kingdom was designed in part to increase the extent to which individuals were free to make their own provision for retirement rather than rely solely on state protection. The British government contended that the scope for individuals to make their own provision for retirement was too restricted and that this infringed upon individual freedom (Dilnot and Webb, 1989).

Italy and Sweden have both announced reforms to start new pension schemes that are commonly considered to be pay-as-you-go defined contribution plans. These schemes, however, have features of both defined benefit and defined contribution plans.

Coverage

Coverage is mandatory for most workers in OECD countries. The average participation rate for workers in OECD countries is 94 per cent (World Bank, 1994, table A.4). However, in some countries the protection for self-employed workers is less than that for employees. In Japan self-employed workers are covered by one part of the social security retirement benefit scheme – the National Pension Programme that covers all residents – but they are not covered by the Employees' Insurance Programme, which is only for employees of firms in commerce and industry. Similarly Denmark includes the self-employed in its universal pension scheme, but excludes them from its employment-related retirement pension scheme. Belgium includes the self-employed in a special scheme that only provides basic protection. Ireland excludes domestic workers from social security coverage. Sometimes public sector employees are excluded because they have their own scheme. For that reason Ireland excludes public employees hired before 1995. Some people who are legally required to be covered are not covered because they fail to make required contributions. Contribution evasion tends to be more prevalent among self-employed workers, domestic workers and workers in the informal sector.

In a number of OECD countries coverage extends beyond the workforce and includes all residents. Countries with coverage that extends beyond the workforce include Australia, Canada, Finland, Japan, the Netherlands, New Zealand, Norway and Sweden.

Social security governance

OECD countries have two traditions of social security governance. In the Anglo-Saxon tradition of Canada, the United Kingdom and the United States governance is done through a government institution, with pluralistic interest groups influencing social security governance through party politics and lobbying. In the western European tradition in Germany and the Netherlands employers and employees have a more direct role in governance through their participation in social security oversight institutions.

In some countries, the governance of mandatory occupational plans involves worker representatives. The mandatory ATP plan in Denmark is governed by a tripartite board of workers, employers and government. In Sweden the LO trade union, which covers most hourly workers, negotiates on their behalf concerning mandatory pension plans. The mandatory plans in Australia and Switzerland have bipartite governance involving both employee and employer representatives.

ISSUES IN SOCIAL SECURITY RETIREMENT INCOME REFORM

OECD countries are concerned about the financial viability of their social security retirement benefit schemes as their populations age. Among the countries of the world the proportion of the population that is aged is highest in the economically developed countries of the OECD.

Actuarial projections indicate that almost all countries in the OECD face sharp increases in social security retirement benefit expenditures. These expenditures are projected to rise to more than 15 per cent of GDP in Germany, Italy and Japan, while they are projected to rise to less than 10 per cent of GDP in Australia, Canada, the United Kingdom and the United States (OECD, 1996). The lower levels in the English-speaking countries are in part the result of less generous social security systems. To keep their social security systems in balance, countries will need either to raise revenues, to reduce benefits, or to raise the age at which benefits are received. Workers, however, are increasingly resisting further increases in contribution rates so it is likely that these countries will cut benefits and attempt to raise the retirement age. Many countries in the OECD have already made some cuts in benefits.

As a consequence of population ageing and slowing economic growth, financial problems for social security schemes in the OECD are expected to increase in the future. The high levels of unemployment in some OECD countries reduce the revenues flowing into the schemes to pay current beneficiaries and have generated pressure on workers either to retire early or to claim invalidity (disability) benefits. The demographic pressure on the financial situation of pension schemes will add to the problems of scheme maturation that already exist in many OECD countries. As systems mature, benefit levels rise because workers have contributed to the scheme for more years.

Estimates of the size of the pension-related unfunded liabilities of the public pension schemes vary. These unfunded liabilities are a form of public sector debt never included in statistics on national debt. In general their inclusion in public debt would greatly increase it. The net present value of unfunded social security retirement benefit liabilities – the difference between the value of benefits promised and the size of the social security trust fund – in the United Kingdom is estimated to equal 4 per cent of gross domestic product (GDP), compared with over 100 per cent in France, Germany, and Japan and 26 per cent in the United States (Budd Campbell et al., 1996). The unfunded liabilities of social security retirement pension benefits in the entire OECD is roughly 145 per cent of the combined GNP of the countries (Peterson, 1996).

Many countries are responding to social security financing problems by increasing the age of entitlement for early or "normal" retirement income benefits, with the expectation that this may increase the age at which workers actually retire. Countries are also looking for other ways to reduce benefits.

Impetus for reform has also come as a result of pressure from employers to lower wage costs, with mandatory social security contributions being an important part of wage costs in some countries. Pressure for reform has also come from the financial sector which would stand to gain considerably from fees it would earn if social security were privatized, with private sector managers handling the funds.

Benefit cuts

A major policy issue in OECD countries is how to share the cost across the population of the increasing retirement dependency ratio. The cost can be borne entirely by the working generation through increased contribution rates, borne entirely by the retired generation through decreased benefit levels, or shared between the two generations by a combination of contribution rate increases and benefit cuts. Most countries are following the last approach, but with greater reliance on benefits cuts. This marks a change from the past, when countries raised both contribution rates and benefit generosity.

A number of OECD countries in western Europe have reduced the cost of their retirement social security schemes in an attempt to ensure their participation in the European Monetary Union (EMU) in 1999. Criteria for inclusion in the EMU are in part that the public sector deficit can be no greater than 3 per cent of GDP. The measures to reduce the budget deficits include reform of the social security system. In order to meet the criteria France and other countries needed to reduce their budget deficit. Because of resistance to raising taxes, the bulk of the changes to reduce budget deficits occurred through benefit cuts.

Benefit cuts can be across the board (an equal percentage for all beneficiaries) or selective with some beneficiaries bearing a higher percentage cut. Selective cuts are usually aimed at higher-income retirees. Because low-income retirees depend relatively more on social security, across the board cuts cause a larger percentage reduction in their retirement income than that for upper-income retirees.

Benefit formula changes

A number of technical changes can be made in social security retirement benefit formulas that result in benefit cuts. Spain has enacted a social security reform that increases the number of years of earnings used in the calculation of benefits. By the bringing of more low-earnings years into the calculation, benefits are reduced. Until 1996 the earnings reference period for calculating pension benefits was the final eight years. With effect from 1997 it increased and will continue doing so until reaching 15 years in 2001. While the old rules allowed workers to retire after 20 years of contributions with benefits equal to 80 per cent of full benefits, the new rules when fully implemented require 25 years of contributions for full benefits.

While increasing the averaging period is a cut that is not explicitly aimed at upper-income workers, it will generally reduce their benefits more than the benefits of lower-income workers. This difference occurs because upper-income workers tend to have more steeply sloped earnings profiles over their careers, so that, for them, increasing the number of years brings in years that are relatively low in comparison to their earnings near retirement.

Starting in 1996 earnings on which the Finnish TEL pension is based will gradually increase to the average of the last ten years. Benefits had been based on the average for the last four years, leaving out the highest and lowest years. In 1993 France changed its benefit formula from the best ten years to the best 25 years, to be phased in from 1994 to 2008. In 1995 Italy changed from the last five years to lifetime earnings for new entrants to social security.

The United Kingdom in 1986 legislated a change that reduces the generosity of the earnings-related pension from the year 2000, with the reduction gradually being phased in over the period from 2000 to 2009. The maximum SERPS benefit will be reduced from 25 per cent of covered earnings to 20 per cent. In addition benefits will be based on earnings over the entire working life, not just the best 20 years. With the ceiling on taxable earnings indexed to prices, and with prices growing less rapidly than earnings, the proportion of individual earnings cut off by the upper earnings limit will increase over time. The amount of pensionable earnings used to calculate pension entitlements will increasingly be determined by the real value of the upper earnings limit, rather than the underlying age-earnings profile of the individual (Creedy and Disney, 1989). Japan by contrast has cut benefits by reducing its benefit accrual rate in its retirement benefit formula (see box RB6.1 for a description of the Japanese pension scheme).

Box RB6.1 The Japanese social security retirement benefit system

Japan established the universal National Pension Insurance scheme in 1961. It provides flat retirement benefits for all elderly residents. Earnings-related benefits are also provided, under several different programmes, for all employees in the public and private sectors (see table RB6.1). Each pension provides a retirement benefit, a disability benefit and a survivor's benefit. A minimum number of years of contributions are required. Each scheme is reviewed every five years to determine if changes are needed. Each year the level of benefits is increased in line with the annual rate of increase in the consumer price index for the previous year. In 1995, social security benefits were 58.7 per cent of the income of all elderly households, and 50.5 per cent of all elderly households relied only on social security benefits.

The National Pension Insurance programme is a universal system requiring contributions by all legal residents age 20 to 60. It provides flat benefits from age 65 with 40 years of contributions, with reduced benefits if contributions were made in less than 40 years but in at least 25 years. No benefits are paid with less than 25 years of contributions.

Several earnings-related schemes cover different occupational groups. The biggest ones are the Employees' Pension Insurance schemes and schemes for central government employees and local government employees. The Employees' Pension Insurance scheme has a mandatory contribution rate of 18.75 per cent of earnings. The average replacement rate it provides beneficiaries was 43 per cent in 1993.

Financing method

The National Pension Insurance scheme is financed by a flat-rate contribution, which in 1997 was 12,800 yen a month (approximately US$130) from all legal residents aged 20 to 60 and by general tax revenues that financed one-third of the benefits and all the administrative costs. Low-income participants are

Table RB6.1   Social security retirement benefits schemes in Japan

Type and name of scheme	Contribution rate	Participants/pensioners
Universal scheme		
• National Pension Insurance	12 800 yen a month	25.0
Earnings-related scheme: private sector		
• Employees' Pension Insurance	18.75%	21.0
• Private School Teachers	13.30%	13.4
• Agriculture and Fishery	19.49%	27.2
• Japan Railway Employees	20.09%	151.3
• NTT Employees	17.35%	55.0
• Japan Tobacco Employees	19.92%	103.5
Earnings-related scheme: public sector		
Central Government Employees	18.39%	50.7
Local Government Employees	16.56%	38.7

Source: Department of Health and Welfare, Pension Division, 1998.

exempt from contributions but will receive reduced benefits. Dependent spouses of employed persons are not required to contribute. If they have earnings greater than 1.41 million yen (approximately US$14,000) a year they are not considered to be dependent and must pay social security contributions.

For the earnings-related pension schemes, contribution rates and benefit amounts differ according to their histories and their government subsidies. In the Employees' Pension Insurance programme employer and employee contribute equally. For workers in this programme its contributions are combined with National Pension programme contributions and are made together.

Contracting out

Employers can voluntarily provide occupational pensions for their employees and receive tax preferences. Most private pensions are defined benefit. To promote private pensions, large employers with 500 employees or more can contract out of the earnings-related part of the Employees' Pension Insurance programme. This means that they can pay a reduced contribution rate to that programme so long as they establish a private pension scheme of sufficient generosity. The financial situation of the Employees' Pension Insurance scheme has deteriorated because only small and medium-sized employers have remained in the scheme and their employees are older than the average for all employees. The financial incentive to contract out, however, has declined considerably over time. The reduction in mandatory contribution rate due to contracting out in 1995 was 18 per cent, compared with 44 to 51 per cent in 1966. Because of the declining advantage of contracting out, in June 1998 the Japan Employers' Association proposed that contracting out be abolished.

In 1997 Austria changed its social security retirement benefit scheme so that benefits were based on the last ten years prior to retirement, rather than the last five. Previous changes in 1996 resulted in a system where the retirement pension equalled 1.9 per cent per year for the first 30 years and 1.5 per cent per year for the next 15 years (maximum 80 per cent). Under new rules, the factors will be 1.83 per cent per year for the first 30 years and 1.675 per cent per year for the next 15 years (maximum 80 per cent). The new rules reduce benefits for those who retire with less than 45 years of service.

Germany in 1992 switched from basing benefits on gross wages to basing them on net wages after taxes and mandatory contributions. Increases in mandatory contribution rates for social security will result in lower net than gross wage increases, which will result in lower pension increases.

In the Netherlands reduction of the growth of the statutory minimum wage lowered social security retirement benefits by 9 per cent in real terms between 1983 and 1986. In 1996 the survivors' insurance scheme was replaced by a new scheme with lower benefits and stricter eligibility requirements. Under the new scheme survivors' benefits will only be available to a surviving partner born before 1950, or who has children under 18 years of age, or who has a disability. The government's rationale for these changes is that private life insurance is widely available.

COLAs

Benefits can be reduced by changing the calculation of cost-of-living adjustments (COLAs). Two other factors have also caused governments to change social security COLAs. First, in some countries prices have risen faster than wages. As a result, pensioners' incomes rose faster than those of workers. Second, as taxes and contribution rates rose as a percentage of earnings, there was a growing gap between gross and net earnings in the working population (Myles and Quadagno, 1997).

COLAs are paid to beneficiaries in order to increase their nominal benefits to offset the effect of inflation eroding the real value of benefits. To reduce benefit expenditures, Austria suspended indexation of benefits for 1997. However low-income beneficiaries received an equalization payment, graded according to income. In 1993 Belgium introduced a policy aimed at avoiding the bankruptcy of the social security system. It included a three-year freeze on benefits. In Germany, starting in 1992, post-retirement increases in benefits were linked to net wages rather than gross wages (Queisser, 1996b). Japan also made this change in 1994. This mechanism distributes the burden of an ageing population among workers and pensioners. With the growth of taxes and social security contribution rates, net wages are growing less rapidly than gross wages.

Increasing the pensionable age

Despite longer life expectancies, early retirement is increasingly common in OECD countries. A striking feature of retirement income policy is that once a pensionable age is determined for the social security scheme, it tends to remain unchanged for many years (ILO, 1989a). The pensionable age is the minimum age at which social security retirement benefits can be received. Many countries, however, at some point during the 1950s to 1980s, lowered their pensionable age. In Switzerland the AVS social security pension for all residents, first legislated in 1946, provided a retirement pension for men and women at age 65. In 1957 the age for women was lowered to 63 and then to 62 in 1964. The pensionable age has not been lowered for men.

Some countries allow for partial retirement with a partial pension benefit. In 1988 France introduced partial pension provisions which enabled workers aged 60 and over having completed 150 quarters of employment to work on a part-time basis while drawing part of their pension from the basic scheme. The pension reform law of 1992 in Germany introduced the option of receiving a partial pension benefit to make the transition from employment to retirement more flexible. The pensioner can choose one-third, half or two-thirds of the regular retirement pension, depending on the amount of income earned. Persons receiving partial pensions and earning income are still required to contribute to the pension scheme, which increases their benefit entitlement for the full pension when they retire altogether (Queisser, 1996b).

In Denmark the basic means-tested retirement pension introduced in 1933 was first paid at age 65 for men and 60 for women. In 1967 these ages were raised to 67 for men and married women and 62 for unmarried women. In 1984 the pensionable age for unmarried women was brought up to 67. In 1987, however, a scheme allowing for provision of partial pensions took effect. This applies to workers aged 60 to 67. Norway lowered the normal pensionable age for the basic pension for residents from 70 to 67 in 1973. France, in 1981, reduced from 65 to 60 the minimum age at which a full retirement pension could be received by employees in the general employees' social security scheme.

Pension reform in the Netherlands permits partial employer-provided pensions from age 55. Under this system an employee, with the employer's agreement, can work part-time and receive a partial pension from the employer's plan. Dutch occupational pension schemes can also provide bridging pensions between the ages of 55 and 65 to compensate an individual taking early retirement for the fact that social security retirement benefits are not payable until age 65. For workers still working at age 65 it is not necessary to retire to receive retirement benefits.

Sweden in 1976 lowered the normal age for both the universal basic pension and the earnings-related pension from 67 to 65, at the same time introducing partial pensions. In 1986, without altering the normal pensionable age, Finland introduced provisions for early retirement under the National Pension Plan. In 1987 a part-time pension was introduced under the statutory supplementary pension scheme. Thus, during the 1980s, there was a move towards allowing greater flexibility in pensionable age by allowing early retirement or retirement with a partial pension (ILO, 1989a).

During the 1990s a new trend emerged. Many countries increased the legislated age for early or normal retirement, although often the increase will not take effect until early in the 2000s. Raising the pensionable age is a non-specific reduction of benefits. It is unclear whether raising the pensionable age will cause workers to retire later or will only result in a benefit cut.

One way to cut benefits is to postpone access to full benefits to a later age, coupled with actuarial reductions in benefits received at an earlier age. This is done by increasing the penalty for retiring early. The major part of any savings to the system occurs after many years as gradually an increasingly large proportion of retirees have been affected by the change. This approach has been followed by Germany, Italy, Japan, Switzerland and the United States. The United States in 1983 cut future benefits by raising the "normal" pensionable age by two years, phased in gradually over 22 years starting for workers aged 62 in the year 2000.

Traditionally most OECD countries have permitted women to retire at younger ages than men. Most countries, however, are taking steps to equalize pensionable ages for men and women. Greece is doing so at 65 with a long phase-in period. It affects people who started working in 1993 or later (Petridou, 1996). Portugal is doing the same, although the process will be completed in 2000.

Switzerland, by contrast, has decided not to equalize the ages, rather raising the pensionable age for women from 62 to 64, with the pensionable age for men staying at 65, phasing in being completed by 2005. Italy, which had low pensionable ages of 55 for women and 60 for men is raising pensionable ages to 60 for women and 65 for men. It formerly also had a seniority pension that a retiree could receive, based solely on years of work, but that pension provision is being terminated.

In Germany the earliest age at which social security pensions can be taken is being raised to 65 for both sexes, phased in between 2000 and 2001 for men (2004 for women). The United Kingdom is equalizing pensionable ages for men and women at the pensionable age for men of 65, with the first increase affecting women reaching age 60 in 2010 with a ten-year phase-in period. Australia is raising the minimum age at which a woman can receive a retirement pension by six months every two years, from age 60 in 1995 to age 65 in 2013. In Belgium the pensionable age, along with the retirement benefit calculation, will be equalized for men and women over a transitional period of 13 years from January 1997. The pensionable age for women was increased to 61 on that date and will increase by one year every three years until it reaches 65 in 2009. The option of a flexible pensionable age between 60 and 65 for both men and women remains, but will become subject to a requirement as to length of employment, starting at a minimum of 20 years in 1997 and rising to a minimum of 35 years in 2005. Austria provides an early retirement pension benefit for long service. Under the previous rules the pension was paid from age 60 for men and age 55 for women to a person with 420 insurance months. This will change to 450 months for men born after 1940 and women born after 1945.

Counter to the trend in other countries, Finland has a labour policy that encourages early retirement to reduce unemployment. An early retirement benefit scheme pension which was introduced in 1986 gives employees the option of retiring between ages 60 and 65. The benefit is actuarially reduced for payment before age 65. Also counter to the trend, unions in France have waged a series of strikes to demand a reduction in the pensionable age to 55.

Selective targeted benefit cuts

Universal flat-rate benefits common in the Nordic and Anglo-Saxon countries (excluding the United States) are on the decline. "Clawbacks" (benefit reductions) from upper- and middle-income households have been implemented in Australia, Canada, Finland, Iceland, Netherlands, New Zealand and Sweden. Only Ireland, Japan, Norway and the United Kingdom still provide universal flat-rate benefits for all citizens who reach a specified age. Need is replacing citizenship as the criterion for eligibility (Myles and Quadagno, 1997).

Four countries, Australia, Canada, Denmark and New Zealand, finance their basic retirement benefit from general revenue, and all four have instituted selective benefit cuts, abandoning the principle of a universal flat benefit. Canada introduced a "clawback" through the income tax for high-income earners in 1989. Denmark introduced an income test in 1994.

In the postwar period Finland, Norway and Sweden introduced universal flat benefit pensions financed from payroll deductions. All three then introduced earnings-related pensions that left little room for private pension schemes. As the earnings-related schemes have matured, the basic universal benefit has been eroded by the introduction of pension testing of those benefits. In 1994 Sweden essentially abolished the universal benefit by introducing a pension test for the entire benefit. Finland followed Sweden and introduced pension testing of the entire basic benefit in 1996. Iceland had preceded these countries, introducing a pension test in the 1970s (Myles and Quadagno, 1997). Starting in 1992, Norway reduced the maximum pension points that can be earned per year from 8.33 to 7.0 (see box 3.1). This reduces the future retirement income benefits of high earners.

Contribution increases

Contribution increases can occur through increases in the contribution rate or in the contribution base.

Increases in contribution rates

Contribution rates have increased in many countries, including Denmark, Finland, France, Sweden and the United States (see table RB6.2). In nearly all OECD countries the mandatory contribution rate is scheduled to increase in the future. The United Kingdom is an exception. Under its reformed system, contribution rates to the National Insurance Fund will fall from 18.25 per cent in 1995 to 15.85 per cent in 2040. Belgium is a further exception, planning to reduce social security contributions over five years to those of its neighbouring countries.

France in 1997 raised the generalized social security contribution rate to 3.4 per cent from 2.4 per cent. In addition the contribution base was extended to cover employer contributions to occupational pension schemes. The contribution rates to the mandatory occupational pension schemes are also increasing. The minimum contribution rate, shared equally by the employer and employee, was raised from 10 per cent in 1994 to 12 per cent in 1995 to 13 per cent in 1996 and to 14 per cent in 1997. It is expected to increase to 16 per cent by 2003.

In Canada the contribution rate rose from 5.6 per cent in 1996 (employer and employee combined) and is expected to rise to 9.9 per cent by the year 2003. The Canada Pension Plan actuary has estimated that the rate will need to increase to 14.2 per cent by 2030 for the scheme to remain solvent.

Table RB6.2   Change in social security pension contribution rates in OECD countries between 1991 and 1997, selected countries

Country	Percentage increase	
	Employee	Employer
Austria	0	0
Belgium	0	0
Canada	30.4	30.4
Germany	27.0	27.0
Italy	21.9	20.0
Japan	19.7 (men)	19.7 (men)
	22.6 (women)	22.6 (women)
Netherlands	38.1	0
Portugal	0	−3.0
Spain	−2.2	−1.6
Switzerland	2.1	2.1
United States	0	0

Note: The figures for Canada are for the Canada Pension Plan.

Changes in the contribution base

Changes in the tax base can be made by raising or eliminating the contribution ceiling or by expanding the definition of compensation to include non-wage compensation. Following the Second World War most social security systems had a ceiling on contributions, exceptions being Italy and Switzerland. Since then an increasing number of countries have removed the ceiling, including Finland, Norway (for employers' contributions first and subsequently for workers' contributions), Portugal and Sweden (ILO, 1984a). The United States has retained the ceiling but raised it to the point that most workers earn less.

In Austria, starting in 1996 contributions must be made in order to receive credit for periods of education. These contributions can be made in arrears. France in 1996 levied a new tax at a rate of 6 per cent on employer-paid premiums for group insurance, complementary savings plans and health coverage through insurance companies that is used to help fund non-contributory retirement benefits. A new fund will be created to amortize social security debt over a period of 13 years. To finance the fund a 0.5 per cent tax will be levied on all income, with few exceptions.

In Japan bonuses were previously not included in the social security contribution calculation, but were covered as of April 1995, at a rate of 1 per cent of the bonus, split evenly between employee and employer. Twice yearly bonuses are an important part of worker compensation in many large Japanese firms. In the United States social security benefits have been made liable to income taxation for high-income beneficiaries, with the tax used to help finance social security. In addition employee contributions to a popular type of defined plan, the 401(k) plan, are subject to mandatory social security contributions.

Gender equality

A social rather than a fiscal cause for some social security reforms is a move towards gender equality in social security provisions. This trend goes beyond the equalization of retirement ages. Most of the social security systems in the OECD were established at a time when relatively few women worked in the labour market. Many systems have had features based on the traditional pattern of men working in the labour market and women working at home. Rising divorce rates and increased female labour force participation, as well as a strong politically motivated demand for equality of treatment of men and women, have generated a number of reforms in survivor benefit schemes. Many countries have introduced widower's benefits on an equivalent basis to widow's benefits, while at the same time subjecting survivor benefits to an income test or to the survivor's unavailability for work owing to rearing children, invalidity or advanced age.

In 1984 Denmark significantly reformed its social security system, eliminating differential treatment of men and women. Differential treatment of men and women has also been eliminated from the United States social security system. Belgium is moving towards gender-neutral accrual rates. The accrual rate for men is one forty-fifth per year of coverage. The accrual rate for women was lowered from one fortieth per year of coverage to one forty-first in 1997 and is scheduled to reduce in steps to one forty-fifth in 2009.

Switzerland has introduced a child-rearing credit for either the father or mother who is raising a dependent child age 16 or younger. Under former Swiss law, survivor's pensions were only payable to a widow with a dependent child; under the reform, a survivor's pension is payable to either a widow or widower with a dependent child. More significantly Switzerland has also introduced earnings sharing in determining retirement benefits. Each partner of a married couple is credited with 50 per cent of the total earnings of the couple.

Encouraging private provision

A further strategy to reduce the demographic pressures on social security schemes is to give more responsibility for pension provision to employers and employees. It has always been the intention in Denmark, Ireland, the Netherlands and the United Kingdom that the social security pension should serve as a guarantee of a minimum income in retirement.

In the United Kingdom there has been increasing success in getting people to provide for themselves, particularly since 1987, by means of individual defined contribution pensions. There has been a considerable growth of interest in encouraging funded complementary pension schemes in countries that have not had such a tradition.

Privatizing social security

Using a broad definition of privatization that includes mandatory occupational pensions, nearly a third of the OECD countries discussed in this brief have partially privatized their social security systems. They have done this by making employer-provided pensions mandatory (six countries) or by allowing contracting out from the social security system (two countries). The essential aspect of all the privatized systems is that they are managed in the private sector.

Mandatory employer-provided pensions

In several OECD countries where widespread employer-sponsored pension schemes have long existed on a voluntary basis these schemes have become the foundation for a mandatory second tier. Denmark has a mandatory employer-provided scheme, the ATP scheme. All employees between the ages of 16 and 66 who work at least ten hours a week must participate. Both the employer and employee are required to contribute, with the contribution based on hours worked rather than earnings. The ATP is a defined contribution scheme. Its importance is limited, however, because the contributions and benefits are small.

In 1962 the principal mandatory pension scheme in Finland (TEL) was introduced. It covers about 50 per cent of the private sector workforce. There are eight other mandatory pension schemes, all similar to TEL. While the social security scheme acts as a national safety net, the mandatory pension schemes provide pension benefits for employed persons. Beginning in 1996 the Finnish social security pension scheme became income tested. Thus the social security pension benefit is reduced by amounts payable under TEL and other occupational pensions.

France has mandatory industry-wide pay-as-you-go schemes (see box 7.2). These are financed by employer and employee contributions. In 1985 Switzerland made occupational pension schemes mandatory for all wage earners. A security fund, mutually financed by income from the occupational pension schemes, guarantees the payment of benefits (ILO, 1989a).

Australia has introduced a privatized retirement income scheme through mandatory contributions to private pension schemes. For most employees the scheme will eventually replace at least partially the social security pension benefit. The Australian means-tested social security pension scheme will continue, but, with the projected accumulation of private pension funds its importance will decrease. The system will take several decades to mature. At the point that new retirees have spent their entire working career under the system, it will substantially replace the social security pension. Since the social security pension is unfunded, the change replaces an unfunded with a funded scheme. The scheme is being phased in, and by the fiscal year 2002/3 the total contribution to the scheme from employees, employers and government will equal 15 per cent of salary. The funds that manage the investment of the contributions are private. They are predominantly defined contribution schemes. In establishing the schemes, the government has been able to use a well-developed financial infrastructure that was already in place.

Two other OECD countries have mandatory pension schemes that cover a large fraction, but not all, of the workforce. The Netherlands has widespread pension coverage as a consequence of many industries having mandatory pension schemes. In the Netherlands there are 81 industry-wide pension funds, of which 66 are compulsory (Lutjens, 1996). Compulsory supplementary pension coverage is also widespread in Greece and covers the majority of the labour force. This has been particularly so since 1987 when the supplementary scheme for the rural population was established (Petridou, 1996).

Contracting out

Both Japan and the United Kingdom allow contracting out of the state-sponsored social security scheme. With contracting out an employee or employer, depending on the scheme rules, may withdraw from part of social security mandatory contributions if the employee participates in a plan of sufficient generosity. Together Japan and the United Kingdom have more than 50 years' experience of contracting out schemes. In both Japan and the United Kingdom the social security scheme has a flat-rate benefit and an earnings-related benefit. Contracting out permits the employee to withdraw from the earnings-related part of the social security scheme. In both countries employers can substitute an occupational pension for the earnings-related tier of the contributory component. In the United Kingdom, since 1988, individuals can opt out of either the private or public plan by starting a personal pension plan. This option is unavailable in Japan.

Notional defined contribution plans

In a notional defined contribution plan the worker has an individual account that is credited with his contributions plus interest. However the accumulation is notional rather than actual since the money paid in by workers is immediately paid out to pensioners rather than being invested, so the system remains pay-as-you-go. For each individual the account balance is based on bookkeeping entries recording contributions to the system and interest earnings credited to it.

The notional account system in Italy is commonly described as a defined contribution scheme, but it could also be characterized as a revalued career average defined benefit scheme, with entitlement depending directly on the relevant contribution record (Daykin, 1996). Under the old system pension benefits were a proportion of earnings on the basis of formulas, which differed considerably from one scheme to another. Under the new system, the amount of contributions paid is entered in the individual's account record. The amount is revalued each year in relation to nominal GDP (the average nominal GDP over the past five years) and, at the end of working life, the pension benefit is calculated by multiplying the total amount obtained by a conversion factor determined by the scheme. The value of the conversion factor varies according to age at which employment ceases. This can be between 57 and 65 years, with the factor varying from 4.72 per cent for retirement at 57 years to 6.13 per cent for retirement at 65 years. The pension benefit is then revalued according to changes in prices.

The conversion factor is a key parameter of the new system. It determines the pension benefit based on the accumulated and revalued amount of contributions paid. The conversion factor may be modified every ten years by the Ministry of Labour and Social Security to accommodate demographic change and the growth rate of GDP.

Sweden has adopted the notional account scheme, with the first benefits to be paid in 2001. The contributions will directly determine the entitlements in two ways. Part of the contribution, two percentage points, will be invested and the eventual sum will be determined by the investment performance of the fund. The rest of the contribution, 16.5 percentage points of earnings, will be revalued by means of an index, which is designed to ensure that pension entitlements only keep pace with cost-of-living changes if the economy grows at a target rate, gaining in real value if it grows faster and suffering negative real growth if it grows more slowly. The accumulated amount available at retirement will be annuitized using a factor which is expected will increase steadily in order to reflect improving life expectancy.

CONCLUSIONS: TRENDS IN SOCIAL SECURITY

A number of trends in the development of social security systems in OECD countries can be identified.

- *Trend towards cutting benefits.* In order to finance the increased benefits costs due to the increase in the retirement dependency rate, many countries are cutting benefits. Benefit cuts are being made both across the board and aimed at higher-income workers. One aspect of benefit cuts is a trend towards including more years in calculating benefits in defined benefit schemes.

- *Trend towards higher mandatory contribution rates.* The burden of an increased retirement dependency rate is being shared between workers and retirees. Workers are paying higher mandatory contribution rates.

- *Trend towards higher minimum and "normal" pensionable ages.* With the increasing longevity of populations, there is a trend towards raising pensionable ages. This is being implemented in some countries by raising the minimum pensionable age for women so that it equals that of men.

- *Trend towards equal treatment of men and women.* A number of countries are making changes designed to improve fairness between men and women.

- *Trend towards convergence of benefit formulas.* Most countries with a flat benefit only have added an earnings-related benefit. Some countries with an earnings-related benefit only have added a minimum benefit.
- *Trend towards national schemes.* Countries have generally moved towards a single national social security retirement benefits scheme covering all workers.
- *Trend towards defined contribution schemes.* Several countries are moving towards defined contribution or notional defined contribution plans.

This review indicates that the defined benefit social security pension systems in the OECD countries are subject to change through the political process. However the policy of raising the minimum pensionable age in a number of countries exemplifies that typically major changes occur with a long phase-in period.

THE QUANTITATIVE MODELLING OF PENSION REFORM AND DEVELOPMENT

Financial planning in the social sector is an essential part of responsible governance and can be greatly assisted by the development of quantitative models giving a reasonable assessment of the expected financial development of a programme.

Pension models can be used to project pension expenditure, to study alternative financing options and to assess the implications of the pension scheme for the distribution of income, both for contributors and beneficiaries. Pension schemes are major economic and redistributive systems which often have a considerable impact on public budgets and on the financial status of other social protection programmes. Therefore a proper analysis of a pension scheme also should place the pension scheme in the context of the national social protection system in order to reflect the interrelationships between the different branches of the social protection system,[1] to better understand how the available resources are allocated, and to assess the implications of potential changes for public sector budgets. It is also necessary to assess how the whole social protection system reacts to changing economic and demographic conditions.

Future economic conditions and the behavioural implications of changes to social legislations are difficult to predict and the inherent degree of uncertainty contained in projections increases as the projection period extends into the future. Thus models should be considered as providing the analytical framework needed for decision making, rather than exact figures and straightforward conclusions. This means that they should provide consistent results for alternative policy options, based on reasonable assumptions which can be subjected to alternative scenarios to test the results' sensitivity and to identify the main determinants for future financial development.[2]

This brief provides a general overview of how models work and how they should be used to analyse pension schemes properly. It stresses both the importance of modelling as a means of sound governance and planning and the relevance of a comprehensive quantitative modelling even for the analysis of a single branch of a national social protection system. The ILO uses three types of models for the study of pension reforms:

- a social budget model which maps the macro socioeconomic environment as well as the social protection environment of pension schemes;
- a pension model which assesses the long-term financial implications of alternative benefit provisions and alternative financing options;
- an income distribution model which determines the redistributive aspects of a pension scheme or reform options.

THE SOCIAL BUDGET MODEL

Objectives and overview

The social budget model sets the demographic and the macroeconomic framework needed for a detailed analysis of the pension scheme. It provides a consolidated view of the financial status of the social protection system. It supports the political decision-making process by:

- describing how the present system of social protection would behave in financial terms if the provisions and the financing were not changed (status quo projections);
- assessing the implications for public sector budgets;
- measuring the impact of changes to the social protection provisions, taking into account the interrelationships between the different branches of protection;
- testing the sensitivity of the system to different scenarios on the future demographic and economic development.

The model allows decision makers to understand what level of expenditure and social protection the country might need, and how that would be allocated between the different branches of protection and the different categories of beneficiaries. It also provides information on the sources of financing and the level of social security funds or deficits, and it may be used to measure the financial effect of reform options.

The exact content of national social budgets varies from country to country depending on both the benefits offered and the organization of the national social protection system. Nevertheless there are core elements which normally appear in national social budgets. The expenditure side includes pensions, health care, short-term cash benefits, family benefits, social assistance and unemployment benefits. The income side includes all resources used to finance the above expenditures: social security contributions, taxes (general and earmarked) and government subsidies, private or collective insurance contributions and investment income.

A social budget encompasses the income and the expenditure of the social security institutions as well as other government and (to a lesser extent) private expenditure and income pertaining to social protection. It therefore makes it possible to understand better the financial situation of each fund or institution. It may also provide relevant information on the mix between public and private mechanisms of social protection

The social budgeting process includes accounting for past years and projections in the future for a medium-term period. Social expenditure and income are often projected over a horizon of five to ten years, but projections over longer periods could be necessary to assess the impact of long-term structural changes.

Modelling the socioeconomic environment

Demographic and economic assumptions on the future development of a country are required before undertaking projections. The key assumptions concern population, economic growth, labour force and wages. Assumptions on the future rate of return on investments may also be important if substantial reserves are accumulating. Complementary behavioural assumptions are also needed, such as the enforcement of contribution payments, and the periodical ad hoc adjustments of benefits or contribution ceilings to account for inflation.

Possible interrelationships between these assumptions should be properly taken into account to ensure their consistency. For instance, the assumption on the development of wages cannot be defined without reference to the assumptions on economic growth and the development of employment and unemployment.

The selection of assumptions should take into account recent experience to the extent that information is available and applicable but, in recognition of the nature of the schemes (especially the pension schemes), the assumptions should reflect long-term trends rather than give undue weight to recent experience.

Modelling the social protection system

Indicators are developed to measure the impact of the provisions of the schemes, the characteristics of the covered population and the demographic and economic environment on the financial situation of the social protection system. They help to better understand the financial determinants of the system and to estimate future expenditure and income.

The three principal indicators are the coverage ratio, since expenditure and income are a function of the extent of coverage of the scheme; the beneficiary ratio related to the proportion of beneficiaries in the covered population; and the replacement rate related to the level of benefits provided by the scheme.[3] These indicators are calculated for all types of cash benefits: pensions, sickness benefits, unemployment benefits. For benefits in kind such as health care or social assistance, further refinements must be introduced to reflect better the utilization of the different types of services and their unit costs. The methodology used for cash benefits will be discussed below, paying special attention to pensions.

The coverage ratio measures the percentage of wages that are covered by the social security system. It is a function of both the proportion of the population covered and the level of covered earnings. In the case of pension schemes covering wage earners, the coverage ratio can be split into three components:

- the coverage rate, which is the proportion of the employed population insured under the scheme;

- the wage share of GDP, which is the proportion of national income paid to wage earners;

- the catchment factor, which is the proportion of individual wages covered by the scheme and usually subject to the application of a ceiling on covered earnings.

The coverage rate is a key indicator of the effective level of protection provided by pension schemes, especially in developing countries where coverage is usually limited to people in urban areas. Variation in the coverage rate will have an immediate impact on the amount of total contributory income. However there is a time lag before the impact on expenditure can be felt, especially in the case of retirement pensions, where the individual history of covered earnings is used to calculate the pension to be received at a much later stage.

The beneficiary ratio measures the proportion of the covered population receiving benefits. It varies according to the entitlement conditions specified in the provisions and according to factors such as the employment record and the population age structure in the case of retirement pensions.

The replacement rate compares the average level of individual benefits to the average individual level of earnings. It depends on the initial replacement rate when benefits are first paid and in the case of pensions on the indexation provisions during the payment period. The individual initial replacement rate may vary according to the benefit provisions, the employment record (or residence record for universal pensions) and the individual's earnings during the working years.[4] Following the introduction of new provisions, there may also be a slow progression of the average initial replacement rate as it may take years for a pension scheme to mature.

The effective replacement rate also depends on the mechanism of indexation of benefits in payment, that is whether it is linked to changes in prices or wages. Individual replacement rates would fall if benefits were only partially indexed.

It is also necessary to look at the catchment factor to get a clear picture of the level of protection. Pension schemes with adequate replacement rates and periodic indexation could fail to provide adequate protection for covered people if the ceiling on covered earnings was too low, or not properly indexed.

THE PENSION MODEL

Objectives and overview

Pension models are used to estimate the future value of the indicators for pension schemes and to project pension income and expenditure. The pension model is used to assess the financial viability of a pension scheme either to confirm that income and expenditure are expected to remain in balance over a period of time or to make recommendations on the necessity to revise the contribution rate and the structure of benefits. It is also used to examine the financial impact of alternative options for reforming a pension scheme to assist policy makers in the design of sound benefit provisions and to make recommendations on the financing of the scheme. More specifically the pension model is used for the following:

- to project expenditure and contributions under status quo conditions and for different reform proposals;
- to assess the relevance of building up a contingency or funding reserve;
- to propose schedules of contribution rates consistent with the funding objective;
- to test how the system reacts to changing economic and demographic conditions.

The pension model is used primarily to project the salary base of contributors and the benefit expenditure. Then schedules of contribution rates can be calculated for different financing options based on projected contributions and benefits. The cost of a scheme (benefit expenditure plus administration) depends on the benefit provisions as well as the demographic and economic environment. The choice of a financing system aims to allocate the financing of the cost of the scheme over the years and among the participants in an orderly and rational manner. The financial system should be established taking into account the economic, financial, fiscal and political objectives and constraints.

Pension model inputs

The demographic and macroeconomic assumptions are defined with a longer time perspective in the pension model than for social budgeting purposes. Assumptions specific to the scheme, such as the contribution collection rate and the incidence rates of retirement and invalidity, must also be specified. They are defined by looking primarily at the scheme provisions and the scheme's historical experience.

Information on the covered population at valuation date is needed, such as insurable wages, credited past service and pensions in payments. The data must be desegregated on a basis maintaining the homogeneous characteristics of each group of insured persons. Separate calculations are made for males and females, and for populations covered by distinct schemes or provisions. Within each group assumptions on the salary distribution and the employment distribution are formulated on an age-specific basis.

Finally information on the existing scheme assets, if any, is needed to project the annual cash flows of investment income. An interest rate assumption based on the nature of the assets, the past returns and the investment policy must be formulated. This assumption is established in relation to the assumptions of economic growth and wage development.

Projection methodology

Based on the insured population data and the set of assumptions, pension projections are performed following a year-by-year cohort methodology. The simulation ages the existing population and gradually replaces it with the successive cohorts of participants on an annual basis according to the demographic and coverage assumptions. The projections of insurable earnings and expenditure are then performed according to the economic assumptions and the scheme provisions.

Pension reforms should be introduced following a proper assessment of the long-term financial implications. Reform proposals may only become fully effective many years after their implementation. The objective is to check the financial viability of the scheme, the relative balance between future income and expenditure, using consistent and reasonable assumptions. The model will provide the necessary contribution rates. Whether they are acceptable or not is a matter of political decision.

Financing system

As mentioned in Chapter 9, an important aspect of the financing of social insurance schemes is how to plan and manage the raising of resources systematically, so as to meet the costs of benefits and administration as they arise. For short-term benefits, such as sickness or maternity benefits, entitlement is based on participation history over a short period of time and are payable only for a limited number of weeks. Therefore the annual cost attains a stable level in relation to the insured wage bill in a relatively short time and the financing method which suggests itself is the pay-as-you-go system under which resources raised year by year balance the expected cost year by year. A small margin is often allowed in order to build up a contingency reserve, the purpose of which is to help meet an unforeseen rise in expenditure or fall in income.

Long-term pension benefits have a future expenditure pattern quite different from that of short-term benefits. The following factors generally contribute to a pattern of annually increasing expenditures on pensions in absolute terms, in proportion to total annual insured earnings and as an average amount per insured person.

- Each year a new group of insured persons, or their dependants, qualify for pensions. This results in annual increases in the number of pensions in payment for many years after the inception of the scheme.

- Pension benefits generally increase with the years of service of the insured person at the time the benefit becomes payable and until all workers have been covered for their full working life. The longer a pension scheme operates, the greater will be the average years of service applied to determine new pension benefits.

- When the pension is based on an insured person's earnings, at or near the time he or she qualified for a pension, the average annual pension will generally increase each year.

- Beneficiaries of pensions awarded in previous years will continue to receive pensions and, because longevity generally increases, future pension beneficiaries will receive them for increasingly long periods.

- Pensions already in payment may be increased in accordance with increases in the level of wages or cost of living.

Given the pattern of rising annual expenditures, the pay-as-you-go contribution rate (as a percentage of insured earnings) would be low at the inception of the scheme and would increase annually for many years thereafter.

At the other extreme, the contribution rate could be set with the objective of ensuring financial equilibrium between the income and disbursements of the scheme over a very long period of time (more than 50 years). This is the general average premium financial system. Since, in a typical pension scheme, annual disbursements are an increasing percentage of insured earnings, the contribution rate will exceed the rate which would apply under the pay-as-you-go system in the early years (and generally for many years) of operation of the scheme. Consequently, during this period, the annual contribution and investment income of the scheme will exceed its annual disbursements. This excess forms a reserve which is invested, and the interest on it supplements contribution income when annual disbursements eventually exceed the annual contributions.

There is also the possibility of an intermediate financial system that lies between the pay-as-you-go system and the general average premium system. The financial system is then characterized by the length of the equilibrium period as well as by a funding objective at the end of the equilibrium period.

With partially funded schemes (also called "scaled premium system"), reserves are accumulated (a) to level out the contribution rate needed during the equilibrium period to finance the expected expenditure and to cope with unanticipated shortfalls in revenue or increases in expenditure, and (b) to generate investment revenue to finance part of the expenditure. The longer the period of equilibrium, the higher is the contribution rate and the greater the accumulation of reserve funds. Until a scheme reaches a mature state or with population ageing, increases in the contribution rate must occur from time to time.

Actuarial valuations are needed under any financial system, but they are of particular interest when it is necessary to estimate over a long period of time the value of future earnings and future expenditure in order to establish the current contribution rate. The contribution rate is sensitive to the actuarial assumptions used and deviations between expected values and real values could lead to a revision of the contribution rate. In other words funding a longer equilibrium period contributes to a greater stability of the contribution rate in a context of scheme maturing or population ageing, but it makes the scheme more sensitive to other parameters, such as the economic parameters. The capacity of the economy and its institutions to absorb and manage pension funds in an effective and profitable way also has to be taken into account when establishing a financial system.

To summarize, the modelling exercise should serve two objectives:

- to simulate schedules of contribution rates, and the corresponding liabilities if applicable, for different financing options and different scenarios of economic and demographic development (including the necessary revisions to the assumptions over the years);
- to assist decision makers in the determination of an optimal financing strategy considering the situation of the scheme, the financing objectives and the environment.

MODELLING DISTRIBUTIONAL EFFECTS

Objectives and overview

The primary objective of the modelling of distributional effects is to assess the implications of the expenditure and financing of the social security benefit scheme for the distribution of household income, both for contributors and beneficiaries. Since there are limits to the level of redistribution societies want, the distributional impact of pensions also has to be analysed in the overall context of the social protection system. More specifically, the distribution model is used:

- to assess the effect of alternative benefit and contribution provisions on the current income of contributors and pensioners at a point in time;
- to compare the effect of pension provisions on lifetime earnings for successive generations of participants or for persons with different socioeconomic characteristics;
- to measure the effect of the development of social expenditure on the development of net earnings of different categories of contributors, taking the various sources of financing of the social protection system into account.

The objective is to estimate the direction and magnitude of redistribution for typical individual cases and for different economic and demographic scenarios. This is needed to evaluate whether the pension scheme achieves the desired redistributive social policy objectives.

Indicators of distributional effects

The redistributive effect of pensions may be first assessed by comparing the effect of alternative pension and contribution provisions on the income of contributors and pensioners at a point in time. This is called the "individual current income effect". It is also possible to compare the values of contributions and benefits over the lifetime of an insured person. Finally the impact of the development of total social expenditure on the progression of net earnings of contributors with different characteristics may be measured.

Current redistribution

The redistributive impact of alternative provisions may be assessed by calculating and comparing replacement rates and effective contribution rates for hypothetical individuals at a given point in time. Calculations are made for different earnings levels as the contribution rate and the benefit rate may vary with the earnings level. The contributory periods are defined on the basis of employment patterns, and different employment patterns, such as full-time work and part-time work, might imply different redistribution patterns.[5] The specification of different employment patterns also allows the measurement of the redistributive impact of provisions granting credits under specific circumstances, such as child care, disability or unemployment.

Calculations are made at given points in time, either during the years following the introduction of new provisions or once the scheme has reached maturity. In order to assess properly different policy options, the benefits provided by all the mandatory tiers of the pension scheme might have to be considered: in addition to the mandatory pension or savings scheme, amounts of flat-rate universal pensions, social assistance benefits and state guarantees to individuals (such as a minimum rate of return) might have to be estimated. Finally the redistributive effect of pension taxation might be estimated by calculating replacement rates and contribution rates on both a gross and a net basis.

Lifetime redistribution

The actuarial balance is the difference between the present value of lifetime benefits and the present value of lifetime contributions.[6] When calculated for different categories of individuals and different policy options, it indicates who benefits from an increase in lifetime income and who suffers a decrease as a result of the pension scheme. It is also possible to calculate the equilibrium rates of return at which the actuarial balance is in equilibrium (the present value of benefits equals the present value of contributions).

Actuarial balance or equilibrium rates of return can be calculated for different earnings levels and employment patterns, as well as for successive cohorts of participants. Assumptions specific to each group may be used if there are significant differences or if the assumptions vary over time. This is particularly important for economic assumptions, but specific demographic assumptions may also be used, for instance, to reflect mortality differentials between income groups and mortality improvement over time.

Calculating the actuarial balance, or equilibrium rates of return, to compare pension funding methods deserves special notice. When pensions are funded, the contribution rate (for a defined benefit scheme) or the benefit level (for a defined contribution scheme) depends on the interest rate and a prospective calculation of an equilibrium rate simply replicates the interest rate used as assumption. Interest rates depend on the other economic and demographic variables: savings by large cohorts of young people and dissavings by large cohorts of old people could affect the rate of return on investments and have distributional consequences. Using generational accounting to compare the rate of return for successive generations and for different funding methods may be misleading unless those dynamic effects are properly accounted for.

Finally calculations of actuarial balance and equilibrium rates have to be put in a proper context to ensure a sound interpretation of the results. The different components of the pension scheme are not designed only to maximize the rate of return. For instance, proper management of the pension risks (investment risk, longevity risk) is also necessary to achieve an objective of income replacement and security in retirement and the implementation of a pension scheme may be the expression of other concerns such as social solidarity and social cohesion. This means that income redistribution between subgroups might be a positive feature of a social security pension scheme and all subgroups should not have the same actuarial balance. Calculations of actuarial balance or equilibrium rates of interest are a tool to check whether the results conform to the policy objectives. Nevertheless it is important to make a clear distinction between the tools, the means and the end.

Net income effect

The projection of total social expenditure using the social budget model indicates the absolute level of transfers that take place via the social protection system. The net income effect is the measure of the proportion of future increase in gross income which would be taken away by increased levels of social transfers.[7]

The rate of growth of net income (as a proportion of the rate of growth of gross income) depends on both the level of social expenditure and the way it is financed. The financing of a scheme by contributions on covered earnings allocates the cost between the participants, usually as a fixed percentage of earnings up to a ceiling. Alternatively taxation financing spreads the cost across all income earners but at different rates according to the tax rules and schedules. The tax status of social contributions and benefits also has to be taken into account to assess the impact of the development of social expenditure on the progression of net income.[8]

Notes

[1] There are significant interactions which have to be accounted for when evaluating different reform proposals. For instance, there are interactions between early retirement provisions, on the one hand, and the labour market situation, the system of unemployment benefits and active labour market programmes, on the other hand. There are also interactions between invalidity pensions, sickness benefits and unemployment benefits. The utilization of social assistance benefits clearly depends on the level of old-age, survivor and invalidity benefits provided by the national pension schemes.

[2] The degree of sophistication of the projection models may vary considerably depending on the exact purpose of the projections, the information available and the degree of uncertainty of future demographic and economic developments. In theory, models could include endogenous behavioural responses to social or economic policies. Although great attention is devoted to determining the assumptions in a consistent and reasonable manner, the models discussed in this brief do not integrate such behavioural equations.

[3] The beneficiary ratio and the benefit ratio are used to calculate the pay-as-you-go cost rate. The coverage ratio makes it possible to express social expenditure and income as a percentage of total wages or total GDP.

[4] The replacement rate may also be reduced in the case of early retirement and increased for deferred retirement, but a system of flexible retirement age also has an impact on the beneficiary ratio. There should be no net effect if the system is actuarially neutral.

[5] Links may be established between earnings levels and contributory periods to measure properly redistribution between persons at different levels of earnings.

[6] Pension contributions paid by employers and employees are normally considered when estimating the present value of contributions, but government subsidies financed from general taxation can also be taken into account.

[7] Assuming an unchanged level of public deficit and no change to the other public policy and fiscal measures.

[8] The objective is not to test the impact of alternative fiscal rules, but rather to test alternative pension financing options considering the current fiscal rules. Therefore average effective taxation rates might be estimated for different income levels, different categories of taxpayers or different sources of income in order to be able to make the necessary calculations without having to develop a complete taxation model.

SOCIAL SECURITY CONVENTIONS AND RECOMMENDATIONS OF THE ILO

Since its beginning in 1919, the International Labour Organization has viewed social security as one of its main concerns. The preamble of the Constitution of the ILO set forth the following goals in this field: the prevention of unemployment, the "protection of workers against sickness, disease and injury arising out of their employment, the protection of children, young persons and women, the provision of retirement and injury benefits" and "protection of the interests of workers when employed in countries other than their own".

The Declaration of Philadelphia of 1944 recognized the "solemn obligation" of the ILO to further encourage among the nations of the world programmes that will achieve, *inter alia*, the extension of social security measures to provide a basic income to all in need of such protection and comprehensive medical care, as well as provision for child welfare and maternity protection.

One of the ways in which the ILO strives to achieve these objectives is through the setting of International Labour Standards which are adopted by the International Labour Conference after consultation with all the ILO's member States. The standards take the form of either Conventions or Recommendations and cover all areas which are related to the objectives of the ILO. Conventions are designed to be ratified. When a member State ratifies a Convention, the State becomes subject to legally binding international obligations. Recommendations are not open for ratification, but lay down general or technical guidelines and they often supplement corresponding Conventions. The significance of the standards lies in their practical effect. A country that has ratified a Convention is obliged to report regularly on the measures taken to give effect to ratified Conventions. The government's reports are carefully examined and evaluated by the Committee of Experts on the Application of Conventions and Recommendations, an independent organ of the ILO.

In this respect, the social security Conventions not only serve as guidelines for the establishment of new social security schemes, or the reform of existing schemes, but, when ratified, they also offer an international guarantee that the Conventions and Recommendations will be maintained. They are often regarded as containing an internationally accepted definition of the very idea of social security.

The first Convention in the field of social security, the Maternity Protection Convention (No. 3), was adopted in 1919 at the very first session of the International Labour Conference, and the most recent social security Convention, the Employment Promotion and Protection against Unemployment Convention (No. 168), was adopted in 1988. The International Labour Conference adopted 45 social security standards, of which 30 are Conventions and 15 are Recommendations (see table TB2.1). The social security Conventions thus account for nearly 17 per cent of the 182 Conventions which the International Labour Conference has adopted during the first 80 years of its existence. In addition a number of Conventions and Recommendations not dealing exclusively with social security contain special provisions have been included to deal with matters of this kind.

Historically and conceptually ILO social security instruments can be divided into three main groups or generations.

1. The first generation of social security standards corresponds to those adopted before the Second World War. These Conventions pertain to the "social insurance era", when compulsory insurance schemes were progressively elaborated for each of the principal contingencies (maternity, unemployment, industrial accidents, occupational diseases, sickness, retirement, invalidity or death) and covered particular categories of workers (industrial workers, wage earners and so on).

2. The instruments of the second generation pertain to the social security era. During the 1940s new concepts were developed whose practical application was to transform the prewar social insurance schemes. These concepts, expressed in the Beveridge report in the United Kingdom (Beveridge, 1942), included universal and comprehensive coverage, unification of social security schemes and guaranteed income security and medical care for the entire population. This new era began with the Income Security Recommendation, 1944 (No. 67), and culminated with the adoption in 1952 of the Social Security (Minimum Standards) Convention (No. 102), which introduced the objective of a basic level of social security that should be progressively attained everywhere in the world.

Convention No. 102 differs from the prewar Conventions by virtue of its comprehensiveness, flexibility regarding means, and precision regarding aims. It is comprehensive because it defines and brings together in a single instrument all nine branches of social security which cover all the standard contingencies in which workers are prevented from providing for themselves and their dependants or have to meet additional expenses (see below). It is the first and only Convention which covers family allowances as a branch of social security. As to the scope of protection, the Convention is comprehensive in that it no longer defines classes of persons to be protected in purely legal terms, that is

Table TB2.1 Instruments of the International Labour Organization concerning social insurance and social security

A.	Conventions	Entry into force
No. 3	Maternity Protection Convention, 1919	1921
No. 8	Unemployment, Indemnity (Shipwreck) Convention, 1920	1921
No. 12	Workmen's Compensation (Agriculture) Convention, 1921	1923
No. 17	Workmen's Compensation (Accidents) Convention, 1925	1927
No. 18	Workmen's Compensation (Occupational Diseases) Convention, 1925	1927
No. 19	Equality of Treatment (Accident Compensation) Convention, 1925	1926
No. 24	Sickness Insurance (Industry) Convention, 1927	1928
No. 25	Sickness Insurance (Agriculture) Convention, 1927	1928
No. 35	Retirement Insurance (Industry, etc.) Convention, 1933	1937
No. 36	Retirement Insurance (Agriculture) Convention, 1933	1937
No. 37	Invalidity Insurance (Industry, etc.) Convention, 1933	1937
No. 38	Invalidity (Agriculture) Convention, 1933	1937
No. 39	Survivors' Insurance (Industry, etc.) Convention, 1933	1946
No. 40	Survivors' Insurance (Agriculture) Convention, 1933	1949
No. 42	Workmen's Compensation (Occupation Diseases) Convention (Revised), 1934	1936
No. 44	Unemployment Provision Convention, 1934	1938
No. 48	Maintenance of Migrants' Pension Rights Convention, 1935	1938
No. 55	Shipowners' Liability (Sick and Injured Seamen) Convention, 1936	1939
No. 56	Sickness Insurance (Sea) Convention, 1936	1949
No. 70	Social Security (Seafarers) Convention, 1946	
No. 71	Seafarers' Pensions Convention, 1946	1962
No. 102	Social Security (Minimum Standards) Convention, 1952	1955
No. 103	Maternity Protection (Revised) Convention, 1952	1955
No. 118	Equality of Treatment (Social Security) Convention, 1962	1964
No. 121	Employment Injury Benefits Convention, 1964 [Schedule I amended in 1980]	1965
No. 128	Invalidity, Old-Age and Survivors' Benefits Convention, 1967	1969
No. 130	Medical Care and Sickness Benefits Convention, 1969	1972
No. 157	Maintenance of Social Security Rights Convention, 1982	1986
No. 165	Social Security (Seafarers) Convention (Revised), 1987	1992
No. 168	Employment Promotion and Protection against Unemployment Convention, 1988	1991

Remarks: Convention No. 70 has not received the required number of ratifications for entry into force. It is no longer open for ratification since the entry into force of Convention No. 165, 1987.

Table TB2.1 Continued

B.	Recommendations	Date of adoption
No. 10	Unemployment Insurance (Seamen) Recommendation	1920
No. 23	Workmen's Compensation (Jurisdiction) Recommendation	1925
No. 25	Equality of Treatment (Accident Compensation) Recommendation	1925
No. 44	Unemployment Provision Recommendation	1934
No. 67	Income Security Recommendation	1944
No. 68	Social Security (Armed Forces) Recommendation	1944
No. 69	Medical Care Recommendation	1944
No. 75	Seafarers' Social Security (Agreements) Recommendation	1946
No. 76	Seafarers' (Medical Care for Dependants) Recommendation	1946
No. 95	Maternity Protection Recommendation	1952
No. 121	Employment Injury Benefits Recommendation	1964
No. 131	Invalidity, Old-Age and Survivors' Benefits Recommendation	1967
No. 134	Medical Care and Sickness Benefits Recommendation	1969
No. 167	Maintenance of Social Security Rights Recommendation	1983
No. 176	Employment Promotion and Protection against Unemployment Recommendation	1988

in terms of type of contract and branch of economic activity. Instead Convention No. 102 simply requires that a specific percentage of the population be protected. The scope of protection is also comprehensive in such a way that it not only covers the insured person but extends its protection to the family members of the insured. The ratifying State is thus free to develop the scope of its system by extending coverage successively to different occupations and regions and to make such exceptions as appear expedient in its particular circumstances.

Convention No. 102 also displays considerable flexibility. First, a ratifying State is not obliged to accept all contingencies covered by the Convention, but can confine its ratification to just three of the nine branches of social security, provided they include at least one of the following: unemployment, employment injury, retirement, invalidity and survivors' benefits. In addition the Convention provides for temporary exceptions for countries "whose economy and medical facilities are insufficiently developed". Finally the third, and perhaps most important, element of flexibility is that the Convention no longer prescribes a rigid model of administrative and financial organization laid down in prewar Conventions, but allows for a variety of forms and structures.

3. Convention No. 102 has subsequently been supplemented by a number of Conventions, which set higher standards covering wider categories of the population and, at the same time, revise all prewar Conventions on social insurance. These Conventions, adopted after Convention No. 102, belong to the third generation of social security standards. The Conventions and Recommendations of this third generation formed inside the general social security scheme

four well-defined subsystems: one consisting of branches providing long-term benefits (invalidity, retirement and survivors), another regrouping short-term benefits (medical care and sickness, as well as maternity benefits), accompanied by two other subsystems dealing with employment injury and unemployment benefits.

Three Conventions deal exclusively with the principle of equality of treatment between nationals and non-nationals, which underlines the character of social security schemes: the Equality of Treatment (Accident Compensation) Convention, 1925 (No. 19); the Equality of Treatment (Social Security) Convention, 1962 (No. 118), concerning equality of treatment between migrant workers and national workers in the field of social security which stipulates that non-national workers shall have the same rights in social security as national workers; and the Maintenance of Social Security Rights Convention 1982, (No. 157), which is a complex instrument on transferring and accumulating credits and sharing costs between the states in which the persons were working.

SOCIAL SECURITY (MINIMUM STANDARDS) CONVENTION, 1952 (NO. 102)

This section explains Convention No. 102. (See also ILO, 1984c.)

Contingencies

The contingencies covered by Convention No. 102 include all nine branches of social security, namely medical care, sickness benefit, unemployment benefit, retirement benefit, employment injury benefit, family benefit, maternity benefit, invalidity benefit and survivors' benefit.

Personal scope of protection

The personal scope of protection does not relate to categories of protected persons in purely juridical terms (that is, in terms of type of labour contract) like the previous Conventions. Instead it fixes percentages of the population which have to be covered. These percentages relate either to all employed persons, to the whole working population (including self-employed persons) or to all residents. For pensions the Convention stipulates a minimum coverage of at least 50 per cent of all employees, or at least 20 per cent of all residents, or all residents whose means during the contingency do not exceed prescribed limits.

Survivors

According to the Convention, survivors are the widow(s) and children of the insured person.

Qualifying period

A qualifying period may be a period of contributions, of employment, or of residence preceding the contingency. A full retirement pension should be made available subject to a qualifying period of no more than 30 years of contributions or employment, or 20 years of residence. A reduced pension should be secured, however, after 15 years of contributions or employment. Where a contributory scheme covers, in principle, all economically active persons, there is an alternative formula: a prescribed yearly average number of contributions over a prescribed period.

Similarly a full invalidity and survivors' pension should be available after not more than 15 years of contributions or employment, or ten years of residence. A reduced pension should be secured, however, after at least five years of contributions or employment. In the comprehensive contributory scheme, there is an alternative formula: a prescribed yearly average number of contributions over a period of three years.

Kind of benefits and their duration

All pensions provided for in the Convention have to be paid in cash, as periodic payments. The Convention does not allow the payment of lump-sum benefits. Furthermore the benefit has to be granted for the duration of the contingency.

Minimum standards for determining rates of periodical cash benefits

The guidelines for determining the standard minimum rates of benefit are tied to a schedule of standard beneficiaries and indicated percentages (see table TB2.2). The standard beneficiary is a family unit the composition of which varies according to the contingency. In case of retirement benefit, the standard beneficiary is a man with wife of pensionable age. In case of invalidity benefit, it is a man with wife and two children, and in case of survivors' benefit it is a widow with two children. The percentages indicated in the table may relate either to the wage of a "skilled manual male employee" or to the wage of an "ordinary adult male labourer" according to the pension formula which a state is using for the calculation of the pensions. The Convention allows the calculation of the pensions in three different ways.

1. Where the rate of benefit is according to the national legislation calculated by reference to the previous earnings of the beneficiary or covered person, the rate of benefit payable to a standard beneficiary, together with any family allowance involved, should be not less than the indicated percentage of the previous earnings plus family allowance. Formal rules should be described for the calculation of the previous earnings. An upper limit may be set to the rate of the benefit, or to the level of reckonable earnings. This level should not be set below the earnings of a skilled manual male employee (the

Table TB2.2   Rate of periodical cash benefits (percentages)

Contingency	Standard beneficiary	Minimum standards Convention 102 (%)	Higher standards (%)
Sickness	Man with wife and two children	45	60 (C.130)
Unemployment	Man with wife and two children	45	50 (C.168)
Retirement	Man with wife of pensionable age	40	45[1] (C.128)
Employment injury:			
Incapacity for work	Man with wife and two children	50	60 (C.121)
Invalidity	Man with wife and two children	50	60 (C.121)
Survivors	Widow with two children	40	50 (C.121)
Maternity	Woman	45	66 (C.103)
Invalidity	Man with wife and two children	40[1]	50[2] (C.121)
Survivors	Widow with two children	40[2]	45[2] (C.128)

Notes: The replacement rate of the benefit (including family allowances) is related in case of an earnings-related scheme, to the former earnings for which the reference earnings are the earnings of a skilled manual male employee (including family allowances) in the country concerned; or the earnings of a person whose earnings are equal to, or greater than, the earnings of 75 per cent of all persons protected (including family allowances) in the country concerned; or the earnings of a person whose earnings are equal to 125 per cent of the average earnings of all persons protected (including family allowances) in the country concerned. In the case of a flat-rate benefit it is related to the earnings of an unskilled labourer (including family allowances) in the country concerned.

[1] These rates are required only for a protected person who has completed a qualifying period of 30 years of contribution or employment or 20 years of residence. At least a reduced benefit shall be secured after 15 years of contribution or employment. [2] These rates are required only for a protected person who has completed or whose breadwinner has completed a qualifying period of 15 years of contribution or employment or 10 years of residence. At least a reduced benefit shall be secured after 5 years of contribution or employment.

Convention gives an earnings level "equal to 125 per cent of the average earnings of all the persons protected" as one of the alternatives).

2. In countries where the pensions are at a flat rate, the rate of benefit payable to a standard beneficiary, together with any family allowance involved, should be not less than the indicated percentage of the wage, plus family allowance, of an ordinary adult male labourer. The latter is defined either as a person deemed typical of unskilled labour in the manufacture of machinery other than electrical machinery, or as an unskilled labourer employed in the major group of economic activities with the largest workforce covered for the benefit.

3. In countries where all residents are covered, the rate of benefit may be determined by taking into account the means of the beneficiary and his family, according to a prescribed scale. Substantial amounts of the other means of the family should be disregarded before the benefit is reduced. The total of the benefit, and other means (if any) above the amount disregarded, should be comparable to the benefit calculated elsewhere under the flat-rate formula.

Retirement, invalidity and survivors' pensions shall not be less than 40 per cent of the earnings of the standard beneficiary or, if pensions are paid at a flat rate, not less than 40 per cent of the average wage of an ordinary adult male labourer.

Adjustment of benefits

According to the Convention, the rates of current periodic payments in respect of all retirement, invalidity and survivors' benefit shall be reviewed following substantial changes in the general level of earnings where these result from substantial changes in the cost of living.

Equality of treatment

The Convention requires that in principle, non-national residents should have the same rights in social security as national residents. However, where the benefits are paid wholly or mainly from public funds, national legislation may apply special qualifying rules to persons who were born outside the territory. Also, in the case where benefits are payable under a social insurance scheme, the rights of nationals of another country may be made subject to the terms of a reciprocal agreement between the countries concerned.

Financing of the schemes

The Convention requires that the cost of benefits and the costs of the administration have to be borne collectively in such a way that hardship of persons with small means is avoided, that the economic situation of a country, and the classes of persons protected, are taken into account and that in branches covered by social insurance arrangements the total of the employees' contributions should not exceed 50 per cent of the total cost.

Administration of the schemes

The Convention does not impose specific terms of administration of a scheme, but it obliges the states to accept general responsibility for the administration of social security and for securing and monitoring the financial soundness of the social security funds. Furthermore it provides for associating representatives of the protected persons, and employers, with the management of social security institutions where appropriate.

Right of appeal

Claimants should have a right of appeal against the refusal of benefit, or in respect of its quality or quantity.

Suspension of benefits

The Convention allows that benefits may be suspended in the following cases:

- during absence abroad;

- while the person is maintained at public expense in an institution;
- if a person is simultaneously entitled to two forms of cash benefit (the beneficiary should receive not less than the amount of the larger of the two conflicting benefits);
- where the contingency was caused by wilful misconduct or a criminal offence on the part of the claimant, or the claim was fraudulent;
- where a person neglects to make use of medical or rehabilitation services, or fails to observe prescribed rules of behaviour during the contingency;
- in the case of survivor's benefit, where a widow is living with a man as his wife. In the cases and within the limits prescribed, part of the benefit otherwise due shall be paid to the dependants of the person concerned.

PENSIONS FOR PUBLIC SECTOR EMPLOYEES

In many developing countries with low social security coverage an important part of retirement income coverage is provided by programmes for public sector employees. Civil servants and members of the armed forces in most countries were among the first occupational groups to obtain pension benefits. The creation of these schemes by statute provided the workers covered by them with a security similar to a vested right. For this reason, in many countries public employees were excluded from newly created social security schemes.

Since the Second World War, however, support for operating separate retirement schemes or providing preferences for public employees has decreased, especially in developed countries. Public employees (including the military) in the United Kingdom, for example, are covered by separate occupational schemes, but workers may switch either to the state earnings-related pension scheme or into a personal pension plan.[1] Elsewhere pensions for civil servants or other public employees in such OECD countries as the Netherlands, Sweden and Switzerland are provided on an occupational basis that supplements the universal flat-rate pension available to all citizens.

By contrast, separate civil service pension systems in developing countries – many originating under colonial rule – have been largely retained. This continues to be the case particularly in Africa, with the exception of Liberia, Tanzania, and Zimbabwe. Meanwhile the situation for public sector pension provision in Latin America appears to be changing. Pensions for civil servants and other public sector workers still tend to be managed separately, but a regional trend towards almost universal pension schemes, which allows for at least some partial privatization, is unmistakable. The recent treatment of pensions for public sector workers in Argentina, Bolivia, Chile, Colombia and Peru exemplifies that trend.[2]

THE VARIETY OF RETIREMENT SCHEMES AVAILABLE TO EMPLOYEES IN THE PUBLIC SECTOR

Public sector occupations granted preferential treatment under separate pension schemes often include the armed forces, police, teachers and high government officials. At least 75 out of 158 countries with social security schemes continue to operate a separate pension programme for civil servants or other (non-military) public sector employees (US Social Security Administration, 1997). Most of the published literature on public sector schemes omits descriptions of military benefits and, for security reasons, avoids discussing that covered group.

When providing retirement benefits for public sector workers, most countries display a marked preference for defined benefit earnings-related plans over defined contribution plans. Among OECD countries there are some mixed defined benefit plus defined contribution combinations operating in Greece, Mexico and the United States, and many more instances of multi-tiered arrangements, which incorporate flat-rate benefits, as found in Finland, Japan, Netherlands, Norway, Switzerland and the United Kingdom. Varied degrees of favouritism towards civil servants can be found in a number of countries. In Africa the countries of Madagascar, Mali and Togo make a prominent distinction on the basis of both wage and pension. Government employees in Togo are hired either as civil servants, permanent employees or non-permanent contractuals. Civil servants enjoy higher pay and a Treasury-managed pension fund. Permanent employees work under a much lower juridical status and less exacting civil service guidelines, and are covered by the ordinary social security fund. Non-permanent contractuals are also covered by the social security fund.

LINKAGE TO NATIONAL PENSION SCHEMES: SEPARATE OR INTEGRATED?

A review of civil service pension schemes conducted by a joint initiative of the OECD and European Union[3] notes the advantage of increased labour mobility resulting from the inclusion of public sector employees in a national system of retirement income. The integration of public sector schemes is often accomplished via an occupational supplement. If the social security scheme covers public sector employees through a minimum or flat-rate pension, the intended coverage will require some rules to guide the coordination of benefits. A more complicated approach incorporates an offset formula. Here the public sector pension plan administrator calculates an employee's pension benefit based on the plan's benefit formula and some proportion of that benefit is reduced in consideration of the benefit to be obtained from the social security scheme. Where integration is effectively complete, public employees become a subset of the labour force falling under national social security norms.

About one-third of the countries shown in Appendix I to this brief operate public sector pension plans that are integrated in some fashion (occupational supplements and offsets) into their national social security schemes. The proportion of systems reflecting some level of integration ranges from above 50 per cent among OECD countries to a third in the Latin American region and to even lower percentages in Africa and Asia. Integration of civil servants and other government employees among former centrally planned economies in the former Soviet bloc was effected systematically throughout the socialist period, although certain occupations received preferences, such as early retirement provisions – a practice in decline.

Since the Second World War an increasing number of countries have social security schemes. According to the seminal ILO report on social security for public employees, *Report III of the Joint Committee on the Public Service* of 1988, systems in every region of the world can be found where integration has occurred on at least a partial basis. Citations in that report include countries in Latin America such as Bolivia (since 1949), Costa Rica (since 1947), Ecuador (since 1963) and Panama (since 1941); the African countries of Algeria (since 1984), Libyan Arab Jamahiriya (since 1981) and Rwanda (since 1962); the countries of Kuwait (since 1976) and Malaysia (since 1975) and the United States (since 1983). More recent actions taken in Latin America, in the context of far-reaching pension reform measures, have pushed integration almost to the point of completion, with the exception of military personnel. Besides Chile (1981), these countries include Argentina (1993), Bolivia (1997), Colombia (1994), El Salvador (1996) and Peru (1993).

PENSION COVERAGE

Appendix II to this brief provides figures on public sector pension coverage for a limited number of non-OECD countries where data are available. The relative coverage of public sector employees versus social security schemes is indicated through the use of ratios for workers and retirees for each category.[4]

The ratio of public to social security scheme coverage is nearly always higher for retirees than for covered workers. This relationship can be explained in at least two ways: (a) more favourable provisions that increase the likelihood of public sector employees obtaining a pension (lower retirement age or service period) or (b) an established civil service tradition resulting in more mature public sector scheme(s) versus relatively younger social security schemes.

Public sector employee pensions account for a higher level of coverage relative to social security coverage in developing countries than in developed countries. This is expected, given that formal sectors in many developing countries are still relatively small. At the same time public sector system maturity and preferences towards public sector employees tend to be more attenuated in the developing group.

Public worker coverage rises slightly above 20 per cent of the social security scheme in Mexico and Portugal, countries with histories of significant state involvement in economic affairs. In consideration of past measures in Portugal to integrate their public sector schemes into the social security scheme, worker ratios should decline there.

Among the sample of developing countries, five countries – Brazil, Cameroon, Mauritius, Peru and the Philippines – have public sector to social security scheme ratios of 10–20 per cent. Figures for three countries, Mali, Syria and Trinidad and Tobago, range from 25 to 42 per cent, while Tunisia recorded a covered worker ratio of nearly 65 per cent. In the late 1990s, changes or policy discussions in Brazil, Mali and Peru indicated that lower ratios are expected. The 1988 ILO report on public sector pensions mentions changes in the late 1980s for Tunisia that would be expected to bring about harmonization of provisions between public sector and social security schemes. It is expected that more recent data will reflect those steps.[5]

Among the non-OECD retiree ratios, high figures for Mali and Syria are consistent with the earlier review of covered workers.

PUBLIC SECTOR TRENDS AND POLICY ISSUES

Trends in public sector financing in the late 1990s may influence public sector pension benefits and coverage. These trends include the following:

- matching public sector parameters to social security standards: steps taken in Finland and Peru, in addition to options under consideration by Mali, provide evidence of this trend;

- meeting the Maastricht guidelines for fiscal criteria: members of the European Union intending to participate in the European Monetary Union, in part through convergence towards limits on overall deficit and gross debt of the national government, have discovered that financial burdens associated with public sector pensions might complicate meeting these targets. Developments in France, Germany and Italy indicate some methods to deal with public sector pension costs;

- moving to defined contribution schemes to maintain public sector pensions: some countries have moved to defined contribution schemes in an effort to secure the long-term viability of public sector pensions. New Zealand (separate government agency defined contribution schemes) and Thailand (creation of a provident fund) offer two examples of countries choosing this route;

- reducing the generosity of public sector pensions by integrating schemes into social security schemes: overgenerous public sector pensions translate into relatively higher expenditures that are becoming less tolerable in many countries. The situation in Portugal and the United States offers a contrast in the approach to integrating an established public sector scheme within the larger social security scheme;

- dealing with public sector pension finance at the subnational level: when a nation's political structure undergoes restructuring, tensions created by fiscal interactions among levels of government can arise. The role played by public sector pensions in the macroeconomic stability of Argentina and Brazil gives some insight into a larger financial picture when pension obligations shift to the national level;

- preserving separate public sector pension schemes despite their associated fiscal pressures: many developing countries seek to maintain exclusive pension schemes for civil servants or other public sector employees. Reform agendas in Pakistan, Sri Lanka, and Zambia present a range of options for achieving that objective.

A review of these trends raises at least two important points. First, the operation of separate public sector, chiefly civil service, pension schemes with relatively favourable provisions is typically extended to compensate for a lifetime commitment to government service, relatively lower pay than is available in the private sector in some countries, or certain job-related constraints. In a climate of tighter fiscal guidelines, it may become difficult to justify such preferential treatment. That point brings us to a second area relating to current efforts in many countries to restore fiscal balance. Policy initiatives, which include pension reform as part of planned public sector rationalization, may provide the opportunity to integrate public sector schemes within larger national retirement schemes. Extending social security coverage to public sector schemes can lead to increased labour mobility of public sector employees.

Countries around the world normally extend preferential treatment towards the retirement needs of public sector workers, usually for civil servants and almost always for military personnel. The frequency of these schemes can be generalized on a regional basis: OECD countries increasingly seek to narrow the gap between public and private sectors, while developing countries have largely maintained preferences towards public sector workers (chiefly civil servants). Integrated systems, however, are becoming more common in every region of the world. Schemes for public sector employees are an important aspect of government-provided retirement benefits in some developing countries.

Notes

[1] Appendix I provides tables containing this information for both OECD and non-OECD countries (the latter on a regional basis). These tables are an expanded revision of the 1988 ILO *Report III of the Joint Committee on the Public Service*.

[2] Only in Bolivia, however, is the provision for pensions of military personnel integrated into the national retirement system.

[3] Support for Improvement in Governance and Management in Central and Eastern European Countries (SIGMA) Programme.

[4] One caveat requiring our attention concerns the reliability of country entries whenever fiscal reform efforts influence public sector employment levels. Civil service reform and ancillary steps taken to "downsize" government or privatize state assets can result in lower public sector coverage and/or a shift in the coverage ratio away from a public scheme towards the social security scheme.

[5] One explanation of the high ratio recorded in Tunisia would relate to the high level of public sector employment. World Bank data for the second half of the 1980s show that the ratio of government employment, combined civil service and other public sector workers equalled 23.4 per cent.

Table TB3.1 Public sector retirement schemes in the OECD countries

Country	Scheme design	Year of legislation	Separate or integrated	Public sector coverage[11]
Austria[1]	DB	1965	Separate	Public servants (Federation)
Belgium[1]	DB	1984	Separate	Several schemes[6]
Canada[1,2]	DB	1965	Integrated only after age 65	Federal public service employees
Finland[1,3]	Flat + DB	1969	Integrated flat; DB separate	Public servants
France[1,5]	DB	1964	Separate	Employees w/ civil servant status & military
Germany[1,4,5]	DB	1976	Separate	Lifetime state/fed'l public servants & military
Greece[1]	DB + DC supplement	1979	Separate	Public servants/employees w/ official status
Ireland[2,3,4]	DB	1976	Separate	Public servants
Italy[1,2]	Flat	1995	Integrated	All employed workers
	DB + supplement	1995	Separate	Public servants and military
Japan[1]	DB	1960	Separate	Pre-1986 public servant recruits
	Flat + DB	1986	Flat only integrated	Post-1985, flat: citizens; DB: public servants
Luxembourg[1]	DB	1954	Separate	Civil servants & other (railway) state workers
Mexico[1,2]	DB + DC[7]	1992	DB not integrated	Civil servants & other public employees
Netherlands[1,2,5]	Flat + DB supplement	1966	Only DB supplement separate	Flat: citizens; DB: public sector employees
Norway[1]	Flat + DB	1966	Only DB separate	Public employees
Portugal[2,4]	DB	n/a	Separate	Pre-10/93 public servants/admin. employees
	DB	1993	Integrated	Public servants & administration employees
Spain[1,2]	DB + DB supplement	1987	DB separate, DB supplement integrated	DB: civil & military pension; DB supplement: civil servant
Sweden[1,5]	Flat + DB supplement	1962	DB supplement only separate	Public employees, local employees, & military
	DC + DB supplement	2000(?)	DB supplement still separate	Post-1999 public employees
Switzerland[1,2]	Flat + DB	1946	Only separate DB	Flat: all citizens; DB: public servants & federal employees
Turkey[3]	DB	n/a	Separate	Public employees
United Kingdom[1,2,5]	Flat + occup. scheme[8]	1975	Occupational only separate	Flat: citizens; occup.: public servants & military
United States[1,3,4]	DB	1920	Separate	Pre-1984 entrants for federal public service
	DB(2)[9] + DC optional[10]	1983	DB integrated, DC separate	Post-1983 entrants for federal public service

Notes: DB = defined benefit; DC = defined contribution; n/a = not available.

[1] ILO (1988). [2] US Social Security Administration (1997). [3] World Bank staff. [4] Country-specific sources. [5] OECD-Phare, *Civil service pension schemes*, Sigma Paper No. 10. [6] ILO report specifies over 200 public sector schemes, although most managed under one plan. [7] Supplementary private savings system (SAR) mandated by 1992 legislation. [8] Since separate DB occupational schemes for various public servants & military are not compulsory, participants may choose to opt out and into DC plans. [9] Current participants are covered by social security and a basic annuity plan in addition to the DC scheme. [10] DC scheme allows employees to contribute up to 10 per cent of tax-deferred earnings, with the State matching the first 5 per cent. [11] An attempt has been made to standardize the terminology used in this column. These descriptions reflect the information reported by government ministries and social security institutions.

Table TB3.2   Public sector retirement schemes in Africa

Country	Scheme design	Recent law	Separate or integrated	Public sector coverage
Benin[1]	DB	1966	Separate	Public employees
Burkina Faso[2,3]	DB	n/a	Separate	Public employees
Burundi[1,2]	DB	1980	Separate	Public servants
Côte d'Ivoire[1]	DB	1962	Separate	Public servants
Gabon[1]	DB	1978	Separate	Non-contractual public servants
Liberia[2]	DB	1988	Integrated	Public employees & employers with 5+ workers
Madagascar[1]	DB	n/a	Separate	Public employees
Mali[3]	DB	1961	Separate	Civil servants & military
Morocco[1]	DB	1971	Separate	Noncontractual public servants
	DB	1977	Separate	Local staff & public contractuals
Nigeria[1]	DB	1974	Separate	Pensionable public employees
Senegal[1]	DB	1981	Separate	Public servants
Tanzania[2]	DC	1964	Integrated	Employed persons in public & private sectors
Togo[1]	DB	1963	Separate	Public servants not on contractual basis
Tunisia[1,4]	DB	1985	Separate	Public servants/employees & police
Zimbabwe[1,3]	DB	1980	Separate	State employees
	DB	1993	Integrated	State employees

Notes: DB = defined benefit; DC = defined contribution; n/a = not available.

[1] ILO (1988). [2] US Social Security Administration (1997). [3] World Bank staff. [4] Country-specific sources.

Table TB3.3   Public sector retirement schemes in Asia and Eurasia

Country	Scheme design	Recent law	Separate or integrated	Public sector coverage
Bangladesh[1]	DB	1974	Separate	State employees
India[1]	DB	1981	Separate	Central government public servants
Indonesia[1]	DB	1969	Separate	Public servants
Malaysia[1]	DB	1980	Separate	Public servants
Myanmar[1,2]	DB	1954	Sole national pension scheme	Only coverage for public servants
Nepal[2]	DC	1991	Integrated	Public employees & employers w/10+ workers
Pakistan[1,3]	DB + lump-sum option	1972	Separate	Public employees
Philippines[1]	DB	1977	Separate	Government and state employees
Sri Lanka[3,4]	DB	1990	Separate	Civil servants
Albania[2]	Flat + DB; also supplement	1993	Supplement only separate	Employed persons and self-employed
Bahrain[1]	DB	1975	Separate	Public servants & state salaried employees
Cyprus[1]	DB	1980	Integrated after age 65	Public servants

Notes: DB = defined benefit; DC = defined contribution.

[1] ILO (1988). [2] US Social Security Administration (1997). [3] World Bank staff. [4] Country-specific sources.

Table TB3.4 Public sector retirement schemes in Latin America

Country	Scheme design	Recent law	Separate or integrated	Public sector coverage
Argentina[1,2]	Flat + optional DC/DB[5]	1993	Integrated: flat & optional DB	All workers except military and provincial workers
Barbados[1]	DB or lump-sum option	1975	Separate	Civil servants
Bolivia[1]	DC	1997	Integrated	All workers including military personnel
Brazil	DB	1988	Separate: various schemes	National & provincial civil servants
Chile[1,3]	DC	1981	Integrated	Workers except military pre-reform schemes
	DB	1968	Separate	Military and pre-reform public schemes
Colombia[1,2,4]	DB or DC option	1994	Integrated	Most public sector employees[6]
	DB	Varied	Separate schemes	Oil workers, teachers, and armed forces
Costa Rica[1]	DB	1992	Separate	Teachers, legislators, and public employees
El Salvador[1,4]	DB	1995	Integrated	Employed workers in private and public sector
	DB	n/a	Separate	Public servants and judiciary
Peru[1,2,3]	Special: DB	1996	Integrated	All private, public & municipal sector workers
	Gen'l: optional DB/DC	1974	Separate	Special: pre-1980 military & public empl. recruits
		1993	Integrated	Gen'l: employees in public and private sectors
Surinam[4]	DB	1972	Separate	Public servants & teachers in state schools
Trinidad & Tobago[3]	DB	n/a	Separate	Public servants
Venezuela[4]	DB	n/a	Separate	Public servants

Notes: DB = defined benefit; DC = defined contribution; n/a = not available.

[1] US Social Security Administration (1997). [2] World Bank staff. [3] Country-specific sources. [4] ILO (1988). [5] 1993 reform of Argentine system allowed individuals to participate in either a DB public system or a private DC system, and DB pension base covered period after July 1994. [6] US Social Security Administration (1995) is unclear about categories covered under the special public servant scheme shown in the ILO report, and it appears that the 1994 reform integrated some public employees into the national system.

Social security pensions: Development and reform

Table TB3.5   Pension coverage for public and private sectors in OECD countries

Country	Public sector scheme(s)		Social security		Relative coverage ratios	
	Covered workers (1)	Retirees (2)	Covered workers (3)	Retirees (4)	(1)/(3)	(2)/(4)
Australia (1989)[1]	453 282	94 785	–	1 334 310	–	.071
Austria (1989)	–	97 807	–	786 763	–	.124
Germany (1989)	2 493 000	1 174 000	33 206 000	8 616 000	.075	.136
Mexico (1989)	1 826 476	136 565	8 790 957	321 176	.208	.425
Portugal (1993)	1 000 000E	–	4 300 000E	–	.233	–
Spain (1989)	902 800	318 200	12 128 000	3 478 400	.074	.091
United States (1995)[2]	6 100 000	7 522 300	112 000 000E	35 023 000E	.054	.215

Notes: Years are those of reported employment data; E = estimate; – denotes absence of data.

[1] Includes military. [2] Includes approximately 1.6 million workers who are partially covered by the social security scheme.

APPENDIX II

Table TB3.6 Pension coverage for public and private sectors in non-OECD countries

Country	Public sector scheme(s)		Social security		Relative coverage ratios	
	Covered workers (1)	Retirees (2)	Covered workers (3)	Retirees (4)	(1)/(3)	(2)/(4)
Barbados[1] (1996)	–	5 300	–	28 061	–	0.189
Brazil[2] (1989/97)	2 534 788	–	16 000 000E	–	0.158	–
Cameroon[3,4] (1989)	70 537	–	420 879	–	0.168	–
Mali[5] (1995–96)	35 205	23 615	87 655	32 013	0.402	0.737
Mauritius[3] (1989)	50 700	12 800	270 000	103 200	0.188	0.124
Philippines[3] (1989)	1 134 000	76 848	11 468 314	144 303	0.099	0.533
Peru[2] (1996)	–	–	–	–	–	–
Civil servant CV	250 000	50 000	–	–	–	–
Private sector SNP	–	–	980 000	320 000	0.105	0.156
Fully funded SPP	–	–	1 400 000	–	–	–
Syria[3] (1989)	192 772	44 476	464 341	18 662	0.415	2.383
Trinidad & Tobago[2] (1992)	60 000	8 000	235 878	32 246	0.254	0.248
Tunisia[3] (1989)	408 700	–	631 825	–	0.647	–

Notes: E = estimate; – denotes absence of data.

[1] World Bank. [2] IMF staff. [3] ILO data. [4] Retirement scheme figures unavailable and proxied by injury compensation programme numbers. [5] National authorities

THE IMPACT OF DEMOGRAPHY

CASE-BASED PROJECTION FOR IMMATURE SCHEMES

A simple pension projection model demonstrates the typical cost development of a pension scheme as well as the relative impact of different factors. All potential factors are listed in table TB4.1. This model can be used to analyse possibilities for the extension of coverage. The case used for the modelling is a typical new pension scheme in Africa. The selection of an African case has the advantage that it is a typical and realistic development of a scheme that starts with no pensioners.

The typical relative cost development of a hypothetical pension scheme in Africa has been simulated under three key assumptions.

1. *Demographic:* The population structure of Zimbabwe is used as the basis for the model. The determinants of the future mortality and fertility are also based on the projections of demographic indicators for Zimbabwe.[1]

2. *Economic:* It is assumed that the economy has a 3 per cent real growth rate per year. The assumed wage share of GDP is 44 per cent. Labour force participation rates and employment rates are those of Zimbabwe.[2]

3. *Governance:* It is assumed that the scheme has a benchmark replacement rate of 40 per cent of career average earnings (approximated by a ten-year average of revalued earnings) subject to a minimum replacement rate of 20 per cent. The 40 per cent roughly corresponds to the requirements of the Social Security (Minimum Standards) Convention, 1952 (No. 102). Shorter periods of employment lead to a reduction of the pension level by about 1.33 per cent per year. This is a fairly conservative pension formula which does not reflect the more generous formulas in Francophone Africa. In the base case, pensions in payment are adjusted in line with insurable wages. Invalidity pensions are paid at the benchmark rate and survivors' pensions are paid at a rate of 60 per cent of the entitlement of the deceased.

Table TB4.1 Summary of factors influencing the financial equilibrium of a pension scheme

	Impact on income	Impact on expenditure
Economic factors		
(1) Growth	Increase in insured persons and wages	Increase in entitlements and beneficiaries
(2) Employment growth (most likely depends on (1))	Increase in insured persons	Increase in beneficiaries
(3) Wage share and wages increase (might depend on (1))	Increase in insurable earnings	Increase in benefit amounts
(4) Wage increase/inflation	Increase in insurable earnings	Increase in benefit amounts
(5) Interest rate increase	Increase in investment income	
Demographic factors		
(1) Initial population age	Relationship of actives to beneficiaries	Same
(2) Mortality decrease		Increase in the number of beneficiaries and longer service of benefits
(3) Fertility increase	Increase in the number of contributors (long run) if economic development permits	Increase in the number of beneficiaries (long run)
Governance factors		
(1) Design	Contribution provisions	Pension formula and entitlement conditions determining the number and amount of benefits
(2) Maintenance (adjustment)	Ceiling on insurable earnings	Benefit levels
(3) Administrative efficiency		
(4) Administration cost decrease	Increase of income	Decrease in expenditure on administration
(5) Increase in registration compliance	Short-term direct increase in insurable earnings	Direct long-term increase in beneficiaries
(6) Increase in wage compliance	Short-term direct increase in insurable earnings	Long-term increase in benefits

It is assumed that the population registration compliance rate increases from an initial value of 10 per cent to 80 per cent after 35 years and stays constant thereafter. Wage compliance increases from 50 per cent to 80 per cent after 15 years and stays constant thereafter.

TYPICAL COST DEVELOPMENTS

Under the above assumptions, the two basic cost indicators develop as follows: under the simulated new scheme, as well as under a simulated conversion option. The conversion case is simulated on the basis of the assumption that a provident fund has operated for about 30 years and that all new pensioners

Figure TB4.1   Pay-as-you-go and national pension cost of a typical African pension scheme, 1992–2057

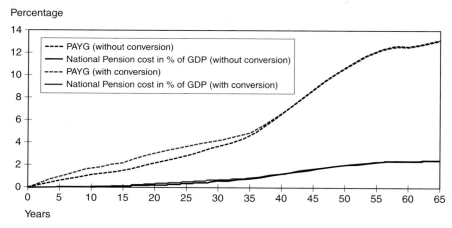

in the start year will convert 100 per cent of their balance into pensions. The conversion case simulates a policy option which many African governments are currently exploring.

The results (see figure TB4.1) show that, under conservative assumptions concerning the pension formula and with a slowly ageing population, the overall cost of the pension scheme remains at fairly low levels for at least six-and-a-half decades, provided the scheme is managed soundly. But the pay-as-you-go cost development also shows the characteristic curve of increasing expenditure which is typical of all national pension schemes. As pension schemes mature, and each new cohort of insured with increasing pension entitlement retires, the relative cost of the scheme will increase until it reaches a stage of relative maturity; that is, a stage at which the pension entitlement relative to average insured wages is virtually constant and where the ratio of pensioners to insured is also relatively stable (except for future demographic shifts). The stage is called the relative stationary state. The relatively stationary state is probably reached between the 60th and 80th year of a scheme's existence provided that the scheme started out with an almost complete coverage of the population to be insured by law and at a fairly high stage of economic development. Relative maturity is generally reached when the first cohort of insured persons entering the scheme at the age of entry into the labour force has almost completely died. Pension schemes can never be in a perfect stationary state, however, since career patterns, demographic structures and the benefit conditions of a scheme change over the course of decades. In developing countries the time until full final population coverage is reached should be added to the above period of maturation. This implies generally that the labour market must have reached its final stage of full formalization.

The bad news in this case is that, on the basis of assumptions which are thought to be realistic, even after six decades only about 17 per cent of the labour force would be covered and only about 20 per cent of the total population over age 60 would benefit from a pension (if one assumes that at least two persons over the age of 60 per household benefit from a pension).

If one were to assume that the formalization of the labour market and the economy was to occur much faster, and reach European levels in six decades, the overall estimated cost of the pension scheme would be 6–7 per cent of GDP, considerably lower than in OECD countries because of the younger population and the not fully mature scheme.

Health and social assistance schemes could take up another 10 per cent of GDP (the OECD average for 1990). In total the national social protection scheme in this case could, at the end of six decades, cost as much as Greece and Portugal allocated to their social protection schemes in 1994. It is hoped that economic progress will occur much faster. A 10 per cent average growth could bring typical developing countries in Africa up to present lower OECD standards in about three decades. For some fast-growing Asian countries this period would be even shorter.

It is worthwhile to discuss briefly whether the above typical country in Africa could already now afford a much better social protection scheme, for example a universal tax-financed pension scheme for all invalids and persons over 70 years. Even a modest benefit of 20 per cent of the present average wage in the formal sector would go a long way towards combating poverty. In order to present a complete simulation, future economic developments must be projected. The result is that a modest benefit paid to eligible persons not currently covered by the national social insurance scheme would initially cost about 2 per cent of GDP. The cost would drop to about 1.3 per cent of GDP after 30 years if growth rates and the increase in formal sector employment (which would bring more people into formal social insurance and reduce the cost of this residual benefit) materialized as assumed. A figure of 2 per cent of GDP appears not to be expensive, but it would require either savings in present expenditure or additional resources of about 6 per cent of the present total government revenues. This could be achieved by an increase in average income tax of 2.2 per cent or a new consumption tax of 3.6 per cent. These figures appear to be small but they would require a substantial political effort at a time when the budget of the model country is already in deficit by 7 per cent of GDP. Whether this modest additional social protection scheme is affordable depends on whether the government and the public are willing to set different priorities in their present public spending or whether they would accept the collection and payment of additional taxes. Acceptability of such a programme might be higher in about 25 years, when the economy and the tax bases will have grown (see discussion in box TB4.1).

Box TB4.1 Can a typical African economy afford a basic universal benefit system for the disabled and the old?

The following model calculation is built on the demographic structure of Zimbabwe and the typical structure of southern African economies. The growth rates assumed are first 3 per cent and then 4 per cent, which do not appear to be unrealistic in the region. The country is assumed to have a short-term benefit system for the formal sector workforce. Present pension benefits (which do not exist, but only cover a part of the formal sector) have been ignored. The assumption of a labour productivity growth rate of only 1 per cent per annum automatically leads to a steep increase in formal sector employment.

In order to introduce a benefits system like this, the government would have to increase the formal sector income tax by 2.2 percentage points which, in relative terms, is equivalent to a hike in income tax of 15 per cent. Whether the solidarity between the formal and informal sector in this country would be strong enough to accept this remains questionable. Alternatively the government could try to finance the measure through an increase in the consumption taxes which would make all citizens contribute, at least to some extent, to the financing of the benefit. Indirect consumption taxes would have to increase at least initially by about 14 per cent in relative terms or by 3.6 percentage points. If this was unpopular, the government would face the risk that the population would attempt to evade taxes to an even greater extent than at present. In the case of income taxes, employers and employees might collude and underdeclare incomes. As a result the overall tax base might decrease, with a negative effect on the government deficit and thus indirectly on economic performance. The government might find that the financing of this improvement of health services might roughly cost the same amount of money and be much more popular and lead to less negative side effects. The actual degree of acceptance, and hence affordability, of any social protection measure has to be tested and explored in each specific case.

SENSITIVITY TESTING

Once the typical pattern of the financial development of a national pension scheme in Africa is established, the planning and design of any national pension scheme requires an understanding of the uncertainty of projections, particularly as concerns the relative impact of demographic development, economic development and governance on the typical pattern and hence on the specific national projections.

Table TB4.2 provides the results of a sensitivity test on some of the parameters. From the sensitivity tests it is clear that the determinants which have the most direct impact on the financial development of the scheme with respect to the base case are the governance parameters. This theoretical exercise in a developing country context thus confirms the statistical observations in OECD countries.

Table TB4.2   Base case and sensitivity test results on the financial development of a typical African pension scheme, 1992–2057

	PAYG rate (percentage of total insurable earnings)			General average premium	National pension cost (percentage of GDP)		
	2010 t = 18	2030 t = 38	2057 t = 65		2010 t = 18	2030 t = 38	2057 t = 65
Base case	1.9	5.69	13.17	7.1	0.21	1.09	2.53
Sensitivity tests							
Demographic parameters							
Increase in life expectancy variation by 10%	1.91	5.76	13.69	7.26	0.21	1.11	2.63
Economic parameters							
GDP growth by 10% (including interest rate)	1.89	5.61	12.82	6.96	0.21	1.08	2.46
Productivity growth by 10%	1.91	5.72	13.29	7.15	0.21	1.1	2.55
Governance parameters							
Increase of benchmark replacement rate by 10%	2.05	6.26	14.49	7.8	0.23	1.2	2.78
Excess adjustment of pensions by 1% point (which is equal to a gradual increase of the replacement rate to about 11% in the final year)	1.95	5.96	14.35	7.56	0.22	1.15	2.76
Increase in compliance registration by 10%	1.9	5.69	13.17	7.1	0.23	1.2	2.78
Increase in wage compliance by 10%	1.9	5.69	13.17	7.1	0.23	1.2	2.78

Among the governance determinants the increase in the benchmark replacement rate by 10 per cent (and implicitly the assumed accrual rate) increases the pay-as-you-go cost and the national pension cost and the general average premium[3] by 10 per cent after 65 years. The effects of the increase in this benchmark rate take effect immediately, with an increase in the pay-as-you-go cost of 8 per cent after 18 years as pension benefits paid out increase without a growth in insurable wages. An increase in the registration compliance, as well as the wage compliance, affects both the income of the scheme, through higher contribution income, and the expenditure of the scheme, through pensions calculated on higher reference wages; therefore the pay-as-you-go cost and the general average premium do not change with respect to the base case if the increases take effect immediately. The national pension cost, however, increases as the overall expenditure volume increases.

A growth of GDP by 10 per cent, while the productivity per worker remains unchanged with respect to the base case, generates a higher total employment level, which in turn increases the wage base of the scheme. However, in the long run there is also an increase in the number of beneficiaries. Therefore, after 65 years the general average premium decreases by only 2 per cent with respect to the base case scenario. In the opposite case, however, where there is an increase in the productivity of workers, with GDP unchanged with respect to the base case, there is a decrease in employment. This decrease in active contributors generates a decrease in the contribution income and, only after some time lag, a decline in the future number of beneficiaries.

The increase in life expectancy affects the length of time during which benefits are paid to the insured and, therefore, the cost of the scheme. In the sensitivity test the life expectancy increases by two years over a 65-year time span and generates a pay-as-you-go cost and a national pension cost increase of 3.9 per cent.

Notes

[1] Indicated in United Nations (1996).

[2] ILO, *Yearbook of Labour Statistics 1995*, 54th issue, Geneva, 1995.

[3] A general average premium can be regarded as the "average" pay-as-you-go contribution rate throughout the projection period.

STATISTICAL ANNEX

THE DEMOGRAPHY OF PENSIONS

Table A.1 Demographic indicators for pensions: A regional summary, 1950–2050

	Africa	Arab states	Asia and Pacific	Central and Eastern Europe and Central Asia	Latin America and the Caribbean	OECD countries	World
Life expectancy at birth							
1950–55	38	42	40	64	51	66	47
1970–75	46	55	56	69	61	71	58
1990–95	52	64	64	69	69	76	64
Annual rates of total population growth (%)							
1975–2000	2.8	3.5	1.7	0.5	1.9	0.7	1.6
2000–2025	2.3	2.5	1.0	0.0	1.2	0.3	1.1
2025–2050	1.4	1.4	0.5	−0.1	0.6	−0.1	0.6
Old-age dependency ratios **Elderly** [1]							
1975	6	6	7	14	8	17	10
2000	6	5	9	17	9	21	11
2025	7	8	14	24	14	32	15
2050	12	13	25	34	27	42	24

Notes: [1] (65 and over)/(15–64).

Source: United Nations, *Demographic Yearbook*, various issues, New York.

Table A.2 Life expectancy by sex at specified ages, by country or territory, 1985–95

Country or territory	Year	Male 1985–95*						Female 1985–95*					
		Age 0	50	55	60	65	70	Age 0	50	55	60	65	70
Africa													
Algeria	1987	65.8	24.4	20.2	16.3	12.7	9.3	66.3	25.7	21.4	17.5	13.7	10.1
Egypt	1991	62.9	21.6	18.0	14.9	12.0	9.4	66.4	24.4	20.3	16.5	12.9	10.0
Malawi	1992–7	43.5	20.6	17.3	14.1	11.2	8.6	46.8	22.2	18.6	15.1	11.9	9.2
Mali	1987	55.2	28.0	24.4	20.7	17.6	14.4	58.7	24.0	26.1	22.1	18.6	15.1
Mauritius	1992–4	66.4	21.9	18.3	15.1	12.3	9.8	74.0	27.6	23.4	19.5	15.9	12.8
Group simple average		*58.8*	*23.3*	*19.6*	*16.2*	*13.1*	*10.3*	*62.4*	*24.8*	*22.0*	*18.1*	*14.6*	*11.4*
Arab states													
Bahrain	1986–91	66.8	–	–	–	–	–	69.4	–	–	–	–	–
Iraq	1990	77.4	32.4	28.8	24.8	21.3	18.0	78.2	31.1	26.6	22.0	17.7	12.9
Kuwait	1992–3	71.8	25.6	21.4	17.3	14.1	10.8	73.3	25.5	21.1	16.8	13.3	10.0
Group simple average		*72.0*	*29.0*	*25.1*	*21.1*	*17.7*	*14.4*	*73.7*	*28.3*	*23.9*	*19.4*	*15.5*	*11.4*
Asia and Pacific													
Bangladesh	1988	56.9	23.1	19.2	15.5	12.2	9.6	56.0	23.6	19.7	15.8	12.0	8.0
Cyprus	1992–3	74.6	27.7	23.4	19.2	15.5	12.3	79.1	30.9	26.3	21.8	17.5	13.5
India	1986–90	57.7	21.7	18.0	14.7	11.9	9.4	58.1	23.7	19.8	16.1	12.9	10.1
Macau	1988	75.0	27.6	23.4	19.5	15.9	12.5	80.3	32.3	27.8	23.3	18.9	14.8
Maldives	1992	67.2	24.3	20.4	16.8	13.5	10.5	66.6	22.6	18.7	15.4	12.2	9.4
New Caledonia	1994	67.7	23.5	–	15.8	–	10.1	73.9	27.4	–	19.5	–	12.7
Philippines	1991	63.1	22.9	19.1	15.5	12.3	9.5	66.7	25.2	21.2	17.3	13.7	10.6
Singapore	1994	74.2	26.5	22.2	18.2	14.8	11.8	78.5	30.0	25.6	21.3	17.3	13.6
Thailand	1985–6	63.8	23.0	19.1	15.5	12.5	9.7	68.9	26.2	22.1	18.6	15.2	12.0
Group simple average		*66.7*	*24.5*	*20.6*	*16.7*	*13.6*	*10.6*	*69.8*	*26.9*	*22.6*	*18.8*	*14.9*	*11.6*

Central and Eastern Europe and Central Asia

Albania	1988–9	69.6	—	—	—	—	—	75.5	—	—	—	—	—
Armenia	1991–2	68.7	24.1	20.6	16.9	14.0	10.9	75.5	28.6	24.3	20.1	16.2	12.7
Azerbaijan	1989	66.6	—	—	—	—	—	74.2	—	—	—	—	—
Belarus	1993	63.8	20.8	17.6	14.6	12.0	9.5	74.4	27.6	23.4	19.4	15.6	12.1
Bulgaria	1991–3	67.7	23.2	19.5	16.0	12.8	10.0	74.7	27.9	23.5	19.3	15.4	11.8
Czech Republic	1994	69.5	23.4	19.5	16.0	12.9	10.1	76.6	28.9	24.4	20.2	16.2	12.6
Estonia	1992	64.1	21.1	17.7	14.4	11.6	9.3	75.0	28.3	24.0	19.8	16.0	12.4
Georgia	1989	68.1	—	—	—	—	—	75.7	—	—	—	—	—
Hungary	1994	64.8	20.8	17.6	14.7	12.0	9.6	74.2	27.4	23.3	19.3	15.6	12.1
Kazakhstan	1990	63.8	21.7	18.3	15.1	12.4	10.0	73.1	27.9	23.7	19.7	16.2	12.9
Kyrgyzstan	1992	64.2	22.6	19.1	15.6	12.3	9.8	72.2	27.9	23.8	19.8	15.7	12.4
Latvia	1994	60.7	21.3	18.6	16.2	14.1	12.2	72.9	27.4	23.4	19.7	16.3	13.2
Lithuania	1993	63.3	21.3	18.2	15.2	12.5	10.1	75.0	28.6	24.5	20.4	16.5	13.0
Moldova, Rep. Of	1991	64.3	21.4	18.0	14.8	11.8	9.1	71.0	25.3	21.3	17.6	14.0	10.9
Poland	1993	67.4	22.4	18.8	15.5	12.5	9.9	76.0	28.7	24.3	20.1	16.2	12.6
Romania	1992–4	65.9	22.5	19.0	15.8	12.8	10.0	73.3	27.4	23.2	19.0	15.2	11.6
Russian Federation	1994	57.6	17.8	15.1	12.6	10.4	8.4	71.2	26.0	22.0	18.3	14.6	11.3
Slovakia	1994	68.3	22.8	19.1	15.8	12.9	10.4	76.5	29.0	24.6	20.4	16.5	12.9
Slovenia	1993–4	69.6	23.8	19.9	16.4	13.3	10.4	77.4	29.6	25.1	20.9	16.8	13.0
Tajikistan	1992	65.4	25.0	—	17.7	—	11.7	71.1	28.4	—	20.4	—	13.5
Turkmenistan	1989	61.8	—	—	—	—	—	68.4	—	—	—	—	—
Ukraine	1992–3	63.5	20.8	17.6	14.5	11.8	9.4	73.7	27.2	22.9	19.0	15.2	11.8
Uzbekistan	1989	66.0	—	—	—	—	—	72.1	—	—	—	—	—
Group simple average		*65.4*	*22.0*	*18.5*	*15.4*	*12.5*	*10.0*	*73.9*	*27.9*	*23.6*	*19.6*	*15.8*	*12.4*

Latin America and the Caribbean

Argentina	1990–1	68.2	23.9	20.0	16.5	13.3	10.4	73.1	28.4	24.2	20.0	16.1	12.5
Bahamas	1989–91	68.3	25.1	21.6	18.2	15.0	12.3	75.3	29.7	25.6	21.6	17.9	14.5
Brazil[1]	1995	63.8	23.4	19.8	16.4	13.3	10.5	70.4	26.7	22.6	18.7	15.1	11.8
Belize	1991	70.0	26.7	22.6	18.9	15.2	12.2	74.1	29.8	25.5	21.5	17.3	13.8
Chile	1995	71.8	26.4	22.3	18.5	15.0	11.8	77.8	30.6	26.2	22.0	18.1	14.5
Colombia	1990–5	66.4	25.2	21.3	17.7	14.4	11.6	72.3	27.5	23.3	19.4	15.8	12.7
Costa Rica	1990–5	72.9	27.1	22.8	18.8	15.1	11.8	77.6	30.6	26.2	21.9	17.9	14.1
Cuba	1988	72.9	27.6	23.5	19.6	16.0	12.7	76.8	30.2	25.9	21.8	17.9	14.3
Ecuador[1]	1995	67.3	26.7	22.7	18.9	15.4	12.1	72.5	29.9	25.6	21.5	17.7	14.2
El Salvador	1985	50.7	—	—	—	—	—	63.9	—	—	—	—	—
Guatemala	1979–80	55.1	23.4	19.9	16.6	13.5	10.3	59.4	25.0	21.1	17.5	14.2	11.4

(continued)

Table A.2 Life expectancy by sex at specified ages (continued)

Country or territory	Year	Male 1985–95*						Female 1985–95*					
		Age 0	50	55	60	65	70	Age 0	50	55	60	65	70
Latin America and the Caribbean													
Netherlands Antilles[2]	1981–91	72.3	26.1	22.0	18.3	14.8	11.9	77.9	30.9	26.6	22.3	18.3	14.6
Nicaragua	1990–5	64.8	25.8	21.8	18.0	14.5	11.4	67.7	27.6	23.5	19.6	15.9	12.5
Panama[1]	1990–5	70.9	27.0	22.9	18.9	15.3	12.1	75.0	30.0	25.6	21.5	17.5	13.8
Peru[1]	1990–5	62.7	24.3	20.3	16.5	13.1	9.9	66.6	26.9	22.6	18.5	14.6	11.1
Puerto Rico	1990–2	69.6	26.8	23.0	19.3	16.0	12.9	78.5	31.6	27.2	22.9	18.9	15.2
Trinidad and Tobago	1990	68.4	23.6	19.9	16.5	13.5	10.8	73.2	26.9	22.9	19.3	15.9	12.8
Uruguay	1984–6	68.4	24.0	20.2	16.7	13.5	10.7	74.9	29.2	25.0	21.0	17.3	14.0
Venezuela[1]	1985	66.7	24.8	20.9	17.3	14.2	11.4	72.8	28.4	24.2	20.3	16.7	13.5
Group simple average		66.9	25.4	21.5	17.9	14.5	11.5	72.6	28.9	24.7	20.6	16.8	13.4
OECD countries													
Australia	1994	75.0	28.0	23.6	19.4	15.7	12.3	80.9	33.0	28.5	24.0	19.7	15.7
Austria	1994	73.3	26.7	22.6	18.6	15.1	11.9	79.7	31.7	27.2	22.8	18.6	14.6
Belgium	1988–90	72.4	25.8	21.5	17.6	14.0	10.9	79.1	31.3	26.8	22.5	18.3	14.4
Canada	1985–7	73.0	26.5	22.3	18.4	14.9	11.8	79.8	31.9	27.5	23.2	19.2	15.4
Denmark	1992–3	72.5	25.7	21.5	17.6	14.1	11.1	77.8	29.8	25.5	21.4	17.6	14.0
Finland	1994	72.8	26.3	22.1	18.2	14.6	11.4	80.2	31.9	27.4	22.9	18.6	14.5
France	1992	72.9	27.0	23.0	19.2	15.7	12.5	81.2	33.3	28.8	24.4	20.1	16.0
Germany	1992–4	72.8	26.0	21.8	18.0	14.5	11.4	79.3	31.2	26.7	22.4	18.2	14.3
Greece	1990–1	74.6	—	—	—	—	—	80.0	—	—	—	—	—
Iceland	1992–3	76.9	29.2	24.8	20.5	16.7	13.2	80.8	32.2	27.8	23.3	19.1	15.1
Ireland	1990–2	72.3	25.2	20.9	17.0	13.4	10.4	77.9	29.8	25.4	21.1	17.1	13.5
Italy	1992	73.8	27.0	22.7	18.7	15.1	11.9	80.4	32.2	27.6	23.2	18.9	14.9
Japan	1994	76.6	28.9	24.6	20.4	16.7	13.1	83.0	34.5	29.9	25.3	21.0	16.8
Luxembourg	1985–7	70.6	24.2	20.2	16.4	13.1	10.1	77.9	30.1	25.6	21.3	17.2	13.3
Netherlands	1992–3	74.2	26.7	22.3	18.2	14.6	11.3	80.2	32.0	27.5	23.2	19.0	15.1
New Zealand	1990–2	72.9	26.6	22.4	18.4	14.8	11.7	78.7	31.1	26.7	22.5	18.5	14.8
Norway	1993	74.2	26.9	22.6	18.5	14.8	11.5	80.3	31.9	27.3	22.9	18.8	14.8

Portugal	1993–4	71.2	25.7	21.6	17.7	14.2	11.0	78.2	30.7	.26.2	21.8	17.6	13.6
Spain	1990–1	73.4	27.3	23.2	19.2	15.5	12.2	80.5	32.6	28.0	23.5	19.2	15.1
Sweden	1994	76.1	28.4	24.0	19.9	16.0	12.5	81.4	32.9	28.4	24.0	19.8	15.7
Switzerland	1993–4	75.1	28.3	24.0	19.8	16.0	12.6	81.6	33.5	28.9	24.5	20.2	16.1
United Kingdom	1994	74.2	26.7	22.4	18.3	14.7	11.5	79.4	31.2	26.7	22.4	18.4	14.7
United States	1993	72.2	26.7	22.6	18.8	15.3	12.2	78.8	31.4	27.0	22.8	18.9	15.3
Group simple average		*73.6*	*26.8*	*22.6*	*18.6*	*15.0*	*11.7*	*79.9*	*31.8*	*27.3*	*23.0*	*18.8*	*14.9*

Notes: – = figures not available. *Expectation of life estimated for years within this decennial period, data based on national survey. [1] Excluding some Indian population (such as nomadic or tribal population). [2] Including Aruba.

Sources: United Nations, *Demographic Yearbook*, various issues, New York: United Nations, *Demographic Yearbook 1991 Special Issue*, New York.

Table A.3 Population growth and proportion of total population in older age groups, by country or territory, 1975–2050

Country or territory	Annual rates of population growth (%)						Proportion of total population in older age groups (%)							
	Total population			Elderly (65 and over)			60 and over				65 and over			
	1975–2000	2000–2025	2025–2050	1975–2000	2000–2025	2025–2050	1975	2000	2025	2050	1975	2000	2025	2050
World total	**1.6**	**1.1**	**0.6**	**2.4**	**2.7**	**2.3**	**8.5**	**9.9**	**14.6**	**20.7**	**5.6**	**6.8**	**10.0**	**15.1**
Africa	**2.8**	**2.3**	**1.4**	**3.0**	**3.4**	**4.0**	**4.9**	**5.0**	**6.5**	**11.8**	**3.1**	**3.2**	**4.2**	**7.9**
Algeria	2.8	1.6	0.9	2.3	3.8	4.1	6.1	5.7	10.3	19.6	4.2	3.8	6.4	14.0
Angola	3.0	2.8	1.7	2.9	3.1	4.1	4.9	4.5	4.7	8.6	2.9	2.8	3.0	5.5
Benin	2.9	2.8	1.6	1.9	3.7	4.3	5.4	4.2	5.5	10.5	3.5	2.8	3.5	6.8
Botswana	3.1	1.9	1.0	3.6	3.9	4.8	3.3	4.0	6.3	14.4	2.1	2.4	3.9	9.9
Burkina Faso	2.8	2.7	1.7	2.6	2.5	4.7	4.6	4.3	4.1	8.4	2.8	2.7	2.5	5.3
Burundi	2.6	2.3	1.3	1.6	3.5	4.0	5.5	4.1	5.8	10.8	3.4	2.7	3.6	7.0
Cameroon	2.8	2.6	1.6	2.9	2.9	4.2	5.7	5.5	6.0	11.2	3.6	3.6	4.0	7.6
Cape Verde	1.8	1.8	1.0	1.0	1.6	5.6	8.1	6.4	8.3	18.2	5.4	4.4	4.2	13.0
Central African Republic	2.3	2.0	1.3	2.3	2.3	3.6	6.4	6.0	6.5	11.6	3.9	4.0	4.3	7.7
Chad	2.4	2.2	1.4	2.4	2.5	3.7	5.8	5.6	6.0	10.1	3.6	3.6	3.9	6.7
Comoros	3.3	2.6	1.3	3.1	3.7	4.7	4.3	4.0	5.3	11.4	2.6	2.5	3.3	7.4
Congo	2.9	2.7	1.7	2.7	2.6	4.3	5.5	5.0	5.0	9.3	3.4	3.2	3.2	6.1
Congo, Dem Rep. of the	3.3	2.9	1.8	3.3	3.2	4.3	4.6	4.5	4.7	8.7	2.8	2.9	3.1	5.6
Côte d'Ivoire	3.3	1.9	1.1	4.2	3.1	4.4	4.1	4.8	6.2	13.8	2.4	3.0	4.0	9.0
Djibouti	5.0	2.0	1.1	6.1	3.4	3.7	4.2	5.3	7.2	12.4	2.5	3.2	4.5	8.4
Egypt	2.3	1.4	0.8	2.5	3.7	3.1	6.5	6.8	11.9	20.4	4.2	4.5	8.0	14.2
Equatorial Guinea	2.8	2.3	1.5	2.5	2.5	3.5	6.8	6.0	6.3	10.3	4.3	3.9	4.1	6.7
Eritrea	2.4	2.2	1.2	3.2	3.3	3.8	4.2	5.0	6.4	11.8	2.5	3.1	4.1	7.8
Ethiopia	2.9	2.9	1.8	3.2	3.5	3.9	4.4	4.5	5.0	8.3	2.8	2.8	3.2	5.4
Gabon	3.0	2.2	1.3	2.7	2.0	2.6	9.4	8.6	8.0	11.3	6.1	5.7	5.5	7.6
Gambia	3.3	1.9	1.1	3.7	3.7	2.9	4.8	5.2	7.6	11.5	2.9	3.1	4.8	7.5
Ghana	2.9	2.4	1.4	3.3	3.9	4.1	4.4	4.8	6.6	12.4	2.7	3.0	4.3	8.2
Guinea	2.6	2.7	1.6	2.5	3.4	4.0	4.4	4.2	4.8	8.5	2.6	2.6	3.0	5.4
Guinea-Bissau	2.6	2.0	1.3	3.0	1.9	3.2	6.5	6.5	6.3	10.0	3.7	4.2	4.1	6.5
Kenya	3.2	2.0	1.1	2.3	3.2	5.2	5.5	4.3	6.2	15.7	3.7	2.9	3.9	10.6

Lesotho	2.7	2.3	1.4	3.2	3.0	3.7	5.7	6.2	7.2	12.7	3.6	4.0	4.8	8.7
Liberia	2.9	2.8	1.7	2.8	3.3	4.0	5.5	5.3	6.0	10.4	3.7	3.6	4.1	7.2
Libyan Arab Jamahiriya	3.9	2.8	1.6	5.0	4.4	4.1	3.7	4.7	6.1	11.3	2.2	2.9	4.1	7.6
Madagascar	3.3	2.8	1.6	3.0	3.8	4.4	4.5	4.1	5.3	10.3	2.2	2.7	3.3	6.5
Malawi	3.0	2.5	1.5	3.9	2.8	4.6	3.7	4.2	4.5	9.3	2.5	2.5	2.8	6.0
Mali	2.9	2.7	1.6	2.9	3.4	4.3	4.2	4.1	4.9	8.8	3.0	3.3	3.0	5.6
Mauritania	2.6	2.2	1.3	3.0	3.3	3.9	5.0	5.0	6.8	12.3	2.7	6.0	4.4	8.4
Mauritius	1.1	0.9	0.4	4.3	3.6	2.1	4.5	8.8	17.5	22.8	3.7	4.3	11.7	17.5
Morocco	2.1	1.3	0.7	2.8	3.6	3.6	5.2	6.6	11.8	21.7	3.1	3.2	7.7	15.7
Mozambique	2.5	2.4	1.5	2.7	2.7	3.9	5.2	5.1	5.4	9.5	3.5	3.8	3.4	6.2
Namibia	2.7	2.2	1.3	3.0	2.9	3.8	5.5	5.8	6.8	12.2	2.4	2.4	4.5	8.3
Niger	3.3	3.0	1.8	3.3	3.5	4.2	4.1	3.9	4.5	8.0	2.5	2.9	2.8	5.1
Nigeria	2.9	2.5	1.4	3.5	3.7	3.8	4.2	4.6	6.0	10.5	3.8	6.7	3.8	6.9
Réunion	1.5	1.0	0.5	3.8	3.4	2.5	6.1	9.9	17.5	25.2	2.4	2.4	11.9	19.5
Rwanda	2.3	2.1	1.1	2.2	3.0	5.0	4.0	3.8	4.8	11.6	3.0	3.0	2.9	7.6
Senegal	2.8	2.3	1.3	3.0	3.4	4.0	4.7	4.7	6.1	11.3	3.1	2.6	3.9	7.4
Sierra Leone	2.0	2.1	1.3	1.8	2.6	3.6	5.3	4.8	5.3	9.0	3.0	4.5	3.3	5.8
Somalia	3.0	2.9	1.7	2.4	3.4	4.2	5.0	4.2	4.6	8.2	3.8	3.2	2.9	5.3
South Africa	2.4	1.8	1.0	3.1	3.4	3.3	6.0	6.8	10.1	16.5	2.7	2.7	6.7	11.7
Sudan	2.5	1.8	1.0	3.2	3.7	3.9	4.5	5.1	7.8	14.7	2.9	2.6	5.0	10.3
Swaziland	2.9	2.2	1.1	2.7	4.3	4.5	4.7	4.5	7.1	14.7	2.3	3.1	4.5	10.3
Tanzania, United Rep. of	3.0	2.5	1.4	3.6	3.5	4.6	3.8	4.2	5.3	10.9	3.1	4.9	3.3	7.2
Togo	2.9	2.5	1.5	2.9	2.8	4.2	5.1	4.8	5.1	10.0	3.5	2.2	3.3	6.5
Tunisia	2.2	1.3	0.7	3.6	3.4	3.4	5.8	7.4	12.9	22.3	2.5	2.3	8.2	16.3
Uganda	2.8	2.8	1.6	2.3	2.7	5.1	4.1	3.4	3.5	8.1	2.6	2.7	5.8	12.0
Zambia	2.6	2.3	1.2	2.0	2.4	5.9	4.3	3.5	3.8	11.0	2.6	5.8	2.3	7.1
Zimbabwe	2.9	1.8	1.0	3.0	3.1	4.8	4.2	4.1	5.9	13.8	3.0	2.3	3.7	9.2
Arab states	*3.5*	*2.5*	*1.4*	*3.4*	*4.7*	*3.9*	*4.7*	*4.6*	*7.6*	*13.4*	*3.0*	*2.9*	*4.9*	*9.1*
Bahrain	3.3	1.3	0.3	4.5	7.4	1.7	3.6	4.9	19.6	24.3	2.3	3.0	12.8	17.8
Gaza Strip	3.7	3.8	2.3	3.0	4.1	4.7	4.3	3.3	4.3	7.1	2.8	2.4	2.5	4.5
Iraq	3.0	2.4	1.2	4.0	4.3	4.2	4.1	4.9	7.5	14.7	2.5	3.1	4.9	10.1
Jordan	3.6	2.6	1.4	3.7	3.8	4.9	4.3	4.6	6.6	13.4	2.8	2.9	3.9	9.2
Kuwait	2.7	1.6	0.6	3.7	8.5	2.8	2.6	3.6	16.0	24.7	1.6	2.0	10.3	17.7
Lebanon	0.7	1.2	0.6	1.3	2.3	3.5	7.5	8.2	12.2	21.4	5.0	5.8	7.7	15.5
Oman	4.6	3.6	2.1	4.1	5.6	3.6	4.4	3.9	5.5	8.4	2.6	2.3	3.8	5.5
Qatar	5.1	1.1	0.4	5.5	9.9	-0.6	3.1	4.8	24.1	19.8	2.0	2.2	17.9	14.0
Saudi Arabia	4.5	2.7	1.4	4.3	5.8	3.1	4.8	4.6	8.8	13.3	3.0	2.9	6.1	9.2

(continued)

Table A.3 Population growth and proportion of total population in older age groups (continued)

Country or territory	Annual rates of population growth (%)						Proportion of total population in older age (%)							
	Total population			Elderly (65 and over)			60 and over				65 and over			
	1975–2000	2000–2025	2025–2050	1975–2000	2000–2025	2025–2050	1975	2000	2025	2050	1975	2000	2025	2050
Arab states														
Syrian Arab Republic	3.1	2.0	1.1	2.4	3.7	5.1	5.3	4.7	7.7	18.1	3.7	3.1	4.6	12.2
United Arab Emirates	6.5	1.2	0.4	7.4	9.3	0.3	3.4	5.0	22.7	23.4	2.0	2.5	17.2	16.9
Yemen	3.9	3.2	1.8	3.5	3.3	5.3	4.4	3.7	4.3	8.8	2.6	2.3	2.4	5.7
Asia and Pacific	*1.7*	*1.0*	*0.5*	*3.1*	*3.2*	*2.7*	*6.3*	*8.2*	*14.1*	*22.0*	*3.9*	*5.5*	*9.3*	*15.8*
Afghanistan	2.1	2.3	1.2	2.7	3.5	3.8	4.2	4.6	6.1	9.9	2.4	2.7	3.6	6.9
Bangladesh	2.1	1.4	0.8	1.7	3.7	4.2	5.7	5.2	9.0	19.9	3.6	3.3	5.8	13.4
Bhutan	2.3	2.4	1.4	2.5	3.2	3.6	5.1	5.2	6.3	10.6	3.1	3.2	4.0	6.9
Brunei Darussalam	2.9	1.3	0.5	2.5	6.8	2.0	5.6	5.2	17.9	23.8	3.5	3.3	12.1	17.4
Cambodia	1.8	1.7	0.9	2.2	4.1	3.1	4.7	4.8	8.7	14.6	2.8	3.0	5.4	9.3
China	1.3	0.6	0.1	3.0	3.0	1.9	6.9	10.0	18.5	26.2	4.4	6.7	12.2	19.2
Cyprus	1.1	0.7	0.3	1.6	2.4	1.1	13.9	15.3	22.3	26.1	9.8	11.1	16.8	20.1
East Timor	1.1	1.2	0.7	0.8	4.4	3.1	4.5	4.4	9.1	16.3	2.7	2.5	5.4	10.0
Fiji	1.6	1.3	0.7	3.7	4.3	3.1	4.5	7.2	13.8	22.5	2.7	4.5	9.3	16.7
French Polynesia	2.5	1.4	0.7	4.1	4.5	2.9	4.9	6.8	13.7	21.7	2.9	4.3	9.2	15.7
Guam	2.2	1.1	0.5	5.7	4.2	1.8	3.8	8.0	16.8	20.9	2.3	5.3	11.3	15.4
India	2.0	1.1	0.6	3.0	3.3	3.0	6.2	7.6	12.6	21.3	3.8	5.0	8.4	15.2
Indonesia	1.8	1.0	0.6	3.4	3.4	3.2	5.3	7.4	12.7	21.6	3.2	4.7	8.3	15.8
Iran, Islamic Rep. of	3.4	2.1	1.1	4.3	3.2	4.1	5.1	5.8	8.0	16.5	3.3	4.1	5.4	11.2
Israel	2.3	1.1	0.5	3.1	2.5	1.9	11.8	12.7	18.1	24.4	7.8	9.5	13.4	18.8
Korea, Dem. Peo. Rep. of	1.5	0.9	0.4	3.6	4.1	2.4	5.1	8.1	17.1	24.0	3.2	5.3	11.4	18.8
Korea, Rep. of	1.1	0.5	0.0	3.6	3.7	1.8	5.8	10.5	21.8	28.8	3.6	6.7	14.7	23.1
Lao People's Dem. Rep.	2.6	2.4	1.2	3.0	3.4	3.8	4.6	4.8	6.0	11.0	2.7	2.9	3.8	7.0
Macau	2.6	0.6	-0.1	3.2	4.9	0.8	8.5	8.9	27.1	30.4	5.6	6.6	18.9	23.3
Malaysia	2.4	1.4	0.8	2.8	4.3	3.2	5.6	6.5	12.5	21.1	3.7	4.1	8.3	15.0
Maldives	3.2	2.7	1.4	2.0	3.2	4.4	6.9	5.0	5.9	12.1	4.4	3.3	3.8	7.9
Mongolia	2.6	1.6	0.8	3.7	3.4	4.3	4.7	5.6	10.0	20.2	2.9	3.8	5.9	14.0

Myanmar	2.0	1.3	0.7	2.6	2.9	3.4	6.2	7.0	10.8	18.8	3.8	4.6	6.8	13.2
Nepal	2.6	2.1	1.1	2.9	3.2	3.8	6.6	8.6	15.5	23.3	4.3	5.5	10.8	17.5
Pakistan	3.0	2.2	1.1	3.3	4.3	3.9	4.8	4.9	8.2	15.1	3.0	3.2	5.3	10.3
Papua New Guinea	2.3	1.8	1.0	2.1	3.5	4.1	5.2	5.0	7.2	14.4	3.1	3.6	4.5	9.7
Philippines	2.3	1.4	0.9	3.5	4.2	3.4	4.3	5.7	10.9	18.7	2.7	3.6	7.2	13.2
Samoa	0.6	1.5	0.9	3.1	2.7	4.5	4.3	7.3	9.7	21.7	2.7	4.9	6.5	15.5
Singapore	1.9	0.6	0.0	4.1	4.8	0.7	6.7	10.4	27.8	29.1	4.1	7.1	19.8	23.6
Solomon Islands	3.4	2.6	1.4	3.0	4.3	4.5	4.9	4.7	6.9	13.7	3.3	3.0	4.5	9.5
Sri Lanka	1.3	1.0	0.5	3.3	3.4	2.5	6.1	9.6	17.0	25.2	4.1	6.6	11.9	19.4
Thailand	1.5	0.5	0.2	4.2	3.5	2.6	4.7	8.7	17.9	28.1	3.0	5.8	12.1	21.7
Vanuatu	2.6	2.2	1.2	4.1	4.1	3.8	3.8	4.9	8.1	14.4	2.3	3.3	5.2	9.7
Viet Nam	2.1	1.3	0.7	3.1	2.7	3.8	6.4	7.3	11.9	22.1	4.0	5.2	7.5	16.1
Central and Eastern Europe and Central Asia	*0.5*	*0.0*	*-0.1*	*1.5*	*1.2*	*1.0*	*13.5*	*17.0*	*21.7*	*28.1*	*9.1*	*11.7*	*15.7*	*20.8*
Albania	1.5	0.8	0.4	2.6	3.1	2.3	6.9	9.0	16.0	23.0	4.5	6.0	10.4	16.7
Armenia	1.0	0.5	0.2	2.7	2.4	1.7	8.3	13.2	20.2	27.6	5.8	8.7	13.7	20.1
Azerbaijan	1.3	0.9	0.5	2.2	2.5	2.6	7.9	10.7	16.1	24.3	5.6	6.9	10.4	17.8
Belarus	0.4	-0.3	-0.4	1.7	0.8	0.7	14.2	19.5	25.0	31.8	10.0	13.8	18.0	23.9
Bosnia and Herzegovina	0.6	0.0	-0.5	3.0	2.5	0.8	8.1	14.9	26.5	33.4	5.5	9.9	18.6	25.4
Bulgaria	-0.2	-0.4	-0.4	1.3	0.4	0.6	16.1	21.2	25.7	32.3	10.9	15.8	19.4	25.0
Croatia	0.2	-0.2	-0.2	1.3	0.9	0.3	15.5	20.5	25.9	29.2	11.0	14.6	19.5	22.5
Czech Republic	0.1	-0.2	-0.5	0.0	1.3	0.8	18.3	17.0	24.9	32.3	12.9	12.6	18.6	25.3
Estonia	0.0	-0.5	-0.6	0.5	0.8	0.6	17.1	19.7	26.2	34.8	12.2	13.9	19.3	26.0
Georgia	0.4	0.2	0.2	2.0	1.1	1.1	12.4	18.3	22.0	25.9	8.5	12.6	15.7	19.8
Hungary	-0.3	-0.5	-0.5	0.3	0.6	0.5	18.3	19.6	24.4	30.8	12.6	14.5	18.9	24.1
Kazakhstan	0.7	0.7	0.4	1.6	2.7	2.0	8.5	11.4	16.8	23.4	5.7	7.1	11.5	16.9
Kyrgyzstan	1.3	1.1	0.8	1.3	2.3	3.1	8.5	8.9	12.2	20.3	5.9	6.0	8.0	14.2
Latvia	-0.1	-0.5	-0.4	0.4	0.4	0.5	17.8	20.3	25.1	31.0	12.7	14.3	18.2	22.8
Lithuania	0.4	-0.2	-0.3	1.2	0.9	0.7	15.1	18.6	24.5	30.0	11.1	13.5	17.6	22.6
Moldova, Rep. of	0.6	0.4	0.2	2.1	1.7	1.3	10.8	14.2	19.2	24.8	6.8	9.8	13.8	18.0
Poland	0.5	0.1	0.0	1.4	1.7	0.8	13.8	16.2	22.8	27.8	9.5	11.8	17.2	21.2
Romania	0.2	-0.3	-0.4	1.5	0.9	1.1	14.3	18.6	22.7	33.2	9.6	13.2	17.5	25.2
Russian Federation	0.3	-0.4	-0.6	1.8	1.0	0.5	13.6	18.7	24.9	31.8	8.9	12.7	18.0	23.3
Slovakia	0.5	0.1	-0.2	1.1	1.6	1.2	13.8	15.1	22.5	30.2	9.6	11.1	16.5	23.3
Slovenia	0.4	-0.4	-0.7	1.4	1.2	0.7	15.4	19.6	28.0	36.4	11.0	14.2	21.0	29.3
Tajikistan	2.5	1.7	1.0	2.4	2.9	4.0	6.7	6.8	9.6	18.8	4.7	4.6	6.1	12.8
TFYR of Macedonia	1.2	0.5	0.2	2.9	2.6	1.3	9.2	13.8	21.6	26.7	6.2	9.5	15.6	20.5

(continued)

Table A.3 Population growth and proportion of total population in older age groups (continued)

Country or territory	Annual rates of population growth (%)						Proportion of total population in old-age (%)							
	Total population			Elderly (65 and over)			60 and over				65 and over			
	1975–2000	2000–2025	2025–2050	1975–2000	2000–2025	2025–2050	1975	2000	2025	2050	1975	2000	2025	2050
Central and Eastern Europe and Central Asia														
Turkmenistan	2.3	1.5	0.8	2.1	3.3	3.7	6.8	6.5	10.5	19.1	4.5	4.2	6.6	13.1
Ukraine	0.1	-0.4	-0.5	1.4	0.6	0.6	15.8	21.2	25.3	32.2	10.5	14.3	18.6	24.4
Uzbekistan	2.4	1.5	0.8	1.6	3.1	3.7	7.8	6.9	10.6	19.4	5.5	4.6	6.8	13.5
Yugoslavia	0.6	0.1	0.1	2.1	1.1	0.7	12.9	18.6	22.8	25.9	9.2	13.3	17.0	19.7
Latin America and the Caribbean	*1.9*	*1.2*	*0.6*	*2.8*	*3.5*	*2.9*	*6.5*	*8.0*	*14.1*	*22.2*	*4.3*	*5.4*	*9.6*	*16.7*
Argentina	1.4	1.0	0.6	2.4	1.9	2.1	11.4	13.3	16.6	23.4	7.6	9.7	12.3	17.8
Bahamas	1.9	1.0	0.4	3.3	4.3	2.6	5.9	8.1	18.1	26.7	3.8	5.4	12.0	20.6
Barbados	0.3	0.5	0.1	0.9	1.9	1.5	13.6	14.5	23.2	29.0	9.9	11.4	16.2	23.0
Belize	2.4	1.8	1.0	2.2	3.0	4.9	6.8	6.0	9.4	20.6	4.5	4.3	5.8	15.1
Bolivia	2.3	1.8	1.0	2.9	3.6	3.7	5.5	6.2	8.9	16.4	3.4	4.0	6.1	11.6
Brazil	1.8	1.0	0.5	2.9	3.8	2.7	6.0	7.9	15.3	23.8	3.9	5.2	10.3	17.9
Chile	1.6	1.0	0.5	2.8	3.3	1.9	7.9	10.2	18.2	23.5	5.3	7.2	12.7	17.9
Colombia	2.0	1.2	0.7	3.1	4.2	2.8	5.5	6.8	14.4	22.0	3.5	4.6	9.7	16.4
Costa Rica	2.7	1.6	0.8	4.4	4.2	2.8	5.2	7.5	14.3	21.0	3.4	5.1	9.7	15.6
Cuba	0.7	0.2	-0.2	2.2	2.5	1.5	9.9	13.7	25.0	32.7	6.7	9.6	17.1	26.0
Dominican Republic	2.1	1.1	0.7	3.8	4.1	3.1	4.7	6.8	14.2	22.8	3.0	4.5	9.4	17.1
Ecuador	2.4	1.4	0.7	3.1	3.8	3.3	6.1	6.9	12.6	21.9	4.0	4.7	8.6	16.3
El Salvador	1.7	1.5	0.8	3.7	3.1	4.2	4.5	6.9	10.1	21.1	2.9	4.7	7.0	15.9
Guadaloupe	1.3	0.9	0.4	2.8	2.9	2.1	8.7	11.5	19.3	25.8	5.8	8.4	13.5	20.7
Guatemala	2.9	2.3	1.2	4.0	3.5	3.9	4.4	5.5	7.4	13.9	2.8	3.7	4.9	9.5
Guyana	0.7	1.0	0.4	1.2	4.0	3.1	5.5	6.3	14.4	22.7	3.7	4.2	8.9	16.9
Haiti	1.9	1.9	1.4	1.1	2.2	3.5	7.0	5.8	6.5	10.5	4.6	3.8	4.1	7.0
Honduras	3.1	2.0	1.1	4.2	4.1	4.2	4.2	5.2	8.6	17.4	2.6	3.4	5.7	12.4
Jamaica	1.0	1.1	0.6	1.4	2.6	3.4	8.5	8.8	14.9	24.1	5.8	6.4	9.4	18.7
Martinique	0.8	0.7	0.3	3.0	2.1	1.7	9.3	14.4	21.3	26.5	6.2	10.7	15.1	21.1

Mexico	2.1	1.1	0.7	2.8	3.9	3.3	5.7	6.9	13.5	23.3	4.0	4.7	9.3	17.8
Netherlands Antilles	0.8	0.7	0.3	2.3	3.7	0.8	8.6	12.0	23.0	25.6	5.7	8.2	17.1	19.5
Nicaragua	2.7	2.0	1.1	3.7	4.3	4.4	4.0	4.8	8.4	17.7	2.5	3.2	5.6	12.7
Panama	2.0	1.1	0.6	3.1	3.7	2.8	6.5	8.1	15.4	23.7	4.3	5.5	10.5	17.9
Paraguay	2.9	2.2	1.2	1.4	4.6	3.6	7.2	5.3	9.4	16.0	5.1	3.5	6.2	11.3
Peru	2.1	1.3	0.7	3.4	3.7	3.4	5.6	7.2	12.6	22.4	3.5	4.8	8.6	16.6
Puerto Rico	1.1	0.7	0.4	3.2	2.3	1.6	9.2	14.3	20.5	26.4	6.3	10.5	15.4	21.1
Suriname	0.9	1.2	0.6	2.2	2.5	3.9	5.8	7.9	12.8	22.9	3.9	5.4	7.5	16.6
Trinidad and Tobago	1.1	0.9	0.5	2.2	3.4	2.5	7.6	9.3	17.4	26.1	4.9	6.5	11.8	19.8
Uruguay	0.6	0.5	0.3	1.7	0.7	1.5	14.1	17.0	18.4	23.3	9.6	12.7	13.4	17.9
Venezuela	2.6	1.5	0.8	4.0	4.4	3.1	4.9	6.6	13.2	21.4	3.1	4.4	9.0	15.7
OECD countries	*0.7*	*0.3*	*-0.1*	*1.7*	*1.8*	*0.7*	*15.4*	*18.8*	*26.8*	*30.6*	*10.9*	*14.1*	*20.1*	*24.6*
Australia	1.2	1.0	0.2	2.5	2.5	1.2	12.8	15.9	23.5	28.0	8.7	11.9	17.4	22.3
Austria	0.4	0.0	-0.4	0.2	1.5	0.9	20.4	19.8	29.2	35.7	14.9	14.4	21.0	29.0
Belgium	0.2	0.0	-0.2	0.9	1.2	0.3	19.1	21.4	29.4	30.9	13.9	16.4	22.0	25.0
Canada	1.1	0.7	0.0	2.8	2.7	0.7	12.3	16.7	27.7	30.6	8.4	12.6	20.5	24.5
Denmark	0.2	0.0	-0.1	0.5	1.2	0.2	18.7	19.6	26.5	26.4	13.4	14.7	19.7	21.1
Finland	0.4	0.1	-0.1	1.7	1.8	0.0	15.5	19.6	28.8	28.3	10.6	14.6	22.3	22.6
France	0.5	0.1	-0.1	1.2	1.4	0.5	18.3	20.8	29.0	32.5	13.5	16.2	22.5	26.4
Germany	0.2	-0.1	-0.6	0.5	1.2	0.6	20.4	22.6	30.2	36.5	14.8	15.9	21.8	29.2
Greece	0.6	-0.2	-0.4	2.2	0.9	0.6	17.4	23.8	30.1	36.3	12.2	17.8	23.2	30.4
Iceland	1.0	0.7	0.3	1.9	2.4	1.2	12.7	14.9	23.2	27.0	9.2	11.5	17.2	21.5
Ireland	0.5	0.2	0.1	0.6	1.9	1.4	15.5	15.4	23.4	30.0	11.0	11.4	17.6	24.3
Italy	0.1	-0.4	-0.8	1.7	1.1	0.5	17.4	23.6	34.0	42.0	12.0	17.7	25.6	35.7
Japan	0.5	-0.2	-0.4	3.5	1.6	0.2	11.7	22.6	32.1	36.0	7.9	16.5	25.9	30.4
Luxembourg	0.7	0.3	0.0	1.1	1.6	0.7	18.6	19.4	26.5	29.0	13.1	14.3	19.6	23.4
Netherlands	0.6	0.1	-0.3	1.5	2.1	0.3	15.1	18.2	30.2	32.4	10.8	13.6	22.4	26.3
New Zealand	0.8	1.0	0.3	1.9	2.4	1.3	12.7	15.3	21.5	26.2	8.7	11.3	15.9	20.4
Norway	0.4	0.0	0.0	0.8	1.3	0.4	19.1	19.2	25.9	27.1	13.7	15.0	19.5	21.6
Portugal	0.3	-0.1	-0.3	2.2	0.9	0.8	14.3	21.0	27.4	33.1	9.9	15.7	20.5	27.4
Spain	0.4	-0.2	-0.7	2.5	1.0	1.0	14.4	21.4	30.6	40.7	10.0	16.5	22.7	34.6
Sweden	0.3	0.3	0.0	0.7	1.3	0.3	21.0	21.6	27.8	29.1	15.1	16.7	21.6	23.2
Switzerland	0.6	0.1	-0.4	1.2	1.9	0.4	17.5	19.5	31.3	33.9	12.6	14.7	23.0	27.8
Turkey	2.0	1.1	0.5	3.1	3.2	3.1	6.9	8.7	14.7	23.9	4.5	5.9	9.9	18.6
United Kingdom	0.1	0.1	-0.1	0.6	1.1	0.5	19.6	20.7	27.3	29.2	14.0	15.8	20.3	23.2
United States	0.9	0.7	0.2	1.6	2.3	0.8	14.8	16.3	24.7	27.1	10.5	12.4	18.3	21.2

Source: United Nations, *World Population Prospects 1950–2050, 1996 revision, medium variant projections.* New York, 1997.

Table A.4 Dependency ratios (%), by country or territory, 1975–2050

Country or territory	Elderly dependency ratio[1]				Total dependency ratio[2]				Needs-weighted dependency ratio[3]			
	1975	2000	2025	2050	1975	2000	2025	2050	1975	2000	2025	2050
World total	10	11	15	23	74	58	52	55	23	20	21	26
Africa	6	6	7	12	92	86	65	47	26	24	20	18
Algeria	9	6	9	21	107	68	44	52	31	20	16	24
Angola	5	6	5	8	87	101	78	46	25	28	22	16
Benin	7	5	6	10	91	97	71	46	26	27	21	17
Botswana	4	4	6	15	109	80	54	49	30	22	16	20
Burkina Faso	6	5	4	8	98	99	76	46	27	27	21	15
Burundi	7	5	6	10	96	91	67	45	27	25	20	16
Cameroon	7	7	7	11	88	89	69	48	25	26	21	18
Cape Verde	11	8	6	20	109	77	44	52	33	23	14	23
Central African Republic	7	7	7	11	80	84	65	47	24	25	20	17
Chad	7	7	5	10	83	87	69	47	24	25	21	17
Comoros	5	5	5	11	99	91	62	46	27	25	18	17
Congo	7	6	6	9	92	96	74	47	26	27	21	16
Congo, Dem. Rep. of the	5	6	5	8	92	104	78	47	26	29	22	16
Côte d'Ivoire	5	6	6	13	93	85	54	47	26	24	17	18
Djibouti	5	6	7	12	86	77	61	47	24	22	19	18
Egypt	8	7	12	22	79	65	47	52	24	20	17	24
Equatorial Guinea	8	7	7	10	80	89	70	47	24	26	21	17
Eritrea	5	6	7	11	89	88	64	47	25	25	19	17
Ethiopia	5	6	6	8	94	99	80	47	26	28	23	16
Gabon	10	11	9	11	65	83	69	46	21	26	22	17
Gambia	5	6	8	11	82	80	64	45	23	23	20	17
Ghana	5	5	7	12	93	87	65	48	26	25	20	18
Guinea	5	5	5	8	92	98	77	47	26	27	22	16
Guinea-Bissau	6	8	7	10	72	85	70	47	21	25	21	17
Kenya	8	5	6	16	112	86	50	49	32	24	15	20
Lesotho	7	7	8	13	83	82	64	48	24	24	20	18

Liberia	7	7	11	91	90	75	48	26	26	22	17	
Libyan Arab Jamahiriya	4	5	11	93	91	69	46	26	25	21	17	
Madagascar	5	5	10	94	94	69	45	26	26	20	16	
Malawi	4	5	9	98	97	74	46	27	27	21	16	
Mali	5	5	8	94	99	75	46	26	27	21	16	
Mauritania	6	7	12	86	81	63	47	24	23	19	18	
Mauritius	5	9	28	74	48	50	59	21	17	21	29	
Morocco	7	7	24	103	62	45	55	30	19	17	26	
Mozambique	6	6	9	89	92	72	47	25	26	21	16	
Namibia	6	7	12	86	83	64	47	25	24	20	18	
Niger	5	5	7	95	104	80	46	26	29	22	15	
Nigeria	5	5	10	90	92	69	46	25	26	21	16	
Réunion	7	10	32	84	52	50	63	25	18	22	32	
Rwanda	5	4	11	103	89	62	47	28	24	18	17	
Senegal	5	6	11	91	87	66	46	25	25	20	17	
Sierra Leone	6	6	8	84	88	72	46	24	25	21	16	
Somalia	6	5	8	94	102	78	46	26	28	22	15	
South Africa	7	10	18	81	69	54	51	24	21	19	22	
Sudan	5	8	15	89	72	55	50	25	21	18	20	
Swaziland	6	7	15	94	80	54	50	26	22	17	20	
Tanzania, United Rep. of	5	6	10	101	91	67	46	28	25	20	17	
Togo	6	6	9	90	95	71	45	25	25	21	16	
Tunisia	7	8	25	90	59	45	56	26	19	17	27	
Uganda	5	5	7	100	106	76	44	27	29	21	15	
Western Sahara	6	8	18	90	71	45	49	25	21	15	21	
Zambia	5	4	10	97	95	62	46	27	26	18	17	
Zimbabwe	5	6	14	107	86	51	47	29	24	15	18	
Arab states	*6*	*5*	*13*	*98*	*81*	*63*	*47*	*28*	*23*	*20*	*19*	
Bahrain	4	4	28	83	48	51	58	23	14	22	29	
Gaza Strip	6	5	7	100	119	90	50	28	32	25	16	
Iraq	5	6	15	96	80	58	49	27	23	18	20	
Jordan	6	6	14	100	86	59	48	28	24	18	19	
Kuwait	3	3	28	85	54	50	60	23	15	20	29	
Lebanon	9	9	24	86	63	45	55	26	20	17	26	
Oman	5	5	8	89	100	85	47	25	27	25	16	
Qatar	3	3	22	55	40	68	54	15	11	32	24	
Saudi Arabia	6	5	13	90	77	68	46	25	22	22	18	

(continued)

Table A.4 Dependency ratios *(continued)*

Country or territory	Elderly dependency ratio[1]				Total dependency ratio[2]				Needs-weighted dependency ratio[3]			
	1975	2000	2025	2050	1975	2000	2025	2050	1975	2000	2025	2050
Arab states												
Syrian Arab Republic	8	5	7	18	109	78	46	51	31	22	15	22
United Arab Emirates	3	4	28	27	43	44	63	58	12	13	30	28
Yemen	6	5	4	8	115	103	74	43	32	28	21	15
Asia and Pacific	*7*	*9*	*14*	*24*	*80*	*56*	*47*	*55*	*24*	*18*	*19*	*26*
Afghanistan	4	5	6	10	86	80	65	42	24	22	19	15
Bangladesh	7	5	8	20	98	64	44	51	28	19	15	23
Bhutan	6	6	7	10	79	86	66	45	22	25	20	16
Brunei Darussalam	6	5	19	27	77	54	53	58	23	16	22	28
Cambodia	5	5	8	14	82	77	54	47	23	22	18	18
China	8	10	18	31	78	46	46	61	23	16	21	31
Cyprus	15	17	27	33	56	55	59	64	22	22	28	32
East Timor	5	4	8	15	81	71	48	47	23	20	16	19
Fiji	5	7	14	26	74	56	47	57	21	17	19	27
French Polynesia	5	7	14	24	82	59	48	55	23	18	19	26
Guam	4	8	17	24	66	58	51	54	18	19	21	25
India	7	8	12	23	77	61	45	53	23	19	17	25
Indonesia	6	7	12	25	82	55	45	56	24	17	17	26
Iran, Islamic Republic of	6	8	8	17	95	89	51	49	27	26	17	21
Israel	13	15	21	30	68	60	54	61	24	23	24	30
Korea, Dem. Peo. Rep. of	6	8	17	30	90	48	47	60	26	16	20	30
Korea, Rep. of	6	9	22	39	71	39	47	68	21	14	22	36
Lao People's Dem. Rep.	5	6	6	10	81	94	61	45	23	26	18	16
Macau	9	9	30	39	54	43	57	68	18	16	29	37
Malaysia	7	7	12	23	85	65	47	53	25	20	18	25
Maldives	8	7	6	12	86	97	61	47	26	28	18	18
Mongolia	5	6	9	21	88	67	44	52	25	20	15	24
Myanmar	7	7	10	20	80	63	44	51	24	19	16	23
Nepal	6	6	7	13	84	84	56	46	24	24	18	18

(continued)

New Caledonia	8	9	16	28	76	54	49	59	23	18	20	29
Pakistan	6	6	8	15	94	82	56	48	26	23	18	20
Papua New Guinea	6	5	7	14	82	72	52	47	23	20	16	19
Philippines	5	6	11	20	86	68	47	51	24	20	17	23
Samoa	6	8	9	24	111	69	45	54	31	21	16	26
Singapore	7	10	31	40	59	42	59	69	18	16	31	37
Solomon Islands	7	6	7	14	104	85	61	49	29	24	19	19
Sri Lanka	7	10	18	32	77	49	50	63	23	17	22	32
Thailand	6	8	18	36	92	45	46	68	26	15	20	35
Vanuatu	4	6	8	14	93	81	59	48	26	23	19	19
Viet Nam	8	9	11	25	91	65	45	55	27	21	17	26
Central and Eastern *Europe and Central Asia*	*14*	*17*	*24*	*34*	*54*	*49*	*50*	*63*	*20*	*21*	*24*	*33*
Albania	8	9	15	26	80	55	48	56	24	18	20	27
Armenia	10	13	20	33	67	50	49	63	22	19	23	32
Azerbaijan	10	11	15	28	84	57	48	59	26	20	20	29
Belarus	15	21	27	40	55	49	51	68	22	22	26	37
Bosnia and Herzegovina	9	14	28	43	57	40	50	70	19	17	26	39
Bulgaria	16	24	29	43	49	49	52	70	20	24	26	39
Croatia	16	21	30	38	48	47	56	68	20	23	28	36
Czech Republic	20	18	28	43	54	43	50	70	23	20	26	39
Estonia	18	20	29	44	51	46	51	70	21	22	27	39
Georgia	14	19	24	32	58	53	56	64	21	23	26	32
Hungary	19	21	29	40	49	46	52	68	22	22	27	37
Kazakhstan	9	21	17	27	68	53	51	58	22	19	21	28
Kyrgyzstan	11	10	12	22	85	69	47	53	27	22	18	24
Latvia	19	21	28	38	51	48	52	65	22	23	27	35
Lithuania	18	20	27	38	58	49	52	67	23	22	26	36
Moldova, Rep. of	11	15	21	29	55	50	52	60	19	20	24	30
Poland	14	17	27	35	51	46	54	66	20	20	27	34
Romania	15	19	26	43	53	46	48	70	21	21	25	39
Russian Federation	13	18	27	39	47	44	50	65	18	20	26	36
Slovakia	15	16	25	39	56	45	49	68	21	19	25	37
Slovenia	17	20	32	52	53	43	52	77	22	21	29	45
Tajikistan	9	8	9	19	100	79	48	51	30	21	17	22
TFYR of Macedonia	10	14	24	34	58	46	54	65	20	24	26	33
Turkmenistan	9	7	10	20	92	71	45	50	27	21	16	23

Table A.4 Dependency ratios (continued)

Country or territory	Elderly dependency ratio[1]				Total dependency ratio[2]				Needs-weighted dependency ratio[3]			
	1975	2000	2025	2050	1975	2000	2025	2050	1975	2000	2025	2050
Central and Eastern Europe and Central Asia												
Ukraine	16	21	28	41	50	47	51	68	20	22	27	37
Uzbekistan	11	8	10	20	96	73	46	51	29	22	17	23
Yugoslavia	14	20	27	33	51	50	55	67	20	22	27	33
Latin America and the Caribbean	*8*	*9*	*14*	*26*	*84*	*58*	*50*	*58*	*25*	*19*	*20*	*28*
Argentina	12	16	19	29	58	60	53	60	21	23	23	29
Bahamas	7	8	18	34	82	46	49	66	24	16	21	34
Barbados	17	17	25	39	70	50	53	70	26	21	26	37
Belize	9	8	8	23	107	79	44	54	31	23	15	25
Bolivia	6	7	9	17	87	77	54	50	25	23	18	21
Brazil	7	8	15	29	79	51	48	61	23	17	20	30
Chile	9	11	19	29	73	55	54	60	23	19	23	29
Colombia	7	7	15	26	87	59	50	58	25	19	20	27
Costa Rica	6	8	15	25	84	62	54	57	24	20	21	26
Cuba	12	14	25	46	79	45	49	75	26	18	25	41
Dominican Republic	6	7	14	27	94	60	49	58	26	19	19	28
Ecuador	8	8	13	26	92	63	48	57	27	19	18	27
El Salvador	6	8	10	25	95	68	47	57	27	21	17	27
Guadeloupe	11	13	20	34	92	50	51	66	28	19	23	34
Guatemala	5	7	8	14	94	87	60	48	26	25	19	19
Guyana	7	6	13	27	92	52	45	58	26	16	18	28
Haiti	8	7	7	10	84	78	67	46	25	23	20	17
Honduras	5	6	9	19	102	82	52	51	28	24	17	22
Jamaica	12	10	14	30	104	58	46	61	32	20	18	30
Martinique	12	16	23	35	87	53	54	66	28	21	25	34
Mexico	8	8	14	28	102	61	48	60	30	19	19	29
Netherlands Antilles	9	12	27	32	63	49	60	63	20	18	29	32
Nicaragua	5	6	8	19	102	79	51	52	28	22	17	23

	1	2	3	4	5	6	7	8	9	10	11	12
Panama	8	9	16	29	89	58	49	60	26	19	20	29
Paraguay	10	6	10	17	95	75	58	50	29	22	19	21
Peru	7	8	13	26	88	62	48	57	25	19	18	27
Puerto Rico	10	16	24	35	66	53	56	66	22	21	26	34
Suriname	8	9	11	26	106	61	45	57	31	20	17	27
Trinidad and Tobago	9	10	18	32	75	48	49	64	23	17	21	32
Uruguay	15	20	20	29	60	58	53	60	23	24	23	29
Venezuela	6	7	13	25	87	63	50	56	25	19	19	26
OECD countries												
Australia	17	21	32	42	57	49	59	72	23	23	31	39
Austria	14	18	28	38	57	49	58	69	21	21	28	36
Belgium	24	21	32	52	62	46	54	80	27	22	30	46
Canada	22	25	36	43	57	51	62	74	25	25	33	40
Denmark	13	18	33	42	53	47	61	73	20	21	32	39
Finland	21	22	32	35	56	50	60	65	25	23	31	34
France	16	22	37	38	48	49	67	69	20	23	35	36
Germany	22	25	37	47	60	53	64	77	26	26	34	43
Greece	23	23	34	52	57	45	54	77	26	23	30	45
Iceland	19	27	37	56	57	49	59	84	24	26	33	49
Ireland	15	18	27	36	65	54	59	67	24	22	28	35
Italy	19	17	28	43	73	48	57	75	28	20	28	40
Japan	19	26	41	69	57	47	59	93	24	25	35	58
Korea	12	24	43	56	47	46	66	86	18	24	38	50
Luxembourg	20	21	31	40	53	48	60	71	23	23	31	38
Netherlands	17	20	36	46	57	47	61	75	23	22	33	42
New Zealand	14	17	25	33	63	52	57	64	23	22	27	33
Norway	22	23	31	36	60	54	61	67	26	25	31	35
Portugal	16	23	32	49	61	48	55	77	23	24	30	44
Spain	16	24	35	66	60	46	54	91	23	24	31	56
Sweden	24	26	36	39	56	56	66	70	26	27	34	37
Switzerland	19	22	37	50	54	47	61	79	23	22	34	45
Turkey	8	9	14	30	81	52	46	61	24	18	19	30
United Kingdom	22	24	33	39	59	53	61	70	26	25	32	37
United States	16	19	29	35	55	51	61	66	22	22	30	34

Notes: [1] (65 and over)/(15 – 64). [2] [(0 – 14) + (65 and over)]/(15 – 64). [3] [0.25 × (0 – 14) + 0.75(65 and over)]/(15 – 64).

Source: United Nations, *World Population Prospects 1950–2050*, 1996 revision, medium variant projections, New York, 1997.

2

EMPLOYMENT AND RETIREMENT OF OLDER WORKERS

Table A.5 Qualifying conditions for old-age benefit, by country or territory, 1997

Country or territory	Normal retirement age M–W	Covered years required for pension M–W	Early retirement provisions	Retirement necessary to receive benefits
Africa				
Algeria	60–55	17	Age 50 (M), 45 (W) and 20 years' employment	Yes
Benin	55	20	Age 50 if prematurely aged	Yes
Burkina Faso	55	15	Age 50 if prematurely aged, 53 if civil servant	Yes
Burundi	55	15	Age 50 if prematurely aged, 45 if arduous conditions	No
Central African Republic	55–50	20	5 years earlier if prematurely aged	Yes
Congo, Dem. Rep. of the	63–60	5	Age 55 if prematurely aged	Yes
Congo	55	20[1]	5 years if prematurely aged	Yes
Côte d'Ivoire	55	10	Age 50–54 with 5% reduction per year	Yes
Egypt	60	10	If 20 years of contribution, full pension at age 55 and reduced pension from 40	Yes
Gabon	55	20	5 years earlier if prematurely aged	Yes
Gambia	55	–	Age 45 if no employment for 2 years	–
Ghana	60	20	Age 55–59 with reduction, unless hazardous employment	–
Guinea	55	15	From age 50 if unable to work or reduction 5%-10% per year	Yes
Kenya	55	–	At age 50 if out of insured employment	Yes
Liberia	60	8 yrs. 4 mths	–	Up to 65
Libyan Arab Jamahiriya	65	20	Age 60 if hazardous or unhealthy occupation	Yes
Madagascar	60–55	15	Age 55–50 if incapacity to work or seamen	Yes
Mali	55	10	At age 50: unreduced if incapacity, otherwise 5% reduction per year	Yes
Mauritania	60–55	20	5 years earlier if prematurely aged	Yes
Morocco	60	15	–	Yes
Niger	60	20	5 years earlier if prematurely aged	Yes
Nigeria	60	10	–	Yes
Rwanda	55	20	5 years earlier if prematurely aged	Yes
Senegal	55	1	2 years earlier (5% reduction per year)	Yes
South Africa	65–60	–	–	Means-tested
Sudan	60–55	12	Arduous work. Reduced pension at age 45 with 12 years' contribution	–
Tanzania, United Rep. of	55	–	If unemployed or in non-contributory employment	Yes
Togo	55	20	30 years of coverage: age 50 if prematurely aged	Yes
Tunisia	60	10	Unemployed, or prematurely aged because of arduous work, or large families. Reduced pension (2% year) from age 50 if 30 years of coverage	Yes
Zimbabwe	60	10	Age 55 for workers in arduous employment	–

(*continued*)

Table A.5 Qualifying conditions for old-age benefit (*continued*)

Country or territory	Normal retirement age M–W	Covered years required for pension M–W	Early retirement provisions	Retirement necessary to receive benefits
Arab states				
Iraq	60–55	20	Any age if 30 years' (M) or 25 years' (W) contributions	Yes
Jordan	60–55	10	Reduced pension from age 46, if 15 years' coverage	–
Kuwait	50	15	Age 45 (M) and 40 (W) if 20 years' coverage; 15 years for women with children[2]	Yes (at least up to 50)
Oman	60–55	15–10	Reduced pension if 20 years (M) or 15 years (W) of contributions	–
Saudi Arabia	60	10	–	Yes
Syrian Arab Republic	60	15	Age 55 with 20 years' coverage	Earnings test
Asia and Pacific				
Afghanistan	60–55	25–20	–	–
China	60–55	10	Arduous/unhealthy work or totally disabled	–
Cyprus	65	–	Age 63 if average earnings at least equal to 70 % of basic earnings	–
Fiji	55	10	–	–
India	58	10	Between 50 and 57, and 20 years' covered employment, with a reduction of 3% per year	Yes
Indonesia	55	5 yrs. 5 mths	–	–
Iran, Islamic Republic of	60–55	10	Any age if 30 years of work: lower age if unhealthy work	Yes
Israel	65–60	12 (or 5 in last 10)	–	Earnings test
Korea, Rep. of	60	20	Reduced pension age 55–59	Up to 65
Malaysia	55	–	–	Yes
Pakistan	60–55	15	Reduced pension payable 5 years earlier (6% per year)	No
Papua New Guinea	55	–	At any age if 15 years of coverage	Yes
Philippines	60	10	–	–
Singapore	55	–	–	–
Sri Lanka	55–50	–	–	Yes
Viet Nam	60–55	20	Reduced by up to 5 years if hazardous or arduous work	–
Central and Eastern Europe and Central Asia				
Albania	60–55	20	Large families: reduced by up to 5 years for women with large families	Yes
Armenia	60–55	25	Age 50 with 20 years' coverage if hazardous work or large families/ disabled children	Yes
Belarus	60–55	25[3]	Hazardous work, large families, war veterans/disabled children	–
Bulgaria	60–55	25–20	Hazardous work, large families, teachers and military	–

Table A.5 Qualifying conditions for old-age benefit (*continued*)

Country or territory	Normal retirement age M–W	Covered years required for pension M–W	Early retirement provisions	Retirement necessary to receive benefits
Central and Eastern Europe and Central Asia				
Croatia	60–55	20	Any age with 40–35 years' coverage. Arduous or unhealthy employment. Reduced pension: age 55 and 35 years (M) or age 50 and 30 years (W)	–
Czech Republic (2007)	62–61[4]	25	Reduced pension up to 5 years earlier. Large families	First 2 years
Estonia (2007)	65–60[4]	15	Large families/disabled children. Arduous work (up to 10 years)	–
Georgia	60–55	25–20	Large families/disabled children. Hazardous/arduous work	Earnings test
Hungary (2003)	60[5]	20	Unhealthy work. Reduced pension up to 5 years earlier (contribution requirement)	–
Kyrgyzstan	60–55	25–20	Large families/disabled children. Hazardous work	–
Moldova, Republic of				
Poland	65–60	25–20	Special groups and special conditions	Partial
Romania	60–55	30–25	Large families. Arduous/dangerous work. Up to 5 years earlier under certain conditions	–
Russian Federation	60–55	25–20[6]	2 years earlier if unemployed. Hazardous/dangerous/northern work, large families/disabled children	–
Slovakia	60–57	25–20	Large families	–
Slovenia	–	–	Varies with the number of years	Yes
Latin America and the Caribbean				
Argentina (2001)	65–60[4]	30	Reduced up to 10 years for hazardous work	No if full benefits
Bahamas	65	2.9	–	–
Barbados	65	9.6	–	–
Belize	60	9.6	–	Up to 65
Bolivia (new scheme)	65	–	Replaced rate of 70% rural employees, arduous employment	–
Brazil	65–60	8[7]	30 years (reduced pension after 25 years)	–
Chile	65–60	20 yrs. (minimum benefit)	Replacement rate of 50% and pension greater than 110% of minimum pension	–
Costa Rica	62–60	38.5[8]	–	No
Cuba	60–55	25	Reduced up to 5 years if arduous work	Income ceiling
Dominica				
Dominican Republic	60	15.4	–	Up to 65
Ecuador	55	30	Any age if 35 years of contributions. Age 45 with 25 years and 6 months of unemployment	Yes

(*continued*)

Table A.5 Qualifying conditions for old-age benefit (*continued*)

Country or territory	Normal retirement age M–W	Covered years required for pension M–W	Early retirement provisions	Retirement necessary to receive benefits
Latin America and the Caribbean				
El Salvador	60–55	14.4	Any age if 30 years of contributions. If pension equals 70% of basic earnings and 160% of minimum pension	–
Guatemala	60	15	–	Yes from lost employment. Earnings test
Guyana	60	14.4	–	No
Haiti	55	20	–	–
Honduras	65–60	15	–	Yes
Jamaica	65–60	3	–	Until 70 (M), 65 (W)
Mexico (new system)	65	24	–	–
Nicaragua	60	14.4	Age 55 if physically or mentally impaired	–
Panama	62–57	15	–	Yes
Paraguay	60	25	At age 55 if 30 years of contributions	–
Peru	65	20	Replacement rate of 50% and pension greater than 110% of minimum pension[9]	–
Saint Lucia	60	10	–	Yes
Trinidad and Tobago	60	14.4	–	Up to 65
Uruguay (2003) new scheme	60[5]	35	–	Yes
Venezuela	60–55	14.4	Unhealthy/arduous occupations	No
OECD countries				
Australia (2013)	65[10]	–	–	Means-tested
Austria	65–60	15	Age 60–55 if 35 years insurance after 1 year of sickness/unemployment	Earnings ceiling on early pension
Belgium	65	45	–	–
Canada	65	1	Age 60–64 with 6% reduction per year	Up to 65
Denmark	67	–	Inability to work	Flat-rate pension, income-tested
Finland	65	–	Age 58–64 if inability to work. Age 60–64 with 4%–6% reduction per year	Yes
France	60	–	–	–
Germany	65	5	From age 60 (W) and 63 (M) reduced by 3.6% per year unless satisfies contribution, disability or unemployment requirements	–
Greece	65–60	15	From age 60 (M) and 55 (W) reduced by 6% per year unless satisfies contribution requirements, hazardous employment, dependent/disabled children (W)	Earnings tested

Table A.5 Qualifying conditions for old-age benefit (*continued*).

Country or territory	Normal retirement age M–W	Covered years required for pension M–W	Early retirement provisions	Retirement necessary to receive benefits
OECD countries				
Iceland	67	–	Age 65	No
Ireland	65	3	No	Up to 66
Italy (new system)[11]	62	5	Reduced pension (defined contribution) from age 57	Yes
Japan	65[12]	25	Age 60–64 with actuarial reduction	Earnings test up to 65
Luxembourg	65	10	Age 57 or 60 (2 programmes) if 40 years of coverage	–
Netherlands	65	49	–	No
New Zealand (2001)	65[13]	–	–	No, but subject to additional tax
Norway	67	3	–	
Portugal (1999)	65[14]	15	Special groups at 60 if unemployment benefit depleted	Up to 70
Spain	65	15	Age 60–64 with 8% reduction per year. Dangerous/unhealthy work	–
Switzerland	65–62[15]	1	Up to two years before the NRA (6.8% reduction per year)	Up to 70
Sweden	65	3	Reduced pension from age 60[16]	–
Turkey	55–50	15	Any age if 25 years of insurance	–
United Kingdom	65–60[17]	–	No	–
United States	65[18]	10	Reduced pension from the age of 62	Earnings test, up to 70

Notes: [1]Pension reduced if between 5 and 20 years of coverage. [2]Age to be increased to 55 (M) and 50 (W) in 2020. [3]Or pension at least equal to 50% of minimum pension. [4]Currently rising from an age of 60 for men and 55 for women. [5]Currently rising from an age of 55 for women. [6]Or pension at least equal to 2/3 of minimum old-age pension. [7]To reach 15 years in 2011. [8]Down to 20 years at age 65. [9]For the private system. [10] Currently rising from an age of 60 for women. [11] For new hires from 1 January 1996. [12]Pension payable from the age of 60, will gradually be phased out. [13]Currently rising from an age of 60. [14]Currently rising from an age of 62 for women. [15]To be raised to 64 for women between 2001 and 2005. [16]In a new system, to be implemented gradually, pension will be payable from the age of 61. [17] To be raised to 65 over the period 2010–20. [18] To be raised to 67 between 2000 and 2027.

Sources: US Social Security Administration, 1997; Mercer, 1997; ILO reports.

Table A.6 Coverage rules, by country or territory, 1996

Country or territory	Coverage of employees		Coverage of self-employed	Groups covered by special systems
	Basic rule	Exclusions		
Africa				
Algeria	Employed persons	–	Yes	Military
Benin	Employed persons	–	–	Public employees
Burkina Faso	Employed persons, technical students and apprentices	Temporary workers	Voluntary to persons previously covered as employees	Public employees
Burundi	Employed persons	Casual or temporary labour	–	Public employees
Cape Verde	Employed persons	–	–	Public employees
Chad	Salaried workers regulated by the Labour Code	–	–	–
Congo	Employed persons	–	–	Public employees
Congo, Dem. Rep. of the	Employed persons	–	Voluntary if at least 5 years of covered employment	Public employees
Côte d'Ivoire	Employed persons	Categories of agricultural workers	No	Public employees
Gabon	Employed persons	–	Separate system	Public employees
Ghana	Employed persons	–	Voluntary	Military
Guinea	Employed persons	–	–	–
Kenya	Employed persons	Casual workers	–	Public employees
Liberia	Establishments with 5 or more employees; voluntary in smaller firms	Casual workers, family labour, domestic employees	Voluntary	–
Libyan Arab Jamahiriya	All residents	–		Military
Madagascar	Employed persons	Temporary and casual workers	–	Public employees
Mali	Employed persons	–	–	Public employees
Mauritius	Universal pension – all residents; earnings related – all employees	–	–	Public employees and certain occupations with equivalent private programme

Morocco	Employees and apprentices in industry, commerce, agriculture, cooperatives, artisans and liberal professions	–	No	Public employees and certain other categories
Rwanda	Employed persons	–	Voluntary	–
Sudan	Employees of establishments with 5 or more employees	Domestic servants, homeworkers, family labour	No	Public employees and military
Arab states				
Bahrain	Establishments with 10 or more workers; voluntary in smaller firms	Domestic servants, certain agricultural workers, casual workers, temporary non-citizen workers	–	Public employees
Iraq	Establishments with 5 or more workers	Agricultural and temporary employees, domestic servants and family labour	–	Public employees, domestic servants, temporary employees, and family labour
Kuwait	Employed persons	Foreign workers	Special system	Self-employed and military
Lebanon	Employees in industry, commerce and agriculture	Temporarily agricultural employees, Aliens from countries not providing reciprocity	–	Public employees and teachers
Oman	Employed citizens aged 15–59 in the private sector under permanent work contract	Foreign workers, domestic servants and artisans	–	–
Saudi Arabia	Employees of enterprises with 10 or more workers; voluntary in smaller firms	Foreign workers, farmers, seamen, domestic workers, family labour and casual workers	–	Public employees
Syrian Arab Republic	Employees in industry and commerce; agricultural workers	Domestic servants, temporary and casual employees, family labour	–	Public employees

(continued)

Table A.6 Coverage rules (*continued*)

Country or territory	Coverage of employees		Coverage of self-employed	Groups covered by special systems
	Basic rule	Exclusions		
Asia and Pacific				
Cyprus	Employed persons	–	Yes	–
India	Establishments in specified industries established 3 years or more with 20 or more workers	Employees earning over 5000 rupees a month. Possible contracting-out	No	Miners, railway, public employees.
Indonesia	Entreprises with 10 or more employees or a payroll of Rp. 1 million or more a month (gradual extension)	–	No	Public employees and military
Iran, Islamic Republic of	Specific occupations and geographical areas	–	Official licence holders are covered, optional for others	Public employees and military
Israel	Residents aged 18 and over	Persons who immigrated after age 60	Yes	–
Korea, Rep. of	Voluntary for firms with less than 5 workers and employees under 18	–	Voluntary	Public employees, military and private schools teachers
Malaysia	Provident Fund: all employees, voluntary coverage of domestic workers; disability insurance; voluntary for employees earning more than 2000M/mth	–	Provident Fund: voluntary; disability: excluded	Public employees
Nepal	Compulsory for government employees; voluntary for organizations with 10 or more employees	–		

Country				
Pakistan	Employees in enterprises with 10 or more workers	Family labour	No	Public employees, police, military, statutory bodies, bank and railway employees
Philippines	Employed persons	Family labour	If income above a threshold	Public employees
Singapore	Employed persons subject to a floor of income	Members of approved equivalent private plans (virtually non-existent)	Some self-employed workers	Public employees
Sri Lanka	Employed persons	Family labour and employees under approved private provident funds	—	Public employees
Thailand	Employees of enterprises with 10 or more employees	—	Voluntary	Public employees and private school teachers
Central and Eastern Europe and Central Asia				
Albania	Employed persons	—	Yes	—
Belarus	Employed permanent residents	—	—	Aviators, teachers, artists
Croatia	Employed in industries, commerce or services, public employees and apprentices	—	Special systems	—
Estonia	All persons residing in Estonia	—	—	—
Georgia	Employed persons residing in Georgia	—	—	Teachers, professional athletes, test pilots
Kazakhstan	Employed persons residing in the country	—	—	Special provisions for government employees, teachers, professional athletes, artists, etc.
Latvia	Wage and salary earners, entrepreneurs and rural workers	—	—	—

(continued)

Table A.6 Coverage rules (continued)

Country or territory	Coverage of employees		Coverage of self-employed	Groups covered by special systems
	Basic rule	Exclusions		
Central and Eastern Europe and Central Asia				
Romania	Employed persons; voluntary insurance for farmers	–	–	Lawyers and other professional categories
Russian Federation	Employed citizens and independent farmers	–	Yes	Professional athletes, cosmonauts, military and other groups
Slovakia	Employed members of cooperatives and some special groups	–	Yes	–
Turkmenistan	Employed persons	–	–	–
Ukraine	Employed persons	–	–	Victims of Chernobyl disaster
Latin America and the Caribbean				
Argentina	Employed persons	–	Yes	Military
Bahamas	Employed persons	–	Yes	–
Belize	Employed persons aged 14–64	Casual labour, family labour, military personnel, persons employed few hours a week	Voluntary for workers entering self-employment	–
Brazil	Employed persons in industry, commerce and agriculture, domestic servants and clerics	–	Yes	Public employees and military
Chile (new system)	Employed persons	–	Voluntary	Military
Colombia	Employed persons	Agricultural workers in some regions	Voluntary	State oil company, teachers, military and national police

			Voluntary Special system	
Costa Rica	Employed persons	—	—	Military, Interior Ministry, self-employed, artists, agricultural cooperatives
Cuba	All wage earners	—	—	Government employees
Dominican Republic	Persons aged 14–59 in government-owned corporations	White-collar workers earning over a limit, family labour, apprentices	No	—
El Salvador (new system)	Employees in private, public and municipal sectors	—	—	—
Guatemala	All employees, including agricultural workers	—	—	—
Guyana	Employed persons, aged 16–59, with minimum earnings	Casual and subsidiary employment, familiy labour	Yes	Public employees
Haiti	Employees of industrial, commercial and agricultural firms	Unpaid family labour and members of religious communities	—	—
Paraguay	Employed persons	—	Yes	Railroad, banking and public employees
Uruguay	Employed persons	—	Yes	Banks, notaries, university graduates, military and police
OECD countries				
Austria	Employed persons	—	Special systems for self-employed in trade, industry and agriculture	Miners, notaries, public employees
Belgium	Employed persons	—	Special system	Public employees
Canada	Universal pension – residents; earnings-related pension – employed persons with minimum earnings	—	Yes	—
Denmark	Universal pension – residents; employment-related pension – employed persons aged 16–66	—	No	—

(continued)

671

Table A.6 Coverage rules (*continued*)

Country or territory	Coverage of employees		Coverage of self-employed	Groups covered by special systems
	Basic rule	Exclusions		
OECD countries				
France	Employed persons	—	Special systems	Different sectors
Germany	Employed persons	—	Yes	Self-employed, miners, public employees, farmers
Greece	Employees in industry, commerce and related occupations	Equivalent approved occupational and establishment funds	Certain urban self-employed workers	Agricultural workers, public employees, tradesmen and craftsmen
Iceland	Universal pension – residents; occupational pension – employed persons	—	Yes	—
Ireland	Employed persons aged 16–65 with minimum earnings	Domestic workers	Old-age and survivor benefits	—
Italy	Employed persons	—	Special systems	Different groups
Luxembourg	All employees	—	Yes	Public employees and railway
Norway	Universal pension – residents; earnings-related pension – employed persons earning over base amount	—	Yes	Seamen, fishermen, forestry workers, railway and public employees
Portugal	Employed persons	—	Yes	Miners, longshoremen, railway workers, fishermen and merchant seamen (to be unified with general system)

672

Country				
Switzerland	Basic pension – residents gainfully employed (voluntary for those abroad); occupational pension – employees earning over social security offset		Voluntary	–
Sweden	Universal pension – residents; earnings-related pension – employed persons earning over base amount		Yes	–
Turkey	Employees in industry, commerce and service sector; voluntary for aliens who work for a foreign company		Special system	Public employees, the self-employed, farmers and agricultural workers, financial services industry
United Kingdom	Employees earning over base amount; possible contracting out of earnings-related pension		Basic pension	–
United States	Employed persons	Casual, agricultural, and domestic employment	Yes (if earnings over base amount)	Government employees and railroad employees

Note: – = nil or negligible.

Source: US Social Security Administration, 1997.

673

3

PENSION COVERAGE

Table A.7 Percentage of total labour force in wage and salary employment, by country or territory, *c.* 1990–95[1]

Country or territory	Year	Percentage of total labour force in paid employment			Total employment in agriculture (% of labour force)
		non-agriculture	agriculture	total	
Africa					
Benin	1992	–	–	1.3	–
Botswana	1991	50.2	1.4	51.6	–
Burkina Faso	1991	–	–	3.5	–
Burundi	1991	1.4	0.2	1.6	–
Côte d'Ivoire	1990	7.5	1.2	8.7	–
Egypt	1995	42.9	6.2	49.2	29.4
Eritrea	1996	2.6	0.1	2.8	–
Ethiopia	1992	2.5	0.4	2.9	–
Gambia	1990	–	–	6.7	–
Ghana	1990	2.4	0.2	2.7	–
Kenya	1990	10.4	2.4	12.8	–
Madagascar	1990	3.5	1.3	4.8	–
Malawi	1995	5.9	6.2	12.0	–
Mauritius	1995	54.6	7.0	61.6	13.4
Niger	1990	0.6	0.1	0.6	–
Réunion	1990	–	–	31.9	–
South Africa	1991	–	–	42.6	–
Swaziland	1995	21.4	7.2	28.6	–
Zambia	1990	10.9	1.3	12.2	–
Zimbabwe	1995	18.2	6.4	24.6	–
Group simple average		*15.7*	*2.8*	*18.1*	–
Asia and Pacific					
China	1996	19.3	0.8	20.1	44.7
Fiji	1993	37.9	0.7	38.5	–
India	1996	6.4	0.4	6.8	–
Israel	1996	77.5	1.1	78.6	2.9
Korea, Rep. of	1995	60.4	0.9	61.2	12.2
Macau	1996	–	–	76.5	–
Philippines	1993	12.0	0.5	12.5	41.7
Singapore	1996	82.7	0.1	82.8	0.2
Solomon Islands	1992	11.6	3.6	15.2	–
Viet Nam	1995	–	–	8.0	–
Group simple average		*38.5*	*1.0*	*40.0*	*20.3*
Central and Eastern Europe and Central Asia					
Albania	1991	41.8	13.3	55.1	–
Bulgaria	1996	57.5	18.9	76.4	–
Croatia	1995	49.8	2.7	52.6	–
Czech Republic	1996	78.7	3.6	82.4	5.9
Estonia	1995	73.7	9.1	82.8	11.0
Hungary	1996	58.9	4.1	63.0	7.5
Kazakhstan	1995	51.8	14.8	66.6	–
Latvia	1996	63.7	5.6	69.3	18.6
Lithuania	1996	60.0	6.4	66.4	20.9
Poland	1996	59.9	1.9	61.8	19.4
Romania	1996	54.4	3.8	58.2	35.4
Slovakia	1994	53.1	6.9	60.0	8.5

Table A.7   Total labour force in wage and salary employment (*continued*)

Country or territory	Year	Percentage of total labour force in paid employment			Total employment in agriculture (% of labour force)
		non-agriculture	agriculture	total	
Central and Eastern Europe and Central Asia					
Slovenia	1993	82.3	8.4	90.7	10.7
Ukraine	1990	–	–	73.4	–
Group simple average		*60.4*	*7.7*	*68.5*	*15.3*
Latin America and the Caribbean					
Bolivia	1996	49.9	0.3	50.3	2.0
Brazil	1995	48.6	6.5	55.0	24.5
Colombia	1996	57.9	0.7	58.6	1.1
Costa Rica	1996	54.7	12.1	66.8	20.3
El Salvador	1994	–	–	14.4	25.8
Jamaica	1990	–	–	14.7	23.4
Mexico	1996	50.7	6.1	56.8	21.7
Nicaragua	1996	13.5	1.2	14.7	–
Panama	1995	51.7	6.3	58.0	17.9
Paraguay	1994	–	–	59.2	3.7
Peru	1996	32.0	1.5	33.5	4.2
Puerto Rico	1993	–	–	12.5	3.0
Trinidad and Tobago	1995	–	–	57.2	8.8
Group simple average		*44.9*	*4.3*	*42.4*	*13.0*
OECD countries					
Belgium	1990	–	–	76.1	2.5
Canada	1996	73.9	1.5	75.3	3.7
Denmark	1996	82.6	1.8	84.4	3.7
Finland	1996	70.4	1.5	71.9	5.8
France	1994	74.0	1.0	75.0	4.1
Germany	1996	80.2	1.4	81.6	2.7
Greece	1995	47.6	0.9	48.5	18.4
Iceland	1996	73.8	5.0	78.8	9.2
Ireland	1996	71.2	1.5	72.6	9.7
Italy	1995	59.9	2.4	62.3	6.5
Japan	1996	78.6	0.7	79.3	5.3
Netherlands	1996	80.6	1.6	82.3	3.5
Norway	1996	85.2	1.7	86.9	4.9
Portugal	1996	64.4	1.7	66.1	11.3
Spain	1996	56.0	2.2	58.3	6.8
Sweden	1996	81.0	0.9	81.9	2.7
Turkey	1995	19.0	0.2	19.3	44.7
United Kingdom	1996	75.8	0.9	76.7	1.8
United States	1996	–	–	89.2	2.7
Group simple average		*69.1*	*1.6*	*73.7*	*7.7*

Notes: [1] Wage and salary employment refers to persons who, during the reference period, performed some work for wage or salary, in cash or in kind; or to persons who, having already worked in their present job, were temporarily not at work during the reference period and had a formal attachment to their job.

– = figures not available.

Due to rounding figures may not add up.

Sources: ILO, *Yearbook or.Labour Statistics, 1992–1997,* Geneva; OECD, *Labour Force Statistics, 1976–1996,* Paris.

Table A.8 Effective coverage rates of pension systems, by country, *c.* 1995 (ratios as percentages)

Country	Year	Contributors, labour force	Old-age pensioners, persons 60 and over	All pensioners, persons 60 and over
Africa				
Benin[1]	1996	3.8	2.7	4.4
Burkina Faso	1993	2.5		2.8
Burundi	1993	3.2		8.7
Gabon	1991	15.6		18.2
Ghana	1993	7.8		
Guinea	1993	1.6	1.6	2.3
Kenya	1993	18.9		
Morocco[2]	1995	19.5	17.2	
Niger[1]	1992	1.3		
Nigeria	1993	1.3		0.1
Sudan	1991	12.1		
Togo	1996	15.9	24.4	43.3
Zambia	1994	8.2		5.8
Arab states				
Bahrain	1993	12.2		45.0
Jordan	1996	27.1		
Kuwait[3]	1996	22.9	82.7	156.7
Saudi Arabia	1996/7	20.9	1.9	3.7
Asia and Pacific				
China[4]	1996	11.9	2.0	2.0
Cyprus	1996	74.9	45.6	67.8
Israel	1993	100.0		79.4
Korea, Republic of	1996	37.0	1.2	2.4
Malaysia	1996	92.1		
Singapore[5]	1996	66.3	34.3	38.2
Turkey		42.1	41.4	69.2
Central and Eastern Europe and Central Asia				
Belarus	1996	77.9	107.7	135.2
Bulgaria	1994	58.0	116.7	133.7
Croatia	1995		50.4	99.9
Czech Republic	1996		93.7	160.1
Latvia	1992	87.9	106.4	
Lithuania	1996	74.3	102.2	137.2
Moldova, Republic of	1996	34.5		
Romania	1993	90.2		84.2
Ukraine	1993	92.2	45.5	58.0
Latin America and the Caribbean				
Argentina[6]	1996	53.3	44.0	70.6
Barbados	1993	67.3		33.7
Bolivia	1992	46.7		
Brazil[7]	1996	38.4	65.7	121.5
Colombia	1992	68.9		
Dominica	1996		19.3	27.4
Ecuador	1996	36.9		27.8

Table A.8   Effective coverage rates of pension systems (*continued*)

Country	Year	Contributors, labour force	Old-age pensioners, persons 60 and over	All pensioners, persons 60 and over
Latin America and the Caribbean				
Mexico	1992	36.0		
Nicaragua	1992	15.3		
Uruguay	1992	69.0		

Notes: [1]Excluding public employees. [2]Part of the data is from 1992. [3]Excluding the military. [4]Government employees only. [5]Contributors to the central provident fund. [6]Public scheme only. [7]Including the beneficiaries of the length of service pension.

Sources: ILO, *International Inquiry into the Cost of Social Security* (various years); ILO, *World Labour Reports* (various years); ILO, technical cooperation reports; ILO, *Economically active population, 1950–2000*, Geneva, 1996; United Nations, *Demographic Yearbook 1995*, New York, 1997; United Nations, *World Population Prospects*, 1996 revision, New York, 1997.

4

SOURCES AND LEVEL OF RETIREMENT INCOME

Table A.9 Target replacement rates and indexation provisions of pension systems, by country or territory, 1997

Country or territory	Replacement rate (30 years' coverage) (%)	Reference period	Indexation (adjustment of pension in payment)
Africa			
Algeria	75	Highest 3 years	—
Benin	60	Last 3 or 5 years (whichever is higher)	Cost-of-living changes, depending on the financial resources of the system, prices
Burkina Faso	40	Last 3 or 5 years (whichever is higher)	Cost of living changes, prices
Burundi	60	Last 3 or 5 years (whichever is higher)	—
Cameroon	45	Last 3 or 5 years (whichever is higher)	—
Cape Verde	65	Highest 36 months in last 5 years	—
Central African Republic	40	Last 3 or 5 years (whichever is higher)	—
Chad	48	Last 3 or 5 years (whichever is higher)	—
Congo	60	Last 3 or 5 years (whichever is higher)[1]	Cost of living changes, prices
Congo, Dem. Rep. of the	50		Wage index
Côte d'Ivoire	40	Average earnings	—
Egypt	67	Last 2 years	—
Equatorial Guinea	80	Last 2 years	—
Eritrea	50		—
Ethiopia	50	Last 3 years	—
Gabon	50	Last 3 or 5 years (whichever is higher)	—
Ghana	65	Highest 3 years	—
Guinea	60	Average earnings	—
Liberia	51	Average earnings	—
Libyan Arab Jamahiriya	70	Last 3 years	Changes in wages
Madagascar		Last 10 years	Automatically, cost of living, prices
Mali	50	Last 5 years	Periodic, cost of living
Mauritania	40	Last 3 or 5 years (whichever is higher)	Each year by ministerial decree
Mauritius			Ad hoc revaluation of benefits
Morocco	70	Last 3 or 5 years (whichever is higher)	—
Niger	40	Last 3 or 5 years (whichever is higher)	—
Nigeria	60		—
Rwanda	45	Last 3 or 5 years (whichever is higher)	Cost of living, prices
Sudan	60	Average earnings	—

(continued)

683

Table A.9 Target replacement rates and indexation provisions (*continued*)

Country or territory	Replacement rate (30 years' coverage) (%)	Reference period	Indexation (adjustment of pension in payment)
Africa			
Togo	40	Last 3 or 5 years (whichever is higher)	Cost of living
Tunisia	80; not exceeding 6 times minimum wage	Last 3 or 5 years (whichever is higher)	–
Zimbabwe	40		–
Arab states			
Bahrain	60	Last 2 years	–
Iraq	75	Last 3 years	–
Jordan	60	Last 2 years	–
Kuwait	95	Last monthly earnings	–
Oman	50	Last 2 years	–
Saudi Arabia	60	Last 2 years	–
Syrian Arab Republic	66.6	Last 2 years (or 5 successive years in the last 10 if higher)	–
Yemen	75	Last 2 years	–
Asia and Pacific			
Cyprus			Once a year according to change in wage
Iran, Islamic Rep. of	99.9	Last 2 years	–
Israel			Automatic adjustment of benefits for changes in average wage
Pakistan	60	Last year	–
Philippines			Periodic, based on price and wage changes
Singapore			Rate is linked to average commercial savings and fixed deposit rates adjusted every 1 January and 1 July
Viet Nam	Max: 75	Last 10 years	–
Central and Eastern Europe and Central Asia			
Armenia	65 of wage base (M), 70 (W)	Highest 5 consecutive years in last 15 years	Periodic, cost of living
Belarus	60 (M), 65 (W)	Highest 5 consecutive years in last 15 years	Benefit adjustment when average wage increases by more than 15 per cent

Bulgaria	65 (M), 75 (W)	Highest 3 consecutive years in the last 15 years	–
Croatia		Best consecutive 10 years of insurance coverage	Salaries adjusted by increase in average salary, periodic adjustment
Estonia			Cost of living
Georgia	60 (M), 65 (W)	Last 1 or 5 years (whichever is higher)	Periodic, cost of living
Hungary	68	Best 4 years in last 5 years	Semi-annual adjustment according to estimated change in national average wage levels
Kazakhstan	65 (M), 70 (W)		Periodic, cost of living
Kyrgyzstan	60 of average monthly wage (M), 65 (W)	Highest 5 consecutive years in last 15 years	Periodic, cost of living
Latvia	54 to 85 of reference wage, according to work categories and wage levels		Changes in the earnings index
Romania		Best 5 consecutive years during last 10 years	–
Russian Federation	60 (M), 65 (W)	2 years preceding retirement or any continuous 5-year period	Quarterly review of pensions according to cost of living
Slovakia	54	Highest 5 of last 10 years	
Slovenia	55 (M), 60–70 (W)	10 highest paid consecutive years in insured period from 1970	Monthly adjustment of pensions for changes in average wages plus cost-of-living adjustment in February
Turkmenistan	60 (M), 65 (W)	Best 5 consecutive years in last 15 years	Periodic, cost of living
Ukraine	60 (M), 65 (W)	Gross average earnings in last 2 years or best 5 consecutive years during worker's career	Periodic, cost of living
Uzbekistan	85	Average wage over any 5-year period	Periodic, cost of living
Latin America and the Caribbean			
Bahamas	Maximum of 60	1 750 weeks	–
Barbados	61	Best 3 years of 15	–
Belize	60	Highest 3 years of earnings in last 15 years	–
Brazil	97	Last 36 months	Adjusted to changes in index that determines changes in minimum salary for the following month
Colombia	85	10 years prior to received pension	CPI
Costa Rica	70	Last five years of coverage	Twice a year (January and July)
Cuba	55	Highest 5 of last 10 years	–

(continued)

Table A.9 Target replacement rates and indexation provisions (*continued*)

Country or territory	Replacement rate (30 years' coverage) (%)	Reference period	Indexation (adjustment of pension in payment)
Latin America and the Caribbean			
Dominica	56	Best 3 years of the last 10	—
Dominican Republic	64	Last 2 years	—
Ecuador	75	5 highest earnings years (need not be consecutive)	Periodic, cost of living
Guatemala	70	Last 5 years of contribution	—
Guyana	56	Highest 3 years out of the last 5 years of work before age 60	—
Haiti	33	Last 10 years	—
Honduras	65		
Nicaragua	82	Last 5, 4 or 3 years (based on contributions of 15, 20 or 25 years)	Periodic, wage changes
Panama	79	Highest 7 years	Ad hoc basis depending on economic conditions
Paraguay	100	Last 3 years	—
Peru (social insurance system)	90	Last 5, 4 or 3 years (contribution periods of 20–25, 25–30 and 30+)	Quarterly, cost of living in Lima
Venezuela	46 + 9 000 boli-/month	Last 5 or the highest 5 years in the last 10 years (whichever is higher)	Occasional adjustments of benefits for changes in prices and wages
OECD countries			
Australia	—		Adjusted in March and September according to price index
Austria	55	In best 15 years for each of first 30 insurance years	Automatic annual adjustment of benefits for changes in national average covered earnings
Belgium	60 (or 75 for married couple)	Average earnings	Automatic periodic adjustment of pensions for retail price changes
Canada	—		Automatic, CPI
Finland	—	—	Cost of living (universal pension), 20% of the annual average increase in wage and 80% of annual average increase in price changes

Country		Earnings base	Adjustment
France	–	Best 25 years (as of 2000)	Cost of living
Germany	–	–	Annually for changes in the real value of pensions compared to changes in earnings
Greece	–	Last 5 years	Indexed to pensions of civil servants
Iceland	–	–	Changes in workers' wages
Italy	–	–	Average increase in GDP within the last 5 years
Japan	–	–	Automatic annual cost of living
Luxembourg	–	–	Automatic indexation of pensions to changes in cost of living and periodic adjustments according to wage changes
Netherlands	–	–	Automatic adjustment of all pensions twice a year for changes in net minimum wages
New Zealand	–	–	Annual review of income-tested benefits
Norway	–	–	Recorded earnings, wage limits and pensions in force adjusted automatically for changes in general price and income levels
Portugal	60	Highest 10 of last 15 years	Cost of living
Spain	90	Benefit base	Periodic according to CPI
Sweden	–	–	Annual automatic adjustment of benefits as the base amount is adjusted
Switzerland	–	–	Benefits adjusted for price increases at same time as base pension
Turkey	85	Indexed earnings during last 5 or 7 years	Periodically, change in price and wages
United Kingdom	–	–	Annually according to price changes
United States	–	Based on covered earnings averaged over period after 1950 (or age 21, if later) up to age 62 or death, excluding 5 years with the lowest earnings	Automatic cost-of-living adjustment

Notes: − = nil or negligible. [1] Must have occurred in the ten-year period prior to the date of eligibility.

Source: US Social Security Administration, 1997.

Table A.10 Shares of various kinds of income in total gross household income of all pensioner households (%), OECD countries, c. 1990

Country (year of reference)	Income from							
	Wages, salaries	Self-employment	Interest profits	Pensions	Unemployment benefits	Other transfers	Other sources	Total[1]
Belgium (1992)	10.8	–	0.4	86.1	1.7	0.8	0.1	100
Canada (1991)	13.3	1.6	13.4	63.5	1.4	5.2	1.5	100
Denmark (1992)	7.9	1.8	8.2	74.9	0.9	5.8	0.6	100
France (1989)	7.8	2.1	4.3	80.9	1.7	2.5	0.7	100
Germany (1989)	9.8	1.0	4.2	83.3	0.3	0.9	0.5	100
Greece (1987/88)[2]	10.3	24.0	8.0	55.9	–	0.4	1.4	100
Ireland (1987)	17.1	5.5	3.4	36.5[3]	1.8	35.7[4]	0.1	100
Italy (1989)	15.5	2.8	21.1	58	–	2.3	0.3	100
Luxembourg (1985)	8.7	1.5	3.5	83.8	0.1	1.8	0.7	100
Netherlands (1991)	4.2	0.6	5.1	87.1	0.2	2.1	0.8	100
Portugal (1989/90)	27.5	–	4	35.7	–	0.5	32.4[5]	100
Spain (1990)	14.4	3.4	2.6	75.2	1.3	1.8	1.2	100
United Kingdom (1991)	10.0	1.3	11.1	67.7	0.2	9.6	0.3	100
United States (1991)	14.0	1.4	13.4	66.9	0.4	3.7	0.3	100

Notes: – = nil or negligible. [1]Differences due to rounding. [2]Including pensioner households with head of household 42 – 54 years and *main* income from pensions. [3]Retirement and old-age contributory pensions. [4]Includes non-contributory pensions. [5]Including income in kind of farmers, etc.

Sources: Hauser (1997); Joint ILO-OECD Workshop, Development and Reform of Pension Schemes.

Table A.11 Pension expenditure and social security expenditure, by country, c. 1995

Country	Year	Social security expenditure (% GDP)			Pension expenditure/ total expenditure (%)	Administration / total expenditure[1]		
		Pension	Other branches	Total		Pension (%)	Other branches (%)	Total (%)
Africa								
Benin[2]	1996	0.3	0.1	0.4	74	24	25	24
Ghana	1993	0.3	0.0	0.3	100	78	–	78
Kenya	1992/93	1.4	0.5	1.9	74	72	10	47
Mauritius	1992/93	3.1	0.8	4.0	78	4	14	5
Morocco	1992	1.5	0.5	2.0	74	14	17	16
Namibia	1996/97	0.0	0.1	0.1	0	–	11	11
Togo	1996	0.8	0.9	1.7	46	21	46	34
Tunisia	1992	3.3	2.3	5.7	59	6	26	15
Zambia	1993	0.2	0.1	0.2	63	93	90	92
Arab States								
Bahrain	1992	1.1	0.3	1.5	75	25	18	23
Kuwait	1996	4.9	–	–	–	3	–	–
Saudi Arabia[3]	1996/97	0.2	0.0	0.2	77	–	–	10
Asia and Pacific								
China[4]	1996	1.8	–	–	–	–	–	–
Cyprus	1996	7.4	4.1	11.6	64	1	–	2
Israel	1992	4.2	9.0	13.3	32	2	11	9
Korea, Rep. of	1996	0.1	2.7	2.8	2	36	13	14
Philippines	1993	2.6	0.5	3.0	85	8	24	13
Singapore	1996	1.4	0.3	1.8	80	–	–	4
Thailand	1996	0.0	0.2	0.2	4	–	–	6
Central and Eastern Europe and Central Asia								
Belarus	1996	8.6	1.6	10.2	84	–	–	1
Bulgaria								
Croatia	1996	9.2	2.0	11.2	82	–	–	2
Czech Republic	1996	8.8	1.6	10.4	85	–	–	3
Hungary	1995	9.9	18.7	28.6	35	–	–	–

(*continued*)

Table A.11 Pension expenditure and social security expenditure (continued)

Country	Year	Social security expenditure (% GDP)			Pension expenditure/ total expenditure (%)	Administration / total expenditure[1]		Total (%)
		Pension	Other branches	Total		Pension (%)	Other branches (%)	
Central and Eastern Europe and Central Asia								
Latvia	1994	12.0	5.2	17.2	70	–	–	2
Lithuania	1996	7.4	3.0	10.4	71	–	–	4
Moldova, Rep. of	1996	14.3	2.3	16.6	86	–	–	39
Romania	1992	6.2	10.5	17.0	37	–	–	1
Latin America and the Caribbean								
Argentina	1996	4.1	0.3	4.4	94	2	–	–
Dominica	1996			4.7		27	–	–
Ecuador	1996	1.9	0.9	2.9	67	–	–	–
Panama						–	–	–
Trinidad and Tobago	1996/97	0.8	0.1	0.9	91	–	–	16
OECD countries								
Austria	1995	–	–	29.7	–	–	–	2
Belgium	1995	14.2	15.5	29.7	48	–	–	4
Canada	1993	5.7	16.6	22.3	26	1	3	2
Denmark	1995	–	–	34.3	–	–	–	3
Finland	1996	13.6	16.8	30.5	45	–	–	3
France	1995	–	–	30.6	–	–	–	4
Germany	1995	–	–	29.4	–	–	–	4
Greece	1995	12.2	8.7	21.1	58	–	–	5
Iceland	1996	3.2	3.7	6.9	46	–	–	1
Ireland	1995	–	–	19.9	–	–	–	4
Italy	1995	–	–	24.6	–	–	–	3
Luxembourg	1995	–	–	25.3	–	–	–	3
Netherlands	1995	–	–	31.6	–	–	–	4
Portugal	1995	–	–	20.7	–	–	–	5
Spain	1995	10.6	10.9	21.8	49	–	–	2
Sweden	1995	–	–	35.6	–	–	–	1

Turkey	1996	4.8	0.6	5.5	89	2
United Kingdom	1994	–	–	27.7	–	4
United States	1994/95	6.8	8.0	14.9	46	2

Notes: – = data not available. [1] This refers to the main social security schemes excluding the benefit expenditure and administration expenditure of special schemes. [2] Excluding public employees. [3] Data on administration costs refer to 1993. [4] Excluding administration cost.

Sources: ILO, *International Inquiry into the Cost of Social Security* (various years), ILO reports.

Table A.12 Sources of financing[1] of pension and social security systems, by country, c. 1995

Country	Year	Pensions Total receipts (% GDP)	Contributions	State financing	Income from capital	Other receipts	Social security Total receipts (% GDP)	Contributions	State financing	Income from capital	Other receipts
Africa											
Benin	1996	0.3	100	0	0	0	0.7	100	0	0	0
Burundi	1991	0.7	72	0	28	0	1.4	82	0	18	0
Ghana	1993	2.7	82	0	17	1	2.7	82	0	17	0
Kenya	1993	2.5	18	0	81	0	3.2	24	11	65	0
Mauritius	1992/93	4.5	25	47	28	0	6.2	42	38	20	0
Namibia	1996/97						0.1	69	0	0	31
Togo	1996	0.5	68	0	32	0	1.9	66	0	34	0
Tunisia	1992	4.5	93	0	7	0	6.8	82	0	8	11
Zambia	1993						0.6	83	0	17	0
Arab states											
Bahrain	1992	1.9	58	0	42	0	2.4	58	0	42	0
Jordan	1992	2.6	64	0	35	1	2.9	65	0	34	1
Kuwait	1996	8.8	21	49	27	3					
Saudi Arabia	1993	0.3	100	0	0	0					
Syrian Arab Republic	1991	0.4	95	0	0	5	1.0	84	0	12	5
Yemen	1994	0.3	77	0	23	0					
Asia and Pacific											
China	1996	2.0	92	0	0	8	8.4	58	18	23	1
Cyprus	1996	8.0	57	18	24	1	1.0	51	5	44	0
India	1992						0.3	66	0	33	1
Indonesia	1996	0.2	75	0	24	1	13.7	46	45	7	1
Israel[2]	1992	4.1	40	50	10	0	3.1	80	11	0	8
Korea, Rep. of	1996	1.4	91	9	0	0	1.8	10	73	6	10
Pakistan	1993						12.7	82	0	15	2
Singapore[3]	1996						0.4	82	0	15	2
Thailand	1995						0.4	47	32	0	21

Region / Country	Year										
Central and Eastern Europe and Central Asia											
Belarus	1996	10.6	100	0	0	0	20.8	100	0	0	0
Bulgaria	1992	12.5	91	7	0	2	13.0	100	0	0	0
Croatia[4]	1996	11.4	100	0	0	0	16.3	100	0	0	0
Czech Republic	1993	9.0	100	0	0	0					
Estonia	1993	9.8	0	94	0	6					
Latvia	1994						15.4	88	10	0	2
Lithuania	1996						8.3	99	0	0	1
Moldova, Rep. of	1996						10.0	96	3	0	1
Romania	1992						19.5	54	46	0	0
Slovenia	1991	12.8	91	1	1	7					
Latin America and the Caribbean											
Argentina[5]	1996	3.3	62	38	0	0	3.8	66	34	0	0
Brazil	1996						5.9	66	24	0	10
Chile	1993	18.2	20	28	51	1	22.9	29	29	41	1
Dominica	1996	3.4	69	0	31	0	5.1	73	0	27	0
Guatemala	1993	0.5	76	0	0	24	1.4	87	0	0	13
Nicaragua	1992	0.2	91	4	4	0	0.5	76	11	2	11
Trinidad and Tobago	1995						1.5	49	0	51	0
OECD countries											
Canada	1994	5.3	31	53	15	1	23.8	26	64	10	0
Denmark	1993	10.0	5	85	10	0	33.2	9	88	3	0
Finland	1996	16.2	76	24	0	0	32.7	51	49	0	0
Iceland	1996	3.2	51	49	0	0	6.9	37	63	0	0
Luxembourg	1993	14.8	56	32	12	0	30.8	56	37	7	1
Netherlands	1993	15.2	68	20	12	0	33.6	65	22	13	0
New Zealand	1992	7.4	0	98	0	2	20.1	1	95	3	1
Norway	1992						20.9	62	33	4	1
Spain	1995	5.8	200	97	0	3	21.9	67	33	0	1
Sweden	1993	16.9	60	40	0	0	38.2	44	56	0	0
Switzerland	1993	21.0	62	12	21	4	28.2	66	12	19	4
Turkey[6]	1996	4.0	68	0	9	23	4.9	73	0	8	19
United States	1994/95	9.4	64	14	2	0	17.7	48	39	13	0

Notes: [1] Excluding possible transfers between schemes. [2] Without civil servants. [3] Central provident fund. [4] Includes employment injury programme. [5] Public schemes only. [6] Insured persons contributions to Civil Servants' Fund covers old-age, survivors and invalidity, and sickness and health.

Source: ILO, *International Inquiry into the Cost of Social Security* (various years).

Table A.13 System dependency ratio, by country, c. 1995

Country	Year	Demography ratio (%)		Financial ratio (%)		Cost rate (%)[1]	
		Old-age	Total	Old-age	Total	Old-age	Total
Africa							
Cameroon	1989	1.5	–	34.8	–	0.5	–
Guinea	1991	17.0	24.0	18.4	13.9	3.1	3.3
Madagascar	1995	11.5	–	27.0	–	3.1	–
Morocco	1995	4.6	–	73.0	–	3.4	–
Togo	1994	11.5	–	46.3	–	5.3	–
Zambia	1997	27.9	–	–	–	–	–
Asia and Pacific							
Fiji[2]	1996	1.7	2.0	53.9	49.9	–	–
Iran (Islamic Rep. of)	1995	5.9	–	83.0	–	4.9	–
Mongolia	1993	36.4	45.6	67.1	66.4	24.4	30.3
Turkey	1995	–	43.0	–	93.0	–	40.0
Viet Nam	1996	38.5	57.2	79.0	65.0	30.4	37.2
Central and Eastern Europe and Central Asia							
Albania	1993/94	56.6	–	54.2	–	30.7	–
Belarus	1994	–	–	34.7	–	–	–
Bulgaria	1994	79.0	91.0	38.9	37.9	30.7	34.5
Croatia	1993	43.0	–	62.0	–	26.7	–
Czech Republic	1993/94	51	–	46.8	–	23.9	–
Estonia	1994	–	–	38.9	–	–	–
Hungary	1993/94	66	–	56.9	–	37.6	–
Latvia	1993	41.0	–	32.0	–	13.1	–
Lithuania	1992/94	57.5	–	45.9	–	26.4	–
Moldova, Rep. of	1994	–	–	53.5	–	–	–
Poland	1993/94	53	–	74.8	–	39.6	–
Romania	1993/94	49	–	49.2	–	24.1	–
Russian Federation	1994	–	52.4	–	35.0	–	–
Slovakia	1993	24.6	51.5	44.0	41.0	10.8	18.3
Slovenia	1994	–	–	75.4	–	–	21.1

TFYR of Macedonia	1993	28.0	–	82.3	–	23.0
Turkmenistan	1994	19.0	24.5	–	45.0	–
Ukraine	1993	45.5	58.6	39.0	37.0	17.7
Latin America and the Caribbean						
Barbados	1993	15.5	–	35.0	–	5.4
Dominica	1996	9.0	–	38.0	–	3.4
Panama	1997	11.5	–	89.0	–	10.2
Saint Lucia	1996	3.4	–	57.0	–	1.9
Trinidad and Tobago	1995	10.8	16.9	41.7	35.4	4.5

Notes: – = data not available. [1] This cost rate gives an approximation to the PAYG cost rate. However they are not equal because the cost rate calculated here does not include administration fees and benefits paid as lump sum payments. [2] A majority of beneficiaries opt for a lump-sum payment rather than a pension.

Sources: Regional Monitoring Report No. 3, Florence, UNICEF; for Croatia and the Former Yugoslav Republic of Macedonia, *The financing of pension systems in Central and Eastern Europe,* Washington, DC, World Bank, 1996; for Poland, ILO calculations based on Polish statistical data; *Averting the Old Age Crisis,* Washington, DC, World Bank, 1994.

Table A.14 Legal provisions on contributions and state financing, by country or territory, 1996

Country or territory	Type of schemes					Social security contributions (%)			Pension contribution (%)			State contribution to pension financing
	Pension	Sickness and/or maternity	Workers' compensation	Unemployment insurance	Family allowance	Worker	Employer	Total	Worker	Employer	Total	
Africa												
Algeria	x	x o	x	x	2	7.5	24	31.5	4.5[1]	8[1]	12.5[1]	None
Benin	x	x	x		x	3.6	16.4–19.4	20–23	3.6	6.4	10	None
Cameroon	x	x	x		x	2.8	13–16.2	15.8–19	2.8	4.2	7	None
Congo	x	x	x		x	2.4	16.1	18.5	2.4	3.6	6	None
Côte d'Ivoire	x	x	x		x	1.6	9.9–12.9	11.5–14.5	1.6	2.4	4	None
Egypt	x	x o	x	x		12–15	33–35	45–50	11–14	24–26	35–40	1% of payroll plus any deficit
Ethiopia	x	x				4	6	10	4	6	10	None
Gabon	x	x o	1		x	2.5	20.1	22.6	2.5	5	7.5	None
Ghana	x	1				5	12.5	17.5	5	12.5	17.5	None
Madagascar	x	x	1		x	1	13	14	1	3.5	4.5	None
Mali	x	x	x		x	3.6	16.4–19.4	20–23	3.6	5.4	9	None
Morocco	x	x	1		x	3.5	16.4	19.1	3.3	6.5	9.8	None
South Africa	2	x	1	x		1	1	2	…	…	…	Entire cost (social assistance)
Sudan	x	x	x			8	19	27	8	17	25	None
Tanzania, United Rep. of	x	1, 2	1	1		10	10	20	10	10	20	None
Uganda	x	1	1			5	10	15	5	10	15	None
Zambia	x	1	1			5	5	10	5	5	10	None
Zimbabwe	x	1, 2	1			3	3	6	3	3	6	None
Arab states												
Jordan	x	x				5	10	15	5	8	13	Any deficit
Kuwait	x	2				5	10	15	5	10	15	Annual subsidy equal to 10% of payroll
Lebanon	x	x o	1		x	3	27.5–35.5	30.5–38.5	…	8.5	8.5	None
Saudi Arabia	x	1	x			5	10	15	5	8	13	Cost of administration (initial phase), annual subsidy and any operating deficit
Syrian Arab Republic	x	x	x			7	17	24	7	14	21	None
Yemen	x	x	x			6	13	19	6	9	15	None

Asia and Pacific

Country												Government contribution
Cyprus	x	x	x o	x		2	6.3	6.3	12.6	...	...	...	4% of earnings, full cost of social old-age pension
Fiji	x		x	1			11.75	7	14	7	7	14	None
India	x	x	x o	x	1		2	19.9	31.7	10	10.7	20.7	1.16% of payroll
Indonesia	x	x	o	x	x		7	7.2–11.7	9.2–13.7	2	4	6	None
Iran, Islamic Rep. of	x	x	x o	x	x	x	7	23	30				3% of payroll, employers' contribution for the first 5 employees in small industrial and technical workshops (not for the pension branch only), full cost of social assistance benefits, other subsidies
Israel	x	x	x o	x	x	x	5.7–9.7	4.9	10.6–14.6	2.2–4.1	2.3	4.5–6.4	1% of earnings, reduced contributions on lower earnings
Korea, Rep. of[2]	x	x	x o	x			4–7	7.6–40	11.6–47	3	6	9	Partial cost of administration and of programmes for special clientele
Malaysia	x	2	x				11.5	13.8	25.3	11.5	12.5	24	None
Nepal	x	x		1			10	10	20	10	10	20	None
Papua New Guinea	x	2	x	1			5	7	12	5	7	12	
Philippines	x	x	x o	x			4.6	7.3	11.9	—	—	—	Any deficit
Sri Lanka	x	2	x	1			8	12	20	8	12	20	None
Viet Nam	x	x	x	x		2	5	20	25	5	10	15	Subsidizes whole of benefit expenditures for employees in covered employment until implementation of programme by employer

Central and Eastern Europe and Central Asia

Country												Government contribution
Albania	x	x o	x			2	11.7	32.5	44.2	—	—	—	Cost of those in compulsory military service
Belarus	x	x o	x			x	1	5.7–36[3]	6.7–3.7	—	—	—	Cost of social pension and special subsidies as needed
Bulgaria	x	x	x			x	2	42[3]	47	—	—	—	Any deficit
Croatia	x	x	x			x	22.8	20.6	43.4	—	—	—	Any deficit
Czech Republic	x	x	x			x 2	12.5	35	47.5	—	—	—	Full cost of social pension, subsidies as needed
Georgia	x	x	x			x	1	40	41	—	—	—	Any deficit
Hungary	x	x	x			2	11.5	44.5	56	—	—	—	Any deficit
Latvia	x	x	x			2	9	28	37	—	—	—	Employed persons in agriculture

(continued)

Table A.14 Legal provisions on contributions and state financing (*continued*)

Country or territory	Type of schemes					Social security contributions (%)			Pension contribution (%)			State contribution to pension financing
	Pension	Sickness and/or maternity	Workers' compensation	Unemployment insurance	Family allowance	Worker	Employer	Total	Worker	Employer	Total	
Central and Eastern Europe and Central Asia												
Lithuania	x	x	x	x	2	1	23	24				Any deficit
Poland	x	x	x	x	2	...	48	48				Any deficit
Russian Federation	x	x	x	x[4]	x,2	1	39	40	—	—	—	Full cost of social pension, subsidies as needed
Turkmenistan	x	x	x	x	x	1	39	40				Full cost of social pension, subsidies as needed
Latin America and the Caribbean												
Argentina	x	x	1	x	x	15	31.9	46.9	11	16	27	Contribution to the social insurance system through general revenues, investments and earmarked taxes
Bolivia (new pension system)	x	x	x	1	1	12.5	11.5	24.00	12.50		12.5	Payment of pension under the old system and social assistance under the new system
Brazil	x	x	x	2	x	8–10	30–34	38–44	8–10[5]	20[5]	28–30[5]	Administrative costs, deficits
Chile (new pension system)	x	x	x	2	2	20	0.9–7.7	20.9–27.7	13[6]	—	13[6]	Guaranteed minimum pension
Colombia	x	x	x	1	x	7.4–8.4	23.5–31.8	30.9–40.2	3.4–4.4	10.1	13.5–14.5	Partial subsidy to solidarity fund
Costa Rica	x	x	1			8	19	27	2.5	4.75	7.25	0.25% of total covered earnings
Ecuador	x	x	x	x		8–10	7.6–9.6	15.6–19.6	6–8	0.4–2.4	6.4–10.4	40% subsidy
El Salvador (new private system)	x	x	x			6	12	18.0	3[7]	4.5[7]	7.5[7]	Value of insured person's contributions under the old system and minimum pension under the new system
Guatemala	x	x	x			4.5	10	14.5	1.5	3	4.5	25% of cost of benefits paid
Honduras	x	x	x	1		3.5	7	10.5	1	2	3	1% of payroll
Jamaica	x	x	x			2.5	2.5	5	—	—	—	Administrative expenses

Country											Government's contribution / source
(Latin America)											
Mexico	x	x	1	1	4.9	12.85–23.7[8]	17.75–28.6[8]	1.75	3.75–4.9	6.7	10% of employers' contribution (guarantees minimum pension)
Nicaragua	x	x	x	1	4	11.1	15.1	—	—	—	0.25% of earnings
Paraguay	x	x			9.5	13	22.5	—	—	—	1.5% of earnings
Peru	x	x					23–32[9]	13		13	Guarantees minimum pension
Venezuela	x	x	x	x	8.7	14.75–18.75	23.5–27.5	4	9–11	13–15	At least 1.5% of total taxable earnings, covering cost of administration
OECD countries											
Australia	2	x	2	2	1.3		1.3				Entire cost from general revenues
Austria	x	x	x	x	17.2	27.7	44.9	10.3	12.6	22.8	Any deficits; nursing care insurance and income-tested allowance
Belgium	x	x	x	x	13.1	24.9	37.9	7.5	8.9	16.4	Annual subsidies
Canada	x	x	x	2	5.9	8.13–11.6[10]	14.0–17.5	3	3	6	Whole cost of universal pension and income-tested benefits
Denmark	x	x	2	2	[11]	[11]	[11]	[11]	[11]	[11]	Whole cost of universal pension
Finland	x[1]	x	2	2	7.9–10.3	22.3–33.3	30.2–43.6	4.5	19.2–21.7	23.7–26.2	Part of cost of universal pension; cost of earnings related pension for self-employed and farmers
France	x	x	x	x	15.3	35.4	50.7	6.7	9.8	16.5	Variable subsidies
Germany	x	x	x	2	20.2	21.7	41.9	10.2	10.2	20.3	Annual subsidy of about 20% of total cost of pension insurance
Greece	x	x	x	x	12	23.9	35.9	6.7	13.3	20	10%
Iceland	x[2]	x[2]	x	2	4	11.2–13.7	15.2–17.7	—	—	—	Remaining cost of universal pension
Ireland	x	x	2	2	5.5–7.8	8.8–12.3	14.3–20	—	—	—	Full cost of means-tested allowance, any deficit
Italy	x	x	x	x	10.7	43.1	53.8	8.9	19.4	28.3	Full cost of means-tested allowance, any deficit
Japan	x	x	x	x	13.4	14.4	27.8	8.7	8.7	17.3	Administration costs and 1/3 of national pension
Luxembourg	x	x	2	2	13.1–15.1	11.1–18.6	24.2–33.7	8	8	16	8% of earnings (1/3 of cost)
Netherlands	x[12]	x	2	2	44.7	10.6	55.3	32.3	0	32.3	Funds needed to bring low benefits up to social minimum, lump-sum contributions for disability scheme, any deficit

(continued)

Table A.14 Legal provisions on contributions and state financing (*continued*)

Country or territory	Type of schemes					Social security contributions (%)			Pension contribution (%)			State contribution to pension financing
	Pension	Sickness and/or maternity	Workers' compensation	Unemployment insurance	Family allowance	Worker	Employer	Total	Worker	Employer	Total	
New Zealand	2	2	x	2	2	0	0	0	0	0	0	Entire cost financed from general revenues
Norway	x	x	x	x	2	7.8	14.1	21.9	–	–	–	Any deficits
Portugal	x	x	1,x	x	x	11	26.8	37.8	11	23.8[13]	34.8[13]	Subsidy for social pension
Spain	x	x	x	x	x	6.3	31.8	38.1	–	–	–	Annual subsidy
Switzerland	x	x	1	x	x	6.4	6.5–22.2	12.9–28.6	4.9	4.9	9.8	Annual subsidies to social insurance system (20% of cost for old age, 50% of cost for disability)
Sweden	x	x	x	x	2	6	29.9	35.9	1	19.1	20.1	About 25% of cost of universal pension
Turkey	x	x	x	1	2	14	19.5–27	33.5–41	9	11–13	20–22	None
United Kingdom	x	x	x	x	2	2–10	3–10	15–22	–	–	–	Full cost of means-tested allowances and other non-contributory benefits
United States	x	x	1	x	2	7.7	10.5	18.2	6.2	6.2	12.4	Full cost of means-tested allowances and cost of special old-age benefit for people aged 72 before 1968

Notes: [1]Disability and survivors' benefit financed under sickness and maternity programme. [2]Average social security contributions, workers: 4.5%, employers:9.2%. [3]Up to 57% for unusually arduous and unhealthy work. [4]Includes early pension paid to unemployed older workers. [5]These contributions also finance sickness and maternity, and family allowance. [6]Assuming a total charge of 3% for disability and survivors' insurance and the commission. [7]Additional cost for disability and survivors' pension. [8]Includes medical benefits. [9]Average 24%. [10]Excluding work injury. [11]Portion of set amount for old age, disability, death. Central and local government and other types of contributions for other programmes. [12]No specific work-injury insurance since 1967. Sickness and disability programmes apply to all incapacities, whether work-connected or not. [13]Plus flat amount for unemployment. – = figures not available. x = benefit provided and financed at least partially from social security contributions. o = medical care and/or hospitalization are provided in addition to cash sickness and/or maternity benefits. 1 = benefits are financed by the employer, through direct provision of benefits, private insurance, etc. 2 = benefits are financed by the government.

Source: US Social Security Administration, 1997.

5

INVESTMENTS AND CAPITAL MARKETS

Table A.15   Capitalization of stock markets, by country, 1997

Country or territory	Market capitalization[1]		Share of world stock market capitalization (%)
	US $ (millions)	% of GDP	
World total	**20 177 662.00**	**70.60**	**100.00**
Africa			
Botswana	326.00	6.60	<0.1
Côte d'Ivoire	914.00	8.60	<0.1
Egypt	20 830.00	20.90	0.10
Ghana	1 492.00	23.50	<0.1
Kenya	1 846.00	20.00	<0.1
Mauritius	1 676.00	39.00	<0.1
Morocco	12 177.00	23.60	<0.1
Namibia	473.00	14.60	<0.1
Nigeria	3 646.00	11.10	<0.1
South Africa	232 069.00	191.30	1.15
Tunisia	4 263.00	21.80	<0.1
Zambia	229.00	6.80	<0.1
Zimbabwe	1 969.00	48.10	<0.1
Group simple average	*21 685.38*	*33.53*	*0.63*
Arab states			
Jordan	5 446.00	62.70	<0.1
Kuwait	18 817.00	51.10	<0.1
Oman	2 673.00	16.40	<0.1
Saudi Arabia	40 961.00	32.70	0.20
Group simple average	*16 974.25*	*40.73*	*0.20*
Asia and Pacific			
Bangladesh	4 551.00	14.30	<0.1
China	206 366.00	14.00	1.02
India	128 466.00	34.40	0.64
Indonesia	29 105.00	40.30	0.14
Iran, Islamic Rep. of	17 008.00	–	<0.1
Israel	45 268.00	39.60	0.22
Korea, Rep. of	41 881.00	28.60	0.21
Malaysia	93 608.00	309.60	0.46
Nepal	208.00	4.70	<0.1
Pakistan	10 966.00	16.40	<0.1
Philippines	31 361.00	96.20	0.16
Singapore	150 215.00	159.70	0.74
Sri Lanka	2 096.00	13.30	<0.1
Thailand	23 538.00	53.90	0.12
Group simple average	*56 045.50*	*63.46*	*0.41*
Central and Eastern Europe and Central Asia			
Armenia	7.00	0.20	<0.1
Bulgaria	7.00	0.10	<0.1
Croatia	581.00	3.20	<0.1
Czech Republic	12 786.00	32.90	<0.1
Hungary	14 975.00	11.80	<0.1
Kyrgyzstan	5.00	0.30	<0.1
Latvia	148.00	2.90	<0.1

Table A.15 Capitalization of stock markets (*continued*)

Country or territory	Market capitalization[1]		Share of world stock market capitalization (%)
	US $ (millions)	% of GDP	
Central and Eastern Europe and Central Asia			
Lithuania	900.00	11.60	<0.1
Poland	12 135.00	6.20	<0.1
Romania	61.00	0.20	<0.1
Russian Federation	128 207.00	8.50	0.64
Slovakia	1 826.00	11.50	<0.1
Slovenia	663.00	3.60	<0.1
Uzbekistan	128.00	0.50	<0.1
Group simple average	*12 316.36*	*6.68*	*0.64*
Latin America and the Caribbean			
Argentina	59 252.00	15.20	0.29
Bolivia	114.00	1.60	<0.1
Brazil	255 478.00	29.00	1.27
Chile	72 046.00	88.80	0.36
Colombia	19 530.00	20.10	<0.1
Costa Rica	782.00	8.70	<0.1
Ecuador	1 946.00	10.20	<0.1
El Salvador	450.00	4.30	<0.1
Guatemala	168.00	1.10	<0.1
Honduras	338.00	8.50	<0.1
Jamaica	1 887.00	42.60	<0.1
Mexico	156 595.00	31.80	0.78
Panama	831.00	10.50	<0.1
Paraguay	383.00	4.00	<0.1
Peru	17 586.00	20.20	<0.1
Trinidad and Tobago	1 405.00	25.70	<0.1
Uruguay	266.00	1.50	<0.1
Venezuela	14 581.00	14.90	<0.1
Group simple average	*33 535.44*	*18.82*	*0.67*
OECD countries			
Australia	311 988.00	79.50	1.55
Austria	33 953.00	15.00	0.17
Belgium	119 831.00	45.30	0.59
Canada	486 268.00	83.90	2.41
Denmark	71 688.00	41.10	0.36
Finland	63 078.00	50.90	0.31
France	591 123.00	38.40	2.93
Germany	670 997.00	28.50	3.33
Greece	34 164.00	19.70	0.17
Ireland	12 243.00	17.60	<0.1
Italy	258 160.00	21.40	1.28
Japan	3 088 850.00	67.20	15.31
Netherlands	378 721.00	96.50	1.88
New Zealand	38 288.00	58.80	0.19
Norway	57 423.00	36.40	0.28
Portugal	38 954.00	23.70	0.19
Spain	242 779.00	41.70	1.20

Table A.15 Capitalization of stock markets (*continued*)

Country or territory	Market capitalization[1]		Share of world stock market capitalization (%)
	US $ (millions)	% of GDP	
OECD countries			
Sweden	247 217.00	98.80	1.23
Switzerland	402 104.00	137.00	1.99
Turkey	61 090.00	16.50	0.30
United Kingdom	1 740 246.00	151.90	8.62
United States	8 484 433.00	115.60	42.05
Group simple average	*792 436.27*	*58.43*	*4.11*

Notes: <0.1 means less than 0.1% of world stock. [1] Market value of shares times the number of shares.

Source: World Bank, *1998 World Development Indicators*.

GLOSSARY

The book discusses social security pension schemes. A "scheme" is equivalent to a "plan" in North American pension terminology. Four social security pension schemes are discussed: old-age benefits schemes, survivors' benefits schemes, invalidity benefits schemes and social assistance benefits schemes. Invalidity benefits are equivalent to disability benefits in North American terminology. The four schemes together are referred to as the social security pension system.

Actuarial assumptions: factors which actuaries use in estimating the cost of funding a defined benefit pension plan. Examples are rate of return on plan investments, mortality rates and the rates at which plan participants are expected to leave the plan because of retirement, disability and voluntary or involuntary termination of employment.

Actuarial equivalent: benefit having the same present value as the benefit it replaces. Also the amount of annuity that can be provided at the same present value cost as a specified annuity of a different type or a specified annuity payable from a different age. For example, a lifetime monthly benefit of $67.50 beginning at age 60 (on a given set of actuarial assumptions) may be said to be the actuarial equivalent of $100 per month beginning at age 65.

Actuarial valuation: an examination of a pension plan by applying an actuarial cost method to determine whether contributions are being made at a rate sufficient to provide the funds out of which the promised pensions can be paid when due.

Actuary: a person professionally trained in the technical and mathematical aspects of insurance, pensions and related fields. The actuary estimates how much money must be contributed to a pension fund each year in order to provide the benefits that will become payable in the future.

Annuity: an arrangement to provide an income for a specified number of years, or for the remaining lifetime of an individual, or the remaining lifetime of more than one individual.

Asset allocation: the division of the pension assets among various investment media, such as stocks, bonds and real estate.

Beneficiary: the person designated to receive benefits under an employee benefit plan in the event of the death of the person covered by the plan.

Contracted-out: a contracted-out pension plan provides a portion of the social security benefit, in exchange for a lower contribution rate to the social security system. Both Japan and the United Kingdom allow pension plans to contract out of the earnings-related portion of their social security systems under specified conditions.

Contributory earnings-related pension: a pension based on earnings that is financed by payroll tax contributions from employees and/or employers.

Contributory flat-rate pension: a pension of uniform amount or based on years of service or residence but independent of earnings that is financed by payroll tax contributions from employees and/or employers.

Contributory scheme: a scheme to which participants contribute as well as the employer. Under certain contributory plans participants may be required to contribute as a condition of eligibility.

Defined benefit scheme: a pension plan providing a definite benefit formula for calculating benefit amounts, such as a flat amount per year of service or a percentage of salary or a percentage of salary times years of service.

Defined contribution scheme: a pension plan in which the contributions are made to an individual account for each employee. The retirement benefit is dependent upon the account balance at retirement. The balance depends upon amounts contributed, investment experience and, in the case of profit sharing plans, amounts which may be allocated to the amount owing to forfeitures by terminating employees.

Early retirement age: an age defined by the terms of a defined benefit pension plan, which is earlier than normal retirement age, at which a participant may receive an immediate, possibly reduced, pension under the plan.

Eligibility requirements: (1) conditions which an employee must satisfy to participate in a plan; (2) conditions which an employee must satisfy to obtain a benefit.

Fiduciary: (1) indicates the relationship of trust and confidence where one person (the fiduciary) holds or controls property for the benefit of another person; (2) anyone who exercises power and control, management or disposition with regard to a fund's assets, or who has authority to do so or who has authority or responsibility in the plan's administration.

Flat-rate benefit: pension benefits that are unrelated to earnings. They are sometimes structured to be higher for workers with long years of work or for people with long years of residence in the country.

Funding: a systematic programme under which contributions are made to a pension plan in amounts and at times approximately concurrent with the accruing of benefit rights under a retirement system.

Gatekeepers: administrators responsible for controlling entry into the disability benefit system.

Index funds: stock or bond portfolios structured so that their risk levels and expected returns closely approximate those of stock or bond market indexes.

Integration with social security: in order for private pension benefits not to be duplicative with social security, defined benefit plans often provide that part of the social security pension be subtracted from the private annuity. Defined benefit or defined contribution plans can provide that lower pension accruals be applied to employees' earnings below a specified level (generally the social security taxable wage base).

Invalidity: disability.

Joint and survivor annuity: a provision that enables a plan participant to take annuity payments with continuing payments of all or part of the benefits after his or her death going to a designated beneficiary. The annual pension benefits of the participant electing to have such a survivor annuity are generally reduced to provide for the survivor.

Locked-in benefits: accrued pension benefits which cannot be refunded to the employee in cash before retirement age.

Lump-sum payment: payment within one taxable year to the recipient of the entire balance payable to the participant from a trust which forms part of a qualified pension or employee annuity plan.

Mandatory private pension system: a system requiring employers, by law, to provide private/occupational pensions.

Mandatory savings system: a compulsory defined contribution pension system which pays benefits either as a lump sum or as an annuity based on employee, and in some cases employer contributions and returns on investment of funds, including both publicly managed provident funds and privately managed systems such as that in Chile.

Money purchase scheme: a defined contribution pension plan in which the employer's contributions are determined for, and allocated with respect to, each participant, usually as a percentage of compensation.

Non-contributory flat-rate universal pension: a pension of uniform amount, or based on years of service but independent of earnings, that is paid to residents or citizens who meet age or disability requirements and that is financed with no contributions from employers or employees.

Non-contributory means-tested pension: a pension paid to eligible persons whose own or family income and/or assets fall below designated levels that is generally financed through government contributions with no contributions from employers or employees.

Non-contributory pension scheme: a plan in which the employer pays the entire cost of the pension, with the employee not contributing.

Normal cost: annual cost for a pension plan for the benefits accrued that year by employees.

Normal retirement age: the age, as established by a plan, when unreduced benefits can be received.

Notional defined contribution scheme: a pay-as-you-go scheme. Each participant has an individual account in which benefit rights are accumulated in a similar manner to that in a funded defined contribution scheme. The worker's contributions are credited to his or her account but no funds are deposited in the account. The worker's account balance is periodically revalued upwards, just as if a funded account were being credited with interest.

Occupational pension scheme: a pension plan offered through an individual's employment to private or public sector employees. Benefits are generally paid as an annuity, but could also be paid as a lump sum.

OECD: the Organization for Economic Cooperation and Development, which seeks to encourage economic cooperation among the leading economies.

Opt-out: individuals may choose not to contribute to (opt out of) the state earnings-related pension scheme in the United Kingdom if they establish an appropriate personal pension plan.

Participant: an employee participating in, receiving benefits or eligible to receive benefits from, an employee pension plan.

Pay-as-you-go: the payment of pension benefits out of current revenues without an advance accumulation of funds, thus an unfunded scheme.

Pension scheme: an employee benefit scheme which provides retirement benefits by the purchase of insurance or annuity contracts or the establishment of a trust fund, or a combination of both. A pension scheme may pay benefits either as an annuity or as a lump sum.

Private pension scheme: pension schemes established by private (in contrast to governmental) agencies, including commercial, industrial, labour and service organizations, non-profit organizations, and non-profit religious, educational, and charitable institutions.

Privatization of social security: the process of converting a government-managed social security programme to one managed in the private sector.

Provident fund: a fully funded, defined contribution scheme in which funds are managed by the public sector.

Prudent man (person) rule: a requirement that plan fiduciaries carry out their duties with the care, skill, prudence and diligence which a prudent man acting in a like capacity and familiar with such matters would use under conditions prevailing at the time.

Recognition bond: a bond issued by the government to individual workers in some countries that have converted from a pay-as-you-go social security pension to a defined contribution pension. The bond is issued in recognition of the worker's contributions to the former pay-as-you-go system, and it becomes a source of income at retirement.

Replacement rate: that portion of a reference salary, either final earnings or an average over several years, replaced by the pension.

Scheme: pension scheme, British terminology, equivalent to plan in American pension terminology.

Social assistance: a cash payment provided to poor people and based on need.

Social partners: employees and employers.

Superannuation scheme: a pension plan offering retirement benefits which may be paid as a pension or as a lump sum (Australia).

Survivor annuity: see joint and survivor annuity.

Target benefit scheme: a defined contribution plan for which contributions are based upon an actuarial valuation designed to provide a target benefit for each participant upon retirement.

Vesting: the right of an employee to the benefits he or she has accrued, or some portion of them, even if employment under the plan terminates. An employee who has met the vesting requirements of a pension plan is said to have a "vested" right.

BIBLIOGRAPHY

Aaron, Henry J. 1966. "The social insurance paradox", *Canadian Journal of Economic and Political Science*, no. 32, pp. 371–77.

— 1982. *The economic effects of social security* (Washington, DC, Brookings Institution Press).

Aarts, Leo J.M.; de Jong, Philip. 1997. "Private provision of disability insurance: How does the Dutch policy of privatizing disability insurance compare with US experiences in workers' compensation", presented at the Fourth International Research Seminar on Issues in Social Security (Sigtuna, Sweden, 14–17 June).

Aarts, Leo J.M.; de Jong, Philip; Burkhauser, Richard V.B. (eds). 1996. *Curing the Dutch disease: An international perspective on disability policy reform* (Aldershot, Avebury).

Administradoras de fondos de jubilaciones y pensiones. 1997. *El régimen de capitalización a tres años de la reforma previsional* (Buenos Aires, AFJP).

Aguilar Gutiérrez, Róger; Durán Valverde, Fabio. 1996. "La reforma del sistema nacional de pensiones en Costa Rica", *Seguridad social* (Mexico City), vol. 202, pp. 135–50.

Ahmad, S.E.; Drèze, J.; Hills, J.; Sen, A. (eds). 1991. *Social security in developing countries* (Oxford, Clarendon Press).

Alm, James. 1996. "Explaining tax compliance", in S. Pozo (ed.), *Exploring the underground economy: Studies of illegal and unreported activity* (Kalamazoo, Michigan, W.E. Upjohn Institute for Employment Research), pp. 103–28.

Altman, Nancy. 1992. "Government regulation: Enhancing the equity, adequacy and security of pension benefits", in *Private pensions and public policy* (Paris, Organisation for Economic Cooperation and Development).

American Academy of Actuaries' Committee on Social Insurance. 1996. "Privatizing social security", *Contingencies* (Washington, DC), no. 8, pp. 24–30.

Amzallag, Jacques. 1995. *Replacement ratios: comparability and trends*, International Social Security Association, 25th General Assembly, Report no. 2 (Nusa Dua, Indonesia).

Análisis Laboral. 1996. *Sistema privado de pensiones, revisitado*, (Lima), vol. 20, no. 223, pp. 27–34.

Anderson, Joseph M. 1997a. *The pension system of the Republic of Kazakhstan: Analysis and proposals for reform* (Bethesda, Maryland, Development Alternatives Inc.).

— 1997b. *The pension system of the Republic of Kazakhstan: Policy, structure, operations, reform* (Bethesda, Maryland, Development Alternatives Inc.).

Andrews, Emily S. 1993. *Private pensions in the United States*, OECD Series on Private pensions and Public Policy, no. 10 (Paris, Organisation for Economic Cooperation and Development).

Andrews, Emily S.; Rashid, Mansora. 1996. *The financing of pension systems in Central and Eastern Europe: An overview of major trends and their determinants, 1990–1993* (Washington, DC, World Bank).

Antal, Ilona. 1998. "The pension reform in Hungary", in *Evaluation and prospects of social security reforms: Papers of the Meeting for social security organizations in Central and Eastern Europe, Prague, 10–12 February* (Geneva, ISSA).

Arrau, Patricio; Schmidt-Hebbel, Klaus. 1994. "Pension systems and reforms: Country experiences and research issues", *Revista de análisis económico* (Santiago, Chile), vol. 9, no. 1, pp. 3–20.

Asher, Mukul G. 1998a. "Financial crisis and its implications for pension funds in South-East Asia", paper presented at World Bank Economic Development Institute conference (Hangzhou, China).

— 1998b. "The future of retirement protection in Southeast Asia", *International Social Security Review* (Oxford), vol. 51, no. 1, pp. 3–30.

Association of British Insurers. 1997. *Pensions – a long term strategy* (London, ABI).

Attias-Donfut, Claudine; Wolff, François-Charles. 1997. "Transferts publics et privés entre générations: Incidence sur les inégalités sociales", *Retraite et société* (Paris), no. 20, pp. 20–39.

Augusztinovics, M. 1995. "The long-term financial balance of the pension system: Microsimulation", in E. Ehrlick and G. Revloz (eds), *Human resources and social stability during transition in Hungary* (San Francisco, International Center for Growth).

Babeau, André. 1997. "The problems raised by the introduction of pension funds in France, in *Comparing social welfare systems in Southern Europe* (Paris, MIRE), pp. 267–80.

Bagdy, Gusztav. 1996. "Policies for national consensus and reform", in W. van Ginneken (ed.), *Finding the balance: Financing and coverage of social protection in Europe*, Occasional Papers on Social Security (Geneva, ISSA), pp. 149–65.

Bahr, Holger; Kater, Ulrich. 1997. "Umlageverfahren versus Kapitaldeckungsverfahren: Quo vadis Rentenversicherung?", *Wirtschaftsdienst: Zeitschrift für Wirtschaftspolitik* (Hamburg), vol. 77, no. 4, pp. 212–19.

Bahrain. 1997. *General organization for social insurance: The twentieth annual report for the year 1996* (Manama, Bahrain, The General Organisation for Social Insurance).

Bailey, Clive. 1994. *Extension of social security to small establishments and the non-wage earning population*, African Series, no. 14 (Geneva ISSA), pp. 37–56.

Bailey, Clive; Turner, John A. 1997. *Social security and contribution evasion* (Geneva, ILO).

Bailey, Clive; Queisser, Monika; Woodall, John. 1997. *Reforming pensions in Zambia: An analysis of existing schemes and options for reforms*, Policy Research Working Paper No. 1716 (Washington, DC, World Bank).

Bajtelsmit, Vickie. 1996. "Conservative pension investment: How much difference does it make?", *Benefits Quarterly* (Brookfield, Wisconsin), vol. 12, no. 29, pp. 35–39.

Banco de Previsión Social. 1997. *La seguridad social en el Uruguay de hoy: Una visión social* (Montevideo).

Bandrès, Eduardo; Cuenco, Alain. 1997. "Annuities and transfers in Spanish social security systems", in *Comparing social welfare systems in Southern Europe* (Paris, MIRE), pp. 281–301.

Banting, Keith G.; Boadway, Robin. 1996. "Reforming retirement income policy: The issues", in *Reform of retirement income policy: International and Canadian perspectives* (Kingston, Ontario, Queen's University), pp. 1–26.

Barco, Robert J. 1974. "Are government bonds net wealth?", *Journal of Political Economy*, vol. 82, no. 6, pp. 1095–117.

Barr, Nicholas. 1997. "Pension reform in Central and Eastern Europe: Some comments", in *The politics of welfare: Between governmental policy and local initiative* (Vienna, Institut für die Wissenschaft vom Menschen).

Barrientos, Armando. 1998. "Pension reform, personal pensions and gender differences in pension coverage", *World Development* (Washington, DC), vol. 26, no. 1, pp. 125–37.

Bateman, Hazel; Piggott, John. 1997. "Mandatory retirement saving: Australia and Malaysia compared", in S. Valdés-Prieto (ed.), *The economics of pensions: Principles, policies and international experience* (Cambridge, Cambridge University Press), pp. 318–49.

Bateman, Hazel et al. 1998. *Promoting pension reform: A critical assessment of the policy agenda: Proceedings of the APEC Regional Forum on Pension Reform, Cancun, Mexico, 4–6 February* (Manila, Asian Development Bank).

Baumol, William J.; Turner, John A. 1997. "A portfolio model of retirement income including social security" (Fort Collins, Colorado State University), unpublished.

Baumol, William J.; Bernasek, Alexandra; Jianakoplos, Nancy A. 1997. "Gender differences in pension investment allocation decision", working paper (Fort Collins, Colorado State University).

Baumol, William J.; Goldfeld, Stephen M.; Gordon, Lilli A.; Koehn, Michael F. 1990. *The Economics of Mutual Fund Markets: Competition Versus Regulation* (New York, Kluwer Academic Publishers).

Beattie, Roger; McGillivray, Warren. 1995. "A risky strategy: Reflections on the World Bank Report *Averting the old age crisis*", *International Social Security Review* (Geneva), vol. 48, no. 3/4, pp. 5–22.

Besharov, D.J. 1998. "Social welfare's twin dilemmas: Universalism versus Targeting and Support versus Dependency", in ISSA, *International Research Conference on Social Security, Summing up the evidence: The impact of incentives and targeting in social security,* Conference volume (Jerusalem), January.

Besley, T.; Coate, S. 1998. "Centralised versus decentralised provision of local public goods" (London, London School of Economics), mimeo.

Beveridge, Sir William. 1942. *Social insurance and allied services* (London, HM Stationery Office).

Beye, Claus-Jürgen. 1997. "Bericht der Leitung der Fachvereinigung Mathematische Sachverständige", *Betriebliche Altersversorgung* (Heidelberg), vol. 52, no. 5, pp. 154–63.

Blake, D. 1994. "Pension schemes as options on pension fund assets: Implications for pension fund asset management" (London, Birkbeck College), mimeo.

— 1995. *Pension funds and pension schemes in the United Kingdom* (Oxford, Oxford University Press).

— 1997. *Pension funds and capital markets,* Discussion Paper No. PI-9706 (London, Birkbeck College, The Pensions Institute).

— 1998. "Pension schemes as options on pension fund assets: Implications for pension fund management." *Insurance mathematics and economics,* vol. 23, no. 3, pp. 263–86.

Blanchard, Olivier J. 1993. "The vanishing equity premium", in R. O'Brien (ed.), *Finance and the international economy* (Oxford, Oxford University Press).

Blommestein, Hans J. 1998. "Pension funds and financial markets", *The OECD Observer* (Paris), no. 212, pp. 23–27.

Blöndal, Sveinbjörn; Pearson, Mark. 1995. "Unemployment and other non-employment benefits", *Oxford Review of Economic Policy* (Oxford), vol. 11, no. 1, pp. 136–69.

Blöndal, Sveinbjörn; Scarpetta, Stephano. 1998a. "Retire early, stay at work?", *The OECD Observer* (Paris), no. 212, pp. 15–19.

— 1998b. "The retirement decision in OECD countries", OECD Working Papers vol. 6, no. 38 (Paris, OECD).

Blondeau, Jacques; Dubois, David. 1997. "Financing old-age dependency in Europe: Towards overall management of old age", *Geneva Papers on Risk and Insurance: Issues and practice* (Geneva), no. 82, pp. 46–59.

Bodie, Zvi. 1990. "Pensions as retirement income insurance", *Journal of Economic Literature* (Nashville), vol. 28, pp. 28–49.

Bodie, Zvi; Merton, Robert C. 1992. "Pension benefit guarantees in the United States; a functional analysis", in R. Schmitt (ed.), *The future of pensions in the United States* (Philadelphia, University of Pennsylvania Press).

Bodie, Zvi; Mitchell, Olivia. 1996. "Pension security in an aging world", in Z. Bodie, O. Mitchell and J. Turner (eds), *Securing employer-based pensions: An international perspective* (Philadelphia, University of Pennsylvania Press), pp. 1–30.

Bodie, Zvi; Mitchell, Olivia; Turner, John (eds). 1996. *Securing employer-based pensions: An international perspective* (Philadelphia, University of Pennsylvania Press).

Bonilla García, Alejandro. 1995. "Reformas a los sistemas de pensiones", *Seguridad Social* (Mexico City), vol. 196, pp. 207–27.

Bonilla García, Alejandro; Conte-Grand, Alfredo H. 1997. "Pension reforms in Latin America: Chronicle and reflections", paper presented at the ILO regional social security seminar in Lima, Peru (October).

Borowczyk, Ewa. 1998. *Social insurance institution in reform: Information, facts* (Warsaw, Social Insurance Institution).

Borzutsky, Silvia. 1997. "Privatizing social security: Relevance of the Chilean experience", in J. Midgley; M.W. Sherraden (eds), *Alternatives to social security: An international inquiry* (Westport, Connecticut, Auburn House), pp. 75–90.

Bosworth, Barry; Burtless, Gary (eds). 1998. *Aging societies: The global dimension* (Washington, DC, The Brookings Institution Press).

Bradshaw, J.; Terum, L. 1997. "How Nordic is the Nordic model? Social assistance in a comparative perspective", *Scandinavian Journal of Social Welfare*, vol. 6, pp. 247–56.

Breyer, Friedrich. 1996. "Zur Kombination von Kapitaldeckungs- und Umlageverfahren in der deutschen Rentenversicherung", in *Die Alterssicherungssysteme vor der demographischen Herausforderung: das Säulen-Modell der Weltbank als Lösungsansatz*, Veranstaltung der GVG und der Weltbank, Berlin, 15–17 April (Cologne, Gesellschaft für Versicherungswissenschaft und -gestaltung).

Brocas, A.M.; Cailloux, A.M.; Oget, V. 1990. *Women and social security: Progress towards equality of treatment* (Geneva, ILO).

Budd, Alan; Campbell, Nigel; Chan, Alexi. 1996. "Pensions system in the United Kingdom", paper presented at the National Bureau of Economic Research (cf. Edey and Simon, 1996).

Bundesarbeitsblatt.1997. "Handeln im Sozialbereich: Europäischer Vergleich", *Bundesarbeitsblatt* (Bonn), vol. 5, pp. 7–17.

— 1998. "Gesetz zur Reform der gesetzlichen Rentenversicherung", *Bundesarbeitsblatt* (Bonn), no. 2, pp. 56–82.

Burgess, R.S.L.; Drèze, J.; Ferriera, F.; Hussain, A.; Thomas, J.J. 1993. "Social protection and structural adjustment", in C. Colclough (ed.), *Financing Health and Education* (Oxford, Oxford University Press).

Burkhauser, Richard V.; Daly, Mary C. 1996. "Employment and economic well-being following the onset of a disability: The role for public policy", in J. Mashaw et al. (eds), *Disability, work and cash benefits* (Kalamazoo, Michigan, W.E. Upjohn Institute for Employment Research), pp. 59–102.

— 1998. "Disability and work: The experience of German and American men", *Federal Reserve Bank of San Francisco Economic Review*, vol. 2, pp. 17–29.

Burkhauser, Richard V.; Haveman, Robert H. 1982. *Disability and work: The economics of American policy* (Baltimore, Massachusetts, Johns Hopkins University Press).

Burkhauser, Richard V.; Turner, John A. 1978. "A time series analysis on social security and its effect on the market work of men at younger ages", *Journal of Political Economy* (Chicago), no. 86, pp. 701–15.

— 1985. "Is the social security payroll tax a tax?", *Public Finance Quarterly*, vol. 13, pp. 253–67.

Campbell, G. Ricardo. 1994a. "Brazil Constitutional reform points to reform of social security pensions", *IBIS Review* (Chicago), vol. 8, no. 7, p. 28.

— 1994b. "Chilean Government Worried By Pension Fund Noncompliance", *IBIS Review* (Chicago), vol. 9, no. 22, September.

Canada Pension Plan. 1997. *Sixteenth Actuarial Report*.

Canadian Institute of Actuaries. 1996. *Loi sur la "Caisse de dépôt et placement du Québec"*, Report of the Task Force on the Future of the Canada Pension Plan and the Quebec Pension Plan.

Cantello Branco, Marta de. 1998. *Pension reform in the Baltics, Russia and other countries of the Former Soviet Union* (Washington, DC, IMF).

Castro Gutiérrez, Alvaro et al. 1996. *Current pension systems evolution*, Study Series no. 22 (Mexico City, Inter-American Conference on Social Security).

Cerda, Luis. 1997a. "Reforma al sistema de seguridad social de México", *Seguridad social* (Mexico City), no. 204, pp. 136–66.

— 1997b. "Reform to the social security system of Mexico", *Seguridad social* (Mexico City), no. 204, pp. 167–94.

Chand, Sheetal K.; Jaeger, Albert. 1996. *Aging populations and public pension schemes*, Occasional Paper 147 (Washington, DC, IMF).

Charlton, Roger; McKinnon, Roddy; Munro, Harry T. 1997. "Exploring the future for pensions pillarisation", *Futures* (Paris), vol. 29, no. 1, pp. 159–76.

Christensen, Bent Jesper; Datta Gupta, Nabanita. 1998. "The effects of pension systems reform on married couples' retirement: Evidence from Denmark", working paper, Aarhaus, Denmark.

Cichon, Michael; Samuel, Lenia. 1994. *Making social protection work, the challenge of tripartism in social governance for countries in transition* (Budapest, ILO; Nicosia, Ministry of Labour and Social Insurance).

Cichon, Michael; Hopkins, M.; Hagemejer, Krzysztof. 1994. *Technical assistance to the social security sector of the Slovak Republic: Social protection expenditure in Slovakia – results of a quantitative analysis* (Geneva and Turin, ILO, International Training Centre).

Cichon, Michael; Pal, Karuna; Latulippe, Denis. 1999. *Debating the affordability of social protection systems and pension schemes*, ILO discussion paper (Geneva).

Cifuentes, Rodrigo; Valdés-Prieto, Salvador. 1996. "Fiscal effects of pension reform. A simple simulation model", paper presented at the World Bank Conference on Pension systems: From crisis to reform (Washington, DC).

Clark, Robert. 1993. "Population aging and work rates of older persons: an international comparison", in O.S. Mitchell (ed.), *As the workforce ages* (Ithaca, New York, ILR Press).

Commander, S.; Schankerman, M. 1995. "Enterprise restructuring and the efficient provison of social benefits" (Washington, DC, World Bank), mimeo.

Congressional Budget Office. 1996. *The economic and budget outlook: Fiscal years 1997–2006* (Washington, DC).

Cooper, Glenn; Scherer, Peter. 1998. "Can we afford to grow old?", *The OECD Observer* (Paris), no. 212, pp. 20–22.

Coppini, Mario Alberto. 1997. "El método contributivo para el cálculo de las pensiones: Una verificación actuarial", *Estudios de la Seguridad Social* (Buenos Aires), vol. 82, pp. 51–74.

Corden, A. 1995. "Changing Perspectives on Benefit Take-up", *SPRU Papers* (London, HMSO).

Córdova Macías, Ricardo. 1995. "Tendencias internacionales de reforma a los sistemas de pensiones: El caso de América Latina", *Seguridad Social* (Mexico), vol. 196, pp. 155–81.

Corsetti, Giancarlo; Schmidt-Hebbel, Klaus. 1994. "Pension reform and growth", in S. Valdés-Prieto (ed.), *The economics of pensions* (Cambridge, Cambridge University Press).

Cottani, Joaquin A.; Demarco, Gustavo C. 1996. "The shift to a funded social security system: The case of Argentina", NBER Social Security Project (Washington, DC).

Cowell, Frank A. 1990. *Cheating the Government: The economics of evasion* (London, MIT Press).

Craig, P. 1991. "Costs and benefits: a review of take-up of income-related benefits", *Journal of Social Policy,* vol. 20, no. 4, pp. 537–66.

Creedy, John; Disney, Richard. 1989. "The new pension scheme in Britain", in A. Dilnot; I. Walker (eds), *The economics of social security* (Oxford, Oxford University Press).

Crombrugghe, Alain de. 1997. *Wage and pension pressure on the Polish budget* (Washington, DC, World Bank).

Cutler, Neal. 1996. *Selected results from Financial Literacy 2000* (Philadelphia, University of Pennsylvania).

Davanne, O.; Pujol, T. 1997. "Analyse économique de la retraite par répartition", *Revue française d'économie* (Paris), vol. 12, no. 1, pp. 33–116.

Davies, Bryn. 1996. "Equity within and between generations in pensions", paper presented at a conference on "Pensions in the European Union: Adapting to economic and social changes", organized by the Association for Social Security Research and Policy and the European Network for Research on Supplementary Pensions (Münster, Germany, 13–16 June).

Davis, E. Philip. 1995a. *Pension funds, retirement-income security and capital markets: An international perspective* (Oxford, Oxford University Press).

— 1995b. "International investment of pension funds in Europe, scope and implications for financial stability", *Finanzmarkt und Portfolio Management,* vol. 9, pp. 162–86.

— 1995c. "An international comparison of the financing of occupational pensions", in Z. Bodie, O. Mitchell and J. Turner (eds), *Securing employer-based pensions: An international perspective* (Philadelphia, University of Pennsylvania Press). Also published as Special Paper No. 62 (London, London School of Economics, Financial Markets Group).

— 1995d. "Institutional investors, unstable financial markets and monetary policy", in F. Bruni, D. Fair and R. O'Brien (eds), *Risk management in volatile financial markets* (Amsterdam, Kluwer). Also published as Special Paper No. 75 (London, London School of Economics, Financial Markets Group).

— 1996a. "Pension Fund Investments", in B. Steil et al. (eds), *The European equity markets, the state of the union and an agenda for the millennium* (London, The Royal Institute of International Affairs).

— 1996b. *Pension funds, retirement-income security and capital markets: An international perspective* (Oxford, Clarendon Press).

— 1996c. "The role of institutional investors in the evolution of financial structure and behaviour", in *The future of the financial system,* proceedings of a conference held at the Reserve Bank of Australia (Sydney).

— 1997. *Private pensions in OECD countries: The United Kingdom* (Paris, OECD).

— 1998a. *Regulation of pension fund assets* (Paris, OECD).

— 1998b. *Pensions in the corporate sector* (Kiel, Institute for World Economics).

Daykin, Christopher D. 1995a. "Occupational pension provision in the United Kingdom", in Z. Bodie, O. Mitchell and J. Turner (eds), *Securing employer-based pensions: An international perspective* (Philadelphia, University of Pennsylvania Press), pp. 33–68.

— 1996a. *Can we avert the old-age crisis?* (London).

— 1996b. "Europe – an ageing continent", *Benefits and Compensation International* (London), vol. 26, no. 1, pp. 14–23.

Dean, Andrew; Durand, Fallon; Hoeller, Peter, 1990. "Saving trends and behaviour in OECD countries", *OECD Economic Studies* (Paris), no. 14, Spring, pp. 7–59.

Dei, Henry. 1997. "Ghana: Meeting the challenge of conversion: Ghana's provident fund becomes a pension scheme", *International Social Security Review* (Geneva, ISSA), vol. 50, no. 2, pp. 63–71.

Delsen, Lei; Reday-Mulvey, Geneviève (eds). 1996. *Gradual retirement in the OECD countries: Macro and micro issues and policies* (Aldershot, Dartmouth).

Demirguc-Kunt, A.; Levine, R. 1996. "Stock markets, corporate finance and economic growth", *World Bank Economic Review* (Washington, DC), no. 10, pp. 223–39.

Department of Social Security. 1994. *Income related benefits: Estimates of take-up in 1990 and 1991* (London, HMSO).

Deutsche Bank Research. 1995. *Von der Pensionsrückstellung zum Pensionsfonds: Eine Chance für den deutschen Finanzmarkt* (Frankfurt, Deutsche Bank).

Diamond, Peter A. 1993. *Privatisation of social security; lessons from Chile*, Working Paper no. 4510 (Cambridge, Massachusetts, National Bureau of Economic Research).

Diamond, Peter A.; Valdés-Prieto, Salvador. 1994. "Social security reforms", in B.P. Bosworter; R. Dornbusch; R. Labán (eds), *The Chilean economy: Lessons and challenges* (Washington, DC, The Brookings Institution), pp. 257–327.

Dilnot, Andrew; Webb, Steven. 1989. "The 1988 social security reforms", in A. Dilnot; I. Walker (eds), *The economics of social security* (Oxford, Oxford University Press), pp. 239–68.

Ditch, John; Barnes, Helen. 1996. "Social assistance coverage and administration", in W. van Ginneken (ed.), *Finding the balance: Financing and coverage of social protection in Europe* (Geneva, ISSA), Occasional Papers on Social Security, pp. 109–29.

Ditch, John; Oldfield, N.; Astin, M. 1998. *Social Assistance Data Base* (Department of Social Security; University of Essex).

Ditch, John; Bradshaw, J.; Clasen J.; Huby, M.; Moodie, M. 1997. *Comparative Social assistance: Localisation and Discretion* (Aldershot, Ashgate), pp. 98.

Documentación de la Seguridad Social: Serie Americana. 1997. "Problemas normativos y financieros de la reforma de las pensiones" (Geneva, ISSA), no. 18.

Doescher, Tabitha; Turner, John. 1988. "Social security benefits and the baby boom generation", *American Economic Review* (Nashville, Tennessee), vol. 78, pp. 76–80.

Dorsey, Stuart; Macpherson, David A. 1997. "Pensions and training", *Industrial Relations* (Berkeley, California), vol. 36, no. 1, pp. 81–96.

Dorsey, Stuart; Cornwell, Christopher; Macpherson, David. 1998. *Pensions and productivity* (Kalamazoo, Michigan, W.E. Upjohn Institute).

Dostal, Jaroslav. 1998. "Basic information on the pension scheme reform and the current structure of the system", in *Evaluation and prospects of social security reforms: Papers of the Meeting for Social Security Organizations in Central and Eastern Europe, Prague, 10–12 February* (Geneva, ISSA).

Drèze, J.; Sen, A. 1989. *Hunger and public action* (Oxford, Clarendon).

— 1991. "Public action for social security: Foundations and strategy", in A. Ehtisham; J. Drèze; J. Hills; A. Sen (eds), *Social security in developing countries* (Oxford, Clarendon).

Eardley, T.; Bradshaw, J.; Ditch, J.; Gough, I.; Whiteford, P. 1996. *Social Assistance in OECD countries, Volume 1, Synthesis Report and Volume 2, Country Reports,* Department of Social Security Research Report, no. 46 (London, HMSO).

Economic Bulletin for Europe. 1996. Vol. 48.

Economist Intelligence Unit. 1996. *Investing and trading (Chile)* (London, EIU).

Edey, M.; Simon, J. 1996. *Australia's retirement income system: Implications for saving and capital markets,* Working Paper No. 5799 (Cambridge, Massachusetts, National Bureau of Economic Research).

Edwards, Sebastian. 1996. *The Chilean pension reform: A pioneering programme,* Working Paper No. 5811 (Cambridge, Massachusetts, National Bureau of Economic Research).

Einerhand, Marcel; Melis, Tom; Rovers, Michel. 1994. *Social security and taxes: A study on an international comparability of statistics with regard to some aspects of social security* (The Hague, Ministry of Social Affairs and Employment).

Eisner, Robert. 1997. *The great deficit scores: The federal budget, trade and social security* (New York, Century Foundation Press).

— 1998. *Social security: More, not less* (New York, Century Foundation Press).

Espina, Alvaro. 1996. "Reform of pension schemes in the OECD countries", *International Labour Review,* vol. 135, no. 2, pp. 181–206.

Estudios de la Seguridad Social. 1998. "La organización y la gestión de los regímenes de pensiones: hacia la optimización de los servicios y de los resultados" (Buenos Aires), vol. 83, VII Conferencia Regional Americana de la AISS, Montevideo, 1997.

European Bank for Reconstruction and Development. 1996. *Transition Report* (London, EBRD).

European Federation for Retirement Provision. 1996. *European pension funds: Their impact on European capital markets and competitiveness* (London, EFRP).

Euzéby, A.; van Langendonck, J. 1995. *Neo-liberalism: The question of privatization in EEC countries* (Geneva, ILO).

Fassina, Stefano. 1996. "Le pensioni in Italia tra riforma e contrariforma", *L'Assistenza sociale: Problemi della sicurezza sociale e del lavoro* (Rome), vol. 4, pp. 127–44.

Feldstein, Martin. 1974. "Social security, induced retirement and aggregate capital accumulation." *Journal of Political Economy,* vol. 82, no. 5, pp. 756–66.

— 1996. "The missing piece in policy analysis: Social security reform", *American Economic Review* vol. 86, no. 2, pp. 1–14.

Ferge, Zsuzsa. 1997. "The actors of the Hungarian pension reform", *The politics of welfare: Between governmental policy and local initiative* (Vienna, Institut für die Wissenschaft vom Menschen), Fifth European Forum, 24–26 October, Vienna.

Ferrara, Peter J.; Goodman, John C.; Matthews (Jr.), Merrill. 1995. *Private alternatives to social security in other countries,* Report no. 200 (National Center for Policy Analysis, Dallas, Texas).

Field, Frank; Owen, Matthew. 1994. *National pensions saving plan: Universalising private pension provision* (London, Fabian Society).

Fischer, Simon; Easterly, William. 1990. "The economics of the government budget constraint", *World Bank Research Observer* (Washington, DC), vol. 5, no. 2, pp. 127–42.

Flückiger, Yves. 1996. "Nouvelles pistes pour le financement des assurances sociales", *Aspects de la sécurité sociale* (Lausanne), no. 2/3, pp. 47–62.

Fontaine, Juan Andrés. 1997. "Are there good macroeconomic reasons for limiting external investments by pension funds? The Chilean experience", in S. Valdés-Prieto (ed.), *The economics of pensions: principles, politics and international experience* (Cambridge, Cambridge University Press), pp. 251–74.

Forney, Matt; Fany, Bay. 1998. "Chômage et retraites: Deux enjeux de la réforme de la protection sociale", *Problèmes économiques* (Paris), no. 2557, pp. 18–23.

Freinkman, L.; Starodubrovskaya, I. 1996. *Restructuring of enterprise social assets in Russia: trends, problems, possible solutions.* Police Research Working Paper No. 1635 (Washington, DC, World Bank).

Friedman, B. et al. 1996. *How can China provide income security for its rapidly aging population?,* Policy Research Working Paper No. 1674 (Washington, DC, World Bank).

Frijns, Jean; Petersen, Carel. 1992. "Financing, administration and portfolio management: How secure is the pension promise?", in *Private pensions and public policy* (Paris, Organisation for Economic Cooperation and Development), pp. 97–113.

Fry, V.; Stark, G. 1987. "The take-up of supplementary benefit: gaps in the safety net", *Fiscal Studies*, vol. 8, pp. 1–14.

Gapic, M. 1997. "Basic principles of old-age pension and disability insurance", *Yugoslav Survey* (Belgrade), vol. 38, no. 1, pp. 97–118.

Gentz, Manfred. 1997. "Die Bedeutung von Aktien in der Altersversorgung aus Sicht eines Industrieunternehmens", *Betriebliche Altersversorgung* (Heidelberg), vol. 52, no. 6, pp. 242–47.

Gerencsér, László. 1997. *Hungarian pension reform: Brief information* (Budapest).

Giersch, Herbert (ed.). 1997. *Reforming the welfare state* (Berlin, Springer).

Gillion, Colin; Bonilla García, Alejandro. 1992. "Analysis of a national private pension scheme: The case of Chile", *International Labour Review*, vol. 131, no. 2, pp. 171–95.

Glancy, Simon. 1996. *European retirement provision in the 21st Century: Harnessing the potential of the savings and pension markets* (Dublin, Lafferty Publications).

Glassner, Thomas Charles; Valdés-Prieto, Salvador. 1996. *Pension reform in small developing countries* (Washington, DC, World Bank).

Gleizes, Michel; Plessis, Catherine. 1997. "La retraite des salariés du secteur privé en 2015", *Retraite et société* (Paris), no. 20, pp. 6–19.

Goldman, Sachs. 1993. "The nature and scale of economically targeted investments by the 104 largest public United States pension plans", mimeo.

— 1996. *The international diversification of insurance and pension assets*, report by the European Pension and Insurance Group.

Gordon, Michael S.; Mitchell, Olivia S.; Twinney, Marc M. (eds.). 1997. *Positioning pensions for the year 2000* (Philadelphia, University of Pennsylvania Press).

Götting, Ulrike. 1998. *Transformation der Wohlfahrtsstaaten in Mittel- und Osteuropa* (Opladen, Eine Zwischenbilanz Leske and Budrich).

Greenwald, B.C.; Stiglitz, J.E. 1990. *Information, finance and markets: The architecture of allocative mechanisms*, Working Paper No. 3652 (Cambridge, Massachusetts, National Bureau of Economic Research).

Greisler, Peter. 1996. "Die private Altersvorsorge im gegliederten System der Alterssicherung", in *Die Alterssicherungssysteme vor der demographischen Herausforderung: das Säulen-Modell der Weltbank als Lösungsansatz,* Veranstaltung der GVG und der Weltbank, Berlin, 15–17 April (Cologne, Gesellschaft für Versicherungswissenschaft und -gestaltung).

Grigorescu, Constantin. 1997. "Pension system reform in Romania", *Studii si cercetari economice* (Bucharest), no. 4.

Gruat, Jean-Victor. 1997. "Review of policy issues", in *Extending coverage under basic pension schemes – General and Chinese considerations*, Issues in Social Security, Discussion Paper No. 4 (Geneva, ILO, Social Security Department), pp. 1–18.

Grubbs, Donald S. 1995. "Comment on James and Vittas", in Z. Bodie, O. Mitchell and J. Turner (eds), *Securing employer-based pensions, an international perspective* (Philadelphia, University of Pennsylvania Press).

Guhan, S. 1994. "Social security options for developing countries", *International Labour Review* (Geneva), vol. 133, no. 1, pp. 35–53.

Guillemard, Anne-Marie. 1997. "The changing age of labour force withdrawal", *Observatoire des Retraites Newsletter*, vol. 9, pp. 9–10.

Gupta, R.C. 1994. *NGO experiences in social security* (New Delhi, Friedrich Ebert Stiftung).

Habitat. 1991. *Diez años de historia del Sistema de AFP* (Santiago, Chile, AFP Habitat S.A.).

Hannah, Leslie. 1986. *Occupational pension funds; getting the long-term answers right*, Discussion Paper No. 99 (Manchester, Centre for Economic Policy Research).

Hansell, S. 1992. "The new wave in old-age pensions", *Institutional Investor*, November, pp. 57–64.

Hauser, Richard. 1997. "Adequacy and poverty among the retired", paper presented for Joint ILO-OECD Workshop on Development and Reform of Pension Schemes (OECD, Paris, 15–17 December).

Hausner, Jerzy. 1997. "Security through diversity: Conditions for the successful reform of the pension system in Poland", *The politics of welfare: Between governmental policy and local initiative* (Vienna, Institut für die Wissenschaft vom Menschen), Fifth European Forum, 24–26 October, Vienna.

Hecker, Wilhelm. 1997. "Die künftige Bedeutung und Rolle der betrieblichen Altersversorgung in Deutschland", *Betriebliche Altersversorgung* (Heidelberg), vol. 52, no. 4, pp. 118–23.

Heller, Peter S. 1998. *Rethinking public pension reform initiatives*, Working Paper No. 98/61 (Washington, DC, IMF).

Hemming, R. 1998. *Should public pensions be funded?*, Working Paper No. 98/35 (Washington, DC, IMF).

Hennessy, Patrick. 1997. "The growing risk of dependency in old age: What role for families and for social security?", *International Social Security Review* (Geneva), vol. 50, no. 1, pp. 23–39.

Hepp, S. 1990. *The Swiss pension funds* (Berne, Verlag Paul Haupt).

Heubeck, Klaus. 1996. "Die betriebliche Altersversorgung zwischen gesetzlicher Rentenversicherung und privater Eigenvorsorge", in *Die Alterssicherungssysteme vor der demographischen Herausforderung: das Säulen-Modell der Weltbank als Lösungsansatz,* Veranstaltung der GVG und der Weltbank, Berlin, 15–17 April (Cologne, Gesellschaft für Versicherungswissenschaft und -gestaltung).

Hicks, Peter. 1998. "The policy challenge of ageing populations", *The OECD Observer* (Paris), no. 212, pp. 7–9.

Hinz, Richard; McCarthy, David; Turner, John. 1997. "Are women conservative investors? Gender differences in participant directed pension investments", in M.S Gordon; O.S. Mitchell; M.M. Twinney (eds), *Positioning pensions for the year 2000* (Philadelphia, University of Pennsylvania Press), pp. 91–106.

Holzmann, Robert. 1997a. *On the economic benefits and fiscal requirements of moving from unfunded to funded pensions* (Washington, DC, American Institute for Contemporary German Studies).

— 1997b. *Fiscal alternatives of moving from unfunded to funded pensions* (Paris, OECD).

— 1997c. *Pension reform, financial market development and economic growth: Preliminary evidence from Chile*, Staff Papers 44/2 (Washington, DC, IMF).

— 1997d. *Pension reform in Central and Eastern Europe: Necessity, approaches and open questions* (Saarbrücken, European Institute).

Hoskins, Dalmer D. 1997. "The example of pension reform", *The politics of welfare: Between governmental policy and local initiative* (Vienna, Institut für die Wissenschaft vom Menschen), Fifth European Forum, 24–26 October, Vienna.

Hoynes, Hillary W.; Moffitt, Robert. 1996. "The effectiveness of financial work incentives in Social Security Disability Insurance and Supplemental Security Income", in J. Mashaw et al. (eds) *Disability, work and cash benefits* (Kalamazoo, Michigan, W.E. Upjohn Institute for Employment Research), pp. 189–222.

Hu, Aidi. 1997. "Reforming China's social security system: Facts and perspectives", *International Social Security Review* (Geneva, ISSA), vol. 50, no. 3, pp. 45–65.

Hu, X., Cai, R.; Zhu, X. Forthcoming. "Extending the coverage of social security protection in China", in W. van Ginneken (ed.), *Basic social security for all. Case-studies of developing countries* (Geneva).

Hudson, Robert B. 1995. "The evolution of the welfare state: Shifting rights and responsibilities for the old", *International Social Security Review* (Geneva), vol. 48, no. 1, pp. 3–17.

Hughes, Gerard. 1996. "Pension financing, the substitution effect and national savings", paper presented at a conference on "Pensions in the European Union: Adapting to economic and social change", organized by the Association for Social Security Research and Policy and the European Network for Research on Supplementary Pensions (Münster, Germany, 13–16 June).

Hujo, Katja. 1997. "Die Reform der Rentenversicherung in Argentinien", *Lateinamerika: Analysen, Daten, Dokumentation* (Hamburg), no. 36, pp. 65–79.

Ibbotson Associates. 1997. *Investment Analyst Software* (Chicago, Ibbotson Associates).

IDS (Incomes Data Services). 1993. "Europe focuses on the role of older workers", *European Report* (May), pp. 9–17.

Improta, C. 1996. "Italie: La réforme des retraites du 8 août 1995", *Retraite et société* (Paris), no. 16, pp. 91–103.

Inada, Yoshihisa; Ogawa, Kazuo; Tamaoka, Masayuki; Tokutsu, Ichiro. 1994. "Quantitive analysis of the pension system – in connection with the growth path of the Japanese economy", *Review of social policy* (Tokyo), no. 3, pp. 61–82.

Inter-American Development Bank and Institute of the Americas. 1995. "Realizing the full potential of reform", Second Hemispheric Conference on Social Security, Pension Reform and Capital Markets Development (Washington, DC).

International Finance Corporation. 1996. *Emerging Stock Markets Factbook 1996* (Washington, DC).

International Labour Office (ILO). 1984a. *Financing social security: The options. An international analysis* (Geneva).

— 1984b. *Into the twenty-first century: The development of social security* (Geneva).

— 1984c. *Introduction to social security* (Geneva), pp. 177–81.

— 1988. *Report III of the Joint Committee on the Public Service* (Geneva).

— 1989a. *From pyramid to pillar: Population change and social security in Europe* (Geneva).

— 1989b. "Rapport au gouvernement de la République camerounaise sur l'extension de la protection sociale aux populations non salariées" (Geneva), unpublished document.

— 1990. "Extension de la protection sociale au secteur de l'artisanat au Maroc" (Geneva), unpublished document.

— 1992. *Report of the Director-General: Appendix on the experiences of a number of countries in the area of social security*, 13th Conference of American States Members of the International Labour Organization (Caracas).

— 1993a. *Report of the Director-General,* 8th African Regional Conference, Mauritius, January 1994 (Geneva).

— 1993b. "Social insurance and social protection: Report of the Director-General: Part I", International Labour Conference, 80th Session (Geneva).

— 1994a. *Making social protection work. The challenge of tripartism in social governance for countries in transition.* Cichon, Michael; Samuel, Lenia. (Geneva).

— 1994b. *Report of the Director-General* (Geneva).

— 1994c. *Technical assistance to the social security sector of the Slovak Republic: Social protection expenditure in Slovakia – results of a quantitative analysis* (Geneva), Turin, ILO, International Training Centre.

— 1994d. *The Bulgarian challenge: Reforming labour market and social policy* (Budapest, ILO-CEET).

— 1995a. *Social protection in the Viségrad countries*, ILO-CEET Report no. 13 (Budapest).

— 1995b. *Technical assistance to the social security sector of the Slovak Republic: Actuarial valuation of the present and the proposed reforms of the social insurance pension scheme* (Geneva).

— 1995c. *Yearbook of labour statistics*, 54th edition (Geneva).

— 1996a. *The cost of social security. Fourteenth international inquiry, 1987–1989* (Geneva).

— 1996b. *Development of social security*, Report of an ILO technical appraisal mission (Geneva).

— 1996c. *The ILO social budget model* (Geneva).

— 1996d. *Social protection for the unorganized sector in India*, Report prepared for the UNDP under Technical Support Services-1 (New Delhi, ILO/SAAT draft).

— 1996e. *Social security reform project in Turkey: Model results* (Geneva).

— 1996f. *Supplementary modelling report – prepared for the Government of Turkey for the social security and health insurance reform project* (Geneva).

— 1996g. *Economically active population, 1950–2000* (Geneva).

— 1997a. "Regular adjustment of financial parameters of social protection systems in volatile inflationary environments", *International Social Security Review* (Geneva), vol. 51, no. 1, pp. 47–71.

— 1997b. *The ILO pension model* (Geneva).

— 1997c. *Hungary – Country Review* (Budapest, ILO-CEET).

— 1997d. *Informe técnico preliminar: Valuación actuarial y financiero de la Caja de Seguro Social y Cuentas Sociales de Panamá.*

— 1997e. *Expected pension and social expenditure in OECD and Eastern and Central European countries. An operational framework for pension reform, Budapest* (Geneva).

— 1997f. *Short-term budget projections for the National Social Security Institute of Bulgaria* (Geneva).

— 1997g. *Ageing in Asia: The growing need for social protection* (Bangkok, ILO/EASMAT).

— 1997h. *Report III of the Joint Committee on the Public Service* of 1988 (Geneva).

— 1997i. *Social security financing* (Turin).

— 1997j. *The Lao People's Democratic Republic. Report to the Government on a preparatory assistance project relating to the development of social security* (Geneva).

— 1997k. *Jobs for Africa: A policy framework for an employment-intensive growth strategy*, Report of the ILO/UNDP on employment generation and poverty reduction (Geneva).

Institut de recherches économiques et sociales. 1997. "L'avenir des retraités en Europe", *Questions de sécurité sociale: le mensuel de la protection sociale* (Champigny, France), vol. 49, no. 12, pp. 21–27.

International Monetary Fund (IMF). 1997a. *Government Finance Statistics* (Washington, DC, IMF).

— 1997b. *International Statistical Yearbook 1997* (Washington, DC, IMF).

— 1998. *World Economic Outlook, May 1998* (Washington, DC, IMF).

International Social Security Association. 1989. *Autonomous management of social security institutions* (Geneva).

— 1992. *Survivors' benefits in a changing world.* Studies and Research no. 31 (Geneva).

— 1995a. *Accountability of the partners in social security* (Geneva), European series.

— 1995b. "Report of the ISSA regional meeting for Asia and the Pacific on the extension of social security protection to the entire population", *Social Security Documentation: Asia and Pacific series* (New Delhi), no. 17.

— 1995c. *Social security financing: Issues and perspectives* (Geneva).

— 1995d. *Social security tomorrow: Permanence and change* (Geneva). *Social security: A time for redefinition*, Vienna, 9–11 November 1994.

— 1996a. *Developments and trends in social security throughout the world, 1993–1995: Social security in the 90s: The imperatives of change*, 25th General Assembly, Nusa Dua, Indonesia, 13–19 November 1995 (Geneva).

— 1996b. *Social protection in Europe: Outline of social security programmes, 1996* (Geneva).

— 1997a. "Current social security issues in Asia and the Pacific", *Social Security Documentation: Asia and Pacific Series* (New Delhi), vol. 21.

— 1997b. European Commission. Phare Programme. *Pension systems and reforms – Britain, Hungary, Italy, Poland, Sweden* (Budapest, Institute of Economics).

— 1997c. *Problemas normativos y financieros de la reforma de las pensiones* (Geneva).

— 1997d. *Social Security Advisory Council Report.*

— 1997e. (ILO, ISSA.) *Training Manual: Pensions schemes* (Turin, International Training Centre).

— 1998. *The social security reform debate: In search of a new consensus; a summary* (Geneva).

Iyer, Subramaniam. 1993. "Pension reform in developing countries", Joint/Brazil seminar on social security, *International Labour Review,* vol. 132, no. 2.

Jain, S. 1999. "Basic social security in India", in W. van Ginneken (ed.), *Social security for the excluded majority: Case-studies of developing countries* (Geneva, ILO).

James, Estelle. 1996a. "Providing better protection and promoting growth: A defence of *Averting the old-age crisis*", *International Social Security Review* (Geneva), vol. 49, no. 3, pp. 3–20.

— 1996b. "The World Bank's three-pillar system: Will it provide income security to the world's aging population?", in *Die Alterssicherungssysteme vor der demographischen Herausforderung: das Säulen-Modell der Weltbank als Lösungsansatz*, Veranstaltung der GVG und der Weltbank, Berlin, 15–17 April (Cologne, Gesellschaft für Versicherungswissenschaft und -gestaltung), pp. 43–62.

— 1997a. *New systems for old age security: Theory, practice, and empirical evidence*, Policy Research Working Paper No. 1766 (Washington, DC, World Bank).

— 1997b. *Pension reform: Is there a tradeoff between efficiency and equity?*, Policy Research Working Paper No. 1767 (Washington, DC, World Bank).

— 1997c. "Public pension plans in international perspective: Problems, reforms and research issues", in S. Valdés-Prieto (ed.), *The economics of pensions: Principles, policies and international experience* (Cambridge, Cambridge University Press), pp. 350–70.

James, Estelle; Palacios, Robert. 1995. "Costs of administering public and private pension plans" in IMF, *Finance and Development* (Washington, DC, IMF), pp. 12–15.

James, Estelle; Vittas, Dimitri. 1995. "Mandatory saving schemes; are they the answer to the old-age security problem?", in Zvi Bodie; Olivia Mitchell; John Turner (eds), *Securing employer-based pensions, an international perspective* (Philadelphia, University of Pennsylvania Press), pp. 151–82.

Jenkins, Michael. 1992. Discussion in the Report of the ISSA Regional Meeting for Asia and the Pacific on the Extension of Social Security Protection to the Entire Population, Manila, 8–10 June 1992 (29–31), reproduced as "Extending social security protection to the entire population: Problems and issues", *International Social Security Review*, vol. 46, no. 2, pp. 3–20 (see especially pp. 14–15).

Jollans, Alastair. 1998. *Pensions and the ageing population* (Oxford, Institute of Actuaries).

de Jong, David S.; Jakabin, Ann Gray. 1997. *J.K. Lasser's year-round tax strategies: 1998* (New York, Simon & Schuster).

Jordan. 1997. *Social Security Corporation Annual Report 1996* (Amman).

Kellner, Gundula. 1998. *Die chilenische Rentenreform und ihre Bedeutung für die inländische Kapitalbildung* (Tectum, Edition Wissenschaft 21).

Kemp, P. 1997. *A comparative study of housing allowances*, DSS Research Report (London, The Stationery Office).

Kenny, Lawrence W.; Toma, Mark. 1997. "The role of tax bases and collection costs in the determination of income tax rates, seigniorage and inflation", *Public Choice*, vol. 92, pp. 75–90.

Kerr, S. 1983. *Making ends meet: an investigation into the non-claiming of supplementary pensions* (London, Bedford Square Press).

Kiefer, Manfred. 1998. "Die Rentenreform in Peru", *Auswirkungen auf soziale Sicherung, Sinanzmärkte und Staatsfinanzen* (Frankfurt, Peter Lang).

Kingson, Eric R.; Schulz, James H. (eds). 1997. *Social security in the 21st century* (New York, Oxford University Press).

Korczyk, Sophie M. 1990. *The NRECA Study of Spending, Saving and Retirement* (Washington, DC: National Rural Electric Cooperative Association).

— 1998. *How America Saves*, Report to the American Association of Retired Persons, (Washington, DC).

Kotlikoff, Laurence J. 1988. "Intergenerational transfers and savings", *Journal of Economic Perspectives*, vol. 2, pp. 41–58.

Kotlikoff, Laurence J.; Smetters, Kent; Walliser, Jan. 1996. "Privatizing US social security – A simulation study", paper presented at the World Bank Conference on "Pension systems: From crisis to reform" (Washington, DC).

Lacey, Robert. 1996. "Pension reform in Latin America: Current and future challenges and the role of the World Bank", *Economic Notes*, no. 5.

Laczko, Frank; Payne, Katrina (eds). 1994. *Older people in eastern and central Europe: the price of transition to a market economy* (London, HelpAge International).

La Porta, R., 1993. "Retirement policy – an international perspective", *Transactions* (Schaumburg), vol. 45, pp. 187–211.

La Porta, R.; Turner, John A. 1998. "Partial retirement in OECD countries: What works?", ILO working paper.

La Porta, R.; Lopez-de-Silanes, F.; Schleifer, A.; Vishny, R. 1996. *Legal determinants of external finance*, Working Paper No. 5661 (Cambridge, Massachusetts, NBER).

Latulippe, Denis. 1996. "Effective retirement age and duration of retirement in the industrial countries between 1950 and 1990", *Issues in Social protection. Discussion Paper No. 2,* Social Security Department, International Labour Office (Geneva).

— 1997. *Expected pension and social expenditure in OECD and Eastern and Central European countries. An operational framework for pension reform, Budapest* (Geneva, ILO).

Leechor, C. 1996. *Reforming Indonesia's pension system*, Policy Research Working Paper No. 1677 (Washington, DC, World Bank, East Asia and Pacific, Country Dept. III).

Legal & General. 1997. *Pensions News* (London) February/March.

Leibfried, S. 1993. "Towards a European Welfare State", in C. Jones (ed.), *New Perspectives on Welfare States in Europe* (London, Routledge).

Leibfritz, Willi; Roseveare, D.; Fore, D.; Wurzel, Eckhard. 1995. *Ageing populations, pension systems and government budgets: How do they affect saving?*, OECD Economics Department Working Papers No. 156 (Paris).

Leimer, Dean R. 1995. "A guide to social security money's worth issues", *Social Security Bulletin* (Washington, DC), no. 58, pp. 3–20.

Leimer, Dean R.; Lesnoy, Selig D. 1982. "Social security and private savings: new time decries evidence". *Journal of Political Economy*, vol. 90, pp. 606–42.

Leonesio, Michael V. 1996. "The economics of retirement: A nontechnical guide," *Social Security Bulletin* (Washington, DC), no. 59, pp. 29–50.

Lewis, David. 1998. *Pension reform and the funding alternatives* (Geneva, ISSA).

Lloyd-Sherlock, Peter; Johnson, Paul (eds). 1996. *Ageing and social policy: Global comparisons* (London, Suntory and Toyota International Centres for Economics and Related Disciplines).

Lumsdaine, Robin L. 1996. "Factors affecting labor supply decisions and retirement income," in Eric A. Hanushek; Nancy L. Mariato (eds), *Assessing knowledge of retirement behavior* (Washington, DC, National Academy Press), pp. 61–122.

Lutjens, Erik. 1996. "Supplementary pensions in the Netherlands", in E. Reynaud; L. apRoberts; B. Davies; Gerard Hughes (eds), with the collaboration of T. Ghilarducci and J. Turner, *International perspectives on supplementary pensions: Actors and issues* (Westport, Connecticut, Quorum Books), pp. 16–23.

Mabbett, Deborah. 1997. "Reforming social security in economies in transition: Problems and policies in the former Soviet Republic of Moldova", in *International Social Security Review* (Geneva), vol. 50, no. 1, pp. 57–74.

Mackenzie, G.A.; Gerson, Philip; Cuevas, Alfredo, 1997. "Can public pension reform increase saving?", *Finance and Development* (Washington, DC), pp. 46–49.

Magnussen, Knut A. 1996. *Old-age pensions, retirement behaviour and personal saving: A discussion of the literature* (London, The Pensions Institute, Birbeck College, University of London).

Maia, Fernando. 1997. *A reforma do sistema de pensoes em Portugal: Uma pluraidade de razoes* (Lisbon, OISS).

Manchester, Joyce. 1997. "Taxing issues for social security", paper presented at the 1997 Pension Research Council Symposium, May 12 and 13, 1997, "Prospects for social security reform" (Philadephia, University of Pennsylvania).

Marschler, Hans-Christian. 1997. "Die Fortentwicklung der Direktversicherung als flexibles personalwirtschaftliches Versorgungsinstrument für die Praxis", *Betriebliche Altersversorgung* (Heidelberg), vol. 52, no. 2, pp. 51–60.

Marsh, A.; McKay, S. 1993. *Families, work and benefits* (London, Policy Studies Institute).

Martin, Jean Pierre. 1996. *Measures of replacement rates for the purpose of international comparisons: A note* (Paris, OECD).

Mathew, T.I. 1973. "Social security for the rural population. A study of some social services in selected rural areas of India", *International Labour Review* (Geneva), vol. 108, no. 4, pp. 313–28.

McCarthy, F.D.; Zheng, K. 1996. *Population aging and pension systems: Reform options for China*, Policy Research Working Paper No. 1607 (Washington, DC).

McKinnon, Roddy; Charlton, Roger; Munro, Harry T. 1997. "The national provident fund model: An analytical and evaluative reassessment", *International Social Security Review* (Geneva, ISSA), vol. 50, no. 2, pp. 43–61.

Mehra, R.; Prescott, E.C. 1985. "The equity premium: A puzzle", *Journal of Monetary Economics* (Amsterdam), vol. 15, pp. 145–61.

Mercer W.M. 1997. *International benefits guidelines 1997*, 20th edition (New York).

Mesa-Lago, Carmelo. 1991a. *Social security and prospects for equity in Latin America*, Discussion Paper (Washington, DC, World Bank).

— 1991b. "Social security and economic adjustment restructuring in Latin America and the Caribbean: A comparative assessment", in A. Ehtisham; J. Drèze; J. Hills; A. Sen (eds), *Social security in developing countries* (Oxford, Clarendon Press), pp. 356–94.

— 1994. "Expansion of social security protection to the rural population in Latin America", in T.S. Sankaran; R.K.A Subrahmanya; S.K. Wadhawan (eds), *Social security in developing countries* (New Delhi, Har-Anand Publications), pp. 34–62.

— 1996a. "Las reformas de las pensiones de seguridad social en América Latina: sistemas públicos, privados, mixtos y paralelos", *Estudios de la Seguridad Social* (Buenos Aires), no. 80, pp. 58–85.

— 1996b. "Pension system reforms in Latin America: The position of the international organizations", *CEPAL Review* (New York), no. 60, pp. 73–98.

— 1997a. "Comparative analysis of structural pension reform in eight Latin American countries: Description, evaluation and lessons", paper presented at the ILO regional social security seminar in Lima, October.

— 1997b. *Modelos alternativos de la reforma de la seguridad social en América Latina: comparación y evaluación* (San Salvador, Fundación Friedrich Ebert).

— 1997c. "Die Reform der Renten in Lateinamerika und die Position der internationalen Organisationen", *Zeitschrift für ausländisches und internationales Sozialrecht* (Trier), vol. 11, no. 3, pp. 161–274.

Mesa-Lago, Carmelo; Arenas de Mesa, Alberto. 1997. "Fünfzehn Jahre nach der Privatisierung des Rentensystems in Chile: Evaluation, Lehre und zukünftige Aufgaben", *Deutsche Rentenversicherung* (Frankfurt), vol. 7, pp. 405–26.

Mesa-Lago, Carmelo; Santamaría, Sergio; López, Rosa María. 1997. *La seguridad social en Nicaragua: Diagnóstico y propuesta de reforma: Versión preliminar* (Managua, Friedrich Ebert Stiftung).

Midgley, James; Sherraden, Martin W. (eds). 1997. *Alternatives to social security: An international inquiry* (Westport, Connecticut, Auburn House), pp. 75–90.

Midgley, James; Tracy, Martin B. 1996. *Challenges to social security: An international exploration* (Westport, Connecticut, Auburn House).

Midwinter, Eric. 1997. *Pensioned off: Retirement and income examined* (Buckingham, United Kingdom, Open University Press).

Miles, David. 1997. "Financial markets, ageing and social welfare", *Fiscal studies* (London), vol. 18, part 2, pp. 161–87.

Ministry of Health and Social Affairs (Sweden). 1994. *Reformerat Pensionssystem* (A reformed pension system) (Stockholm, Allmänna Förlaget).

— 1998. "Lägesrapport av pensionsreformen" (A summary of the pension reform) (Stockholm), mimeo.

Ministry of Labour (Czech Republic). 1996. *Pensions: Basic Information* (Prague).

Ministry of Labour, Social Affairs and Family (Slovakia). 1993. *Social policy of Slovakia* (Bratislava).

Mitchell, Olivia. 1996. *Administrative costs in public and private retirement systems*, National Bureau of Economic Research Working Paper Series (Working Paper No. 5734) (Cambridge, Massachusetts, NBER).

— 1997. *Building an environment for pension reform in developing countries*, Working Paper (Philadelphia, Pension Research Council, The Wharton School).

Mitchell, Olivia; Barreto, F.A. 1997. *After Chile, what? Second round pension reforms in Latin America*, Working Paper No. 6316 (Cambridge, Massachusetts, NBER).

Mitchell, Olivia; Hsin, Ping-Lung. 1994. *Public pension governance and performance*, Working Paper No. 4632 (Cambridge, Massachusetts, NBER).

Mitchell, Olivia; Poterba, James S.; Warshawsky, Mark; Brown, Jeff. 1998. *New evidence on the money's worth of individual annuities*, working paper (Cambridge, Massachusetts).

Modigliani, Franco. 1986. "Life cycles, individual thrift and the wealth of nations", *American Economic Review*, vol. 70, pp. 297–313.

Moles, Ricardo R. 1997. "Los modelos de pensiones en América Latina", *Reforma de los Sistemas de Pensiones en América Latina* (Buenos Aires), no. 2.

Mouton, Pierre. 1984. "Methods of financing social security in industrial countries: An international analysis", *Financing social security: The options. An international analysis* (Geneva, ILO), pp. 3–32.

Mouton, Pierre; Yahiel, Michel. 1997. "Les pays d'Europe centrale et orientale face à la réforme des systèmes de retraite", *Retraite et société* (Paris), no. 18, pp. 34–47.

Munnel, Alicia; Yohn, Frederick O. 1992. "What is the impact of pensions on savings?", in Zvi Bodie; Alicia Munnell (eds), *Pensions and the economy: Sources, uses and limitations of data* (Philadelphia, University of Pennsylvania Press).

Murakami, Kiyoshi. 1997. "Pension problems and proposals for future reform in Japan", *Benefits and Compensation International* (London), vol. 26, no. 8, pp. 14–21.

Myers, Robert J. 1992. "Chile's Social Security Reform, After Ten Years", *Benefits Quarterly* (Brookfield, Wisconsin), 8 (Third Quarter), pp. 41–55.

Myles, John; Quadagno, Jill. 1997. "Recent trends in public pension reform: A comparative view", in K. Banting; R. Boadway (eds), *Reform of retirement income policy: International and Canadian perspectives* (Kingston, Ontario, Queen's University, School of Policy Studies).

Nagi, Saad. 1991. "Disability concepts revisited: Implications to prevention", in A.M. Pope; A.R. Tarlove (eds), *Disability in America: Toward a national agenda for prevention* (Washington, DC, National Academy Press), Appendix A.

National Pension Corporation, Republic of Korea. *Report for 1996 – National Pension Scheme* (Seoul).

Nitsch, Manfred; Schwarzer, Helmut. 1996. *Recent developments in financing social security in Latin America*, Issues in Social Security, Discussion Paper No. 1 (Geneva, ILO, Social Security Department).

Oeter, Ferdinand. 1997. "Die vier Säulen sozialer Gerechtigkeit und Sicherheit", *Zeitschrift für Sozialreform* (Wiesbaden), vol. 43, no. 5, pp. 397–406.

Office of the Government Plenipotentiary for Social Security Reform (Poland) 1997. *Security through diversity: Reform in the pension system in Poland* (Warsaw).

Organization for Economic Cooperation and Development. 1985. *Social Expenditures: 1960–1990* (Paris).

— 1994a. *The OECD jobs study: Facts, analysis, strategies* (Paris).

— 1994b. *Taxation and household saving* (Paris).

— 1995a. *Ageing population, pension systems and government budgets: How do they affect saving?*, OECD Working Paper, vol. III, no. 68.

— 1995b. *OECD Economic Outlook* (Paris), no. 58, December.

— 1995c. *The transition from work to retirement* (Paris).

— 1996. *Ageing in OECD countries: A critical policy challenge* (Paris).

— 1997. *Private pensions in OECD countries: The United Kingdom* (Paris).

Orsmond, D.W.H. 1996. "Ukraine: Agenda for fiscal reform over the medium term", paper prepared for joint Fund/Bank seminar on accelerating Ukraine's transition to a market economy: Credible macro-economic adjustment and systematic reforms (Washington, DC).

Ostrup, Finn. 1996. "The development of supplementary pensions in Denmark", in E. Reynaud; L. apRoberts; B. Davies; G. Hughes (eds), with the collaboration of T. Ghilarducci; J. Turner, *International perspectives on supplementary pensions: Actors and issues* (Westport, Connecticut, Quorum Books), pp. 127–36.

Owen, Matthew; Field, Frank. 1997. "Pension reform in Britain: Alternative modes of provision", in J. Midgley; M.W. Sherraden (eds) *Alternatives to social security: An international inquiry* (Westport, Connecticut, Auburn House), pp. 91–103.

Palmer, Edward. 1987. "Public and private pensions and saving in Sweden", *Conjugating public and private: The case of pensions*, Studies and Research Report no. 24 (Geneva, ISSA).

— 1997. "Formas de financiación de la seguridad social en un contexto de disminución del total de las cotizaciones", *Estudios de la Seguridad Social* (Buenos Aires), no. 82, pp. 22–50.

Paredes, Oscar. 1997. "La reforma pensional colombiana", *Documentación de la Seguridad Social* (Geneva), no. 18, pp. 79–98.

Paribas Report. 1995. *An Ageing Europe: The implications for the financial markets* (Paribas Capital Markets).

Patel, Urjit R. 1997. "Aspects of pension fund reform: Lessons for India", *Economic and Political Weekly* (Mumbai, India), vol. 32, no. 38, pp. 2395–2402.

Paulsdorff, Jürgen. 1997. "Generationenvertrag: Quo vadis?", *Die Angestelltenversicherung* (Berlin), vol. 44, no. 3, pp. 116–19.

Pedersen, Peder J.; Smith, Nina. 1995. "The retirement decision", in G.V. Mogensen (ed.), Work incentives in the Danish Welfare State (Aarhus, The Rockwool Foundation, Aarhus University Press), pp. 227–44.

— "Early exit in the Danish labour market – the development in recent years", in E. Wadensjo (ed.), The Nordic labour markets in the 1990s (Amsterdam, Elsevier Science B.V.), vol. 2, pp. 33–67.

Pemberton, J. 1997. *National and international privatisation of pensions* (Reading, University of Reading, Department of Economics).

Pene, D. 1997. *Dynamique de la retraite: Une menace pour l'Europe* (Paris, Economica).

Peterson, Peter G. 1996. "Global pension crisis", Remarks to the Council on Foreign Relations (New York).

Petridou, Helene. 1996. "Supplementary pensions in Greece", in E. Reynaud; L. apRoberts; B. Davies; G. Hughes (eds), with the collaboration of T. Ghilarducci and J. Turner, *International perspectives on supplementary pensions: Actors and issues* (Westport, Connecticut, Quorum Books), pp. 24–32.

Pigou, A.C. 1920. *The economics of welfare* (London, MacMillan).

Pinera, José. 1998. *Pensionsreform: Das chilenische Modell* (Vienna, Manz).

Poland. Office of the Government Plenipotentiary for Social Security Reform. 1997. *Security through diversity: Reform of the pension system in Poland* (Warsaw).

Poortvliet, W.G.; Laine, T.P. 1994. "A global trend: Privatization and reform of social security pensions plans", *Geneva Papers on Risk and Insurance* (Geneva), vol. 19, no. 72, pp. 257–86.

Pophal, Roger. 1997. "Direktversicherung als Beitrags- oder Leistungszusage", *Betriebliche Altersversorgung* (Heidelberg), vol. 52, part 5, pp. 174–78.

Poterba, James M.; Wise, David A. 1996. *Individual financial decisions in retirement saving plans and the provision of resources for retirement*, working paper (Cambridge, Massachusetts, NBER).

Poterba, James M.; Wise, David A.;Venti, S.F. 1996. *Personal retirement saving programs and asset accumulation: Reconciling the evidence*, working paper (Cambridge, Massachusetts, NBER).

Pritchett, Lant. 1997. "Divergence, big time", *Journal of Economic Perspectives*, no. 11, pp. 3–17.

Queisser, Monika. 1995. "Chile and beyond: The second-generation pension reforms in Latin America", *International Social Security Review* (Geneva), vol. 48, no. 3/4, pp. 23–39.

— 1996a. "Bandbreite der Weltbank-projekte zur Unterstützung der Reformen im Bereich der Alterssicherung", in *Die Alterssicherungssysteme vor der demographischen Herausforderung: das Säulen-Modell der Weltbank als Lösungsansatz,*Veranstaltung der GVG und der Weltbank, Berlin, 15–17 April (Cologne, Gesellschaft für Versicherungswissenschaft und -gestaltung).

— 1996b. *Pensions in Germany*, World Bank Policy Research Working Paper No. 1664 (Washington, DC).

— 1997a. *Pension reform and private pension funds in Peru and Colombia*, Policy Research Working Paper No. 1853 (Washington, DC, World Bank).

— 1997. "Reforma de previdência: Depois do Chile: A segunda geração de reformas na América Latina", *Conjuntura social: Previdência e justiça social* (Brasilia), vol. 8, no. 3, pp. 13–26.

— 1998. "Regulation and supervision of pension funds: Principles and practice", *International Social Security Review* (Geneva, ISSA), vol. 51, no. 2, pp. 39–55.

Ramírez, Victor A. 1997. "La reforma al sistema de pensiones de El Salvador: principales procesos de cambio", *ISSA and CISS joint conference on reengineering of social security organizations* (Geneva, ISSA).

Rawls, John. 1971. *A theory of justice* (Cambridge, Massachusetts, Belknap).

Reimers, Cordelia; Honig, Marjorie. 1997. "Responses to social security by men and women: Myopic and far-sighted behavior", *Journal of Human Resources* (Madison), vol. 31, no. 2, pp. 359–82.

Rein, Martin; Turner, John. 1999. "Work, family, state and market: Income at the last stages of the working career", *International Social Security Review* (Geneva).

Reisen, Helmut. 1997. "Liberalizing foreign investments by pension funds: Positive and normative aspects", *World development* (Oxford), vol. 25, no. 7, pp. 1173–82.

Research Programme on Social Security, Insurance and Savings. 1997. "Le futur des retraités en Europe: Une synthèse des principales réformes récentes du premier pilier", *The Four Pillars,* (Geneva), no. 21bis.

Revollo, Alfonso. 1995. "The proposed Bolivian pension system reform", a presentation made at the Second Hemispheric Conference on Social Security, Pension Reform and Capital Markets Development, Realizing the full potential of reform, co-sponsored by the Inter-American Development Bank and the Institute of the Americas (Washington, DC).

Reynaud, Emmanuel. 1995. "Financing retirement pensions: Pay-as-you-go and funded systems in the European Union", *International Social Security Review* (Geneva), no. 48, vol. 3/4, pp. 41–58.

— 1996. "Financing models for pay-as-you-go systems", in E. Reynaud; L. apRoberts; B. Davies; G. Hughes (eds), with the collaboration of I. Ghilarducci and J. Turner, *International perspectives on supplementary pensions: Actors and issues* (Westport, Connecticut, Quorom Books), pp. 82–96.

— 1997a. "L'avenir des retraités en débat", *Chronique internationale de l'IRES* (Noisy-le-Grand, France), vol. 48, September, pp. 5–16.

— 1997b. "France: A national and contractual second tier", in M. Rein; E. Wadensjöm (eds), *Enterprise and the welfare state* (Cheltenham, Edward Elgar), pp. 65–98.

— 1997c. *Private pensions in OECD countries: France* (Paris, OECD).

— 1997d. "Reforma da previdência: Financiamento da previdência: Repartição e capitalizaço na União Européia", *Conjuntura social: Previdência e justiça social* (Brasilia), vol. 8, no. 3, pp. 57–70.

— 1998a. "Pensions in the European Union: Adapting to economic and social change", *International Social Security Review* (Geneva), vol. 51, no. 1, pp. 31–46.

— 1998b. *Les retraites dans l'Union Européenne: Adaptation aux évolutions économiques et sociales* (Paris, L'Harmattan).

— 2000. *Social dialogue and pension reform: United Kingdom, United States, Germany, Japan, Sweden, Italy, Spain* (Geneva, ILO).

Reynaud, Emmanuel; Hege, Adelheid. 1996. "Italy: A fundamental transformation of the pension system", *International Social Security Review* (Geneva), vol. 49, no. 3, pp. 65–74.

Ribe, Frederick. 1994. "Funded social security systems: A review of issues in four East Asian countries", *Revista de Análisis Económico* (Santiago), vol. 9, no. 1, pp. 169–82.

Riboud, M.; Chu, H. 1997. *Pension reforms and growth in Ukraine: An analysis focusing on labor market constraints*, Policy Research Working Paper No. 1731 (Washington, DC, World Bank).

Richards, Anthony J. 1996. *Volatility and predictability in national stock markets: How do emerging and mature markets differ?* (Washington, DC, IMF).

Richter, Rudolf; Schlieper, Ulrich; Friedmann, Willy. 1981. *Makroökonomik. Eine Einführung*, 4th ed. (Berlin, Heidelberg, New York, Springer-Verlag), p. 275.

Rimachevskaia, N. 1997. "Troisième âge et la transition en Russie", *Courrier des pays de l'est* (Paris), no. 420, pp. 34–46.

Rische, Herbert; Sailer, Markus. 1996. "Die Alterssicherung in Mittel- und Osteuropa, Herkunft, Reformbedarf und aktuelle Entwicklungen", *Deutsche Rentenversicherung* (Frankfurt), vol. 5–6, pp. 367–75.

Rische, Herbert et al. (eds). 1996. *Die Alterssicherungssysteme vor der demographischen Herausforderung: das Säulen-Modell der Weltbank als Lösungsansatz*, Veranstaltung der GVG und der Weltbank, Berlin, 15–17 April (Cologne, Gesellschaft für Versicherungswissenschaft und -gestaltung).

Rodríguez, Renán. 1997. "La reforma de la previsión social en Uruguay", *Documentación de la Seguridad Social* (Geneva, ISSA), no. 18, pp. 123–56.

Romero Montes; Francisco Javier. 1997. "La reforma del sistema de pensiones en el Perú", *Documentación de la Seguridad Social* (Geneva, ISSA), no. 18, pp. 99–121.

Rosenberg, Peter. 1996. "Umlageverfahren versus Kapitaldeckungsverfahren: Vorschlag zu einer optimalen Kombination", in *Die Alterssicherungssysteme vor der demographischen Herausforderung: das Säulen-Modell der Weltbank als Lösungsansatz,*Veranstaltung der GVG und der Weltbank, Berlin, 15–17 April (Cologne, Gesellschaft für Versicherungswissenschaft und -gestaltung).

Rosenman, Linda S. 1997. "The social security approach and retirement pensions in Australia", in J. Midgley and M.W. Sherraden, (eds) *Alternatives to social security: An international inquiry* (Westport, Connecticut, Auburn House), pp. 17–32.

Rosenman, Linda S.; Warburton, Jeni. 1996. "Restructuring Australian retirement incomes: Implications of changing work and retirement patterns", *International Social Security Review* (Geneva), vol. 49, no. 4, pp. 5–24.

Ross, S. 1996. *Overview of social security and taxation systems interactions* (Sigtuna, Sweden, ISSA Symposium).

Royal Norwegian Ministry of Finance. 1997. *The National Budget: 1998* (Oslo).

Ruland, Franz. 1996. "Die Rentenversicherung: Zukunftssicher, weil anpassungsfähig", in *Die Alterssicherungssysteme vor der demographischen Herausforderung: das Säulen-Modell der Weltbank als Lösungsansatz,*Veranstaltung der GVG und der Weltbank, Berlin, 15–17 April (Cologne: Gesellschaft für Versicherungswissenschaft und -gestaltung).

Rupp, Kalman; Stapleton, David (eds). 1998. *Growth in disability benefits* (Kalamazoo, Michigan, W.E. Upjohn Institute for Employment Research).

Rutkowski, M. 1996. *Changes in the wage structure during economic transition in Central and Eastern Europe* (Washington, DC, World Bank).

Salafia, Antonio. 1995. *La riforma previdenziale ed italiana a confronto* (Rome).

Sales-Sarrapy, C.; Solis-Soberon, F.; Villagomez-Amezcua, A. 1996. *Pension system reform: The Mexican case*, NBER Working Paper Series (Cambridge, Massachusetts, NBER).

Samorodov, Alexander. 1998. *Ageing and labour markets for older workers* (Geneva, ILO).

Samuelson, Paul A. 1958. "An exact consumption loan model of interest with or without the social contrivance of money", *Journal of Political Economy*, no. 66, pp. 467–82.

Samuelson, Paul A.; Nordhaus, William D. with the assistance of Mandel, Michael J. 1995. *Economics,* 15th ed. (New York, St. Louis, McGraw-Hill), pp. 627–28.

Sankaran, T.S. 1998. "Social assistance: Evidence and policy issues", in W. van Ginneken (ed.), *Social security for all Indians* (New Delhi, Oxford University Press), pp. 57–76.

Saunier, Jean-Marie. 1994. *Les régimes obligatoires de retraite en France, en Allemagne et au Royaume-Uni: Essai de mesure des écarts entre catégories de salaires* (Paris, Solidarité santé).

Scherman, Karl Gustaf. 1996. "Die reform der Alterssicherung in Schweden: Hintergründe, Konzept und Auswirkungen", *Deutsche Rentenversicherung* (Frankfurt), no. 5/6, pp. 356–66.

Scherman, Karl Gustaf; Smedmark, Göran. 1997. "The Swedish pension reform", in *Reports to the International conference on problems developing and reforming social security schemes* Alma-Ata, 2–5 September (Geneva, ISSA).

Schewe, Dieter. 1997. "Die 'Lebenserwartung' als Rentenfaktor oder als Anstoß zum Krieg der Generationen: 17 Thesen", *Sozialer Fortschritt* (Bonn), vol. 46, no. 8, pp. 173–75.

Schieber, Sylvestor; Shoven, John. 1997. "The consequences of population ageing for private pension fund savings and asset markets", in Michael D. Hurd; Naohiro Zashiro (eds), *The economic effects of ageing in the United States and Japan* (Chicago, University of Chicago Press).

Schmähl, Winfried. 1996. "Die Alterissicherungssysteme aus gesamtwirtschaftlicher und ordnungspolitischer Sicht", in *Die Alterssicherungssysteme vor der demographischen Herausforderung: das Säulen-Modell der Weltbank als Lösungsansatz,* Veranstaltung der GVG und der Weltbank, Berlin, 15–17 April (Cologne, Gesellschaft für Versicherungswissenschaft und -gestaltung); also published in *Wirtschaftsdienst: Zeitschrift für Wirtschaftspolitik*, vol. 76, no. 8, pp. 409–17.

— 1997. "Rentenreformen brauchen konzeptionsgeleibebe Entscheidungen", *Wirtschaftsdienst: Zeitschrift für Wirtschaftspolitik*, vol. 77, no. 6, pp. 319–22.

Schmidt-Hebbel, Klaus. 1995. *Colombia's pension reform: Fiscal and macroeconomic effects,* Discussion Paper No. 314 (Washington, DC, World Bank).

Schneider, Jacques-André. 1997. "Difficultés et défis des caisses de pensions", *Aspects de la Sécurité Sociale: Bulletin de la FEAS* (Geneva), no. 2, pp. 5–11.

Scholz, Wolfgang; Hagemejer, Krzyszstof; Cichon, Michael. 2000. *Social budgeting* (Geneva, ILO).

Schulz, James H. 1997. *Ageing in Asia: The growing need for social protection* (Bangkok, ILO/EASMAT).

Schuppisser, H.R. 1997. "Financer les assurances sociales par le salaire ou par l'impôt?", *Aspects de la Sécurité Sociale: Bulletin de la FEAS* (Geneva), no. 2, pp. 32–37.

Seguridad Social (Mexico). 1997. "La reforma de los sistemas de seguridad social en América Latina", *Seguridad Social* (Mexico City), vol. 206, pp. 7–31.

Shah, Hemant. 1997. *Toward better regulation of private pension funds,* Policy Research Working Paper No. 1791 (Washington, DC, World Bank).

Sheffrin, Steven M.; Triest, Robert K. 1992. "Can brute deterrence backfire? Perceptions and attitudes in taxpayer compliance", in J. Slemrod (ed.), *Why people pay taxes* (Ann Arbor, Michigan, University of Michigan Press), pp. 193–218.

Shigehara, Kumiharu. 1998. "New policies for dealing with ageing", *The OECD Observer* (Paris), no. 212, pp. 5–6.

Shoven, John B. 1996. "Are we ready for the aging baby boomers?", *Actuarial Futures*, pp. 3–11.

Siebert, Horst (ed.). 1998. *Redesigning social security* (Tübingen, Mohr Siebeck).

Siegal, Jeremy J. 1994. *Stocks for the long run* (Burr Ridge, Illinois, Irwin Professional Publishing).

Simanovits, A. 1997. "The Case of Hungary", in M. Augusztinovics (ed.), *Pension systems and reforms: Britain, Hungary, Italy, Poland, Sweden*, Final report, European Commission PHARE ACE Programme (Budapest).

Sinfield, Adrian. 1993. "Reverse targeting and upside down benefits – How Perverse Policies Perpetuate Poverty", in Adrian Sinfield (ed.), *Poverty, inequality and justice* (Edinburgh, New Waverly Papers), pp. 39–48.

— 1998. "Social protection versus tax benefits", in D. Pieters (ed.), *Social protection of the next generation* (The Hague, Kluwer Law International), pp. 111–52.

Singh, Ajit. 1997. "Pension reform, the stock market, capital formation and economic growth: A critical commentary on the World Bank's proposals", *International Social Security Review* (Geneva), vol. 49, no. 3, pp. 21–43.

Singh, H. 1994. "ISSA studies on extension of social security to unprotected groups in Asia and the Pacific", in T.S. Sankaran; R.K.A. Subrahmanya; S.K. Wadhawan (eds), *Social security in developing countries* (New Delhi, Har-Ahnand Publications), pp. 19–33.

Slemrod, Joel (ed.). 1992. *Why people pay taxes* (Ann Arbor, Michigan, University of Michigan Press).

Slodky, Javier. 1997. "The reform to social security in Argentina", in *Social security in America towards the end of the XX Century* (Mexico, Interamerican Conference on Social Security) Studies series no. 36, pp. 85–108.

Smeeding, Timothy M. 1997. *Reshuffling responsibilities in old age: The United States in a comparative perspective*, Luxembourg Income Study Working Paper Series (Luxembourg).

Smith, Kent W. 1992. "Reciprocity and fairness: Positive incentives for tax compliance", in J. Slemrod (ed.), *Why people pay taxes* (Ann Arbor, Michigan, University of Michigan Press), pp. 223–50.

Solnik, B.H. 1988. *International Investments* (Reading, Massachusetts, Addison Wesley).

Ståhlberg, Ann-Charlotte. 1990. "Lifecycle income redistribution of the public sector: Inter- and intragenerational effects", in Persson (ed.), *Generating equality in the welfare state* (Oslo, Norwegian University Press).

— 1995. "Pension reform in Sweden", *Scandinavian Journal of Social Welfare*, no. 4, pp. 267–73.

Steuerle, Eugene and Bakija, Jon. 1994. *Retooling social security for the 21st century: Right and wrong approaches to reform* (Washington, DC, Urban Institute Press).

Steuerle, Eugene and Bakija, Jon. 1997. "Retooling social security for the 21st century", *Social Security Bulletin* (Washington, DC), vol. 60, no. 2, pp. 37–60.

Stiglitz, Joseph E. 1993. *Financial systems for Eastern Europe's emerging economies* (San Francisco, ICS Press).

Storm, Andreas. 1997. "Für eine belastungsgerechte Erneuerung des Generationsvertrages: Konzeptionelle Überlegungen für eine tragfähige Reform der gesetzlichen Rentenversicherung. 12 Thesen", *Deutsche Rentenversicherung* (Frankfurt). No. 1/2, pp. 122–25.

Stropnik, Nada. 1997. *Social and economic aspects of ageing societies* (Ljubljana, Institute for Economic Research).

Stufetti, Daniel. 1997. "Aktuelle Probleme der zweiten Säule aus der Sicht des Bundesamt für Sozialversicherung", *Soziale Sicherheit* (Berne), vol. 4, pp. 199–205.

Superintendencia de Administradoras de Fondos de Jubilaciones y Pensiones. 1997. *Estudios Sobre el Régimen de Capitalización Argentino* (Buenos Aires).

Syvia, A. 1989. *Managerial problems in the administration of social security schemes*, Social Security Documentation: African Series, no. 11 (Geneva, ISSA), pp. 41–58.

Tajika, Eiji and Hayashi, Fumiko. 1997. "A comparison of the rates of return offered by the National Pension Fund, post office pensions, and personal pension plans of life insurance companies", *Review of Social Policy* (Tokyo), vol. 6, pp. 65–86.

Tamagno, Edward. 1997. *Financing and Managing Pension Plans: A Case Study of Canada* (Geneva, ISSA).

Tambouri, Giovanni. 1998. "Motivation, purpose and processes in pension reform", Third Leo Wildmann Symposium, International Social Security Association, 26th General Assembly (Marrakech, Morocco).

Tang, K.L. 1997. "Non-contributory pensions in Hong Kong: An alternative to social security?", in J. Midgley and M.W. Sherraden (eds), *Alternatives to social security: An international inquiry* (Westport, Connecticut, Auburn House), pp. 61–74.

Tanzi, Vito. 1996. "The fiscal dimensions of public pension systems", in *Protecting retirement incomes: Options for reform*, ISSA Studies and Research, No. 37 (Geneva), pp. 27–38.

Tanzi, Vito; Shome, Parathasarathi. 1993. *A primer on tax evasion*, working paper (Washington, DC, IMF).

Tepper, Irwin. 1992. "Comments on Bodie and Papke", in Z. Bodie; A. Munnell (eds), *Pensions and the United States economy* (Philadelphia, Pension Research Council, University of Pennsylvania).

Terwey, Franz. 1997. "Les aspects socio-économiques du système par répartition de la protection sociale", *Retraite et société* (Paris), pp. 16–23.

Thelen, Peter. 1996. "Vollbesteuerung der Renten bleibt in der Diskussion", *Die Angestelltenversicherung* (Berlin), vol. 43, no. 2, pp. 575–78.

Thompson, K. 1997. "Review of strategic and technical issues", in *Extending coverage under basic pension schemes – Géneral and Chinese considerations*, Issues in Social Security Discussion Paper No.4 (Geneva, ILO), pp. 19–33.

Thompson, Lawrence H. 1992. "Social security surpluses", in *New Palgrave Dictionary of Money and Finance* (London, Macmillan).

— 1994. "Advantages and disadvantages of different social welfare strategies", *Social Security Bulletin* (Washington, DC), vol. 57, no. 3, pp. 3–11; also published in *International Social Security Review* (Geneva), vol. 48, no. 3–4, pp. 59–75.

— 1995. "Principles of financing social security pensions", *International Social Security Review* (Geneva), vol. 49, no. 3, pp. 45–63.

— 1996. "Garantizar ingresos de jubilación suficientes: Parametros para enfoques aceptables", *Revista de Trabajo y de la Seguridad Social* (Buenos Aires), vol. 3, no. 9, pp. 47–53.

— 1998. *Older and wiser: The economics of public pensions* (Washington, DC, The Urban Institute Press).

Thornton, John E. et al. 1996. *People in pensions, 1997* (London, Pendragon).

Topinska, Irena. 1996. "Financing social protection: Challenges of transition", in W. van Ginneken (ed.), *Finding the balance: Financing and coverage of social protection in Europe*, Occasional Papers on Social Security (Geneva, ISSA), pp. 131–48.

Turner, John. 1984. "Population age structure and the size of social security", *Southern Economic Journal*, vol. 50, pp. 1131–46.

— 1992. *Trends in pensions 1992* (Washington, DC, US Government Printing Office).

Turner, John; Beller, Daniel J. 1989. *Trends in pensions* (Washington, DC, US Government Printing Office).

Turner, John; Rajnes, David M. 1995a. "Can private pensions fill the gap?", *Ageing International* (Washington), vol. 22, no. 2, pp. 38–43.

— 1995b. "Private pension systems in transition economies", in Z. Bodie, O. Mitchell and J. Turner (eds), *Securing employer-based pensions: An international perspective* (Philadelphia, University of Pennsylvania Press), pp. 193–210.

— 1996. "Retirement income system reform in Central and Eastern Europe", *Benefits Quarterly*, (Brookfield, Wisconsin), pp. 49–58.

Turner, John; Watanabe, Noriyasu. 1995. *Private pension policies in industrialized countries* (Kalamazoo, Michigan, W.E. Upjohn Institute for Employment Research).

— 1996. *Poverty, children and policy: Responses for a brighter future*, Economies in Transition Studies, Regional Monitoring Report (Florence), no. 4.

United Nations. 1969. *A system of national accounts* (New York).

— 1995. *Demographic Yearbook* (New York).

— 1996. *World Population Prospects 1950–2050* (New York).

United Nations Children's Fund (UNICEF). 1995. *Poverty, children and policy: Responses for a brighter future*, Economies in Transition Studies, Regional Monitoring Report (Florence), no. 3.

United Nations Development Programme (UNDP). 1997. *Human development report* (New York).

Urban Institute. 1997. "The declining importance of class: A roundtable on intergenerational mobility", *Update*, vol. 26.

US Department of Commerce. 1996. *Global aging into the 21st Century* (Washington, DC, National Institute on Aging).

US Department of Labor. 1993. "Abstract of 1993 Form 5500 Annual Reports", *Private Pension Plan Bulletin* 6, Winter (Washington, DC).

— 1994. *Pension and health benefits of American workers* (Washington, DC).

— 1997. "Abstract of 1992 Form 5500 Annual Reports", Private Pension Plan Bulletin. (Washington, DC).

US General Accounting Office. 1996a. "Issues in classifying workers as employees or independent contractors", Statement of Natar M. Gandhi (20 June).

— 1996b. "Issues in tax compliance burden", statement of Natwar M. Gandhi (3 April).

— 1996c. "Internal Revenue Service: Results of nonfiler strategy and opportunities to improve future efforts" (May).

US Social Security Administration. 1995. *Social security programs throughout the world – 1995* (Washington, DC).

— 1997. *Social security programs throughout the world – 1997* (Washington, DC).

Uthoff, Andra. 1995. "Pension system reform in Latin America", *CEPAL Review* (Santiago), no. 59, pp. 43–60.

Van der Hoeven, Rolph; Sziraczki, Gyorgy. 1997. *Lessons from privatization: Labour issues in developing and transitional countries* (Geneva, ILO).

Van Ginneken, Wouter (ed.). 1996a. *Finding the balance: Financing and coverage of social protection in Europe*, Occasional Papers on Social Security (Geneva, ISSA).

— 1996b. *Social security for the informal sector: Issues, options and tasks ahead*, Working Paper for the Interdepartmental Project on the Urban Informal Sector (Geneva, ILO).

— 1997. *Social security for the informal sector: Investigating the feasibility of pilot projects in Benin, India, El Salvador and Tanzania*, Issues in Social Security Discussion Paper No. 5 (Geneva, ILO).

— (ed.). 1998. *Social security for all Indians* (New Delhi, Oxford University Press).

Van Oorschot, W. 1991. Non take-up of social security benefits in Europe, *Journal of European Social Policy*, vol. 1, no. 1, pp. 15–30.

— 1995. *Take it or leave it: A study on non-take-up of social security benefits* (Aldershot: Avebury).

Van Oorschot, W. and Schell, J. 1991. "Means testing in Europe; A growing concern", in M. Adler, C. Bell, J. Clasen and A. Sinfield (eds). *The sociology of social security* (Edinburgh, Edinburgh University Press), pp. 187–211.

Van Oorschot, W. and Smolenaas, E. 1993. "Local income assistance policies: The Dutch case and a European impression" (Tilburg, University, Work and Organisation Research Centre).

Vanston, Nicholas. 1998. "The economic impacts of ageing", *The OECD Observer* (Paris), no. 212, pp. 10–14.

— 1997a. "Financial design of pensions and the mandate to annuities" (Washington, DC, World Bank), mimeo.

— 1997b. *The economics of pensions: Principles, policies and international experience* (Cambridge, Cambridge University Press).

— 1998. "The private sector in social security: Latin American lessons for APEC", paper presented at the APEC regional forum for pension fund reforms (Cancun, Mexico, 4–6 February).

Verzekeringskamer. 1997. *Financiële Gegevens Pensioenfondsen* (Apeldoorn, Netherlands).

Vittas, Dimitri. 1993. *Swiss Chilanpore: the way forward in pension reform?*, World Bank Discussion Paper No. WPS 1093 (Washington, DC); also published as *The implications for social security of structural adjustment policies*, Studies and Research No. 34 (Geneva, ISSA), pp. 113–35.

— 1994. *Sequencing social security, pension and insurance reform,* Discussion Paper No. WPS 1551 (Washington, DC, World Bank).

— 1996. *Private pension funds in Hungary: Early performance and regulatory issues*, Policy Research Working Paper No. 1638 (Washington, DC, World Bank).

— 1997a. "Links between pension reform, insurance and financial markets: Sequencing social security, pension and insurance reform", in *Eleventh Regional Conference for Asia and the Pacific, Manila, 24–27 Nov.* (Manila, ISSA).

— 1997b. *Private pension funds in Argentina's new integrated pension system*, Policy Research Working Paper No. 1820 (Washington, DC, World Bank).

— 1997c. *The Argentine pension reform and its relevance for Eastern Europe* (Washington, DC, World Bank).

Vittas, Dimitri and Iglesias, Augusto. 1991. "The rationale and performance of personal pension plans in Chile" (Washington, DC, World Bank), mimeo.

Vittas, Dimitri and Michelitsch, R. 1994. *Pension funds in central Europe and Russia: Their prospects and potential role in corporate governance*, Discussion Paper (Washington, DC, World Bank).

Voirin, Michel. 1994. "Une grille de lecture pour la comparaison internationale des régimes privés de pensions en relation avec les régimes publics", *Cahiers genevois de sécurité sociale* (Geneva), vol. 12, pp. 7–57.

— 1995. "Private and public pension schemes: Elements of a comparative approach", *International Social Security Review* (Geneva), vol. 48, no. 3/4, pp. 91–141.

Vroman,Wayne. 1996. "Pension fund revenue enhancement: Suggested initiatives for Kazakhstan", unpublished report, Kazakhstan Pension Reform Project, USAID financial support, (Washington, DC).

Wadhawan, Sahdev K. 1989. *Social security for workers in the informal sector in India* (Geneva, ILO).

Walford, J. 1993. *Personal Pensions 1994* (London, Financial Times Business Enterprises).

Wang, X. 1996. "Sozialversicherungsrecht der VR China im Wandel", *Zeitschrift für ausländisches und internationales Arbeits- und Sozialrecht* (Munich), vol. 10, no. 3, pp. 285–95.

Warshàwsky, Mark J. 1988. "Private annuity markets in the United States, 1919–1984", *Journal of Risk and Insurance*, vol. 40, pp. 518–28.

Weaver, Carolyn. 1993. *Guarantees of private pension benefits: Current problems and likely future prospects* (Washington, DC, American Enterprise Institute).

Wenruo, Hou. 1997. "Urban and rural pension insurance in China", in United Nations (ed.), *Sustaining social security* (New York).

Wheeler, Peter M.; Kearney, John R. 1996. "Income protection for the aged in the 21st century: A framework to help inform the debate", *Social Security Bulletin*, (Washington, DC), no. 59, pp. 3–19.

Whiteford, P. 1995. "Use of replacement rates in international comparisons of benefit systems", *International Social Security Review* (Geneva), vol. 48, no. 2, pp. 3–30.

World Bank. 1991. *Lessons of tax reform*, (Washington, DC).

— 1994. *Averting the old-age crisis: Policies to protect the old and promote growth* (Oxford, Oxford University Press).

— 1995a. *Fiscal management in the Russian Federation*, report (Washington, DC).

— 1995b. *Poverty in Russia: An assessment* (Washington, DC).

— 1996a. *World Development Report 1996: From Plan to Market* (Washington, DC).

— 1996b. *Estonia – Poverty assessment* (Washington, DC).

— 1996c. "The financing of pension systems in Central and Eastern Europe: An overview of major trends and their determinants, 1990–1993", Technical Paper No. 339, Social Challenges of Transition Series (Washington, DC).

— 1997. *Old age security: Pension reform in China* (Washington, DC).

— 1998. *World development indicators* (Washington, DC).

Yashiro, N. 1997. "Aging of the population in Japan and its implications to the other countries", *Journal of Asian Economics* (London), vol. 8, no. 2, pp. 245–61.

Yi, Lin. 1997. *Pension system reform in China* (Croydon, United Kingdom, Sedgwick Noble Lowndes).

Zukowski, Maciej. 1996. "Alterssicherungssystem in Polen: Geschichte, gegenwärtige Lage, Umgestaltung", *Zeitschrift für ausländisches und internationales Arbeits- und Sozialrecht* (Munich), vol. 10, no. 2, pp. 89–141.

INDEX

Note: Page numbers in **bold** refer to major text sections, those in *italic* to tables, figures and boxes. The letter *g* appended to a page number indicates a glossary entry. Subscript numbers appended to a page number indicate a footnote reference. Concatenated page numbers (eg 17–19) do not necessarily indicate continuous treatment.

accounting 173, *174*, 177–9, **367–70**, *374*, *384–7*, 386, 388

actuarial process 133–5, 138, 150–52, *221–2*, 479–80, 486_{10}, 606–7, 707g

administration *see* governance and administration

advance-funded schemes 356, 360–64

Afghanistan *648, 654, 662*

Africa 20, 82–3, **515–31**, *661*
   benefits 46–7, 51, 63, 516, 524–5, *683–4*
   coverage *194*, 203, 404, 413, 515, 517, 519–20, 526–8, 530, *666–7, 679*
   defined benefit schemes 47, 516, 528, *626*
   demographics 518, *519, 641–2, 646–7, 652–3, 677, 694*
   economic development 339, 517–18
   evasion 251–2
   financing 131, 139, 388_3, *689, 692, 696*
   governance 234, 236–8, 520, 522–4, 530–31
   investment 172, 354, 522–4, *703*
   pension development 3, **525–31**
   performance projection model 22, **630–o36**
   private sector 516, 529, 531
   provident funds 516, 524, 528–9
   public sector 618, 620, *626*
   retirement age 41–3, *42*, 346, *661*
   retirement income *286, 288–9*, 290, *683–4*
   see also individual regions/countries

age at retirement *see* retirement age

Albania *558, 560, 567, 626, 662, 669*
   demographics 553, *559, 643, 649, 655, 677, 694*
   financing *561, 697*
   invalidity benefits *558*, 567
   pension development 562, 567
   retirement age 567, *662*

Algeria 73, 515, 517, 620, *661, 683, 696*
   coverage 519, *666*
   demographics *642, 646, 652*
   retirement age 445, *661*

Angola 516, 525, *646, 652*

annuities **56–62**, *60*, 66, 315, *542–3*, 707g
   defined benefit schemes 5, *57–8*, 59
   defined contribution schemes 5, 27, 55, 59, 309, *311–14*

anti-poverty benefits *see* social assistance

Antigua and Barbuda 533, 535

Arab Labour Organization 546

Arab states (Middle East) 20–21, **546–52**, *662, 703*
   benefits 549–51, *684*
   coverage 548, *667, 679*
   demographics 547, *641–2, 647–8, 653–4*
   financing 546, 551–2, *551, 689, 692, 696*
   retirement age 41–3, *42*, 549, *662*
   retirement income *286, 684*
   see also individual countries; Middle East

coverage 203, *204*, 582, *671*
demographics *644, 651, 657, 678*
entitlement 579, *664*
financing *138*, 139, *248, 360, 371*, 372,
380, *381*, 579, 581, *690, 693, 699*
governance *235, 248*, 463, 583
pension development 578, 589, 591,
593–4
private sector 594
retirement age 42, *346*, 445, *446–7*,
451–2, 589, *664*
retirement income 295, 300₁₇, *688*
social assistance 99, *100–101*, 104, *106*,
112–13, *114, 120, 123–4*
dependency, establishing (survivors'
benefits) 90–91
dependency ratios 273, 278–9, 557, 559,
559, 577, 641, 652–7, 694–5
developed countries 25
coverage 405, 420
economic effects *see* economic effects
invalidity benefits 74–6, *74*, 82
pension structure 464, 469, 472–3, 478
private sector 30–31
public sector 4, 30–31, 618
retirement age 43, 438–9, *441–2*, 442
see also individual countries
developing countries *60*, 62–4, 82–3, 398–
9, 402
coverage 8, 14, 199, 213–14, 246, 307,
404–5, 409, 417, 421, 620–21
evasion 266
financing 131, 401
governance 14, 24, 229, 426–7, 429,
431, 433, 458, 464, *466*, 484
investment **158–65**, 178, 181–5
pension models 468–9, *469–72*
public sector 4, 29–30, 618, 620–22
retirement age 43, 438–9
see also individual countries
discrimination *see* equality of treatment
divorced people, survivors' benefits *92–3*,
94–6
Djibouti *646, 652*
Dominica *663, 679, 686, 690, 693, 695*
Dominican Republic 533, 535, 537, *650,
656, 663, 671, 686*

early retirement *446–7*, 549, 577, *661–5*,
708*g*
minimum age 41–3, 347, 351, 437–43,
440, 443, 445, 451–2, 549–50
economic considerations 439, 442

factors affecting 63, 351, 442
life cycle model 439–40
and life expectancy 43, 439, 442,
445, 449
pay-as-you-go financing 440, 442
policy considerations 443–5
policy options 443
pathways to 75, 78, 338, 345–50, **445**,
447–9, 451–2
and redistribution of income 270–71
see also retirement age
earnings
irregular 319, 324–5
misreporting 47, 246, 252–3, *257*, 262,
318
see also income; wages
earnings test *42*, 44–5, 66, 347–8, 350,
352, 580
see also means test
earnings-related benefits *42*, 46–9, *54*,
194, *194*, 404, 412–13, 468–9, *469*,
484, 562, 578–80, *586–7*, 591
East Asia 194, 196, 237, 499–500
East Germany, former 581
East Timor *648, 654*
Eastern Europe *see* Central and Eastern
Europe and Central Asia
economic development 195–6, 499–500,
517–18
see also transition countries
economic effects (pension schemes) 13–14,
336–66
capital market 339–41
defined benefit 13, 336–7, 340, 342–6,
346–51, 352–3, 365
defined contribution 13–14, 336–8,
342–5, 351–3, 363, 365
desired **337–41**
financial markets 363–4
labour market 307–8, 339–41, **341–53**
competitiveness 344
defined benefit schemes **346–51**
defined contribution schemes 351–2
demand/supply **341–4**, 352
earnings test 347–8, 352
invalidity benefits 345
investments 352–3
retirement age 344–9, *346*
saving *see* saving
social security retirement
benefits 345–6
unemployment benefits 345
link between national saving and
economic growth *see* saving

social assistance (*cont.*)
   treatment of resources 104, *105–10*,
     111–12
   taxonomy 98–9
   see also low-income workers; means
     tests; poverty
social budget model **599–601**
social insurance 70–71, 73, *80–81*, 82, *84–
   5*, 99, **455–8**
social protection, structure 217–18,
   600–601
social security boards, relationship with
   chief executive 242, *243*
social security institutions *see* governance
   and administration
social security, philosophy of **455–8**
social security systems, sources of
   financing *692–3*
Social Security Technical Programme
   (ILO) 224
socioeconomic environment,
   modelling 600
solidarity principle (pension provision)
   136, 136₆, 400–401
Solomon Islands *649, 655, 677*
Somalia 516, 525, *647, 653*
South Africa 3, 236–7, *466*, 516–17, 525,
   661, 703
   coverage 203, 418, 519
   demographics *647, 653, 677*
   financing 139, *371*, 516, *696*
   invalidity benefits 71, 82
South America 239, 252, 456, 532–3,
   540–41
South Asia 194, 215
South Yemen 548, 552
South-East Asia 194, 196, 237–8, 500
south-Eastern Europe 560, *560–61*
southern Africa 529–30
Southern Europe *441*
Soviet Union, former 178–9, 230–31, 249,
   448, 560, *560–61*, 620
Spain *592, 665, 704*
   benefits 579, 585, *687*
   coverage *204–5, 207*, 581, *628*
   demographics *645, 651, 657, 678*
   financing *371, 690, 693, 700*
   pension development 581, 585, *592*
   private sector 35, *628*

public sector 35, *371, 625, 628*
retirement age *346, 665*
retirement income 580, *687–8*
social assistance *100–101*, 103, *109*,
   112, *116, 120*, 123, *123–4*
Sri Lanka 238–9, 622, *626, 662, 697, 703*
   contributions *141*
   coverage *669*
   demographics *649, 655*
   invalidity benefits 71, 83
stabilization funds 46
stakeholders *see* governance and
   administration
state-owned enterprises, pension
   liabilities **510–12**
stock markets *see* securities markets
structure (pension schemes) 17–18,
   295–7, **453–86**
   defined benefit vs defined contribution
     schemes **475–7**
   social assistance *see* social assistance
   determinants **455–64**
     administrative costs *see* governance
       and administration
     goals 456–8
     governance capability 455, 458
     political philosophies **455–8**
     rates of return 455, 459–61
     risk 455, 459–61
   tiers 18, 27, 407, 454, 464–5, 478
     first tier 465, **468–73**, 475–6
     second tier 465, **473–5**, 476
     third tier 465
   see also individual subjects
sub-Saharan Africa 194, 196, 215, 249,
   515, 517–18, 530
subsidies 4, 32–3, 474, *475*
Sudan 71, *141, 647, 653, 661, 667, 679,
   683, 696*
Suriname *627, 651, 657*
survivors' benefits 5–6, **87–96**, 710g
   annuity options 60
   children 88–91, *92–4*
   coverage **91–5**, 95–6
   determining survivors 89–90, 613
   divorced people *92–3*, 94–6
   entitlement **87–96**, 614
   equity **91–6**
   establishing dependency 90–91
   gender specific 6, 88–91, *92–4*, 94–6,
     593
   provident funds 90
   rates 91, 614–16, *615*